THIRD EDITION

Python Cookbook

David Beazley and Brian K. Jones

O'REILLY®

Beijing · Cambridge · Farnham · Köln · Sebastopol · Tokyo

Python Cookbook, Third Edition

by David Beazley and Brian K. Jones

Copyright © 2013 David Beazley and Brian Jones. All rights reserved.

Printed in the United States of America.

Published by O'Reilly Media, Inc., 1005 Gravenstein Highway North, Sebastopol, CA 95472.

O'Reilly books may be purchased for educational, business, or sales promotional use. Online editions are also available for most titles (*http://my.safaribooksonline.com*). For more information, contact our corporate/institutional sales department: 800-998-9938 or *corporate@oreilly.com*.

Editors: Meghan Blanchette and Rachel Roumeliotis	**Indexer:** WordCo Indexing Services
Production Editor: Kristen Borg	**Cover Designer:** Karen Montgomery
Copyeditor: Jasmine Kwityn	**Interior Designer:** David Futato
Proofreader: BIM Proofreading Services	**Illustrator:** Robert Romano

May 2013:   Third Edition

Revision History for the Third Edition:

2013-05-08:   First release

See *http://oreilly.com/catalog/errata.csp?isbn=9781449340377* for release details.

Nutshell Handbook, the Nutshell Handbook logo, and the O'Reilly logo are registered trademarks of O'Reilly Media, Inc. *Python Cookbook*, the image of a springhaas, and related trade dress are trademarks of O'Reilly Media, Inc.

Many of the designations used by manufacturers and sellers to distinguish their products are claimed as trademarks. Where those designations appear in this book, and O'Reilly Media, Inc., was aware of a trademark claim, the designations have been printed in caps or initial caps.

While every precaution has been taken in the preparation of this book, the publisher and authors assume no responsibility for errors or omissions, or for damages resulting from the use of the information contained herein.

ISBN: 978-1-449-34037-7

[LSI]

Table of Contents

Preface

Since 2008, the Python world has been watching the slow evolution of Python 3. It was always known that the adoption of Python 3 would likely take a long time. In fact, even at the time of this writing (2013), most working Python programmers continue to use Python 2 in production. A lot has been made about the fact that Python 3 is not backward compatible with past versions. To be sure, backward compatibility is an issue for anyone with an existing code base. However, if you shift your view toward the future, you'll find that Python 3 offers much more than meets the eye.

Just as Python 3 is about the future, this edition of the *Python Cookbook* represents a major change over past editions. First and foremost, this is meant to be a very forward looking book. All of the recipes have been written and tested with Python 3.3 without regard to past Python versions or the "old way" of doing things. In fact, many of the recipes will only work with Python 3.3 and above. Doing so may be a calculated risk, but the ultimate goal is to write a book of recipes based on the most modern tools and idioms possible. It is hoped that the recipes can serve as a guide for people writing new code in Python 3 or those who hope to modernize existing code.

Needless to say, writing a book of recipes in this style presents a certain editorial challenge. An online search for Python recipes returns literally thousands of useful recipes on sites such as ActiveState's Python recipes (*http://code.activestate.com/recipes/langs/python*) or Stack Overflow (*http://stackoverflow.com/questions/tagged/python*). However, most of these recipes are steeped in history and the past. Besides being written almost exclusively for Python 2, they often contain workarounds and hacks related to differences between old versions of Python (e.g., version 2.3 versus 2.4). Moreover, they often use outdated techniques that have simply become a built-in feature of Python 3.3. Finding recipes exclusively focused on Python 3 can be a bit more difficult.

Rather than attempting to seek out Python 3-specific recipes, the topics of this book are merely inspired by existing code and techniques. Using these ideas as a springboard, the writing is an original work that has been deliberately written with the most modern

Python programming techniques possible. Thus, it can serve as a reference for anyone who wants to write their code in a modern style.

In choosing which recipes to include, there is a certain realization that it is simply impossible to write a book that covers every possible thing that someone might do with Python. Thus, a priority has been given to topics that focus on the core Python language as well as tasks that are common to a wide variety of application domains. In addition, many of the recipes aim to illustrate features that are new to Python 3 and more likely to be unknown to even experienced programmers using older versions. There is also a certain preference to recipes that illustrate a generally applicable programming technique (i.e., programming patterns) as opposed to those that narrowly try to address a very specific practical problem. Although certain third-party packages get coverage, a majority of the recipes focus on the core language and standard library.

Who This Book Is For

This book is aimed at more experienced Python programmers who are looking to deepen their understanding of the language and modern programming idioms. Much of the material focuses on some of the more advanced techniques used by libraries, frameworks, and applications. Throughout the book, the recipes generally assume that the reader already has the necessary background to understand the topic at hand (e.g., general knowledge of computer science, data structures, complexity, systems programming, concurrency, C programming, etc.). Moreover, the recipes are often just skeletons that aim to provide essential information for getting started, but which require the reader to do more research to fill in the details. As such, it is assumed that the reader knows how to use search engines and Python's excellent online documentation.

Many of the more advanced recipes will reward the reader's patience with a much greater insight into how Python actually works under the covers. You will learn new tricks and techniques that can be applied to your own code.

Who This Book Is Not For

This is not a book designed for beginners trying to learn Python for the first time. In fact, it already assumes that you know the basics that might be taught in a Python tutorial or more introductory book. This book is also not designed to serve as a quick reference manual (e.g., quickly looking up the functions in a specific module). Instead, the book aims to focus on specific programming topics, show possible solutions, and serve as a springboard for jumping into more advanced material you might find online or in a reference.

Conventions Used in This Book

The following typographical conventions are used in this book:

Italic
> Indicates new terms, URLs, email addresses, filenames, and file extensions.

`Constant width`
> Used for program listings, as well as within paragraphs to refer to program elements such as variable or function names, databases, data types, environment variables, statements, and keywords.

`Constant width bold`
> Shows commands or other text that should be typed literally by the user.

`Constant width italic`
> Shows text that should be replaced with user-supplied values or by values determined by context.

 This icon signifies a tip, suggestion, or general note.

 This icon indicates a warning or caution.

Online Code Examples

Almost all of the code examples in this book are available online at *http://github.com/ dabeaz/python-cookbook*. The authors welcome bug fixes, improvements, and comments.

Using Code Examples

This book is here to help you get your job done. In general, if this book includes code examples, you may use the code in this book in your programs and documentation. You do not need to contact us for permission unless you're reproducing a significant portion of the code. For example, writing a program that uses several chunks of code from this book does not require permission. Selling or distributing a CD-ROM of examples from O'Reilly books does require permission. Answering a question by citing this book and quoting example code does not require permission. Incorporating a significant amount of example code from this book into your product's documentation does require permission.

We appreciate, but do not require, attribution. An attribution usually includes the title, author, publisher, and ISBN. For example: *Python Cookbook*, 3rd edition, by David Beazley and Brian K. Jones (O'Reilly). Copyright 2013 David Beazley and Brian Jones, 978-1-449-34037-7.

If you feel your use of code examples falls outside fair use or the permission given here, feel free to contact us at *permissions@oreilly.com*.

Safari® Books Online

 Safari Books Online is an on-demand digital library that delivers expert content in both book and video form from the world's leading authors in technology and business.

Technology professionals, software developers, web designers, and business and creative professionals use Safari Books Online as their primary resource for research, problem solving, learning, and certification training.

Safari Books Online offers a range of product mixes and pricing programs for organizations, government agencies, and individuals. Subscribers have access to thousands of books, training videos, and prepublication manuscripts in one fully searchable database from publishers like O'Reilly Media, Prentice Hall Professional, Addison-Wesley Professional, Microsoft Press, Sams, Que, Peachpit Press, Focal Press, Cisco Press, John Wiley & Sons, Syngress, Morgan Kaufmann, IBM Redbooks, Packt, Adobe Press, FT Press, Apress, Manning, New Riders, McGraw-Hill, Jones & Bartlett, Course Technology, and dozens more. For more information about Safari Books Online, please visit us online.

How to Contact Us

Please address comments and questions concerning this book to the publisher:

O'Reilly Media, Inc.
1005 Gravenstein Highway North
Sebastopol, CA 95472
800-998-9938 (in the United States or Canada)
707-829-0515 (international or local)
707-829-0104 (fax)

We have a web page for this book, where we list errata, examples, and any additional information. You can access this page at *http://oreil.ly/python_cookbook_3e*.

To comment or ask technical questions about this book, send email to *bookques tions@oreilly.com*.

For more information about our books, courses, conferences, and news, see our website at *http://www.oreilly.com*.

Find us on Facebook: *http://facebook.com/oreilly*

Follow us on Twitter: *http://twitter.com/oreillymedia*

Watch us on YouTube: *http://www.youtube.com/oreillymedia*

Acknowledgments

We would like to acknowledge the technical reviewers, Jake Vanderplas, Robert Kern, and Andrea Crotti, for their very helpful comments, as well as the general Python community for their support and encouragement. We would also like to thank the editors of the prior edition, Alex Martelli, Anna Ravenscroft, and David Ascher. Although this edition is newly written, the previous edition provided an initial framework for selecting the topics and recipes of interest. Last, but not least, we would like to thank readers of the early release editions for their comments and suggestions for improvement.

David Beazley's Acknowledgments

Writing a book is no small task. As such, I would like to thank my wife Paula and my two boys for their patience and support during this project. Much of the material in this book was derived from content I developed teaching Python-related training classes over the last six years. Thus, I'd like to thank all of the students who have taken my courses and ultimately made this book possible. I'd also like to thank Ned Batchelder, Travis Oliphant, Peter Wang, Brian Van de Ven, Hugo Shi, Raymond Hettinger, Michael Foord, and Daniel Klein for traveling to the four corners of the world to teach these courses while I stayed home in Chicago to work on this project. Meghan Blanchette and Rachel Roumeliotis of O'Reilly were also instrumental in seeing this project through to completion despite the drama of several false starts and unforeseen delays. Last, but not least, I'd like to thank the Python community for their continued support and putting up with my flights of diabolical fancy.

David M. Beazley

http://www.dabeaz.com

https://twitter.com/dabeaz

Brian Jones' Acknowledgments

I would like to thank both my coauthor, David Beazley, as well as Meghan Blanchette and Rachel Roumeliotis of O'Reilly, for working with me on this project. I would also like to thank my amazing wife, Natasha, for her patience and encouragement in this project, and her support in all of my ambitions. Most of all, I'd like to thank the Python community at large. Though I have contributed to the support of various open source projects, languages, clubs, and the like, no work has been so gratifying and rewarding as that which has been in the service of the Python community.

Brian K. Jones

http://www.protocolostomy.com

https://twitter.com/bkjones

## CHAPTER 1

Data Structures and Algorithms

Python provides a variety of useful built-in data structures, such as lists, sets, and dictionaries. For the most part, the use of these structures is straightforward. However, common questions concerning searching, sorting, ordering, and filtering often arise. Thus, the goal of this chapter is to discuss common data structures and algorithms involving data. In addition, treatment is given to the various data structures contained in the collections module.

1.1. Unpacking a Sequence into Separate Variables

Problem

You have an N-element tuple or sequence that you would like to unpack into a collection of N variables.

Solution

Any sequence (or iterable) can be unpacked into variables using a simple assignment operation. The only requirement is that the number of variables and structure match the sequence. For example:

```
>>> p = (4, 5)
>>> x, y = p
>>> x
4
>>> y
5
>>>

>>> data = [ 'ACME', 50, 91.1, (2012, 12, 21) ]
>>> name, shares, price, date = data
>>> name
```

```
'ACME'
>>> date
(2012, 12, 21)

>>> name, shares, price, (year, mon, day) = data
>>> name
'ACME'
>>> year
2012
>>> mon
12
>>> day
21
>>>
```

If there is a mismatch in the number of elements, you'll get an error. For example:

```
>>> p = (4, 5)
>>> x, y, z = p
Traceback (most recent call last):
  File "<stdin>", line 1, in <module>
ValueError: need more than 2 values to unpack
>>>
```

Discussion

Unpacking actually works with any object that happens to be iterable, not just tuples or lists. This includes strings, files, iterators, and generators. For example:

```
>>> s = 'Hello'
>>> a, b, c, d, e = s
>>> a
'H'
>>> b
'e'
>>> e
'o'
>>>
```

When unpacking, you may sometimes want to discard certain values. Python has no special syntax for this, but you can often just pick a throwaway variable name for it. For example:

```
>>> data = [ 'ACME', 50, 91.1, (2012, 12, 21) ]
>>> _, shares, price, _ = data
>>> shares
50
>>> price
91.1
>>>
```

However, make sure that the variable name you pick isn't being used for something else already.

1.2. Unpacking Elements from Iterables of Arbitrary Length

Problem

You need to unpack N elements from an iterable, but the iterable may be longer than N elements, causing a "too many values to unpack" exception.

Solution

Python "star expressions" can be used to address this problem. For example, suppose you run a course and decide at the end of the semester that you're going to drop the first and last homework grades, and only average the rest of them. If there are only four assignments, maybe you simply unpack all four, but what if there are 24? A star expression makes it easy:

```python
def drop_first_last(grades):
    first, *middle, last = grades
    return avg(middle)
```

As another use case, suppose you have user records that consist of a name and email address, followed by an arbitrary number of phone numbers. You could unpack the records like this:

```python
>>> record = ('Dave', 'dave@example.com', '773-555-1212', '847-555-1212')
>>> name, email, *phone_numbers = user_record
>>> name
'Dave'
>>> email
'dave@example.com'
>>> phone_numbers
['773-555-1212', '847-555-1212']
>>>
```

It's worth noting that the phone_numbers variable will always be a list, regardless of how many phone numbers are unpacked (including none). Thus, any code that uses phone_numbers won't have to account for the possibility that it might not be a list or perform any kind of additional type checking.

The starred variable can also be the first one in the list. For example, say you have a sequence of values representing your company's sales figures for the last eight quarters. If you want to see how the most recent quarter stacks up to the average of the first seven, you could do something like this:

```python
*trailing_qtrs, current_qtr = sales_record
trailing_avg = sum(trailing_qtrs) / len(trailing_qtrs)
return avg_comparison(trailing_avg, current_qtr)
```

Here's a view of the operation from the Python interpreter:

```
>>> *trailing, current = [10, 8, 7, 1, 9, 5, 10, 3]
>>> trailing
[10, 8, 7, 1, 9, 5, 10]
>>> current
3
```

Discussion

Extended iterable unpacking is tailor-made for unpacking iterables of unknown or arbitrary length. Oftentimes, these iterables have some known component or pattern in their construction (e.g. "everything after element 1 is a phone number"), and star unpacking lets the developer leverage those patterns easily instead of performing acrobatics to get at the relevant elements in the iterable.

It is worth noting that the star syntax can be especially useful when iterating over a sequence of tuples of varying length. For example, perhaps a sequence of tagged tuples:

```
records = [
    ('foo', 1, 2),
    ('bar', 'hello'),
    ('foo', 3, 4),
]

def do_foo(x, y):
    print('foo', x, y)

def do_bar(s):
    print('bar', s)

for tag, *args in records:
    if tag == 'foo':
        do_foo(*args)
    elif tag == 'bar':
        do_bar(*args)
```

Star unpacking can also be useful when combined with certain kinds of string processing operations, such as splitting. For example:

```
>>> line = 'nobody:*:-2:-2:Unprivileged User:/var/empty:/usr/bin/false'
>>> uname, *fields, homedir, sh = line.split(':')
>>> uname
'nobody'
>>> homedir
'/var/empty'
>>> sh
'/usr/bin/false'
>>>
```

Sometimes you might want to unpack values and throw them away. You can't just specify a bare * when unpacking, but you could use a common throwaway variable name, such as _ or ign (ignored). For example:

```
>>> record = ('ACME', 50, 123.45, (12, 18, 2012))
>>> name, *_, (*_, year) = record
>>> name
'ACME'
>>> year
2012
>>>
```

There is a certain similarity between star unpacking and list-processing features of various functional languages. For example, if you have a list, you can easily split it into head and tail components like this:

```
>>> items = [1, 10, 7, 4, 5, 9]
>>> head, *tail = items
>>> head
1
>>> tail
[10, 7, 4, 5, 9]
>>>
```

One could imagine writing functions that perform such splitting in order to carry out some kind of clever recursive algorithm. For example:

```
>>> def sum(items):
...     head, *tail = items
...     return head + sum(tail) if tail else head
...
>>> sum(items)
36
>>>
```

However, be aware that recursion really isn't a strong Python feature due to the inherent recursion limit. Thus, this last example might be nothing more than an academic curiosity in practice.

1.3. Keeping the Last N Items

Problem

You want to keep a limited history of the last few items seen during iteration or during some other kind of processing.

Solution

Keeping a limited history is a perfect use for a collections.deque. For example, the following code performs a simple text match on a sequence of lines and yields the matching line along with the previous N lines of context when found:

```
from collections import deque

def search(lines, pattern, history=5):
    previous_lines = deque(maxlen=history)
    for line in lines:
        if pattern in line:
            yield line, previous_lines
        previous_lines.append(line)

# Example use on a file
if __name__ == '__main__':
    with open('somefile.txt') as f:
        for line, prevlines in search(f, 'python', 5):
            for pline in prevlines:
                print(pline, end='')
            print(line, end='')
            print('-'*20)
```

Discussion

When writing code to search for items, it is common to use a generator function involving yield, as shown in this recipe's solution. This decouples the process of searching from the code that uses the results. If you're new to generators, see Recipe 4.3.

Using deque(maxlen=N) creates a fixed-sized queue. When new items are added and the queue is full, the oldest item is automatically removed. For example:

```
>>> q = deque(maxlen=3)
>>> q.append(1)
>>> q.append(2)
>>> q.append(3)
>>> q
deque([1, 2, 3], maxlen=3)
>>> q.append(4)
>>> q
deque([2, 3, 4], maxlen=3)
>>> q.append(5)
>>> q
deque([3, 4, 5], maxlen=3)
```

Although you could manually perform such operations on a list (e.g., appending, deleting, etc.), the queue solution is far more elegant and runs a lot faster.

More generally, a deque can be used whenever you need a simple queue structure. If you don't give it a maximum size, you get an unbounded queue that lets you append and pop items on either end. For example:

```
>>> q = deque()
>>> q.append(1)
>>> q.append(2)
>>> q.append(3)
>>> q
```

```
deque([1, 2, 3])
>>> q.appendleft(4)
>>> q
deque([4, 1, 2, 3])
>>> q.pop()
3
>>> q
deque([4, 1, 2])
>>> q.popleft()
4
```

Adding or popping items from either end of a queue has O(1) complexity. This is unlike a list where inserting or removing items from the front of the list is O(N).

1.4. Finding the Largest or Smallest N Items

Problem

You want to make a list of the largest or smallest N items in a collection.

Solution

The heapq module has two functions—nlargest() and nsmallest()—that do exactly what you want. For example:

```
import heapq

nums = [1, 8, 2, 23, 7, -4, 18, 23, 42, 37, 2]
print(heapq.nlargest(3, nums))  # Prints [42, 37, 23]
print(heapq.nsmallest(3, nums)) # Prints [-4, 1, 2]
```

Both functions also accept a key parameter that allows them to be used with more complicated data structures. For example:

```
portfolio = [
    {'name': 'IBM', 'shares': 100, 'price': 91.1},
    {'name': 'AAPL', 'shares': 50, 'price': 543.22},
    {'name': 'FB', 'shares': 200, 'price': 21.09},
    {'name': 'HPQ', 'shares': 35, 'price': 31.75},
    {'name': 'YHOO', 'shares': 45, 'price': 16.35},
    {'name': 'ACME', 'shares': 75, 'price': 115.65}
]

cheap = heapq.nsmallest(3, portfolio, key=lambda s: s['price'])
expensive = heapq.nlargest(3, portfolio, key=lambda s: s['price'])
```

Discussion

If you are looking for the N smallest or largest items and N is small compared to the overall size of the collection, these functions provide superior performance. Underneath the covers, they work by first converting the data into a list where items are ordered as a heap. For example:

```
>>> nums = [1, 8, 2, 23, 7, -4, 18, 23, 42, 37, 2]
>>> import heapq
>>> heap = list(nums)
>>> heapq.heapify(heap)
>>> heap
[-4, 2, 1, 23, 7, 2, 18, 23, 42, 37, 8]
>>>
```

The most important feature of a heap is that `heap[0]` is always the smallest item. Moreover, subsequent items can be easily found using the `heapq.heappop()` method, which pops off the first item and replaces it with the next smallest item (an operation that requires O(log N) operations where N is the size of the heap). For example, to find the three smallest items, you would do this:

```
>>> heapq.heappop(heap)
-4
>>> heapq.heappop(heap)
1
>>> heapq.heappop(heap)
2
```

The `nlargest()` and `nsmallest()` functions are most appropriate if you are trying to find a relatively small number of items. If you are simply trying to find the single smallest or largest item (N=1), it is faster to use `min()` and `max()`. Similarly, if N is about the same size as the collection itself, it is usually faster to sort it first and take a slice (i.e., use `sorted(items)[:N]` or `sorted(items)[-N:]`). It should be noted that the actual implementation of `nlargest()` and `nsmallest()` is adaptive in how it operates and will carry out some of these optimizations on your behalf (e.g., using sorting if N is close to the same size as the input).

Although it's not necessary to use this recipe, the implementation of a heap is an interesting and worthwhile subject of study. This can usually be found in any decent book on algorithms and data structures. The documentation for the `heapq` module also discusses the underlying implementation details.

1.5. Implementing a Priority Queue

Problem

You want to implement a queue that sorts items by a given priority and always returns the item with the highest priority on each pop operation.

Solution

The following class uses the `heapq` module to implement a simple priority queue:

```
import heapq

class PriorityQueue:
    def __init__(self):
        self._queue = []
        self._index = 0

    def push(self, item, priority):
        heapq.heappush(self._queue, (-priority, self._index, item))
        self._index += 1

    def pop(self):
        return heapq.heappop(self._queue)[-1]
```

Here is an example of how it might be used:

```
>>> class Item:
...     def __init__(self, name):
...         self.name = name
...     def __repr__(self):
...         return 'Item({!r})'.format(self.name)
...
>>> q = PriorityQueue()
>>> q.push(Item('foo'), 1)
>>> q.push(Item('bar'), 5)
>>> q.push(Item('spam'), 4)
>>> q.push(Item('grok'), 1)
>>> q.pop()
Item('bar')
>>> q.pop()
Item('spam')
>>> q.pop()
Item('foo')
>>> q.pop()
Item('grok')
>>>
```

Observe how the first `pop()` operation returned the item with the highest priority. Also observe how the two items with the same priority (`foo` and `grok`) were returned in the same order in which they were inserted into the queue.

Discussion

The core of this recipe concerns the use of the `heapq` module. The functions `heapq.heappush()` and `heapq.heappop()` insert and remove items from a list `_queue` in a way such that the first item in the list has the smallest priority (as discussed in Recipe 1.4). The `heappop()` method always returns the "smallest" item, so that is the key to making the queue pop the correct items. Moreover, since the push and pop operations have O(log N) complexity where N is the number of items in the heap, they are fairly efficient even for fairly large values of N.

In this recipe, the queue consists of tuples of the form (-priority, index, item). The priority value is negated to get the queue to sort items from highest priority to lowest priority. This is opposite of the normal heap ordering, which sorts from lowest to highest value.

The role of the index variable is to properly order items with the same priority level. By keeping a constantly increasing index, the items will be sorted according to the order in which they were inserted. However, the index also serves an important role in making the comparison operations work for items that have the same priority level.

To elaborate on that, instances of Item in the example can't be ordered. For example:

```
>>> a = Item('foo')
>>> b = Item('bar')
>>> a < b
Traceback (most recent call last):
  File "<stdin>", line 1, in <module>
TypeError: unorderable types: Item() < Item()
>>>
```

If you make (priority, item) tuples, they can be compared as long as the priorities are different. However, if two tuples with equal priorities are compared, the comparison fails as before. For example:

```
>>> a = (1, Item('foo'))
>>> b = (5, Item('bar'))
>>> a < b
True
>>> c = (1, Item('grok'))
>>> a < c
Traceback (most recent call last):
  File "<stdin>", line 1, in <module>
TypeError: unorderable types: Item() < Item()
>>>
```

By introducing the extra index and making (priority, index, item) tuples, you avoid this problem entirely since no two tuples will ever have the same value for index (and Python never bothers to compare the remaining tuple values once the result of comparison can be determined):

```
>>> a = (1, 0, Item('foo'))
>>> b = (5, 1, Item('bar'))
>>> c = (1, 2, Item('grok'))
>>> a < b
True
>>> a < c
```

```
True
>>>
```

If you want to use this queue for communication between threads, you need to add appropriate locking and signaling. See Recipe 12.3 for an example of how to do this.

The documentation for the `heapq` module has further examples and discussion concerning the theory and implementation of heaps.

1.6. Mapping Keys to Multiple Values in a Dictionary

Problem

You want to make a dictionary that maps keys to more than one value (a so-called "multidict").

Solution

A dictionary is a mapping where each key is mapped to a single value. If you want to map keys to multiple values, you need to store the multiple values in another container such as a list or set. For example, you might make dictionaries like this:

```
d = {
    'a' : [1, 2, 3],
    'b' : [4, 5]
}

e = {
    'a' : {1, 2, 3},
    'b' : {4, 5}
}
```

The choice of whether or not to use lists or sets depends on intended use. Use a list if you want to preserve the insertion order of the items. Use a set if you want to eliminate duplicates (and don't care about the order).

To easily construct such dictionaries, you can use `defaultdict` in the `collections` module. A feature of `defaultdict` is that it automatically initializes the first value so you can simply focus on adding items. For example:

```
from collections import defaultdict

d = defaultdict(list)
d['a'].append(1)
d['a'].append(2)
d['b'].append(4)
...

d = defaultdict(set)
```

```
d['a'].add(1)
d['a'].add(2)
d['b'].add(4)
...
```

One caution with `defaultdict` is that it will automatically create dictionary entries for keys accessed later on (even if they aren't currently found in the dictionary). If you don't want this behavior, you might use `setdefault()` on an ordinary dictionary instead. For example:

```
d = {}      # A regular dictionary
d.setdefault('a', []).append(1)
d.setdefault('a', []).append(2)
d.setdefault('b', []).append(4)
...
```

However, many programmers find `setdefault()` to be a little unnatural—not to mention the fact that it always creates a new instance of the initial value on each invocation (the empty list [ ] in the example).

Discussion

In principle, constructing a multivalued dictionary is simple. However, initialization of the first value can be messy if you try to do it yourself. For example, you might have code that looks like this:

```
d = {}
for key, value in pairs:
    if key not in d:
        d[key] = []
    d[key].append(value)
```

Using a `defaultdict` simply leads to much cleaner code:

```
d = defaultdict(list)
for key, value in pairs:
    d[key].append(value)
```

This recipe is strongly related to the problem of grouping records together in data processing problems. See Recipe 1.15 for an example.

1.7. Keeping Dictionaries in Order

Problem

You want to create a dictionary, and you also want to control the order of items when iterating or serializing.

Solution

To control the order of items in a dictionary, you can use an `OrderedDict` from the `collections` module. It exactly preserves the original insertion order of data when iterating. For example:

```
from collections import OrderedDict

d = OrderedDict()
d['foo'] = 1
d['bar'] = 2
d['spam'] = 3
d['grok'] = 4

# Outputs "foo 1", "bar 2", "spam 3", "grok 4"
for key in d:
    print(key, d[key])
```

An `OrderedDict` can be particularly useful when you want to build a mapping that you may want to later serialize or encode into a different format. For example, if you want to precisely control the order of fields appearing in a JSON encoding, first building the data in an `OrderedDict` will do the trick:

```
>>> import json
>>> json.dumps(d)
'{"foo": 1, "bar": 2, "spam": 3, "grok": 4}'
>>>
```

Discussion

An `OrderedDict` internally maintains a doubly linked list that orders the keys according to insertion order. When a new item is first inserted, it is placed at the end of this list. Subsequent reassignment of an existing key doesn't change the order.

Be aware that the size of an `OrderedDict` is more than twice as large as a normal dictionary due to the extra linked list that's created. Thus, if you are going to build a data structure involving a large number of `OrderedDict` instances (e.g., reading 100,000 lines of a CSV file into a list of `OrderedDict` instances), you would need to study the requirements of your application to determine if the benefits of using an `OrderedDict` outweighed the extra memory overhead.

1.8. Calculating with Dictionaries

Problem

You want to perform various calculations (e.g., minimum value, maximum value, sorting, etc.) on a dictionary of data.

Solution

Consider a dictionary that maps stock names to prices:

```python
prices = {
    'ACME': 45.23,
    'AAPL': 612.78,
    'IBM': 205.55,
    'HPQ': 37.20,
    'FB': 10.75
}
```

In order to perform useful calculations on the dictionary contents, it is often useful to invert the keys and values of the dictionary using zip(). For example, here is how to find the minimum and maximum price and stock name:

```python
min_price = min(zip(prices.values(), prices.keys()))
# min_price is (10.75, 'FB')

max_price = max(zip(prices.values(), prices.keys()))
# max_price is (612.78, 'AAPL')
```

Similarly, to rank the data, use zip() with sorted(), as in the following:

```python
prices_sorted = sorted(zip(prices.values(), prices.keys()))
# prices_sorted is [(10.75, 'FB'), (37.2, 'HPQ'),
#                   (45.23, 'ACME'), (205.55, 'IBM'),
#                   (612.78, 'AAPL')]
```

When doing these calculations, be aware that zip() creates an iterator that can only be consumed once. For example, the following code is an error:

```python
prices_and_names = zip(prices.values(), prices.keys())
print(min(prices_and_names))    # OK
print(max(prices_and_names))    # ValueError: max() arg is an empty sequence
```

Discussion

If you try to perform common data reductions on a dictionary, you'll find that they only process the keys, not the values. For example:

```python
min(prices)    # Returns 'AAPL'
max(prices)    # Returns 'IBM'
```

This is probably not what you want because you're actually trying to perform a calculation involving the dictionary values. You might try to fix this using the values() method of a dictionary:

```python
min(prices.values())    # Returns 10.75
max(prices.values())    # Returns 612.78
```

Unfortunately, this is often not exactly what you want either. For example, you may want to know information about the corresponding keys (e.g., which stock has the lowest price?).

You can get the key corresponding to the min or max value if you supply a key function to `min()` and `max()`. For example:

```
min(prices, key=lambda k: prices[k])   # Returns 'FB'
max(prices, key=lambda k: prices[k])   # Returns 'AAPL'
```

However, to get the minimum value, you'll need to perform an extra lookup step. For example:

```
min_value = prices[min(prices, key=lambda k: prices[k])]
```

The solution involving `zip()` solves the problem by "inverting" the dictionary into a sequence of `(value, key)` pairs. When performing comparisons on such tuples, the `value` element is compared first, followed by the key. This gives you exactly the behavior that you want and allows reductions and sorting to be easily performed on the dictionary contents using a single statement.

It should be noted that in calculations involving `(value, key)` pairs, the key will be used to determine the result in instances where multiple entries happen to have the same value. For instance, in calculations such as `min()` and `max()`, the entry with the smallest or largest key will be returned if there happen to be duplicate values. For example:

```
>>> prices = { 'AAA' : 45.23, 'ZZZ': 45.23 }
>>> min(zip(prices.values(), prices.keys()))
(45.23, 'AAA')
>>> max(zip(prices.values(), prices.keys()))
(45.23, 'ZZZ')
>>>
```

1.9. Finding Commonalities in Two Dictionaries

Problem

You have two dictionaries and want to find out what they might have in common (same keys, same values, etc.).

Solution

Consider two dictionaries:

```
a = {
    'x' : 1,
    'y' : 2,
    'z' : 3
}
```

```
b = {
    'w' : 10,
    'x' : 11,
    'y' : 2
}
```

To find out what the two dictionaries have in common, simply perform common set operations using the keys() or items() methods. For example:

```
# Find keys in common
a.keys() & b.keys()   # { 'x', 'y' }

# Find keys in a that are not in b
a.keys() - b.keys()   # { 'z' }

# Find (key,value) pairs in common
a.items() & b.items() # { ('y', 2) }
```

These kinds of operations can also be used to alter or filter dictionary contents. For example, suppose you want to make a new dictionary with selected keys removed. Here is some sample code using a dictionary comprehension:

```
# Make a new dictionary with certain keys removed
c = {key:a[key] for key in a.keys() - {'z', 'w'}}
# c is {'x': 1, 'y': 2}
```

Discussion

A dictionary is a mapping between a set of keys and values. The keys() method of a dictionary returns a keys-view object that exposes the keys. A little-known feature of keys views is that they also support common set operations such as unions, intersections, and differences. Thus, if you need to perform common set operations with dictionary keys, you can often just use the keys-view objects directly without first converting them into a set.

The items() method of a dictionary returns an items-view object consisting of (key, value) pairs. This object supports similar set operations and can be used to perform operations such as finding out which key-value pairs two dictionaries have in common.

Although similar, the values() method of a dictionary does not support the set operations described in this recipe. In part, this is due to the fact that unlike keys, the items contained in a values view aren't guaranteed to be unique. This alone makes certain set operations of questionable utility. However, if you must perform such calculations, they can be accomplished by simply converting the values to a set first.

1.10. Removing Duplicates from a Sequence while Maintaining Order

Problem

You want to eliminate the duplicate values in a sequence, but preserve the order of the remaining items.

Solution

If the values in the sequence are hashable, the problem can be easily solved using a set and a generator. For example:

```
def dedupe(items):
    seen = set()
    for item in items:
        if item not in seen:
            yield item
            seen.add(item)
```

Here is an example of how to use your function:

```
>>> a = [1, 5, 2, 1, 9, 1, 5, 10]
>>> list(dedupe(a))
[1, 5, 2, 9, 10]
>>>
```

This only works if the items in the sequence are hashable. If you are trying to eliminate duplicates in a sequence of unhashable types (such as dicts), you can make a slight change to this recipe, as follows:

```
def dedupe(items, key=None):
    seen = set()
    for item in items:
        val = item if key is None else key(item)
        if val not in seen:
            yield item
            seen.add(val)
```

Here, the purpose of the key argument is to specify a function that converts sequence items into a hashable type for the purposes of duplicate detection. Here's how it works:

```
>>> a = [ {'x':1, 'y':2}, {'x':1, 'y':3}, {'x':1, 'y':2}, {'x':2, 'y':4}]
>>> list(dedupe(a, key=lambda d: (d['x'],d['y'])))
[{'x': 1, 'y': 2}, {'x': 1, 'y': 3}, {'x': 2, 'y': 4}]
>>> list(dedupe(a, key=lambda d: d['x']))
[{'x': 1, 'y': 2}, {'x': 2, 'y': 4}]
>>>
```

This latter solution also works nicely if you want to eliminate duplicates based on the value of a single field or attribute or a larger data structure.

Discussion

If all you want to do is eliminate duplicates, it is often easy enough to make a set. For example:

```
>>> a
[1, 5, 2, 1, 9, 1, 5, 10]
>>> set(a)
{1, 2, 10, 5, 9}
>>>
```

However, this approach doesn't preserve any kind of ordering. So, the resulting data will be scrambled afterward. The solution shown avoids this.

The use of a generator function in this recipe reflects the fact that you might want the function to be extremely general purpose—not necessarily tied directly to list processing. For example, if you want to read a file, eliminating duplicate lines, you could simply do this:

```
with open(somefile,'r') as f:
    for line in dedupe(f):
        ...
```

The specification of a key function mimics similar functionality in built-in functions such as sorted(), min(), and max(). For instance, see Recipes 1.8 and 1.13.

1.11. Naming a Slice

Problem

Your program has become an unreadable mess of hardcoded slice indices and you want to clean it up.

Solution

Suppose you have some code that is pulling specific data fields out of a record string with fixed fields (e.g., from a flat file or similar format):

```
######     012345678901234567890123456789012345678901234567890123456789'
record = '....................100          .......513.25     ..........'
cost = int(record[20:32]) * float(record[40:48])
```

Instead of doing that, why not name the slices like this?

```
SHARES = slice(20,32)
PRICE  = slice(40,48)

cost = int(record[SHARES]) * float(record[PRICE])
```

In the latter version, you avoid having a lot of mysterious hardcoded indices, and what you're doing becomes much clearer.

Discussion

As a general rule, writing code with a lot of hardcoded index values leads to a readability and maintenance mess. For example, if you come back to the code a year later, you'll look at it and wonder what you were thinking when you wrote it. The solution shown is simply a way of more clearly stating what your code is actually doing.

In general, the built-in slice() creates a slice object that can be used anywhere a slice is allowed. For example:

```
>>> items = [0, 1, 2, 3, 4, 5, 6]
>>> a = slice(2, 4)
>>> items[2:4]
[2, 3]
>>> items[a]
[2, 3]
>>> items[a] = [10,11]
>>> items
[0, 1, 10, 11, 4, 5, 6]
>>> del items[a]
>>> items
[0, 1, 4, 5, 6]
```

If you have a slice instance s, you can get more information about it by looking at its s.start, s.stop, and s.step attributes, respectively. For example:

```
>>> a = slice(10, 50, 2)
>>> a.start
10
>>> a.stop
50
>>> a.step
2
>>>
```

In addition, you can map a slice onto a sequence of a specific size by using its indices(size) method. This returns a tuple (start, stop, step) where all values have been suitably limited to fit within bounds (as to avoid IndexError exceptions when indexing). For example:

```
>>> s = 'HelloWorld'
>>> a.indices(len(s))
(5, 10, 2)
>>> for i in range(*a.indices(len(s))):
...     print(s[i])
...
W
r
```

```
d
>>>
```

1.12. Determining the Most Frequently Occurring Items in a Sequence

Problem

You have a sequence of items, and you'd like to determine the most frequently occurring items in the sequence.

Solution

The `collections.Counter` class is designed for just such a problem. It even comes with a handy `most_common()` method that will give you the answer.

To illustrate, let's say you have a list of words and you want to find out which words occur most often. Here's how you would do it:

```python
words = [
    'look', 'into', 'my', 'eyes', 'look', 'into', 'my', 'eyes',
    'the', 'eyes', 'the', 'eyes', 'the', 'eyes', 'not', 'around', 'the',
    'eyes', "don't", 'look', 'around', 'the', 'eyes', 'look', 'into',
    'my', 'eyes', "you're", 'under'
]

from collections import Counter
word_counts = Counter(words)
top_three = word_counts.most_common(3)
print(top_three)
# Outputs [('eyes', 8), ('the', 5), ('look', 4)]
```

Discussion

As input, `Counter` objects can be fed any sequence of hashable input items. Under the covers, a `Counter` is a dictionary that maps the items to the number of occurrences. For example:

```python
>>> word_counts['not']
1
>>> word_counts['eyes']
8
>>>
```

If you want to increment the count manually, simply use addition:

```python
>>> morewords = ['why','are','you','not','looking','in','my','eyes']
>>> for word in morewords:
...     word_counts[word] += 1
```

```
...
>>> word_counts['eyes']
9
>>>
```

Or, alternatively, you could use the `update()` method:

```
>>> word_counts.update(morewords)
>>>
```

A little-known feature of `Counter` instances is that they can be easily combined using various mathematical operations. For example:

```
>>> a = Counter(words)
>>> b = Counter(morewords)
>>> a
Counter({'eyes': 8, 'the': 5, 'look': 4, 'into': 3, 'my': 3, 'around': 2,
        "you're": 1, "don't": 1, 'under': 1, 'not': 1})
>>> b
Counter({'eyes': 1, 'looking': 1, 'are': 1, 'in': 1, 'not': 1, 'you': 1,
        'my': 1, 'why': 1})

>>> # Combine counts
>>> c = a + b
>>> c
Counter({'eyes': 9, 'the': 5, 'look': 4, 'my': 4, 'into': 3, 'not': 2,
        'around': 2, "you're": 1, "don't": 1, 'in': 1, 'why': 1,
        'looking': 1, 'are': 1, 'under': 1, 'you': 1})

>>> # Subtract counts
>>> d = a - b
>>> d
Counter({'eyes': 7, 'the': 5, 'look': 4, 'into': 3, 'my': 2, 'around': 2,
        "you're": 1, "don't": 1, 'under': 1})
>>>
```

Needless to say, `Counter` objects are a tremendously useful tool for almost any kind of problem where you need to tabulate and count data. You should prefer this over manually written solutions involving dictionaries.

1.13. Sorting a List of Dictionaries by a Common Key

Problem

You have a list of dictionaries and you would like to sort the entries according to one or more of the dictionary values.

Solution

Sorting this type of structure is easy using the `operator` module's `itemgetter` function. Let's say you've queried a database table to get a listing of the members on your website, and you receive the following data structure in return:

```
rows = [
    {'fname': 'Brian', 'lname': 'Jones', 'uid': 1003},
    {'fname': 'David', 'lname': 'Beazley', 'uid': 1002},
    {'fname': 'John', 'lname': 'Cleese', 'uid': 1001},
    {'fname': 'Big', 'lname': 'Jones', 'uid': 1004}
]
```

It's fairly easy to output these rows ordered by any of the fields common to all of the dictionaries. For example:

```
from operator import itemgetter

rows_by_fname = sorted(rows, key=itemgetter('fname'))
rows_by_uid = sorted(rows, key=itemgetter('uid'))

print(rows_by_fname)
print(rows_by_uid)
```

The preceding code would output the following:

```
[{'fname': 'Big', 'uid': 1004, 'lname': 'Jones'},
 {'fname': 'Brian', 'uid': 1003, 'lname': 'Jones'},
 {'fname': 'David', 'uid': 1002, 'lname': 'Beazley'},
 {'fname': 'John', 'uid': 1001, 'lname': 'Cleese'}]

[{'fname': 'John', 'uid': 1001, 'lname': 'Cleese'},
 {'fname': 'David', 'uid': 1002, 'lname': 'Beazley'},
 {'fname': 'Brian', 'uid': 1003, 'lname': 'Jones'},
 {'fname': 'Big', 'uid': 1004, 'lname': 'Jones'}]
```

The `itemgetter()` function can also accept multiple keys. For example, this code

```
rows_by_lfname = sorted(rows, key=itemgetter('lname','fname'))
print(rows_by_lfname)
```

Produces output like this:

```
[{'fname': 'David', 'uid': 1002, 'lname': 'Beazley'},
 {'fname': 'John', 'uid': 1001, 'lname': 'Cleese'},
 {'fname': 'Big', 'uid': 1004, 'lname': 'Jones'},
 {'fname': 'Brian', 'uid': 1003, 'lname': 'Jones'}]
```

Discussion

In this example, `rows` is passed to the built-in `sorted()` function, which accepts a keyword argument key. This argument is expected to be a callable that accepts a single item from rows as input and returns a value that will be used as the basis for sorting. The itemgetter() function creates just such a callable.

The operator.itemgetter() function takes as arguments the lookup indices used to extract the desired values from the records in rows. It can be a dictionary key name, a numeric list element, or any value that can be fed to an object's __getitem__() method. If you give multiple indices to itemgetter(), the callable it produces will return a tuple with all of the elements in it, and sorted() will order the output according to the sorted order of the tuples. This can be useful if you want to simultaneously sort on multiple fields (such as last and first name, as shown in the example).

The functionality of itemgetter() is sometimes replaced by lambda expressions. For example:

```
rows_by_fname = sorted(rows, key=lambda r: r['fname'])
rows_by_lfname = sorted(rows, key=lambda r: (r['lname'],r['fname']))
```

This solution often works just fine. However, the solution involving itemgetter() typically runs a bit faster. Thus, you might prefer it if performance is a concern.

Last, but not least, don't forget that the technique shown in this recipe can be applied to functions such as min() and max(). For example:

```
>>> min(rows, key=itemgetter('uid'))
{'fname': 'John', 'lname': 'Cleese', 'uid': 1001}
>>> max(rows, key=itemgetter('uid'))
{'fname': 'Big', 'lname': 'Jones', 'uid': 1004}
>>>
```

1.14. Sorting Objects Without Native Comparison Support

Problem

You want to sort objects of the same class, but they don't natively support comparison operations.

Solution

The built-in sorted() function takes a key argument that can be passed a callable that will return some value in the object that sorted will use to compare the objects. For example, if you have a sequence of User instances in your application, and you want to sort them by their user_id attribute, you would supply a callable that takes a User instance as input and returns the user_id. For example:

```
>>> class User:
...     def __init__(self, user_id):
...         self.user_id = user_id
```

```
...        def __repr__(self):
...            return 'User({})'.format(self.user_id)
...
>>> users = [User(23), User(3), User(99)]
>>> users
[User(23), User(3), User(99)]
>>> sorted(users, key=lambda u: u.user_id)
[User(3), User(23), User(99)]
>>>
```

Instead of using `lambda`, an alternative approach is to use `operator.attrgetter()`:

```
>>> from operator import attrgetter
>>> sorted(users, key=attrgetter('user_id'))
[User(3), User(23), User(99)]
>>>
```

Discussion

The choice of whether or not to use `lambda` or `attrgetter()` may be one of personal preference. However, `attrgetter()` is often a tad bit faster and also has the added feature of allowing multiple fields to be extracted simultaneously. This is analogous to the use of `operator.itemgetter()` for dictionaries (see Recipe 1.13). For example, if User instances also had a `first_name` and `last_name` attribute, you could perform a sort like this:

```
by_name = sorted(users, key=attrgetter('last_name', 'first_name'))
```

It is also worth noting that the technique used in this recipe can be applied to functions such as `min()` and `max()`. For example:

```
>>> min(users, key=attrgetter('user_id')
User(3)
>>> max(users, key=attrgetter('user_id')
User(99)
>>>
```

1.15. Grouping Records Together Based on a Field

Problem

You have a sequence of dictionaries or instances and you want to iterate over the data in groups based on the value of a particular field, such as date.

Solution

The `itertools.groupby()` function is particularly useful for grouping data together like this. To illustrate, suppose you have the following list of dictionaries:

```
rows = [
    {'address': '5412 N CLARK', 'date': '07/01/2012'},
    {'address': '5148 N CLARK', 'date': '07/04/2012'},
    {'address': '5800 E 58TH', 'date': '07/02/2012'},
    {'address': '2122 N CLARK', 'date': '07/03/2012'},
    {'address': '5645 N RAVENSWOOD', 'date': '07/02/2012'},
    {'address': '1060 W ADDISON', 'date': '07/02/2012'},
    {'address': '4801 N BROADWAY', 'date': '07/01/2012'},
    {'address': '1039 W GRANVILLE', 'date': '07/04/2012'},
]
```

Now suppose you want to iterate over the data in chunks grouped by date. To do it, first sort by the desired field (in this case, date) and then use `itertools.groupby()`:

```
from operator import itemgetter
from itertools import groupby

# Sort by the desired field first
rows.sort(key=itemgetter('date'))

# Iterate in groups
for date, items in groupby(rows, key=itemgetter('date')):
    print(date)
    for i in items:
        print('    ', i)
```

This produces the following output:

```
07/01/2012
    {'date': '07/01/2012', 'address': '5412 N CLARK'}
    {'date': '07/01/2012', 'address': '4801 N BROADWAY'}
07/02/2012
    {'date': '07/02/2012', 'address': '5800 E 58TH'}
    {'date': '07/02/2012', 'address': '5645 N RAVENSWOOD'}
    {'date': '07/02/2012', 'address': '1060 W ADDISON'}
07/03/2012
    {'date': '07/03/2012', 'address': '2122 N CLARK'}
07/04/2012
    {'date': '07/04/2012', 'address': '5148 N CLARK'}
    {'date': '07/04/2012', 'address': '1039 W GRANVILLE'}
```

Discussion

The `groupby()` function works by scanning a sequence and finding sequential "runs" of identical values (or values returned by the given key function). On each iteration, it returns the value along with an iterator that produces all of the items in a group with the same value.

An important preliminary step is sorting the data according to the field of interest. Since `groupby()` only examines consecutive items, failing to sort first won't group the records as you want.

If your goal is to simply group the data together by dates into a large data structure that allows random access, you may have better luck using `defaultdict()` to build a multidict, as described in Recipe 1.6. For example:

```
from collections import defaultdict
rows_by_date = defaultdict(list)
for row in rows:
    rows_by_date[row['date']].append(row)
```

This allows the records for each date to be accessed easily like this:

```
>>> for r in rows_by_date['07/01/2012']:
...     print(r)
...
{'date': '07/01/2012', 'address': '5412 N CLARK'}
{'date': '07/01/2012', 'address': '4801 N BROADWAY'}
>>>
```

For this latter example, it's not necessary to sort the records first. Thus, if memory is no concern, it may be faster to do this than to first sort the records and iterate using `groupby()`.

1.16. Filtering Sequence Elements

Problem

You have data inside of a sequence, and need to extract values or reduce the sequence using some criteria.

Solution

The easiest way to filter sequence data is often to use a list comprehension. For example:

```
>>> mylist = [1, 4, -5, 10, -7, 2, 3, -1]
>>> [n for n in mylist if n > 0]
[1, 4, 10, 2, 3]
>>> [n for n in mylist if n < 0]
[-5, -7, -1]
>>>
```

One potential downside of using a list comprehension is that it might produce a large result if the original input is large. If this is a concern, you can use generator expressions to produce the filtered values iteratively. For example:

```
>>> pos = (n for n in mylist if n > 0)
>>> pos
<generator object <genexpr> at 0x1006a0eb0>
>>> for x in pos:
...     print(x)
...
```

```
1
4
10
2
3
>>>
```

Sometimes, the filtering criteria cannot be easily expressed in a list comprehension or generator expression. For example, suppose that the filtering process involves exception handling or some other complicated detail. For this, put the filtering code into its own function and use the built-in `filter()` function. For example:

```python
values = ['1', '2', '-3', '-', '4', 'N/A', '5']

def is_int(val):
    try:
        x = int(val)
        return True
    except ValueError:
        return False

ivals = list(filter(is_int, values))
print(ivals)
# Outputs ['1', '2', '-3', '4', '5']
```

`filter()` creates an iterator, so if you want to create a list of results, make sure you also use `list()` as shown.

Discussion

List comprehensions and generator expressions are often the easiest and most straightforward ways to filter simple data. They also have the added power to transform the data at the same time. For example:

```python
>>> mylist = [1, 4, -5, 10, -7, 2, 3, -1]
>>> import math
>>> [math.sqrt(n) for n in mylist if n > 0]
[1.0, 2.0, 3.1622776601683795, 1.4142135623730951, 1.7320508075688772]
>>>
```

One variation on filtering involves replacing the values that don't meet the criteria with a new value instead of discarding them. For example, perhaps instead of just finding positive values, you want to also clip bad values to fit within a specified range. This is often easily accomplished by moving the filter criterion into a conditional expression like this:

```python
>>> clip_neg = [n if n > 0 else 0 for n in mylist]
>>> clip_neg
[1, 4, 0, 10, 0, 2, 3, 0]
>>> clip_pos = [n if n < 0 else 0 for n in mylist]
>>> clip_pos
```

```
[0, 0, -5, 0, -7, 0, 0, -1]
>>>
```

Another notable filtering tool is `itertools.compress()`, which takes an iterable and an accompanying Boolean selector sequence as input. As output, it gives you all of the items in the iterable where the corresponding element in the selector is `True`. This can be useful if you're trying to apply the results of filtering one sequence to another related sequence. For example, suppose you have the following two columns of data:

```
addresses = [
    '5412 N CLARK',
    '5148 N CLARK',
    '5800 E 58TH',
    '2122 N CLARK'
    '5645 N RAVENSWOOD',
    '1060 W ADDISON',
    '4801 N BROADWAY',
    '1039 W GRANVILLE',
]

counts = [ 0, 3, 10, 4, 1, 7, 6, 1]
```

Now suppose you want to make a list of all addresses where the corresponding count value was greater than 5. Here's how you could do it:

```
>>> from itertools import compress
>>> more5 = [n > 5 for n in counts]
>>> more5
[False, False, True, False, False, True, True, False]
>>> list(compress(addresses, more5))
['5800 E 58TH', '4801 N BROADWAY', '1039 W GRANVILLE']
>>>
```

The key here is to first create a sequence of Booleans that indicates which elements satisfy the desired condition. The `compress()` function then picks out the items corresponding to `True` values.

Like `filter()`, `compress()` normally returns an iterator. Thus, you need to use `list()` to turn the results into a list if desired.

1.17. Extracting a Subset of a Dictionary

Problem

You want to make a dictionary that is a subset of another dictionary.

Solution

This is easily accomplished using a dictionary comprehension. For example:

```
prices = {
    'ACME': 45.23,
    'AAPL': 612.78,
    'IBM': 205.55,
    'HPQ': 37.20,
    'FB': 10.75
}

# Make a dictionary of all prices over 200
p1 = { key:value for key, value in prices.items() if value > 200 }

# Make a dictionary of tech stocks
tech_names = { 'AAPL', 'IBM', 'HPQ', 'MSFT' }
p2 = { key:value for key,value in prices.items() if key in tech_names }
```

Discussion

Much of what can be accomplished with a dictionary comprehension might also be done by creating a sequence of tuples and passing them to the dict() function. For example:

```
p1 = dict((key, value) for key, value in prices.items() if value > 200)
```

However, the dictionary comprehension solution is a bit clearer and actually runs quite a bit faster (over twice as fast when tested on the prices dictionary used in the example).

Sometimes there are multiple ways of accomplishing the same thing. For instance, the second example could be rewritten as:

```
# Make a dictionary of tech stocks
tech_names = { 'AAPL', 'IBM', 'HPQ', 'MSFT' }
p2 = { key:prices[key] for key in prices.keys() & tech_names }
```

However, a timing study reveals that this solution is almost 1.6 times slower than the first solution. If performance matters, it usually pays to spend a bit of time studying it. See Recipe 14.13 for specific information about timing and profiling.

1.18. Mapping Names to Sequence Elements

Problem

You have code that accesses list or tuple elements by position, but this makes the code somewhat difficult to read at times. You'd also like to be less dependent on position in the structure, by accessing the elements by name.

Solution

`collections.namedtuple()` provides these benefits, while adding minimal overhead over using a normal tuple object. `collections.namedtuple()` is actually a factory method that returns a subclass of the standard Python `tuple` type. You feed it a type name, and the fields it should have, and it returns a class that you can instantiate, passing in values for the fields you've defined, and so on. For example:

```
>>> from collections import namedtuple
>>> Subscriber = namedtuple('Subscriber', ['addr', 'joined'])
>>> sub = Subscriber('jonesy@example.com', '2012-10-19')
>>> sub
Subscriber(addr='jonesy@example.com', joined='2012-10-19')
>>> sub.addr
'jonesy@example.com'
>>> sub.joined
'2012-10-19'
>>>
```

Although an instance of a `namedtuple` looks like a normal class instance, it is interchangeable with a tuple and supports all of the usual tuple operations such as indexing and unpacking. For example:

```
>>> len(sub)
2
>>> addr, joined = sub
>>> addr
'jonesy@example.com'
>>> joined
'2012-10-19'
>>>
```

A major use case for named tuples is decoupling your code from the position of the elements it manipulates. So, if you get back a large list of tuples from a database call, then manipulate them by accessing the positional elements, your code could break if, say, you added a new column to your table. Not so if you first cast the returned tuples to namedtuples.

To illustrate, here is some code using ordinary tuples:

```
def compute_cost(records):
    total = 0.0
    for rec in records:
        total += rec[1] * rec[2]
    return total
```

References to positional elements often make the code a bit less expressive and more dependent on the structure of the records. Here is a version that uses a `namedtuple`:

```
from collections import namedtuple

Stock = namedtuple('Stock', ['name', 'shares', 'price'])
```

```
def compute_cost(records):
    total = 0.0
    for rec in records:
        s = Stock(*rec)
        total += s.shares * s.price
    return total
```

Naturally, you can avoid the explicit conversion to the Stock namedtuple if the records sequence in the example already contained such instances.

Discussion

One possible use of a namedtuple is as a replacement for a dictionary, which requires more space to store. Thus, if you are building large data structures involving dictionaries, use of a namedtuple will be more efficient. However, be aware that unlike a dictionary, a namedtuple is immutable. For example:

```
>>> s = Stock('ACME', 100, 123.45)
>>> s
Stock(name='ACME', shares=100, price=123.45)
>>> s.shares = 75
Traceback (most recent call last):
  File "<stdin>", line 1, in <module>
AttributeError: can't set attribute
>>>
```

If you need to change any of the attributes, it can be done using the _replace() method of a namedtuple instance, which makes an entirely new namedtuple with specified values replaced. For example:

```
>>> s = s._replace(shares=75)
>>> s
Stock(name='ACME', shares=75, price=123.45)
>>>
```

A subtle use of the _replace() method is that it can be a convenient way to populate named tuples that have optional or missing fields. To do this, you make a prototype tuple containing the default values and then use _replace() to create new instances with values replaced. For example:

```
from collections import namedtuple

Stock = namedtuple('Stock', ['name', 'shares', 'price', 'date', 'time'])

# Create a prototype instance
stock_prototype = Stock('', 0, 0.0, None, None)

# Function to convert a dictionary to a Stock
def dict_to_stock(s):
    return stock_prototype._replace(**s)
```

Here is an example of how this code would work:

```
>>> a = {'name': 'ACME', 'shares': 100, 'price': 123.45}
>>> dict_to_stock(a)
Stock(name='ACME', shares=100, price=123.45, date=None, time=None)
>>> b = {'name': 'ACME', 'shares': 100, 'price': 123.45, 'date': '12/17/2012'}
>>> dict_to_stock(b)
Stock(name='ACME', shares=100, price=123.45, date='12/17/2012', time=None)
>>>
```

Last, but not least, it should be noted that if your goal is to define an efficient data structure where you will be changing various instance attributes, using namedtuple is not your best choice. Instead, consider defining a class using __slots__ instead (see Recipe 8.4).

1.19. Transforming and Reducing Data at the Same Time

Problem

You need to execute a reduction function (e.g., sum(), min(), max()), but first need to transform or filter the data.

Solution

A very elegant way to combine a data reduction and a transformation is to use a generator-expression argument. For example, if you want to calculate the sum of squares, do the following:

```
nums = [1, 2, 3, 4, 5]
s = sum(x * x for x in nums)
```

Here are a few other examples:

```
# Determine if any .py files exist in a directory
import os
files = os.listdir('dirname')
if any(name.endswith('.py') for name in files):
    print('There be python!')
else:
    print('Sorry, no python.')

# Output a tuple as CSV
s = ('ACME', 50, 123.45)
print(','.join(str(x) for x in s))

# Data reduction across fields of a data structure
portfolio = [
    {'name':'GOOG', 'shares': 50},
    {'name':'YHOO', 'shares': 75},
    {'name':'AOL', 'shares': 20},
```

```
    {'name':'SCOX', 'shares': 65}
]
min_shares = min(s['shares'] for s in portfolio)
```

Discussion

The solution shows a subtle syntactic aspect of generator expressions when supplied as the single argument to a function (i.e., you don't need repeated parentheses). For example, these statements are the same:

```
s = sum((x * x for x in nums))    # Pass generator-expr as argument
s = sum(x * x for x in nums)      # More elegant syntax
```

Using a generator argument is often a more efficient and elegant approach than first creating a temporary list. For example, if you didn't use a generator expression, you might consider this alternative implementation:

```
nums = [1, 2, 3, 4, 5]
s = sum([x * x for x in nums])
```

This works, but it introduces an extra step and creates an extra list. For such a small list, it might not matter, but if nums was huge, you would end up creating a large temporary data structure to only be used once and discarded. The generator solution transforms the data iteratively and is therefore much more memory-efficient.

Certain reduction functions such as min() and max() accept a key argument that might be useful in situations where you might be inclined to use a generator. For example, in the portfolio example, you might consider this alternative:

```
# Original: Returns 20
min_shares = min(s['shares'] for s in portfolio)

# Alternative: Returns {'name': 'AOL', 'shares': 20}
min_shares = min(portfolio, key=lambda s: s['shares'])
```

1.20. Combining Multiple Mappings into a Single Mapping

Problem

You have multiple dictionaries or mappings that you want to logically combine into a single mapping to perform certain operations, such as looking up values or checking for the existence of keys.

Solution

Suppose you have two dictionaries:

```
a = {'x': 1, 'z': 3 }
b = {'y': 2, 'z': 4 }
```

Now suppose you want to perform lookups where you have to check both dictionaries (e.g., first checking in a and then in b if not found). An easy way to do this is to use the ChainMap class from the collections module. For example:

```
from collections import ChainMap
c = ChainMap(a,b)
print(c['x'])       # Outputs 1  (from a)
print(c['y'])       # Outputs 2  (from b)
print(c['z'])       # Outputs 3  (from a)
```

Discussion

A ChainMap takes multiple mappings and makes them logically appear as one. However, the mappings are not literally merged together. Instead, a ChainMap simply keeps a list of the underlying mappings and redefines common dictionary operations to scan the list. Most operations will work. For example:

```
>>> len(c)
3
>>> list(c.keys())
['x', 'y', 'z']
>>> list(c.values())
[1, 2, 3]
>>>
```

If there are duplicate keys, the values from the first mapping get used. Thus, the entry c['z'] in the example would always refer to the value in dictionary a, not the value in dictionary b.

Operations that mutate the mapping always affect the first mapping listed. For example:

```
>>> c['z'] = 10
>>> c['w'] = 40
>>> del c['x']
>>> a
{'w': 40, 'z': 10}
>>> del c['y']
Traceback (most recent call last):
...
KeyError: "Key not found in the first mapping: 'y'"
>>>
```

A ChainMap is particularly useful when working with scoped values such as variables in a programming language (i.e., globals, locals, etc.). In fact, there are methods that make this easy:

```
>>> values = ChainMap()
>>> values['x'] = 1
>>> # Add a new mapping
>>> values = values.new_child()
>>> values['x'] = 2
>>> # Add a new mapping
>>> values = values.new_child()
>>> values['x'] = 3
>>> values
ChainMap({'x': 3}, {'x': 2}, {'x': 1})
>>> values['x']
3
>>> # Discard last mapping
>>> values = values.parents
>>> values['x']
2
>>> # Discard last mapping
>>> values = values.parents
>>> values['x']
1
>>> values
ChainMap({'x': 1})
>>>
```

As an alternative to ChainMap, you might consider merging dictionaries together using the update() method. For example:

```
>>> a = {'x': 1, 'z': 3 }
>>> b = {'y': 2, 'z': 4 }
>>> merged = dict(b)
>>> merged.update(a)
>>> merged['x']
1
>>> merged['y']
2
>>> merged['z']
3
>>>
```

This works, but it requires you to make a completely separate dictionary object (or destructively alter one of the existing dictionaries). Also, if any of the original dictionaries mutate, the changes don't get reflected in the merged dictionary. For example:

```
>>> a['x'] = 13
>>> merged['x']
1
```

A ChainMap uses the original dictionaries, so it doesn't have this behavior. For example:

```
>>> a = {'x': 1, 'z': 3 }
>>> b = {'y': 2, 'z': 4 }
>>> merged = ChainMap(a, b)
>>> merged['x']
1
>>> a['x'] = 42
>>> merged['x']    # Notice change to merged dicts
42
>>>
```

## CHAPTER 2

Strings and Text

Almost every useful program involves some kind of text processing, whether it is parsing data or generating output. This chapter focuses on common problems involving text manipulation, such as pulling apart strings, searching, substitution, lexing, and parsing. Many of these tasks can be easily solved using built-in methods of strings. However, more complicated operations might require the use of regular expressions or the creation of a full-fledged parser. All of these topics are covered. In addition, a few tricky aspects of working with Unicode are addressed.

2.1. Splitting Strings on Any of Multiple Delimiters

Problem

You need to split a string into fields, but the delimiters (and spacing around them) aren't consistent throughout the string.

Solution

The `split()` method of string objects is really meant for very simple cases, and does not allow for multiple delimiters or account for possible whitespace around the delimiters. In cases when you need a bit more flexibility, use the `re.split()` method:

```
>>> line = 'asdf fjdk; afed, fjek,asdf,    foo'
>>> import re
>>> re.split(r'[;,\s]\s*', line)
['asdf', 'fjdk', 'afed', 'fjek', 'asdf', 'foo']
```

Discussion

The `re.split()` function is useful because you can specify multiple patterns for the separator. For example, as shown in the solution, the separator is either a comma (,), semicolon (;), or whitespace followed by any amount of extra whitespace. Whenever that pattern is found, the entire match becomes the delimiter between whatever fields lie on either side of the match. The result is a list of fields, just as with `str.split()`.

When using `re.split()`, you need to be a bit careful should the regular expression pattern involve a capture group enclosed in parentheses. If capture groups are used, then the matched text is also included in the result. For example, watch what happens here:

```
>>> fields = re.split(r'(;|,|\s)\s*', line)
>>> fields
['asdf', ' ', 'fjdk', ';', 'afed', ',', 'fjek', ',', 'asdf', ',', 'foo']
>>>
```

Getting the split characters might be useful in certain contexts. For example, maybe you need the split characters later on to reform an output string:

```
>>> values = fields[::2]
>>> delimiters = fields[1::2] + ['']
>>> values
['asdf', 'fjdk', 'afed', 'fjek', 'asdf', 'foo']
>>> delimiters
[' ', ';', ',', ',', ',', '']

>>> # Reform the line using the same delimiters
>>> ''.join(v+d for v,d in zip(values, delimiters))
'asdf fjdk;afed,fjek,asdf,foo'
>>>
```

If you don't want the separator characters in the result, but still need to use parentheses to group parts of the regular expression pattern, make sure you use a noncapture group, specified as `(?:...)`. For example:

```
>>> re.split(r'(?:,|;|\s)\s*', line)
['asdf', 'fjdk', 'afed', 'fjek', 'asdf', 'foo']
>>>
```

2.2. Matching Text at the Start or End of a String

Problem

You need to check the start or end of a string for specific text patterns, such as filename extensions, URL schemes, and so on.

Solution

A simple way to check the beginning or end of a string is to use the `str.starts with()` or `str.endswith()` methods. For example:

```
>>> filename = 'spam.txt'
>>> filename.endswith('.txt')
True
>>> filename.startswith('file:')
False
>>> url = 'http://www.python.org'
>>> url.startswith('http:')
True
>>>
```

If you need to check against multiple choices, simply provide a tuple of possibilities to
startswith() or endswith():

```
>>> import os
>>> filenames = os.listdir('.')
>>> filenames
[ 'Makefile', 'foo.c', 'bar.py', 'spam.c', 'spam.h' ]
>>> [name for name in filenames if name.endswith(('.c', '.h')) ]
['foo.c', 'spam.c', 'spam.h'
>>> any(name.endswith('.py') for name in filenames)
True
>>>
```

Here is another example:

```
from urllib.request import urlopen

def read_data(name):
    if name.startswith(('http:', 'https:', 'ftp:')):
        return urlopen(name).read()
    else:
        with open(name) as f:
            return f.read()
```

Oddly, this is one part of Python where a tuple is actually required as input. If you happen
to have the choices specified in a list or set, just make sure you convert them using
tuple() first. For example:

```
>>> choices = ['http:', 'ftp:']
>>> url = 'http://www.python.org'
>>> url.startswith(choices)
Traceback (most recent call last):
  File "<stdin>", line 1, in <module>
TypeError: startswith first arg must be str or a tuple of str, not list
>>> url.startswith(tuple(choices))
True
>>>
```

Discussion

The `startswith()` and `endswith()` methods provide a very convenient way to perform basic prefix and suffix checking. Similar operations can be performed with slices, but are far less elegant. For example:

```
>>> filename = 'spam.txt'
>>> filename[-4:] == '.txt'
True
>>> url = 'http://www.python.org'
>>> url[:5] == 'http:' or url[:6] == 'https:' or url[:4] == 'ftp:'
True
>>>
```

You might also be inclined to use regular expressions as an alternative. For example:

```
>>> import re
>>> url = 'http://www.python.org'
>>> re.match('http:|https:|ftp:', url)
<_sre.SRE_Match object at 0x101253098>
>>>
```

This works, but is often overkill for simple matching. Using this recipe is simpler and runs faster.

Last, but not least, the `startswith()` and `endswith()` methods look nice when combined with other operations, such as common data reductions. For example, this statement that checks a directory for the presence of certain kinds of files:

```
if any(name.endswith(('.c', '.h')) for name in listdir(dirname)):
    ...
```

2.3. Matching Strings Using Shell Wildcard Patterns

Problem

You want to match text using the same wildcard patterns as are commonly used when working in Unix shells (e.g., `*.py`, `Dat[0-9]*.csv`, etc.).

Solution

The `fnmatch` module provides two functions—`fnmatch()` and `fnmatchcase()`—that can be used to perform such matching. The usage is simple:

```
>>> from fnmatch import fnmatch, fnmatchcase
>>> fnmatch('foo.txt', '*.txt')
True
>>> fnmatch('foo.txt', '?oo.txt')
True
>>> fnmatch('Dat45.csv', 'Dat[0-9]*')
```

```
True
>>> names = ['Dat1.csv', 'Dat2.csv', 'config.ini', 'foo.py']
>>> [name for name in names if fnmatch(name, 'Dat*.csv')]
['Dat1.csv', 'Dat2.csv']
>>>
```

Normally, fnmatch() matches patterns using the same case-sensitivity rules as the system's underlying filesystem (which varies based on operating system). For example:

```
>>> # On OS X (Mac)
>>> fnmatch('foo.txt', '*.TXT')
False

>>> # On Windows
>>> fnmatch('foo.txt', '*.TXT')
True
>>>
```

If this distinction matters, use fnmatchcase() instead. It matches exactly based on the lower- and uppercase conventions that you supply:

```
>>> fnmatchcase('foo.txt', '*.TXT')
False
>>>
```

An often overlooked feature of these functions is their potential use with data processing of nonfilename strings. For example, suppose you have a list of street addresses like this:

```
addresses = [
    '5412 N CLARK ST',
    '1060 W ADDISON ST',
    '1039 W GRANVILLE AVE',
    '2122 N CLARK ST',
    '4802 N BROADWAY',
]
```

You could write list comprehensions like this:

```
>>> from fnmatch import fnmatchcase
>>> [addr for addr in addresses if fnmatchcase(addr, '* ST')]
['5412 N CLARK ST', '1060 W ADDISON ST', '2122 N CLARK ST']
>>> [addr for addr in addresses if fnmatchcase(addr, '54[0-9][0-9] *CLARK*')]
['5412 N CLARK ST']
>>>
```

Discussion

The matching performed by fnmatch sits somewhere between the functionality of simple string methods and the full power of regular expressions. If you're just trying to provide a simple mechanism for allowing wildcards in data processing operations, it's often a reasonable solution.

If you're actually trying to write code that matches filenames, use the glob module instead. See Recipe 5.13.

2.4. Matching and Searching for Text Patterns

Problem

You want to match or search text for a specific pattern.

Solution

If the text you're trying to match is a simple literal, you can often just use the basic string methods, such as str.find(), str.endswith(), str.startswith(), or similar. For example:

```
>>> text = 'yeah, but no, but yeah, but no, but yeah'

>>> # Exact match
>>> text == 'yeah'
False

>>> # Match at start or end
>>> text.startswith('yeah')
True
>>> text.endswith('no')
False

>>> # Search for the location of the first occurrence
>>> text.find('no')
10
>>>
```

For more complicated matching, use regular expressions and the re module. To illustrate the basic mechanics of using regular expressions, suppose you want to match dates specified as digits, such as "11/27/2012." Here is a sample of how you would do it:

```
>>> text1 = '11/27/2012'
>>> text2 = 'Nov 27, 2012'
>>>
>>> import re
>>> # Simple matching: \d+ means match one or more digits
>>> if re.match(r'\d+/\d+/\d+', text1):
...     print('yes')
... else:
...     print('no')
...
yes
>>> if re.match(r'\d+/\d+/\d+', text2):
...     print('yes')
... else:
```

```
...        print('no')
...
no
>>>
```

If you're going to perform a lot of matches using the same pattern, it usually pays to precompile the regular expression pattern into a pattern object first. For example:

```
>>> datepat = re.compile(r'\d+/\d+/\d+')
>>> if datepat.match(text1):
...        print('yes')
... else:
...        print('no')
...
yes
>>> if datepat.match(text2):
...        print('yes')
... else:
...        print('no')
...
no
>>>
```

match() always tries to find the match at the start of a string. If you want to search text for all occurrences of a pattern, use the findall() method instead. For example:

```
>>> text = 'Today is 11/27/2012. PyCon starts 3/13/2013.'
>>> datepat.findall(text)
['11/27/2012', '3/13/2013']
>>>
```

When defining regular expressions, it is common to introduce capture groups by enclosing parts of the pattern in parentheses. For example:

```
>>> datepat = re.compile(r'(\d+)/(\d+)/(\d+)')
>>>
```

Capture groups often simplify subsequent processing of the matched text because the contents of each group can be extracted individually. For example:

```
>>> m = datepat.match('11/27/2012')
>>> m
<_sre.SRE_Match object at 0x1005d2750>

>>> # Extract the contents of each group
>>> m.group(0)
'11/27/2012'
>>> m.group(1)
'11'
>>> m.group(2)
'27'
>>> m.group(3)
'2012'
>>> m.groups()
```

```
('11', '27', '2012')
>>> month, day, year = m.groups()
>>>

>>> # Find all matches (notice splitting into tuples)
>>> text
'Today is 11/27/2012. PyCon starts 3/13/2013.'
>>> datepat.findall(text)
[('11', '27', '2012'), ('3', '13', '2013')]
>>> for month, day, year in datepat.findall(text):
...     print('{}-{}-{}'.format(year, month, day))
...
2012-11-27
2013-3-13
>>>
```

The findall() method searches the text and finds all matches, returning them as a list. If you want to find matches iteratively, use the finditer() method instead. For example:

```
>>> for m in datepat.finditer(text):
...     print(m.groups())
...
('11', '27', '2012')
('3', '13', '2013')
>>>
```

Discussion

A basic tutorial on the theory of regular expressions is beyond the scope of this book. However, this recipe illustrates the absolute basics of using the re module to match and search for text. The essential functionality is first compiling a pattern using re.compile() and then using methods such as match(), findall(), or finditer().

When specifying patterns, it is relatively common to use raw strings such as r'(\d+)/(\d+)/(\d+)'. Such strings leave the backslash character uninterpreted, which can be useful in the context of regular expressions. Otherwise, you need to use double backslashes such as '(\\d+)/(\\d+)/(\\d+)'.

Be aware that the match() method only checks the beginning of a string. It's possible that it will match things you aren't expecting. For example:

```
>>> m = datepat.match('11/27/2012abcdef')
>>> m
<_sre.SRE_Match object at 0x1005d27e8>
>>> m.group()
'11/27/2012'
>>>
```

If you want an exact match, make sure the pattern includes the end-marker ($), as in the following:

```
>>> datepat = re.compile(r'(\d+)/(\d+)/(\d+)$')
>>> datepat.match('11/27/2012abcdef')
>>> datepat.match('11/27/2012')
<_sre.SRE_Match object at 0x1005d2750>
>>>
```

Last, if you're just doing a simple text matching/searching operation, you can often skip the compilation step and use module-level functions in the re module instead. For example:

```
>>> re.findall(r'(\d+)/(\d+)/(\d+)', text)
[('11', '27', '2012'), ('3', '13', '2013')]
>>>
```

Be aware, though, that if you're going to perform a lot of matching or searching, it usually pays to compile the pattern first and use it over and over again. The module-level functions keep a cache of recently compiled patterns, so there isn't a huge performance hit, but you'll save a few lookups and extra processing by using your own compiled pattern.

2.5. Searching and Replacing Text

Problem

You want to search for and replace a text pattern in a string.

Solution

For simple literal patterns, use the str.replace() method. For example:

```
>>> text = 'yeah, but no, but yeah, but no, but yeah'

>>> text.replace('yeah', 'yep')
'yep, but no, but yep, but no, but yep'
>>>
```

For more complicated patterns, use the sub() functions/methods in the re module. To illustrate, suppose you want to rewrite dates of the form "11/27/2012" as "2012-11-27." Here is a sample of how to do it:

```
>>> text = 'Today is 11/27/2012. PyCon starts 3/13/2013.'
>>> import re
>>> re.sub(r'(\d+)/(\d+)/(\d+)', r'\3-\1-\2', text)
'Today is 2012-11-27. PyCon starts 2013-3-13.'
>>>
```

The first argument to sub() is the pattern to match and the second argument is the replacement pattern. Backslashed digits such as \3 refer to capture group numbers in the pattern.

If you're going to perform repeated substitutions of the same pattern, consider compiling it first for better performance. For example:

```
>>> import re
>>> datepat = re.compile(r'(\d+)/(\d+)/(\d+)')
>>> datepat.sub(r'\3-\1-\2', text)
'Today is 2012-11-27. PyCon starts 2013-3-13.'
>>>
```

For more complicated substitutions, it's possible to specify a substitution callback function instead. For example:

```
>>> from calendar import month_abbr
>>> def change_date(m):
...     mon_name = month_abbr[int(m.group(1))]
...     return '{} {} {}'.format(m.group(2), mon_name, m.group(3))
...
>>> datepat.sub(change_date, text)
'Today is 27 Nov 2012. PyCon starts 13 Mar 2013.'
>>>
```

As input, the argument to the substitution callback is a match object, as returned by match() or find(). Use the .group() method to extract specific parts of the match. The function should return the replacement text.

If you want to know how many substitutions were made in addition to getting the replacement text, use re.subn() instead. For example:

```
>>> newtext, n = datepat.subn(r'\3-\1-\2', text)
>>> newtext
'Today is 2012-11-27. PyCon starts 2013-3-13.'
>>> n
2
>>>
```

Discussion

There isn't much more to regular expression search and replace than the sub() method shown. The trickiest part is specifying the regular expression pattern—something that's best left as an exercise to the reader.

2.6. Searching and Replacing Case-Insensitive Text

Problem

You need to search for and possibly replace text in a case-insensitive manner.

Solution

To perform case-insensitive text operations, you need to use the re module and supply the re.IGNORECASE flag to various operations. For example:

```
>>> text = 'UPPER PYTHON, lower python, Mixed Python'
>>> re.findall('python', text, flags=re.IGNORECASE)
['PYTHON', 'python', 'Python']
>>> re.sub('python', 'snake', text, flags=re.IGNORECASE)
'UPPER snake, lower snake, Mixed snake'
>>>
```

The last example reveals a limitation that replacing text won't match the case of the matched text. If you need to fix this, you might have to use a support function, as in the following:

```
def matchcase(word):
    def replace(m):
        text = m.group()
        if text.isupper():
            return word.upper()
        elif text.islower():
            return word.lower()
        elif text[0].isupper():
            return word.capitalize()
        else:
            return word
    return replace
```

Here is an example of using this last function:

```
>>> re.sub('python', matchcase('snake'), text, flags=re.IGNORECASE)
'UPPER SNAKE, lower snake, Mixed Snake'
>>>
```

Discussion

For simple cases, simply providing the re.IGNORECASE is enough to perform case-insensitive matching. However, be aware that this may not be enough for certain kinds of Unicode matching involving case folding. See Recipe 2.10 for more details.

2.7. Specifying a Regular Expression for the Shortest Match

Problem

You're trying to match a text pattern using regular expressions, but it is identifying the longest possible matches of a pattern. Instead, you would like to change it to find the shortest possible match.

Solution

This problem often arises in patterns that try to match text enclosed inside a pair of starting and ending delimiters (e.g., a quoted string). To illustrate, consider this example:

```
>>> str_pat = re.compile(r'\"(.*)\"')
>>> text1 = 'Computer says "no."'
>>> str_pat.findall(text1)
['no.']
>>> text2 = 'Computer says "no." Phone says "yes."'
>>> str_pat.findall(text2)
['no." Phone says "yes.']
>>>
```

In this example, the pattern r'\"(.*)\"' is attempting to match text enclosed inside quotes. However, the * operator in a regular expression is greedy, so matching is based on finding the longest possible match. Thus, in the second example involving text2, it incorrectly matches the two quoted strings.

To fix this, add the ? modifier after the * operator in the pattern, like this:

```
>>> str_pat = re.compile(r'\"(.*?)\"')
>>> str_pat.findall(text2)
['no.', 'yes.']
>>>
```

This makes the matching nongreedy, and produces the shortest match instead.

Discussion

This recipe addresses one of the more common problems encountered when writing regular expressions involving the dot (.) character. In a pattern, the dot matches any character except a newline. However, if you bracket the dot with starting and ending text (such as a quote), matching will try to find the longest possible match to the pattern. This causes multiple occurrences of the starting or ending text to be skipped altogether and included in the results of the longer match. Adding the ? right after operators such as * or + forces the matching algorithm to look for the shortest possible match instead.

2.8. Writing a Regular Expression for Multiline Patterns

Problem

You're trying to match a block of text using a regular expression, but you need the match to span multiple lines.

Solution

This problem typically arises in patterns that use the dot (.) to match any character but forget to account for the fact that it doesn't match newlines. For example, suppose you are trying to match C-style comments:

```
>>> comment = re.compile(r'/\*(.*?)\*/')
>>> text1 = '/* this is a comment */'
>>> text2 = '''/* this is a
...             multiline comment */
... '''
>>>
>>> comment.findall(text1)
[' this is a comment ']
>>> comment.findall(text2)
[]
>>>
```

To fix the problem, you can add support for newlines. For example:

```
>>> comment = re.compile(r'/\*((?:.|\n)*?)\*/')
>>> comment.findall(text2)
[' this is a\n             multiline comment ']
>>>
```

In this pattern, (?:.|\n) specifies a noncapture group (i.e., it defines a group for the purposes of matching, but that group is not captured separately or numbered).

Discussion

The re.compile() function accepts a flag, re.DOTALL, which is useful here. It makes the . in a regular expression match all characters, including newlines. For example:

```
>>> comment = re.compile(r'/\*(.*?)\*/', re.DOTALL)
>>> comment.findall(text2)
[' this is a\n             multiline comment ']
```

Using the re.DOTALL flag works fine for simple cases, but might be problematic if you're working with extremely complicated patterns or a mix of separate regular expressions that have been combined together for the purpose of tokenizing, as described in Recipe 2.18. If given a choice, it's usually better to define your regular expression pattern so that it works correctly without the need for extra flags.

2.9. Normalizing Unicode Text to a Standard Representation

Problem

You're working with Unicode strings, but need to make sure that all of the strings have the same underlying representation.

Solution

In Unicode, certain characters can be represented by more than one valid sequence of code points. To illustrate, consider the following example:

```
>>> s1 = 'Spicy Jalape\u00f1o'
>>> s2 = 'Spicy Jalapen\u0303o'
>>> s1
'Spicy Jalapeño'
>>> s2
'Spicy Jalapeño'
>>> s1 == s2
False
>>> len(s1)
14
>>> len(s2)
15
>>>
```

Here the text "Spicy Jalapeño" has been presented in two forms. The first uses the fully composed "ñ" character (U+00F1). The second uses the Latin letter "n" followed by a "~" combining character (U+0303).

Having multiple representations is a problem for programs that compare strings. In order to fix this, you should first normalize the text into a standard representation using the `unicodedata` module:

```
>>> import unicodedata
>>> t1 = unicodedata.normalize('NFC', s1)
>>> t2 = unicodedata.normalize('NFC', s2)
>>> t1 == t2
True
>>> print(ascii(t1))
'Spicy Jalape\xf1o'

>>> t3 = unicodedata.normalize('NFD', s1)
>>> t4 = unicodedata.normalize('NFD', s2)
>>> t3 == t4
True
>>> print(ascii(t3))
'Spicy Jalapen\u0303o'
>>>
```

The first argument to `normalize()` specifies how you want the string normalized. NFC means that characters should be fully composed (i.e., use a single code point if possible). NFD means that characters should be fully decomposed with the use of combining characters.

Python also supports the normalization forms NFKC and NFKD, which add extra compatibility features for dealing with certain kinds of characters. For example:

```
>>> s = '\ufb01'   # A single character
>>> s
'fi'
>>> unicodedata.normalize('NFD', s)
'fi'

# Notice how the combined letters are broken apart here
>>> unicodedata.normalize('NFKD', s)
'fi'
>>> unicodedata.normalize('NFKC', s)
'fi'
>>>
```

Discussion

Normalization is an important part of any code that needs to ensure that it processes Unicode text in a sane and consistent way. This is especially true when processing strings received as part of user input where you have little control of the encoding.

Normalization can also be an important part of sanitizing and filtering text. For example, suppose you want to remove all diacritical marks from some text (possibly for the purposes of searching or matching):

```
>>> t1 = unicodedata.normalize('NFD', s1)
>>> ''.join(c for c in t1 if not unicodedata.combining(c))
'Spicy Jalapeno'
>>>
```

This last example shows another important aspect of the `unicodedata` module—namely, utility functions for testing characters against character classes. The `combining()` function tests a character to see if it is a combining character. There are other functions in the module for finding character categories, testing digits, and so forth.

Unicode is obviously a large topic. For more detailed reference information about normalization, visit Unicode's page on the subject (*http://www.unicode.org/faq/normaliza tion.html*). Ned Batchelder has also given an excellent presentation on Python Unicode handling issues at his website (*http://nedbatchelder.com/text/unipain.html*).

2.10. Working with Unicode Characters in Regular Expressions

Problem

You are using regular expressions to process text, but are concerned about the handling of Unicode characters.

Solution

By default, the re module is already programmed with rudimentary knowledge of certain Unicode character classes. For example, \d already matches any unicode digit character:

```
>>> import re
>>> num = re.compile('\d+')
>>> # ASCII digits
>>> num.match('123')
<_sre.SRE_Match object at 0x1007d9ed0>

>>> # Arabic digits
>>> num.match('\u0661\u0662\u0663')
<_sre.SRE_Match object at 0x101234030>
>>>
```

If you need to include specific Unicode characters in patterns, you can use the usual escape sequence for Unicode characters (e.g., \uFFFF or \UFFFFFFFF). For example, here is a regex that matches all characters in a few different Arabic code pages:

```
>>> arabic = re.compile('[\u0600-\u06ff\u0750-\u077f\u08a0-\u08ff]+')
>>>
```

When performing matching and searching operations, it's a good idea to normalize and possibly sanitize all text to a standard form first (see Recipe 2.9). However, it's also important to be aware of special cases. For example, consider the behavior of case-insensitive matching combined with case folding:

```
>>> pat = re.compile('stra\u00dfe', re.IGNORECASE)
>>> s = 'straße'
>>> pat.match(s)              # Matches
<_sre.SRE_Match object at 0x10069d370>
>>> pat.match(s.upper())      # Doesn't match
>>> s.upper()                 # Case folds
'STRASSE'
>>>
```

Discussion

Mixing Unicode and regular expressions is often a good way to make your head explode. If you're going to do it seriously, you should consider installing the third-party `regex` library (*http://pypi.python.org/pypi/regex*), which provides full support for Unicode case folding, as well as a variety of other interesting features, including approximate matching.

2.11. Stripping Unwanted Characters from Strings

Problem

You want to strip unwanted characters, such as whitespace, from the beginning, end, or middle of a text string.

Solution

The `strip()` method can be used to strip characters from the beginning or end of a string. `lstrip()` and `rstrip()` perform stripping from the left or right side, respectively. By default, these methods strip whitespace, but other characters can be given. For example:

```
>>> # Whitespace stripping
>>> s = '   hello world   \n'
>>> s.strip()
'hello world'
>>> s.lstrip()
'hello world   \n'
>>> s.rstrip()
'   hello world'
>>>

>>> # Character stripping
>>> t = '-----hello====='
>>> t.lstrip('-')
'hello====='
>>> t.strip('-=')
'hello'
>>>
```

Discussion

The various `strip()` methods are commonly used when reading and cleaning up data for later processing. For example, you can use them to get rid of whitespace, remove quotations, and other tasks.

Be aware that stripping does not apply to any text in the middle of a string. For example:

```
>>> s = '   hello        world   \n'
>>> s = s.strip()
>>> s
'hello        world'
>>>
```

If you needed to do something to the inner space, you would need to use another technique, such as using the `replace()` method or a regular expression substitution. For
example:

```
>>> s.replace(' ', '')
'helloworld'
>>> import re
>>> re.sub('\s+', ' ', s)
'hello world'
>>>
```

It is often the case that you want to combine string stripping operations with some other
kind of iterative processing, such as reading lines of data from a file. If so, this is one
area where a generator expression can be useful. For example:

```
with open(filename) as f:
    lines = (line.strip() for line in f)
    for line in lines:
        ...
```

Here, the expression `lines = (line.strip() for line in f)` acts as a kind of data
transform. It's efficient because it doesn't actually read the data into any kind of temporary list first. It just creates an iterator where all of the lines produced have the stripping operation applied to them.

For even more advanced stripping, you might turn to the `translate()` method. See the
next recipe on sanitizing strings for further details.

2.12. Sanitizing and Cleaning Up Text

Problem

Some bored script kiddie has entered the text "pýthöñ" into a form on your web page
and you'd like to clean it up somehow.

Solution

The problem of sanitizing and cleaning up text applies to a wide variety of problems
involving text parsing and data handling. At a very simple level, you might use basic
string functions (e.g., `str.upper()` and `str.lower()`) to convert text to a standard case.
Simple replacements using `str.replace()` or `re.sub()` can focus on removing or

changing very specific character sequences. You can also normalize text using `unicode data.normalize()`, as shown in Recipe 2.9.

However, you might want to take the sanitation process a step further. Perhaps, for example, you want to eliminate whole ranges of characters or strip diacritical marks. To do so, you can turn to the often overlooked `str.translate()` method. To illustrate, suppose you've got a messy string such as the following:

```
>>> s = 'pýthöñ\fis\tawesome\r\n'
>>> s
'pýthöñ\x0cis\tawesome\r\n'
>>>
```

The first step is to clean up the whitespace. To do this, make a small translation table and use `translate()`:

```
>>> remap = {
...     ord('\t') : ' ',
...     ord('\f') : ' ',
...     ord('\r') : None      # Deleted
... }
>>> a = s.translate(remap)
>>> a
'pýthöñ is awesome\n'
>>>
```

As you can see here, whitespace characters such as \t and \f have been remapped to a single space. The carriage return \r has been deleted entirely.

You can take this remapping idea a step further and build much bigger tables. For example, let's remove all combining characters:

```
>>> import unicodedata
>>> import sys
>>> cmb_chrs = dict.fromkeys(c for c in range(sys.maxunicode)
...                          if unicodedata.combining(chr(c)))
...
>>> b = unicodedata.normalize('NFD', a)
>>> b
'pýthöñ is awesome\n'
>>> b.translate(cmb_chrs)
'python is awesome\n'
>>>
```

In this last example, a dictionary mapping every Unicode combining character to None is created using the `dict.fromkeys()`.

The original input is then normalized into a decomposed form using `unicodedata.nor malize()`. From there, the translate function is used to delete all of the accents. Similar techniques can be used to remove other kinds of characters (e.g., control characters, etc.).

As another example, here is a translation table that maps all Unicode decimal digit characters to their equivalent in ASCII:

```
>>> digitmap = { c: ord('0') + unicodedata.digit(chr(c))
...             for c in range(sys.maxunicode)
...             if unicodedata.category(chr(c)) == 'Nd' }
...
>>> len(digitmap)
460
>>> # Arabic digits
>>> x = '\u0661\u0662\u0663'
>>> x.translate(digitmap)
'123'
>>>
```

Yet another technique for cleaning up text involves I/O decoding and encoding functions. The idea here is to first do some preliminary cleanup of the text, and then run it through a combination of encode() or decode() operations to strip or alter it. For example:

```
>>> a
'pýthön is awesome\n'
>>> b = unicodedata.normalize('NFD', a)
>>> b.encode('ascii', 'ignore').decode('ascii')
'python is awesome\n'
>>>
```

Here the normalization process decomposed the original text into characters along with separate combining characters. The subsequent ASCII encoding/decoding simply discarded all of those characters in one fell swoop. Naturally, this would only work if getting an ASCII representation was the final goal.

Discussion

A major issue with sanitizing text can be runtime performance. As a general rule, the simpler it is, the faster it will run. For simple replacements, the str.replace() method is often the fastest approach—even if you have to call it multiple times. For instance, to clean up whitespace, you could use code like this:

```
def clean_spaces(s):
    s = s.replace('\r', '')
    s = s.replace('\t', ' ')
    s = s.replace('\f', ' ')
    return s
```

If you try it, you'll find that it's quite a bit faster than using translate() or an approach using a regular expression.

On the other hand, the translate() method is very fast if you need to perform any kind of nontrivial character-to-character remapping or deletion.

In the big picture, performance is something you will have to study further in your particular application. Unfortunately, it's impossible to suggest one specific technique that works best for all cases, so try different approaches and measure it.

Although the focus of this recipe has been text, similar techniques can be applied to bytes, including simple replacements, translation, and regular expressions.

2.13. Aligning Text Strings

Problem

You need to format text with some sort of alignment applied.

Solution

For basic alignment of strings, the `ljust()`, `rjust()`, and `center()` methods of strings can be used. For example:

```
>>> text = 'Hello World'
>>> text.ljust(20)
'Hello World         '
>>> text.rjust(20)
'         Hello World'
>>> text.center(20)
'    Hello World     '
>>>
```

All of these methods accept an optional fill character as well. For example:

```
>>> text.rjust(20,'=')
'=========Hello World'
>>> text.center(20,'*')
'****Hello World*****'
>>>
```

The `format()` function can also be used to easily align things. All you need to do is use the <, >, or ^ characters along with a desired width. For example:

```
>>> format(text, '>20')
'         Hello World'
>>> format(text, '<20')
'Hello World         '
>>> format(text, '^20')
'    Hello World     '
>>>
```

If you want to include a fill character other than a space, specify it before the alignment character:

```
>>> format(text, '=>20s')
'=========Hello World'
```

```
>>> format(text, '*^20s')
'****Hello World*****'
>>>
```

These format codes can also be used in the `format()` method when formatting multiple values. For example:

```
>>> '{:>10s} {:>10s}'.format('Hello', 'World')
'     Hello      World'
>>>
```

One benefit of `format()` is that it is not specific to strings. It works with any value, making it more general purpose. For instance, you can use it with numbers:

```
>>> x = 1.2345
>>> format(x, '>10')
'    1.2345'
>>> format(x, '^10.2f')
'   1.23   '
>>>
```

Discussion

In older code, you will also see the `%` operator used to format text. For example:

```
>>> '%-20s' % text
'Hello World         '
>>> '%20s' % text
'         Hello World'
>>>
```

However, in new code, you should probably prefer the use of the `format()` function or method. `format()` is a lot more powerful than what is provided with the `%` operator. Moreover, `format()` is more general purpose than using the `jlust()`, `rjust()`, or `center()` method of strings in that it works with any kind of object.

For a complete list of features available with the `format()` function, consult the online Python documentation (*http://docs.python.org/3/library/string.html#formatspec*).

2.14. Combining and Concatenating Strings

Problem

You want to combine many small strings together into a larger string.

Solution

If the strings you wish to combine are found in a sequence or iterable, the fastest way to combine them is to use the `join()` method. For example:

```
>>> parts = ['Is', 'Chicago', 'Not', 'Chicago?']
>>> ' '.join(parts)
'Is Chicago Not Chicago?'
>>> ','.join(parts)
'Is,Chicago,Not,Chicago?'
>>> ''.join(parts)
'IsChicagoNotChicago?'
>>>
```

At first glance, this syntax might look really odd, but the join() operation is specified as a method on strings. Partly this is because the objects you want to join could come from any number of different data sequences (e.g., lists, tuples, dicts, files, sets, or generators), and it would be redundant to have join() implemented as a method on all of those objects separately. So you just specify the separator string that you want and use the join() method on it to glue text fragments together.

If you're only combining a few strings, using + usually works well enough:

```
>>> a = 'Is Chicago'
>>> b = 'Not Chicago?'
>>> a + ' ' + b
'Is Chicago Not Chicago?'
>>>
```

The + operator also works fine as a substitute for more complicated string formatting operations. For example:

```
>>> print('{} {}'.format(a,b))
Is Chicago Not Chicago?
>>> print(a + ' ' + b)
Is Chicago Not Chicago?
>>>
```

If you're trying to combine string literals together in source code, you can simply place them adjacent to each other with no + operator. For example:

```
>>> a = 'Hello' 'World'
>>> a
'HelloWorld'
>>>
```

Discussion

Joining strings together might not seem advanced enough to warrant an entire recipe, but it's often an area where programmers make programming choices that severely impact the performance of their code.

The most important thing to know is that using the + operator to join a lot of strings together is grossly inefficient due to the memory copies and garbage collection that occurs. In particular, you never want to write code that joins strings together like this:

```
s = ''
for p in parts:
    s += p
```

This runs quite a bit slower than using the join() method, mainly because each +=
operation creates a new string object. You're better off just collecting all of the parts first
and then joining them together at the end.

One related (and pretty neat) trick is the conversion of data to strings and concatenation
at the same time using a generator expression, as described in Recipe 1.19. For example:

```
>>> data = ['ACME', 50, 91.1]
>>> ','.join(str(d) for d in data)
'ACME,50,91.1'
>>>
```

Also be on the lookout for unnecessary string concatenations. Sometimes programmers
get carried away with concatenation when it's really not technically necessary. For example, when printing:

```
print(a + ':' + b + ':' + c)       # Ugly
print(':'.join([a, b, c]))         # Still ugly

print(a, b, c, sep=':')            # Better
```

Mixing I/O operations and string concatenation is something that might require study
in your application. For example, consider the following two code fragments:

```
# Version 1 (string concatenation)
f.write(chunk1 + chunk2)

# Version 2 (separate I/O operations)
f.write(chunk1)
f.write(chunk2)
```

If the two strings are small, the first version might offer much better performance due
to the inherent expense of carrying out an I/O system call. On the other hand, if the two
strings are large, the second version may be more efficient, since it avoids making a large
temporary result and copying large blocks of memory around. Again, it must be stressed
that this is something you would have to study in relation to your own data in order to
determine which performs best.

Last, but not least, if you're writing code that is building output from lots of small strings,
you might consider writing that code as a generator function, using yield to emit fragments. For example:

```
def sample():
    yield 'Is'
    yield 'Chicago'
    yield 'Not'
    yield 'Chicago?'
```

The interesting thing about this approach is that it makes no assumption about how the fragments are to be assembled together. For example, you could simply join the fragments using `join()`:

```
text = ''.join(sample())
```

Or you could redirect the fragments to I/O:

```
for part in sample():
    f.write(part)
```

Or you could come up with some kind of hybrid scheme that's smart about combining I/O operations:

```
def combine(source, maxsize):
    parts = []
    size = 0
    for part in source:
        parts.append(part)
        size += len(part)
        if size > maxsize:
            yield ''.join(parts)
            parts = []
            size = 0
    yield ''.join(parts)

for part in combine(sample(), 32768):
    f.write(part)
```

The key point is that the original generator function doesn't have to know the precise details. It just yields the parts.

2.15. Interpolating Variables in Strings

Problem

You want to create a string in which embedded variable names are substituted with a string representation of a variable's value.

Solution

Python has no direct support for simply substituting variable values in strings. However, this feature can be approximated using the `format()` method of strings. For example:

```
>>> s = '{name} has {n} messages.'
>>> s.format(name='Guido', n=37)
'Guido has 37 messages.'
>>>
```

Alternatively, if the values to be substituted are truly found in variables, you can use the combination of format_map() and vars(), as in the following:

```
>>> name = 'Guido'
>>> n = 37
>>> s.format_map(vars())
'Guido has 37 messages.'
>>>
```

One subtle feature of vars() is that it also works with instances. For example:

```
>>> class Info:
...     def __init__(self, name, n):
...         self.name = name
...         self.n = n
...
>>> a = Info('Guido',37)
>>> s.format_map(vars(a))
'Guido has 37 messages.'
>>>
```

One downside of format() and format_map() is that they do not deal gracefully with missing values. For example:

```
>>> s.format(name='Guido')
Traceback (most recent call last):
  File "<stdin>", line 1, in <module>
KeyError: 'n'
>>>
```

One way to avoid this is to define an alternative dictionary class with a __miss ing__() method, as in the following:

```
class safesub(dict):
    def __missing__(self, key):
        return '{' + key + '}'
```

Now use this class to wrap the inputs to format_map():

```
>>> del n       # Make sure n is undefined
>>> s.format_map(safesub(vars()))
'Guido has {n} messages.'
>>>
```

If you find yourself frequently performing these steps in your code, you could hide the variable substitution process behind a small utility function that employs a so-called "frame hack." For example:

```
import sys

def sub(text):
    return text.format_map(safesub(sys._getframe(1).f_locals))
```

Now you can type things like this:

```
>>> name = 'Guido'
>>> n = 37
>>> print(sub('Hello {name}'))
Hello Guido
>>> print(sub('You have {n} messages.'))
You have 37 messages.
>>> print(sub('Your favorite color is {color}'))
Your favorite color is {color}
>>>
```

Discussion

The lack of true variable interpolation in Python has led to a variety of solutions over the years. As an alternative to the solution presented in this recipe, you will sometimes see string formatting like this:

```
>>> name = 'Guido'
>>> n = 37
>>> '%(name) has %(n) messages.' % vars()
'Guido has 37 messages.'
>>>
```

You may also see the use of template strings:

```
>>> import string
>>> s = string.Template('$name has $n messages.')
>>> s.substitute(vars())
'Guido has 37 messages.'
>>>
```

However, the format() and format_map() methods are more modern than either of these alternatives, and should be preferred. One benefit of using format() is that you also get all of the features related to string formatting (alignment, padding, numerical formatting, etc.), which is simply not possible with alternatives such as Template string objects.

Parts of this recipe also illustrate a few interesting advanced features. The little-known __missing__() method of mapping/dict classes is a method that you can define to handle missing values. In the safesub class, this method has been defined to return missing values back as a placeholder. Instead of getting a KeyError exception, you would see the missing values appearing in the resulting string (potentially useful for debugging).

The sub() function uses sys._getframe(1) to return the stack frame of the caller. From that, the f_locals attribute is accessed to get the local variables. It goes without saying that messing around with stack frames should probably be avoided in most code. However, for utility functions such as a string substitution feature, it can be useful. As an aside, it's probably worth noting that f_locals is a dictionary that is a copy of the local variables in the calling function. Although you can modify the contents of f_locals, the modifications don't actually have any lasting effect. Thus, even though accessing a different stack frame might look evil, it's not possible to accidentally overwrite variables or change the local environment of the caller.

2.16. Reformatting Text to a Fixed Number of Columns

Problem

You have long strings that you want to reformat so that they fill a user-specified number of columns.

Solution

Use the `textwrap` module to reformat text for output. For example, suppose you have the following long string:

```
s = "Look into my eyes, look into my eyes, the eyes, the eyes, \
the eyes, not around the eyes, don't look around the eyes, \
look into my eyes, you're under."
```

Here's how you can use the `textwrap` module to reformat it in various ways:

```
>>> import textwrap
>>> print(textwrap.fill(s, 70))
Look into my eyes, look into my eyes, the eyes, the eyes, the eyes,
not around the eyes, don't look around the eyes, look into my eyes,
you're under.

>>> print(textwrap.fill(s, 40))
Look into my eyes, look into my eyes,
the eyes, the eyes, the eyes, not around
the eyes, don't look around the eyes,
look into my eyes, you're under.

>>> print(textwrap.fill(s, 40, initial_indent='    '))
    Look into my eyes, look into my
eyes, the eyes, the eyes, the eyes, not
around the eyes, don't look around the
eyes, look into my eyes, you're under.

>>> print(textwrap.fill(s, 40, subsequent_indent='    '))
Look into my eyes, look into my eyes,
    the eyes, the eyes, the eyes, not
    around the eyes, don't look around
    the eyes, look into my eyes, you're
    under.
```

Discussion

The `textwrap` module is a straightforward way to clean up text for printing—especially if you want the output to fit nicely on the terminal. On the subject of the terminal size, you can obtain it using `os.get_terminal_size()`. For example:

```
>>> import os
>>> os.get_terminal_size().columns
80
>>>
```

The `fill()` method has a few additional options that control how it handles tabs, sentence endings, and so on. Look at the documentation for the `textwrap.TextWrapper` class (*http://docs.python.org/3.3/library/textwrap.html#textwrap.TextWrapper*) for further details.

2.17. Handling HTML and XML Entities in Text

Problem

You want to replace HTML or XML entities such as `&entity;` or `&#code;` with their corresponding text. Alternatively, you need to produce text, but escape certain characters (e.g., <, >, or &).

Solution

If you are producing text, replacing special characters such as < or > is relatively easy if you use the `html.escape()` function. For example:

```
>>> s = 'Elements are written as "<tag>text</tag>".'
>>> import html
>>> print(s)
Elements are written as "<tag>text</tag>".
>>> print(html.escape(s))
Elements are written as &quot;&lt;tag&gt;text&lt;/tag&gt;&quot;.

>>> # Disable escaping of quotes
>>> print(html.escape(s, quote=False))
Elements are written as "&lt;tag&gt;text&lt;/tag&gt;".
>>>
```

If you're trying to emit text as ASCII and want to embed character code entities for non-ASCII characters, you can use the `errors='xmlcharrefreplace'` argument to various I/O-related functions to do it. For example:

```
>>> s = 'Spicy Jalapeño'
>>> s.encode('ascii', errors='xmlcharrefreplace')
b'Spicy Jalape&#241;o'
>>>
```

To replace entities in text, a different approach is needed. If you're actually processing HTML or XML, try using a proper HTML or XML parser first. Normally, these tools will automatically take care of replacing the values for you during parsing and you don't need to worry about it.

If, for some reason, you've received bare text with some entities in it and you want them replaced manually, you can usually do it using various utility functions/methods associated with HTML or XML parsers. For example:

```
>>> s = 'Spicy &quot;Jalape&#241;o&quot.'
>>> from html.parser import HTMLParser
>>> p = HTMLParser()
>>> p.unescape(s)
'Spicy "Jalapeño".'
>>>

>>> t = 'The prompt is &gt;&gt;&gt;'
>>> from xml.sax.saxutils import unescape
>>> unescape(t)
'The prompt is >>>'
>>>
```

Discussion

Proper escaping of special characters is an easily overlooked detail of generating HTML or XML. This is especially true if you're generating such output yourself using `print()` or other basic string formatting features. Using a utility function such as `html.escape()` is an easy solution.

If you need to process text in the other direction, various utility functions, such as `xml.sax.saxutils.unescape()`, can help. However, you really need to investigate the use of a proper parser. For example, if processing HTML or XML, using a parsing module such as `html.parser` or `xml.etree.ElementTree` should already take care of details related to replacing entities in the input text for you.

2.18. Tokenizing Text

Problem

You have a string that you want to parse left to right into a stream of tokens.

Solution

Suppose you have a string of text such as this:

```
text = 'foo = 23 + 42 * 10'
```

To tokenize the string, you need to do more than merely match patterns. You need to have some way to identify the kind of pattern as well. For instance, you might want to turn the string into a sequence of pairs like this:

```
tokens = [('NAME', 'foo'), ('EQ','='), ('NUM', '23'), ('PLUS','+'),
          ('NUM', '42'), ('TIMES', '*'), ('NUM', 10)]
```

To do this kind of splitting, the first step is to define all of the possible tokens, including whitespace, by regular expression patterns using named capture groups such as this:

```
import re
NAME  = r'(?P<NAME>[a-zA-Z_][a-zA-Z_0-9]*)'
NUM   = r'(?P<NUM>\d+)'
PLUS  = r'(?P<PLUS>\+)'
TIMES = r'(?P<TIMES>\*)'
EQ    = r'(?P<EQ>=)'
WS    = r'(?P<WS>\s+)'

master_pat = re.compile('|'.join([NAME, NUM, PLUS, TIMES, EQ, WS]))
```

In these re patterns, the ?P<TOKENNAME> convention is used to assign a name to the pattern. This will be used later.

Next, to tokenize, use the little-known scanner() method of pattern objects. This method creates a scanner object in which repeated calls to match() step through the supplied text one match at a time. Here is an interactive example of how a scanner object works:

```
>>> scanner = master_pat.scanner('foo = 42')
>>> scanner.match()
<_sre.SRE_Match object at 0x100677738>
>>> _.lastgroup, _.group()
('NAME', 'foo')
>>> scanner.match()
<_sre.SRE_Match object at 0x100677738>
>>> _.lastgroup, _.group()
('WS', ' ')
>>> scanner.match()
<_sre.SRE_Match object at 0x100677738>
>>> _.lastgroup, _.group()
('EQ', '=')
>>> scanner.match()
<_sre.SRE_Match object at 0x100677738>
>>> _.lastgroup, _.group()
('WS', ' ')
>>> scanner.match()
<_sre.SRE_Match object at 0x100677738>
>>> _.lastgroup, _.group()
('NUM', '42')
>>> scanner.match()
>>>
```

To take this technique and put it into code, it can be cleaned up and easily packaged into a generator like this:

```
from collections import namedtuple

Token = namedtuple('Token', ['type','value'])

def generate_tokens(pat, text):
    scanner = pat.scanner(text)
    for m in iter(scanner.match, None):
        yield Token(m.lastgroup, m.group())

# Example use
for tok in generate_tokens(master_pat, 'foo = 42'):
    print(tok)

# Produces output
# Token(type='NAME', value='foo')
# Token(type='WS', value=' ')
# Token(type='EQ', value='=')
# Token(type='WS', value=' ')
# Token(type='NUM', value='42')
```

If you want to filter the token stream in some way, you can either define more generator functions or use a generator expression. For example, here is how you might filter out all whitespace tokens.

```
tokens = (tok for tok in generate_tokens(master_pat, text)
          if tok.type != 'WS')
for tok in tokens:
    print(tok)
```

Discussion

Tokenizing is often the first step for more advanced kinds of text parsing and handling. To use the scanning technique shown, there are a few important details to keep in mind. First, you must make sure that you identify every possible text sequence that might appear in the input with a correponding re pattern. If any nonmatching text is found, scanning simply stops. This is why it was necessary to specify the whitespace (WS) token in the example.

The order of tokens in the master regular expression also matters. When matching, re tries to match pattens in the order specified. Thus, if a pattern happens to be a substring of a longer pattern, you need to make sure the longer pattern goes first. For example:

```
LT = r'(?P<LT><)'
LE = r'(?P<LE><=)'
EQ = r'(?P<EQ>=)'

master_pat = re.compile('|'.join([LE, LT, EQ]))    # Correct
# master_pat = re.compile('|'.join([LT, LE, EQ]))  # Incorrect
```

The second pattern is wrong because it would match the text <= as the token LT followed by the token EQ, not the single token LE, as was probably desired.

Last, but not least, you need to watch out for patterns that form substrings. For example, suppose you have two pattens like this:

```
PRINT = r'(P<PRINT>print)'
NAME  = r'(P<NAME>[a-zA-Z_][a-zA-Z_0-9]*)'

master_pat = re.compile('|'.join([PRINT, NAME]))

for tok in generate_tokens(master_pat, 'printer'):
    print(tok)

# Outputs :
#  Token(type='PRINT', value='print')
#  Token(type='NAME', value='er')
```

For more advanced kinds of tokenizing, you may want to check out packages such as PyParsing (*http://pyparsing.wikispaces.com*) or PLY (*http://www.dabeaz.com/ply/index.html*). An example involving PLY appears in the next recipe.

2.19. Writing a Simple Recursive Descent Parser

Problem

You need to parse text according to a set of grammar rules and perform actions or build an abstract syntax tree representing the input. The grammar is small, so you'd prefer to just write the parser yourself as opposed to using some kind of framework.

Solution

In this problem, we're focused on the problem of parsing text according to a particular grammar. In order to do this, you should probably start by having a formal specification of the grammar in the form of a BNF or EBNF. For example, a grammar for simple arithmetic expressions might look like this:

```
expr ::= expr + term
     |   expr - term
     |   term

term ::= term * factor
     |   term / factor
     |   factor

factor ::= ( expr )
       |   NUM
```

Or, alternatively, in EBNF form:

```
expr ::= term { (+|-) term }*

term ::= factor { (*|/) factor }*

factor ::= ( expr )
         |   NUM
```

In an EBNF, parts of a rule enclosed in { ... }* are optional. The * means zero or more repetitions (the same meaning as in a regular expression).

Now, if you're not familiar with the mechanics of working with a BNF, think of it as a specification of substitution or replacement rules where symbols on the left side can be replaced by the symbols on the right (or vice versa). Generally, what happens during parsing is that you try to match the input text to the grammar by making various substitutions and expansions using the BNF. To illustrate, suppose you are parsing an expression such as 3 + 4 * 5. This expression would first need to be broken down into a token stream, using the techniques described in Recipe 2.18. The result might be a sequence of tokens like this:

```
NUM + NUM * NUM
```

From there, parsing involves trying to match the grammar to input tokens by making substitutions:

```
expr
expr ::= term { (+|-) term }*
expr ::= factor { (*|/) factor }* { (+|-) term }*
expr ::= NUM { (*|/) factor }* { (+|-) term }*
expr ::= NUM { (+|-) term }*
expr ::= NUM + term { (+|-) term }*
expr ::= NUM + factor { (*|/) factor }* { (+|-) term }*
expr ::= NUM + NUM { (*|/) factor}* { (+|-) term }*
expr ::= NUM + NUM * factor { (*|/) factor }* { (+|-) term }*
expr ::= NUM + NUM * NUM { (*|/) factor }* { (+|-) term }*
expr ::= NUM + NUM * NUM { (+|-) term }*
expr ::= NUM + NUM * NUM
```

Following all of the substitution steps takes a bit of coffee, but they're driven by looking at the input and trying to match it to grammar rules. The first input token is a NUM, so substitutions first focus on matching that part. Once matched, attention moves to the next token of + and so on. Certain parts of the righthand side (e.g., { (*/) factor }*) disappear when it's determined that they can't match the next token. In a successful parse, the entire righthand side is expanded completely to match the input token stream.

With all of the preceding background in place, here is a simple recipe that shows how to build a recursive descent expression evaluator:

```
import re
import collections
```

```python
# Token specification
NUM     = r'(?P<NUM>\d+)'
PLUS    = r'(?P<PLUS>\+)'
MINUS   = r'(?P<MINUS>-)'
TIMES   = r'(?P<TIMES>\*)'
DIVIDE  = r'(?P<DIVIDE>/)'
LPAREN  = r'(?P<LPAREN>\()'
RPAREN  = r'(?P<RPAREN>\))'
WS      = r'(?P<WS>\s+)'

master_pat = re.compile('|'.join([NUM, PLUS, MINUS, TIMES,
                                  DIVIDE, LPAREN, RPAREN, WS]))

# Tokenizer
Token = collections.namedtuple('Token', ['type','value'])

def generate_tokens(text):
    scanner = master_pat.scanner(text)
    for m in iter(scanner.match, None):
        tok = Token(m.lastgroup, m.group())
        if tok.type != 'WS':
            yield tok

# Parser
class ExpressionEvaluator:
    '''
    Implementation of a recursive descent parser.   Each method
    implements a single grammar rule.  Use the ._accept() method
    to test and accept the current lookahead token.  Use the ._expect()
    method to exactly match and discard the next token on on the input
    (or raise a SyntaxError if it doesn't match).
    '''

    def parse(self,text):
        self.tokens = generate_tokens(text)
        self.tok = None            # Last symbol consumed
        self.nexttok = None        # Next symbol tokenized
        self._advance()            # Load first lookahead token
        return self.expr()

    def _advance(self):
        'Advance one token ahead'
        self.tok, self.nexttok = self.nexttok, next(self.tokens, None)

    def _accept(self,toktype):
        'Test and consume the next token if it matches toktype'
        if self.nexttok and self.nexttok.type == toktype:
            self._advance()
            return True
        else:
            return False
```

```python
    def _expect(self,toktype):
        'Consume next token if it matches toktype or raise SyntaxError'
        if not self._accept(toktype):
            raise SyntaxError('Expected ' + toktype)

    # Grammar rules follow

    def expr(self):
        "expression ::= term { ('+'|'-') term }*"

        exprval = self.term()
        while self._accept('PLUS') or self._accept('MINUS'):
            op = self.tok.type
            right = self.term()
            if op == 'PLUS':
                exprval += right
            elif op == 'MINUS':
                exprval -= right
        return exprval

    def term(self):
        "term ::= factor { ('*'|'/') factor }*"

        termval = self.factor()
        while self._accept('TIMES') or self._accept('DIVIDE'):
            op = self.tok.type
            right = self.factor()
            if op == 'TIMES':
                termval *= right
            elif op == 'DIVIDE':
                termval /= right
        return termval

    def factor(self):
        "factor ::= NUM | ( expr )"

        if self._accept('NUM'):
            return int(self.tok.value)
        elif self._accept('LPAREN'):
            exprval = self.expr()
            self._expect('RPAREN')
            return exprval
        else:
            raise SyntaxError('Expected NUMBER or LPAREN')
```

Here is an example of using the ExpressionEvaluator class interactively:

```
>>> e = ExpressionEvaluator()
>>> e.parse('2')
2
>>> e.parse('2 + 3')
5
```

```
>>> e.parse('2 + 3 * 4')
14
>>> e.parse('2 + (3 + 4) * 5')
37
>>> e.parse('2 + (3 + * 4)')
Traceback (most recent call last):
  File "<stdin>", line 1, in <module>
  File "exprparse.py", line 40, in parse
    return self.expr()
  File "exprparse.py", line 67, in expr
    right = self.term()
  File "exprparse.py", line 77, in term
    termval = self.factor()
  File "exprparse.py", line 93, in factor
    exprval = self.expr()
  File "exprparse.py", line 67, in expr
    right = self.term()
  File "exprparse.py", line 77, in term
    termval = self.factor()
  File "exprparse.py", line 97, in factor
    raise SyntaxError("Expected NUMBER or LPAREN")
SyntaxError: Expected NUMBER or LPAREN
>>>
```

If you want to do something other than pure evaluation, you need to change the
ExpressionEvaluator class to do something else. For example, here is an alternative
implementation that constructs a simple parse tree:

```
class ExpressionTreeBuilder(ExpressionEvaluator):
    def expr(self):
        "expression ::= term { ('+'|'-') term }"

        exprval = self.term()
        while self._accept('PLUS') or self._accept('MINUS'):
            op = self.tok.type
            right = self.term()
            if op == 'PLUS':
                exprval = ('+', exprval, right)
            elif op == 'MINUS':
                exprval = ('-', exprval, right)
        return exprval

    def term(self):
        "term ::= factor { ('*'|'/') factor }"

        termval = self.factor()
        while self._accept('TIMES') or self._accept('DIVIDE'):
            op = self.tok.type
            right = self.factor()
            if op == 'TIMES':
                termval = ('*', termval, right)
            elif op == 'DIVIDE':
```

```
            termval = ('/', termval, right)
        return termval

    def factor(self):
        'factor ::= NUM | ( expr )'

        if self._accept('NUM'):
            return int(self.tok.value)
        elif self._accept('LPAREN'):
            exprval = self.expr()
            self._expect('RPAREN')
            return exprval
        else:
            raise SyntaxError('Expected NUMBER or LPAREN')
```

The following example shows how it works:

```
>>> e = ExpressionTreeBuilder()
>>> e.parse('2 + 3')
('+', 2, 3)
>>> e.parse('2 + 3 * 4')
('+', 2, ('*', 3, 4))
>>> e.parse('2 + (3 + 4) * 5')
('+', 2, ('*', ('+', 3, 4), 5))
>>> e.parse('2 + 3 + 4')
('+', ('+', 2, 3), 4)
>>>
```

Discussion

Parsing is a huge topic that generally occupies students for the first three weeks of a
compilers course. If you are seeking background knowledge about grammars, parsing
algorithms, and other information, a compilers book is where you should turn. Needless
to say, all of that can't be repeated here.

Nevertheless, the overall idea of writing a recursive descent parser is generally simple.
To start, you take every grammar rule and you turn it into a function or method. Thus,
if your grammar looks like this:

```
expr ::= term { ('+'|'-') term }*

term ::= factor { ('*'|'/') factor }*

factor ::= '(' expr ')'
         |   NUM
```

You start by turning it into a set of methods like this:

```
class ExpressionEvaluator:
    ...
    def expr(self):
        ...
```

```
def term(self):
    ...

def factor(self):
    ...
```

The task of each method is simple—it must walk from left to right over each part of the grammar rule, consuming tokens in the process. In a sense, the goal of the method is to either consume the rule or generate a syntax error if it gets stuck. To do this, the following implementation techniques are applied:

- If the next symbol in the rule is the name of another grammar rule (e.g., term or factor), you simply call the method with the same name. This is the "descent" part of the algorithm—control descends into another grammar rule. Sometimes rules will involve calls to methods that are already executing (e.g., the call to expr in the factor ::= '(' expr ')' rule). This is the "recursive" part of the algorithm.

- If the next symbol in the rule has to be a specific symbol (e.g., ()), you look at the next token and check for an exact match. If it doesn't match, it's a syntax error. The _expect() method in this recipe is used to perform these steps.

- If the next symbol in the rule could be a few possible choices (e.g., + or -), you have to check the next token for each possibility and advance only if a match is made. This is the purpose of the _accept() method in this recipe. It's kind of like a weaker version of the _expect() method in that it will advance if a match is made, but if not, it simply backs off without raising an error (thus allowing further checks to be made).

- For grammar rules where there are repeated parts (e.g., such as in the rule expr ::= term { ('+'|'-') term }*), the repetition gets implemented by a while loop. The body of the loop will generally collect or process all of the repeated items until no more are found.

- Once an entire grammar rule has been consumed, each method returns some kind of result back to the caller. This is how values propagate during parsing. For example, in the expression evaluator, return values will represent partial results of the expression being parsed. Eventually they all get combined together in the topmost grammar rule method that executes.

Although a simple example has been shown, recursive descent parsers can be used to implement rather complicated parsers. For example, Python code itself is interpreted by a recursive descent parser. If you're so inclined, you can look at the underlying grammar by inspecting the file *Grammar/Grammar* in the Python source. That said, there are still numerous pitfalls and limitations with making a parser by hand.

One such limitation of recursive descent parsers is that they can't be written for grammar rules involving any kind of left recursion. For example, suppose you need to translate a rule like this:

```
items ::= items ',' item
        | item
```

To do it, you might try to use the `items()` method like this:

```
def items(self):
    itemsval = self.items()
    if itemsval and self._accept(','):
        itemsval.append(self.item())
    else:
        itemsval = [ self.item() ]
```

The only problem is that it doesn't work. In fact, it blows up with an infinite recursion error.

You can also run into tricky issues concerning the grammar rules themselves. For example, you might have wondered whether or not expressions could have been described by this more simple grammar:

```
expr ::= factor { ('+'|'-'|'*'|'/') factor }*

factor ::= '(' expression ')'
         | NUM
```

This grammar technically "works," but it doesn't observe the standard arithmetic rules concerning order of evaluation. For example, the expression "3 + 4 * 5" would get evaluated as "35" instead of the expected result of "23." The use of separate "expr" and "term" rules is there to make evaluation work correctly.

For really complicated grammars, you are often better off using parsing tools such as PyParsing (*http://pyparsing.wikispaces.com*) or PLY (*http://www.dabeaz.com/ply/ index.html*). This is what the expression evaluator code looks like using PLY:

```
from ply.lex import lex
from ply.yacc import yacc

# Token list
tokens = [ 'NUM', 'PLUS', 'MINUS', 'TIMES', 'DIVIDE', 'LPAREN', 'RPAREN' ]

# Ignored characters

t_ignore = ' \t\n'

# Token specifications (as regexs)
t_PLUS   = r'\+'
t_MINUS  = r'-'
t_TIMES  = r'\*'
t_DIVIDE = r'/'
```

```python
t_LPAREN = r'\('
t_RPAREN = r'\)'

# Token processing functions
def t_NUM(t):
    r'\d+'
    t.value = int(t.value)
    return t

# Error handler
def t_error(t):
    print('Bad character: {!r}'.format(t.value[0]))
    t.skip(1)

# Build the lexer
lexer = lex()

# Grammar rules and handler functions
def p_expr(p):
    '''
    expr : expr PLUS term
         | expr MINUS term
    '''
    if p[2] == '+':
        p[0] = p[1] + p[3]
    elif p[2] == '-':
        p[0] = p[1] - p[3]

def p_expr_term(p):
    '''
    expr : term
    '''
    p[0] = p[1]

def p_term(p):
    '''
    term : term TIMES factor
         | term DIVIDE factor
    '''
    if p[2] == '*':
        p[0] = p[1] * p[3]
    elif p[2] == '/':
        p[0] = p[1] / p[3]

def p_term_factor(p):
    '''
    term : factor
    '''
    p[0] = p[1]

def p_factor(p):
    '''
```

```
    factor : NUM
    '''
    p[0] = p[1]

def p_factor_group(p):
    '''
    factor : LPAREN expr RPAREN
    '''
    p[0] = p[2]

def p_error(p):
    print('Syntax error')

parser = yacc()
```

In this code, you'll find that everything is specified at a much higher level. You simply write regular expressions for the tokens and high-level handling functions that execute when various grammar rules are matched. The actual mechanics of running the parser, accepting tokens, and so forth is implemented entirely by the library.

Here is an example of how the resulting parser object gets used:

```
>>> parser.parse('2')
2
>>> parser.parse('2+3')
5
>>> parser.parse('2+(3+4)*5')
37
>>>
```

If you need a bit more excitement in your programming, writing parsers and compilers can be a fun project. Again, a compilers textbook will have a lot of low-level details underlying theory. However, many fine resources can also be found online. Python's own ast module is also worth a look.

2.20. Performing Text Operations on Byte Strings

Problem

You want to perform common text operations (e.g., stripping, searching, and replacement) on byte strings.

Solution

Byte strings already support most of the same built-in operations as text strings. For example:

```
>>> data = b'Hello World'
>>> data[0:5]
b'Hello'
>>> data.startswith(b'Hello')
True
>>> data.split()
[b'Hello', b'World']
>>> data.replace(b'Hello', b'Hello Cruel')
b'Hello Cruel World'
>>>
```

Such operations also work with byte arrays. For example:

```
>>> data = bytearray(b'Hello World')
>>> data[0:5]
bytearray(b'Hello')
>>> data.startswith(b'Hello')
True
>>> data.split()
[bytearray(b'Hello'), bytearray(b'World')]
>>> data.replace(b'Hello', b'Hello Cruel')
bytearray(b'Hello Cruel World')
>>>
```

You can apply regular expression pattern matching to byte strings, but the patterns themselves need to be specified as bytes. For example:

```
>>>
>>> data = b'FOO:BAR,SPAM'
>>> import re
>>> re.split('[:,]',data)
Traceback (most recent call last):
  File "<stdin>", line 1, in <module>
  File "/usr/local/lib/python3.3/re.py", line 191, in split
    return _compile(pattern, flags).split(string, maxsplit)
TypeError: can't use a string pattern on a bytes-like object

>>> re.split(b'[:,]',data)      # Notice: pattern as bytes
[b'FOO', b'BAR', b'SPAM']
>>>
```

Discussion

For the most part, almost all of the operations available on text strings will work on byte strings. However, there are a few notable differences to be aware of. First, indexing of byte strings produces integers, not individual characters. For example:

```
>>> a = 'Hello World'     # Text string
>>> a[0]
'H'
>>> a[1]
'e'
>>> b = b'Hello World'     # Byte string
```

```
>>> b[0]
72
>>> b[1]
101
>>>
```

This difference in semantics can affect programs that try to process byte-oriented data on a character-by-character basis.

Second, byte strings don't provide a nice string representation and don't print cleanly unless first decoded into a text string. For example:

```
>>> s = b'Hello World'
>>> print(s)
b'Hello World'                # Observe b'...'
>>> print(s.decode('ascii'))
Hello World
>>>
```

Similarly, there are no string formatting operations available to byte strings.

```
>>> b'%10s %10d %10.2f' % (b'ACME', 100, 490.1)
Traceback (most recent call last):
  File "<stdin>", line 1, in <module>
TypeError: unsupported operand type(s) for %: 'bytes' and 'tuple'

>>> b'{} {} {}'.format(b'ACME', 100, 490.1)
Traceback (most recent call last):
  File "<stdin>", line 1, in <module>
AttributeError: 'bytes' object has no attribute 'format'
>>>
```

If you want to do any kind of formatting applied to byte strings, it should be done using normal text strings and encoding. For example:

```
>>> '{:10s} {:10d} {:10.2f}'.format('ACME', 100, 490.1).encode('ascii')
b'ACME              100     490.10'
>>>
```

Finally, you need to be aware that using a byte string can change the semantics of certain operations—especially those related to the filesystem. For example, if you supply a filename encoded as bytes instead of a text string, it usually disables filename encoding/decoding. For example:

```
>>> # Write a UTF-8 filename
>>> with open('jalape\xf1o.txt', 'w') as f:
...     f.write('spicy')
...

>>> # Get a directory listing
>>> import os
>>> os.listdir('.')             # Text string (names are decoded)
['jalapeño.txt']
```

```
>>> os.listdir(b'.')          # Byte string (names left as bytes)
[b'jalapen\xcc\x83o.txt']
>>>
```

Notice in the last part of this example how giving a byte string as the directory name caused the resulting filenames to be returned as undecoded bytes. The filename shown in the directory listing contains raw UTF-8 encoding. See Recipe 5.15 for some related issues concerning filenames.

As a final comment, some programmers might be inclined to use byte strings as an alternative to text strings due to a possible performance improvement. Although it's true that manipulating bytes tends to be slightly more efficient than text (due to the inherent overhead related to Unicode), doing so usually leads to very messy and nonidiomatic code. You'll often find that byte strings don't play well with a lot of other parts of Python, and that you end up having to perform all sorts of manual encoding/decoding operations yourself to get things to work right. Frankly, if you're working with text, use normal text strings in your program, not byte strings.

## CHAPTER 3

Numbers, Dates, and Times

Performing mathematical calculations with integers and floating-point numbers is easy in Python. However, if you need to perform calculations with fractions, arrays, or dates and times, a bit more work is required. The focus of this chapter is on such topics.

3.1. Rounding Numerical Values

Problem

You want to round a floating-point number to a fixed number of decimal places.

Solution

For simple rounding, use the built-in `round(value, ndigits)` function. For example:

```
>>> round(1.23, 1)
1.2
>>> round(1.27, 1)
1.3
>>> round(-1.27, 1)
-1.3
>>> round(1.25361,3)
1.254
>>>
```

When a value is exactly halfway between two choices, the behavior of round is to round to the nearest even digit. That is, values such as 1.5 or 2.5 both get rounded to 2.

The number of digits given to `round()` can be negative, in which case rounding takes place for tens, hundreds, thousands, and so on. For example:

```
>>> a = 1627731
>>> round(a, -1)
1627730
```

```
>>> round(a, -2)
1627700
>>> round(a, -3)
1628000
>>>
```

Discussion

Don't confuse rounding with formatting a value for output. If your goal is simply to output a numerical value with a certain number of decimal places, you don't typically need to use round(). Instead, just specify the desired precision when formatting. For example:

```
>>> x = 1.23456
>>> format(x, '0.2f')
'1.23'
>>> format(x, '0.3f')
'1.235'
>>> 'value is {:0.3f}'.format(x)
'value is 1.235'
>>>
```

Also, resist the urge to round floating-point numbers to "fix" perceived accuracy problems. For example, you might be inclined to do this:

```
>>> a = 2.1
>>> b = 4.2
>>> c = a + b
>>> c
6.300000000000001
>>> c = round(c, 2)      # "Fix" result (???)
>>> c
6.3
>>>
```

For most applications involving floating point, it's simply not necessary (or recommended) to do this. Although there are small errors introduced into calculations, the behavior of those errors are understood and tolerated. If avoiding such errors is important (e.g., in financial applications, perhaps), consider the use of the decimal module, which is discussed in the next recipe.

3.2. Performing Accurate Decimal Calculations

Problem

You need to perform accurate calculations with decimal numbers, and don't want the small errors that naturally occur with floats.

Solution

A well-known issue with floating-point numbers is that they can't accurately represent all base-10 decimals. Moreover, even simple mathematical calculations introduce small errors. For example:

```
>>> a = 4.2
>>> b = 2.1
>>> a + b
6.300000000000001
>>> (a + b) == 6.3
False
>>>
```

These errors are a "feature" of the underlying CPU and the IEEE 754 arithmetic performed by its floating-point unit. Since Python's float data type stores data using the native representation, there's nothing you can do to avoid such errors if you write your code using `float` instances.

If you want more accuracy (and are willing to give up some performance), you can use the `decimal` module:

```
>>> from decimal import Decimal
>>> a = Decimal('4.2')
>>> b = Decimal('2.1')
>>> a + b
Decimal('6.3')
>>> print(a + b)
6.3
>>> (a + b) == Decimal('6.3')
True
>>>
```

At first glance, it might look a little weird (i.e., specifying numbers as strings). However, `Decimal` objects work in every way that you would expect them to (supporting all of the usual math operations, etc.). If you print them or use them in string formatting functions, they look like normal numbers.

A major feature of `decimal` is that it allows you to control different aspects of calculations, including number of digits and rounding. To do this, you create a local context and change its settings. For example:

```
>>> from decimal import localcontext
>>> a = Decimal('1.3')
>>> b = Decimal('1.7')
>>> print(a / b)
0.7647058823529411764705882353
>>> with localcontext() as ctx:
...     ctx.prec = 3
...     print(a / b)
...
```

```
0.765
>>> with localcontext() as ctx:
...         ctx.prec = 50
...         print(a / b)
...
0.76470588235294117647058823529411764705882352941176
>>>
```

Discussion

The `decimal` module implements IBM's "General Decimal Arithmetic Specification." Needless to say, there are a huge number of configuration options that are beyond the scope of this book.

Newcomers to Python might be inclined to use the `decimal` module to work around perceived accuracy problems with the `float` data type. However, it's really important to understand your application domain. If you're working with science or engineering problems, computer graphics, or most things of a scientific nature, it's simply more common to use the normal floating-point type. For one, very few things in the real world are measured to the 17 digits of accuracy that floats provide. Thus, tiny errors introduced in calculations just don't matter. Second, the performance of native floats is significantly faster—something that's important if you're performing a large number of calculations.

That said, you can't ignore the errors completely. Mathematicians have spent a lot of time studying various algorithms, and some handle errors better than others. You also have to be a little careful with effects due to things such as subtractive cancellation and adding large and small numbers together. For example:

```
>>> nums = [1.23e+18, 1, -1.23e+18]
>>> sum(nums)    # Notice how 1 disappears
0.0
>>>
```

This latter example can be addressed by using a more accurate implementation in `math.fsum()`:

```
>>> import math
>>> math.fsum(nums)
1.0
>>>
```

However, for other algorithms, you really need to study the algorithm and understand its error propagation properties.

All of this said, the main use of the `decimal` module is in programs involving things such as finance. In such programs, it is extremely annoying to have small errors creep into the calculation. Thus, `decimal` provides a way to avoid that. It is also common to encounter `Decimal` objects when Python interfaces with databases—again, especially when accessing financial data.

3.3. Formatting Numbers for Output

Problem

You need to format a number for output, controlling the number of digits, alignment, inclusion of a thousands separator, and other details.

Solution

To format a single number for output, use the built-in `format()` function. For example:

```
>>> x = 1234.56789

>>> # Two decimal places of accuracy
>>> format(x, '0.2f')
'1234.57'

>>> # Right justified in 10 chars, one-digit accuracy
>>> format(x, '>10.1f')
'    1234.6'

>>> # Left justified
>>> format(x, '<10.1f')
'1234.6    '

>>> # Centered
>>> format(x, '^10.1f')
'  1234.6  '

>>> # Inclusion of thousands separator
>>> format(x, ',')
'1,234.56789'
>>> format(x, '0,.1f')
'1,234.6'
>>>
```

If you want to use exponential notation, change the f to an e or E, depending on the case you want used for the exponential specifier. For example:

```
>>> format(x, 'e')
'1.234568e+03'
>>> format(x, '0.2E')
'1.23E+03'
>>>
```

The general form of the width and precision in both cases is `'[<>^]?width[,]?(.dig its)?'` where `width` and `digits` are integers and ? signifies optional parts. The same format codes are also used in the `.format()` method of strings. For example:

```
>>> 'The value is {:0,.2f}'.format(x)
'The value is 1,234.57'
>>>
```

Discussion

Formatting numbers for output is usually straightforward. The technique shown works for both floating-point numbers and `Decimal` numbers in the `decimal` module.

When the number of digits is restricted, values are rounded away according to the same rules of the `round()` function. For example:

```
>>> x
1234.56789
>>> format(x, '0.1f')
'1234.6'
>>> format(-x, '0.1f')
'-1234.6'
>>>
```

Formatting of values with a thousands separator is not locale aware. If you need to take that into account, you might investigate functions in the `locale` module. You can also swap separator characters using the `translate()` method of strings. For example:

```
>>> swap_separators = { ord('.'):',', ord(','):'.' }
>>> format(x, ',').translate(swap_separators)
'1.234,56789'
>>>
```

In a lot of Python code, numbers are formatted using the % operator. For example:

```
>>> '%0.2f' % x
'1234.57'
>>> '%10.1f' % x
'    1234.6'
>>> '%-10.1f' % x
'1234.6    '
>>>
```

This formatting is still acceptable, but less powerful than the more modern `format()` method. For example, some features (e.g., adding thousands separators) aren't supported when using the % operator to format numbers.

3.4. Working with Binary, Octal, and Hexadecimal Integers

Problem

You need to convert or output integers represented by binary, octal, or hexadecimal digits.

Solution

To convert an integer into a binary, octal, or hexadecimal text string, use the bin(), oct(), or hex() functions, respectively:

```
>>> x = 1234
>>> bin(x)
'0b10011010010'
>>> oct(x)
'0o2322'
>>> hex(x)
'0x4d2'
>>>
```

Alternatively, you can use the format() function if you don't want the 0b, 0o, or 0x prefixes to appear. For example:

```
>>> format(x, 'b')
'10011010010'
>>> format(x, 'o')
'2322'
>>> format(x, 'x')
'4d2'
>>>
```

Integers are signed, so if you are working with negative numbers, the output will also include a sign. For example:

```
>>> x = -1234
>>> format(x, 'b')
'-10011010010'
>>> format(x, 'x')
'-4d2'
>>>
```

If you need to produce an unsigned value instead, you'll need to add in the maximum value to set the bit length. For example, to show a 32-bit value, use the following:

```
>>> x = -1234
>>> format(2**32 + x, 'b')
'11111111111111111111101100101110'
>>> format(2**32 + x, 'x')
```

```
'fffffb2e'
>>>
```

To convert integer strings in different bases, simply use the int() function with an appropriate base. For example:

```
>>> int('4d2', 16)
1234
>>> int('10011010010', 2)
1234
>>>
```

Discussion

For the most part, working with binary, octal, and hexadecimal integers is straightforward. Just remember that these conversions only pertain to the conversion of integers to and from a textual representation. Under the covers, there's just one integer type.

Finally, there is one caution for programmers who use octal. The Python syntax for specifying octal values is slightly different than many other languages. For example, if you try something like this, you'll get a syntax error:

```
>>> import os
>>> os.chmod('script.py', 0755)
  File "<stdin>", line 1
    os.chmod('script.py', 0755)
                            ^
SyntaxError: invalid token
>>>
```

Make sure you prefix the octal value with 0o, as shown here:

```
>>> os.chmod('script.py', 0o755)
>>>
```

3.5. Packing and Unpacking Large Integers from Bytes

Problem

You have a byte string and you need to unpack it into an integer value. Alternatively, you need to convert a large integer back into a byte string.

Solution

Suppose your program needs to work with a 16-element byte string that holds a 128-bit integer value. For example:

```
data = b'\x00\x124V\x00x\x90\xab\x00\xcd\xef\x01\x00#\x004'
```

To interpret the bytes as an integer, use int.from_bytes(), and specify the byte ordering like this:

```
>>> len(data)
16
>>> int.from_bytes(data, 'little')
69120565666575113957766354792709489108
>>> int.from_bytes(data, 'big')
94522842520747284487117727783387188
>>>
```

To convert a large integer value back into a byte string, use the int.to_bytes() method, specifying the number of bytes and the byte order. For example:

```
>>> x = 94522842520747284487117727783387188
>>> x.to_bytes(16, 'big')
b'\x00\x124V\x00x\x90\xab\x00\xcd\xef\x01\x00#\x004'
>>> x.to_bytes(16, 'little')
b'4\x00#\x00\x01\xef\xcd\x00\xab\x90x\x00V4\x12\x00'
>>>
```

Discussion

Converting large integer values to and from byte strings is not a common operation. However, it sometimes arises in certain application domains, such as cryptography or networking. For instance, IPv6 network addresses are represented as 128-bit integers. If you are writing code that needs to pull such values out of a data record, you might face this problem.

As an alternative to this recipe, you might be inclined to unpack values using the struct module, as described in Recipe 6.11. This works, but the size of integers that can be unpacked with struct is limited. Thus, you would need to unpack multiple values and combine them to create the final value. For example:

```
>>> data
b'\x00\x124V\x00x\x90\xab\x00\xcd\xef\x01\x00#\x004'
>>> import struct
>>> hi, lo = struct.unpack('>QQ', data)
>>> (hi << 64) + lo
94522842520747284487117727783387188
>>>
```

The specification of the byte order (little or big) just indicates whether the bytes that make up the integer value are listed from the least to most significant or the other way around. This is easy to view using a carefully crafted hexadecimal value:

```
>>> x = 0x01020304
>>> x.to_bytes(4, 'big')
b'\x01\x02\x03\x04'
>>> x.to_bytes(4, 'little')
```

```
b'\x04\x03\x02\x01'
>>>
```

If you try to pack an integer into a byte string, but it won't fit, you'll get an error. You can use the int.bit_length() method to determine how many bits are required to store a value if needed:

```
>>> x = 523 ** 23
>>> x
335381300113661875107536852714019056160355655333978849017944067
>>> x.to_bytes(16, 'little')
Traceback (most recent call last):
  File "<stdin>", line 1, in <module>
OverflowError: int too big to convert
>>> x.bit_length()
208
>>> nbytes, rem = divmod(x.bit_length(), 8)
>>> if rem:
...      nbytes += 1
...
>>>
>>> x.to_bytes(nbytes, 'little')
b'\x03X\xf1\x82iT\x96\xac\xc7c\x16\xf3\xb9\xcf...\xd0'
>>>
```

3.6. Performing Complex-Valued Math

Problem

Your code for interacting with the latest web authentication scheme has encountered a singularity and your only solution is to go around it in the complex plane. Or maybe you just need to perform some calculations using complex numbers.

Solution

Complex numbers can be specified using the complex(real, imag) function or by floating-point numbers with a j suffix. For example:

```
>>> a = complex(2, 4)
>>> b = 3 - 5j
>>> a
(2+4j)
>>> b
(3-5j)
>>>
```

The real, imaginary, and conjugate values are easy to obtain, as shown here:

```
>>> a.real
2.0
```

```
>>> a.imag
4.0
>>> a.conjugate()
(2-4j)
>>>
```

In addition, all of the usual mathematical operators work:

```
>>> a + b
(5-1j)
>>> a * b
(26+2j)
>>> a / b
(-0.4117647058823529+0.6470588235294118j)
>>> abs(a)
4.47213595499958
>>>
```

To perform additional complex-valued functions such as sines, cosines, or square roots,
use the cmath module:

```
>>> import cmath
>>> cmath.sin(a)
(24.83130584894638-11.356612711218174j)
>>> cmath.cos(a)
(-11.36423470640106-24.814651485634187j)
>>> cmath.exp(a)
(-4.829809383269385-5.5920560936409816j)
>>>
```

Discussion

Most of Python's math-related modules are aware of complex values. For example, if
you use numpy, it is straightforward to make arrays of complex values and perform
operations on them:

```
>>> import numpy as np
>>> a = np.array([2+3j, 4+5j, 6-7j, 8+9j])
>>> a
array([ 2.+3.j,   4.+5.j,   6.-7.j,   8.+9.j])
>>> a + 2
array([ 4.+3.j,   6.+5.j,   8.-7.j,  10.+9.j])
>>> np.sin(a)
array([    9.15449915  -4.16890696j,    -56.16227422 -48.50245524j,
         -153.20827755-526.47684926j,   4008.42651446-589.49948373j])
>>>
```

Python's standard mathematical functions do not produce complex values by default,
so it is unlikely that such a value would accidentally show up in your code. For example:

```
>>> import math
>>> math.sqrt(-1)
Traceback (most recent call last):
```

```
    File "<stdin>", line 1, in <module>
ValueError: math domain error
>>>
```

If you want complex numbers to be produced as a result, you have to explicitly use cmath or declare the use of a complex type in libraries that know about them. For example:

```
>>> import cmath
>>> cmath.sqrt(-1)
1j
>>>
```

3.7. Working with Infinity and NaNs

Problem

You need to create or test for the floating-point values of infinity, negative infinity, or NaN (not a number).

Solution

Python has no special syntax to represent these special floating-point values, but they can be created using float(). For example:

```
>>> a = float('inf')
>>> b = float('-inf')
>>> c = float('nan')
>>> a
inf
>>> b
-inf
>>> c
nan
>>>
```

To test for the presence of these values, use the math.isinf() and math.isnan() functions. For example:

```
>>> math.isinf(a)
True
>>> math.isnan(c)
True
>>>
```

Discussion

For more detailed information about these special floating-point values, you should refer to the IEEE 754 specification. However, there are a few tricky details to be aware of, especially related to comparisons and operators.

Infinite values will propagate in calculations in a mathematical manner. For example:

```
>>> a = float('inf')
>>> a + 45
inf
>>> a * 10
inf
>>> 10 / a
0.0
>>>
```

However, certain operations are undefined and will result in a NaN result. For example:

```
>>> a = float('inf')
>>> a/a
nan
>>> b = float('-inf')
>>> a + b
nan
>>>
```

NaN values propagate through all operations without raising an exception. For example:

```
>>> c = float('nan')
>>> c + 23
nan
>>> c / 2
nan
>>> c * 2
nan
>>> math.sqrt(c)
nan
>>>
```

A subtle feature of NaN values is that they never compare as equal. For example:

```
>>> c = float('nan')
>>> d = float('nan')
>>> c == d
False
>>> c is d
False
>>>
```

Because of this, the only safe way to test for a NaN value is to use `math.isnan()`, as shown in this recipe.

Sometimes programmers want to change Python's behavior to raise exceptions when operations result in an infinite or NaN result. The `fpectl` module can be used to adjust this behavior, but it is not enabled in a standard Python build, it's platform-dependent, and really only intended for expert-level programmers. See the online Python documentation (*http://docs.python.org/3/library/fpectl.html*) for further details.

3.8. Calculating with Fractions

Problem

You have entered a time machine and suddenly find yourself working on elementary-level homework problems involving fractions. Or perhaps you're writing code to make calculations involving measurements made in your wood shop.

Solution

The `fractions` module can be used to perform mathematical calculations involving fractions. For example:

```
>>> from fractions import Fraction
>>> a = Fraction(5, 4)
>>> b = Fraction(7, 16)
>>> print(a + b)
27/16
>>> print(a * b)
35/64

>>> # Getting numerator/denominator
>>> c = a * b
>>> c.numerator
35
>>> c.denominator
64

>>> # Converting to a float
>>> float(c)
0.546875

>>> # Limiting the denominator of a value
>>> print(c.limit_denominator(8))
4/7

>>> # Converting a float to a fraction
>>> x = 3.75
>>> y = Fraction(*x.as_integer_ratio())
>>> y
Fraction(15, 4)
>>>
```

Discussion

Calculating with fractions doesn't arise often in most programs, but there are situations where it might make sense to use them. For example, allowing a program to accept units of measurement in fractions and performing calculations with them in that form might alleviate the need for a user to manually make conversions to decimals or floats.

3.9. Calculating with Large Numerical Arrays

Problem

You need to perform calculations on large numerical datasets, such as arrays or grids.

Solution

For any heavy computation involving arrays, use the NumPy library (*http://www.numpy.org*). The major feature of NumPy is that it gives Python an array object that is much more efficient and better suited for mathematical calculation than a standard Python list. Here is a short example illustrating important behavioral differences between lists and NumPy arrays:

```
>>> # Python lists
>>> x = [1, 2, 3, 4]
>>> y = [5, 6, 7, 8]
>>> x * 2
[1, 2, 3, 4, 1, 2, 3, 4]
>>> x + 10
Traceback (most recent call last):
  File "<stdin>", line 1, in <module>
TypeError: can only concatenate list (not "int") to list
>>> x + y
[1, 2, 3, 4, 5, 6, 7, 8]

>>> # Numpy arrays
>>> import numpy as np
>>> ax = np.array([1, 2, 3, 4])
>>> ay = np.array([5, 6, 7, 8])
>>> ax * 2
array([2, 4, 6, 8])
>>> ax + 10
array([11, 12, 13, 14])
>>> ax + ay
array([ 6,  8, 10, 12])
>>> ax * ay
array([ 5, 12, 21, 32])
>>>
```

As you can see, basic mathematical operations involving arrays behave differently. Specifically, scalar operations (e.g., `ax * 2` or `ax + 10`) apply the operation on an element-by-element basis. In addition, performing math operations when both operands are arrays applies the operation to all elements and produces a new array.

The fact that math operations apply to all of the elements simultaneously makes it very easy and fast to compute functions across an entire array. For example, if you want to compute the value of a polynomial:

```
>>> def f(x):
...     return 3*x**2 - 2*x + 7
...
>>> f(ax)
array([ 8, 15, 28, 47])
>>>
```

NumPy provides a collection of "universal functions" that also allow for array operations. These are replacements for similar functions normally found in the math module.
For example:

```
>>> np.sqrt(ax)
array([ 1.        ,  1.41421356,  1.73205081,  2.        ])
>>> np.cos(ax)
array([ 0.54030231, -0.41614684, -0.9899925 , -0.65364362])
>>>
```

Using universal functions can be hundreds of times faster than looping over the array
elements one at a time and performing calculations using functions in the math module.
Thus, you should prefer their use whenever possible.

Under the covers, NumPy arrays are allocated in the same manner as in C or Fortran.
Namely, they are large, contiguous memory regions consisting of a homogenous data
type. Because of this, it's possible to make arrays much larger than anything you would
normally put into a Python list. For example, if you want to make a two-dimensional
grid of 10,000 by 10,000 floats, it's not an issue:

```
>>> grid = np.zeros(shape=(10000,10000), dtype=float)
>>> grid
array([[ 0.,  0.,  0., ...,  0.,  0.,  0.],
       [ 0.,  0.,  0., ...,  0.,  0.,  0.],
       [ 0.,  0.,  0., ...,  0.,  0.,  0.],
       ...,
       [ 0.,  0.,  0., ...,  0.,  0.,  0.],
       [ 0.,  0.,  0., ...,  0.,  0.,  0.],
       [ 0.,  0.,  0., ...,  0.,  0.,  0.]])
>>>
```

All of the usual operations still apply to all of the elements simultaneously:

```
>>> grid += 10
>>> grid
array([[ 10.,  10.,  10., ...,  10.,  10.,  10.],
       [ 10.,  10.,  10., ...,  10.,  10.,  10.],
       [ 10.,  10.,  10., ...,  10.,  10.,  10.],
       ...,
       [ 10.,  10.,  10., ...,  10.,  10.,  10.],
       [ 10.,  10.,  10., ...,  10.,  10.,  10.],
       [ 10.,  10.,  10., ...,  10.,  10.,  10.]])
>>> np.sin(grid)
array([[-0.54402111, -0.54402111, -0.54402111, ..., -0.54402111,
        -0.54402111, -0.54402111],
```

```
       [-0.54402111, -0.54402111, -0.54402111, ..., -0.54402111,
         -0.54402111, -0.54402111],
       [-0.54402111, -0.54402111, -0.54402111, ..., -0.54402111,
         -0.54402111, -0.54402111],
       ...,
       [-0.54402111, -0.54402111, -0.54402111, ..., -0.54402111,
         -0.54402111, -0.54402111],
       [-0.54402111, -0.54402111, -0.54402111, ..., -0.54402111,
         -0.54402111, -0.54402111],
       [-0.54402111, -0.54402111, -0.54402111, ..., -0.54402111,
         -0.54402111, -0.54402111]])
>>>
```

One extremely notable aspect of NumPy is the manner in which it extends Python's list indexing functionality—especially with multidimensional arrays. To illustrate, make a simple two-dimensional array and try some experiments:

```
>>> a = np.array([[1, 2, 3, 4], [5, 6, 7, 8], [9, 10, 11, 12]])
>>> a
array([[ 1,  2,  3,  4],
       [ 5,  6,  7,  8],
       [ 9, 10, 11, 12]])

>>> # Select row 1
>>> a[1]
array([5, 6, 7, 8])

>>> # Select column 1
>>> a[:,1]
array([ 2,  6, 10])

>>> # Select a subregion and change it
>>> a[1:3, 1:3]
array([[ 6,  7],
       [10, 11]])
>>> a[1:3, 1:3] += 10
>>> a
array([[ 1,  2,  3,  4],
       [ 5, 16, 17,  8],
       [ 9, 20, 21, 12]])

>>> # Broadcast a row vector across an operation on all rows
>>> a + [100, 101, 102, 103]
array([[101, 103, 105, 107],
       [105, 117, 119, 111],
       [109, 121, 123, 115]])
>>> a
array([[ 1,  2,  3,  4],
       [ 5, 16, 17,  8],
       [ 9, 20, 21, 12]])

>>> # Conditional assignment on an array
```

```
>>> np.where(a < 10, a, 10)
array([[ 1,  2,  3,  4],
       [ 5, 10, 10,  8],
       [ 9, 10, 10, 10]])
>>>
```

Discussion

NumPy is the foundation for a huge number of science and engineering libraries in Python. It is also one of the largest and most complicated modules in widespread use. That said, it's still possible to accomplish useful things with NumPy by starting with simple examples and playing around.

One note about usage is that it is relatively common to use the statement `import numpy as np`, as shown in the solution. This simply shortens the name to something that's more convenient to type over and over again in your program.

For more information, you definitely need to visit *http://www.numpy.org*.

3.10. Performing Matrix and Linear Algebra Calculations

Problem

You need to perform matrix and linear algebra operations, such as matrix multiplication, finding determinants, solving linear equations, and so on.

Solution

The NumPy library (*http://www.numpy.org*) has a `matrix` object that can be used for this purpose. Matrices are somewhat similar to the array objects described in Recipe 3.9, but follow linear algebra rules for computation. Here is an example that illustrates a few essential features:

```
>>> import numpy as np
>>> m = np.matrix([[1,-2,3],[0,4,5],[7,8,-9]])
>>> m
matrix([[ 1, -2,  3],
        [ 0,  4,  5],
        [ 7,  8, -9]])

>>> # Return transpose
>>> m.T
matrix([[ 1,  0,  7],
        [-2,  4,  8],
        [ 3,  5, -9]])

>>> # Return inverse
>>> m.I
```

```
matrix([[ 0.33043478, -0.02608696,  0.09565217],
        [-0.15217391,  0.13043478,  0.02173913],
        [ 0.12173913,  0.09565217, -0.0173913 ]])

>>> # Create a vector and multiply
>>> v = np.matrix([[2],[3],[4]])
>>> v
matrix([[2],
        [3],
        [4]])
>>> m * v
matrix([[ 8],
        [32],
        [ 2]])
>>>
```

More operations can be found in the numpy.linalg subpackage. For example:

```
>>> import numpy.linalg

>>> # Determinant
>>> numpy.linalg.det(m)
-229.99999999999983

>>> # Eigenvalues
>>> numpy.linalg.eigvals(m)
array([-13.11474312,   2.75956154,   6.35518158])

>>> # Solve for x in mx = v
>>> x = numpy.linalg.solve(m, v)
>>> x
matrix([[ 0.96521739],
        [ 0.17391304],
        [ 0.46086957]])
>>> m * x
matrix([[ 2.],
        [ 3.],
        [ 4.]])
>>> v
matrix([[2],
        [3],
        [4]])
>>>
```

Discussion

Linear algebra is obviously a huge topic that's far beyond the scope of this cookbook. However, if you need to manipulate matrices and vectors, NumPy is a good starting point. Visit *http://www.numpy.org* for more detailed information.

3.11. Picking Things at Random

Problem

You want to pick random items out of a sequence or generate random numbers.

Solution

The `random` module has various functions for random numbers and picking random items. For example, to pick a random item out of a sequence, use `random.choice()`:

```
>>> import random
>>> values = [1, 2, 3, 4, 5, 6]
>>> random.choice(values)
2
>>> random.choice(values)
3
>>> random.choice(values)
1
>>> random.choice(values)
4
>>> random.choice(values)
6
>>>
```

To take a sampling of N items where selected items are removed from further consideration, use `random.sample()` instead:

```
>>> random.sample(values, 2)
[6, 2]
>>> random.sample(values, 2)
[4, 3]
>>> random.sample(values, 3)
[4, 3, 1]
>>> random.sample(values, 3)
[5, 4, 1]
>>>
```

If you simply want to shuffle items in a sequence in place, use `random.shuffle()`:

```
>>> random.shuffle(values)
>>> values
[2, 4, 6, 5, 3, 1]
>>> random.shuffle(values)
>>> values
[3, 5, 2, 1, 6, 4]
>>>
```

To produce random integers, use `random.randint()`:

```
>>> random.randint(0,10)
2
```

```
>>> random.randint(0,10)
5
>>> random.randint(0,10)
0
>>> random.randint(0,10)
7
>>> random.randint(0,10)
10
>>> random.randint(0,10)
3
>>>
```

To produce uniform floating-point values in the range 0 to 1, use random.random():

```
>>> random.random()
0.9406677561675867
>>> random.random()
0.133129581343897
>>> random.random()
0.4144991136919316
>>>
```

To get N random-bits expressed as an integer, use random.getrandbits():

```
>>> random.getrandbits(200)
335837000776573622800628485064121869519521710558559406913275
>>>
```

Discussion

The random module computes random numbers using the Mersenne Twister algorithm. This is a deterministic algorithm, but you can alter the initial seed by using the random.seed() function. For example:

```
random.seed()            # Seed based on system time or os.urandom()
random.seed(12345)       # Seed based on integer given
random.seed(b'bytedata') # Seed based on byte data
```

In addition to the functionality shown, random() includes functions for uniform, Gaussian, and other probability distributions. For example, random.uniform() computes uniformly distributed numbers, and random.gauss() computes normally distributed numbers. Consult the documentation for information on other supported distributions.

Functions in random() should not be used in programs related to cryptography. If you need such functionality, consider using functions in the ssl module instead. For example, ssl.RAND_bytes() can be used to generate a cryptographically secure sequence of random bytes.

3.12. Converting Days to Seconds, and Other Basic Time Conversions

Problem

You have code that needs to perform simple time conversions, like days to seconds, hours to minutes, and so on.

Solution

To perform conversions and arithmetic involving different units of time, use the `date time` module. For example, to represent an interval of time, create a `timedelta` instance, like this:

```
>>> from datetime import timedelta
>>> a = timedelta(days=2, hours=6)
>>> b = timedelta(hours=4.5)
>>> c = a + b
>>> c.days
2
>>> c.seconds
37800
>>> c.seconds / 3600
10.5
>>> c.total_seconds() / 3600
58.5
>>>
```

If you need to represent specific dates and times, create `datetime` instances and use the standard mathematical operations to manipulate them. For example:

```
>>> from datetime import datetime
>>> a = datetime(2012, 9, 23)
>>> print(a + timedelta(days=10))
2012-10-03 00:00:00
>>>
>>> b = datetime(2012, 12, 21)
>>> d = b - a
>>> d.days
89
>>> now = datetime.today()
>>> print(now)
2012-12-21 14:54:43.094063
>>> print(now + timedelta(minutes=10))
2012-12-21 15:04:43.094063
>>>
```

When making calculations, it should be noted that `datetime` is aware of leap years. For example:

```
>>> a = datetime(2012, 3, 1)
>>> b = datetime(2012, 2, 28)
>>> a - b
datetime.timedelta(2)
>>> (a - b).days
2
>>> c = datetime(2013, 3, 1)
>>> d = datetime(2013, 2, 28)
>>> (c - d).days
1
>>>
```

Discussion

For most basic date and time manipulation problems, the datetime module will suffice. If you need to perform more complex date manipulations, such as dealing with time zones, fuzzy time ranges, calculating the dates of holidays, and so forth, look at the dateutil module (*http://pypi.python.org/pypi/python-dateutil*).

To illustrate, many similar time calculations can be performed with the dateutil.rel ativedelta() function. However, one notable feature is that it fills in some gaps pertaining to the handling of months (and their differing number of days). For instance:

```
>>> a = datetime(2012, 9, 23)
>>> a + timedelta(months=1)
Traceback (most recent call last):
  File "<stdin>", line 1, in <module>
TypeError: 'months' is an invalid keyword argument for this function
>>>

>>> from dateutil.relativedelta import relativedelta
>>> a + relativedelta(months=+1)
datetime.datetime(2012, 10, 23, 0, 0)
>>> a + relativedelta(months=+4)
datetime.datetime(2013, 1, 23, 0, 0)
>>>

>>> # Time between two dates
>>> b = datetime(2012, 12, 21)
>>> d = b - a
>>> d
datetime.timedelta(89)
>>> d = relativedelta(b, a)
>>> d
relativedelta(months=+2, days=+28)
>>> d.months
2
>>> d.days
28
>>>
```

3.13. Determining Last Friday's Date

Problem

You want a general solution for finding a date for the last occurrence of a day of the week. Last Friday, for example.

Solution

Python's datetime module has utility functions and classes to help perform calculations like this. A decent, generic solution to this problem looks like this:

```
from datetime import datetime, timedelta

weekdays = ['Monday', 'Tuesday', 'Wednesday', 'Thursday',
            'Friday', 'Saturday', 'Sunday']

def get_previous_byday(dayname, start_date=None):
    if start_date is None:
        start_date = datetime.today()
    day_num = start_date.weekday()
    day_num_target = weekdays.index(dayname)
    days_ago = (7 + day_num - day_num_target) % 7
    if days_ago == 0:
        days_ago = 7
    target_date = start_date - timedelta(days=days_ago)
    return target_date
```

Using this in an interpreter session would look like this:

```
>>> datetime.today()  # For reference
datetime.datetime(2012, 8, 28, 22, 4, 30, 263076)
>>> get_previous_byday('Monday')
datetime.datetime(2012, 8, 27, 22, 3, 57, 29045)
>>> get_previous_byday('Tuesday') # Previous week, not today
datetime.datetime(2012, 8, 21, 22, 4, 12, 629771)
>>> get_previous_byday('Friday')
datetime.datetime(2012, 8, 24, 22, 5, 9, 911393)
>>>
```

The optional start_date can be supplied using another datetime instance. For example:

```
>>> get_previous_byday('Sunday', datetime(2012, 12, 21))
datetime.datetime(2012, 12, 16, 0, 0)
>>>
```

Discussion

This recipe works by mapping the start date and the target date to their numeric position in the week (with Monday as day 0). Modular arithmetic is then used to figure out how many days ago the target date last occurred. From there, the desired date is calculated from the start date by subtracting an appropriate `timedelta` instance.

If you're performing a lot of date calculations like this, you may be better off installing the `python-dateutil` package (*http://pypi.python.org/pypi/python-dateutil*) instead. For example, here is an example of performing the same calculation using the `rela tivedelta()` function from `dateutil`:

```
>>> from datetime import datetime
>>> from dateutil.relativedelta import relativedelta
>>> from dateutil.rrule import *
>>> d = datetime.now()
>>> print(d)
2012-12-23 16:31:52.718111

>>> # Next Friday
>>> print(d + relativedelta(weekday=FR))
2012-12-28 16:31:52.718111
>>>

>>> # Last Friday
>>> print(d + relativedelta(weekday=FR(-1)))
2012-12-21 16:31:52.718111
>>>
```

3.14. Finding the Date Range for the Current Month

Problem

You have some code that needs to loop over each date in the current month, and want an efficient way to calculate that date range.

Solution

Looping over the dates doesn't require building a list of all the dates ahead of time. You can just calculate the starting and stopping date in the range, then use `datetime.time delta` objects to increment the date as you go.

Here's a function that takes any `datetime` object, and returns a tuple containing the first date of the month and the starting date of the next month:

```
from datetime import datetime, date, timedelta
import calendar
```

```
def get_month_range(start_date=None):
    if start_date is None:
        start_date = date.today().replace(day=1)
    _, days_in_month = calendar.monthrange(start_date.year, start_date.month)
    end_date = start_date + timedelta(days=days_in_month)
    return (start_date, end_date)
```

With this in place, it's pretty simple to loop over the date range:

```
>>> a_day = timedelta(days=1)
>>> first_day, last_day = get_month_range()
>>> while first_day < last_day:
...     print(first_day)
...     first_day += a_day
...
2012-08-01
2012-08-02
2012-08-03
2012-08-04
2012-08-05
2012-08-06
2012-08-07
2012-08-08
2012-08-09
#... and so on...
```

Discussion

This recipe works by first calculating a date correponding to the first day of the month. A quick way to do this is to use the `replace()` method of a `date` or `datetime` object to simply set the `days` attribute to 1. One nice thing about the `replace()` method is that it creates the same kind of object that you started with. Thus, if the input was a `date` instance, the result is a `date`. Likewise, if the input was a `datetime` instance, you get a `datetime` instance.

After that, the `calendar.monthrange()` function is used to find out how many days are in the month in question. Any time you need to get basic information about calendars, the `calendar` module can be useful. `monthrange()` is only one such function that returns a tuple containing the day of the week along with the number of days in the month.

Once the number of days in the month is known, the ending date is calculated by adding an appropriate `timedelta` to the starting date. It's subtle, but an important aspect of this recipe is that the ending date is not to be included in the range (it is actually the first day of the next month). This mirrors the behavior of Python's slices and range operations, which also never include the end point.

To loop over the date range, standard math and comparison operators are used. For example, `timedelta` instances can be used to increment the date. The `<` operator is used to check whether a date comes before the ending date.

Ideally, it would be nice to create a function that works like the built-in range() function, but for dates. Fortunately, this is extremely easy to implement using a generator:

```
def date_range(start, stop, step):
    while start < stop:
        yield start
        start += step
```

Here is an example of it in use:

```
>>> for d in date_range(datetime(2012, 9, 1), datetime(2012,10,1),
                        timedelta(hours=6)):
...     print(d)
...
2012-09-01 00:00:00
2012-09-01 06:00:00
2012-09-01 12:00:00
2012-09-01 18:00:00
2012-09-02 00:00:00
2012-09-02 06:00:00
...
>>>
```

Again, a major part of the ease of implementation is that dates and times can be manipulated using standard math and comparison operators.

3.15. Converting Strings into Datetimes

Problem

Your application receives temporal data in string format, but you want to convert those strings into datetime objects in order to perform nonstring operations on them.

Solution

Python's standard datetime module is typically the easy solution for this. For example:

```
>>> from datetime import datetime
>>> text = '2012-09-20'
>>> y = datetime.strptime(text, '%Y-%m-%d')
>>> z = datetime.now()
>>> diff = z - y
>>> diff
datetime.timedelta(3, 77824, 177393)
>>>
```

Discussion

The datetime.strptime() method supports a host of formatting codes, like %Y for the four-digit year and %m for the two-digit month. It's also worth noting that these formatting placeholders also work in reverse, in case you need to represent a `datetime` object in string output and make it look nice.

For example, let's say you have some code that generates a datetime object, but you need to format a nice, human-readable date to put in the header of an auto-generated letter or report:

```
>>> z
datetime.datetime(2012, 9, 23, 21, 37, 4, 177393)
>>> nice_z = datetime.strftime(z, '%A %B %d, %Y')
>>> nice_z
'Sunday September 23, 2012'
>>>
```

It's worth noting that the performance of `strptime()` is often much worse than you might expect, due to the fact that it's written in pure Python and it has to deal with all sorts of system locale settings. If you are parsing a lot of dates in your code and you know the precise format, you will probably get much better performance by cooking up a custom solution instead. For example, if you knew that the dates were of the form "YYYY-MM-DD," you could write a function like this:

```
from datetime import datetime
def parse_ymd(s):
    year_s, mon_s, day_s = s.split('-')
    return datetime(int(year_s), int(mon_s), int(day_s))
```

When tested, this function runs over seven times faster than `datetime.strptime()`. This is probably something to consider if you're processing large amounts of data involving dates.

3.16. Manipulating Dates Involving Time Zones

Problem

You had a conference call scheduled for December 21, 2012, at 9:30 a.m. in Chicago. At what local time did your friend in Bangalore, India, have to show up to attend?

Solution

For almost any problem involving time zones, you should use the `pytz` module (*http://pypi.python.org/pypi/pytz*). This package provides the Olson time zone database, which is the de facto standard for time zone information found in many languages and operating systems.

A major use of `pytz` is in localizing simple dates created with the `datetime` library. For example, here is how you would represent a date in Chicago time:

```
>>> from datetime import datetime
>>> from pytz import timezone
>>> d = datetime(2012, 12, 21, 9, 30, 0)
>>> print(d)
2012-12-21 09:30:00
>>>

>>> # Localize the date for Chicago
>>> central = timezone('US/Central')
>>> loc_d = central.localize(d)
>>> print(loc_d)
2012-12-21 09:30:00-06:00
>>>
```

Once the date has been localized, it can be converted to other time zones. To find the same time in Bangalore, you would do this:

```
>>> # Convert to Bangalore time
>>> bang_d = loc_d.astimezone(timezone('Asia/Kolkata'))
>>> print(bang_d)
2012-12-21 21:00:00+05:30
>>>
```

If you are going to perform arithmetic with localized dates, you need to be particularly aware of daylight saving transitions and other details. For example, in 2013, U.S. standard daylight saving time started on March 13, 2:00 a.m. local time (at which point, time skipped ahead one hour). If you're performing naive arithmetic, you'll get it wrong. For example:

```
>>> d = datetime(2013, 3, 10, 1, 45)
>>> loc_d = central.localize(d)
>>> print(loc_d)
2013-03-10 01:45:00-06:00
>>> later = loc_d + timedelta(minutes=30)
>>> print(later)
2013-03-10 02:15:00-06:00        # WRONG! WRONG!
>>>
```

The answer is wrong because it doesn't account for the one-hour skip in the local time. To fix this, use the normalize() method of the time zone. For example:

```
>>> from datetime import timedelta
>>> later = central.normalize(loc_d + timedelta(minutes=30))
>>> print(later)
2013-03-10 03:15:00-05:00
>>>
```

Discussion

To keep your head from completely exploding, a common strategy for localized date handling is to convert all dates to UTC time and to use that for all internal storage and manipulation. For example:

```
>>> print(loc_d)
2013-03-10 01:45:00-06:00
>>> utc_d = loc_d.astimezone(pytz.utc)
>>> print(utc_d)
2013-03-10 07:45:00+00:00
>>>
```

Once in UTC, you don't have to worry about issues related to daylight saving time and other matters. Thus, you can simply perform normal date arithmetic as before. Should you want to output the date in localized time, just convert it to the appropriate time zone afterward. For example:

```
>>> later_utc = utc_d + timedelta(minutes=30)
>>> print(later_utc.astimezone(central))
2013-03-10 03:15:00-05:00
>>>
```

One issue in working with time zones is simply figuring out what time zone names to use. For example, in this recipe, how was it known that "Asia/Kolkata" was the correct time zone name for India? To find out, you can consult the `pytz.country_timezones` dictionary using the ISO 3166 country code as a key. For example:

```
>>> pytz.country_timezones['IN']
['Asia/Kolkata']
>>>
```

 By the time you read this, it's possible that the `pytz` module will be deprecated in favor of improved time zone support, as described in PEP 431 (*http://www.python.org/dev/peps/pep-0431*). Many of the same issues will still apply, however (e.g., advice using UTC dates, etc.).

## CHAPTER 4

Iterators and Generators

Iteration is one of Python's strongest features. At a high level, you might simply view iteration as a way to process items in a sequence. However, there is so much more that is possible, such as creating your own iterator objects, applying useful iteration patterns in the `itertools` module, making generator functions, and so forth. This chapter aims to address common problems involving iteration.

4.1. Manually Consuming an Iterator

Problem

You need to process items in an iterable, but for whatever reason, you can't or don't want to use a `for` loop.

Solution

To manually consume an iterable, use the `next()` function and write your code to catch the `StopIteration` exception. For example, this example manually reads lines from a file:

```
with open('/etc/passwd') as f:
    try:
        while True:
            line = next(f)
            print(line, end='')
    except StopIteration:
        pass
```

Normally, `StopIteration` is used to signal the end of iteration. However, if you're using `next()` manually (as shown), you can also instruct it to return a terminating value, such as `None`, instead. For example:

```
with open('/etc/passwd') as f:
    while True:
        line = next(f, None)
        if line is None:
            break
        print(line, end='')
```

Discussion

In most cases, the for statement is used to consume an iterable. However, every now and then, a problem calls for more precise control over the underlying iteration mechanism. Thus, it is useful to know what actually happens.

The following interactive example illustrates the basic mechanics of what happens during iteration:

```
>>> items = [1, 2, 3]
>>> # Get the iterator
>>> it = iter(items)     # Invokes items.__iter__()
>>> # Run the iterator
>>> next(it)             # Invokes it.__next__()
1
>>> next(it)
2
>>> next(it)
3
>>> next(it)
Traceback (most recent call last):
  File "<stdin>", line 1, in <module>
StopIteration
>>>
```

Subsequent recipes in this chapter expand on iteration techniques, and knowledge of the basic iterator protocol is assumed. Be sure to tuck this first recipe away in your memory.

4.2. Delegating Iteration

Problem

You have built a custom container object that internally holds a list, tuple, or some other iterable. You would like to make iteration work with your new container.

Solution

Typically, all you need to do is define an __iter__() method that delegates iteration to the internally held container. For example:

```
class Node:
    def __init__(self, value):
        self._value = value
        self._children = []

    def __repr__(self):
        return 'Node({!r})'.format(self._value)

    def add_child(self, node):
        self._children.append(node)

    def __iter__(self):
        return iter(self._children)

# Example
if __name__ == '__main__':
    root = Node(0)
    child1 = Node(1)
    child2 = Node(2)
    root.add_child(child1)
    root.add_child(child2)
    for ch in root:
        print(ch)
    # Outputs Node(1), Node(2)
```

In this code, the __iter__() method simply forwards the iteration request to the internally held _children attribute.

Discussion

Python's iterator protocol requires __iter__() to return a special iterator object that implements a __next__() method to carry out the actual iteration. If all you are doing is iterating over the contents of another container, you don't really need to worry about the underlying details of how it works. All you need to do is to forward the iteration request along.

The use of the iter() function here is a bit of a shortcut that cleans up the code. iter(s) simply returns the underlying iterator by calling s.__iter__(), much in the same way that len(s) invokes s.__len__().

4.3. Creating New Iteration Patterns with Generators

Problem

You want to implement a custom iteration pattern that's different than the usual built-in functions (e.g., range(), reversed(), etc.).

Solution

If you want to implement a new kind of iteration pattern, define it using a generator function. Here's a generator that produces a range of floating-point numbers:

```
def frange(start, stop, increment):
    x = start
    while x < stop:
        yield x
        x += increment
```

To use such a function, you iterate over it using a for loop or use it with some other function that consumes an iterable (e.g., sum(), list(), etc.). For example:

```
>>> for n in frange(0, 4, 0.5):
...     print(n)
...
...
0
0.5
1.0
1.5
2.0
2.5
3.0
3.5
>>> list(frange(0, 1, 0.125))
[0, 0.125, 0.25, 0.375, 0.5, 0.625, 0.75, 0.875]
>>>
```

Discussion

The mere presence of the yield statement in a function turns it into a generator. Unlike a normal function, a generator only runs in response to iteration. Here's an experiment you can try to see the underlying mechanics of how such a function works:

```
>>> def countdown(n):
...     print('Starting to count from', n)
...     while n > 0:
...         yield n
...         n -= 1
...     print('Done!')
...

>>> # Create the generator, notice no output appears
>>> c = countdown(3)
>>> c
<generator object countdown at 0x1006a0af0>

>>> # Run to first yield and emit a value
>>> next(c)
Starting to count from 3
3
```

```
>>> # Run to the next yield
>>> next(c)
2

>>> # Run to next yield
>>> next(c)
1

>>> # Run to next yield (iteration stops)
>>> next(c)
Done!
Traceback (most recent call last):
  File "<stdin>", line 1, in <module>
StopIteration
>>>
```

The key feature is that a generator function only runs in response to "next" operations carried out in iteration. Once a generator function returns, iteration stops. However, the for statement that's usually used to iterate takes care of these details, so you don't normally need to worry about them.

4.4. Implementing the Iterator Protocol

Problem

You are building custom objects on which you would like to support iteration, but would like an easy way to implement the iterator protocol.

Solution

By far, the easiest way to implement iteration on an object is to use a generator function. In Recipe 4.2, a Node class was presented for representing tree structures. Perhaps you want to implement an iterator that traverses nodes in a depth-first pattern. Here is how you could do it:

```
class Node:
    def __init__(self, value):
        self._value = value
        self._children = []

    def __repr__(self):
        return 'Node({!r})'.format(self._value)

    def add_child(self, node):
        self._children.append(node)

    def __iter__(self):
        return iter(self._children)
```

```
    def depth_first(self):
        yield self
        for c in self:
            yield from c.depth_first()

# Example
if __name__ == '__main__':
    root = Node(0)
    child1 = Node(1)
    child2 = Node(2)
    root.add_child(child1)
    root.add_child(child2)
    child1.add_child(Node(3))
    child1.add_child(Node(4))
    child2.add_child(Node(5))

    for ch in root.depth_first():
        print(ch)
    # Outputs Node(0), Node(1), Node(3), Node(4), Node(2), Node(5)
```

In this code, the depth_first() method is simple to read and describe. It first yields
itself and then iterates over each child yielding the items produced by the child's
depth_first() method (using yield from).

Discussion

Python's iterator protocol requires __iter__() to return a special iterator object that
implements a __next__() operation and uses a StopIteration exception to signal
completion. However, implementing such objects can often be a messy affair. For example, the following code shows an alternative implementation of the depth_first()
method using an associated iterator class:

```
class Node:
    def __init__(self, value):
        self._value = value
        self._children = []

    def __repr__(self):
        return 'Node({!r})'.format(self._value)

    def add_child(self, other_node):
        self._children.append(other_node)

    def __iter__(self):
        return iter(self._children)

    def depth_first(self):
        return DepthFirstIterator(self)

class DepthFirstIterator(object):
```

```
'''
Depth-first traversal
'''
def __init__(self, start_node):
    self._node = start_node
    self._children_iter = None
    self._child_iter = None

def __iter__(self):
    return self

def __next__(self):
    # Return myself if just started; create an iterator for children
    if self._children_iter is None:
        self._children_iter = iter(self._node)
        return self._node

    # If processing a child, return its next item
    elif self._child_iter:
        try:
            nextchild = next(self._child_iter)
            return nextchild
        except StopIteration:
            self._child_iter = None
            return next(self)

    # Advance to the next child and start its iteration
    else:
        self._child_iter = next(self._children_iter).depth_first()
        return next(self)
```

The DepthFirstIterator class works in the same way as the generator version, but it's a mess because the iterator has to maintain a lot of complex state about where it is in the iteration process. Frankly, nobody likes to write mind-bending code like that. Define your iterator as a generator and be done with it.

4.5. Iterating in Reverse

Problem

You want to iterate in reverse over a sequence.

Solution

Use the built-in reversed() function. For example:

```
>>> a = [1, 2, 3, 4]
>>> for x in reversed(a):
...     print(x)
...
```

```
4
3
2
1
```

Reversed iteration only works if the object in question has a size that can be determined or if the object implements a __reversed__() special method. If neither of these can be satisfied, you'll have to convert the object into a list first. For example:

```
# Print a file backwards
f = open('somefile')
for line in reversed(list(f)):
    print(line, end='')
```

Be aware that turning an iterable into a list as shown could consume a lot of memory if it's large.

Discussion

Many programmers don't realize that reversed iteration can be customized on user-defined classes if they implement the __reversed__() method. For example:

```
class Countdown:
    def __init__(self, start):
        self.start = start

    # Forward iterator
    def __iter__(self):
        n = self.start
        while n > 0:
            yield n
            n -= 1

    # Reverse iterator
    def __reversed__(self):
        n = 1
        while n <= self.start:
            yield n
            n += 1
```

Defining a reversed iterator makes the code much more efficient, as it's no longer necessary to pull the data into a list and iterate in reverse on the list.

4.6. Defining Generator Functions with Extra State

Problem

You would like to define a generator function, but it involves extra state that you would like to expose to the user somehow.

Solution

If you want a generator to expose extra state to the user, don't forget that you can easily implement it as a class, putting the generator function code in the __iter__() method. For example:

```
from collections import deque

class linehistory:
    def __init__(self, lines, histlen=3):
        self.lines = lines
        self.history = deque(maxlen=histlen)

    def __iter__(self):
        for lineno, line in enumerate(self.lines,1):
            self.history.append((lineno, line))
            yield line

    def clear(self):
        self.history.clear()
```

To use this class, you would treat it like a normal generator function. However, since it creates an instance, you can access internal attributes, such as the history attribute or the clear() method. For example:

```
with open('somefile.txt') as f:
    lines = linehistory(f)
    for line in lines:
        if 'python' in line:
            for lineno, hline in lines.history:
                print('{}:{}'.format(lineno, hline), end='')
```

Discussion

With generators, it is easy to fall into a trap of trying to do everything with functions alone. This can lead to rather complicated code if the generator function needs to interact with other parts of your program in unusual ways (exposing attributes, allowing control via method calls, etc.). If this is the case, just use a class definition, as shown. Defining your generator in the __iter__() method doesn't change anything about how you write your algorithm. The fact that it's part of a class makes it easy for you to provide attributes and methods for users to interact with.

One potential subtlety with the method shown is that it might require an extra step of calling iter() if you are going to drive iteration using a technique other than a for loop. For example:

```
>>> f = open('somefile.txt')
>>> lines = linehistory(f)
>>> next(lines)
Traceback (most recent call last):
```

```
    File "<stdin>", line 1, in <module>
TypeError: 'linehistory' object is not an iterator

>>> # Call iter() first, then start iterating
>>> it = iter(lines)
>>> next(it)
'hello world\n'
>>> next(it)
'this is a test\n'
>>>
```

4.7. Taking a Slice of an Iterator

Problem

You want to take a slice of data produced by an iterator, but the normal slicing operator doesn't work.

Solution

The itertools.islice() function is perfectly suited for taking slices of iterators and generators. For example:

```
>>> def count(n):
...     while True:
...             yield n
...             n += 1
...
>>> c = count(0)
>>> c[10:20]
Traceback (most recent call last):
  File "<stdin>", line 1, in <module>
TypeError: 'generator' object is not subscriptable

>>> # Now using islice()
>>> import itertools
>>> for x in itertools.islice(c, 10, 20):
...     print(x)
...
10
11
12
13
14
15
16
17
18
19
>>>
```

Discussion

Iterators and generators can't normally be sliced, because no information is known about their length (and they don't implement indexing). The result of islice() is an iterator that produces the desired slice items, but it does this by consuming and discarding all of the items up to the starting slice index. Further items are then produced by the islice object until the ending index has been reached.

It's important to emphasize that islice() will consume data on the supplied iterator. Since iterators can't be rewound, that is something to consider. If it's important to go back, you should probably just turn the data into a list first.

4.8. Skipping the First Part of an Iterable

Problem

You want to iterate over items in an iterable, but the first few items aren't of interest and you just want to discard them.

Solution

The itertools module has a few functions that can be used to address this task. The first is the itertools.dropwhile() function. To use it, you supply a function and an iterable. The returned iterator discards the first items in the sequence as long as the supplied function returns True. Afterward, the entirety of the sequence is produced.

To illustrate, suppose you are reading a file that starts with a series of comment lines. For example:

```
>>> with open('/etc/passwd') as f:
...     for line in f:
...         print(line, end='')
...
##
# User Database
#
# Note that this file is consulted directly only when the system is running
# in single-user mode.  At other times, this information is provided by
# Open Directory.
...
##
nobody:*:-2:-2:Unprivileged User:/var/empty:/usr/bin/false
root:*:0:0:System Administrator:/var/root:/bin/sh
...
>>>
```

If you want to skip all of the initial comment lines, here's one way to do it:

```
>>> from itertools import dropwhile
>>> with open('/etc/passwd') as f:
...     for line in dropwhile(lambda line: line.startswith('#'), f):
...         print(line, end='')
...
nobody:*:-2:-2:Unprivileged User:/var/empty:/usr/bin/false
root:*:0:0:System Administrator:/var/root:/bin/sh
...
>>>
```

This example is based on skipping the first items according to a test function. If you happen to know the exact number of items you want to skip, then you can use iter tools.islice() instead. For example:

```
>>> from itertools import islice
>>> items = ['a', 'b', 'c', 1, 4, 10, 15]
>>> for x in islice(items, 3, None):
...     print(x)
...
1
4
10
15
>>>
```

In this example, the last None argument to islice() is required to indicate that you want everything *beyond* the first three items as opposed to only the first three items (e.g., a slice of [3:] as opposed to a slice of [:3]).

Discussion

The dropwhile() and islice() functions are mainly convenience functions that you can use to avoid writing rather messy code such as this:

```
with open('/etc/passwd') as f:
    # Skip over initial comments
    while True:
        line = next(f, '')
        if not line.startswith('#'):
            break

    # Process remaining lines
    while line:
        # Replace with useful processing
        print(line, end='')
        line = next(f, None)
```

Discarding the first part of an iterable is also slightly different than simply filtering all of it. For example, the first part of this recipe might be rewritten as follows:

```
with open('/etc/passwd') as f:
    lines = (line for line in f if not line.startswith('#'))
```

```
for line in lines:
    print(line, end='')
```

This will obviously discard the comment lines at the start, but will also discard all such lines throughout the entire file. On the other hand, the solution only discards items until an item no longer satisfies the supplied test. After that, all subsequent items are returned with no filtering.

Last, but not least, it should be emphasized that this recipe works with all iterables, including those whose size can't be determined in advance. This includes generators, files, and similar kinds of objects.

4.9. Iterating Over All Possible Combinations or Permutations

Problem

You want to iterate over all of the possible combinations or permutations of a collection of items.

Solution

The `itertools` module provides three functions for this task. The first of these— `iter tools.permutations()`—takes a collection of items and produces a sequence of tuples that rearranges all of the items into all possible permutations (i.e., it shuffles them into all possible configurations). For example:

```
>>> items = ['a', 'b', 'c']
>>> from itertools import permutations
>>> for p in permutations(items):
...     print(p)
...
('a', 'b', 'c')
('a', 'c', 'b')
('b', 'a', 'c')
('b', 'c', 'a')
('c', 'a', 'b')
('c', 'b', 'a')
>>>
```

If you want all permutations of a smaller length, you can give an optional length argument. For example:

```
>>> for p in permutations(items, 2):
...     print(p)
...
('a', 'b')
('a', 'c')
```

```
('b', 'a')
('b', 'c')
('c', 'a')
('c', 'b')
>>>
```

Use `itertools.combinations()` to produce a sequence of combinations of items taken from the input. For example:

```
>>> from itertools import combinations
>>> for c in combinations(items, 3):
...     print(c)
...
('a', 'b', 'c')
>>> for c in combinations(items, 2):
...     print(c)
...
('a', 'b')
('a', 'c')
('b', 'c')
>>> for c in combinations(items, 1):
...     print(c)
...
('a',)
('b',)
('c',)
>>>
```

For `combinations()`, the actual order of the elements is not considered. That is, the combination `('a', 'b')` is considered to be the same as `('b', 'a')` (which is not produced).

When producing combinations, chosen items are removed from the collection of possible candidates (i.e., if `'a'` has already been chosen, then it is removed from consideration). The `itertools.combinations_with_replacement()` function relaxes this, and allows the same item to be chosen more than once. For example:

```
>>> for c in combinations_with_replacement(items, 3):
...     print(c)
...
('a', 'a', 'a')
('a', 'a', 'b')
('a', 'a', 'c')
('a', 'b', 'b')
('a', 'b', 'c')
('a', 'c', 'c')
('b', 'b', 'b')
('b', 'b', 'c')
('b', 'c', 'c')
('c', 'c', 'c')
>>>
```

Discussion

This recipe demonstrates only some of the power found in the `itertools` module. Although you could certainly write code to produce permutations and combinations yourself, doing so would probably require more than a fair bit of thought. When faced with seemingly complicated iteration problems, it always pays to look at `itertools` first. If the problem is common, chances are a solution is already available.

4.10. Iterating Over the Index-Value Pairs of a Sequence

Problem

You want to iterate over a sequence, but would like to keep track of which element of the sequence is currently being processed.

Solution

The built-in `enumerate()` function handles this quite nicely:

```
>>> my_list = ['a', 'b', 'c']
>>> for idx, val in enumerate(my_list):
...     print(idx, val)
...
0 a
1 b
2 c
```

For printing output with canonical line numbers (where you typically start the numbering at 1 instead of 0), you can pass in a `start` argument:

```
>>> my_list = ['a', 'b', 'c']
>>> for idx, val in enumerate(my_list, 1):
...     print(idx, val)
...
1 a
2 b
3 c
```

This case is especially useful for tracking line numbers in files should you want to use a line number in an error message:

```
def parse_data(filename):
    with open(filename, 'rt') as f:
        for lineno, line in enumerate(f, 1):
            fields = line.split()
            try:
                count = int(fields[1])
                ...
            except ValueError as e:
                print('Line {}: Parse error: {}'.format(lineno, e))
```

enumerate() can be handy for keeping track of the offset into a list for occurrences of certain values, for example. So, if you want to map words in a file to the lines in which they occur, it can easily be accomplished using enumerate() to map each word to the line offset in the file where it was found:

```
word_summary = defaultdict(list)

with open('myfile.txt', 'r') as f:
    lines = f.readlines()

for idx, line in enumerate(lines):
    # Create a list of words in current line
    words = [w.strip().lower() for w in line.split()]
    for word in words:
        word_summary[word].append(idx)
```

If you print word_summary after processing the file, it'll be a dictionary (a default dict to be precise), and it'll have a key for each word. The value for each word-key will be a list of line numbers that word occurred on. If the word occurred twice on a single line, that line number will be listed twice, making it possible to identify various simple metrics about the text.

Discussion

enumerate() is a nice shortcut for situations where you might be inclined to keep your own counter variable. You could write code like this:

```
lineno = 1
for line in f:
    # Process line
    ...
    lineno += 1
```

But it's usually much more elegant (and less error prone) to use enumerate() instead:

```
for lineno, line in enumerate(f):
    # Process line
    ...
```

The value returned by enumerate() is an instance of an enumerate object, which is an iterator that returns successive tuples consisting of a counter and the value returned by calling next() on the sequence you've passed in.

Although a minor point, it's worth mentioning that sometimes it is easy to get tripped up when applying enumerate() to a sequence of tuples that are also being unpacked. To do it, you have to write code like this:

```
data = [ (1, 2), (3, 4), (5, 6), (7, 8) ]

# Correct!
for n, (x, y) in enumerate(data):
```

```
    ...
# Error!
for n, x, y in enumerate(data):
    ...
```

4.11. Iterating Over Multiple Sequences Simultaneously

Problem

You want to iterate over the items contained in more than one sequence at a time.

Solution

To iterate over more than one sequence simultaneously, use the zip() function. For example:

```
>>> xpts = [1, 5, 4, 2, 10, 7]
>>> ypts = [101, 78, 37, 15, 62, 99]
>>> for x, y in zip(xpts, ypts):
...     print(x,y)
...
1 101
5 78
4 37
2 15
10 62
7 99
>>>
```

zip(a, b) works by creating an iterator that produces tuples (x, y) where x is taken from a and y is taken from b. Iteration stops whenever one of the input sequences is exhausted. Thus, the length of the iteration is the same as the length of the shortest input. For example:

```
>>> a = [1, 2, 3]
>>> b = ['w', 'x', 'y', 'z']
>>> for i in zip(a,b):
...     print(i)
...
(1, 'w')
(2, 'x')
(3, 'y')
>>>
```

If this behavior is not desired, use itertools.zip_longest() instead. For example:

```
>>> from itertools import zip_longest
>>> for i in zip_longest(a,b):
...     print(i)
...
```

```
(1, 'w')
(2, 'x')
(3, 'y')
(None, 'z')
>>> for i in zip_longest(a, b, fillvalue=0):
...     print(i)
...
(1, 'w')
(2, 'x')
(3, 'y')
(0, 'z')
>>>
```

Discussion

zip() is commonly used whenever you need to pair data together. For example, suppose you have a list of column headers and column values like this:

```
headers = ['name', 'shares', 'price']
values = ['ACME', 100, 490.1]
```

Using zip(), you can pair the values together to make a dictionary like this:

```
s = dict(zip(headers,values))
```

Alternatively, if you are trying to produce output, you can write code like this:

```
for name, val in zip(headers, values):
    print(name, '=', val)
```

It's less common, but zip() can be passed more than two sequences as input. For this case, the resulting tuples have the same number of items in them as the number of input sequences. For example:

```
>>> a = [1, 2, 3]
>>> b = [10, 11, 12]
>>> c = ['x','y','z']
>>> for i in zip(a, b, c):
...     print(i)
...
(1, 10, 'x')
(2, 11, 'y')
(3, 12, 'z')
>>>
```

Last, but not least, it's important to emphasize that zip() creates an iterator as a result. If you need the paired values stored in a list, use the list() function. For example:

```
>>> zip(a, b)
<zip object at 0x1007001b8>
>>> list(zip(a, b))
[(1, 10), (2, 11), (3, 12)]
>>>
```

4.12. Iterating on Items in Separate Containers

Problem

You need to perform the same operation on many objects, but the objects are contained in different containers, and you'd like to avoid nested loops without losing the readability of your code.

Solution

The `itertools.chain()` method can be used to simplify this task. It takes a list of iterables as input, and returns an iterator that effectively masks the fact that you're really acting on multiple containers. To illustrate, consider this example:

```
>>> from itertools import chain
>>> a = [1, 2, 3, 4]
>>> b = ['x', 'y', 'z']
>>> for x in chain(a, b):
...     print(x)
...
1
2
3
4
x
y
z
>>>
```

A common use of `chain()` is in programs where you would like to perform certain operations on all of the items at once but the items are pooled into different working sets. For example:

```
# Various working sets of items
active_items = set()
inactive_items = set()

# Iterate over all items
for item in chain(active_items, inactive_items):
    # Process item
    ...
```

This solution is much more elegant than using two separate loops, as in the following:

```
for item in active_items:
    # Process item
    ...

for item in inactive_items:
    # Process item
    ...
```

Discussion

`itertools.chain()` accepts one or more iterables as arguments. It then works by creating an iterator that successively consumes and returns the items produced by each of the supplied iterables you provided. It's a subtle distinction, but `chain()` is more efficient than first combining the sequences and iterating. For example:

```
# Inefficent
for x in a + b:
    ...

# Better
for x in chain(a, b):
    ...
```

In the first case, the operation a + b creates an entirely new sequence and additionally requires a and b to be of the same type. `chain()` performs no such operation, so it's far more efficient with memory if the input sequences are large and it can be easily applied when the iterables in question are of different types.

4.13. Creating Data Processing Pipelines

Problem

You want to process data iteratively in the style of a data processing pipeline (similar to Unix pipes). For instance, you have a huge amount of data that needs to be processed, but it can't fit entirely into memory.

Solution

Generator functions are a good way to implement processing pipelines. To illustrate, suppose you have a huge directory of log files that you want to process:

```
foo/
    access-log-012007.gz
    access-log-022007.gz
    access-log-032007.gz
    ...
    access-log-012008
bar/
    access-log-092007.bz2
    ...
    access-log-022008
```

Suppose each file contains lines of data like this:

```
124.115.6.12 - - [10/Jul/2012:00:18:50 -0500] "GET /robots.txt ..." 200 71
210.212.209.67 - - [10/Jul/2012:00:18:51 -0500] "GET /ply/ ..." 200 11875
210.212.209.67 - - [10/Jul/2012:00:18:51 -0500] "GET /favicon.ico ..." 404 369
```

```
61.135.216.105 - - [10/Jul/2012:00:20:04 -0500] "GET /blog/atom.xml ..." 304 -
...
```

To process these files, you could define a collection of small generator functions that perform specific self-contained tasks. For example:

```python
import os
import fnmatch
import gzip
import bz2
import re

def gen_find(filepat, top):
    '''
    Find all filenames in a directory tree that match a shell wildcard pattern
    '''
    for path, dirlist, filelist in os.walk(top):
        for name in fnmatch.filter(filelist, filepat):
            yield os.path.join(path,name)

def gen_opener(filenames):
    '''
    Open a sequence of filenames one at a time producing a file object.
    The file is closed immediately when proceeding to the next iteration.
    '''
    for filename in filenames:
        if filename.endswith('.gz'):
            f = gzip.open(filename, 'rt')
        elif filename.endswith('.bz2'):
            f = bz2.open(filename, 'rt')
        else:
            f = open(filename, 'rt')
        yield f
        f.close()

def gen_concatenate(iterators):
    '''
    Chain a sequence of iterators together into a single sequence.
    '''
    for it in iterators:
        yield from it

def gen_grep(pattern, lines):
    '''
    Look for a regex pattern in a sequence of lines
    '''
    pat = re.compile(pattern)
    for line in lines:
        if pat.search(line):
            yield line
```

You can now easily stack these functions together to make a processing pipeline. For example, to find all log lines that contain the word *python*, you would just do this:

```
lognames = gen_find('access-log*', 'www')
files = gen_opener(lognames)
lines = gen_concatenate(files)
pylines = gen_grep('(?i)python', lines)
for line in pylines:
    print(line)
```

If you want to extend the pipeline further, you can even feed the data in generator expressions. For example, this version finds the number of bytes transferred and sums the total:

```
lognames = gen_find('access-log*', 'www')
files = gen_opener(lognames)
lines = gen_concatenate(files)
pylines = gen_grep('(?i)python', lines)
bytecolumn = (line.rsplit(None,1)[1] for line in pylines)
bytes = (int(x) for x in bytecolumn if x != '-')
print('Total', sum(bytes))
```

Discussion

Processing data in a pipelined manner works well for a wide variety of other problems, including parsing, reading from real-time data sources, periodic polling, and so on.

In understanding the code, it is important to grasp that the yield statement acts as a kind of data producer whereas a for loop acts as a data consumer. When the generators are stacked together, each yield feeds a single item of data to the next stage of the pipeline that is consuming it with iteration. In the last example, the sum() function is actually driving the entire program, pulling one item at a time out of the pipeline of generators.

One nice feature of this approach is that each generator function tends to be small and self-contained. As such, they are easy to write and maintain. In many cases, they are so general purpose that they can be reused in other contexts. The resulting code that glues the components together also tends to read like a simple recipe that is easily understood.

The memory efficiency of this approach can also not be overstated. The code shown would still work even if used on a massive directory of files. In fact, due to the iterative nature of the processing, very little memory would be used at all.

There is a bit of extreme subtlety involving the gen_concatenate() function. The purpose of this function is to concatenate input sequences together into one long sequence of lines. The itertools.chain() function performs a similar function, but requires that all of the chained iterables be specified as arguments. In the case of this particular recipe, doing that would involve a statement such as lines = iter tools.chain(*files), which would cause the gen_opener() generator to be fully consumed. Since that generator is producing a sequence of open files that are immediately closed in the next iteration step, chain() can't be used. The solution shown avoids this issue.

Also appearing in the gen_concatenate() function is the use of yield from to delegate to a subgenerator. The statement yield from it simply makes gen_concatenate() emit all of the values produced by the generator it. This is described further in Recipe 4.14.

Last, but not least, it should be noted that a pipelined approach doesn't always work for every data handling problem. Sometimes you just need to work with all of the data at once. However, even in that case, using generator pipelines can be a way to logically break a problem down into a kind of workflow.

David Beazley has written extensively about these techniques in his "Generator Tricks for Systems Programmers" tutorial presentation (*http://www.dabeaz.com/generators*). Consult that for even more examples.

4.14. Flattening a Nested Sequence

Problem

You have a nested sequence that you want to flatten into a single list of values.

Solution

This is easily solved by writing a recursive generator function involving a yield from statement. For example:

```
from collections import Iterable

def flatten(items, ignore_types=(str, bytes)):
    for x in items:
        if isinstance(x, Iterable) and not isinstance(x, ignore_types):
            yield from flatten(x)
        else:
            yield x

items = [1, 2, [3, 4, [5, 6], 7], 8]

# Produces 1 2 3 4 5 6 7 8
for x in flatten(items):
    print(x)
```

In the code, the isinstance(x, Iterable) simply checks to see if an item is iterable. If so, yield from is used to emit all of its values as a kind of subroutine. The end result is a single sequence of output with no nesting.

The extra argument `ignore_types` and the check for `not isinstance(x, ig nore_types)` is there to prevent strings and bytes from being interpreted as iterables and expanded as individual characters. This allows nested lists of strings to work in the way that most people would expect. For example:

```
>>> items = ['Dave', 'Paula', ['Thomas', 'Lewis']]
>>> for x in flatten(items):
...     print(x)
...
Dave
Paula
Thomas
Lewis
>>>
```

Discussion

The `yield from` statement is a nice shortcut to use if you ever want to write generators that call other generators as subroutines. If you don't use it, you need to write code that uses an extra `for` loop. For example:

```
def flatten(items, ignore_types=(str, bytes)):
    for x in items:
        if isinstance(x, Iterable) and not isinstance(x, ignore_types):
            for i in flatten(x):
                yield i
        else:
            yield x
```

Although it's only a minor change, the `yield from` statement just feels better and leads to cleaner code.

As noted, the extra check for strings and bytes is there to prevent the expansion of those types into individual characters. If there are other types that you don't want expanded, you can supply a different value for the `ignore_types` argument.

Finally, it should be noted that `yield from` has a more important role in advanced programs involving coroutines and generator-based concurrency. See Recipe 12.12 for another example.

4.15. Iterating in Sorted Order Over Merged Sorted Iterables

Problem

You have a collection of sorted sequences and you want to iterate over a sorted sequence of them all merged together.

Solution

The `heapq.merge()` function does exactly what you want. For example:

```
>>> import heapq
>>> a = [1, 4, 7, 10]
>>> b = [2, 5, 6, 11]
>>> for c in heapq.merge(a, b):
...     print(c)
...
1
2
4
5
6
7
10
11
```

Discussion

The iterative nature of `heapq.merge` means that it never reads any of the supplied sequences all at once. This means that you can use it on very long sequences with very little overhead. For instance, here is an example of how you would merge two sorted files:

```
import heapq

with open('sorted_file_1', 'rt') as file1, \
     open('sorted_file_2') 'rt' as file2, \
     open('merged_file', 'wt') as outf:

    for line in heapq.merge(file1, file2):
        outf.write(line)
```

It's important to emphasize that `heapq.merge()` requires that all of the input sequences already be sorted. In particular, it does not first read all of the data into a heap or do any preliminary sorting. Nor does it perform any kind of validation of the inputs to check if they meet the ordering requirements. Instead, it simply examines the set of items from the front of each input sequence and emits the smallest one found. A new item from the chosen sequence is then read, and the process repeats itself until all input sequences have been fully consumed.

4.16. Replacing Infinite while Loops with an Iterator

Problem

You have code that uses a while loop to iteratively process data because it involves a function or some kind of unusual test condition that doesn't fall into the usual iteration pattern.

Solution

A somewhat common scenario in programs involving I/O is to write code like this:

```
CHUNKSIZE = 8192

def reader(s):
    while True:
        data = s.recv(CHUNKSIZE)
        if data == b'':
            break
        process_data(data)
```

Such code can often be replaced using iter(), as follows:

```
def reader(s):
    for chunk in iter(lambda: s.recv(CHUNKSIZE), b''):
        process_data(data)
```

If you're a bit skeptical that it might work, you can try a similar example involving files. For example:

```
>>> import sys
>>> f = open('/etc/passwd')
>>> for chunk in iter(lambda: f.read(10), ''):
...     n = sys.stdout.write(chunk)
...
nobody:*:-2:-2:Unprivileged User:/var/empty:/usr/bin/false
root:*:0:0:System Administrator:/var/root:/bin/sh
daemon:*:1:1:System Services:/var/root:/usr/bin/false
_uucp:*:4:4:Unix to Unix Copy Protocol:/var/spool/uucp:/usr/sbin/uucico
...
>>>
```

Discussion

A little-known feature of the built-in iter() function is that it optionally accepts a zero-argument callable and sentinel (terminating) value as inputs. When used in this way, it creates an iterator that repeatedly calls the supplied callable over and over again until it returns the value given as a sentinel.

This particular approach works well with certain kinds of repeatedly called functions, such as those involving I/O. For example, if you want to read data in chunks from sockets or files, you usually have to repeatedly execute read() or recv() calls followed by an end-of-file test. This recipe simply takes these two features and combines them together into a single iter() call. The use of lambda in the solution is needed to create a callable that takes no arguments, yet still supplies the desired size argument to recv() or read().

## CHAPTER 5

Files and I/O

All programs need to perform input and output. This chapter covers common idioms for working with different kinds of files, including text and binary files, file encodings, and other related matters. Techniques for manipulating filenames and directories are also covered.

5.1. Reading and Writing Text Data

Problem

You need to read or write text data, possibly in different text encodings such as ASCII, UTF-8, or UTF-16.

Solution

Use the open() function with mode rt to read a text file. For example:

```
# Read the entire file as a single string
with open('somefile.txt', 'rt') as f:
    data = f.read()

# Iterate over the lines of the file
with open('somefile.txt', 'rt') as f:
    for line in f:
        # process line
        ...
```

Similarly, to write a text file, use open() with mode wt to write a file, clearing and overwriting the previous contents (if any). For example:

```
# Write chunks of text data
with open('somefile.txt', 'wt') as f:
    f.write(text1)
```

```
    f.write(text2)
    ...

# Redirected print statement
with open('somefile.txt', 'wt') as f:
    print(line1, file=f)
    print(line2, file=f)
    ...
```

To append to the end of an existing file, use open() with mode at.

By default, files are read/written using the system default text encoding, as can be found in sys.getdefaultencoding(). On most machines, this is set to utf-8. If you know that the text you are reading or writing is in a different encoding, supply the optional encoding parameter to open(). For example:

```
with open('somefile.txt', 'rt', encoding='latin-1') as f:
    ...
```

Python understands several hundred possible text encodings. However, some of the more common encodings are ascii, latin-1, utf-8, and utf-16. UTF-8 is usually a safe bet if working with web applications. ascii corresponds to the 7-bit characters in the range U+0000 to U+007F. latin-1 is a direct mapping of bytes 0-255 to Unicode characters U+0000 to U+00FF. latin-1 encoding is notable in that it will never produce a decoding error when reading text of a possibly unknown encoding. Reading a file as latin-1 might not produce a completely correct text decoding, but it still might be enough to extract useful data out of it. Also, if you later write the data back out, the original input data will be preserved.

Discussion

Reading and writing text files is typically very straightforward. However, there are a number of subtle aspects to keep in mind. First, the use of the with statement in the examples establishes a context in which the file will be used. When control leaves the with block, the file will be closed automatically. You don't need to use the with statement, but if you don't use it, make sure you remember to close the file:

```
f = open('somefile.txt', 'rt')
data = f.read()
f.close()
```

Another minor complication concerns the recognition of newlines, which are different on Unix and Windows (i.e., \n versus \r\n). By default, Python operates in what's known as "universal newline" mode. In this mode, all common newline conventions are recognized, and newline characters are converted to a single \n character while reading. Similarly, the newline character \n is converted to the system default newline character on output. If you don't want this translation, supply the `newline=''` argument to `open()`, like this:

```
# Read with disabled newline translation
with open('somefile.txt', 'rt', newline='') as f:
    ...
```

To illustrate the difference, here's what you will see on a Unix machine if you read the contents of a Windows-encoded text file containing the raw data `hello world!\r\n`:

```
>>> # Newline translation enabled (the default)
>>> f = open('hello.txt', 'rt')
>>> f.read()
'hello world!\n'

>>> # Newline translation disabled
>>> g = open('hello.txt', 'rt', newline='')
>>> g.read()
'hello world!\r\n'
>>>
```

A final issue concerns possible encoding errors in text files. When reading or writing a text file, you might encounter an encoding or decoding error. For instance:

```
>>> f = open('sample.txt', 'rt', encoding='ascii')
>>> f.read()
Traceback (most recent call last):
  File "<stdin>", line 1, in <module>
  File "/usr/local/lib/python3.3/encodings/ascii.py", line 26, in decode
    return codecs.ascii_decode(input, self.errors)[0]
UnicodeDecodeError: 'ascii' codec can't decode byte 0xc3 in position
12: ordinal not in range(128)
>>>
```

If you get this error, it usually means that you're not reading the file in the correct encoding. You should carefully read the specification of whatever it is that you're reading and check that you're doing it right (e.g., reading data as UTF-8 instead of Latin-1 or whatever it needs to be). If encoding errors are still a possibility, you can supply an optional `errors` argument to `open()` to deal with the errors. Here are a few samples of common error handling schemes:

```
>>> # Replace bad chars with Unicode U+fffd replacement char
>>> f = open('sample.txt', 'rt', encoding='ascii', errors='replace')
>>> f.read()
'Spicy Jalape?o!'
>>> # Ignore bad chars entirely
>>> g = open('sample.txt', 'rt', encoding='ascii', errors='ignore')
>>> g.read()
'Spicy Jalapeo!'
>>>
```

If you're constantly fiddling with the encoding and errors arguments to open() and doing lots of hacks, you're probably making life more difficult than it needs to be. The number one rule with text is that you simply need to make sure you're always using the proper text encoding. When in doubt, use the default setting (typically UTF-8).

5.2. Printing to a File

Problem

You want to redirect the output of the print() function to a file.

Solution

Use the file keyword argument to print(), like this:

```
with open('somefile.txt', 'rt') as f:
    print('Hello World!', file=f)
```

Discussion

There's not much more to printing to a file other than this. However, make sure that the file is opened in text mode. Printing will fail if the underlying file is in binary mode.

5.3. Printing with a Different Separator or Line Ending

Problem

You want to output data using print(), but you also want to change the separator character or line ending.

Solution

Use the sep and end keyword arguments to print() to change the output as you wish. For example:

```
>>> print('ACME', 50, 91.5)
ACME 50 91.5
>>> print('ACME', 50, 91.5, sep=',')
ACME,50,91.5
>>> print('ACME', 50, 91.5, sep=',', end='!!\n')
ACME,50,91.5!!
>>>
```

Use of the end argument is also how you suppress the output of newlines in output. For example:

```
>>> for i in range(5):
...     print(i)
...
0
1
2
3
4
>>> for i in range(5):
...     print(i, end=' ')
...
0 1 2 3 4 >>>
```

Discussion

Using `print()` with a different item separator is often the easiest way to output data when you need something other than a space separating the items. Sometimes you'll see programmers using `str.join()` to accomplish the same thing. For example:

```
>>> print(','.join('ACME','50','91.5'))
ACME,50,91.5
>>>
```

The problem with `str.join()` is that it only works with strings. This means that it's often necessary to perform various acrobatics to get it to work. For example:

```
>>> row = ('ACME', 50, 91.5)
>>> print(','.join(row))
Traceback (most recent call last):
  File "<stdin>", line 1, in <module>
TypeError: sequence item 1: expected str instance, int found
>>> print(','.join(str(x) for x in row))
ACME,50,91.5
>>>
```

Instead of doing that, you could just write the following:

```
>>> print(*row, sep=',')
ACME,50,91.5
>>>
```

5.4. Reading and Writing Binary Data

Problem

You need to read or write binary data, such as that found in images, sound files, and so on.

Solution

Use the open() function with mode rb or wb to read or write binary data. For example:

```
# Read the entire file as a single byte string
with open('somefile.bin', 'rb') as f:
    data = f.read()

# Write binary data to a file
with open('somefile.bin', 'wb') as f:
    f.write(b'Hello World')
```

When reading binary, it is important to stress that all data returned will be in the form of byte strings, not text strings. Similarly, when writing, you must supply data in the form of objects that expose data as bytes (e.g., byte strings, bytearray objects, etc.).

Discussion

When reading binary data, the subtle semantic differences between byte strings and text strings pose a potential gotcha. In particular, be aware that indexing and iteration return integer byte values instead of byte strings. For example:

```
>>> # Text string
>>> t = 'Hello World'
>>> t[0]
'H'
>>> for c in t:
...     print(c)
...
H
e
l
l
o
...
>>> # Byte string
>>> b = b'Hello World'
>>> b[0]
72
>>> for c in b:
...     print(c)
...
72
101
108
108
111
...
>>>
```

If you ever need to read or write text from a binary-mode file, make sure you remember to decode or encode it. For example:

```
with open('somefile.bin', 'rb') as f:
    data = f.read(16)
    text = data.decode('utf-8')

with open('somefile.bin', 'wb') as f:
    text = 'Hello World'
    f.write(text.encode('utf-8'))
```

A lesser-known aspect of binary I/O is that objects such as arrays and C structures can be used for writing without any kind of intermediate conversion to a bytes object. For example:

```
import array
nums = array.array('i', [1, 2, 3, 4])
with open('data.bin','wb') as f:
    f.write(nums)
```

This applies to any object that implements the so-called "buffer interface," which directly exposes an underlying memory buffer to operations that can work with it. Writing binary data is one such operation.

Many objects also allow binary data to be directly read into their underlying memory using the readinto() method of files. For example:

```
>>> import array
>>> a = array.array('i', [0, 0, 0, 0, 0, 0, 0, 0])
>>> with open('data.bin', 'rb') as f:
...     f.readinto(a)
...
16
>>> a
array('i', [1, 2, 3, 4, 0, 0, 0, 0])
>>>
```

However, great care should be taken when using this technique, as it is often platform specific and may depend on such things as the word size and byte ordering (i.e., big endian versus little endian). See Recipe 5.9 for another example of reading binary data into a mutable buffer.

5.5. Writing to a File That Doesn't Already Exist

Problem

You want to write data to a file, but only if it doesn't already exist on the filesystem.

Solution

This problem is easily solved by using the little-known x mode to open( ) instead of the usual w mode. For example:

```
>>> with open('somefile', 'wt') as f:
...     f.write('Hello\n')
...
>>> with open('somefile', 'xt') as f:
...     f.write('Hello\n')
...
Traceback (most recent call last):
  File "<stdin>", line 1, in <module>
FileExistsError: [Errno 17] File exists: 'somefile'
>>>
```

If the file is binary mode, use mode xb instead of xt.

Discussion

This recipe illustrates an extremely elegant solution to a problem that sometimes arises when writing files (i.e., accidentally overwriting an existing file). An alternative solution is to first test for the file like this:

```
>>> import os
>>> if not os.path.exists('somefile'):
...     with open('somefile', 'wt') as f:
...         f.write('Hello\n')
... else:
...     print('File already exists!')
...
File already exists!
>>>
```

Clearly, using the x file mode is a lot more straightforward. It is important to note that the x mode is a Python 3 specific extension to the open( ) function. In particular, no such mode exists in earlier Python versions or the underlying C libraries used in Python's implementation.

5.6. Performing I/O Operations on a String

Problem

You want to feed a text or binary string to code that's been written to operate on file-like objects instead.

Solution

Use the `io.StringIO()` and `io.BytesIO()` classes to create file-like objects that operate on string data. For example:

```
>>> s = io.StringIO()
>>> s.write('Hello World\n')
12
>>> print('This is a test', file=s)
15
>>> # Get all of the data written so far
>>> s.getvalue()
'Hello World\nThis is a test\n'
>>>

>>> # Wrap a file interface around an existing string
>>> s = io.StringIO('Hello\nWorld\n')
>>> s.read(4)
'Hell'
>>> s.read()
'o\nWorld\n'
>>>
```

The `io.StringIO` class should only be used for text. If you are operating with binary data, use the `io.BytesIO` class instead. For example:

```
>>> s = io.BytesIO()
>>> s.write(b'binary data')
>>> s.getvalue()
b'binary data'
>>>
```

Discussion

The `StringIO` and `BytesIO` classes are most useful in scenarios where you need to mimic a normal file for some reason. For example, in unit tests, you might use `StringIO` to create a file-like object containing test data that's fed into a function that would otherwise work with a normal file.

Be aware that `StringIO` and `BytesIO` instances don't have a proper integer file-descriptor. Thus, they do not work with code that requires the use of a real system-level file such as a file, pipe, or socket.

5.7. Reading and Writing Compressed Datafiles

Problem

You need to read or write data in a file with gzip or bz2 compression.

Solution

The `gzip` and `bz2` modules make it easy to work with such files. Both modules provide an alternative implementation of `open()` that can be used for this purpose. For example, to read compressed files as text, do this:

```
# gzip compression
import gzip
with gzip.open('somefile.gz', 'rt') as f:
    text = f.read()

# bz2 compression
import bz2
with bz2.open('somefile.bz2', 'rt') as f:
    text = f.read()
```

Similarly, to write compressed data, do this:

```
# gzip compression
import gzip
with gzip.open('somefile.gz', 'wt') as f:
    f.write(text)

# bz2 compression
import bz2
with bz2.open('somefile.bz2', 'wt') as f:
    f.write(text)
```

As shown, all I/O will use text and perform Unicode encoding/decoding. If you want to work with binary data instead, use a file mode of `rb` or `wb`.

Discussion

For the most part, reading or writing compressed data is straightforward. However, be aware that choosing the correct file mode is critically important. If you don't specify a mode, the default mode is binary, which will break programs that expect to receive text. Both `gzip.open()` and `bz2.open()` accept the same parameters as the built-in `open()` function, including `encoding`, `errors`, `newline`, and so forth.

When writing compressed data, the compression level can be optionally specified using the `compresslevel` keyword argument. For example:

```
with gzip.open('somefile.gz', 'wt', compresslevel=5) as f:
    f.write(text)
```

The default level is 9, which provides the highest level of compression. Lower levels offer better performance, but not as much compression.

Finally, a little-known feature of `gzip.open()` and `bz2.open()` is that they can be layered on top of an existing file opened in binary mode. For example, this works:

```
import gzip

f = open('somefile.gz', 'rb')
with gzip.open(f, 'rt') as g:
    text = g.read()
```

This allows the gzip and bz2 modules to work with various file-like objects such as sockets, pipes, and in-memory files.

5.8. Iterating Over Fixed-Sized Records

Problem

Instead of iterating over a file by lines, you want to iterate over a collection of fixed-sized records or chunks.

Solution

Use the iter() function and functools.partial() using this neat trick:

```
from functools import partial

RECORD_SIZE = 32

with open('somefile.data', 'rb') as f:
    records = iter(partial(f.read, RECORD_SIZE), b'')
    for r in records:
        ...
```

The records object in this example is an iterable that will produce fixed-sized chunks until the end of the file is reached. However, be aware that the last item may have fewer bytes than expected if the file size is not an exact multiple of the record size.

Discussion

A little-known feature of the iter() function is that it can create an iterator if you pass it a callable and a sentinel value. The resulting iterator simply calls the supplied callable over and over again until it returns the sentinel, at which point iteration stops.

In the solution, the functools.partial is used to create a callable that reads a fixed number of bytes from a file each time it's called. The sentinel of b' ' is what gets returned when a file is read but the end of file has been reached.

Last, but not least, the solution shows the file being opened in binary mode. For reading fixed-sized records, this would probably be the most common case. For text files, reading line by line (the default iteration behavior) is more common.

5.9. Reading Binary Data into a Mutable Buffer

Problem

You want to read binary data directly into a mutable buffer without any intermediate copying. Perhaps you want to mutate the data in-place and write it back out to a file.

Solution

To read data into a mutable array, use the `readinto()` method of files. For example:

```python
import os.path

def read_into_buffer(filename):
    buf = bytearray(os.path.getsize(filename))
    with open(filename, 'rb') as f:
        f.readinto(buf)
    return buf
```

Here is an example that illustrates the usage:

```python
>>> # Write a sample file
>>> with open('sample.bin', 'wb') as f:
...     f.write(b'Hello World')
...
>>> buf = read_into_buffer('sample.bin')
>>> buf
bytearray(b'Hello World')
>>> buf[0:5] = b'Hallo'
>>> buf
bytearray(b'Hallo World')
>>> with open('newsample.bin', 'wb') as f:
...     f.write(buf)
...
11
>>>
```

Discussion

The `readinto()` method of files can be used to fill any preallocated array with data. This even includes arrays created from the `array` module or libraries such as `numpy`. Unlike the normal `read()` method, `readinto()` fills the contents of an existing buffer rather than allocating new objects and returning them. Thus, you might be able to use it to avoid making extra memory allocations. For example, if you are reading a binary file consisting of equally sized records, you can write code like this:

```python
record_size = 32          # Size of each record (adjust value)

buf = bytearray(record_size)
with open('somefile', 'rb') as f:
```

```
    while True:
        n = f.readinto(buf)
        if n < record_size:
            break
        # Use the contents of buf
        ...
```

Another interesting feature to use here might be a memoryview, which lets you make
zero-copy slices of an existing buffer and even change its contents. For example:

```
>>> buf
bytearray(b'Hello World')
>>> m1 = memoryview(buf)
>>> m2 = m1[-5:]
>>> m2
<memory at 0x100681390>
>>> m2[:] = b'WORLD'
>>> buf
bytearray(b'Hello WORLD')
>>>
```

One caution with using `f.readinto()` is that you must always make sure to check its
return code, which is the number of bytes actually read.

If the number of bytes is smaller than the size of the supplied buffer, it might indicate
truncated or corrupted data (e.g., if you were expecting an exact number of bytes to be
read).

Finally, be on the lookout for other "into" related functions in various library modules
(e.g., `recv_into()`, `pack_into()`, etc.). Many other parts of Python have support for
direct I/O or data access that can be used to fill or alter the contents of arrays and buffers.

See Recipe 6.12 for a significantly more advanced example of interpreting binary structures and usage of memoryviews.

5.10. Memory Mapping Binary Files

Problem

You want to memory map a binary file into a mutable byte array, possibly for random
access to its contents or to make in-place modifications.

Solution

Use the `mmap` module to memory map files. Here is a utility function that shows how to
open a file and memory map it in a portable manner:

```
import os
import mmap
```

```
def memory_map(filename, access=mmap.ACCESS_WRITE):
    size = os.path.getsize(filename)
    fd = os.open(filename, os.O_RDWR)
    return mmap.mmap(fd, size, access=access)
```

To use this function, you would need to have a file already created and filled with data. Here is an example of how you could initially create a file and expand it to a desired size:

```
>>> size = 1000000
>>> with open('data', 'wb') as f:
...     f.seek(size-1)
...     f.write(b'\x00')
...
>>>
```

Now here is an example of memory mapping the contents using the memory_map() function:

```
>>> m = memory_map('data')
>>> len(m)
1000000
>>> m[0:10]
b'\x00\x00\x00\x00\x00\x00\x00\x00\x00\x00'
>>> m[0]
0
>>> # Reassign a slice
>>> m[0:11] = b'Hello World'
>>> m.close()

>>> # Verify that changes were made
>>> with open('data', 'rb') as f:
...     print(f.read(11))
...
b'Hello World'
>>>
```

The mmap object returned by mmap() can also be used as a context manager, in which case the underlying file is closed automatically. For example:

```
>>> with memory_map('data') as m:
...     print(len(m))
...     print(m[0:10])
...
1000000
b'Hello World'
>>> m.closed
True
>>>
```

By default, the memory_map() function shown opens a file for both reading and writing. Any modifications made to the data are copied back to the original file. If read-only

---

access is needed instead, supply mmap.ACCESS_READ for the access argument. For example:

```
m = memory_map(filename, mmap.ACCESS_READ)
```

If you intend to modify the data locally, but don't want those changes written back to the original file, use mmap.ACCESS_COPY:

```
m = memory_map(filename, mmap.ACCESS_COPY)
```

Discussion

Using mmap to map files into memory can be an efficient and elegant means for randomly accessing the contents of a file. For example, instead of opening a file and performing various combinations of seek(), read(), and write() calls, you can simply map the file and access the data using slicing operations.

Normally, the memory exposed by mmap() looks like a bytearray object. However, you can interpret the data differently using a memoryview. For example:

```
>>> m = memory_map('data')
>>> # Memoryview of unsigned integers
>>> v - memoryview(m).cast('I')
>>> v[0] = 7
>>> m[0:4]
b'\x07\x00\x00\x00'
>>> m[0:4] = b'\x07\x01\x00\x00'
>>> v[0]
263
>>>
```

It should be emphasized that memory mapping a file does not cause the entire file to be read into memory. That is, it's not copied into some kind of memory buffer or array. Instead, the operating system merely reserves a section of virtual memory for the file contents. As you access different regions, those portions of the file will be read and mapped into the memory region as needed. However, parts of the file that are never accessed simply stay on disk. This all happens transparently, behind the scenes.

If more than one Python interpreter memory maps the same file, the resulting mmap object can be used to exchange data between interpreters. That is, all interpreters can read/write data simultaneously, and changes made to the data in one interpreter will automatically appear in the others. Obviously, some extra care is required to synchronize things, but this kind of approach is sometimes used as an alternative to transmitting data in messages over pipes or sockets.

As shown, this recipe has been written to be as general purpose as possible, working on both Unix and Windows. Be aware that there are some platform differences concerning the use of the mmap() call hidden behind the scenes. In addition, there are options to create anonymously mapped memory regions. If this is of interest to you, make sure you carefully read the Python documentation on the subject (*http://docs.python.org/3/library/mmap.html*).

5.11. Manipulating Pathnames

Problem

You need to manipulate pathnames in order to find the base filename, directory name, absolute path, and so on.

Solution

To manipulate pathnames, use the functions in the `os.path` module. Here is an interactive example that illustrates a few key features:

```
>>> import os
>>> path = '/Users/beazley/Data/data.csv'

>>> # Get the last component of the path
>>> os.path.basename(path)
'data.csv'

>>> # Get the directory name
>>> os.path.dirname(path)
'/Users/beazley/Data'

>>> # Join path components together
>>> os.path.join('tmp', 'data', os.path.basename(path))
'tmp/data/data.csv'

>>> # Expand the user's home directory
>>> path = '~/Data/data.csv'
>>> os.path.expanduser(path)
'/Users/beazley/Data/data.csv'

>>> # Split the file extension
>>> os.path.splitext(path)
('~/Data/data', '.csv')
>>>
```

Discussion

For any manipulation of filenames, you should use the `os.path` module instead of trying to cook up your own code using the standard string operations. In part, this is for portability. The `os.path` module knows about differences between Unix and Windows and can reliably deal with filenames such as *Data/data.csv* and *Data\data.csv*. Second, you really shouldn't spend your time reinventing the wheel. It's usually best to use the functionality that's already provided for you.

It should be noted that the os.path module has many more features not shown in this recipe. Consult the documentation for more functions related to file testing, symbolic links, and so forth.

5.12. Testing for the Existence of a File

Problem

You need to test whether or not a file or directory exists.

Solution

Use the os.path module to test for the existence of a file or directory. For example:

```
>>> import os
>>> os.path.exists('/etc/passwd')
True
>>> os.path.exists('/tmp/spam')
False
>>>
```

You can perform further tests to see what kind of file it might be. These tests return False if the file in question doesn't exist:

```
>>> # Is a regular file
>>> os.path.isfile('/etc/passwd')
True

>>> # Is a directory
>>> os.path.isdir('/etc/passwd')
False

>>> # Is a symbolic link
>>> os.path.islink('/usr/local/bin/python3')
True

>>> # Get the file linked to
>>> os.path.realpath('/usr/local/bin/python3')
'/usr/local/bin/python3.3'
>>>
```

If you need to get metadata (e.g., the file size or modification date), that is also available in the os.path module.

```
>>> os.path.getsize('/etc/passwd')
3669
>>> os.path.getmtime('/etc/passwd')
1272478234.0
>>> import time
>>> time.ctime(os.path.getmtime('/etc/passwd'))
```

```
'Wed Apr 28 13:10:34 2010'
>>>
```

Discussion

File testing is a straightforward operation using os.path. Probably the only thing to be aware of when writing scripts is that you might need to worry about permissions—especially for operations that get metadata. For example:

```
>>> os.path.getsize('/Users/guido/Desktop/foo.txt')
Traceback (most recent call last):
  File "<stdin>", line 1, in <module>
  File "/usr/local/lib/python3.3/genericpath.py", line 49, in getsize
    return os.stat(filename).st_size
PermissionError: [Errno 13] Permission denied: '/Users/guido/Desktop/foo.txt'
>>>
```

5.13. Getting a Directory Listing

Problem

You want to get a list of the files contained in a directory on the filesystem.

Solution

Use the os.listdir() function to obtain a list of files in a directory:

```
import os
names = os.listdir('somedir')
```

This will give you the raw directory listing, including all files, subdirectories, symbolic links, and so forth. If you need to filter the data in some way, consider using a list comprehension combined with various functions in the os.path library. For example:

```
import os.path
# Get all regular files
names = [name for name in os.listdir('somedir')
        if os.path.isfile(os.path.join('somedir', name))]

# Get all dirs
dirnames = [name for name in os.listdir('somedir')
            if os.path.isdir(os.path.join('somedir', name))]
```

The startswith() and endswith() methods of strings can be useful for filtering the contents of a directory as well. For example:

```
pyfiles = [name for name in os.listdir('somedir')
            if name.endswith('.py')]
```

For filename matching, you may want to use the glob or fnmatch modules instead. For example:

```
import glob
pyfiles = glob.glob('somedir/*.py')

from fnmatch import fnmatch
pyfiles = [name for name in os.listdir('somedir')
            if fnmatch(name, '*.py')]
```

Discussion

Getting a directory listing is easy, but it only gives you the names of entries in the directory. If you want to get additional metadata, such as file sizes, modification dates, and so forth, you either need to use additional functions in the os.path module or use the os.stat() function. To collect the data. For example:

```
# Example of getting a directory listing

import os
import os.path
import glob

pyfiles = glob.glob('*.py')

# Get file sizes and modification dates
name_sz_date = [(name, os.path.getsize(name), os.path.getmtime(name))
                    for name in pyfiles]

for name, size, mtime in name_sz_date:
    print(name, size, mtime)

# Alternative: Get file metadata
file_metadata = [(name, os.stat(name)) for name in pyfiles]
for name, meta in file_metadata:
    print(name, meta.st_size, meta.st_mtime)
```

Last, but not least, be aware that there are subtle issues that can arise in filename handling related to encodings. Normally, the entries returned by a function such as os.list dir() are decoded according to the system default filename encoding. However, it's possible under certain circumstances to encounter un-decodable filenames. Recipes 5.14 and 5.15 have more details about handling such names.

5.14. Bypassing Filename Encoding

Problem

You want to perform file I/O operations using raw filenames that have not been decoded or encoded according to the default filename encoding.

Solution

By default, all filenames are encoded and decoded according to the text encoding returned by sys.getfilesystemencoding(). For example:

```
>>> sys.getfilesystemencoding()
'utf-8'
>>>
```

If you want to bypass this encoding for some reason, specify a filename using a raw byte string instead. For example:

```
>>> # Wrte a file using a unicode filename
>>> with open('jalape\xf1o.txt', 'w') as f:
...     f.write('Spicy!')
...
6
>>> # Directory listing (decoded)
>>> import os
>>> os.listdir('.')
['jalapeño.txt']

>>> # Directory listing (raw)
>>> os.listdir(b'.')          # Note: byte string
[b'jalapen\xcc\x83o.txt']

>>> # Open file with raw filename
>>> with open(b'jalapen\xcc\x83o.txt') as f:
...     print(f.read())
...
Spicy!
>>>
```

As you can see in the last two operations, the filename handling changes ever so slightly when byte strings are supplied to file-related functions, such as open() and os.list dir().

Discussion

Under normal circumstances, you shouldn't need to worry about filename encoding and decoding—normal filename operations should just work. However, many operating systems may allow a user through accident or malice to create files with names that don't

---

conform to the expected encoding rules. Such filenames may mysteriously break Python programs that work with a lot of files.

Reading directories and working with filenames as raw undecoded bytes has the potential to avoid such problems, albeit at the cost of programming convenience.

See Recipe 5.15 for a recipe on printing undecodable filenames.

5.15. Printing Bad Filenames

Problem

Your program received a directory listing, but when it tried to print the filenames, it crashed with a UnicodeEncodeError exception and a cryptic message about "surrogates not allowed."

Solution

When printing filenames of unknown origin, use this convention to avoid errors:

```python
def bad_filename(filename):
    return repr(filename)[1:-1]

try:
    print(filename)
except UnicodeEncodeError:
    print(bad_filename(filename))
```

Discussion

This recipe is about a potentially rare but very annoying problem regarding programs that must manipulate the filesystem. By default, Python assumes that all filenames are encoded according to the setting reported by sys.getfilesystemencoding(). However, certain filesystems don't necessarily enforce this encoding restriction, thereby allowing files to be created without proper filename encoding. It's not common, but there is always the danger that some user will do something silly and create such a file by accident (e.g., maybe passing a bad filename to open() in some buggy code).

When executing a command such as os.listdir(), bad filenames leave Python in a bind. On the one hand, it can't just discard bad names. On the other hand, it still can't turn the filename into a proper text string. Python's solution to this problem is to take an undecodable byte value \xhh in a filename and map it into a so-called "surrogate encoding" represented by the Unicode character \udchh. Here is an example of how a bad directory listing might look if it contained a filename *bäd.txt*, encoded as Latin-1 instead of UTF-8:

```
>>> import os
>>> files = os.listdir('.')
>>> files
['spam.py', 'b\udce4d.txt', 'foo.txt']
>>>
```

If you have code that manipulates filenames or even passes them to functions such as
open(), everything works normally. It's only in situations where you want to output the
filename that you run into trouble (e.g., printing it to the screen, logging it, etc.). Specifically, if you tried to print the preceding listing, your program will crash:

```
>>> for name in files:
...     print(name)
...
spam.py
Traceback (most recent call last):
  File "<stdin>", line 2, in <module>
UnicodeEncodeError: 'utf-8' codec can't encode character '\udce4' in
position 1: surrogates not allowed
>>>
```

The reason it crashes is that the character \udce4 is technically invalid Unicode. It's
actually the second half of a two-character combination known as a surrogate pair.
However, since the first half is missing, it's invalid Unicode. Thus, the only way to produce successful output is to take corrective action when a bad filename is encountered.
For example, changing the code to the recipe produces the following:

```
>>> for name in files:
...     try:
...         print(name)
...     except UnicodeEncodeError:
...         print(bad_filename(name))
...
spam.py
b\udce4d.txt
foo.txt
>>>
```

The choice of what to do for the bad_filename() function is largely up to you. Another
option is to re-encode the value in some way, like this:

```
def bad_filename(filename):
    temp = filename.encode(sys.getfilesystemencoding(), errors='surrogateescape')
    return temp.decode('latin-1')
```

Using this version produces the following output:

```
>>> for name in files:
...     try:
...         print(name)
...     except UnicodeEncodeError:
...         print(bad_filename(name))
...
```

```
spam.py
bäd.txt
foo.txt
>>>
```

This recipe will likely be ignored by most readers. However, if you're writing mission-critical scripts that need to work reliably with filenames and the filesystem, it's something to think about. Otherwise, you might find yourself called back into the office over the weekend to debug a seemingly inscrutable error.

5.16. Adding or Changing the Encoding of an Already Open File

Problem

You want to add or change the Unicode encoding of an already open file without closing it first.

Solution

If you want to add Unicode encoding/decoding to an already existing file object that's opened in binary mode, wrap it with an `io.TextIOWrapper()` object. For example:

```
import urllib.request
import io

u = urllib.request.urlopen('http://www.python.org')
f = io.TextIOWrapper(u,encoding='utf-8')
text = f.read()
```

If you want to change the encoding of an already open text-mode file, use its `detach()` method to remove the existing text encoding layer before replacing it with a new one. Here is an example of changing the encoding on `sys.stdout`:

```
>>> import sys
>>> sys.stdout.encoding
'UTF-8'
>>> sys.stdout = io.TextIOWrapper(sys.stdout.detach(), encoding='latin-1')
>>> sys.stdout.encoding
'latin-1'
>>>
```

Doing this might break the output of your terminal. It's only meant to illustrate.

Discussion

The I/O system is built as a series of layers. You can see the layers yourself by trying this simple example involving a text file:

```
>>> f = open('sample.txt','w')
>>> f
<_io.TextIOWrapper name='sample.txt' mode='w' encoding='UTF-8'>
>>> f.buffer
<_io.BufferedWriter name='sample.txt'>
>>> f.buffer.raw
<_io.FileIO name='sample.txt' mode='wb'>
>>>
```

In this example, io.TextIOWrapper is a text-handling layer that encodes and decodes Unicode, io.BufferedWriter is a buffered I/O layer that handles binary data, and io.FileIO is a raw file representing the low-level file descriptor in the operating system. Adding or changing the text encoding involves adding or changing the topmost io.TextIOWrapper layer.

As a general rule, it's not safe to directly manipulate the different layers by accessing the attributes shown. For example, see what happens if you try to change the encoding using this technique:

```
>>> f
<_io.TextIOWrapper name='sample.txt' mode='w' encoding='UTF-8'>
>>> f = io.TextIOWrapper(f.buffer, encoding='latin-1')
>>> f
<_io.TextIOWrapper name='sample.txt' encoding='latin-1'>
>>> f.write('Hello')
Traceback (most recent call last):
  File "<stdin>", line 1, in <module>
ValueError: I/O operation on closed file.
>>>
```

It doesn't work because the original value of f got destroyed and closed the underlying file in the process.

The detach() method disconnects the topmost layer of a file and returns the next lower layer. Afterward, the top layer will no longer be usable. For example:

```
>>> f = open('sample.txt', 'w')
>>> f
<_io.TextIOWrapper name='sample.txt' mode='w' encoding='UTF-8'>
>>> b = f.detach()
>>> b
<_io.BufferedWriter name='sample.txt'>
>>> f.write('hello')
Traceback (most recent call last):
  File "<stdin>", line 1, in <module>
ValueError: underlying buffer has been detached
>>>
```

Once detached, however, you can add a new top layer to the returned result. For example:

```
>>> f = io.TextIOWrapper(b, encoding='latin-1')
>>> f
```

```
<_io.TextIOWrapper name='sample.txt' encoding='latin-1'>
>>>
```

Although changing the encoding has been shown, it is also possible to use this technique to change the line handling, error policy, and other aspects of file handling. For example:

```
>>> sys.stdout = io.TextIOWrapper(sys.stdout.detach(), encoding='ascii',
...                               errors='xmlcharrefreplace')
>>> print('Jalape\u00f1o')
Jalape&#241;o
>>>
```

Notice how the non-ASCII character ñ has been replaced by ñ in the output.

5.17. Writing Bytes to a Text File

Problem

You want to write raw bytes to a file opened in text mode.

Solution

Simply write the byte data to the files underlying `buffer`. For example:

```
>>> import sys
>>> sys.stdout.write(b'Hello\n')
Traceback (most recent call last):
  File "<stdin>", line 1, in <module>
TypeError: must be str, not bytes
>>> sys.stdout.buffer.write(b'Hello\n')
Hello
5
>>>
```

Similarly, binary data can be read from a text file by reading from its `buffer` attribute instead.

Discussion

The I/O system is built from layers. Text files are constructed by adding a Unicode encoding/decoding layer on top of a buffered binary-mode file. The `buffer` attribute simply points at this underlying file. If you access it, you'll bypass the text encoding/decoding layer.

The example involving `sys.stdout` might be viewed as a special case. By default, `sys.stdout` is always opened in text mode. However, if you are writing a script that actually needs to dump binary data to standard output, you can use the technique shown to bypass the text encoding.)

5.18. Wrapping an Existing File Descriptor As a File Object

Problem

You have an integer file descriptor correponding to an already open I/O channel on the operating system (e.g., file, pipe, socket, etc.), and you want to wrap a higher-level Python file object around it.

Solution

A file descriptor is different than a normal open file in that it is simply an integer handle assigned by the operating system to refer to some kind of system I/O channel. If you happen to have such a file descriptor, you can wrap a Python file object around it using the open() function. However, you simply supply the integer file descriptor as the first argument instead of the filename. For example:

```
# Open a low-level file descriptor
import os
fd = os.open('somefile.txt', os.O_WRONLY | os.O_CREAT)

# Turn into a proper file
f = open(fd, 'wt')
f.write('hello world\n')
f.close()
```

When the high-level file object is closed or destroyed, the underlying file descriptor will also be closed. If this is not desired, supply the optional closefd=False argument to open(). For example:

```
# Create a file object, but don't close underlying fd when done
f = open(fd, 'wt', closefd=False)
...
```

Discussion

On Unix systems, this technique of wrapping a file descriptor can be a convenient means for putting a file-like interface on an existing I/O channel that was opened in a different way (e.g., pipes, sockets, etc.). For instance, here is an example involving sockets:

```
from socket import socket, AF_INET, SOCK_STREAM

def echo_client(client_sock, addr):
    print('Got connection from', addr)

    # Make text-mode file wrappers for socket reading/writing
    client_in = open(client_sock.fileno(), 'rt', encoding='latin-1',
                        closefd=False)
    client_out = open(client_sock.fileno(), 'wt', encoding='latin-1',
                        closefd=False)
```

```
        # Echo lines back to the client using file I/O
        for line in client_in:
            client_out.write(line)
            client_out.flush()
        client_sock.close()

    def echo_server(address):
        sock = socket(AF_INET, SOCK_STREAM)
        sock.bind(address)
        sock.listen(1)
        while True:
            client, addr = sock.accept()
            echo_client(client, addr)
```

It's important to emphasize that the above example is only meant to illustrate a feature of the built-in open() function and that it only works on Unix-based systems. If you are trying to put a file-like interface on a socket and need your code to be cross platform, use the makefile() method of sockets instead. However, if portability is not a concern, you'll find that the above solution provides much better performance than using make file().

You can also use this to make a kind of alias that allows an already open file to be used in a slightly different way than how it was first opened. For example, here's how you could create a file object that allows you to emit binary data on stdout (which is normally opened in text mode):

```
import sys
# Create a binary-mode file for stdout
bstdout = open(sys.stdout.fileno(), 'wb', closefd=False)
bstdout.write(b'Hello World\n')
bstdout.flush()
```

Although it's possible to wrap an existing file descriptor as a proper file, be aware that not all file modes may be supported and that certain kinds of file descriptors may have funny side effects (especially with respect to error handling, end-of-file conditions, etc.). The behavior can also vary according to operating system. In particular, none of the examples are likely to work on non-Unix systems. The bottom line is that you'll need to thoroughly test your implementation to make sure it works as expected.

5.19. Making Temporary Files and Directories

Problem

You need to create a temporary file or directory for use when your program executes. Afterward, you possibly want the file or directory to be destroyed.

Solution

The tempfile module has a variety of functions for performing this task. To make an unnamed temporary file, use tempfile.TemporaryFile:

```
from tempfile import TemporaryFile

with TemporaryFile('w+t') as f:
    # Read/write to the file
    f.write('Hello World\n')
    f.write('Testing\n')

    # Seek back to beginning and read the data
    f.seek(0)
    data = f.read()

# Temporary file is destroyed
```

Or, if you prefer, you can also use the file like this:

```
f = TemporaryFile('w+t')
# Use the temporary file
...
f.close()
# File is destroyed
```

The first argument to TemporaryFile() is the file mode, which is usually w+t for text and w+b for binary. This mode simultaneously supports reading and writing, which is useful here since closing the file to change modes would actually destroy it. Temporary File() additionally accepts the same arguments as the built-in open() function. For example:

```
with TemporaryFile('w+t', encoding='utf-8', errors='ignore') as f:
    ...
```

On most Unix systems, the file created by TemporaryFile() is unnamed and won't even have a directory entry. If you want to relax this constraint, use NamedTemporary File() instead. For example:

```
from tempfile import NamedTemporaryFile

with NamedTemporaryFile('w+t') as f:
    print('filename is:', f.name)
    ...

# File automatically destroyed
```

Here, the f.name attribute of the opened file contains the filename of the temporary file. This can be useful if it needs to be given to some other code that needs to open the file. As with TemporaryFile(), the resulting file is automatically deleted when it's closed. If you don't want this, supply a delete=False keyword argument. For example:

```
with NamedTemporaryFile('w+t', delete=False) as f:
    print('filename is:', f.name)
    ...
```

To make a temporary directory, use `tempfile.TemporaryDirectory()`. For example:

```
from tempfile import TemporaryDirectory
with TemporaryDirectory() as dirname:
    print('dirname is:', dirname)
    # Use the directory
    ...
# Directory and all contents destroyed
```

Discussion

The `TemporaryFile()`, `NamedTemporaryFile()`, and `TemporaryDirectory()` functions are probably the most convenient way to work with temporary files and directories, because they automatically handle all of the steps of creation and subsequent cleanup. At a lower level, you can also use the `mkstemp()` and `mkdtemp()` to create temporary files and directories. For example:

```
>>> import tempfile
>>> tempfile.mkstemp()
(3, '/var/folders/7W/7WZl5sfZEF0pljrEB1UMWE+++TI/-Tmp-/tmp7feflv')
>>> tempfile.mkdtemp()
'/var/folders/7W/7WZl5sfZEF0pljrEB1UMWE+++TI/-Tmp-/tmp5wvcv6'
>>>
```

However, these functions don't really take care of further management. For example, the `mkstemp()` function simply returns a raw OS file descriptor and leaves it up to you to turn it into a proper file. Similarly, it's up to you to clean up the files if you want.

Normally, temporary files are created in the system's default location, such as */var/tmp* or similar. To find out the actual location, use the `tempfile.gettemp dir()` function. For example:

```
>>> tempfile.gettempdir()
'/var/folders/7W/7WZl5sfZEF0pljrEB1UMWE+++TI/-Tmp-'
>>>
```

All of the temporary-file-related functions allow you to override this directory as well as the naming conventions using the `prefix`, `suffix`, and `dir` keyword arguments. For example:

```
>>> f = NamedTemporaryFile(prefix='mytemp', suffix='.txt', dir='/tmp')
>>> f.name
'/tmp/mytemp8ee899.txt'
>>>
```

Last, but not least, to the extent possible, the `tempfile()` module creates temporary files in the most secure manner possible. This includes only giving access permission to the current user and taking steps to avoid race conditions in file creation. Be aware that there can be differences between platforms. Thus, you should make sure to check the official documentation (*http://docs.python.org/3/library/tempfile.html*) for the finer points.

5.20. Communicating with Serial Ports

Problem

You want to read and write data over a serial port, typically to interact with some kind of hardware device (e.g., a robot or sensor).

Solution

Although you can probably do this directly using Python's built-in I/O primitives, your best bet for serial communication is to use the pySerial package (*http://pyserial.source forge.net*). Getting started with the package is very easy. You simply open up a serial port using code like this:

```
import serial
ser = serial.Serial('/dev/tty.usbmodem641',  # Device name varies
                    baudrate=9600,
                    bytesize=8,
                    parity='N',
                    stopbits=1)
```

The device name will vary according to the kind of device and operating system. For instance, on Windows, you can use a device of 0, 1, and so on, to open up the communication ports such as "COM0" and "COM1." Once open, you can read and write data using read( ), readline( ), and write( ) calls. For example:

```
ser.write(b'G1 X50 Y50\r\n')
resp = ser.readline()
```

For the most part, simple serial communication should be pretty simple from this point forward.

Discussion

Although simple on the surface, serial communication can sometimes get rather messy. One reason you should use a package such as pySerial is that it provides support for advanced features (e.g., timeouts, control flow, buffer flushing, handshaking, etc.). For instance, if you want to enable RTS-CTS handshaking, you simply provide a rtscts=True argument to Serial( ). The provided documentation is excellent, so there's little benefit to paraphrasing it here.

Keep in mind that all I/O involving serial ports is binary. Thus, make sure you write your code to use bytes instead of text (or perform proper text encoding/decoding as needed). The `struct` module may also be useful should you need to create binary-coded commands or packets.

5.21. Serializing Python Objects

Problem

You need to serialize a Python object into a byte stream so that you can do things such as save it to a file, store it in a database, or transmit it over a network connection.

Solution

The most common approach for serializing data is to use the `pickle` module. To dump an object to a file, you do this:

```
import pickle

data = ...    # Some Python object
f = open('somefile', 'wb')
pickle.dump(data, f)
```

To dump an object to a string, use `pickle.dumps()`:

```
s = pickle.dumps(data)
```

To re-create an object from a byte stream, use either the `pickle.load()` or `pickle.loads()` functions. For example:

```
# Restore from a file
f = open('somefile', 'rb')
data = pickle.load(f)

# Restore from a string
data = pickle.loads(s)
```

Discussion

For most programs, usage of the `dump()` and `load()` function is all you need to effectively use pickle. It simply works with most Python data types and instances of user-defined classes. If you're working with any kind of library that lets you do things such as save/restore Python objects in databases or transmit objects over the network, there's a pretty good chance that `pickle` is being used.

`pickle` is a Python-specific self-describing data encoding. By self-describing, the serialized data contains information related to the start and end of each object as well as information about its type. Thus, you don't need to worry about defining records—it simply works. For example, if working with multiple objects, you can do this:

```
>>> import pickle
>>> f = open('somedata', 'wb')
>>> pickle.dump([1, 2, 3, 4], f)
>>> pickle.dump('hello', f)
>>> pickle.dump({'Apple', 'Pear', 'Banana'}, f)
>>> f.close()
>>> f = open('somedata', 'rb')
>>> pickle.load(f)
[1, 2, 3, 4]
>>> pickle.load(f)
'hello'
>>> pickle.load(f)
{'Apple', 'Pear', 'Banana'}
>>>
```

You can pickle functions, classes, and instances, but the resulting data only encodes name references to the associated code objects. For example:

```
>>> import math
>>> import pickle.
>>> pickle.dumps(math.cos)
b'\x80\x03cmath\ncos\nq\x00.'
>>>
```

When the data is unpickled, it is assumed that all of the required source is available. Modules, classes, and functions will automatically be imported as needed. For applications where Python data is being shared between interpreters on different machines, this is a potential maintenance issue, as all machines must have access to the same source code.

pickle.load() should never be used on untrusted data. As a side effect of loading, pickle will automatically load modules and make instances. However, an evildoer who knows how pickle works can create "malformed" data that causes Python to execute arbitrary system commands. Thus, it's essential that pickle only be used internally with interpreters that have some ability to authenticate one another.

Certain kinds of objects can't be pickled. These are typically objects that involve some sort of external system state, such as open files, open network connections, threads, processes, stack frames, and so forth. User-defined classes can sometimes work around these limitations by providing __getstate__() and __setstate__() methods. If defined, pickle.dump() will call __getstate__() to get an object that can be pickled. Similarly, __setstate__() will be invoked on unpickling. To illustrate what's possible, here is a class that internally defines a thread but can still be pickled/unpickled:

```
# countdown.py
import time
import threading

class Countdown:
    def __init__(self, n):
        self.n = n
        self.thr = threading.Thread(target=self.run)
        self.thr.daemon = True
        self.thr.start()

    def run(self):
        while self.n > 0:
            print('T-minus', self.n)
            self.n -= 1
            time.sleep(5)

    def __getstate__(self):
        return self.n

    def __setstate__(self, n):
        self.__init__(n)
```

Try the following experiment involving pickling:

```
>>> import countdown
>>> c = countdown.Countdown(30)
>>> T-minus 30
T-minus 29
T-minus 28
...

>>> # After a few moments
>>> f = open('cstate.p', 'wb')
>>> import pickle
>>> pickle.dump(c, f)
>>> f.close()
```

Now quit Python and try this after restart:

```
>>> f = open('cstate.p', 'rb')
>>> pickle.load(f)
countdown.Countdown object at 0x10069e2d0>
T-minus 19
T-minus 18
...
```

You should see the thread magically spring to life again, picking up where it left off when you first pickled it.

pickle is not a particularly efficient encoding for large data structures such as binary arrays created by libraries like the array module or numpy. If you're moving large amounts of array data around, you may be better off simply saving bulk array data in a file or using a more standardized encoding, such as HDF5 (supported by third-party libraries).

Because of its Python-specific nature and attachment to source code, you probably shouldn't use `pickle` as a format for long-term storage. For example, if the source code changes, all of your stored data might break and become unreadable. Frankly, for storing data in databases and archival storage, you're probably better off using a more standard data encoding, such as XML, CSV, or JSON. These encodings are more standardized, supported by many different languages, and more likely to be better adapted to changes in your source code.

Last, but not least, be aware that `pickle` has a huge variety of options and tricky corner cases. For the most common uses, you don't need to worry about them, but a look at the official documentation (*http://docs.python.org/3/library/pickle.html*) should be required if you're going to build a signficant application that uses `pickle` for serialization.

## CHAPTER 6

Data Encoding and Processing

The main focus of this chapter is using Python to process data presented in different kinds of common encodings, such as CSV files, JSON, XML, and binary packed records. Unlike the chapter on data structures, this chapter is not focused on specific algorithms, but instead on the problem of getting data in and out of a program.

6.1. Reading and Writing CSV Data

Problem

You want to read or write data encoded as a CSV file.

Solution

For most kinds of CSV data, use the `csv` library. For example, suppose you have some stock market data in a file named *stocks.csv* like this:

```
Symbol,Price,Date,Time,Change,Volume
"AA",39.48,"6/11/2007","9:36am",-0.18,181800
"AIG",71.38,"6/11/2007","9:36am",-0.15,195500
"AXP",62.58,"6/11/2007","9:36am",-0.46,935000
"BA",98.31,"6/11/2007","9:36am",+0.12,104800
"C",53.08,"6/11/2007","9:36am",-0.25,360900
"CAT",78.29,"6/11/2007","9:36am",-0.23,225400
```

Here's how you would read the data as a sequence of tuples:

```python
import csv
with open('stocks.csv') as f:
    f_csv = csv.reader(f)
    headers = next(f_csv)
    for row in f_csv:
```

```
# Process row
...
```

In the preceding code, `row` will be a tuple. Thus, to access certain fields, you will need to use indexing, such as `row[0]` (Symbol) and `row[4]` (Change).

Since such indexing can often be confusing, this is one place where you might want to consider the use of named tuples. For example:

```
from collections import namedtuple
with open('stock.csv') as f:
    f_csv = csv.reader(f)
    headings = next(f_csv)
    Row = namedtuple('Row', headings)
    for r in f_csv:
        row = Row(*r)
        # Process row
        ...
```

This would allow you to use the column headers such as `row.Symbol` and `row.Change` instead of indices. It should be noted that this only works if the column headers are valid Python identifiers. If not, you might have to massage the initial headings (e.g., replacing nonidentifier characters with underscores or similar).

Another alternative is to read the data as a sequence of dictionaries instead. To do that, use this code:

```
import csv
with open('stocks.csv') as f:
    f_csv = csv.DictReader(f)
    for row in f_csv:
        # process row
        ...
```

In this version, you would access the elements of each row using the row headers. For example, `row['Symbol']` or `row['Change']`.

To write CSV data, you also use the `csv` module but create a writer object. For example:

```
headers = ['Symbol','Price','Date','Time','Change','Volume']
rows = [('AA', 39.48, '6/11/2007', '9:36am', -0.18, 181800),
        ('AIG', 71.38, '6/11/2007', '9:36am', -0.15, 195500),
        ('AXP', 62.58, '6/11/2007', '9:36am', -0.46, 935000),
        ]

with open('stocks.csv','w') as f:
    f_csv = csv.writer(f)
    f_csv.writerow(headers)
    f_csv.writerows(rows)
```

If you have the data as a sequence of dictionaries, do this:

```
headers = ['Symbol', 'Price', 'Date', 'Time', 'Change', 'Volume']
rows = [{'Symbol':'AA', 'Price':39.48, 'Date':'6/11/2007',
         'Time':'9:36am', 'Change':-0.18, 'Volume':181800},
        {'Symbol':'AIG', 'Price': 71.38, 'Date':'6/11/2007',
         'Time':'9:36am', 'Change':-0.15, 'Volume': 195500},
        {'Symbol':'AXP', 'Price': 62.58, 'Date':'6/11/2007',
         'Time':'9:36am', 'Change':-0.46, 'Volume': 935000},
        ]

with open('stocks.csv','w') as f:
    f_csv = csv.DictWriter(f, headers)
    f_csv.writeheader()
    f_csv.writerows(rows)
```

Discussion

You should almost always prefer the use of the csv module over manually trying to split and parse CSV data yourself. For instance, you might be inclined to just write some code like this:

```
with open('stocks.csv') as f:
    for line in f:
        row = line.split(',')
        # process row
        ...
```

The problem with this approach is that you'll still need to deal with some nasty details. For example, if any of the fields are surrounded by quotes, you'll have to strip the quotes. In addition, if a quoted field happens to contain a comma, the code will break by producing a row with the wrong size.

By default, the csv library is programmed to understand CSV encoding rules used by Microsoft Excel. This is probably the most common variant, and will likely give you the best compatibility. However, if you consult the documentation for csv, you'll see a few ways to tweak the encoding to different formats (e.g., changing the separator character, etc.). For example, if you want to read tab-delimited data instead, use this:

```
# Example of reading tab-separated values
with open('stock.tsv') as f:
    f_tsv = csv.reader(f, delimiter='\t')
    for row in f_tsv:
        # Process row
        ...
```

If you're reading CSV data and converting it into named tuples, you need to be a little careful with validating column headers. For example, a CSV file could have a header line containing nonvalid identifier characters like this:

```
Street Address,Num-Premises,Latitude,Longitude
5412 N CLARK,10,41.980262,-87.668452
```

This will actually cause the creation of a namedtuple to fail with a ValueError exception. To work around this, you might have to scrub the headers first. For instance, carrying a regex substitution on nonvalid identifier characters like this:

```
import re
with open('stock.csv') as f:
    f_csv = csv.reader(f)
    headers = [ re.sub('[^a-zA-Z_]', '_', h) for h in next(f_csv) ]
    Row = namedtuple('Row', headers)
    for r in f_csv:
        row = Row(*r)
        # Process row
        ...
```

It's also important to emphasize that csv does not try to interpret the data or convert it to a type other than a string. If such conversions are important, that is something you'll need to do yourself. Here is one example of performing extra type conversions on CSV data:

```
col_types = [str, float, str, str, float, int]
with open('stocks.csv') as f:
    f_csv = csv.reader(f)
    headers = next(f_csv)
    for row in f_csv:
        # Apply conversions to the row items
        row = tuple(convert(value) for convert, value in zip(col_types, row))
        ...
```

Alternatively, here is an example of converting selected fields of dictionaries:

```
print('Reading as dicts with type conversion')
field_types = [ ('Price', float),
                ('Change', float),
                ('Volume', int) ]

with open('stocks.csv') as f:
    for row in csv.DictReader(f):
        row.update((key, conversion(row[key]))
                    for key, conversion in field_types)
        print(row)
```

In general, you'll probably want to be a bit careful with such conversions, though. In the real world, it's common for CSV files to have missing values, corrupted data, and other issues that would break type conversions. So, unless your data is guaranteed to be error free, that's something you'll need to consider (you might need to add suitable exception handling).

Finally, if your goal in reading CSV data is to perform data analysis and statistics, you might want to look at the Pandas package (*http://pandas.pydata.org*). Pandas includes a convenient pandas.read_csv() function that will load CSV data into a DataFrame object. From there, you can generate various summary statistics, filter the data, and perform other kinds of high-level operations. An example is given in Recipe 6.13.

6.2. Reading and Writing JSON Data

Problem

You want to read or write data encoded as JSON (JavaScript Object Notation).

Solution

The json module provides an easy way to encode and decode data in JSON. The two main functions are json.dumps() and json.loads(), mirroring the interface used in other serialization libraries, such as pickle. Here is how you turn a Python data structure into JSON:

```
import json

data = {
    'name' : 'ACME',
    'shares' : 100,
    'price' : 542.23
}

json_str = json.dumps(data)
```

Here is how you turn a JSON-encoded string back into a Python data structure:

```
data = json.loads(json_str)
```

If you are working with files instead of strings, you can alternatively use json.dump() and json.load() to encode and decode JSON data. For example:

```
# Writing JSON data
with open('data.json', 'w') as f:
    json.dump(data, f)

# Reading data back
with open('data.json', 'r') as f:
    data = json.load(f)
```

Discussion

JSON encoding supports the basic types of None, bool, int, float, and str, as well as lists, tuples, and dictionaries containing those types. For dictionaries, keys are assumed to be strings (any nonstring keys in a dictionary are converted to strings when encoding). To be compliant with the JSON specification, you should only encode Python lists and dictionaries. Moreover, in web applications, it is standard practice for the top-level object to be a dictionary.

The format of JSON encoding is almost identical to Python syntax except for a few minor changes. For instance, True is mapped to true, False is mapped to false, and None is mapped to null. Here is an example that shows what the encoding looks like:

```
>>> json.dumps(False)
'false'
>>> d = {'a': True,
...      'b': 'Hello',
...      'c': None}
>>> json.dumps(d)
'{"b": "Hello", "c": null, "a": true}'
>>>
```

If you are trying to examine data you have decoded from JSON, it can often be hard to ascertain its structure simply by printing it out—especially if the data contains a deep level of nested structures or a lot of fields. To assist with this, consider using the pprint() function in the pprint module. This will alphabetize the keys and output a dictionary in a more sane way. Here is an example that illustrates how you would pretty print the results of a search on Twitter:

```
>>> from urllib.request import urlopen
>>> import json
>>> u = urlopen('http://search.twitter.com/search.json?q=python&rpp=5')
>>> resp = json.loads(u.read().decode('utf-8'))
>>> from pprint import pprint
>>> pprint(resp)
{'completed_in': 0.074,
 'max_id': 264043230692245504,
 'max_id_str': '264043230692245504',
 'next_page': '?page=2&max_id=264043230692245504&q=python&rpp=5',
 'page': 1,
 'query': 'python',
 'refresh_url': '?since_id=264043230692245504&q=python',
 'results': [{'created_at': 'Thu, 01 Nov 2012 16:36:26 +0000',
              'from_user': ...
             },
             {'created_at': 'Thu, 01 Nov 2012 16:36:14 +0000',
              'from_user': ...
             },
             {'created_at': 'Thu, 01 Nov 2012 16:36:13 +0000',
              'from_user': ...
             },
             {'created_at': 'Thu, 01 Nov 2012 16:36:07 +0000',
              'from_user': ...
             }
             {'created_at': 'Thu, 01 Nov 2012 16:36:04 +0000',
              'from_user': ...
             }],
```

```
 'results_per_page': 5,
 'since_id': 0,
 'since_id_str': '0'}
>>>
```

Normally, JSON decoding will create dicts or lists from the supplied data. If you want to create different kinds of objects, supply the object_pairs_hook or object_hook to json.loads(). For example, here is how you would decode JSON data, preserving its order in an OrderedDict:

```
>>> s = '{"name": "ACME", "shares": 50, "price": 490.1}'
>>> from collections import OrderedDict
>>> data = json.loads(s, object_pairs_hook=OrderedDict)
>>> data
OrderedDict([('name', 'ACME'), ('shares', 50), ('price', 490.1)])
>>>
```

Here is how you could turn a JSON dictionary into a Python object:

```
>>> class JSONObject:
...     def __init__(self, d):
...             self.__dict__ = d
...
>>>
>>> data = json.loads(s, object_hook=JSONObject)
>>> data.name
'ACME'
>>> data.shares
50
>>> data.price
490.1
>>>
```

In this last example, the dictionary created by decoding the JSON data is passed as a single argument to __init__(). From there, you are free to use it as you will, such as using it directly as the instance dictionary of the object.

There are a few options that can be useful for encoding JSON. If you would like the output to be nicely formatted, you can use the indent argument to json.dumps(). This causes the output to be pretty printed in a format similar to that with the pprint() function. For example:

```
>>> print(json.dumps(data))
{"price": 542.23, "name": "ACME", "shares": 100}
>>> print(json.dumps(data, indent=4))
{
    "price": 542.23,
    "name": "ACME",
    "shares": 100
}
>>>
```

If you want the keys to be sorted on output, used the `sort_keys` argument:

```
>>> print(json.dumps(data, sort_keys=True))
{"name": "ACME", "price": 542.23, "shares": 100}
>>>
```

Instances are not normally serializable as JSON. For example:

```
>>> class Point:
...     def __init__(self, x, y):
...             self.x = x
...             self.y = y
...
>>> p = Point(2, 3)
>>> json.dumps(p)
Traceback (most recent call last):
  File "<stdin>", line 1, in <module>
  File "/usr/local/lib/python3.3/json/__init__.py", line 226, in dumps
    return _default_encoder.encode(obj)
  File "/usr/local/lib/python3.3/json/encoder.py", line 187, in encode
    chunks = self.iterencode(o, _one_shot=True)
  File "/usr/local/lib/python3.3/json/encoder.py", line 245, in iterencode
    return _iterencode(o, 0)
  File "/usr/local/lib/python3.3/json/encoder.py", line 169, in default
    raise TypeError(repr(o) + " is not JSON serializable")
TypeError: <__main__.Point object at 0x1006f2650> is not JSON serializable
>>>
```

If you want to serialize instances, you can supply a function that takes an instance as input and returns a dictionary that can be serialized. For example:

```
def serialize_instance(obj):
    d = { '__classname__' : type(obj).__name__ }
    d.update(vars(obj))
    return d
```

If you want to get an instance back, you could write code like this:

```
# Dictionary mapping names to known classes
classes = {
    'Point' : Point
}

def unserialize_object(d):
    clsname = d.pop('__classname__', None)
    if clsname:
        cls = classes[clsname]
        obj = cls.__new__(cls)    # Make instance without calling __init__
        for key, value in d.items():
            setattr(obj, key, value)
            return obj
    else:
        return d
```

Here is an example of how these functions are used:

```
>>> p = Point(2,3)
>>> s = json.dumps(p, default=serialize_instance)
>>> s
'{"__classname__": "Point", "y": 3, "x": 2}'
>>> a = json.loads(s, object_hook=unserialize_object)
>>> a
<__main__.Point object at 0x1017577d0>
>>> a.x
2
>>> a.y
3
>>>
```

The json module has a variety of other options for controlling the low-level interpretation of numbers, special values such as NaN, and more. Consult the documentation (*http://docs.python.org/3/library/json.html*) for further details.

6.3. Parsing Simple XML Data

Problem

You would like to extract data from a simple XML document.

Solution

The xml.etree.ElementTree module can be used to extract data from simple XML documents. To illustrate, suppose you want to parse and make a summary of the RSS feed on Planet Python (*http://planet.python.org*). Here is a script that will do it:

```
from urllib.request import urlopen
from xml.etree.ElementTree import parse

# Download the RSS feed and parse it
u = urlopen('http://planet.python.org/rss20.xml')
doc = parse(u)

# Extract and output tags of interest
for item in doc.iterfind('channel/item'):
    title = item.findtext('title')
    date = item.findtext('pubDate')
    link = item.findtext('link')

    print(title)
    print(date)
    print(link)
    print()
```

If you run the preceding script, the output looks similar to the following:

```
Steve Holden: Python for Data Analysis
Mon, 19 Nov 2012 02:13:51 +0000
http://holdenweb.blogspot.com/2012/11/python-for-data-analysis.html

Vasudev Ram: The Python Data model (for v2 and v3)
Sun, 18 Nov 2012 22:06:47 +0000
http://jugad2.blogspot.com/2012/11/the-python-data-model.html

Python Diary: Been playing around with Object Databases
Sun, 18 Nov 2012 20:40:29 +0000
http://www.pythondiary.com/blog/Nov.18,2012/been-...-object-databases.html

Vasudev Ram: Wakari, Scientific Python in the cloud
Sun, 18 Nov 2012 20:19:41 +0000
http://jugad2.blogspot.com/2012/11/wakari-scientific-python-in-cloud.html

Jesse Jiryu Davis: Toro: synchronization primitives for Tornado coroutines
Sun, 18 Nov 2012 20:17:49 +0000
http://feedproxy.google.com/~r/EmptysquarePython/~3/_DOZT2Kd0hQ/
```

Obviously, if you want to do more processing, you need to replace the `print()` statements with something more interesting.

Discussion

Working with data encoded as XML is commonplace in many applications. Not only is XML widely used as a format for exchanging data on the Internet, it is a common format for storing application data (e.g., word processing, music libraries, etc.). The discussion that follows already assumes the reader is familiar with XML basics.

In many cases, when XML is simply being used to store data, the document structure is compact and straightforward. For example, the RSS feed from the example looks similar to the following:

```
<?xml version="1.0"?>
<rss version="2.0" xmlns:dc="http://purl.org/dc/elements/1.1/">
<channel>
  <title>Planet Python</title>
  <link>http://planet.python.org/</link>
  <language>en</language>
  <description>Planet Python - http://planet.python.org/</description>
  <item>
    <title>Steve Holden: Python for Data Analysis</title>
      <guid>http://holdenweb.blogspot.com/...-data-analysis.html</guid>
      <link>http://holdenweb.blogspot.com/...-data-analysis.html</link>
      <description>...</description>
      <pubDate>Mon, 19 Nov 2012 02:13:51 +0000</pubDate>
  </item>
  <item>
```

```
        <title>Vasudev Ram: The Python Data model (for v2 and v3)</title>
        <guid>http://jugad2.blogspot.com/...-data-model.html</guid>
        <link>http://jugad2.blogspot.com/...-data-model.html</link>
        <description>...</description>
        <pubDate>Sun, 18 Nov 2012 22:06:47 +0000</pubDate>
        </item>
      <item>
        <title>Python Diary: Been playing around with Object Databases</title>
        <guid>http://www.pythondiary.com/...-object-databases.html</guid>
        <link>http://www.pythondiary.com/...-object-databases.html</link>
        <description>...</description>
        <pubDate>Sun, 18 Nov 2012 20:40:29 +0000</pubDate>
      </item>
        ...
    </channel>
    </rss>
```

The `xml.etree.ElementTree.parse()` function parses the entire XML document into a document object. From there, you use methods such as `find()`, `iterfind()`, and `findtext()` to search for specific XML elements. The arguments to these functions are the names of a specific tag, such as `channel/item` or `title`.

When specifying tags, you need to take the overall document structure into account. Each find operation takes place relative to a starting element. Likewise, the tagname that you supply to each operation is also relative to the start. In the example, the call to `doc.iterfind('channel/item')` looks for all "item" elements under a "channel" element. `doc` represents the top of the document (the top-level "rss" element). The later calls to `item.findtext()` take place relative to the found "item" elements.

Each element represented by the `ElementTree` module has a few essential attributes and methods that are useful when parsing. The `tag` attribute contains the name of the tag, the `text` attribute contains enclosed text, and the `get()` method can be used to extract attributes (if any). For example:

```
>>> doc
<xml.etree.ElementTree.ElementTree object at 0x101339510>
>>> e = doc.find('channel/title')
>>> e
<Element 'title' at 0x10135b310>
>>> e.tag
'title'
>>> e.text
'Planet Python'
>>> e.get('some_attribute')
>>>
```

It should be noted that `xml.etree.ElementTree` is not the only option for XML parsing. For more advanced applications, you might consider lxml (*http://pypi.python.org/pypi/lxml*). It uses the same programming interface as `ElementTree`, so the example shown in this recipe works in the same manner. You simply need to change the first import to from lxml.etree import parse. lxml provides the benefit of being fully compliant with XML standards. It is also extremely fast, and provides support for features such as validation, XSLT, and XPath.

6.4. Parsing Huge XML Files Incrementally

Problem

You need to extract data from a huge XML document using as little memory as possible.

Solution

Any time you are faced with the problem of incremental data processing, you should think of iterators and generators. Here is a simple function that can be used to incrementally process huge XML files using a very small memory footprint:

```python
from xml.etree.ElementTree import iterparse

def parse_and_remove(filename, path):
    path_parts = path.split('/')
    doc = iterparse(filename, ('start', 'end'))
    # Skip the root element
    next(doc)

    tag_stack = []
    elem_stack = []
    for event, elem in doc:
        if event == 'start':
            tag_stack.append(elem.tag)
            elem_stack.append(elem)
        elif event == 'end':
            if tag_stack == path_parts:
                yield elem
                elem_stack[-2].remove(elem)
            try:
                tag_stack.pop()
                elem_stack.pop()
            except IndexError:
                pass
```

To test the function, you now need to find a large XML file to work with. You can often find such files on government and open data websites. For example, you can download Chicago's pothole database as XML (*http://bit.ly/YQh2Oh*). At the time of this writing, the downloaded file consists of more than 100,000 rows of data, which are encoded like this:

```xml
<response>
  <row>
```

```
<row ...>
  <creation_date>2012-11-18T00:00:00</creation_date>
  <status>Completed</status>
  <completion_date>2012-11-18T00:00:00</completion_date>
  <service_request_number>12-01906549</service_request_number>
  <type_of_service_request>Pot Hole in Street</type_of_service_request>
  <current_activity>Final Outcome</current_activity>
  <most_recent_action>CDOT Street Cut ... Outcome</most_recent_action>
  <street_address>4714 S TALMAN AVE</street_address>
  <zip>60632</zip>
  <x_coordinate>1159494.68618856</x_coordinate>
  <y_coordinate>1873313.83503384</y_coordinate>
  <ward>14</ward>
  <police_district>9</police_district>
  <community_area>58</community_area>
  <latitude>41.808090232127896</latitude>
  <longitude>-87.69053684711305</longitude>
  <location latitude="41.808090232127896"
                  longitude="-87.69053684711305" />
</row>
<row ...>
  <creation_date>2012-11-18T00:00:00</creation_date>
  <status>Completed</status>
  <completion_date>2012-11-18T00:00:00</completion_date>
  <service_request_number>12-01906695</service_request_number>
  <type_of_service_request>Pot Hole in Street</type_of_service_request>
  <current_activity>Final Outcome</current_activity>
  <most_recent_action>CDOT Street Cut ... Outcome</most_recent_action>
  <street_address>3510 W NORTH AVE</street_address>
  <zip>60647</zip>
  <x_coordinate>1152732.14127696</x_coordinate>
  <y_coordinate>1910409.38979075</y_coordinate>
  <ward>26</ward>
  <police_district>14</police_district>
  <community_area>23</community_area>
  <latitude>41.91002084292946</latitude>
  <longitude>-87.71435952353961</longitude>
  <location latitude="41.91002084292946"
                  longitude="-87.71435952353961" />
</row>
  </row>
</response>
```

Suppose you want to write a script that ranks ZIP codes by the number of pothole reports. To do it, you could write code like this:

```
from xml.etree.ElementTree import parse
from collections import Counter

potholes_by_zip = Counter()

doc = parse('potholes.xml')
for pothole in doc.iterfind('row/row'):
```

```
        potholes_by_zip[pothole.findtext('zip')] += 1

    for zipcode, num in potholes_by_zip.most_common():
        print(zipcode, num)
```

The only problem with this script is that it reads and parses the entire XML file into memory. On our machine, it takes about 450 MB of memory to run. Using this recipe's code, the program changes only slightly:

```
from collections import Counter
potholes_by_zip = Counter()

data = parse_and_remove('potholes.xml', 'row/row')
for pothole in data:
    potholes_by_zip[pothole.findtext('zip')] += 1

for zipcode, num in potholes_by_zip.most_common():
    print(zipcode, num)
```

This version of code runs with a memory footprint of only 7 MB—a huge savings!

Discussion

This recipe relies on two core features of the ElementTree module. First, the iter parse() method allows incremental processing of XML documents. To use it, you supply the filename along with an event list consisting of one or more of the following: start, end, start-ns, and end-ns. The iterator created by iterparse() produces tuples of the form (event, elem), where event is one of the listed events and elem is the resulting XML element. For example:

```
>>> data = iterparse('potholes.xml',('start','end'))
>>> next(data)
('start', <Element 'response' at 0x100771d60>)
>>> next(data)
('start', <Element 'row' at 0x100771e68>)
>>> next(data)
('start', <Element 'row' at 0x100771fc8>)
>>> next(data)
('start', <Element 'creation_date' at 0x100771f18>)
>>> next(data)
('end', <Element 'creation_date' at 0x100771f18>)
>>> next(data)
('start', <Element 'status' at 0x1006a7f18>)
>>> next(data)
('end', <Element 'status' at 0x1006a7f18>)
>>>
```

start events are created when an element is first created but not yet populated with any other data (e.g., child elements). end events are created when an element is completed.

Although not shown in this recipe, start-ns and end-ns events are used to handle XML namespace declarations.

In this recipe, the start and end events are used to manage stacks of elements and tags. The stacks represent the current hierarchical structure of the document as it's being parsed, and are also used to determine if an element matches the requested path given to the parse_and_remove() function. If a match is made, yield is used to emit it back to the caller.

The following statement after the yield is the core feature of ElementTree that makes this recipe save memory:

```
elem_stack[-2].remove(elem)
```

This statement causes the previously yielded element to be removed from its parent. Assuming that no references are left to it anywhere else, the element is destroyed and memory reclaimed.

The end effect of the iterative parse and the removal of nodes is a highly efficient incremental sweep over the document. At no point is a complete document tree ever constructed. Yet, it is still possible to write code that processes the XML data in a straightforward manner.

The primary downside to this recipe is its runtime performance. When tested, the version of code that reads the entire document into memory first runs approximately twice as fast as the version that processes it incrementally. However, it requires more than 60 times as much memory. So, if memory use is a greater concern, the incremental version is a big win.

6.5. Turning a Dictionary into XML

Problem

You want to take the data in a Python dictionary and turn it into XML.

Solution

Although the xml.etree.ElementTree library is commonly used for parsing, it can also be used to create XML documents. For example, consider this function:

```
from xml.etree.ElementTree import Element

def dict_to_xml(tag, d):
    '''
    Turn a simple dict of key/value pairs into XML
    '''
    elem = Element(tag)
    for key, val in d.items():
```

```
            child = Element(key)
            child.text = str(val)
            elem.append(child)
        return elem
```

Here is an example:

```
>>> s = { 'name': 'GOOG', 'shares': 100, 'price':490.1 }
>>> e = dict_to_xml('stock', s)
>>> e
<Element 'stock' at 0x1004b64c8>
>>>
```

The result of this conversion is an Element instance. For I/O, it is easy to convert this to a byte string using the tostring() function in xml.etree.ElementTree. For example:

```
>>> from xml.etree.ElementTree import tostring
>>> tostring(e)
b'<stock><price>490.1</price><shares>100</shares><name>GOOG</name></stock>'
>>>
```

If you want to attach attributes to an element, use its set() method:

```
>>> e.set('_id','1234')
>>> tostring(e)
b'<stock _id="1234"><price>490.1</price><shares>100</shares><name>GOOG</name>
</stock>'
>>>
```

If the order of the elements matters, consider making an OrderedDict instead of a normal dictionary. See Recipe 1.7.

Discussion

When creating XML, you might be inclined to just make strings instead. For example:

```
def dict_to_xml_str(tag, d):
    '''
    Turn a simple dict of key/value pairs into XML
    '''
    parts = ['<{}>'.format(tag)]
    for key, val in d.items():
        parts.append('<{0}>{1}</{0}>'.format(key,val))
    parts.append('</{}>'.format(tag))
    return ''.join(parts)
```

The problem is that you're going to make a real mess for yourself if you try to do things manually. For example, what happens if the dictionary values contain special characters like this?

```
>>> d = { 'name' : '<spam>' }
```

```
>>> # String creation
>>> dict_to_xml_str('item',d)
'<item><name><spam></name></item>'

>>> # Proper XML creation
>>> e = dict_to_xml('item',d)
>>> tostring(e)
b'<item><name>&lt;spam&gt;</name></item>'
>>>
```

Notice how in the latter example, the characters < and > got replaced with < and >.

Just for reference, if you ever need to manually escape or unescape such characters, you can use the escape() and unescape() functions in xml.sax.saxutils. For example:

```
>>> from xml.sax.saxutils import escape, unescape
>>> escape('<spam>')
'&lt;spam&gt;'
>>> unescape(_)
'<spam>'
>>>
```

Aside from creating correct output, the other reason why it's a good idea to create Element instances instead of strings is that they can be more easily combined together to make a larger document. The resulting Element instances can also be processed in various ways without ever having to worry about parsing the XML text. Essentially, you can do all of the processing of the data in a more high-level form and then output it as a string at the very end.

6.6. Parsing, Modifying, and Rewriting XML

Problem

You want to read an XML document, make changes to it, and then write it back out as XML.

Solution

The xml.etree.ElementTree module makes it easy to perform such tasks. Essentially, you start out by parsing the document in the usual way. For example, suppose you have a document named *pred.xml* that looks like this:

```
<?xml version="1.0"?>
<stop>
    <id>14791</id>
    <nm>Clark &amp; Balmoral</nm>
    <sri>
        <rt>22</rt>
        <d>North Bound</d>
```

```
        <dd>North Bound</dd>
    </sri>
    <cr>22</cr>
    <pre>
        <pt>5 MIN</pt>
        <fd>Howard</fd>
        <v>1378</v>
        <rn>22</rn>
    </pre>
    <pre>
        <pt>15 MIN</pt>
        <fd>Howard</fd>
        <v>1867</v>
        <rn>22</rn>
    </pre>
</stop>
```

Here is an example of using ElementTree to read it and make changes to the structure:

```
>>> from xml.etree.ElementTree import parse, Element
>>> doc = parse('pred.xml')
>>> root = doc.getroot()
>>> root
<Element 'stop' at 0x100770cb0>

>>> # Remove a few elements
>>> root.remove(root.find('sri'))
>>> root.remove(root.find('cr'))

>>> # Insert a new element after <nm>...</nm>
>>> root.getchildren().index(root.find('nm'))
1
>>> e = Element('spam')
>>> e.text = 'This is a test'
>>> root.insert(2, e)

>>> # Write back to a file
>>> doc.write('newpred.xml', xml_declaration=True)
>>>
```

The result of these operations is a new XML file that looks like this:

```
<?xml version='1.0' encoding='us-ascii'?>
<stop>
    <id>14791</id>
    <nm>Clark &amp; Balmoral</nm>
    <spam>This is a test</spam><pre>
        <pt>5 MIN</pt>
        <fd>Howard</fd>
        <v>1378</v>
        <rn>22</rn>
    </pre>
    <pre>
```

```
        <pt>15 MIN</pt>
        <fd>Howard</fd>
        <v>1867</v>
        <rn>22</rn>
    </pre>
  </stop>
```

Discussion

Modifying the structure of an XML document is straightforward, but you must remember that all modifications are generally made to the parent element, treating it as if it were a list. For example, if you remove an element, it is removed from its immediate parent using the parent's `remove()` method. If you insert or append new elements, you also use `insert()` and `append()` methods on the parent. Elements can also be manipulated using indexing and slicing operations, such as `element[i]` or `element[i:j]`.

If you need to make new elements, use the `Element` class, as shown in this recipe's solution. This is described further in Recipe 6.5.

6.7. Parsing XML Documents with Namespaces

Problem

You need to parse an XML document, but it's using XML namespaces.

Solution

Consider a document that uses namespaces like this:

```
<?xml version="1.0" encoding="utf-8"?>
<top>
  <author>David Beazley</author>
  <content>
      <html xmlns="http://www.w3.org/1999/xhtml">
          <head>
              <title>Hello World</title>
          </head>
          <body>
              <h1>Hello World!</h1>
          </body>
      </html>
  </content>
</top>
```

If you parse this document and try to perform the usual queries, you'll find that it doesn't work so easily because everything becomes incredibly verbose:

```
>>> # Some queries that work
>>> doc.findtext('author')
```

```
'David Beazley'
>>> doc.find('content')
<Element 'content' at 0x100776ec0>

>>> # A query involving a namespace (doesn't work)
>>> doc.find('content/html')

>>> # Works if fully qualified
>>> doc.find('content/{http://www.w3.org/1999/xhtml}html')
<Element '{http://www.w3.org/1999/xhtml}html' at 0x1007767e0>

>>> # Doesn't work
>>> doc.findtext('content/{http://www.w3.org/1999/xhtml}html/head/title')

>>> # Fully qualified
>>> doc.findtext('content/{http://www.w3.org/1999/xhtml}html/'
...     '{http://www.w3.org/1999/xhtml}head/{http://www.w3.org/1999/xhtml}title')
'Hello World'
>>>
```

You can often simplify matters for yourself by wrapping namespace handling up into a
utility class.

```
class XMLNamespaces:
    def __init__(self, **kwargs):
        self.namespaces = {}
        for name, uri in kwargs.items():
            self.register(name, uri)
    def register(self, name, uri):
        self.namespaces[name] = '{'+uri+'}'
    def __call__(self, path):
        return path.format_map(self.namespaces)
```

To use this class, you do the following:

```
>>> ns = XMLNamespaces(html='http://www.w3.org/1999/xhtml')
>>> doc.find(ns('content/{html}html'))
<Element '{http://www.w3.org/1999/xhtml}html' at 0x1007767e0>
>>> doc.findtext(ns('content/{html}html/{html}head/{html}title'))
'Hello World'
>>>
```

Discussion

Parsing XML documents that contain namespaces can be messy. The XMLNamespaces
class is really just meant to clean it up slightly by allowing you to use the shortened
namespace names in subsequent operations as opposed to fully qualified URIs.

Unfortunately, there is no mechanism in the basic ElementTree parser to get further
information about namespaces. However, you can get a bit more information about the
scope of namespace processing if you're willing to use the iterparse() function instead.
For example:

```
>>> from xml.etree.ElementTree import iterparse
>>> for evt, elem in iterparse('ns2.xml', ('end', 'start-ns', 'end-ns')):
...     print(evt, elem)
...
end <Element 'author' at 0x10110de10>
start-ns ('', 'http://www.w3.org/1999/xhtml')
end <Element '{http://www.w3.org/1999/xhtml}title' at 0x1011131b0>
end <Element '{http://www.w3.org/1999/xhtml}head' at 0x1011130a8>
end <Element '{http://www.w3.org/1999/xhtml}h1' at 0x101113310>
end <Element '{http://www.w3.org/1999/xhtml}body' at 0x101113260>
end <Element '{http://www.w3.org/1999/xhtml}html' at 0x10110df70>
end-ns None
end <Element 'content' at 0x10110de68>
end <Element 'top' at 0x10110dd60>
>>> elem        # This is the topmost element
<Element 'top' at 0x10110dd60>
>>>
```

As a final note, if the text you are parsing makes use of namespaces in addition to other advanced XML features, you're really better off using the lxml library (*http://lxml.de*) instead of ElementTree. For instance, lxml provides better support for validating documents against a DTD, more complete XPath support, and other advanced XML features. This recipe is really just a simple fix to make parsing a little easier.

6.8. Interacting with a Relational Database

Problem

You need to select, insert, or delete rows in a relational database.

Solution

A standard way to represent rows of data in Python is as a sequence of tuples. For example:

```
stocks = [
    ('GOOG', 100, 490.1),
    ('AAPL', 50, 545.75),
    ('FB', 150, 7.45),
    ('HPQ', 75, 33.2),
]
```

Given data in this form, it is relatively straightforward to interact with a relational database using Python's standard database API, as described in PEP 249 (*http://www.python.org/dev/peps/pep-0249*). The gist of the API is that all operations on the database are carried out by SQL queries. Each row of input or output data is represented by a tuple.

To illustrate, you can use the `sqlite3` module that comes with Python. If you are using a different database (e.g., MySql, Postgres, or ODBC), you'll have to install a third-party module to support it. However, the underlying programming interface will be virtually the same, if not identical.

The first step is to connect to the database. Typically, you execute a `connect()` function, supplying parameters such as the name of the database, hostname, username, password, and other details as needed. For example:

```
>>> import sqlite3
>>> db = sqlite3.connect('database.db')
>>>
```

To do anything with the data, you next create a cursor. Once you have a cursor, you can start executing SQL queries. For example:

```
>>> c = db.cursor()
>>> c.execute('create table portfolio (symbol text, shares integer, price real)')
<sqlite3.Cursor object at 0x10067a730>
>>> db.commit()
>>>
```

To insert a sequence of rows into the data, use a statement like this:

```
>>> c.executemany('insert into portfolio values (?,?,?)', stocks)
<sqlite3.Cursor object at 0x10067a730>
>>> db.commit()
>>>
```

To perform a query, use a statement such as this:

```
>>> for row in db.execute('select * from portfolio'):
...     print(row)
...
('GOOG', 100, 490.1)
('AAPL', 50, 545.75)
('FB', 150, 7.45)
('HPQ', 75, 33.2)
>>>
```

If you want to perform queries that accept user-supplied input parameters, make sure you escape the parameters using ? like this:

```
>>> min_price = 100
>>> for row in db.execute('select * from portfolio where price >= ?',
                          (min_price,)):
...     print(row)
...
('GOOG', 100, 490.1)
('AAPL', 50, 545.75)
>>>
```

Discussion

At a low level, interacting with a database is an extremely straightforward thing to do. You simply form SQL statements and feed them to the underlying module to either update the database or retrieve data. That said, there are still some tricky details you'll need to sort out on a case-by-case basis.

One complication is the mapping of data from the database into Python types. For entries such as dates, it is most common to use `datetime` instances from the `datetime` module, or possibly system timestamps, as used in the `time` module. For numerical data, especially financial data involving decimals, numbers may be represented as `Decimal` instances from the `decimal` module. Unfortunately, the exact mapping varies by database backend so you'll have to read the associated documentation.

Another extremely critical complication concerns the formation of SQL statement strings. You should never use Python string formatting operators (e.g., `%`) or the `.format()` method to create such strings. If the values provided to such formatting operators are derived from user input, this opens up your program to an SQL-injection attack (see *http://xkcd.com/327*). The special `?` wildcard in queries instructs the database backend to use its own string substitution mechanism, which (hopefully) will do it safely.

Sadly, there is some inconsistency across database backends with respect to the wildcard. Many modules use `?` or `%s`, while others may use a different symbol, such as `:0` or `:1`, to refer to parameters. Again, you'll have to consult the documentation for the database module you're using. The `paramstyle` attribute of a database module also contains information about the quoting style.

For simply pulling data in and out of a database table, using the database API is usually simple enough. If you're doing something more complicated, it may make sense to use a higher-level interface, such as that provided by an object-relational mapper. Libraries such as SQLAlchemy (*http://www.sqlalchemy.org*) allow database tables to be described as Python classes and for database operations to be carried out while hiding most of the underlying SQL.

6.9. Decoding and Encoding Hexadecimal Digits

Problem

You need to decode a string of hexadecimal digits into a byte string or encode a byte string as hex.

Solution

If you simply need to decode or encode a raw string of hex digits, use the `binascii` module. For example:

```
>>> # Initial byte string
>>> s = b'hello'

>>> # Encode as hex
>>> import binascii
>>> h = binascii.b2a_hex(s)
>>> h
b'68656c6c6f'

>>> # Decode back to bytes
>>> binascii.a2b_hex(h)
b'hello'
>>>
```

Similar functionality can also be found in the `base64` module. For example:

```
>>> import base64
>>> h = base64.b16encode(s)
>>> h
b'68656C6C6F'
>>> base64.b16decode(h)
b'hello'
>>>
```

Discussion

For the most part, converting to and from hex is straightforward using the functions shown. The main difference between the two techniques is in case folding. The `base64.b16decode()` and `base64.b16encode()` functions only operate with uppercase hexadecimal letters, whereas the functions in `binascii` work with either case.

It's also important to note that the output produced by the encoding functions is always a byte string. To coerce it to Unicode for output, you may need to add an extra decoding step. For example:

```
>>> h = base64.b16encode(s)
>>> print(h)
b'68656C6C6F'
>>> print(h.decode('ascii'))
68656C6C6F
>>>
```

When decoding hex digits, the `b16decode()` and `a2b_hex()` functions accept either bytes or unicode strings. However, those strings must only contain ASCII-encoded hexadecimal digits.

6.10. Decoding and Encoding Base64

Problem

You need to decode or encode binary data using Base64 encoding.

Solution

The base64 module has two functions—b64encode() and b64decode()—that do exactly what you want. For example:

```
>>> # Some byte data
>>> s = b'hello'
>>> import base64

>>> # Encode as Base64
>>> a = base64.b64encode(s)
>>> a
b'aGVsbG8='

>>> # Decode from Base64
>>> base64.b64decode(a)
b'hello'
>>>
```

Discussion

Base64 encoding is only meant to be used on byte-oriented data such as byte strings and byte arrays. Moreover, the output of the encoding process is always a byte string. If you are mixing Base64-encoded data with Unicode text, you may have to perform an extra decoding step. For example:

```
>>> a = base64.b64encode(s).decode('ascii')
>>> a
'aGVsbG8-'
>>>
```

When decoding Base64, both byte strings and Unicode text strings can be supplied. However, Unicode strings can only contain ASCII characters.

6.11. Reading and Writing Binary Arrays of Structures

Problem

You want to read or write data encoded as a binary array of uniform structures into Python tuples.

Solution

To work with binary data, use the `struct` module. Here is an example of code that writes a list of Python tuples out to a binary file, encoding each tuple as a structure using `struct`:

```
from struct import Struct

def write_records(records, format, f):
    '''
    Write a sequence of tuples to a binary file of structures.
    '''
    record_struct = Struct(format)
    for r in records:
        f.write(record_struct.pack(*r))

# Example
if __name__ == '__main__':
    records = [ (1, 2.3, 4.5),
                (6, 7.8, 9.0),
                (12, 13.4, 56.7) ]

    with open('data.b', 'wb') as f:
        write_records(records, '<idd', f)
```

There are several approaches for reading this file back into a list of tuples. First, if you're going to read the file incrementally in chunks, you can write code such as this:

```
from struct import Struct

def read_records(format, f):
    record_struct = Struct(format)
    chunks = iter(lambda: f.read(record_struct.size), b'')
    return (record_struct.unpack(chunk) for chunk in chunks)

# Example
if __name__ == '__main__':
    with open('data.b','rb') as f:
        for rec in read_records('<idd', f):
            # Process rec
            ...
```

If you want to read the file entirely into a byte string with a single read and convert it piece by piece, you can write the following:

```
from struct import Struct

def unpack_records(format, data):
    record_struct = Struct(format)
    return (record_struct.unpack_from(data, offset)
            for offset in range(0, len(data), record_struct.size))
```

```
# Example
if __name__ == '__main__':
    with open('data.b', 'rb') as f:
        data = f.read()

    for rec in unpack_records('<idd', data):
        # Process rec
        ...
```

In both cases, the result is an iterable that produces the tuples originally stored when the file was created.

Discussion

For programs that must encode and decode binary data, it is common to use the `struct` module. To declare a new structure, simply create an instance of `Struct` such as:

```
# Little endian 32-bit integer, two double precision floats
record_struct = Struct('<idd')
```

Structures are always defined using a set of structure codes such as i, d, f, and so forth [see the Python documentation (*http://docs.python.org/3/library/struct.html*)]. These codes correspond to specific binary data types such as 32-bit integers, 64-bit floats, 32-bit floats, and so forth. The < in the first character specifies the byte ordering. In this example, it is indicating "little endian." Change the character to > for big endian or ! for network byte order.

The resulting `Struct` instance has various attributes and methods for manipulating structures of that type. The `size` attribute contains the size of the structure in bytes, which is useful to have in I/O operations. `pack()` and `unpack()` methods are used to pack and unpack data. For example:

```
>>> from struct import Struct
>>> record_struct = Struct('<idd')
>>> record_struct.size
20
>>> record_struct.pack(1, 2.0, 3.0)
b'\x01\x00\x00\x00\x00\x00\x00\x00\x00\x00\x00@\x00\x00\x00\x00\x00\x00\x08@'
>>> record_struct.unpack(_)
(1, 2.0, 3.0)
>>>
```

Sometimes you'll see the `pack()` and `unpack()` operations called as module-level functions, as in the following:

```
>>> import struct
>>> struct.pack('<idd', 1, 2.0, 3.0)
b'\x01\x00\x00\x00\x00\x00\x00\x00\x00\x00\x00@\x00\x00\x00\x00\x00\x00\x08@'
>>> struct.unpack('<idd', _)
(1, 2.0, 3.0)
>>>
```

This works, but feels less elegant than creating a single Struct instance—especially if the same structure appears in multiple places in your code. By creating a Struct instance, the format code is only specified once and all of the useful operations are grouped together nicely. This certainly makes it easier to maintain your code if you need to fiddle with the structure code (as you only have to change it in one place).

The code for reading binary structures involves a number of interesting, yet elegant programming idioms. In the read_records() function, iter() is being used to make an iterator that returns fixed-sized chunks. See Recipe 5.8. This iterator repeatedly calls a user-supplied callable (e.g., lambda: f.read(record_struct.size)) until it returns a specified value (e.g., b), at which point iteration stops. For example:

```
>>> f = open('data.b', 'rb')
>>> chunks = iter(lambda: f.read(20), b'')
>>> chunks
<callable_iterator object at 0x10069e6d0>
>>> for chk in chunks:
...     print(chk)
...
b'\x01\x00\x00\x00ffffff\x02@\x00\x00\x00\x00\x00\x00\x12@'
b'\x06\x00\x00\x00333333\x1f@\x00\x00\x00\x00\x00\x00"@'
b'\x0c\x00\x00\x00\xcd\xcc\xcc\xcc\xcc\xcc*@\x9a\x99\x99\x99\x99YL@'
>>>
```

One reason for creating an iterable is that it nicely allows records to be created using a generator comprehension, as shown in the solution. If you didn't use this approach, the code might look like this:

```
def read_records(format, f):
    record_struct = Struct(format)
    while True:
        chk = f.read(record_struct.size)
        if chk == b'':
            break
        yield record_struct.unpack(chk)
    return records
```

In the unpack_records() function, a different approach using the unpack_from() method is used. unpack_from() is a useful method for extracting binary data from a larger binary array, because it does so without making any temporary objects or memory copies. You just give it a byte string (or any array) along with a byte offset, and it will unpack fields directly from that location.

If you used unpack() instead of unpack_from(), you would need to modify the code to make a lot of small slices and offset calculations. For example:

```
def unpack_records(format, data):
    record_struct = Struct(format)
    return (record_struct.unpack(data[offset:offset + record_struct.size])
            for offset in range(0, len(data), record_struct.size))
```

In addition to being more complicated to read, this version also requires a lot more work, as it performs various offset calculations, copies data, and makes small slice objects. If you're going to be unpacking a lot of structures from a large byte string you've already read, `unpack_from()` is a more elegant approach.

Unpacking records is one place where you might want to use `namedtuple` objects from the `collections` module. This allows you to set attribute names on the returned tuples. For example:

```
from collections import namedtuple

Record = namedtuple('Record', ['kind','x','y'])

with open('data.p', 'rb') as f:
    records = (Record(*r) for r in read_records('<idd', f))

for r in records:
    print(r.kind, r.x, r.y)
```

If you're writing a program that needs to work with a large amount of binary data, you may be better off using a library such as `numpy`. For example, instead of reading a binary into a list of tuples, you could read it into a structured array, like this:

```
>>> import numpy as np
>>> f = open('data.b', 'rb')
>>> records = np.fromfile(f, dtype='<i,<d,<d')
>>> records
array([(1, 2.3, 4.5), (6, 7.8, 9.0), (12, 13.4, 56.7)],
      dtype=[('f0', '<i4'), ('f1', '<f8'), ('f2', '<f8')])
>>> records[0]
(1, 2.3, 4.5)
>>> records[1]
(6, 7.8, 9.0)
>>>
```

Last, but not least, if you're faced with the task of reading binary data in some known file format (i.e., image formats, shape files, HDF5, etc.), check to see if a Python module already exists for it. There's no reason to reinvent the wheel if you don't have to.

6.12. Reading Nested and Variable-Sized Binary Structures

Problem

You need to read complicated binary-encoded data that contains a collection of nested and/or variable-sized records. Such data might include images, video, shapefiles, and so on.

Solution

The `struct` module can be used to decode and encode almost any kind of binary data structure. To illustrate the kind of data in question here, suppose you have this Python data structure representing a collection of points that make up a series of polygons:

```
polys = [
        [ (1.0, 2.5), (3.5, 4.0), (2.5, 1.5) ],
        [ (7.0, 1.2), (5.1, 3.0), (0.5, 7.5), (0.8, 9.0) ],
        [ (3.4, 6.3), (1.2, 0.5), (4.6, 9.2) ],
        ]
```

Now suppose this data was to be encoded into a binary file where the file started with the following header:

Byte	Type	Description
0	int	File code (0x1234, little endian)
4	double	Minimum x (little endian)
12	double	Minimum y (little endian)
20	double	Maximum x (little endian)
28	double	Maximum y (little endian)
36	int	Number of polygons (little endian)

Following the header, a series of polygon records follow, each encoded as follows:

Byte	Type	Description
0	int	Record length including length (N bytes)
4-N	Points	Pairs of (X,Y) coords as doubles

To write this file, you can use Python code like this:

```python
import struct
import itertools

def write_polys(filename, polys):
    # Determine bounding box
    flattened = list(itertools.chain(*polys))
    min_x = min(x for x, y in flattened)
    max_x = max(x for x, y in flattened)
    min_y = min(y for x, y in flattened)
    max_y = max(y for x, y in flattened)

    with open(filename, 'wb') as f:
        f.write(struct.pack('<iddddi',
                            0x1234,
                            min_x, min_y,
                            max_x, max_y,
                            len(polys)))
```

```
    for poly in polys:
        size = len(poly) * struct.calcsize('<dd')
        f.write(struct.pack('<i', size+4))
        for pt in poly:
            f.write(struct.pack('<dd', *pt))

# Call it with our polygon data
write_polys('polys.bin', polys)
```

To read the resulting data back, you can write very similar looking code using the
`struct.unpack()` function, reversing the operations performed during writing. For
example:

```
import struct

def read_polys(filename):
    with open(filename, 'rb') as f:
        # Read the header
        header = f.read(40)
        file_code, min_x, min_y, max_x, max_y, num_polys = \
            struct.unpack('<iddddi', header)

        polys = []
        for n in range(num_polys):
            pbytes, = struct.unpack('<i', f.read(4))
            poly = []
            for m in range(pbytes // 16):
                pt = struct.unpack('<dd', f.read(16))
                poly.append(pt)
            polys.append(poly)
    return polys
```

Although this code works, it's also a rather messy mix of small reads, struct unpacking,
and other details. If code like this is used to process a real datafile, it can quickly become
even messier. Thus, it's an obvious candidate for an alternative solution that might simplify some of the steps and free the programmer to focus on more important matters.

In the remainder of this recipe, a rather advanced solution for interpreting binary data
will be built up in pieces. The goal will be to allow a programmer to provide a high-level
specification of the file format, and to simply have the details of reading and unpacking
all of the data worked out under the covers. As a forewarning, the code that follows may
be the most advanced example in this entire book, utilizing various object-oriented
programming and metaprogramming techniques. Be sure to carefully read the discussion section as well as cross-references to other recipes.

First, when reading binary data, it is common for the file to contain headers and other
data structures. Although the struct module can unpack this data into a tuple, another
way to represent such information is through the use of a class. Here's some code that
allows just that:

```
import struct

class StructField:
    '''
    Descriptor representing a simple structure field
    '''
    def __init__(self, format, offset):
        self.format = format
        self.offset = offset
    def __get__(self, instance, cls):
        if instance is None:
            return self
        else:
            r = struct.unpack_from(self.format,
                                    instance._buffer, self.offset)
            return r[0] if len(r) == 1 else r

class Structure:
    def __init__(self, bytedata):
        self._buffer = memoryview(bytedata)
```

This code uses a descriptor to represent each structure field. Each descriptor contains a struct-compatible format code along with a byte offset into an underlying memory buffer. In the __get__() method, the struct.unpack_from() function is used to unpack a value from the buffer without having to make extra slices or copies.

The Structure class just serves as a base class that accepts some byte data and stores it as the underlying memory buffer used by the StructField descriptor. The use of a memoryview() in this class serves a purpose that will become clear later.

Using this code, you can now define a structure as a high-level class that mirrors the information found in the tables that described the expected file format. For example:

```
class PolyHeader(Structure):
    file_code = StructField('<i', 0)
    min_x = StructField('<d', 4)
    min_y = StructField('<d', 12)
    max_x = StructField('<d', 20)
    max_y = StructField('<d', 28)
    num_polys = StructField('<i', 36)
```

Here is an example of using this class to read the header from the polygon data written earlier:

```
>>> f = open('polys.bin', 'rb')
>>> phead = PolyHeader(f.read(40))
>>> phead.file_code == 0x1234
True
>>> phead.min_x
0.5
>>> phead.min_y
0.5
```

```
>>> phead.max_x
7.0
>>> phead.max_y
9.2
>>> phead.num_polys
3
>>>
```

This is interesting, but there are a number of annoyances with this approach. For one, even though you get the convenience of a class-like interface, the code is rather verbose and requires the user to specify a lot of low-level detail (e.g., repeated uses of Struct Field, specification of offsets, etc.). The resulting class is also missing common conveniences such as providing a way to compute the total size of the structure.

Any time you are faced with class definitions that are overly verbose like this, you might consider the use of a class decorator or metaclass. One of the features of a metaclass is that it can be used to fill in a lot of low-level implementation details, taking that burden off of the user. As an example, consider this metaclass and slight reformulation of the Structure class:

```python
class StructureMeta(type):
    '''
    Metaclass that automatically creates StructField descriptors
    '''
    def __init__(self, clsname, bases, clsdict):
        fields = getattr(self, '_fields_', [])
        byte_order = ''
        offset = 0
        for format, fieldname in fields:
            if format.startswith(('<','>','!','@')):
                byte_order = format[0]
                format = format[1:]
            format = byte_order + format
            setattr(self, fieldname, StructField(format, offset))
            offset += struct.calcsize(format)
        setattr(self, 'struct_size', offset)

class Structure(metaclass=StructureMeta):
    def __init__(self, bytedata):
        self._buffer = bytedata

    @classmethod
    def from_file(cls, f):
        return cls(f.read(cls.struct_size))
```

Using this new Structure class, you can now write a structure definition like this:

```python
class PolyHeader(Structure):
    _fields_ = [
        ('<i', 'file_code'),
        ('d', 'min_x'),
        ('d', 'min_y'),
```

```
            ('d', 'max_x'),
            ('d', 'max_y'),
            ('i', 'num_polys')
    ]
```

As you can see, the specification is a lot less verbose. The added `from_file()` class method also makes it easier to read the data from a file without knowing any details about the size or structure of the data. For example:

```
>>> f = open('polys.bin', 'rb')
>>> phead = PolyHeader.from_file(f)
>>> phead.file_code == 0x1234
True
>>> phead.min_x
0.5
>>> phead.min_y
0.5
>>> phead.max_x
7.0
>>> phead.max_y
9.2
>>> phead.num_polys
3
>>>
```

Once you introduce a metaclass into the mix, you can build more intelligence into it. For example, suppose you want to support nested binary structures. Here's a reformulation of the metaclass along with a new supporting descriptor that allows it:

```
class NestedStruct:
    '''
    Descriptor representing a nested structure
    '''
    def __init__(self, name, struct_type, offset):
        self.name = name
        self.struct_type = struct_type
        self.offset = offset
    def __get__(self, instance, cls):
        if instance is None:
            return self
        else:
            data = instance._buffer[self.offset:
                            self.offset+self.struct_type.struct_size]
            result = self.struct_type(data)
            # Save resulting structure back on instance to avoid
            # further recomputation of this step
            setattr(instance, self.name, result)
            return result

class StructureMeta(type):
    '''
    Metaclass that automatically creates StructField descriptors
```

```
    '''
    def __init__(self, clsname, bases, clsdict):
        fields = getattr(self, '_fields_', [])
        byte_order = ''
        offset = 0
        for format, fieldname in fields:
            if isinstance(format, StructureMeta):
                setattr(self, fieldname,
                        NestedStruct(fieldname, format, offset))
                offset += format.struct_size
            else:
                if format.startswith(('<','>','!','@')):
                    byte_order = format[0]
                    format = format[1:]
                format = byte_order + format
                setattr(self, fieldname, StructField(format, offset))
                offset += struct.calcsize(format)
        setattr(self, 'struct_size', offset)
```

In this code, the NestedStruct descriptor is used to overlay another structure definition over a region of memory. It does this by taking a slice of the original memory buffer and using it to instantiate the given structure type. Since the underlying memory buffer was initialized as a memoryview, this slicing does not incur any extra memory copies. Instead, it's just an overlay on the original memory. Moreover, to avoid repeated instantiations, the descriptor then stores the resulting inner structure object on the instance using the same technique described in Recipe 8.10.

Using this new formulation, you can start to write code like this:

```
class Point(Structure):
    _fields_ = [
        ('<d', 'x'),
        ('d', 'y')
    ]

class PolyHeader(Structure):
    _fields_ = [
        ('<i', 'file_code'),
        (Point, 'min'),          # nested struct
        (Point, 'max'),          # nested struct
        ('i', 'num_polys')
    ]
```

Amazingly, it will all still work as you expect. For example:

```
>>> f = open('polys.bin', 'rb')
>>> phead = PolyHeader.from_file(f)
>>> phead.file_code == 0x1234
True
>>> phead.min        # Nested structure
<__main__.Point object at 0x1006a48d0>
>>> phead.min.x
```

```
0.5
>>> phead.min.y
0.5
>>> phead.max.x
7.0
>>> phead.max.y
9.2
>>> phead.num_polys
3
>>>
```

At this point, a framework for dealing with fixed-sized records has been developed, but what about the variable-sized components? For example, the remainder of the polygon files contain sections of variable size.

One way to handle this is to write a class that simply represents a chunk of binary data along with a utility function for interpreting the contents in different ways. This is closely related to the code in Recipe 6.11:

```python
class SizedRecord:
    def __init__(self, bytedata):
        self._buffer = memoryview(bytedata)

    @classmethod
    def from_file(cls, f, size_fmt, includes_size=True):
        sz_nbytes = struct.calcsize(size_fmt)
        sz_bytes = f.read(sz_nbytes)
        sz, = struct.unpack(size_fmt, sz_bytes)
        buf = f.read(sz - includes_size * sz_nbytes)
        return cls(buf)

    def iter_as(self, code):
        if isinstance(code, str):
            s = struct.Struct(code)
            for off in range(0, len(self._buffer), s.size):
                yield s.unpack_from(self._buffer, off)
        elif isinstance(code, StructureMeta):
            size = code.struct_size
            for off in range(0, len(self._buffer), size):
                data = self._buffer[off:off+size]
                yield code(data)
```

The `SizedRecord.from_file()` class method is a utility for reading a size-prefixed chunk of data from a file, which is common in many file formats. As input, it accepts a structure format code containing the encoding of the size, which is expected to be in bytes. The optional `includes_size` argument specifies whether the number of bytes includes the size header or not. Here's an example of how you would use this code to read the individual polygons in the polygon file:

```
>>> f = open('polys.bin', 'rb')
>>> phead = PolyHeader.from_file(f)
>>> phead.num_polys
3
>>> polydata = [ SizedRecord.from_file(f, '<i')
...                for n in range(phead.num_polys) ]
>>> polydata
[<__main__.SizedRecord object at 0x1006a4d50>,
 <__main__.SizedRecord object at 0x1006a4f50>,
 <__main__.SizedRecord object at 0x10070da90>]
>>>
```

As shown, the contents of the SizedRecord instances have not yet been interpreted. To do that, use the iter_as() method, which accepts a structure format code or Struc ture class as input. This gives you a lot of flexibility in how to interpret the data. For example:

```
>>> for n, poly in enumerate(polydata):
...     print('Polygon', n)
...     for p in poly.iter_as('<dd'):
...         print(p)
...
Polygon 0
(1.0, 2.5)
(3.5, 4.0)
(2.5, 1.5)
Polygon 1
(7.0, 1.2)
(5.1, 3.0)
(0.5, 7.5)
(0.8, 9.0)
Polygon 2
(3.4, 6.3)
(1.2, 0.5)
(4.6, 9.2)
>>>

>>> for n, poly in enumerate(polydata):
...     print('Polygon', n)
...     for p in poly.iter_as(Point):
...         print(p.x, p.y)
...
Polygon 0
1.0 2.5
3.5 4.0
2.5 1.5
Polygon 1
7.0 1.2
5.1 3.0
0.5 7.5
0.8 9.0
Polygon 2
```

```
3.4 6.3
1.2 0.5
4.6 9.2
>>>
```

Putting all of this together, here's an alternative formulation of the read_polys() function:

```
class Point(Structure):
    _fields_ = [
        ('<d', 'x'),
        ('d', 'y')
        ]

class PolyHeader(Structure):
    _fields_ = [
        ('<i', 'file_code'),
        (Point, 'min'),
        (Point, 'max'),
        ('i', 'num_polys')
        ]

def read_polys(filename):
    polys = []
    with open(filename, 'rb') as f:
        phead = PolyHeader.from_file(f)
        for n in range(phead.num_polys):
            rec = SizedRecord.from_file(f, '<i')
            poly = [ (p.x, p.y)
                        for p in rec.iter_as(Point) ]
            polys.append(poly)
    return polys
```

Discussion

This recipe provides a practical application of various advanced programming techniques, including descriptors, lazy evaluation, metaclasses, class variables, and memory-views. However, they all serve a very specific purpose.

A major feature of the implementation is that it is strongly based on the idea of lazy-unpacking. When an instance of Structure is created, the __init__() merely creates a memoryview of the supplied byte data and does nothing else. Specifically, no unpacking or other structure-related operations take place at this time. One motivation for taking this approach is that you might only be interested in a few specific parts of a binary record. Rather than unpacking the whole file, only the parts that are actually accessed will be unpacked.

To implement the lazy unpacking and packing of values, the StructField descriptor class is used. Each attribute the user lists in _fields_ gets converted to a Struct Field descriptor that stores the associated structure format code and byte offset into

---

the stored buffer. The StructureMeta metaclass is what creates these descriptors auto-matically when various structure classes are defined. The main reason for using a metaclass is to make it extremely easy for a user to specify a structure format with a high-level description without worrying about low-level details.

One subtle aspect of the StructureMeta metaclass is that it makes byte order sticky. That is, if any attribute specifies a byte order (< for little endian or > for big endian), that ordering is applied to all fields that follow. This helps avoid extra typing, but also makes it possible to switch in the middle of a definition. For example, you might have something more complicated, such as this:

```
class ShapeFile(Structure):
    _fields_ = [ ('>i', 'file_code'),      # Big endian
                 ('20s', 'unused'),
                 ('i', 'file_length'),
                 ('<i', 'version'),        # Little endian
                 ('i', 'shape_type'),
                 ('d', 'min_x'),
                 ('d', 'min_y'),
                 ('d', 'max_x'),
                 ('d', 'max_y'),
                 ('d', 'min_z'),
                 ('d', 'max_z'),
                 ('d', 'min_m'),
                 ('d', 'max_m') ]
```

As noted, the use of a memoryview() in the solution serves a useful role in avoiding memory copies. When structures start to nest, memoryviews can be used to overlay different parts of the structure definition on the same region of memory. This aspect of the solution is subtle, but it concerns the slicing behavior of a memoryview versus a normal byte array. If you slice a byte string or byte array, you usually get a copy of the data. Not so with a memoryview—slices simply overlay the existing memory. Thus, this approach is more efficient.

A number of related recipes will help expand upon the topics used in the solution. See Recipe 8.13 for a closely related recipe that uses descriptors to build a type system. Recipe 8.10 has information about lazily computed properties and is related to the implementation of the NestedStruct descriptor. Recipe 9.19 has an example of using a metaclass to initialize class members, much in the same manner as the StructureMeta class. The source code for Python's ctypes library may also be of interest, due to its similar support for defining data structures, nesting of data structures, and similar functionality.

6.13. Summarizing Data and Performing Statistics

Problem

You need to crunch through large datasets and generate summaries or other kinds of statistics.

Solution

For any kind of data analysis involving statistics, time series, and other related techniques, you should look at the Pandas library (*http://pandas.pydata.org*).

To give you a taste, here's an example of using Pandas to analyze the City of Chicago rat and rodent database (*https://data.cityofchicago.org/Service-Requests/311-Service-Requests-Rodent-Baiting/97t6-zrhs*). At the time of this writing, it's a CSV file with about 74,000 entries:

```
>>> import pandas

>>> # Read a CSV file, skipping last line
>>> rats = pandas.read_csv('rats.csv', skip_footer=1)
>>> rats
<class 'pandas.core.frame.DataFrame'>
Int64Index: 74055 entries, 0 to 74054
Data columns:
Creation Date                  74055  non-null values
Status                         74055  non-null values
Completion Date                72154  non-null values
Service Request Number         74055  non-null values
Type of Service Request        74055  non-null values
Number of Premises Baited      65804  non-null values
Number of Premises with Garbage 65600  non-null values
Number of Premises with Rats   65752  non-null values
Current Activity               66041  non-null values
Most Recent Action             66023  non-null values
Street Address                 74055  non-null values
ZIP Code                       73584  non-null values
X Coordinate                   74043  non-null values
Y Coordinate                   74043  non-null values
Ward                           74044  non-null values
Police District                74044  non-null values
Community Area                 74044  non-null values
Latitude                       74043  non-null values
Longitude                      74043  non-null values
Location                       74043  non-null values
dtypes: float64(11), object(9)

>>> # Investigate range of values for a certain field
>>> rats['Current Activity'].unique()
array([nan, Dispatch Crew, Request Sanitation Inspector], dtype=object)
```

```
>>> # Filter the data
>>> crew_dispatched = rats[rats['Current Activity'] == 'Dispatch Crew']
>>> len(crew_dispatched)
65676
>>>

>>> # Find 10 most rat-infested ZIP codes in Chicago
>>> crew_dispatched['ZIP Code'].value_counts()[:10]
60647     3837
60618     3530
60614     3284
60629     3251
60636     2801
60657     2465
60641     2238
60609     2206
60651     2152
60632     2071
>>>

>>> # Group by completion date
>>> dates = crew_dispatched.groupby('Completion Date')
<pandas.core.groupby.DataFrameGroupBy object at 0x10d0a2a10>
>>> len(dates)
472
>>>

>>> # Determine counts on each day
>>> date_counts = dates.size()
>>> date_counts[0:10]
Completion Date
01/03/2011            4
01/03/2012          125
01/04/2011           54
01/04/2012           38
01/05/2011           78
01/05/2012          100
01/06/2011          100
01/06/2012           58
01/07/2011            1
01/09/2012           12
>>>

>>> # Sort the counts
>>> date_counts.sort()
>>> date_counts[-10:]
Completion Date
10/12/2012          313
10/21/2011          314
09/20/2011          316
10/26/2011          319
```

```
02/22/2011          325
10/26/2012          333
03/17/2011          336
10/13/2011          378
10/14/2011          391
10/07/2011          457
>>>
```

Yes, October 7, 2011, was indeed a very busy day for rats.

Discussion

Pandas is a large library that has more features than can be described here. However, if you need to analyze large datasets, group data, perform statistics, or other similar tasks, it's definitely worth a look.

Python for Data Analysis by Wes McKinney (O'Reilly) also contains much more information.

CHAPTER 7
Functions

Defining functions using the def statement is a cornerstone of all programs. The goal of this chapter is to present some more advanced and unusual function definition and usage patterns. Topics include default arguments, functions that take any number of arguments, keyword-only arguments, annotations, and closures. In addition, some tricky control flow and data passing problems involving callback functions are addressed.

7.1. Writing Functions That Accept Any Number of Arguments

Problem

You want to write a function that accepts any number of input arguments.

Solution

To write a function that accepts any number of positional arguments, use a * argument. For example:

```
def avg(first, *rest):
    return (first + sum(rest)) / (1 + len(rest))

# Sample use
avg(1, 2)        # 1.5
avg(1, 2, 3, 4)  # 2.5
```

In this example, rest is a tuple of all the extra positional arguments passed. The code treats it as a sequence in performing subsequent calculations.

To accept any number of keyword arguments, use an argument that starts with **. For example:

```
import html

def make_element(name, value, **attrs):
    keyvals = [' %s="%s"' % item for item in attrs.items()]
    attr_str = ''.join(keyvals)
    element = '<{name}{attrs}>{value}</{name}>'.format(
                    name=name,
                    attrs=attr_str,
                    value=html.escape(value))
    return element

# Example
# Creates '<item size="large" quantity="6">Albatross</item>'
make_element('item', 'Albatross', size='large', quantity=6)

# Creates '<p>&lt;spam&gt;</p>'
make_element('p', '<spam>')
```

Here, `attrs` is a dictionary that holds the passed keyword arguments (if any).

If you want a function that can accept both any number of positional and keyword-only arguments, use * and ** together. For example:

```
def anyargs(*args, **kwargs):
    print(args)      # A tuple
    print(kwargs)    # A dict
```

With this function, all of the positional arguments are placed into a tuple `args`, and all of the keyword arguments are placed into a dictionary `kwargs`.

Discussion

A * argument can only appear as the last positional argument in a function definition. A ** argument can only appear as the last argument. A subtle aspect of function definitions is that arguments can still appear after a * argument.

```
def a(x, *args, y):
    pass

def b(x, *args, y, **kwargs):
    pass
```

Such arguments are known as keyword-only arguments, and are discussed further in Recipe 7.2.

7.2. Writing Functions That Only Accept Keyword Arguments

Problem

You want a function to only accept certain arguments by keyword.

Solution

This feature is easy to implement if you place the keyword arguments after a * argument or a single unnamed *. For example:

```python
def recv(maxsize, *, block):
    'Receives a message'
    pass

recv(1024, True)        # TypeError
recv(1024, block=True)  # Ok
```

This technique can also be used to specify keyword arguments for functions that accept a varying number of positional arguments. For example:

```python
def mininum(*values, clip=None):
    m = min(values)
    if clip is not None:
        m = clip if clip > m else m
    return m

minimum(1, 5, 2, -5, 10)          # Returns -5
minimum(1, 5, 2, -5, 10, clip=0)  # Returns 0
```

Discussion

Keyword-only arguments are often a good way to enforce greater code clarity when specifying optional function arguments. For example, consider a call like this:

```python
msg = recv(1024, False)
```

If someone is not intimately familiar with the workings of the recv(), they may have no idea what the False argument means. On the other hand, it is much clearer if the call is written like this:

```python
msg = recv(1024, block=False)
```

The use of keyword-only arguments is also often preferrable to tricks involving **kwargs, since they show up properly when the user asks for help:

```python
>>> help(recv)
Help on function recv in module __main__:
```

```
recv(maxsize, *, block)
    Receives a message
```

Keyword-only arguments also have utility in more advanced contexts. For example, they can be used to inject arguments into functions that make use of the *args and **kwargs convention for accepting all inputs. See Recipe 9.11 for an example.

7.3. Attaching Informational Metadata to Function Arguments

Problem

You've written a function, but would like to attach some additional information to the arguments so that others know more about how a function is supposed to be used.

Solution

Function argument annotations can be a useful way to give programmers hints about how a function is supposed to be used. For example, consider the following annotated function:

```
def add(x:int, y:int) -> int:
    return x + y
```

The Python interpreter does not attach any semantic meaning to the attached annotations. They are not type checks, nor do they make Python behave any differently than it did before. However, they might give useful hints to others reading the source code about what you had in mind. Third-party tools and frameworks might also attach semantic meaning to the annotations. They also appear in documentation:

```
>>> help(add)
Help on function add in module __main__:

add(x: int, y: int) -> int
>>>
```

Although you can attach any kind of object to a function as an annotation (e.g., numbers, strings, instances, etc.), classes or strings often seem to make the most sense.

Discussion

Function annotations are merely stored in a function's __annotations__ attribute. For example:

```
>>> add.__annotations__
{'y': <class 'int'>, 'return': <class 'int'>, 'x': <class 'int'>}
```

Although there are many potential uses of annotations, their primary utility is probably just documentation. Because Python doesn't have type declarations, it can often be difficult to know what you're supposed to pass into a function if you're simply reading its source code in isolation. An annotation gives someone more of a hint.

See Recipe 9.20 for an advanced example showing how to use annotations to implement multiple dispatch (i.e., overloaded functions).

7.4. Returning Multiple Values from a Function

Problem

You want to return multiple values from a function.

Solution

To return multiple values from a function, simply return a tuple. For example:

```
>>> def myfun():
...     return 1, 2, 3
...
>>> a, b, c = myfun()
>>> a
1
>>> b
2
>>> c
3
```

Discussion

Although it looks like myfun() returns multiple values, a tuple is actually being created. It looks a bit peculiar, but it's actually the comma that forms a tuple, not the parentheses. For example:

```
>>> a = (1, 2)      # With parentheses
>>> a
(1, 2)
>>> b = 1, 2        # Without parentheses
>>> b
(1, 2)
>>>
```

When calling functions that return a tuple, it is common to assign the result to multiple variables, as shown. This is simply tuple unpacking, as described in Recipe 1.1. The return value could also have been assigned to a single variable:

```
>>> x = myfun()
>>> x
```

```
(1, 2, 3)
>>>
```

7.5. Defining Functions with Default Arguments

Problem

You want to define a function or method where one or more of the arguments are optional and have a default value.

Solution

On the surface, defining a function with optional arguments is easy—simply assign values in the definition and make sure that default arguments appear last. For example:

```
def spam(a, b=42):
    print(a, b)

spam(1)        # Ok. a=1, b=42
spam(1, 2)     # Ok. a=1, b=2
```

If the default value is supposed to be a mutable container, such as a list, set, or dictionary, use None as the default and write code like this:

```
# Using a list as a default value
def spam(a, b=None):
    if b is None:
        b = []
    ...
```

If, instead of providing a default value, you want to write code that merely tests whether an optional argument was given an interesting value or not, use this idiom:

```
_no_value = object()

def spam(a, b=_no_value):
    if b is _no_value:
        print('No b value supplied')
    ...
```

Here's how this function behaves:

```
>>> spam(1)
No b value supplied
>>> spam(1, 2)     # b = 2
>>> spam(1, None)  # b = None
>>>
```

Carefully observe that there is a distinction between passing no value at all and passing a value of None.

Discussion

Defining functions with default arguments is easy, but there is a bit more to it than meets the eye.

First, the values assigned as a default are bound only once at the time of function definition. Try this example to see it:

```
>>> x = 42
>>> def spam(a, b=x):
...     print(a, b)
...
>>> spam(1)
1 42
>>> x = 23       # Has no effect
>>> spam(1)
1 42
>>>
```

Notice how changing the variable x (which was used as a default value) has no effect whatsoever. This is because the default value was fixed at function definition time.

Second, the values assigned as defaults should always be immutable objects, such as None, True, False, numbers, or strings. Specifically, never write code like this:

```
def spam(a, b=[]):       # NO!
    ...
```

If you do this, you can run into all sorts of trouble if the default value ever escapes the function and gets modified. Such changes will permanently alter the default value across future function calls. For example:

```
>>> def spam(a, b=[]):
...     print(b)
...     return b
...
>>> x = spam(1)
>>> x
[]
>>> x.append(99)
>>> x.append('Yow!')
>>> x
[99, 'Yow!']
>>> spam(1)        # Modified list gets returned!
[99, 'Yow!']
>>>
```

That's probably not what you want. To avoid this, it's better to assign None as a default and add a check inside the function for it, as shown in the solution.

The use of the is operator when testing for None is a critical part of this recipe. Sometimes people make this mistake:

```
def spam(a, b=None):
    if not b:        # NO! Use 'b is None' instead
        b = []
    ...
```

The problem here is that although None evaluates to False, many other objects (e.g., zero-length strings, lists, tuples, dicts, etc.) do as well. Thus, the test just shown would falsely treat certain inputs as missing. For example:

```
>>> spam(1)        # OK
>>> x = []
>>> spam(1, x)     # Silent error. x value overwritten by default
>>> spam(1, 0)     # Silent error. 0 ignored
>>> spam(1, '')    # Silent error. '' ignored
>>>
```

The last part of this recipe is something that's rather subtle—a function that tests to see whether a value (any value) has been supplied to an optional argument or not. The tricky part here is that you can't use a default value of None, 0, or False to test for the presence of a user-supplied argument (since all of these are perfectly valid values that a user might supply). Thus, you need something else to test against.

To solve this problem, you can create a unique private instance of object, as shown in the solution (the _no_value variable). In the function, you then check the identity of the supplied argument against this special value to see if an argument was supplied or not. The thinking here is that it would be extremely unlikely for a user to pass the _no_value instance in as an input value. Therefore, it becomes a safe value to check against if you're trying to determine whether an argument was supplied or not.

The use of object() might look rather unusual here. object is a class that serves as the common base class for almost all objects in Python. You can create instances of object, but they are wholly uninteresting, as they have no notable methods nor any instance data (because there is no underlying instance dictionary, you can't even set any attributes). About the only thing you can do is perform tests for identity. This makes them useful as special values, as shown in the solution.

7.6. Defining Anonymous or Inline Functions

Problem

You need to supply a short callback function for use with an operation such as sort(), but you don't want to write a separate one-line function using the def statement. Instead, you'd like a shortcut that allows you to specify the function "in line."

Solution

Simple functions that do nothing more than evaluate an expression can be replaced by a lambda expression. For example:

```
>>> add = lambda x, y: x + y
>>> add(2,3)
5
>>> add('hello', 'world')
'helloworld'
>>>
```

The use of lambda here is the same as having typed this:

```
>>> def add(x, y):
...     return x + y
...
>>> add(2,3)
5
>>>
```

Typically, lambda is used in the context of some other operation, such as sorting or a data reduction:

```
>>> names = ['David Beazley', 'Brian Jones',
...          'Raymond Hettinger', 'Ned Batchelder']
>>> sorted(names, key=lambda name: name.split()[-1].lower())
['Ned Batchelder', 'David Beazley', 'Raymond Hettinger', 'Brian Jones']
>>>
```

Discussion

Although lambda allows you to define a simple function, its use is highly restricted. In particular, only a single expression can be specified, the result of which is the return value. This means that no other language features, including multiple statements, conditionals, iteration, and exception handling, can be included.

You can quite happily write a lot of Python code without ever using lambda. However, you'll occasionally encounter it in programs where someone is writing a lot of tiny functions that evaluate various expressions, or in programs that require users to supply callback functions.

7.7. Capturing Variables in Anonymous Functions

Problem

You've defined an anonymous function using lambda, but you also need to capture the values of certain variables at the time of definition.

Solution

Consider the behavior of the following code:

```
>>> x = 10
>>> a = lambda y: x + y
>>> x = 20
>>> b = lambda y: x + y
>>>
```

Now ask yourself a question. What are the values of a(10) and b(10)? If you think the results might be 20 and 30, you would be wrong:

```
>>> a(10)
30
>>> b(10)
30
>>>
```

The problem here is that the value of x used in the lambda expression is a free variable that gets bound at runtime, not definition time. Thus, the value of x in the lambda expressions is whatever the value of the x variable happens to be at the time of execution. For example:

```
>>> x = 15
>>> a(10)
25
>>> x = 3
>>> a(10)
13
>>>
```

If you want an anonymous function to capture a value at the point of definition and keep it, include the value as a default value, like this:

```
>>> x = 10
>>> a = lambda y, x=x: x + y
>>> x = 20
>>> b = lambda y, x=x: x + y
>>> a(10)
20
>>> b(10)
30
>>>
```

Discussion

The problem addressed in this recipe is something that tends to come up in code that tries to be just a little bit too clever with the use of lambda functions. For example, creating a list of lambda expressions using a list comprehension or in a loop of some kind and expecting the lambda functions to remember the iteration variable at the time of definition. For example:

```
>>> funcs = [lambda x: x+n for n in range(5)]
>>> for f in funcs:
...     print(f(0))
...
4
4
4
4
4
>>>
```

Notice how all functions think that n has the last value during iteration. Now compare to the following:

```
>>> funcs = [lambda x, n=n: x+n for n in range(5)]
>>> for f in funcs:
...     print(f(0))
...
0
1
2
3
4
>>>
```

As you can see, the functions now capture the value of n at the time of definition.

7.8. Making an N-Argument Callable Work As a Callable with Fewer Arguments

Problem

You have a callable that you would like to use with some other Python code, possibly as a callback function or handler, but it takes too many arguments and causes an exception when called.

Solution

If you need to reduce the number of arguments to a function, you should use `func tools.partial()`. The `partial()` function allows you to assign fixed values to one or more of the arguments, thus reducing the number of arguments that need to be supplied to subsequent calls. To illustrate, suppose you have this function:

```
def spam(a, b, c, d):
    print(a, b, c, d)
```

Now consider the use of `partial()` to fix certain argument values:

```
>>> from functools import partial
>>> s1 = partial(spam, 1)        # a = 1
>>> s1(2, 3, 4)
1 2 3 4
>>> s1(4, 5, 6)
1 4 5 6
>>> s2 = partial(spam, d=42)        # d = 42
>>> s2(1, 2, 3)
1 2 3 42
>>> s2(4, 5, 5)
4 5 5 42
>>> s3 = partial(spam, 1, 2, d=42) # a = 1, b = 2, d = 42
>>> s3(3)
1 2 3 42
>>> s3(4)
1 2 4 42
>>> s3(5)
1 2 5 42
>>>
```

Observe that `partial()` fixes the values for certain arguments and returns a new callable as a result. This new callable accepts the still unassigned arguments, combines them with the arguments given to `partial()`, and passes everything to the original function.

Discussion

This recipe is really related to the problem of making seemingly incompatible bits of code work together. A series of examples will help illustrate.

As a first example, suppose you have a list of points represented as tuples of (x,y) coordinates. You could use the following function to compute the distance between two points:

```
points = [ (1, 2), (3, 4), (5, 6), (7, 8) ]

import math
def distance(p1, p2):
    x1, y1 = p1
    x2, y2 = p2
    return math.hypot(x2 - x1, y2 - y1)
```

Now suppose you want to sort all of the points according to their distance from some other point. The `sort()` method of lists accepts a `key` argument that can be used to customize sorting, but it only works with functions that take a single argument (thus, `distance()` is not suitable). Here's how you might use `partial()` to fix it:

```
>>> pt = (4, 3)
>>> points.sort(key=partial(distance,pt))
>>> points
[(3, 4), (1, 2), (5, 6), (7, 8)]
>>>
```

As an extension of this idea, `partial()` can often be used to tweak the argument sig-natures of callback functions used in other libraries. For example, here's a bit of code that uses `multiprocessing` to asynchronously compute a result which is handed to a callback function that accepts both the result and an optional logging argument:

```
def output_result(result, log=None):
    if log is not None:
        log.debug('Got: %r', result)

# A sample function
def add(x, y):
    return x + y

if __name__ == '__main__':
    import logging
    from multiprocessing import Pool
    from functools import partial

    logging.basicConfig(level=logging.DEBUG)
    log = logging.getLogger('test')

    p = Pool()
    p.apply_async(add, (3, 4), callback=partial(output_result, log=log))
    p.close()
    p.join()
```

When supplying the callback function using `apply_async()`, the extra logging argu-ment is given using `partial()`. `multiprocessing` is none the wiser about all of this—it simply invokes the callback function with a single value.

As a similar example, consider the problem of writing network servers. The `socket server` module makes it relatively easy. For example, here is a simple echo server:

```
from socketserver import StreamRequestHandler, TCPServer

class EchoHandler(StreamRequestHandler):
    def handle(self):
        for line in self.rfile:
            self.wfile.write(b'GOT:' + line)

serv = TCPServer(('', 15000), EchoHandler)
serv.serve_forever()
```

However, suppose you want to give the `EchoHandler` class an `__init__()` method that accepts an additional configuration argument. For example:

```
class EchoHandler(StreamRequestHandler):
    # ack is added keyword-only argument. *args, **kwargs are
    # any normal parameters supplied (which are passed on)
    def __init__(self, *args, ack, **kwargs):
        self.ack = ack
        super().__init__(*args, **kwargs)
    def handle(self):
        for line in self.rfile:
            self.wfile.write(self.ack + line)
```

If you make this change, you'll find there is no longer an obvious way to plug it into the TCPServer class. In fact, you'll find that the code now starts generating exceptions like this:

```
Exception happened during processing of request from ('127.0.0.1', 59834)
Traceback (most recent call last):
  ...
TypeError: __init__() missing 1 required keyword-only argument: 'ack'
```

At first glance, it seems impossible to fix this code, short of modifying the source code to socketserver or coming up with some kind of weird workaround. However, it's easy to resolve using partial()—just use it to supply the value of the ack argument, like this:

```
from functools import partial
serv = TCPServer(('', 15000), partial(EchoHandler, ack=b'RECEIVED:'))
serv.serve_forever()
```

In this example, the specification of the ack argument in the __init__() method might look a little funny, but it's being specified as a keyword-only argument. This is discussed further in Recipe 7.2.

The functionality of partial() is sometimes replaced with a lambda expression. For example, the previous examples might use statements such as this:

```
points.sort(key=lambda p: distance(pt, p))

p.apply_async(add, (3, 4), callback=lambda result: output_result(result,log))

serv = TCPServer(('', 15000),
                lambda *args, **kwargs: EchoHandler(*args,
                                                    ack=b'RECEIVED:',
                                                    **kwargs))
```

This code works, but it's more verbose and potentially a lot more confusing to someone reading it. Using partial() is a bit more explicit about your intentions (supplying values for some of the arguments).)

7.9. Replacing Single Method Classes with Functions

Problem

You have a class that only defines a single method besides __init__(). However, to simplify your code, you would much rather just have a simple function.

Solution

In many cases, single-method classes can be turned into functions using closures. Consider, as an example, the following class, which allows a user to fetch URLs using a kind of templating scheme.

```
from urllib.request import urlopen

class UrlTemplate:
    def __init__(self, template):
        self.template = template
    def open(self, **kwargs):
        return urlopen(self.template.format_map(kwargs))

# Example use. Download stock data from yahoo
yahoo = UrlTemplate('http://finance.yahoo.com/d/quotes.csv?s={names}&f={fields}')
for line in yahoo.open(names='IBM,AAPL,FB', fields='sl1c1v'):
    print(line.decode('utf-8'))
```

The class could be replaced with a much simpler function:

```
def urltemplate(template):
    def opener(**kwargs):
        return urlopen(template.format_map(kwargs))
    return opener

# Example use
yahoo = urltemplate('http://finance.yahoo.com/d/quotes.csv?s={names}&f={fields}')
for line in yahoo(names='IBM,AAPL,FB', fields='sl1c1v'):
    print(line.decode('utf-8'))
```

Discussion

In many cases, the only reason you might have a single-method class is to store additional state for use in the method. For example, the only purpose of the UrlTemplate class is to hold the template value someplace so that it can be used in the open() method.

Using an inner function or closure, as shown in the solution, is often more elegant. Simply stated, a closure is just a function, but with an extra environment of the variables that are used inside the function. A key feature of a closure is that it remembers the environment in which it was defined. Thus, in the solution, the opener() function remembers the value of the template argument, and uses it in subsequent calls.

Whenever you're writing code and you encounter the problem of attaching additional state to a function, think closures. They are often a more minimal and elegant solution than the alternative of turning your function into a full-fledged class.

7.10. Carrying Extra State with Callback Functions

Problem

You're writing code that relies on the use of callback functions (e.g., event handlers, completion callbacks, etc.), but you want to have the callback function carry extra state for use inside the callback function.

Solution

This recipe pertains to the use of callback functions that are found in many libraries and frameworks—especially those related to asynchronous processing. To illustrate and for the purposes of testing, define the following function, which invokes a callback:

```
def apply_async(func, args, *, callback):
    # Compute the result
    result = func(*args)

    # Invoke the callback with the result
    callback(result)
```

In reality, such code might do all sorts of advanced processing involving threads, processes, and timers, but that's not the main focus here. Instead, we're simply focused on the invocation of the callback. Here's an example that shows how the preceding code gets used:

```
>>> def print_result(result):
...     print('Got:', result)
...
>>> def add(x, y):
...     return x + y
...
>>> apply_async(add, (2, 3), callback=print_result)
Got: 5
>>> apply_async(add, ('hello', 'world'), callback=print_result)
Got: helloworld
>>>
```

As you will notice, the print_result() function only accepts a single argument, which is the result. No other information is passed in. This lack of information can sometimes present problems when you want the callback to interact with other variables or parts of the environment.

One way to carry extra information in a callback is to use a bound-method instead of a simple function. For example, this class keeps an internal sequence number that is incremented every time a result is received:

```python
class ResultHandler:
    def __init__(self):
        self.sequence = 0
    def handler(self, result):
        self.sequence += 1
        print('[{}] Got: {}'.format(self.sequence, result))
```

To use this class, you would create an instance and use the bound method `handler` as the callback:

```python
>>> r = ResultHandler()
>>> apply_async(add, (2, 3), callback=r.handler)
[1] Got: 5
>>> apply_async(add, ('hello', 'world'), callback=r.handler)
[2] Got: helloworld
>>>
```

As an alternative to a class, you can also use a closure to capture state. For example:

```python
def make_handler():
    sequence = 0
    def handler(result):
        nonlocal sequence
        sequence += 1
        print('[{}] Got: {}'.format(sequence, result))
    return handler
```

Here is an example of this variant:

```python
>>> handler = make_handler()
>>> apply_async(add, (2, 3), callback=handler)
[1] Got: 5
>>> apply_async(add, ('hello', 'world'), callback=handler)
[2] Got: helloworld
>>>
```

As yet another variation on this theme, you can sometimes use a coroutine to accomplish the same thing:

```python
def make_handler():
    sequence = 0
    while True:
        result = yield
        sequence += 1
        print('[{}] Got: {}'.format(sequence, result))
```

For a coroutine, you would use its `send()` method as the callback, like this:

```python
>>> handler = make_handler()
>>> next(handler)          # Advance to the yield
```

```
>>> apply_async(add, (2, 3), callback=handler.send)
[1] Got: 5
>>> apply_async(add, ('hello', 'world'), callback=handler.send)
[2] Got: helloworld
>>>
```

Last, but not least, you can also carry state into a callback using an extra argument and partial function application. For example:

```
>>> class SequenceNo:
...     def __init__(self):
...         self.sequence = 0
...
>>> def handler(result, seq):
...     seq.sequence += 1
...     print('[{}] Got: {}'.format(seq.sequence, result))
...
>>> seq = SequenceNo()
>>> from functools import partial
>>> apply_async(add, (2, 3), callback=partial(handler, seq=seq))
[1] Got: 5
>>> apply_async(add, ('hello', 'world'), callback=partial(handler, seq=seq))
[2] Got: helloworld
>>>
```

Discussion

Software based on callback functions often runs the risk of turning into a huge tangled mess. Part of the issue is that the callback function is often disconnected from the code that made the initial request leading to callback execution. Thus, the execution environment between making the request and handling the result is effectively lost. If you want the callback function to continue with a procedure involving multiple steps, you have to figure out how to save and restore the associated state.

There are really two main approaches that are useful for capturing and carrying state. You can carry it around on an instance (attached to a bound method perhaps) or you can carry it around in a closure (an inner function). Of the two techniques, closures are perhaps a bit more lightweight and natural in that they are simply built from functions. They also automatically capture all of the variables being used. Thus, it frees you from having to worry about the exact state needs to be stored (it's determined automatically from your code).

If using closures, you need to pay careful attention to mutable variables. In the solution, the nonlocal declaration is used to indicate that the sequence variable is being modified from within the callback. Without this declaration, you'll get an error.

The use of a coroutine as a callback handler is interesting in that it is closely related to the closure approach. In some sense, it's even cleaner, since there is just a single function. Moreover, variables can be freely modified without worrying about nonlocal declarations. The potential downside is that coroutines don't tend to be as well understood as other parts of Python. There are also a few tricky bits such as the need to call next() on a coroutine prior to using it. That's something that could be easy to forget in practice. Nevertheless, coroutines have other potential uses here, such as the definition of an inlined callback (covered in the next recipe).

The last technique involving partial() is useful if all you need to do is pass extra values into a callback. Instead of using partial(), you'll sometimes see the same thing accomplished with the use of a lambda:

```
>>> apply_async(add, (2, 3), callback=lambda r: handler(r, seq))
[1] Got: 5
>>>
```

For more examples, see Recipe 7.8, which shows how to use partial() to change argument signatures.

7.11. Inlining Callback Functions

Problem

You're writing code that uses callback functions, but you're concerned about the proliferation of small functions and mind boggling control flow. You would like some way to make the code look more like a normal sequence of procedural steps.

Solution

Callback functions can be inlined into a function using generators and coroutines. To illustrate, suppose you have a function that performs work and invokes a callback as follows (see Recipe 7.10):

```
def apply_async(func, args, *, callback):
    # Compute the result
    result = func(*args)

    # Invoke the callback with the result
    callback(result)
```

Now take a look at the following supporting code, which involves an Async class and an inlined_async decorator:

```
from queue import Queue
from functools import wraps

class Async:
    def __init__(self, func, args):
        self.func = func
        self.args = args
```

```
def inlined_async(func):
    @wraps(func)
    def wrapper(*args):
        f = func(*args)
        result_queue = Queue()
        result_queue.put(None)
        while True:
            result = result_queue.get()
            try:
                a = f.send(result)
                apply_async(a.func, a.args, callback=result_queue.put)
            except StopIteration:
                break
    return wrapper
```

These two fragments of code will allow you to inline the callback steps using `yield` statements. For example:

```
def add(x, y):
    return x + y

@inlined_async
def test():
    r = yield Async(add, (2, 3))
    print(r)
    r = yield Async(add, ('hello', 'world'))
    print(r)
    for n in range(10):
        r = yield Async(add, (n, n))
        print(r)
    print('Goodbye')
```

If you call `test()`, you'll get output like this:

```
5
helloworld
0
2
4
6
8
10
12
14
16
18
Goodbye
```

Aside from the special decorator and use of `yield`, you will notice that no callback functions appear anywhere (except behind the scenes).

Discussion

This recipe will really test your knowledge of callback functions, generators, and control flow.

First, in code involving callbacks, the whole point is that the current calculation will suspend and resume at some later point in time (e.g., asynchronously). When the calculation resumes, the callback will get executed to continue the processing. The `apply_async()` function illustrates the essential parts of executing the callback, although in reality it might be much more complicated (involving threads, processes, event handlers, etc.).

The idea that a calculation will suspend and resume naturally maps to the execution model of a generator function. Specifically, the `yield` operation makes a generator function emit a value and suspend. Subsequent calls to the `__next__()` or `send()` method of a generator will make it start again.

With this in mind, the core of this recipe is found in the `inline_async()` decorator function. The key idea is that the decorator will step the generator function through all of its `yield` statements, one at a time. To do this, a result queue is created and initially populated with a value of `None`. A loop is then initiated in which a result is popped off the queue and sent into the generator. This advances to the next yield, at which point an instance of `Async` is received. The loop then looks at the function and arguments, and initiates the asynchronous calculation `apply_async()`. However, the sneakiest part of this calculation is that instead of using a normal callback function, the callback is set to the queue `put()` method.

At this point, it is left somewhat open as to precisely what happens. The main loop immediately goes back to the top and simply executes a `get()` operation on the queue. If data is present, it must be the result placed there by the `put()` callback. If nothing is there, the operation blocks, waiting for a result to arrive at some future time. How that might happen depends on the precise implementation of the `apply_async()` function.

If you're doubtful that anything this crazy would work, you can try it with the multiprocessing library and have async operations executed in separate processes:

```
if __name__ == '__main__':
    import multiprocessing
    pool = multiprocessing.Pool()
    apply_async = pool.apply_async

    # Run the test function
    test()
```

Indeed, you'll find that it works, but unraveling the control flow might require more coffee.

Hiding tricky control flow behind generator functions is found elsewhere in the standard library and third-party packages. For example, the @contextmanager decorator in the contextlib performs a similar mind-bending trick that glues the entry and exit from a context manager together across a yield statement. The popular Twisted package (*http://twistedmatrix.com*) has inlined callbacks that are also similar.

7.12. Accessing Variables Defined Inside a Closure

Problem

You would like to extend a closure with functions that allow the inner variables to be accessed and modified.

Solution

Normally, the inner variables of a closure are completely hidden to the outside world. However, you can provide access by writing accessor functions and attaching them to the closure as function attributes. For example:

```
def sample():
    n = 0
    # Closure function
    def func():
        print('n=', n)

    # Accessor methods for n
    def get_n():
        return n

    def set_n(value):
        nonlocal n
        n = value

    # Attach as function attributes
    func.get_n = get_n
    func.set_n = set_n
    return func
```

Here is an example of using this code:

```
>>> f = sample()
>>> f()
n= 0
>>> f.set_n(10)
>>> f()
n= 10
>>> f.get_n()
10
>>>
```

Discussion

There are two main features that make this recipe work. First, nonlocal declarations make it possible to write functions that change inner variables. Second, function attributes allow the accessor methods to be attached to the closure function in a straightforward manner where they work a lot like instance methods (even though no class is involved).

A slight extension to this recipe can be made to have closures emulate instances of a class. All you need to do is copy the inner functions over to the dictionary of an instance and return it. For example:

```python
import sys
class ClosureInstance:
    def __init__(self, locals=None):
        if locals is None:
            locals = sys._getframe(1).f_locals

        # Update instance dictionary with callables
        self.__dict__.update((key,value) for key, value in locals.items()
                                if callable(value) )
    # Redirect special methods
    def __len__(self):
        return self.__dict__['__len__']()

# Example use
def Stack():
    items = []

    def push(item):
        items.append(item)

    def pop():
        return items.pop()

    def __len__():
        return len(items)

    return ClosureInstance()
```

Here's an interactive session to show that it actually works:

```python
>>> s = Stack()
>>> s
<__main__.ClosureInstance object at 0x10069ed10>
>>> s.push(10)
>>> s.push(20)
>>> s.push('Hello')
>>> len(s)
3
>>> s.pop()
'Hello'
```

```
>>> s.pop()
20
>>> s.pop()
10
>>>
```

Interestingly, this code runs a bit faster than using a normal class definition. For example, you might be inclined to test the performance against a class like this:

```
class Stack2:
    def __init__(self):
        self.items = []

    def push(self, item):
        self.items.append(item)

    def pop(self):
        return self.items.pop()

    def __len__(self):
        return len(self.items)
```

If you do, you'll get results similar to the following:

```
>>> from timeit import timeit
>>> # Test involving closures
>>> s = Stack()
>>> timeit('s.push(1);s.pop()', 'from __main__ import s')
0.9874754269840196
>>> # Test involving a class
>>> s = Stack2()
>>> timeit('s.push(1);s.pop()', 'from __main__ import s')
1.0707052160287276
>>>
```

As shown, the closure version runs about 8% faster. Most of that is coming from streamlined access to the instance variables. Closures are faster because there's no extra self variable involved.

Raymond Hettinger has devised an even more diabolical variant of this idea (*http://bit.ly/11DSni2*). However, should you be inclined to do something like this in your code, be aware that it's still a rather weird substitute for a real class. For example, major features such as inheritance, properties, descriptors, or class methods don't work. You also have to play some tricks to get special methods to work (e.g., see the implementation of __len__() in ClosureInstance).

Lastly, you'll run the risk of confusing people who read your code and wonder why it doesn't look anything like a normal class definition (of course, they'll also wonder why it's faster). Nevertheless, it's an interesting example of what can be done by providing access to the internals of a closure.

In the big picture, adding methods to closures might have more utility in settings where you want to do things like reset the internal state, flush buffers, clear caches, or have some kind of feedback mechanism.

## CHAPTER 8

Classes and Objects

The primary focus of this chapter is to present recipes to common programming patterns related to class definitions. Topics include making objects support common Python features, usage of special methods, encapsulation techniques, inheritance, memory management, and useful design patterns.

8.1. Changing the String Representation of Instances

Problem

You want to change the output produced by printing or viewing instances to something more sensible.

Solution

To change the string representation of an instance, define the `__str__()` and `__repr__()` methods. For example:

```
class Pair:
    def __init__(self, x, y):
        self.x = x
        self.y = y
    def __repr__(self):
        return 'Pair({0.x!r}, {0.y!r})'.format(self)
    def __str__(self):
        return '({0.x!s}, {0.y!s})'.format(self)
```

The `__repr__()` method returns the code representation of an instance, and is usually the text you would type to re-create the instance. The built-in `repr()` function returns this text, as does the interactive interpreter when inspecting values. The `__str__()` method converts the instance to a string, and is the output produced by the `str()` and `print()` functions. For example:

```
>>> p = Pair(3, 4)
>>> p
Pair(3, 4)              # __repr__() output
>>> print(p)
(3, 4)                  # __str__() output
>>>
```

The implementation of this recipe also shows how different string representations may be used during formatting. Specifically, the special !r formatting code indicates that the output of __repr__() should be used instead of __str__(), the default. You can try this experiment with the preceding class to see this:

```
>>> p = Pair(3, 4)
>>> print('p is {0!r}'.format(p))
p is Pair(3, 4)
>>> print('p is {0}'.format(p))
p is (3, 4)
>>>
```

Discussion

Defining __repr__() and __str__() is often good practice, as it can simplify debugging and instance output. For example, by merely printing or logging an instance, a programmer will be shown more useful information about the instance contents.

It is standard practice for the output of __repr__() to produce text such that eval(repr(x)) == x. If this is not possible or desired, then it is common to create a useful textual representation enclosed in < and > instead. For example:

```
>>> f = open('file.dat')
>>> f
<_io.TextIOWrapper name='file.dat' mode='r' encoding='UTF-8'>
>>>
```

If no __str__() is defined, the output of __repr__() is used as a fallback.

The use of format() in the solution might look a little funny, but the format code {0.x} specifies the x-attribute of argument 0. So, in the following function, the 0 is actually the instance self:

```
def __repr__(self):
    return 'Pair({0.x!r}, {0.y!r})'.format(self)
```

As an alternative to this implementation, you could also use the % operator and the following code:

```
def __repr__(self):
    return 'Pair(%r, %r)' % (self.x, self.y)
```

8.2. Customizing String Formatting

Problem

You want an object to support customized formatting through the format() function and string method.

Solution

To customize string formatting, define the __format__() method on a class. For example:

```python
_formats = {
    'ymd' : '{d.year}-{d.month}-{d.day}',
    'mdy' : '{d.month}/{d.day}/{d.year}',
    'dmy' : '{d.day}/{d.month}/{d.year}'
    }

class Date:
    def __init__(self, year, month, day):
        self.year = year
        self.month = month
        self.day = day

    def __format__(self, code):
        if code == '':
            code = 'ymd'
        fmt = _formats[code]
        return fmt.format(d=self)
```

Instances of the Date class now support formatting operations such as the following:

```python
>>> d = Date(2012, 12, 21)
>>> format(d)
'2012-12-21'
>>> format(d, 'mdy')
'12/21/2012'
>>> 'The date is {:ymd}'.format(d)
'The date is 2012-12-21'
>>> 'The date is {:mdy}'.format(d)
'The date is 12/21/2012'
>>>
```

Discussion

The __format__() method provides a hook into Python's string formatting functionality. It's important to emphasize that the interpretation of format codes is entirely up to the class itself. Thus, the codes can be almost anything at all. For example, consider the following from the datetime module:

```
>>> from datetime import date
>>> d = date(2012, 12, 21)
>>> format(d)
'2012-12-21'
>>> format(d,'%A, %B %d, %Y')
'Friday, December 21, 2012'
>>> 'The end is {:%d %b %Y}. Goodbye'.format(d)
'The end is 21 Dec 2012. Goodbye'
>>>
```

There are some standard conventions for the formatting of the built-in types. See the documentation for the string module (*http://docs.python.org/3/library/string.html*) for a formal specification.

8.3. Making Objects Support the Context-Management Protocol

Problem

You want to make your objects support the context-management protocol (the with statement).

Solution

In order to make an object compatible with the with statement, you need to implement __enter__() and __exit__() methods. For example, consider the following class, which provides a network connection:

```
from socket import socket, AF_INET, SOCK_STREAM

class LazyConnection:
    def __init__(self, address, family=AF_INET, type=SOCK_STREAM):
        self.address = address
        self.family = AF_INET
        self.type = SOCK_STREAM
        self.sock = None

    def __enter__(self):
        if self.sock is not None:
            raise RuntimeError('Already connected')
        self.sock = socket(self.family, self.type)
        self.sock.connect(self.address)
        return self.sock

    def __exit__(self, exc_ty, exc_val, tb):
        self.sock.close()
        self.sock = None
```

The key feature of this class is that it represents a network connection, but it doesn't actually do anything initially (e.g., it doesn't establish a connection). Instead, the connection is established and closed using the with statement (essentially on demand). For example:

```
from functools import partial

conn = LazyConnection(('www.python.org', 80))
# Connection closed
with conn as s:
    # conn.__enter__() executes: connection open
    s.send(b'GET /index.html HTTP/1.0\r\n')
    s.send(b'Host: www.python.org\r\n')
    s.send(b'\r\n')
    resp = b''.join(iter(partial(s.recv, 8192), b''))
    # conn.__exit__() executes: connection closed
```

Discussion

The main principle behind writing a context manager is that you're writing code that's meant to surround a block of statements as defined by the use of the with statement. When the with statement is first encountered, the __enter__() method is triggered. The return value of __enter__() (if any) is placed into the variable indicated with the as qualifier. Afterward, the statements in the body of the with statement execute. Finally, the __exit__() method is triggered to clean up.

This control flow happens regardless of what happens in the body of the with statement, including if there are exceptions. In fact, the three arguments to the __exit__() method contain the exception type, value, and traceback for pending exceptions (if any). The __exit__() method can choose to use the exception information in some way or to ignore it by doing nothing and returning None as a result. If __exit__() returns True, the exception is cleared as if nothing happened and the program continues executing statements immediately after the with block.

One subtle aspect of this recipe is whether or not the LazyConnection class allows nested use of the connection with multiple with statements. As shown, only a single socket connection at a time is allowed, and an exception is raised if a repeated with statement is attempted when a socket is already in use. You can work around this limitation with a slightly different implementation, as shown here:

```
from socket import socket, AF_INET, SOCK_STREAM

class LazyConnection:
    def __init__(self, address, family=AF_INET, type=SOCK_STREAM):
        self.address = address
        self.family = AF_INET
        self.type = SOCK_STREAM
        self.connections = []
```

```
    def __enter__(self):
        sock = socket(self.family, self.type)
        sock.connect(self.address)
        self.connections.append(sock)
        return sock

    def __exit__(self, exc_ty, exc_val, tb):
        self.connections.pop().close()

# Example use
from functools import partial

conn = LazyConnection(('www.python.org', 80))
with conn as s1:
    ...
    with conn as s2:
        ...
        # s1 and s2 are independent sockets
```

In this second version, the LazyConnection class serves as a kind of factory for connections. Internally, a list is used to keep a stack. Whenever __enter__() executes, it makes a new connection and adds it to the stack. The __exit__() method simply pops the last connection off the stack and closes it. It's subtle, but this allows multiple connections to be created at once with nested with statements, as shown.

Context managers are most commonly used in programs that need to manage resources such as files, network connections, and locks. A key part of such resources is they have to be explicitly closed or released to operate correctly. For instance, if you acquire a lock, then you have to make sure you release it, or else you risk deadlock. By implementing __enter__(), __exit__(), and using the with statement, it is much easier to avoid such problems, since the cleanup code in the __exit__() method is guaranteed to run no matter what.

An alternative formulation of context managers is found in the contextmanager module. See Recipe 9.22. A thread-safe version of this recipe can be found in Recipe 12.6.

8.4. Saving Memory When Creating a Large Number of Instances

Problem

Your program creates a large number (e.g., millions) of instances and uses a large amount of memory.

Solution

For classes that primarily serve as simple data structures, you can often greatly reduce the memory footprint of instances by adding the __slots__ attribute to the class definition. For example:

```python
class Date:
    __slots__ = ['year', 'month', 'day']
    def __init__(self, year, month, day):
        self.year = year
        self.month = month
        self.day = day
```

When you define __slots__, Python uses a much more compact internal representation for instances. Instead of each instance consisting of a dictionary, instances are built around a small fixed-sized array, much like a tuple or list. Attribute names listed in the __slots__ specifier are internally mapped to specific indices within this array. A side effect of using slots is that it is no longer possible to add new attributes to instances—you are restricted to only those attribute names listed in the __slots__ specifier.

Discussion

The memory saved by using slots varies according to the number and type of attributes stored. However, in general, the resulting memory use is comparable to that of storing data in a tuple. To give you an idea, storing a single Date instance without slots requires 428 bytes of memory on a 64-bit version of Python. If slots is defined, it drops to 156 bytes. In a program that manipulated a large number of dates all at once, this would make a significant reduction in overall memory use.

Although slots may seem like a feature that could be generally useful, you should resist the urge to use it in most code. There are many parts of Python that rely on the normal dictionary-based implementation. In addition, classes that define slots don't support certain features such as multiple inheritance. For the most part, you should only use slots on classes that are going to serve as frequently used data structures in your program (e.g., if your program created millions of instances of a particular class).

A common misperception of __slots__ is that it is an encapsulation tool that prevents users from adding new attributes to instances. Although this is a side effect of using slots, this was never the original purpose. Instead, __slots__ was always intended to be an optimization tool.

8.5. Encapsulating Names in a Class

Problem

You want to encapsulate "private" data on instances of a class, but are concerned about Python's lack of access control.

Solution

Rather than relying on language features to encapsulate data, Python programmers are expected to observe certain naming conventions concerning the intended usage of data and methods. The first convention is that any name that starts with a single leading underscore (_) should always be assumed to be internal implementation. For example:

```python
class A:
    def __init__(self):
        self._internal = 0      # An internal attribute
        self.public = 1         # A public attribute

    def public_method(self):
        '''
        A public method
        '''
        ...

    def _internal_method(self):
        ...
```

Python doesn't actually prevent someone from accessing internal names. However, doing so is considered impolite, and may result in fragile code. It should be noted, too, that the use of the leading underscore is also used for module names and module-level functions. For example, if you ever see a module name that starts with a leading underscore (e.g., _socket), it's internal implementation. Likewise, module-level functions such as sys._getframe() should only be used with great caution.

You may also encounter the use of two leading underscores (__) on names within class definitions. For example:

```python
class B:
    def __init__(self):
        self.__private = 0
    def __private_method(self):
        ...
    def public_method(self):
        ...
        self.__private_method()
        ...
```

The use of double leading underscores causes the name to be mangled to something else. Specifically, the private attributes in the preceding class get renamed to _B__pri vate and _B__private_method, respectively. At this point, you might ask what purpose such name mangling serves. The answer is inheritance—such attributes cannot be overridden via inheritance. For example:

```
class C(B):
    def __init__(self):
        super().__init__()
        self.__private = 1        # Does not override B.__private
    # Does not override B.__private_method()
    def __private_method(self):
        ...
```

Here, the private names __private and __private_method get renamed to _C__pri vate and _C__private_method, which are different than the mangled names in the base class B.

Discussion

The fact that there are two different conventions (single underscore versus double underscore) for "private" attributes leads to the obvious question of which style you should use. For most code, you should probably just make your nonpublic names start with a single underscore. If, however, you know that your code will involve subclassing, and there are internal attributes that should be hidden from subclasses, use the double underscore instead.

It should also be noted that sometimes you may want to define a variable that clashes with the name of a reserved word. For this, you should use a single trailing underscore. For example:

```
lambda_ = 2.0     # Trailing _ to avoid clash with lambda keyword
```

The reason for not using a leading underscore here is that it avoids confusion about the intended usage (i.e., the use of a leading underscore could be interpreted as a way to avoid a name collision rather than as an indication that the value is private). Using a single trailing underscore solves this problem.

8.6. Creating Managed Attributes

Problem

You want to add extra processing (e.g., type checking or validation) to the getting or setting of an instance attribute.

Solution

A simple way to customize access to an attribute is to define it as a "property." For example, this code defines a property that adds simple type checking to an attribute:

```python
class Person:
    def __init__(self, first_name):
        self.first_name = first_name

    # Getter function
    @property
    def first_name(self):
        return self._first_name

    # Setter function
    @first_name.setter
    def first_name(self, value):
        if not isinstance(value, str):
            raise TypeError('Expected a string')
        self._first_name = value

    # Deleter function (optional)
    @first_name.deleter
    def first_name(self):
        raise AttributeError("Can't delete attribute")
```

In the preceding code, there are three related methods, all of which must have the same name. The first method is a getter function, and establishes first_name as being a property. The other two methods attach optional setter and deleter functions to the first_name property. It's important to stress that the @first_name.setter and @first_name.deleter decorators won't be defined unless first_name was already established as a property using @property.

A critical feature of a property is that it looks like a normal attribute, but access automatically triggers the getter, setter, and deleter methods. For example:

```python
>>> a = Person('Guido')
>>> a.first_name        # Calls the getter
'Guido'
>>> a.first_name = 42  # Calls the setter
Traceback (most recent call last):
  File "<stdin>", line 1, in <module>
  File "prop.py", line 14, in first_name
    raise TypeError('Expected a string')
TypeError: Expected a string
>>> del a.first_name
Traceback (most recent call last):
  File "<stdin>", line 1, in <module>
AttributeError: can't delete attribute
>>>
```

When implementing a property, the underlying data (if any) still needs to be stored somewhere. Thus, in the get and set methods, you see direct manipulation of a _first_name attribute, which is where the actual data lives. In addition, you may ask why the __init__() method sets self.first_name instead of self._first_name. In this example, the entire point of the property is to apply type checking when setting an attribute. Thus, chances are you would also want such checking to take place during initialization. By setting self.first_name, the set operation uses the setter method (as opposed to bypassing it by accessing self._first_name).

Properties can also be defined for existing get and set methods. For example:

```python
class Person:
    def __init__(self, first_name):
        self.set_first_name(first_name)

    # Getter function
    def get_first_name(self):
        return self._first_name

    # Setter function
    def set_first_name(self, value):
        if not isinstance(value, str):
            raise TypeError('Expected a string')
        self._first_name = value

    # Deleter function (optional)
    def del_first_name(self):
        raise AttributeError("Can't delete attribute")

    # Make a property from existing get/set methods
    name = property(get_first_name, set_first_name, del_first_name)
```

Discussion

A property attribute is actually a collection of methods bundled together. If you inspect a class with a property, you can find the raw methods in the fget, fset, and fdel attributes of the property itself. For example:

```python
>>> Person.first_name.fget
<function Person.first_name at 0x1006a60e0>
>>> Person.first_name.fset
<function Person.first_name at 0x1006a6170>
>>> Person.first_name.fdel
<function Person.first_name at 0x1006a62e0>
>>>
```

Normally, you wouldn't call fget or fset directly, but they are triggered automatically when the property is accessed.

Properties should only be used in cases where you actually need to perform extra processing on attribute access. Sometimes programmers coming from languages such as Java feel that all access should be handled by getters and setters, and that they should write code like this:

```
class Person:
    def __init__(self, first_name):
        self.first_name = name
    @property
    def first_name(self):
        return self._first_name
    @first_name.setter
    def first_name(self, value):
        self._first_name = value
```

Don't write properties that don't actually add anything extra like this. For one, it makes your code more verbose and confusing to others. Second, it will make your program run a lot slower. Lastly, it offers no real design benefit. Specifically, if you later decide that extra processing needs to be added to the handling of an ordinary attribute, you could promote it to a property without changing existing code. This is because the syntax of code that accessed the attribute would remain unchanged.

Properties can also be a way to define computed attributes. These are attributes that are not actually stored, but computed on demand. For example:

```
import math
class Circle:
    def __init__(self, radius):
        self.radius = radius
    @property
    def area(self):
        return math.pi * self.radius ** 2
    @property
    def perimeter(self):
        return 2 * math.pi * self.radius
```

Here, the use of properties results in a very uniform instance interface in that radius, area, and perimeter are all accessed as simple attributes, as opposed to a mix of simple attributes and method calls. For example:

```
>>> c = Circle(4.0)
>>> c.radius
4.0
>>> c.area            # Notice lack of ()
50.26548245743669
>>> c.perimeter       # Notice lack of ()
25.132741228718345
>>>
```

Although properties give you an elegant programming interface, sometimes you actually may want to directly use getter and setter functions. For example:

```
>>> p = Person('Guido')
>>> p.get_first_name()
'Guido'
>>> p.set_first_name('Larry')
>>>
```

This often arises in situations where Python code is being integrated into a larger infrastructure of systems or programs. For example, perhaps a Python class is going to be plugged into a large distributed system based on remote procedure calls or distributed objects. In such a setting, it may be much easier to work with an explicit get/set method (as a normal method call) rather than a property that implicitly makes such calls.

Last, but not least, don't write Python code that features a lot of repetitive property definitions. For example:

```
class Person:
    def __init__(self, first_name, last_name):
        self.first_name = first_name
        self.last_name = last_name

    @property
    def first_name(self):
        return self._first_name

    @first_name.setter
    def first_name(self, value):
        if not isinstance(value, str):
            raise TypeError('Expected a string')
        self._first_name = value

    # Repeated property code, but for a different name (bad!)
    @property
    def last_name(self):
        return self._last_name

    @last_name.setter
    def last_name(self, value):
        if not isinstance(value, str):
            raise TypeError('Expected a string')
        self._last_name = value
```

Code repetition leads to bloated, error prone, and ugly code. As it turns out, there are much better ways to achieve the same thing using descriptors or closures. See Recipes 8.9 and 9.21.

8.7. Calling a Method on a Parent Class

Problem

You want to invoke a method in a parent class in place of a method that has been overridden in a subclass.

Solution

To call a method in a parent (or superclass), use the `super()` function. For example:

```python
class A:
    def spam(self):
        print('A.spam')

class B(A):
    def spam(self):
        print('B.spam')
        super().spam()      # Call parent spam()
```

A very common use of `super()` is in the handling of the `__init__()` method to make sure that parents are properly initialized:

```python
class A:
    def __init__(self):
        self.x = 0

class B(A):
    def __init__(self):
        super().__init__()
        self.y = 1
```

Another common use of `super()` is in code that overrides any of Python's special methods. For example:

```python
class Proxy:
    def __init__(self, obj):
        self._obj = obj

    # Delegate attribute lookup to internal obj
    def __getattr__(self, name):
        return getattr(self._obj, name)

    # Delegate attribute assignment
    def __setattr__(self, name, value):
        if name.startswith('_'):
            super().__setattr__(name, value)      # Call original __setattr__
        else:
            setattr(self._obj, name, value)
```

In this code, the implementation of __setattr__() includes a name check. If the name starts with an underscore (_), it invokes the original implementation of __setattr__() using super(). Otherwise, it delegates to the internally held object self._obj. It looks a little funny, but super() works even though there is no explicit base class listed.

Discussion

Correct use of the super() function is actually one of the most poorly understood aspects of Python. Occasionally, you will see code written that directly calls a method in a parent like this:

```
class Base:
    def __init__(self):
        print('Base.__init__')

class A(Base):
    def __init__(self):
        Base.__init__(self)
        print('A.__init__')
```

Although this "works" for most code, it can lead to bizarre trouble in advanced code involving multiple inheritance. For example, consider the following:

```
class Base:
    def __init__(self):
        print('Base.__init__')

class A(Base):
    def __init__(self):
        Base.__init__(self)
        print('A.__init__')

class B(Base):
    def __init__(self):
        Base.__init__(self)
        print('B.__init__')

class C(A,B):
    def __init__(self):
        A.__init__(self)
        B.__init__(self)
        print('C.__init__')
```

If you run this code, you'll see that the Base.__init__() method gets invoked twice, as shown here:

```
>>> c = C()
Base.__init__
A.__init__
Base.__init__
```

```
B.__init__
C.__init__
>>>
```

Perhaps double-invocation of `Base.__init__()` is harmless, but perhaps not. If, on the other hand, you change the code to use `super()`, it all works:

```
class Base:
    def __init__(self):
        print('Base.__init__')

class A(Base):
    def __init__(self):
        super().__init__()
        print('A.__init__')

class B(Base):
    def __init__(self):
        super().__init__()
        print('B.__init__')

class C(A,B):
    def __init__(self):
        super().__init__()      # Only one call to super() here
        print('C.__init__')
```

When you use this new version, you'll find that each `__init__()` method only gets called once:

```
>>> c = C()
Base.__init__
B.__init__
A.__init__
C.__init__
>>>
```

To understand why it works, we need to step back for a minute and discuss how Python implements inheritance. For every class that you define, Python computes what's known as a method resolution order (MRO) list. The MRO list is simply a linear ordering of all the base classes. For example:

```
>>> C.__mro__
(<class '__main__.C'>, <class '__main__.A'>, <class '__main__.B'>,
<class '__main__.Base'>, <class 'object'>)
>>>
```

To implement inheritance, Python starts with the leftmost class and works its way left-to-right through classes on the MRO list until it finds the first attribute match.

The actual determination of the MRO list itself is made using a technique known as C3 Linearization. Without getting too bogged down in the mathematics of it, it is actually a merge sort of the MROs from the parent classes subject to three constraints:

- Child classes get checked before parents
- Multiple parents get checked in the order listed.
- If there are two valid choices for the next class, pick the one from the first parent.

Honestly, all you really need to know is that the order of classes in the MRO list "makes sense" for almost any class hierarchy you are going to define.

When you use the super() function, Python continues its search starting with the next class on the MRO. As long as every redefined method consistently uses super() and only calls it once, control will ultimately work its way through the entire MRO list and each method will only be called once. This is why you don't get double calls to Base.__init__() in the second example.

A somewhat surprising aspect of super() is that it doesn't necessarily go to the direct parent of a class next in the MRO and that you can even use it in a class with no direct parent at all. For example, consider this class:

```python
class A:
    def spam(self):
        print('A.spam')
        super().spam()
```

If you try to use this class, you'll find that it's completely broken:

```python
>>> a = A()
>>> a.spam()
A.spam
Traceback (most recent call last):
  File "<stdin>", line 1, in <module>
  File "<stdin>", line 4, in spam
AttributeError: 'super' object has no attribute 'spam'
>>>
```

Yet, watch what happens if you start using the class with multiple inheritance:

```python
>>> class B:
...     def spam(self):
...         print('B.spam')
...
>>> class C(A,B):
...     pass
...
>>> c = C()
>>> c.spam()
A.spam
B.spam
>>>
```

Here you see that the use of super().spam() in class A has, in fact, called the spam() method in class B—a class that is completely unrelated to A! This is all explained by the MRO of class C:

```
>>> C.__mro__
(<class '__main__.C'>, <class '__main__.A'>, <class '__main__.B'>,
<class 'object'>)
>>>
```

Using super() in this manner is most common when defining mixin classes. See Recipes 8.13 and 8.18.

However, because super() might invoke a method that you're not expecting, there are a few general rules of thumb you should try to follow. First, make sure that all methods with the same name in an inheritance hierarchy have a compatible calling signature (i.e., same number of arguments, argument names). This ensures that super() won't get tripped up if it tries to invoke a method on a class that's not a direct parent. Second, it's usually a good idea to make sure that the topmost class provides an implementation of the method so that the chain of lookups that occur along the MRO get terminated by an actual method of some sort.

Use of super() is sometimes a source of debate in the Python community. However, all things being equal, you should probably use it in modern code. Raymond Hettinger has written an excellent blog post "Python's super() Considered Super!" (*http://rhetting er.wordpress.com/2011/05/26/super-considered-super*) that has even more examples and reasons why super() might be super-awesome.

8.8. Extending a Property in a Subclass

Problem

Within a subclass, you want to extend the functionality of a property defined in a parent class.

Solution

Consider the following code, which defines a property:

```
class Person:
    def __init__(self, name):
        self.name = name

    # Getter function
    @property
    def name(self):
        return self._name
```

```
    # Setter function
    @name.setter
    def name(self, value):
        if not isinstance(value, str):
            raise TypeError('Expected a string')
        self._name = value

    # Deleter function
    @name.deleter
    def name(self):
        raise AttributeError("Can't delete attribute")
```

Here is an example of a class that inherits from `Person` and extends the `name` property with new functionality:

```
class SubPerson(Person):
    @property
    def name(self):
        print('Getting name')
        return super().name

    @name.setter
    def name(self, value):
        print('Setting name to', value)
        super(SubPerson, SubPerson).name.__set__(self, value)

    @name.deleter
    def name(self):
        print('Deleting name')
        super(SubPerson, SubPerson).name.__delete__(self)
```

Here is an example of the new class in use:

```
>>> s = SubPerson('Guido')
Setting name to Guido
>>> s.name
Getting name
'Guido'
>>> s.name = 'Larry'
Setting name to Larry
>>> s.name = 42
Traceback (most recent call last):
  File "<stdin>", line 1, in <module>
  File "example.py", line 16, in name
      raise TypeError('Expected a string')
TypeError: Expected a string
>>>
```

If you only want to extend one of the methods of a property, use code such as the following:

```
class SubPerson(Person):
    @Person.name.getter
    def name(self):
```

```
        print('Getting name')
        return super().name
```

Or, alternatively, for just the setter, use this code:

```
class SubPerson(Person):
    @Person.name.setter
    def name(self, value):
        print('Setting name to', value)
        super(SubPerson, SubPerson).name.__set__(self, value)
```

Discussion

Extending a property in a subclass introduces a number of very subtle problems related to the fact that a property is defined as a collection of getter, setter, and deleter methods, as opposed to just a single method. Thus, when extending a property, you need to figure out if you will redefine all of the methods together or just one of the methods.

In the first example, all of the property methods are redefined together. Within each method, super() is used to call the previous implementation. The use of super(Sub Person, SubPerson).name.__set__(self, value) in the setter function is no mistake. To delegate to the previous implementation of the setter, control needs to pass through the __set__() method of the previously defined name property. However, the only way to get to this method is to access it as a class variable instead of an instance variable. This is what happens with the super(SubPerson, SubPerson) operation.

If you only want to redefine one of the methods, it's not enough to use @property by itself. For example, code like this doesn't work:

```
class SubPerson(Person):
    @property                   # Doesn't work
    def name(self):
        print('Getting name')
        return super().name
```

If you try the resulting code, you'll find that the setter function disappears entirely:

```
>>> s = SubPerson('Guido')
Traceback (most recent call last):
  File "<stdin>", line 1, in <module>
  File "example.py", line 5, in __init__
    self.name = name
AttributeError: can't set attribute
>>>
```

Instead, you should change the code to that shown in the solution:

```
class SubPerson(Person):
    @Person.getter
    def name(self):
        print('Getting name')
        return super().name
```

When you do this, all of the previously defined methods of the property are copied, and the getter function is replaced. It now works as expected:

```
>>> s = SubPerson('Guido')
>>> s.name
Getting name
'Guido'
>>> s.name = 'Larry'
>>> s.name
Getting name
'Larry'
>>> s.name = 42
Traceback (most recent call last):
  File "<stdin>", line 1, in <module>
  File "example.py", line 16, in name
    raise TypeError('Expected a string')
TypeError: Expected a string
>>>
```

In this particular solution, there is no way to replace the hardcoded class name Person with something more generic. If you don't know which base class defined a property, you should use the solution where all of the property methods are redefined and super() is used to pass control to the previous implementation.

It's worth noting that the first technique shown in this recipe can also be used to extend a descriptor, as described in Recipe 8.9. For example:

```
# A descriptor
class String:
    def __init__(self, name):
        self.name = name

    def __get__(self, instance, cls):
        if instance is None:
            return self
        return instance.__dict__[self.name]

    def __set__(self, instance, value):
        if not isinstance(value, str):
            raise TypeError('Expected a string')
        instance.__dict__[self.name] = value

# A class with a descriptor
class Person:
    name = String('name')
    def __init__(self, name):
        self.name = name

# Extending a descriptor with a property
class SubPerson(Person):
    @property
    def name(self):
```

```
        print('Getting name')
        return super().name

    @name.setter
    def name(self, value):
        print('Setting name to', value)
        super(SubPerson, SubPerson).name.__set__(self, value)

    @name.deleter
    def name(self):
        print('Deleting name')
        super(SubPerson, SubPerson).name.__delete__(self)
```

Finally, it's worth noting that by the time you read this, subclassing of setter and deleter methods might be somewhat simplified. The solution shown will still work, but the bug reported at Python's issues page (*http://bugs.python.org/issue14965*) might resolve into a cleaner approach in a future Python version.

8.9. Creating a New Kind of Class or Instance Attribute

Problem

You want to create a new kind of instance attribute type with some extra functionality, such as type checking.

Solution

If you want to create an entirely new kind of instance attribute, define its functionality in the form of a descriptor class. Here is an example:

```
# Descriptor attribute for an integer type-checked attribute
class Integer:
    def __init__(self, name):
        self.name = name

    def __get__(self, instance, cls):
        if instance is None:
            return self
        else:
            return instance.__dict__[self.name]

    def __set__(self, instance, value):
        if not isinstance(value, int):
            raise TypeError('Expected an int')
        instance.__dict__[self.name] = value

    def __delete__(self, instance):
        del instance.__dict__[self.name]
```

A descriptor is a class that implements the three core attribute access operations (get, set, and delete) in the form of __get__(), __set__(), and __delete__() special methods. These methods work by receiving an instance as input. The underlying dictionary of the instance is then manipulated as appropriate.

To use a descriptor, instances of the descriptor are placed into a class definition as class variables. For example:

```python
class Point:
    x = Integer('x')
    y = Integer('y')
    def __init__(self, x, y):
        self.x = x
        self.y = y
```

When you do this, all access to the descriptor attributes (e.g., x or y) is captured by the __get__(), __set__(), and __delete__() methods. For example:

```python
>>> p = Point(2, 3)
>>> p.x             # Calls Point.x.__get__(p,Point)
2
>>> p.y = 5         # Calls Point.y.__set__(p, 5)
>>> p.x = 2.3       # Calls Point.x.__set__(p, 2.3)
Traceback (most recent call last):
  File "<stdin>", line 1, in <module>
  File "descrip.py", line 12, in __set__
    raise TypeError('Expected an int')
TypeError: Expected an int
>>>
```

As input, each method of a descriptor receives the instance being manipulated. To carry out the requested operation, the underlying instance dictionary (the __dict__ attribute) is manipulated as appropriate. The self.name attribute of the descriptor holds the dictionary key being used to store the actual data in the instance dictionary.

Discussion

Descriptors provide the underlying magic for most of Python's class features, including @classmethod, @staticmethod, @property, and even the __slots__ specification.

By defining a descriptor, you can capture the core instance operations (get, set, delete) at a very low level and completely customize what they do. This gives you great power, and is one of the most important tools employed by the writers of advanced libraries and frameworks.

One confusion with descriptors is that they can only be defined at the class level, not on a per-instance basis. Thus, code like this will not work:

```python
# Does NOT work
class Point:
```

```
def __init__(self, x, y):
    self.x = Integer('x')      # No! Must be a class variable
    self.y = Integer('y')
    self.x = x
    self.y = y
```

Also, the implementation of the __get__() method is trickier than it seems:

```
# Descriptor attribute for an integer type-checked attribute
class Integer:
    ...
    def __get__(self, instance, cls):
        if instance is None:
            return self
        else:
            return instance.__dict__[self.name]
    ...
```

The reason __get__() looks somewhat complicated is to account for the distinction between instance variables and class variables. If a descriptor is accessed as a class variable, the instance argument is set to None. In this case, it is standard practice to simply return the descriptor instance itself (although any kind of custom processing is also allowed). For example:

```
>>> p = Point(2,3)
>>> p.x          # Calls Point.x.__get__(p, Point)
2
>>> Point.x  # Calls Point.x.__get__(None, Point)
<__main__.Integer object at 0x100671890>
>>>
```

Descriptors are often just one component of a larger programming framework involving decorators or metaclasses. As such, their use may be hidden just barely out of sight. As an example, here is some more advanced descriptor-based code involving a class decorator:

```
# Descriptor for a type-checked attribute
class Typed:
    def __init__(self, name, expected_type):
        self.name = name
        self.expected_type = expected_type

    def __get__(self, instance, cls):
        if instance is None:
            return self
        else:
            return instance.__dict__[self.name]

    def __set__(self, instance, value):
        if not isinstance(value, self.expected_type):
            raise TypeError('Expected ' + str(self.expected_type))
        instance.__dict__[self.name] = value
```

```
        def __delete__(self, instance):
            del instance.__dict__[self.name]

    # Class decorator that applies it to selected attributes
    def typeassert(**kwargs):
        def decorate(cls):
            for name, expected_type in kwargs.items():
                # Attach a Typed descriptor to the class
                setattr(cls, name, Typed(name, expected_type))
            return cls
        return decorate

    # Example use
    @typeassert(name=str, shares=int, price=float)
    class Stock:
        def __init__(self, name, shares, price):
            self.name = name
            self.shares = shares
            self.price = price
```

Finally, it should be stressed that you would probably not write a descriptor if you simply want to customize the access of a single attribute of a specific class. For that, it's easier to use a property instead, as described in Recipe 8.6. Descriptors are more useful in situations where there will be a lot of code reuse (i.e., you want to use the functionality provided by the descriptor in hundreds of places in your code or provide it as a library feature).

8.10. Using Lazily Computed Properties

Problem

You'd like to define a read-only attribute as a property that only gets computed on access. However, once accessed, you'd like the value to be cached and not recomputed on each access.

Solution

An efficient way to define a lazy attribute is through the use of a descriptor class, such as the following:

```
    class lazyproperty:
        def __init__(self, func):
            self.func = func

        def __get__(self, instance, cls):
            if instance is None:
                return self
            else:
```

```
        value = self.func(instance)
        setattr(instance, self.func.__name__, value)
        return value
```

To utilize this code, you would use it in a class such as the following:

```
import math

class Circle:
    def __init__(self, radius):
        self.radius = radius

    @lazyproperty
    def area(self):
        print('Computing area')
        return math.pi * self.radius ** 2

    @lazyproperty
    def perimeter(self):
        print('Computing perimeter')
        return 2 * math.pi * self.radius
```

Here is an interactive session that illustrates how it works:

```
>>> c = Circle(4.0)
>>> c.radius
4.0
>>> c.area
Computing area
50.26548245743669
>>> c.area
50.26548245743669
>>> c.perimeter
Computing perimeter
25.132741228718345
>>> c.perimeter
25.132741228718345
>>>
```

Carefully observe that the messages "Computing area" and "Computing perimeter" only appear once.

Discussion

In many cases, the whole point of having a lazily computed attribute is to improve performance. For example, you avoid computing values unless you actually need them somewhere. The solution shown does just this, but it exploits a subtle feature of descriptors to do it in a highly efficient way.

As shown in other recipes (e.g., Recipe 8.9), when a descriptor is placed into a class definition, its __get__(), __set__(), and __delete__() methods get triggered on attribute access. However, if a descriptor only defines a __get__() method, it has a much weaker binding than usual. In particular, the __get__() method only fires if the attribute being accessed is not in the underlying instance dictionary.

The lazyproperty class exploits this by having the __get__() method store the computed value on the instance using the same name as the property itself. By doing this, the value gets stored in the instance dictionary and disables further computation of the property. You can observe this by digging a little deeper into the example:

```
>>> c = Circle(4.0)
>>> # Get instance variables
>>> vars(c)
{'radius': 4.0}

>>> # Compute area and observe variables afterward
>>> c.area
Computing area
50.26548245743669
>>> vars(c)
{'area': 50.26548245743669, 'radius': 4.0}

>>> # Notice access doesn't invoke property anymore
>>> c.area
50.26548245743669

>>> # Delete the variable and see property trigger again
>>> del c.area
>>> vars(c)
{'radius': 4.0}
>>> c.area
Computing area
50.26548245743669
>>>
```

One possible downside to this recipe is that the computed value becomes mutable after it's created. For example:

```
>>> c.area
Computing area
50.26548245743669
>>> c.area = 25
>>> c.area
25
>>>
```

If that's a concern, you can use a slightly less efficient implementation, like this:

```
def lazyproperty(func):
    name = '_lazy_' + func.__name__
    @property
    def lazy(self):
        if hasattr(self, name):
            return getattr(self, name)
        else:
```

```
            value = func(self)
            setattr(self, name, value)
            return value
        return lazy
```

If you use this version, you'll find that set operations are not allowed. For example:

```
>>> c = Circle(4.0)
>>> c.area
Computing area
50.26548245743669
>>> c.area
50.26548245743669
>>> c.area = 25
Traceback (most recent call last):
  File "<stdin>", line 1, in <module>
AttributeError: can't set attribute
>>>
```

However, a disadvantage is that all get operations have to be routed through the property's getter function. This is less efficient than simply looking up the value in the instance dictionary, as was done in the original solution.

For more information on properties and managed attributes, see Recipe 8.6. Descriptors are described in Recipe 8.9.

8.11. Simplifying the Initialization of Data Structures

Problem

You are writing a lot of classes that serve as data structures, but you are getting tired of writing highly repetitive and boilerplate __init__() functions.

Solution

You can often generalize the initialization of data structures into a single __init__() function defined in a common base class. For example:

```
class Structure:
    # Class variable that specifies expected fields
    _fields= []
    def __init__(self, *args):
        if len(args) != len(self._fields):
            raise TypeError('Expected {} arguments'.format(len(self._fields)))

        # Set the arguments
        for name, value in zip(self._fields, args):
            setattr(self, name, value)
```

```
# Example class definitions
if __name__ == '__main__':
    class Stock(Structure):
        _fields = ['name', 'shares', 'price']

    class Point(Structure):
        _fields = ['x','y']

    class Circle(Structure):
        _fields = ['radius']
        def area(self):
            return math.pi * self.radius ** 2
```

If you use the resulting classes, you'll find that they are easy to construct. For example:

```
>>> s = Stock('ACME', 50, 91.1)
>>> p = Point(2, 3)
>>> c = Circle(4.5)
>>> s2 = Stock('ACME', 50)
Traceback (most recent call last):
  File "<stdin>", line 1, in <module>
  File "structure.py", line 6, in __init__
    raise TypeError('Expected {} arguments'.format(len(self._fields)))
TypeError: Expected 3 arguments
```

Should you decide to support keyword arguments, there are several design options. One choice is to map the keyword arguments so that they only correspond to the attribute names specified in _fields. For example:

```
class Structure:
    _fields= []
    def __init__(self, *args, **kwargs):
        if len(args) > len(self._fields):
            raise TypeError('Expected {} arguments'.format(len(self._fields)))

        # Set all of the positional arguments
        for name, value in zip(self._fields, args):
            setattr(self, name, value)

        # Set the remaining keyword arguments
        for name in self._fields[len(args):]:
            setattr(self, name, kwargs.pop(name))

        # Check for any remaining unknown arguments
        if kwargs:
            raise TypeError('Invalid argument(s): {}'.format(','.join(kwargs)))

# Example use
if __name__ == '__main__':
    class Stock(Structure):
        _fields = ['name', 'shares', 'price']

    s1 = Stock('ACME', 50, 91.1)
```

```
s2 = Stock('ACME', 50, price=91.1)
s3 = Stock('ACME', shares=50, price=91.1)
```

Another possible choice is to use keyword arguments as a means for adding additional attributes to the structure not specified in _fields. For example:

```
class Structure:
    # Class variable that specifies expected fields
    _fields= []
    def __init__(self, *args, **kwargs):
        if len(args) != len(self._fields):
            raise TypeError('Expected {} arguments'.format(len(self._fields)))

        # Set the arguments
        for name, value in zip(self._fields, args):
            setattr(self, name, value)

        # Set the additional arguments (if any)
        extra_args = kwargs.keys() - self._fields
        for name in extra_args:
            setattr(self, name, kwargs.pop(name))
        if kwargs:
            raise TypeError('Duplicate values for {}'.format(','.join(kwargs)))

# Example use
if __name__ == '__main__':
    class Stock(Structure):
        _fields = ['name', 'shares', 'price']

    s1 = Stock('ACME', 50, 91.1)
    s2 = Stock('ACME', 50, 91.1, date='8/2/2012')
```

Discussion

This technique of defining a general purpose __init__() method can be extremely useful if you're ever writing a program built around a large number of small data structures. It leads to much less code than manually writing __init__() methods like this:

```
class Stock:
    def __init__(self, name, shares, price):
        self.name = name
        self.shares = shares
        self.price = price

class Point:
    def __init__(self, x, y):
        self.x = x
        self.y = y

class Circle:
    def __init__(self, radius):
        self.radius = radius
```

```
def area(self):
    return math.pi * self.radius ** 2
```

One subtle aspect of the implementation concerns the mechanism used to set value using the `setattr()` function. Instead of doing that, you might be inclined to directly access the instance dictionary. For example:

```
class Structure:
    # Class variable that specifies expected fields
    _fields= []
    def __init__(self, *args):
        if len(args) != len(self._fields):
            raise TypeError('Expected {} arguments'.format(len(self._fields)))

        # Set the arguments (alternate)
        self.__dict__.update(zip(self._fields,args))
```

Although this works, it's often not safe to make assumptions about the implementation of a subclass. If a subclass decided to use __slots__ or wrap a specific attribute with a property (or descriptor), directly acccessing the instance dictionary would break. The solution has been written to be as general purpose as possible and not to make any assumptions about subclasses.

A potential downside of this technique is that it impacts documentation and help features of IDEs. If a user asks for help on a specific class, the required arguments aren't described in the usual way. For example:

```
>>> help(Stock)
Help on class Stock in module __main__:

class Stock(Structure)
 ...
 |  Methods inherited from Structure:
 |
 |  __init__(self, *args, **kwargs)
 |
 ...
>>>
```

Many of these problems can be fixed by either attaching or enforcing a type signature in the __init__() function. See Recipe 9.16.

It should be noted that it is also possible to automatically initialize instance variables using a utility function and a so-called "frame hack." For example:

```
def init_fromlocals(self):
    import sys
    locs = sys._getframe(1).f_locals
    for k, v in locs.items():
        if k != 'self':
            setattr(self, k, v)
```

```
class Stock:
    def __init__(self, name, shares, price):
        init_fromlocals(self)
```

In this variation, the init_fromlocals() function uses sys._getframe() to peek at the local variables of the calling method. If used as the first step of an __init__() method, the local variables will be the same as the passed arguments and can be easily used to set attributes with the same names. Although this approach avoids the problem of getting the right calling signature in IDEs, it runs more than 50% slower than the solution provided in the recipe, requires more typing, and involves more sophisticated magic behind the scenes. If your code doesn't need this extra power, often times the simpler solution will work just fine.

8.12. Defining an Interface or Abstract Base Class

Problem

You want to define a class that serves as an interface or abstract base class from which you can perform type checking and ensure that certain methods are implemented in subclasses.

Solution

To define an abstract base class, use the abc module. For example:

```
from abc import ABCMeta, abstractmethod

class IStream(metaclass=ABCMeta):
    @abstractmethod
    def read(self, maxbytes=-1):
        pass
    @abstractmethod
    def write(self, data):
        pass
```

A central feature of an abstract base class is that it cannot be instantiated directly. For example, if you try to do it, you'll get an error:

```
a = IStream()    # TypeError: Can't instantiate abstract class
                 # IStream with abstract methods read, write
```

Instead, an abstract base class is meant to be used as a base class for other classes that are expected to implement the required methods. For example:

```
class SocketStream(IStream):
    def read(self, maxbytes=-1):
        ...
    def write(self, data):
        ...
```

A major use of abstract base classes is in code that wants to enforce an expected programming interface. For example, one way to view the IStream base class is as a high-
level specification for an interface that allows reading and writing of data. Code that
explicitly checks for this interface could be written as follows:

```
def serialize(obj, stream):
    if not isinstance(stream, IStream):
        raise TypeError('Expected an IStream')
    ...
```

You might think that this kind of type checking only works by subclassing the abstract
base class (ABC), but ABCs allow other classes to be registered as implementing the
required interface. For example, you can do this:

```
import io

# Register the built-in I/O classes as supporting our interface
IStream.register(io.IOBase)

# Open a normal file and type check
f = open('foo.txt')
isinstance(f, IStream)        # Returns True
```

It should be noted that @abstractmethod can also be applied to static methods, class
methods, and properties. You just need to make sure you apply it in the proper sequence
where @abstractmethod appears immediately before the function definition, as shown
here:

```
from abc import ABCMeta, abstractmethod

class A(metaclass=ABCMeta):
    @property
    @abstractmethod
    def name(self):
        pass

    @name.setter
    @abstractmethod
    def name(self, value):
        pass

    @classmethod
    @abstractmethod
    def method1(cls):
        pass

    @staticmethod
    @abstractmethod
    def method2():
        pass
```

Discussion

Predefined abstract base classes are found in various places in the standard library. The `collections` module defines a variety of ABCs related to containers and iterators (sequences, mappings, sets, etc.), the `numbers` library defines ABCs related to numeric objects (integers, floats, rationals, etc.), and the `io` library defines ABCs related to I/O handling.

You can use the predefined ABCs to perform more generalized kinds of type checking. Here are some examples:

```
import collections

# Check if x is a sequence
if isinstance(x, collections.Sequence):
    ...

# Check if x is iterable
if isinstance(x, collections.Iterable):
    ...

# Check if x has a size
if isinstance(x, collections.Sized):
    ...

# Check if x is a mapping
if isinstance(x, collections.Mapping):
    ...
```

It should be noted that, as of this writing, certain library modules don't make use of these predefined ABCs as you might expect. For example:

```
from decimal import Decimal
import numbers

x = Decimal('3.4')
isinstance(x, numbers.Real)    # Returns False
```

Even though the value 3.4 is technically a real number, it doesn't type check that way to help avoid inadvertent mixing of floating-point numbers and decimals. Thus, if you use the ABC functionality, it is wise to carefully write tests that verify that the behavior is as you intended.

Although ABCs facilitate type checking, it's not something that you should overuse in a program. At its heart, Python is a dynamic language that gives you great flexibility. Trying to enforce type constraints everywhere tends to result in code that is more complicated than it needs to be. You should embrace Python's flexibility.

8.13. Implementing a Data Model or Type System

Problem

You want to define various kinds of data structures, but want to enforce constraints on the values that are allowed to be assigned to certain attributes.

Solution

In this problem, you are basically faced with the task of placing checks or assertions on the setting of certain instance attributes. To do this, you need to customize the setting of attributes on a per-attribute basis. To do this, you should use descriptors.

The following code illustrates the use of descriptors to implement a system type and value checking framework:

```python
# Base class. Uses a descriptor to set a value
class Descriptor:
    def __init__(self, name=None, **opts):
        self.name = name
        for key, value in opts.items():
            setattr(self, key, value)

    def __set__(self, instance, value):
        instance.__dict__[self.name] = value

# Descriptor for enforcing types
class Typed(Descriptor):
    expected_type = type(None)

    def __set__(self, instance, value):
        if not isinstance(value, self.expected_type):
            raise TypeError('expected ' + str(self.expected_type))
        super().__set__(instance, value)

# Descriptor for enforcing values
class Unsigned(Descriptor):
    def __set__(self, instance, value):
        if value < 0:
            raise ValueError('Expected >= 0')
        super().__set__(instance, value)

class MaxSized(Descriptor):
    def __init__(self, name=None, **opts):
        if 'size' not in opts:
            raise TypeError('missing size option')
        super().__init__(name, **opts)

    def __set__(self, instance, value):
        if len(value) >= self.size:
```

```
        raise ValueError('size must be < ' + str(self.size))
    super().__set__(instance, value)
```

These classes should be viewed as basic building blocks from which you construct a data model or type system. Continuing, here is some code that implements some different kinds of data:

```
class Integer(Typed):
    expected_type = int

class UnsignedInteger(Integer, Unsigned):
    pass

class Float(Typed):
    expected_type = float

class UnsignedFloat(Float, Unsigned):
    pass

class String(Typed):
    expected_type = str

class SizedString(String, MaxSized):
    pass
```

Using these type objects, it is now possible to define a class such as this:

```
class Stock:
    # Specify constraints
    name = SizedString('name',size=8)
    shares = UnsignedInteger('shares')
    price = UnsignedFloat('price')
    def __init__(self, name, shares, price):
        self.name = name
        self.shares = shares
        self.price = price
```

With the constraints in place, you'll find that assigning of attributes is now validated. For example:

```
>>> s = Stock('ACME', 50, 91.1)
>>> s.name
'ACME'
>>> s.shares = 75
>>> s.shares = -10
Traceback (most recent call last):
  File "<stdin>", line 1, in <module>
  File "example.py", line 17, in __set__
    super().__set__(instance, value)
  File "example.py", line 23, in __set__
    raise ValueError('Expected >= 0')
ValueError: Expected >= 0
>>> s.price = 'a lot'
```

```
Traceback (most recent call last):
  File "<stdin>", line 1, in <module>
  File "example.py", line 16, in __set__
    raise TypeError('expected ' + str(self.expected_type))
TypeError: expected <class 'float'>
>>> s.name = 'ABRACADABRA'
Traceback (most recent call last):
  File "<stdin>", line 1, in <module>
  File "example.py", line 17, in __set__
    super().__set__(instance, value)
  File "example.py", line 35, in __set__
    raise ValueError('size must be < ' + str(self.size))
ValueError: size must be < 8
>>>
```

There are some techniques that can be used to simplify the specification of constraints in classes. One approach is to use a class decorator, like this:

```
# Class decorator to apply constraints
def check_attributes(**kwargs):
    def decorate(cls):
        for key, value in kwargs.items():
            if isinstance(value, Descriptor):
                value.name = key
                setattr(cls, key, value)
            else:
                setattr(cls, key, value(key))
        return cls
    return decorate


# Example
@check_attributes(name=SizedString(size=8),
                  shares=UnsignedInteger,
                  price=UnsignedFloat)
class Stock:
    def __init__(self, name, shares, price):
        self.name = name
        self.shares = shares
        self.price = price
```

Another approach to simplify the specification of constraints is to use a metaclass. For example:

```
# A metaclass that applies checking
class checkedmeta(type):
    def __new__(cls, clsname, bases, methods):
        # Attach attribute names to the descriptors
        for key, value in methods.items():
            if isinstance(value, Descriptor):
                value.name = key
        return type.__new__(cls, clsname, bases, methods)
```

```
# Example
class Stock(metaclass=checkedmeta):
    name   = SizedString(size=8)
    shares = UnsignedInteger()
    price  = UnsignedFloat()
    def __init__(self, name, shares, price):
        self.name = name
        self.shares = shares
        self.price = price
```

Discussion

This recipe involves a number of advanced techniques, including descriptors, mixin classes, the use of super(), class decorators, and metaclasses. Covering the basics of all those topics is beyond what can be covered here, but examples can be found in other recipes (see Recipes 8.9, 8.18, 9.12, and 9.19). However, there are a number of subtle points worth noting.

First, in the Descriptor base class, you will notice that there is a __set__() method, but no corresponding __get__(). If a descriptor will do nothing more than extract an identically named value from the underlying instance dictionary, defining __get__() is unnecessary. In fact, defining __get__() will just make it run slower. Thus, this recipe only focuses on the implementation of __set__().

The overall design of the various descriptor classes is based on mixin classes. For example, the Unsigned and MaxSized classes are meant to be mixed with the other descriptor classes derived from Typed. To handle a specific kind of data type, multiple inheritance is used to combine the desired functionality.

You will also notice that all __init__() methods of the various descriptors have been programmed to have an identical signature involving keyword arguments **opts. The class for MaxSized looks for its required attribute in opts, but simply passes it along to the Descriptor base class, which actually sets it. One tricky part about composing classes like this (especially mixins), is that you don't always know how the classes are going to be chained together or what super() will invoke. For this reason, you need to make it work with any possible combination of classes.

The definitions of the various type classes such as Integer, Float, and String illustrate a useful technique of using class variables to customize an implementation. The Typed descriptor merely looks for an expected_type attribute that is provided by each of those subclasses.

The use of a class decorator or metaclass is often useful for simplifying the specification by the user. You will notice that in those examples, the user no longer has to type the name of the attribute more than once. For example:

```
# Normal
class Point:
    x = Integer('x')
    y = Integer('y')

# Metaclass
class Point(metaclass=checkedmeta):
    x = Integer()
    y = Integer()
```

The code for the class decorator and metaclass simply scan the class dictionary looking for descriptors. When found, they simply fill in the descriptor name based on the key value.

Of all the approaches, the class decorator solution may provide the most flexibility and sanity. For one, it does not rely on any advanced machinery, such as metaclasses. Second, decoration is something that can easily be added or removed from a class definition as desired. For example, within the decorator, there could be an option to simply omit the added checking altogether. These might allow the checking to be something that could be turned on or off depending on demand (maybe for debugging versus production).

As a final twist, a class decorator approach can also be used as a replacement for mixin classes, multiple inheritance, and tricky use of the super() function. Here is an alternative formulation of this recipe that uses class decorators:

```
# Base class. Uses a descriptor to set a value
class Descriptor:
    def __init__(self, name=None, **opts):
        self.name = name
        for key, value in opts.items():
            setattr(self, key, value)

    def __set__(self, instance, value):
        instance.__dict__[self.name] = value

# Decorator for applying type checking
def Typed(expected_type, cls=None):
    if cls is None:
        return lambda cls: Typed(expected_type, cls)

    super_set = cls.__set__
    def __set__(self, instance, value):
        if not isinstance(value, expected_type):
            raise TypeError('expected ' + str(expected_type))
        super_set(self, instance, value)
    cls.__set__ = __set__
    return cls

# Decorator for unsigned values
def Unsigned(cls):
    super_set = cls.__set__
```

```python
    def __set__(self, instance, value):
        if value < 0:
            raise ValueError('Expected >= 0')
        super_set(self, instance, value)
    cls.__set__ = __set__
    return cls

# Decorator for allowing sized values
def MaxSized(cls):
    super_init = cls.__init__
    def __init__(self, name=None, **opts):
        if 'size' not in opts:
            raise TypeError('missing size option')
        super_init(self, name, **opts)
    cls.__init__ = __init__

    super_set = cls.__set__
    def __set__(self, instance, value):
        if len(value) >= self.size:
            raise ValueError('size must be < ' + str(self.size))
        super_set(self, instance, value)
    cls.__set__ = __set__
    return cls

# Specialized descriptors
@Typed(int)
class Integer(Descriptor):
    pass

@Unsigned
class UnsignedInteger(Integer):
    pass

@Typed(float)
class Float(Descriptor):
    pass

@Unsigned
class UnsignedFloat(Float):
    pass

@Typed(str)
class String(Descriptor):
    pass

@MaxSized
class SizedString(String):
    pass
```

The classes defined in this alternative formulation work in exactly the same manner as before (none of the earlier example code changes) except that everything runs much faster. For example, a simple timing test of setting a typed attribute reveals that the class decorator approach runs almost 100% faster than the approach using mixins. Now aren't you glad you read all the way to the end?

8.14. Implementing Custom Containers

Problem

You want to implement a custom class that mimics the behavior of a common built-in container type, such as a list or dictionary. However, you're not entirely sure what methods need to be implemented to do it.

Solution

The `collections` library defines a variety of abstract base classes that are extremely useful when implementing custom container classes. To illustrate, suppose you want your class to support iteration. To do that, simply start by having it inherit from `col lections.Iterable`, as follows:

```
import collections

class A(collections.Iterable):
    pass
```

The special feature about inheriting from `collections.Iterable` is that it ensures you implement all of the required special methods. If you don't, you'll get an error upon instantiation:

```
>>> a = A()
Traceback (most recent call last):
  File "<stdin>", line 1, in <module>
TypeError: Can't instantiate abstract class A with abstract methods __iter__
>>>
```

To fix this error, simply give the class the required `__iter__()` method and implement it as desired (see Recipes 4.2 and 4.7).

Other notable classes defined in `collections` include Sequence, MutableSequence, Mapping, MutableMapping, Set, and MutableSet. Many of these classes form hierarchies with increasing levels of functionality (e.g., one such hierarchy is Container, Itera ble, Sized, Sequence, and MutableSequence). Again, simply instantiate any of these classes to see what methods need to be implemented to make a custom container with that behavior:

```
>>> import collections
>>> collections.Sequence()
Traceback (most recent call last):
  File "<stdin>", line 1, in <module>
TypeError: Can't instantiate abstract class Sequence with abstract methods \
```

```
__getitem__, __len__
>>>
```

Here is a simple example of a class that implements the preceding methods to create a
sequence where items are always stored in sorted order (it's not a particularly efficient
implementation, but it illustrates the general idea):

```
import collections
import bisect

class SortedItems(collections.Sequence):
    def __init__(self, initial=None):
        self._items = sorted(initial) if initial is None else []

    # Required sequence methods
    def __getitem__(self, index):
        return self._items[index]

    def __len__(self):
        return len(self._items)

    # Method for adding an item in the right location
    def add(self, item):
        bisect.insort(self._items, item)
```

Here's an example of using this class:

```
>>> items = SortedItems([5, 1, 3])
>>> list(items)
[1, 3, 5]
>>> items[0]
1
>>> items[-1]
5
>>> items.add(2)
>>> list(items)
[1, 2, 3, 5]
>>> items.add(-10)
>>> list(items)
[-10, 1, 2, 3, 5]
>>> items[1:4]
[1, 2, 3]
>>> 3 in items
True
>>> len(items)
5
>>> for n in items:
...     print(n)
...
-10
1
2
3
```

```
5
>>>
```

As you can see, instances of SortedItems behave exactly like a normal sequence and support all of the usual operations, including indexing, iteration, len(), containment (the in operator), and even slicing.

As an aside, the bisect module used in this recipe is a convenient way to keep items in a list sorted. The bisect.insert() inserts an item into a list so that the list remains in order.

Discussion

Inheriting from one of the abstract base classes in collections ensures that your custom container implements all of the required methods expected of the container. However, this inheritance also facilitates type checking.

For example, your custom container will satisfy various type checks like this:

```
>>> items = SortedItems()
>>> import collections
>>> isinstance(items, collections.Iterable)
True
>>> isinstance(items, collections.Sequence)
True
>>> isinstance(items, collections.Container)
True
>>> isinstance(items, collections.Sized)
True
>>> isinstance(items, collections.Mapping)
False
>>>
```

Many of the abstract base classes in collections also provide default implementations of common container methods. To illustrate, suppose you have a class that inherits from collections.MutableSequence, like this:

```
class Items(collections.MutableSequence):
    def __init__(self, initial=None):
        self._items = list(initial) if initial is None else []

    # Required sequence methods
    def __getitem__(self, index):
        print('Getting:', index)
        return self._items[index]

    def __setitem__(self, index, value):
        print('Setting:', index, value)
        self._items[index] = value

    def __delitem__(self, index):
```

```
        print('Deleting:', index)
        del self._items[index]

    def insert(self, index, value):
        print('Inserting:', index, value)
        self._items.insert(index, value)

    def __len__(self):
        print('Len')
        return len(self._items)
```

If you create an instance of Items, you'll find that it supports almost all of the core list methods (e.g., append(), remove(), count(), etc.). These methods are implemented in such a way that they only use the required ones. Here's an interactive session that illustrates this:

```
>>> a = Items([1, 2, 3])
>>> len(a)
Len
3
>>> a.append(4)
Len
Inserting: 3 4
>>> a.append(2)
Len
Inserting: 4 2
>>> a.count(2)
Getting: 0
Getting: 1
Getting: 2
Getting: 3
Getting: 4
Getting: 5
2
>>> a.remove(3)
Getting: 0
Getting: 1
Getting: 2
Deleting: 2
>>>
```

This recipe only provides a brief glimpse into Python's abstract class functionality. The numbers module provides a similar collection of abstract classes related to numeric data types. See Recipe 8.12 for more information about making your own abstract base classes.

8.15. Delegating Attribute Access

Problem

You want an instance to delegate attribute access to an internally held instance possibly as an alternative to inheritance or in order to implement a proxy.

Solution

Simply stated, delegation is a programming pattern where the responsibility for implementing a particular operation is handed off (i.e., delegated) to a different object. In its simplest form, it often looks something like this:

```
class A:
    def spam(self, x):
        pass

    def foo(self):
        pass

class B:
    def __init__(self):
        self._a = A()

    def spam(self, x):
        # Delegate to the internal self._a instance
        return self._a.spam(x)

    def foo(self):
        # Delegate to the internal self._a instance
        return self._a.foo()

    def bar(self):
        pass
```

If there are only a couple of methods to delegate, writing code such as that just given is easy enough. However, if there are many methods to delegate, an alternative approach is to define the __getattr__() method, like this:

```
class A:
    def spam(self, x):
        pass

    def foo(self):
        pass

class B:
    def __init__(self):
        self._a = A()
```

```
        def bar(self):
            pass

        # Expose all of the methods defined on class A
        def __getattr__(self, name):
            return getattr(self._a, name)
```

The __getattr__() method is kind of like a catch-all for attribute lookup. It's a method that gets called if code tries to access an attribute that doesn't exist. In the preceding code, it would catch access to undefined methods on B and simply delegate them to A. For example:

```
b = B()
b.bar()    # Calls B.bar() (exists on B)
b.spam(42) # Calls B.__getattr__('spam') and delegates to A.spam
```

Another example of delegation is in the implementation of proxies. For example:

```
# A proxy class that wraps around another object, but
# exposes its public attributes

class Proxy:
    def __init__(self, obj):
        self._obj = obj

    # Delegate attribute lookup to internal obj
    def __getattr__(self, name):
        print('getattr:', name)
        return getattr(self._obj, name)

    # Delegate attribute assignment
    def __setattr__(self, name, value):
        if name.startswith('_'):
            super().__setattr__(name, value)
        else:
            print('setattr:', name, value)
            setattr(self._obj, name, value)

    # Delegate attribute deletion
    def __delattr__(self, name):
        if name.startswith('_'):
            super().__delattr__(name)
        else:
            print('delattr:', name)
            delattr(self._obj, name)
```

To use this proxy class, you simply wrap it around another instance. For example:

```
class Spam:
    def __init__(self, x):
        self.x = x
    def bar(self, y):
        print('Spam.bar:', self.x, y)
```

```
# Create an instance
s = Spam(2)

# Create a proxy around it
p = Proxy(s)

# Access the proxy
print(p.x)      # Outputs 2
p.bar(3)        # Outputs "Spam.bar: 2 3"
p.x = 37        # Changes s.x to 37
```

By customizing the implementation of the attribute access methods, you could customize the proxy to behave in different ways (e.g., logging access, only allowing read-only access, etc.).

Discussion

Delegation is sometimes used as an alternative to inheritance. For example, instead of writing code like this:

```
class A:
    def spam(self, x):
        print('A.spam', x)

    def foo(self):
        print('A.foo')

class B(A):
    def spam(self, x):
        print('B.spam')
        super().spam(x)

    def bar(self):
        print('B.bar')
```

A solution involving delegation would be written as follows:

```
class A:
    def spam(self, x):
        print('A.spam', x)

    def foo(self):
        print('A.foo')

class B:
    def __init__(self):
        self._a = A()

    def spam(self, x):
        print('B.spam', x)
        self._a.spam(x)
```

```
def bar(self):
    print('B.bar')

def __getattr__(self, name):
    return getattr(self._a, name)
```

This use of delegation is often useful in situations where direct inheritance might not make much sense or where you want to have more control of the relationship between objects (e.g., only exposing certain methods, implementing interfaces, etc.).

When using delegation to implement proxies, there are a few additional details to note. First, the __getattr__() method is actually a fallback method that only gets called when an attribute is not found. Thus, when attributes of the proxy instance itself are accessed (e.g., the _obj attribute), this method would not be triggered. Second, the __se tattr__() and __delattr__() methods need a bit of extra logic added to separate attributes from the proxy instance inself and attributes on the internal object _obj. A common convention is for proxies to only delegate to attributes that don't start with a leading underscore (i.e., proxies only expose the "public" attributes of the held instance).

It is also important to emphasize that the __getattr__() method usually does not apply to most special methods that start and end with double underscores. For example, consider this class:

```
class ListLike:
    def __init__(self):
        self._items = []
    def __getattr__(self, name):
        return getattr(self._items, name)
```

If you try to make a ListLike object, you'll find that it supports the common list methods, such as append() and insert(). However, it does not support any of the operators like len(), item lookup, and so forth. For example:

```
>>> a = ListLike()
>>> a.append(2)
>>> a.insert(0, 1)
>>> a.sort()
>>> len(a)
Traceback (most recent call last):
  File "<stdin>", line 1, in <module>
TypeError: object of type 'ListLike' has no len()
>>> a[0]
Traceback (most recent call last):
  File "<stdin>", line 1, in <module>
TypeError: 'ListLike' object does not support indexing
>>>
```

To support the different operators, you have to manually delegate the associated special methods yourself. For example:

```
class ListLike:
    def __init__(self):
        self._items = []
    def __getattr__(self, name):
        return getattr(self._items, name)

    # Added special methods to support certain list operations
    def __len__(self):
        return len(self._items)
    def __getitem__(self, index):
        return self._items[index]
    def __setitem__(self, index, value):
        self._items[index] = value
    def __delitem__(self, index):
        del self._items[index]
```

See Recipe 11.8 for another example of using delegation in the context of creating proxy classes for remote procedure call.

8.16. Defining More Than One Constructor in a Class

Problem

You're writing a class, but you want users to be able to create instances in more than the one way provided by __init__().

Solution

To define a class with more than one constructor, you should use a class method. Here is a simple example:

```
import time

class Date:
    # Primary constructor
    def __init__(self, year, month, day):
        self.year = year
        self.month = month
        self.day = day

    # Alternate constructor
    @classmethod
    def today(cls):
        t = time.localtime()
        return cls(t.tm_year, t.tm_mon, t.tm_mday)
```

To use the alternate constructor, you simply call it as a function, such as Date.to day(). Here is an example:

```
a = Date(2012, 12, 21)      # Primary
b = Date.today()            # Alternate
```

Discussion

One of the primary uses of class methods is to define alternate constructors, as shown in this recipe. A critical feature of a class method is that it receives the class as the first argument (cls). You will notice that this class is used within the method to create and return the final instance. It is extremely subtle, but this aspect of class methods makes them work correctly with features such as inheritance. For example:

```
class NewDate(Date):
    pass

c = Date.today()        # Creates an instance of Date (cls=Date)
d = NewDate.today()     # Creates an instance of NewDate (cls=NewDate)
```

When defining a class with multiple constructors, you should make the __init__() function as simple as possible—doing nothing more than assigning attributes from given values. Alternate constructors can then choose to perform advanced operations if needed.

Instead of defining a separate class method, you might be inclined to implement the __init__() method in a way that allows for different calling conventions. For example:

```
class Date:
    def __init__(self, *args):
        if len(args) == 0:
            t = time.localtime()
            args = (t.tm_year, t.tm_mon, t.tm_mday)
        self.year, self.month, self.day = args
```

Although this technique works in certain cases, it often leads to code that is hard to understand and difficult to maintain. For example, this implementation won't show useful help strings (with argument names). In addition, code that creates Date instances will be less clear. Compare and contrast the following:

```
a = Date(2012, 12, 21)    # Clear. A specific date.
b = Date()                # ??? What does this do?

# Class method version
c = Date.today()          # Clear. Today's date.
```

As shown, the Date.today() invokes the regular Date.__init__() method by instantiating a Date() with suitable year, month, and day arguments. If necessary, instances can be created without ever invoking the __init__() method. This is described in the next recipe.

8.17. Creating an Instance Without Invoking *init*

Problem

You need to create an instance, but want to bypass the execution of the __init__()
method for some reason.

Solution

A bare uninitialized instance can be created by directly calling the __new__() method
of a class. For example, consider this class:

```python
class Date:
    def __init__(self, year, month, day):
        self.year = year
        self.month = month
        self.day = day
```

Here's how you can create a Date instance without invoking __init__():

```python
>>> d = Date.__new__(Date)
>>> d
<__main__.Date object at 0x1006716d0>
>>> d.year
Traceback (most recent call last):
  File "<stdin>", line 1, in <module>
AttributeError: 'Date' object has no attribute 'year'
>>>
```

As you can see, the resulting instance is uninitialized. Thus, it is now your responsibility
to set the appropriate instance variables. For example:

```python
>>> data = {'year':2012, 'month':8, 'day':29}
>>> for key, value in data.items():
...     setattr(d, key, value)
...
>>> d.year
2012
>>> d.month
8
>>>
```

Discussion

The problem of bypassing __init__() sometimes arises when instances are being created in a nonstandard way such as when deserializing data or in the implementation of a class method that's been defined as an alternate constructor. For example, on the Date class shown, someone might define an alternate constructor today() as follows:

```
from time import localtime

class Date:
    def __init__(self, year, month, day):
        self.year = year
        self.month = month
        self.day = day

    @classmethod
    def today(cls):
        d = cls.__new__(cls)
        t = localtime()
        d.year = t.tm_year
        d.month = t.tm_mon
        d.day = t.tm_mday
        return d
```

Similarly, suppose you are deserializing JSON data and, as a result, produce a dictionary like this:

```
data = { 'year': 2012, 'month': 8, 'day': 29 }
```

If you want to turn this into a `Date` instance, simply use the technique shown in the solution.

When creating instances in a nonstandard way, it's usually best to not make too many assumptions about their implementation. As such, you generally don't want to write code that directly manipulates the underlying instance dictionary `__dict__` unless you know it's guaranteed to be defined. Otherwise, the code will break if the class uses `__slots__`, properties, descriptors, or other advanced techniques. By using `se tattr()` to set the values, your code will be as general purpose as possible.

8.18. Extending Classes with Mixins

Problem

You have a collection of generally useful methods that you would like to make available for extending the functionality of other class definitions. However, the classes where the methods might be added aren't necessarily related to one another via inheritance. Thus, you can't just attach the methods to a common base class.

Solution

The problem addressed by this recipe often arises in code where one is interested in the issue of class customization. For example, maybe a library provides a basic set of classes along with a set of optional customizations that can be applied if desired by the user.

To illustrate, suppose you have an interest in adding various customizations (e.g., logging, set-once, type checking, etc.) to mapping objects. Here are a set of mixin classes that do that:

```python
class LoggedMappingMixin:
    '''
    Add logging to get/set/delete operations for debugging.
    '''
    __slots__ = ()

    def __getitem__(self, key):
        print('Getting ' + str(key))
        return super().__getitem__(key)

    def __setitem__(self, key, value):
        print('Setting {} = {!r}'.format(key, value))
        return super().__setitem__(key, value)

    def __delitem__(self, key):
        print('Deleting ' + str(key))
        return super().__delitem__(key)

class SetOnceMappingMixin:
    '''
    Only allow a key to be set once.
    '''
    __slots__ = ()
    def __setitem__(self, key, value):
        if key in self:
            raise KeyError(str(key) + ' already set')
        return super().__setitem__(key, value)

class StringKeysMappingMixin:
    '''
    Restrict keys to strings only
    '''
    __slots__ = ()
    def __setitem__(self, key, value):
        if not isinstance(key, str):
            raise TypeError('keys must be strings')
        return super().__setitem__(key, value)
```

These classes, by themselves, are useless. In fact, if you instantiate any one of them, it does nothing useful at all (other than generate exceptions). Instead, they are supposed to be mixed with other mapping classes through multiple inheritance. For example:

```python
>>> class LoggedDict(LoggedMappingMixin, dict):
...     pass
...
>>> d = LoggedDict()
>>> d['x'] = 23
Setting x = 23
```

```
>>> d['x']
Getting x
23
>>> del d['x']
Deleting x

>>> from collections import defaultdict
>>> class SetOnceDefaultDict(SetOnceMappingMixin, defaultdict):
...     pass
...
>>> d = SetOnceDefaultDict(list)
>>> d['x'].append(2)
>>> d['y'].append(3)
>>> d['x'].append(10)
>>> d['x'] = 23
Traceback (most recent call last):
  File "<stdin>", line 1, in <module>
  File "mixin.py", line 24, in __setitem__
    raise KeyError(str(key) + ' already set')
KeyError: 'x already set'

>>> from collections import OrderedDict
>>> class StringOrderedDict(StringKeysMappingMixin,
...                         SetOnceMappingMixin,
...                         OrderedDict):
...     pass
...
>>> d = StringOrderedDict()
>>> d['x'] = 23
>>> d[42] = 10
Traceback (most recent call last):
  File "<stdin>", line 1, in <module>
  File "mixin.py", line 45, in __setitem__
    '''
TypeError: keys must be strings
>>> d['x'] = 42
Traceback (most recent call last):
  File "<stdin>", line 1, in <module>
  File "mixin.py", line 46, in __setitem__
    __slots__ = ()
  File "mixin.py", line 24, in __setitem__
    if key in self:
KeyError: 'x already set'
>>>
```

In the example, you will notice that the mixins are combined with other existing classes (e.g., dict, defaultdict, OrderedDict), and even one another. When combined, the classes all work together to provide the desired functionality.

Discussion

Mixin classes appear in various places in the standard library, mostly as a means for extending the functionality of other classes similar to as shown. They are also one of the main uses of multiple inheritance. For instance, if you are writing network code, you can often use the `ThreadingMixIn` from the `socketserver` module to add thread support to other network-related classes. For example, here is a multithreaded XML-RPC server:

```
from xmlrpc.server import SimpleXMLRPCServer
from socketserver import ThreadingMixIn
class ThreadedXMLRPCServer(ThreadingMixIn, SimpleXMLRPCServer):
    pass
```

It is also common to find mixins defined in large libraries and frameworks—again, typically to enhance the functionality of existing classes with optional features in some way.

There is a rich history surrounding the theory of mixin classes. However, rather than getting into all of the details, there are a few important implementation details to keep in mind.

First, mixin classes are never meant to be instantiated directly. For example, none of the classes in this recipe work by themselves. They have to be mixed with another class that implements the required mapping functionality. Similarly, the `ThreadingMixIn` from the `socketserver` library has to be mixed with an appropriate server class—it can't be used all by itself.

Second, mixin classes typically have no state of their own. This means there is no `__init__()` method and no instance variables. In this recipe, the specification of `__slots__ = ()` is meant to serve as a strong hint that the mixin classes do not have their own instance data.

If you are thinking about defining a mixin class that has an `__init__()` method and instance variables, be aware that there is significant peril associated with the fact that the class doesn't know anything about the other classes it's going to be mixed with. Thus, any instance variables created would have to be named in a way that avoids name clashes. In addition, the `__init__()` method would have to be programmed in a way that properly invokes the `__init__()` method of other classes that are mixed in. In general, this is difficult to implement since you know nothing about the argument signatures of the other classes. At the very least, you would have to implement something very general using `*arg`, `**kwargs`. If the `__init__()` of the mixin class took any arguments of its own, those arguments should be specified by keyword only and named in such a way to avoid name collisions with other arguments. Here is one possible implementation of a mixin defining an `__init__()` and accepting a keyword argument:

```
class RestrictKeysMixin:
    def __init__(self, *args, _restrict_key_type, **kwargs):
        self.__restrict_key_type = _restrict_key_type
        super().__init__(*args, **kwargs)

    def __setitem__(self, key, value):
        if not isinstance(key, self.__restrict_key_type):
            raise TypeError('Keys must be ' + str(self.__restrict_key_type))
        super().__setitem__(key, value)
```

Here is an example that shows how this class might be used:

```
>>> class RDict(RestrictKeysMixin, dict):
...     pass
...
>>> d = RDict(_restrict_key_type=str)
>>> e = RDict([('name','Dave'), ('n',37)], _restrict_key_type=str)
>>> f = RDict(name='Dave', n=37, _restrict_key_type=str)
>>> f
{'n': 37, 'name': 'Dave'}
>>> f[42] = 10
Traceback (most recent call last):
  File "<stdin>", line 1, in <module>
  File "mixin.py", line 83, in __setitem__
    raise TypeError('Keys must be ' + str(self.__restrict_key_type))
TypeError: Keys must be <class 'str'>
>>>
```

In this example, you'll notice that initializing an RDict() still takes the arguments understood by dict(). However, there is an extra keyword argument restrict_key_type that is provided to the mixin class.

Finally, use of the super() function is an essential and critical part of writing mixin classes. In the solution, the classes redefine certain critical methods, such as __getitem__() and __setitem__(). However, they also need to call the original implementation of those methods. Using super() delegates to the next class on the method resolution order (MRO). This aspect of the recipe, however, is not obvious to novices, because super() is being used in classes that have no parent (at first glance, it might look like an error). However, in a class definition such as this:

```
class LoggedDict(LoggedMappingMixin, dict):
    pass
```

the use of super() in LoggedMappingMixin delegates to the next class over in the multiple inheritance list. That is, a call such as super().__getitem__() in LoggedMapping Mixin actually steps over and invokes dict.__getitem__(). Without this behavior, the mixin class wouldn't work at all.

An alternative implementation of mixins involves the use of class decorators. For example, consider this code:

```
def LoggedMapping(cls):
    cls_getitem = cls.__getitem__
    cls_setitem = cls.__setitem__
    cls_delitem = cls.__delitem__

    def __getitem__(self, key):
        print('Getting ' + str(key))
        return cls_getitem(self, key)

    def __setitem__(self, key, value):
        print('Setting {} = {!r}'.format(key, value))
        return cls_setitem(self, key, value)

    def __delitem__(self, key):
        print('Deleting ' + str(key))
        return cls_delitem(self, key)

    cls.__getitem__ = __getitem__
    cls.__setitem__ = __setitem__
    cls.__delitem__ = __delitem__
    return cls
```

This function is applied as a decorator to a class definition. For example:

```
@LoggedMapping
class LoggedDict(dict):
    pass
```

If you try it, you'll find that you get the same behavior, but multiple inheritance is no longer involved. Instead, the decorator has simply performed a bit of surgery on the class definition to replace certain methods. Further details about class decorators can be found in Recipe 9.12.

See Recipe 8.13 for an advanced recipe involving both mixins and class decorators.

8.19. Implementing Stateful Objects or State Machines

Problem

You want to implement a state machine or an object that operates in a number of different states, but don't want to litter your code with a lot of conditionals.

Solution

In certain applications, you might have objects that operate differently according to some kind of internal state. For example, consider a simple class representing a connection:

```
class Connection:
    def __init__(self):
```

```
            self.state = 'CLOSED'

    def read(self):
        if self.state != 'OPEN':
            raise RuntimeError('Not open')
        print('reading')

    def write(self, data):
        if self.state != 'OPEN':
            raise RuntimeError('Not open')
        print('writing')

    def open(self):
        if self.state == 'OPEN':
            raise RuntimeError('Already open')
        self.state = 'OPEN'

    def close(self):
        if self.state == 'CLOSED':
            raise RuntimeError('Already closed')
        self.state = 'CLOSED'
```

This implementation presents a couple of difficulties. First, the code is complicated by the introduction of many conditional checks for the state. Second, the performance is degraded because common operations (e.g., `read()` and `write()`) always check the state before proceeding.

A more elegant approach is to encode each operational state as a separate class and arrange for the `Connection` class to delegate to the state class. For example:

```
class Connection:
    def __init__(self):
        self.new_state(ClosedConnectionState)

    def new_state(self, newstate):
        self._state = newstate

    # Delegate to the state class
    def read(self):
        return self._state.read(self)

    def write(self, data):
        return self._state.write(self, data)

    def open(self):
        return self._state.open(self)

    def close(self):
        return self._state.close(self)

# Connection state base class
class ConnectionState:
```

```python
    @staticmethod
    def read(conn):
        raise NotImplementedError()

    @staticmethod
    def write(conn, data):
        raise NotImplementedError()

    @staticmethod
    def open(conn):
        raise NotImplementedError()

    @staticmethod
    def close(conn):
        raise NotImplementedError()

# Implementation of different states
class ClosedConnectionState(ConnectionState):
    @staticmethod
    def read(conn):
        raise RuntimeError('Not open')

    @staticmethod
    def write(conn, data):
        raise RuntimeError('Not open')

    @staticmethod
    def open(conn):
        conn.new_state(OpenConnectionState)

    @staticmethod
    def close(conn):
        raise RuntimeError('Already closed')

class OpenConnectionState(ConnectionState):
    @staticmethod
    def read(conn):
        print('reading')

    @staticmethod
    def write(conn, data):
        print('writing')

    @staticmethod
    def open(conn):
        raise RuntimeError('Already open')

    @staticmethod
    def close(conn):
        conn.new_state(ClosedConnectionState)
```

Here is an interactive session that illustrates the use of these classes:

```
>>> c = Connection()
>>> c._state
<class '__main__.ClosedConnectionState'>
>>> c.read()
Traceback (most recent call last):
  File "<stdin>", line 1, in <module>
  File "example.py", line 10, in read
    return self._state.read(self)
  File "example.py", line 43, in read
    raise RuntimeError('Not open')
RuntimeError: Not open
>>> c.open()
>>> c._state
<class '__main__.OpenConnectionState'>
>>> c.read()
reading
>>> c.write('hello')
writing
>>> c.close()
>>> c._state
<class '__main__.ClosedConnectionState'>
>>>
```

Discussion

Writing code that features a large set of complicated conditionals and intertwined states is hard to maintain and explain. The solution presented here avoids that by splitting the individual states into their own classes.

It might look a little weird, but each state is implemented by a class with static methods, each of which take an instance of Connection as the first argument. This design is based on a decision to not store any instance data in the different state classes themselves. Instead, all instance data should be stored on the Connection instance. The grouping of states under a common base class is mostly there to help organize the code and to ensure that the proper methods get implemented. The NotImplementedError exception raised in base class methods is just there to make sure that subclasses provide an implementation of the required methods. As an alternative, you might consider the use of an abstract base class, as described in Recipe 8.12.

An alternative implementation technique concerns direct manipulation of the __class__ attribute of instances. Consider this code:

```
class Connection:
    def __init__(self):
        self.new_state(ClosedConnection)

    def new_state(self, newstate):
        self.__class__ = newstate

    def read(self):
```

```
            raise NotImplementedError()

        def write(self, data):
            raise NotImplementedError()

        def open(self):
            raise NotImplementedError()

        def close(self):
            raise NotImplementedError()

    class ClosedConnection(Connection):
        def read(self):
            raise RuntimeError('Not open')

        def write(self, data):
            raise RuntimeError('Not open')

        def open(self):
            self.new_state(OpenConnection)

        def close(self):
            raise RuntimeError('Already closed')

    class OpenConnection(Connection):
        def read(self):
            print('reading')

        def write(self, data):
            print('writing')

        def open(self):
            raise RuntimeError('Already open')

        def close(self):
            self.new_state(ClosedConnection)
```

The main feature of this implementation is that it eliminates an extra level of indirection. Instead of having separate `Connection` and `ConnectionState` classes, the two classes are merged together into one. As the state changes, the instance will change its type, as shown here:

```
>>> c = Connection()
>>> c
<__main__.ClosedConnection object at 0x1006718d0>
>>> c.read()
Traceback (most recent call last):
  File "<stdin>", line 1, in <module>
  File "state.py", line 15, in read
    raise RuntimeError('Not open')
RuntimeError: Not open
>>> c.open()
```

```
>>> c
<__main__.OpenConnection object at 0x1006718d0>
>>> c.read()
reading
>>> c.close()
>>> c
<__main__.ClosedConnection object at 0x1006718d0>
>>>
```

Object-oriented purists might be offended by the idea of simply changing the instance __class__ attribute. However, it's technically allowed. Also, it might result in slightly faster code since all of the methods on the connection no longer involve an extra delegation step.)

Finally, either technique is useful in implementing more complicated state machines—especially in code that might otherwise feature large if-elif-else blocks. For example:

```
# Original implementation
class State:
    def __init__(self):
        self.state = 'A'
    def action(self, x):
        if state == 'A':
            # Action for A
            ...
            state = 'B'
        elif state == 'B':
            # Action for B
            ...
            state = 'C'
        elif state == 'C':
            # Action for C
            ...
            state = 'A'

# Alternative implementation
class State:
    def __init__(self):
        self.new_state(State_A)

    def new_state(self, state):
        self.__class__ = state

    def action(self, x):
        raise NotImplementedError()

class State_A(State):
    def action(self, x):
        # Action for A
        ...
        self.new_state(State_B)
```

```
class State_B(State):
    def action(self, x):
        # Action for B
        ...
        self.new_state(State_C)

class State_C(State):
    def action(self, x):
        # Action for C
        ...
        self.new_state(State_A)
```

This recipe is loosely based on the state design pattern found in *Design Patterns: Elements of Reusable Object-Oriented Software* by Erich Gamma, Richard Helm, Ralph Johnson, and John Vlissides (Addison-Wesley, 1995).

8.20. Calling a Method on an Object Given the Name As a String

Problem

You have the name of a method that you want to call on an object stored in a string and you want to execute the method.

Solution

For simple cases, you might use getattr(), like this:

```
import math

class Point:
    def __init__(self, x, y):
        self.x = x
        self.y = y

    def __repr__(self):
        return 'Point({!r:},{!r:})'.format(self.x, self.y)

    def distance(self, x, y):
        return math.hypot(self.x - x, self.y - y)

p = Point(2, 3)
d = getattr(p, 'distance')(0, 0)     # Calls p.distance(0, 0)
```

An alternative approach is to use operator.methodcaller(). For example:

```
import operator
operator.methodcaller('distance', 0, 0)(p)
```

`operator.methodcaller()` may be useful if you want to look up a method by name and supply the same arguments over and over again. For instance, if you need to sort an entire list of points:

```
points = [
    Point(1, 2),
    Point(3, 0),
    Point(10, -3),
    Point(-5, -7),
    Point(-1, 8),
    Point(3, 2)
]

# Sort by distance from origin (0, 0)
points.sort(key=operator.methodcaller('distance', 0, 0))
```

Discussion

Calling a method is actually two separate steps involving an attribute lookup and a function call. Therefore, to call a method, you simply look up the attribute using get attr(), as for any other attribute. To invoke the result as a method, simply treat the result of the lookup as a function.

`operator.methodcaller()` creates a callable object, but also fixes any arguments that are going to be supplied to the method. All that you need to do is provide the appropriate `self` argument. For example:

```
>>> p = Point(3, 4)
>>> d = operator.methodcaller('distance', 0, 0)
>>> d(p)
5.0
>>>
```

Invoking methods using names contained in strings is somewhat common in code that emulates case statements or variants of the visitor pattern. See the next recipe for a more advanced example.

8.21. Implementing the Visitor Pattern

Problem

You need to write code that processes or navigates through a complicated data structure consisting of many different kinds of objects, each of which needs to be handled in a different way. For example, walking through a tree structure and performing different actions depending on what kind of tree nodes are encountered.

Solution

The problem addressed by this recipe is one that often arises in programs that build data structures consisting of a large number of different kinds of objects. To illustrate, suppose you are trying to write a program that represents mathematical expressions. To do that, the program might employ a number of classes, like this:

```python
class Node:
    pass

class UnaryOperator(Node):
    def __init__(self, operand):
        self.operand = operand

class BinaryOperator(Node):
    def __init__(self, left, right):
        self.left = left
        self.right = right

class Add(BinaryOperator):
    pass

class Sub(BinaryOperator):
    pass

class Mul(BinaryOperator):
    pass

class Div(BinaryOperator):
    pass

class Negate(UnaryOperator):
    pass

class Number(Node):
    def __init__(self, value):
        self.value - value
```

These classes would then be used to build up nested data structures, like this:

```python
# Representation of 1 + 2 * (3 - 4) / 5
t1 = Sub(Number(3), Number(4))
t2 = Mul(Number(2), t1)
t3 = Div(t2, Number(5))
t4 = Add(Number(1), t3)
```

The problem is not the creation of such structures, but in writing code that processes them later. For example, given such an expression, a program might want to do any number of things (e.g., produce output, generate instructions, perform translation, etc.).

To enable general-purpose processing, a common solution is to implement the so-called "visitor pattern" using a class similar to this:

```
class NodeVisitor:
    def visit(self, node):
        methname = 'visit_' + type(node).__name__
        meth = getattr(self, methname, None)
        if meth is None:
            meth = self.generic_visit
        return meth(node)

    def generic_visit(self, node):
        raise RuntimeError('No {} method'.format('visit_' + type(node).__name__))
```

To use this class, a programmer inherits from it and implements various methods of the form visit_Name(), where Name is substituted with the node type. For example, if you want to evaluate the expression, you could write this:

```
class Evaluator(NodeVisitor):
    def visit_Number(self, node):
        return node.value

    def visit_Add(self, node):
        return self.visit(node.left) + self.visit(node.right)

    def visit_Sub(self, node):
        return self.visit(node.left) - self.visit(node.right)

    def visit_Mul(self, node):
        return self.visit(node.left) * self.visit(node.right)

    def visit_Div(self, node):
        return self.visit(node.left) / self.visit(node.right)

    def visit_Negate(self, node):
        return -node.operand
```

Here is an example of how you would use this class using the previously generated expression:

```
>>> e = Evaluator()
>>> e.visit(t4)
0.6
>>>
```

As a completely different example, here is a class that translates an expression into operations on a simple stack machine:

```
class StackCode(NodeVisitor):
    def generate_code(self, node):
        self.instructions = []
        self.visit(node)
        return self.instructions

    def visit_Number(self, node):
        self.instructions.append(('PUSH', node.value))
```

```
    def binop(self, node, instruction):
        self.visit(node.left)
        self.visit(node.right)
        self.instructions.append((instruction,))

    def visit_Add(self, node):
        self.binop(node, 'ADD')

    def visit_Sub(self, node):
        self.binop(node, 'SUB')

    def visit_Mul(self, node):
        self.binop(node, 'MUL')

    def visit_Div(self, node):
        self.binop(node, 'DIV')

    def unaryop(self, node, instruction):
        self.visit(node.operand)
        self.instructions.append((instruction,))

    def visit_Negate(self, node):
        self.unaryop(node, 'NEG')
```

Here is an example of this class in action:

```
>>> s = StackCode()
>>> s.generate_code(t4)
[('PUSH', 1), ('PUSH', 2), ('PUSH', 3), ('PUSH', 4), ('SUB',),
 ('MUL',), ('PUSH', 5), ('DIV',), ('ADD',)]
>>>
```

Discussion

There are really two key ideas in this recipe. The first is a design strategy where code that manipulates a complicated data structure is decoupled from the data structure itself. That is, in this recipe, none of the various Node classes provide any implementation that does anything with the data. Instead, all of the data manipulation is carried out by specific implementations of the separate NodeVisitor class. This separation makes the code extremely general purpose.

The second major idea of this recipe is in the implementation of the visitor class itself. In the visitor, you want to dispatch to a different handling method based on some value such as the node type. In a naive implementation, you might be inclined to write a huge if statement, like this:

```
class NodeVisitor:
    def visit(self, node):
        nodetype = type(node).__name__
        if nodetype == 'Number':
```

```
            return self.visit_Number(node)
        elif nodetype == 'Add':
            return self.visit_Add(node)
        elif nodetype == 'Sub':
            return self.visit_Sub(node)
        ...
```

However, it quickly becomes apparent that you don't really want to take that approach. Aside from being incredibly verbose, it runs slowly, and it's hard to maintain if you ever add or change the kind of nodes being handled. Instead, it's much better to play a little trick where you form the name of a method and go fetch it with the getattr() function, as shown. The generic_visit() method in the solution is a fallback should no matching handler method be found. In this recipe, it raises an exception to alert the programmer that an unexpected node type was encountered.

Within each visitor class, it is common for calculations to be driven by recursive calls to the visit() method. For example:

```
class Evaluator(NodeVisitor):
    ...
    def visit_Add(self, node):
        return self.visit(node.left) + self.visit(node.right)
```

This recursion is what makes the visitor class traverse the entire data structure. Essentially, you keep calling visit() until you reach some sort of terminal node, such as Number in the example. The exact order of the recursion and other operations depend entirely on the application.

It should be noted that this particular technique of dispatching to a method is also a common way to emulate the behavior of switch or case statements from other languages. For example, if you are writing an HTTP framework, you might have classes that do a similar kind of dispatch:

```
class HTTPHandler:
    def handle(self, request):
        methname = 'do_' + request.request_method
        getattr(self, methname)(request)

    def do_GET(self, request):
        ...
    def do_POST(self, request):
        ...
    def do_HEAD(self, request):
        ...
```

One weakness of the visitor pattern is its heavy reliance on recursion. If you try to apply it to a deeply nested structure, it's possible that you will hit Python's recursion depth limit (see sys.getrecursionlimit()). To avoid this problem, you can make certain choices in your data structures. For example, you can use normal Python lists instead of linked lists or try to aggregate more data in each node to make the data more shallow.

You can also try to employ nonrecursive traversal algorithms using generators or iterators as discussed in Recipe 8.22.

Use of the visitor pattern is extremely common in programs related to parsing and compiling. One notable implementation can be found in Python's own `ast` module. In addition to allowing traversal of tree structures, it provides a variation that allows a data structure to be rewritten or transformed as it is traversed (e.g., nodes added or removed). Look at the source for `ast` for more details. Recipe 9.24 shows an example of using the `ast` module to process Python source code.

8.22. Implementing the Visitor Pattern Without Recursion

Problem

You're writing code that navigates through a deeply nested tree structure using the visitor pattern, but it blows up due to exceeding the recursion limit. You'd like to eliminate the recursion, but keep the programming style of the visitor pattern.

Solution

Clever use of generators can sometimes be used to eliminate recursion from algorithms involving tree traversal or searching. In Recipe 8.21, a visitor class was presented. Here is an alternative implementation of that class that drives the computation in an entirely different way using a stack and generators:

```
import types

class Node:
    pass

import types
class NodeVisitor:
    def visit(self, node):
        stack = [ node ]
        last_result = None
        while stack:
            try:
                last = stack[-1]
                if isinstance(last, types.GeneratorType):
                    stack.append(last.send(last_result))
                    last_result = None
                elif isinstance(last, Node):
                    stack.append(self._visit(stack.pop()))
                else:
                    last_result = stack.pop()
            except StopIteration:
                stack.pop()
        return last_result
```

```
def _visit(self, node):
    methname = 'visit_' + type(node).__name__
    meth = getattr(self, methname, None)
    if meth is None:
        meth = self.generic_visit
    return meth(node)

def generic_visit(self, node):
    raise RuntimeError('No {} method'.format('visit_' + type(node).__name__))
```

If you use this class, you'll find that it still works with existing code that might have used recursion. In fact, you can use it as a drop-in replacement for the visitor implementation in the prior recipe. For example, consider the following code, which involves expression trees:

```
class UnaryOperator(Node):
    def __init__(self, operand):
        self.operand = operand

class BinaryOperator(Node):
    def __init__(self, left, right):
        self.left = left
        self.right = right

class Add(BinaryOperator):
    pass

class Sub(BinaryOperator):
    pass

class Mul(BinaryOperator):
    pass

class Div(BinaryOperator):
    pass

class Negate(UnaryOperator):
    pass

class Number(Node):
    def __init__(self, value):
        self.value = value

# A sample visitor class that evaluates expressions
class Evaluator(NodeVisitor):
    def visit_Number(self, node):
        return node.value

    def visit_Add(self, node):
        return self.visit(node.left) + self.visit(node.right)
```

```
        def visit_Sub(self, node):
            return self.visit(node.left) - self.visit(node.right)

        def visit_Mul(self, node):
            return self.visit(node.left) * self.visit(node.right)

        def visit_Div(self, node):
            return self.visit(node.left) / self.visit(node.right)

        def visit_Negate(self, node):
            return -self.visit(node.operand)

    if __name__ == '__main__':
        # 1 + 2*(3-4) / 5
        t1 = Sub(Number(3), Number(4))
        t2 = Mul(Number(2), t1)
        t3 = Div(t2, Number(5))
        t4 = Add(Number(1), t3)

        # Evaluate it
        e = Evaluator()
        print(e.visit(t4))      # Outputs 0.6
```

The preceding code works for simple expressions. However, the implementation of Evaluator uses recursion and crashes if things get too nested. For example:

```
>>> a = Number(0)
>>> for n in range(1, 100000):
...     a = Add(a, Number(n))
...
>>> e = Evaluator()
>>> e.visit(a)
Traceback (most recent call last):
...
  File "visitor.py", line 29, in _visit
    return meth(node)
  File "visitor.py", line 67, in visit_Add
    return self.visit(node.left) + self.visit(node.right)
RuntimeError: maximum recursion depth exceeded
>>>
```

Now let's change the Evaluator class ever so slightly to the following:

```
class Evaluator(NodeVisitor):
    def visit_Number(self, node):
        return node.value

    def visit_Add(self, node):
        yield (yield node.left) + (yield node.right)

    def visit_Sub(self, node):
        yield (yield node.left) - (yield node.right)
```

```
    def visit_Mul(self, node):
        yield (yield node.left) * (yield node.right)

    def visit_Div(self, node):
        yield (yield node.left) / (yield node.right)

    def visit_Negate(self, node):
        yield -(yield node.operand)
```

If you try the same recursive experiment, you'll find that it suddenly works. It's magic!

```
>>> a = Number(0)
>>> for n in range(1,100000):
...     a = Add(a, Number(n))
...
>>> e = Evaluator()
>>> e.visit(a)
4999950000
>>>
```

If you want to add custom processing into any of the methods, it still works. For example:

```
class Evaluator(NodeVisitor):
    ...
    def visit_Add(self, node):
        print('Add:', node)
        lhs = yield node.left
        print('left=', lhs)
        rhs = yield node.right
        print('right=', rhs)
        yield lhs + rhs
    ...
```

Here is some sample output:

```
>>> e = Evaluator()
>>> e.visit(t4)
Add: <__main__.Add object at 0x1006a8d90>
left= 1
right= -0.4
0.6
>>>
```

Discussion

This recipe nicely illustrates how generators and coroutines can perform mind-bending tricks involving program control flow, often to great advantage. To understand this recipe, a few key insights are required.

First, in problems related to tree traversal, a common implementation strategy for avoiding recursion is to write algorithms involving a stack or queue. For example, depth-first traversal can be implemented entirely by pushing nodes onto a stack when first encountered and then popping them off once processing has finished. The central core of the `visit()` method in the solution is built around this idea. The algorithm starts by pushing the initial node onto the `stack` list and runs until the stack is empty. During execution, the stack will grow according to the depth of the underlying tree structure.

The second insight concerns the behavior of the `yield` statement in generators. When `yield` is encountered, the behavior of a generator is to emit a value and to suspend. This recipe uses this as a replacement for recursion. For example, instead of writing a recursive expression like this:

```
value = self.visit(node.left)
```

you replace it with the following:

```
value = yield node.left
```

Behind the scenes, this sends the node in question (`node.left`) back to the `visit()` method. The `visit()` method then carries out the execution of the appropriate `visit_Name()` method for that node. In some sense, this is almost the opposite of recursion. That is, instead of calling `visit()` recursively to move the algorithm forward, the `yield` statement is being used to temporarily back out of the computation in progress. Thus, the `yield` is essentially a signal that tells the algorithm that the yielded node needs to be processed first before further progress can be made.

The final part of this recipe concerns propagation of results. When generator functions are used, you can no longer use `return` statements to emit values (doing so will cause a `SyntaxError` exception). Thus, the `yield` statement has to do double duty to cover the case. In this recipe, if the value produced by a `yield` statement is a non-Node type, it is assumed to be a value that will be propagated to the next step of the calculation. This is the purpose of the `last_return` variable in the code. Typically, this would hold the last value yielded by a visit method. That value would then be sent into the previously executing method, where it would show up as the return value from a `yield` statement. For example, in this code:

```
value = yield node.left
```

The `value` variable gets the value of `last_return`, which is the result returned by the visitor method invoked for `node.left`.

All of these aspects of the recipe are found in this fragment of code:

```
try:
    last = stack[-1]
    if isinstance(last, types.GeneratorType):
        stack.append(last.send(last_result))
        last_result = None
    elif isinstance(last, Node):
        stack.append(self._visit(stack.pop()))
    else:
        last_result = stack.pop()
```

```
      except StopIteration:
          stack.pop()
```

The code works by simply looking at the top of the stack and deciding what to do next. If it's a generator, then its `send()` method is invoked with the last result (if any) and the result appended onto the stack for further processing. The value returned by `send()` is the same value that was given to the `yield` statement. Thus, in a statement such as `yield node.left`, the `Node` instance `node.left` is returned by `send()` and placed on the top of the stack.

If the top of the stack is a `Node` instance, then it is replaced by the result of calling the appropriate visit method for that node. This is where the underlying recursion is being eliminated. Instead of the various visit methods directly calling `visit()` recursively, it takes place here. As long as the methods use `yield`, it all works out.

Finally, if the top of the stack is anything else, it's assumed to be a return value of some kind. It just gets popped off the stack and placed into `last_result`. If the next item on the stack is a generator, then it gets sent in as a return value for the `yield`. It should be noted that the final return value of `visit()` is also set to `last_result`. This is what makes this recipe work with a traditional recursive implementation. If no generators are being used, this value simply holds the value given to any `return` statements used in the code.

One potential danger of this recipe concerns the distinction between yielding `Node` and non-`Node` values. In the implementation, all `Node` instances are automatically traversed. This means that you can't use a `Node` as a return value to be propagated. In practice, this may not matter. However, if it does, you might need to adapt the algorithm slightly. For example, possibly by introducing another class into the mix, like this:

```python
class Visit:
    def __init__(self, node):
        self.node = node

class NodeVisitor:
    def visit(self, node):
        stack = [ Visit(node) ]
        last_result = None
        while stack:
            try:
                last = stack[-1]
                if isinstance(last, types.GeneratorType):
                    stack.append(last.send(last_result))
                    last_result = None
                elif isinstance(last, Visit):
                    stack.append(self._visit(stack.pop().node))
                else:
                    last_result = stack.pop()
            except StopIteration:
```

```
                stack.pop()
        return last_result

    def _visit(self, node):
        methname = 'visit_' + type(node).__name__
        meth = getattr(self, methname, None)
        if meth is None:
            meth = self.generic_visit
        return meth(node)

    def generic_visit(self, node):
        raise RuntimeError('No {} method'.format('visit_' + type(node).__name__))
```

With this implementation, the various visitor methods would now look like this:

```
class Evaluator(NodeVisitor):
    ...
    def visit_Add(self, node):
        yield (yield Visit(node.left)) + (yield Visit(node.right))

    def visit_Sub(self, node):
        yield (yield Visit(node.left)) - (yield Visit(node.right))
    ...
```

Having seen this recipe, you might be inclined to investigate a solution that doesn't involve yield. However, doing so will lead to code that has to deal with many of the same issues presented here. For example, to eliminate recursion, you'll need to maintain a stack. You'll also need to come up with some scheme for managing the traversal and invoking various visitor-related logic. Without generators, this code ends up being a very messy mix of stack manipulation, callback functions, and other constructs. Frankly, the main benefit of using yield is that you can write nonrecursive code in an elegant style that looks almost exactly like the recursive implementation.

8.23. Managing Memory in Cyclic Data Structures

Problem

Your program creates data structures with cycles (e.g., trees, graphs, observer patterns, etc.), but you are experiencing problems with memory management.

Solution

A simple example of a cyclic data structure is a tree structure where a parent points to its children and the children point back to their parent. For code like this, you should consider making one of the links a weak reference using the weakref library. For example:

```
import weakref

class Node:
    def __init__(self, value):
        self.value = value
        self._parent = None
        self.children = []

    def __repr__(self):
        return 'Node({!r:})'.format(self.value)

    # property that manages the parent as a weak-reference
    @property
    def parent(self):
        return self._parent if self._parent is None else self._parent()

    @parent.setter
    def parent(self, node):
        self._parent = weakref.ref(node)

    def add_child(self, child):
        self.children.append(child)
        child.parent = self
```

This implementation allows the parent to quietly die. For example:

```
>>> root = Node('parent')
>>> c1 = Node('child')
>>> root.add_child(c1)
>>> print(c1.parent)
Node('parent')
>>> del root
>>> print(c1.parent)
None
>>>
```

Discussion

Cyclic data structures are a somewhat tricky aspect of Python that require careful study because the usual rules of garbage collection often don't apply. For example, consider this code:

```
# Class just to illustrate when deletion occurs
class Data:
    def __del__(self):
        print('Data.__del__')

# Node class involving a cycle
class Node:
    def __init__(self):
        self.data = Data()
        self.parent = None
```

```
        self.children = []
    def add_child(self, child):
        self.children.append(child)
        child.parent = self
```

Now, using this code, try some experiments to see some subtle issues with garbage collection:

```
>>> a = Data()
>>> del a                 # Immediately deleted
Data.__del__
>>> a = Node()
>>> del a                 # Immediately deleted
Data.__del__
>>> a = Node()
>>> a.add_child(Node())
>>> del a                 # Not deleted (no message)
>>>
```

As you can see, objects are deleted immediately all except for the last case involving a cycle. The reason is that Python's garbage collection is based on simple reference counting. When the reference count of an object reaches 0, it is immediately deleted. For cyclic data structures, however, this never happens. Thus, in the last part of the example, the parent and child nodes refer to each other, keeping the reference count nonzero.

To deal with cycles, there is a separate garbage collector that runs periodically. However, as a general rule, you never know when it might run. Consequently, you never really know when cyclic data structures might get collected. If necessary, you can force garbage collection, but doing so is a bit clunky:

```
>>> import gc
>>> gc.collect()      # Force collection
Data.__del__
Data.__del__
>>>
```

An even worse problem occurs if the objects involved in a cycle define their own __del__() method. For example, suppose the code looked like this:

```
# Class just to illustrate when deletion occurs
class Data:
    def __del__(self):
        print('Data.__del__')

# Node class involving a cycle
class Node:
    def __init__(self):
        self.data = Data()
        self.parent = None
        self.children = []

    # NEVER DEFINE LIKE THIS.
```

```
        # Only here to illustrate pathological behavior
        def __del__(self):
            del self.data
            del.parent
            del.children

        def add_child(self, child):
            self.children.append(child)
            child.parent = self
```

In this case, the data structures will never be garbage collected at all and your program will leak memory! If you try it, you'll see that the `Data.__del__` message never appears at all—even after a forced garbage collection:

```
>>> a = Node()
>>> a.add_child(Node())
>>> del a               # No message (not collected)
>>> import gc
>>> gc.collect()        # No message (not collected)
>>>
```

Weak references solve this problem by eliminating reference cycles. Essentially, a weak reference is a pointer to an object that does not increase its reference count. You create weak references using the `weakref` library. For example:

```
>>> import weakref
>>> a = Node()
>>> a_ref = weakref.ref(a)
>>> a_ref
<weakref at 0x100581f70; to 'Node' at 0x1005c5410>
>>>
```

To dereference a weak reference, you call it like a function. If the referenced object still exists, it is returned. Otherwise, `None` is returned. Since the reference count of the original object wasn't increased, it can be deleted normally. For example:

```
>>> print(a_ref())
<__main__.Node object at 0x1005c5410>
>>> del a
Data.__del__
>>> print(a_ref())
None
>>>
```

By using weak references, as shown in the solution, you'll find that there are no longer any reference cycles and that garbage collection occurs immediately once a node is no longer being used. See Recipe 8.25 for another example involving weak references.

8.24. Making Classes Support Comparison Operations

Problem

You'd like to be able to compare instances of your class using the standard comparison operators (e.g., >=, !=, <=, etc.), but without having to write a lot of special methods.

Solution

Python classes can support comparison by implementing a special method for each comparison operator. For example, to support the >= operator, you define a __ge__() method in the classes. Although defining a single method is usually no problem, it quickly gets tedious to create implementations of every possible comparison operator.

The functools.total_ordering decorator can be used to simplify this process. To use it, you decorate a class with it, and define __eq__() and one other comparison method (__lt__, __le__, __gt__, or __ge__). The decorator then fills in the other comparison methods for you.

As an example, let's build some houses and add some rooms to them, and then perform comparisons based on the size of the houses:

```python
from functools import total_ordering
class Room:
    def __init__(self, name, length, width):
        self.name = name
        self.length = length
        self.width = width
        self.square_feet = self.length * self.width

@total_ordering
class House:
    def __init__(self, name, style):
        self.name = name
        self.style = style
        self.rooms = list()

    @property
    def living_space_footage(self):
        return sum(r.square_feet for r in self.rooms)

    def add_room(self, room):
        self.rooms.append(room)

    def __str__(self):
        return '{}: {} square foot {}'.format(self.name,
                                              self.living_space_footage,
                                              self.style)
```

```
    def __eq__(self, other):
        return self.living_space_footage == other.living_space_footage

    def __lt__(self, other):
        return self.living_space_footage < other.living_space_footage
```

Here, the House class has been decorated with @total_ordering. Definitions of __eq__() and __lt__() are provided to compare houses based on the total square footage of their rooms. This minimum definition is all that is required to make all of the other comparison operations work. For example:

```
# Build a few houses, and add rooms to them
h1 = House('h1', 'Cape')
h1.add_room(Room('Master Bedroom', 14, 21))
h1.add_room(Room('Living Room', 18, 20))
h1.add_room(Room('Kitchen', 12, 16))
h1.add_room(Room('Office', 12, 12))

h2 = House('h2', 'Ranch')
h2.add_room(Room('Master Bedroom', 14, 21))
h2.add_room(Room('Living Room', 18, 20))
h2.add_room(Room('Kitchen', 12, 16))

h3 = House('h3', 'Split')
h3.add_room(Room('Master Bedroom', 14, 21))
h3.add_room(Room('Living Room', 18, 20))
h3.add_room(Room('Office', 12, 16))
h3.add_room(Room('Kitchen', 15, 17))
houses = [h1, h2, h3]

print('Is h1 bigger than h2?', h1 > h2) # prints True
print('Is h2 smaller than h3?', h2 < h3) # prints True
print('Is h2 greater than or equal to h1?', h2 >= h1) # Prints False
print('Which one is biggest?', max(houses)) # Prints 'h3: 1101-square-foot Split'
print('Which is smallest?', min(houses)) # Prints 'h2: 846-square-foot Ranch'
```

Discussion

If you've written the code to make a class support all of the basic comparison operators, then total_ordering probably doesn't seem all that magical: it literally defines a mapping from each of the comparison-supporting methods to all of the other ones that would be required. So, if you defined __lt__() in your class as in the solution, it is used to build all of the other comparison operators. It's really just filling in the class with methods like this:

```
class House:
    def __eq__(self, other):
        ...
    def __lt__(self, other):
        ...
```

```
# Methods created by @total_ordering
__le__ = lambda self, other: self < other or self == other
__gt__ = lambda self, other: not (self < other or self == other)
__ge__ = lambda self, other: not (self < other)
__ne__ = lambda self, other: not self == other
```

Sure, it's not hard to write these methods yourself, but @total_ordering simply takes the guesswork out of it.

8.25. Creating Cached Instances

Problem

When creating instances of a class, you want to return a cached reference to a previous instance created with the same arguments (if any).

Solution

The problem being addressed in this recipe sometimes arises when you want to ensure that there is only one instance of a class created for a set of input arguments. Practical examples include the behavior of libraries, such as the logging module, that only want to associate a single logger instance with a given name. For example:

```
>>> import logging
>>> a = logging.getLogger('foo')
>>> b = logging.getLogger('bar')
>>> a is b
False
>>> c = logging.getLogger('foo')
>>> a is c
True
>>>
```

To implement this behavior, you should make use of a factory function that's separate from the class itself. For example:

```
# The class in question
class Spam:
    def __init__(self, name):
        self.name = name

# Caching support
import weakref
_spam_cache = weakref.WeakValueDictionary()

def get_spam(name):
    if name not in _spam_cache:
        s = Spam(name)
        _spam_cache[name] = s
    else:
```

```
        s = _spam_cache[name]
    return s
```

If you use this implementation, you'll find that it behaves in the manner shown earlier:

```
>>> a = get_spam('foo')
>>> b = get_spam('bar')
>>> a is b
False
>>> c = get_spam('foo')
>>> a is c
True
>>>
```

Discussion

Writing a special factory function is often a simple approach for altering the normal rules of instance creation. One question that often arises at this point is whether or not a more elegant approach could be taken.

For example, you might consider a solution that redefines the __new__() method of a class as follows:

```
# Note: This code doesn't quite work
import weakref

class Spam:
    _spam_cache = weakref.WeakValueDictionary()
    def __new__(cls, name):
        if name in cls._spam_cache:
            return cls._spam_cache[name]
        else:
            self = super().__new__(cls)
            cls._spam_cache[name] = self
            return self

    def __init__(self, name):
        print('Initializing Spam')
        self.name = name
```

At first glance, it seems like this code might do the job. However, a major problem is that the __init__() method always gets called, regardless of whether the instance was cached or not. For example:

```
>>> s = Spam('Dave')
Initializing Spam
>>> t = Spam('Dave')
Initializing Spam
>>> s is t
True
>>>
```

That behavior is probably not what you want. So, to solve the problem of caching without reinitialization, you need to take a slightly different approach.

The use of weak references in this recipe serves an important purpose related to garbage collection, as described in Recipe 8.23. When maintaining a cache of instances, you often only want to keep items in the cache as long as they're actually being used somewhere in the program. A WeakValueDictionary instance only holds onto the referenced items as long as they exist somewhere else. Otherwise, the dictionary keys disappear when instances are no longer being used. Observe:

```
>>> a = get_spam('foo')
>>> b = get_spam('bar')
>>> c = get_spam('foo')
>>> list(_spam_cache)
['foo', 'bar']
>>> del a
>>> del c
>>> list(_spam_cache)
['bar']
>>> del b
>>> list(_spam_cache)
[]
>>>
```

For many programs, the bare-bones code shown in this recipe will often suffice. However, there are a number of more advanced implementation techniques that can be considered.

One immediate concern with this recipe might be its reliance on global variables and a factory function that's decoupled from the original class definition. One way to clean this up is to put the caching code into a separate manager class and glue things together like this:

```python
import weakref

class CachedSpamManager:
    def __init__(self):
        self._cache = weakref.WeakValueDictionary()
    def get_spam(self, name):
        if name not in self._cache:
            s = Spam(name)
            self._cache[name] = s
        else:
            s = self._cache[name]
        return s

    def clear(self):
        self._cache.clear()

class Spam:
    manager = CachedSpamManager()
```

```
        def __init__(self, name):
            self.name = name

    def get_spam(name):
        return Spam.manager.get_spam(name)
```

One feature of this approach is that it affords a greater degree of potential flexibility. For example, different kinds of management schemes could be be implemented (as separate classes) and attached to the Spam class as a replacement for the default caching implementation. None of the other code (e.g., get_spam) would need to be changed to make it work.

Another design consideration is whether or not you want to leave the class definition exposed to the user. If you do nothing, a user can easily make instances, bypassing the caching mechanism:

```
>>> a = Spam('foo')
>>> b = Spam('foo')
>>> a is b
False
>>>
```

If preventing this is important, you can take certain steps to avoid it. For example, you might give the class a name starting with an underscore, such as _Spam, which at least gives the user a clue that they shouldn't access it directly.

Alternatively, if you want to give users a stronger hint that they shouldn't instantiate Spam instances directly, you can make __init__() raise an exception and use a class method to make an alternate constructor like this:

```
class Spam:
    def __init__(self, *args, **kwargs):
        raise RuntimeError("Can't instantiate directly")

    # Alternate constructor
    @classmethod
    def _new(cls, name):
        self = cls.__new__(cls)
        self.name = name
```

To use this, you modify the caching code to use Spam._new() to create instances instead of the usual call to Spam(). For example:

```
import weakref

class CachedSpamManager:
    def __init__(self):
        self._cache = weakref.WeakValueDictionary()
    def get_spam(self, name):
        if name not in self._cache:
            s = Spam._new(name)        # Modified creation
```

```
            self._cache[name] = s
        else:
            s = self._cache[name]
    return s
```

Although there are more extreme measures that can be taken to hide the visibility of the Spam class, it's probably best to not overthink the problem. Using an underscore on the name or defining a class method constructor is usually enough for programmers to get a hint.

Caching and other creational patterns can often be solved in a more elegant (albeit advanced) manner through the use of metaclasses. See Recipe 9.13.

## CHAPTER 9

Metaprogramming

One of the most important mantras of software development is "don't repeat yourself." That is, any time you are faced with a problem of creating highly repetitive code (or cutting or pasting source code), it often pays to look for a more elegant solution. In Python, such problems are often solved under the category of "metaprogramming." In a nutshell, metaprogramming is about creating functions and classes whose main goal is to manipulate code (e.g., modifying, generating, or wrapping existing code). The main features for this include decorators, class decorators, and metaclasses. However, a variety of other useful topics—including signature objects, execution of code with exec(), and inspecting the internals of functions and classes—enter the picture. The main purpose of this chapter is to explore various metaprogramming techniques and to give examples of how they can be used to customize the behavior of Python to your own whims.

9.1. Putting a Wrapper Around a Function

Problem

You want to put a wrapper layer around a function that adds extra processing (e.g., logging, timing, etc.).

Solution

If you ever need to wrap a function with extra code, define a decorator function. For example:

```
import time
from functools import wraps

def timethis(func):
    '''
    Decorator that reports the execution time.
```

```
    '''
    @wraps(func)
    def wrapper(*args, **kwargs):
        start = time.time()
        result = func(*args, **kwargs)
        end = time.time()
        print(func.__name__, end-start)
        return result
    return wrapper
```

Here is an example of using the decorator:

```
>>> @timethis
... def countdown(n):
...     '''
...     Counts down
...     '''
...     while n > 0:
...             n -= 1
...
>>> countdown(100000)
countdown 0.008917808532714844
>>> countdown(10000000)
countdown 0.87188299392912
>>>
```

Discussion

A decorator is a function that accepts a function as input and returns a new function as output. Whenever you write code like this:

```
@timethis
def countdown(n):
    ...
```

it's the same as if you had performed these separate steps:

```
def countdown(n):
    ...
countdown = timethis(countdown)
```

As an aside, built-in decorators such as @staticmethod, @classmethod, and @proper ty work in the same way. For example, these two code fragments are equivalent:

```
class A:
    @classmethod
    def method(cls):
        pass

class B:
    # Equivalent definition of a class method
    def method(cls):
```

```
    pass
method = classmethod(method)
```

The code inside a decorator typically involves creating a new function that accepts any arguments using *args and **kwargs, as shown with the wrapper() function in this recipe. Inside this function, you place a call to the original input function and return its result. However, you also place whatever extra code you want to add (e.g., timing). The newly created function wrapper is returned as a result and takes the place of the original function.

It's critical to emphasize that decorators generally do not alter the calling signature or return value of the function being wrapped. The use of *args and **kwargs is there to make sure that any input arguments can be accepted. The return value of a decorator is almost always the result of calling func(*args, **kwargs), where func is the original unwrapped function.

When first learning about decorators, it is usually very easy to get started with some simple examples, such as the one shown. However, if you are going to write decorators for real, there are some subtle details to consider. For example, the use of the decorator @wraps(func) in the solution is an easy to forget but important technicality related to preserving function metadata, which is described in the next recipe. The next few recipes that follow fill in some details that will be important if you wish to write decorator functions of your own.

9.2. Preserving Function Metadata When Writing Decorators

Problem

You've written a decorator, but when you apply it to a function, important metadata such as the name, doc string, annotations, and calling signature are lost.

Solution

Whenever you define a decorator, you should always remember to apply the @wraps decorator from the functools library to the underlying wrapper function. For example:

```
import time
from functools import wraps

def timethis(func):
    '''
    Decorator that reports the execution time.
    '''
    @wraps(func)
    def wrapper(*args, **kwargs):
```

```
        start = time.time()
        result = func(*args, **kwargs)
        end = time.time()
        print(func.__name__, end-start)
        return result
    return wrapper
```

Here is an example of using the decorator and examining the resulting function metadata:

```
>>> @timethis
... def countdown(n:int):
...     '''
...     Counts down
...     '''
...     while n > 0:
...         n -= 1
...
>>> countdown(100000)
countdown 0.008917808532714844
>>> countdown.__name__
'countdown'
>>> countdown.__doc__
'\n\tCounts down\n\t'
>>> countdown.__annotations__
{'n': <class 'int'>}
>>>
```

Discussion

Copying decorator metadata is an important part of writing decorators. If you forget to use @wraps, you'll find that the decorated function loses all sorts of useful information. For instance, if omitted, the metadata in the last example would look like this:

```
>>> countdown.__name__
'wrapper'
>>> countdown.__doc__
>>> countdown.__annotations__
{}
>>>
```

An important feature of the @wraps decorator is that it makes the wrapped function available to you in the __wrapped__ attribute. For example, if you want to access the wrapped function directly, you could do this:

```
>>> countdown.__wrapped__(100000)
>>>
```

The presence of the __wrapped__ attribute also makes decorated functions properly expose the underlying signature of the wrapped function. For example:

```
>>> from inspect import signature
>>> print(signature(countdown))
(n:int)
>>>
```

One common question that sometimes arises is how to make a decorator that directly copies the calling signature of the original function being wrapped (as opposed to using *args and **kwargs). In general, this is difficult to implement without resorting to some trick involving the generator of code strings and exec(). Frankly, you're usually best off using @wraps and relying on the fact that the underlying function signature can be propagated by access to the underlying __wrapped__ attribute. See Recipe 9.16 for more information about signatures.

9.3. Unwrapping a Decorator

Problem

A decorator has been applied to a function, but you want to "undo" it, gaining access to the original unwrapped function.

Solution

Assuming that the decorator has been implemented properly using @wraps (see Recipe 9.2), you can usually gain access to the original function by accessing the __wrapped__ attribute. For example:

```
>>> @somedecorator
>>> def add(x, y):
...     return x + y
...
>>> orig_add = add.__wrapped__
>>> orig_add(3, 4)
7
>>>
```

Discussion

Gaining direct access to the unwrapped function behind a decorator can be useful for debugging, introspection, and other operations involving functions. However, this recipe only works if the implementation of a decorator properly copies metadata using @wraps from the functools module or sets the __wrapped__ attribute directly.

If multiple decorators have been applied to a function, the behavior of accessing __wrapped__ is currently undefined and should probably be avoided. In Python 3.3, it bypasses all of the layers. For example, suppose you have code like this:

```
from functools import wraps

def decorator1(func):
    @wraps(func)
    def wrapper(*args, **kwargs):
        print('Decorator 1')
        return func(*args, **kwargs)
    return wrapper

def decorator2(func):
    @wraps(func)
    def wrapper(*args, **kwargs):
        print('Decorator 2')
        return func(*args, **kwargs)
    return wrapper

@decorator1
@decorator2
def add(x, y):
    return x + y
```

Here is what happens when you call the decorated function and the original function through __wrapped__:

```
>>> add(2, 3)
Decorator 1
Decorator 2
5
>>> add.__wrapped__(2, 3)
5
>>>
```

However, this behavior has been reported as a bug (see *http://bugs.python.org/issue17482*) and may be changed to explose the proper decorator chain in a future release.

Last, but not least, be aware that not all decorators utilize @wraps, and thus, they may not work as described. In particular, the built-in decorators @staticmethod and @class method create descriptor objects that don't follow this convention (instead, they store the original function in a __func__ attribute). Your mileage may vary.

9.4. Defining a Decorator That Takes Arguments

Problem

You want to write a decorator function that takes arguments.

Solution

Let's illustrate the process of accepting arguments with an example. Suppose you want to write a decorator that adds logging to a function, but allows the user to specify the logging level and other details as arguments. Here is how you might define the decorator:

```
from functools import wraps
import logging

def logged(level, name=None, message=None):
    '''
    Add logging to a function.  level is the logging
    level, name is the logger name, and message is the
    log message.  If name and message aren't specified,
    they default to the function's module and name.
    '''
    def decorate(func):
        logname = name if name else func.__module__
        log = logging.getLogger(logname)
        logmsg = message if message else func.__name__

        @wraps(func)
        def wrapper(*args, **kwargs):
            log.log(level, logmsg)
            return func(*args, **kwargs)
        return wrapper
    return decorate

# Example use
@logged(logging.DEBUG)
def add(x, y):
    return x + y

@logged(logging.CRITICAL, 'example')
def spam():
    print('Spam!')
```

On first glance, the implementation looks tricky, but the idea is relatively simple. The outermost function `logged()` accepts the desired arguments and simply makes them available to the inner functions of the decorator. The inner function `decorate()` accepts a function and puts a wrapper around it as normal. The key part is that the wrapper is allowed to use the arguments passed to `logged()`.

Discussion

Writing a decorator that takes arguments is tricky because of the underlying calling sequence involved. Specifically, if you have code like this:

```
@decorator(x, y, z)
def func(a, b):
    pass
```

The decoration process evaluates as follows:

```
def func(a, b):
    pass

func = decorator(x, y, z)(func)
```

Carefully observe that the result of `decorator(x, y, z)` must be a callable which, in turn, takes a function as input and wraps it. See Recipe 9.7 for another example of a decorator taking arguments.

9.5. Defining a Decorator with User Adjustable Attributes

Problem

You want to write a decorator function that wraps a function, but has user adjustable attributes that can be used to control the behavior of the decorator at runtime.

Solution

Here is a solution that expands on the last recipe by introducing accessor functions that change internal variables through the use of `nonlocal` variable declarations. The accessor functions are then attached to the wrapper function as function attributes.

```
from functools import wraps, partial
import logging

# Utility decorator to attach a function as an attribute of obj
def attach_wrapper(obj, func=None):
    if func is None:
        return partial(attach_wrapper, obj)
    setattr(obj, func.__name__, func)
    return func

def logged(level, name=None, message=None):
    '''
    Add logging to a function.  level is the logging
    level, name is the logger name, and message is the
    log message.  If name and message aren't specified,
    they default to the function's module and name.
    '''
    def decorate(func):
        logname = name if name else func.__module__
        log = logging.getLogger(logname)
        logmsg = message if message else func.__name__

        @wraps(func)
        def wrapper(*args, **kwargs):
            log.log(level, logmsg)
            return func(*args, **kwargs)
```

```
        # Attach setter functions
        @attach_wrapper(wrapper)
        def set_level(newlevel):
            nonlocal level
            level = newlevel

        @attach_wrapper(wrapper)
        def set_message(newmsg):
            nonlocal logmsg
            logmsg = newmsg

        return wrapper
    return decorate

# Example use
@logged(logging.DEBUG)
def add(x, y):
    return x + y

@logged(logging.CRITICAL, 'example')
def spam():
    print('Spam!')
```

Here is an interactive session that shows the various attributes being changed after definition:

```
>>> import logging
>>> logging.basicConfig(level=logging.DEBUG)
>>> add(2, 3)
DEBUG:__main__:add
5

>>> # Change the log message
>>> add.set_message('Add called')
>>> add(2, 3)
DEBUG:__main__:Add called
5

>>> # Change the log level
>>> add.set_level(logging.WARNING)
>>> add(2, 3)
WARNING:__main__:Add called
5
>>>
```

Discussion

The key to this recipe lies in the accessor functions [e.g., `set_message()` and `set_lev el()`] that get attached to the wrapper as attributes. Each of these accessors allows internal parameters to be adjusted through the use of `nonlocal` assignments.

An amazing feature of this recipe is that the accessor functions will propagate through multiple levels of decoration (if all of your decorators utilize `@functools.wraps`). For example, suppose you introduced an additional decorator, such as the `@timethis` decorator from Recipe 9.2, and wrote code like this:

```
@timethis
@logged(logging.DEBUG)
def countdown(n):
    while n > 0:
        n -= 1
```

You'll find that the accessor methods still work:

```
>>> countdown(10000000)
DEBUG:__main__:countdown
countdown 0.8198461532592773
>>> countdown.set_level(logging.WARNING)
>>> countdown.set_message("Counting down to zero")
>>> countdown(10000000)
WARNING:__main__:Counting down to zero
countdown 0.8225970268249512
>>>
```

You'll also find that it all still works exactly the same way if the decorators are composed in the opposite order, like this:

```
@logged(logging.DEBUG)
@timethis
def countdown(n):
    while n > 0:
        n -= 1
```

Although it's not shown, accessor functions to return the value of various settings could also be written just as easily by adding extra code such as this:

```
...
@attach_wrapper(wrapper)
def get_level():
    return level

# Alternative
wrapper.get_level = lambda: level
...
```

One extremely subtle facet of this recipe is the choice to use accessor functions in the first place. For example, you might consider an alternative formulation solely based on direct access to function attributes like this:

```
    ...
    @wraps(func)
    def wrapper(*args, **kwargs):
        wrapper.log.log(wrapper.level, wrapper.logmsg)
        return func(*args, **kwargs)

    # Attach adjustable attributes
    wrapper.level = level
    wrapper.logmsg = logmsg
    wrapper.log = log
    ...
```

This approach would work to a point, but only if it was the topmost decorator. If you had another decorator applied on top (such as the @timethis example), it would shadow the underlying attributes and make them unavailable for modification. The use of accessor functions avoids this limitation.

Last, but not least, the solution shown in this recipe might be a possible alternative for decorators defined as classes, as shown in Recipe 9.9.

9.6. Defining a Decorator That Takes an Optional Argument

Problem

You would like to write a single decorator that can be used without arguments, such as @decorator, or with optional arguments, such as @decorator(x,y,z). However, there seems to be no straightforward way to do it due to differences in calling conventions between simple decorators and decorators taking arguments.

Solution

Here is a variant of the logging code shown in Recipe 9.5 that defines such a decorator:

```
from functools import wraps, partial
import logging

def logged(func=None, *, level=logging.DEBUG, name=None, message=None):
    if func is None:
        return partial(logged, level=level, name=name, message=message)

    logname = name if name else func.__module__
    log = logging.getLogger(logname)
    logmsg = message if message else func.__name__
```

```
    @wraps(func)
    def wrapper(*args, **kwargs):
        log.log(level, logmsg)
        return func(*args, **kwargs)
    return wrapper

# Example use
@logged
def add(x, y):
    return x + y

@logged(level=logging.CRITICAL, name='example')
def spam():
    print('Spam!')
```

As you can see from the example, the decorator can be used in both a simple form (i.e., @logged) or with optional arguments supplied (i.e., @logged(level=logging.CRITI CAL, name='example')).

Discussion

The problem addressed by this recipe is really one of programming consistency. When using decorators, most programmers are used to applying them without any arguments at all or with arguments, as shown in the example. Technically speaking, a decorator where all arguments are optional could be applied, like this:

```
@logged()
def add(x, y):
    return x+y
```

However, this is not a form that's especially common, and might lead to common usage errors if programmers forget to add the extra parentheses. The recipe simply makes the decorator work with or without parentheses in a consistent way.

To understand how the code works, you need to have a firm understanding of how decorators get applied to functions and their calling conventions. For a simple decorator such as this:

```
# Example use
@logged
def add(x, y):
    return x + y
```

The calling sequence is as follows:

```
def add(x, y):
    return x + y
add = logged(add)
```

In this case, the function to be wrapped is simply passed to logged as the first argument. Thus, in the solution, the first argument of logged() is the function being wrapped. All of the other arguments must have default values.

For a decorator taking arguments such as this:

```
@logged(level=logging.CRITICAL, name='example')
def spam():
    print('Spam!')
```

The calling sequence is as follows:

```
def spam():
    print('Spam!')
spam = logged(level=logging.CRITICAL, name='example')(spam)
```

On the initial invocation of logged(), the function to be wrapped is not passed. Thus, in the decorator, it has to be optional. This, in turn, forces the other arguments to be specified by keyword. Furthermore, when arguments are passed, a decorator is supposed to return a function that accepts the function and wraps it (see Recipe 9.5). To do this, the solution uses a clever trick involving functools.partial. Specifically, it simply returns a partially applied version of itself where all arguments are fixed except for the function to be wrapped. See Recipe 7.8 for more details about using partial().

9.7. Enforcing Type Checking on a Function Using a Decorator

Problem

You want to optionally enforce type checking of function arguments as a kind of assertion or contract.

Solution

Before showing the solution code, the aim of this recipe is to have a means of enforcing type contracts on the input arguments to a function. Here is a short example that illustrates the idea:

```
>>> @typeassert(int, int)
... def add(x, y):
...     return x + y
...
>>>
>>> add(2, 3)
5
>>> add(2, 'hello')
Traceback (most recent call last):
  File "<stdin>", line 1, in <module>
```

```
    File "contract.py", line 33, in wrapper
TypeError: Argument y must be <class 'int'>
>>>
```

Now, here is an implementation of the @typeassert decorator:

```
from inspect import signature
from functools import wraps

def typeassert(*ty_args, **ty_kwargs):
    def decorate(func):
        # If in optimized mode, disable type checking
        if not __debug__:
            return func

        # Map function argument names to supplied types
        sig = signature(func)
        bound_types = sig.bind_partial(*ty_args, **ty_kwargs).arguments

        @wraps(func)
        def wrapper(*args, **kwargs):
            bound_values = sig.bind(*args, **kwargs)
            # Enforce type assertions across supplied arguments
            for name, value in bound_values.arguments.items():
                if name in bound_types:
                    if not isinstance(value, bound_types[name]):
                        raise TypeError(
                            'Argument {} must be {}'.format(name, bound_types[name])
                        )
            return func(*args, **kwargs)
        return wrapper
    return decorate
```

You will find that this decorator is rather flexible, allowing types to be specified for all or a subset of a function's arguments. Moreover, types can be specified by position or by keyword. Here is an example:

```
>>> @typeassert(int, z=int)
... def spam(x, y, z=42):
...     print(x, y, z)
...
>>> spam(1, 2, 3)
1 2 3
>>> spam(1, 'hello', 3)
1 hello 3
>>> spam(1, 'hello', 'world')
Traceback (most recent call last):
  File "<stdin>", line 1, in <module>
  File "contract.py", line 33, in wrapper
TypeError: Argument z must be <class 'int'>
>>>
```

Discussion

This recipe is an advanced decorator example that introduces a number of important and useful concepts.

First, one aspect of decorators is that they only get applied once, at the time of function definition. In certain cases, you may want to disable the functionality added by a decorator. To do this, simply have your decorator function return the function unwrapped. In the solution, the following code fragment returns the function unmodified if the value of the global __debug__ variable is set to False (as is the case when Python executes in optimized mode with the -O or -OO options to the interpreter):

```
...
def decorate(func):
    # If in optimized mode, disable type checking
    if not __debug__:
        return func
    ...
```

Next, a tricky part of writing this decorator is that it involves examining and working with the argument signature of the function being wrapped. Your tool of choice here should be the inspect.signature() function. Simply stated, it allows you to extract signature information from a callable. For example:

```
>>> from inspect import signature
>>> def spam(x, y, z=42):
...     pass
...
>>> sig = signature(spam)
>>> print(sig)
(x, y, z=42)
>>> sig.parameters
mappingproxy(OrderedDict([('x', <Parameter at 0x10077a050 'x'>),
('y', <Parameter at 0x10077a158 'y'>), ('z', <Parameter at 0x10077a1b0 'z'>)]))
>>> sig.parameters['z'].name
'z'
>>> sig.parameters['z'].default
42
>>> sig.parameters['z'].kind
<_ParameterKind: 'POSITIONAL_OR_KEYWORD'>
>>>
```

In the first part of our decorator, we use the bind_partial() method of signatures to perform a partial binding of the supplied types to argument names. Here is an example of what happens:

```
>>> bound_types = sig.bind_partial(int,z=int)
>>> bound_types
<inspect.BoundArguments object at 0x10069bb50>
>>> bound_types.arguments
```

```
OrderedDict([('x', <class 'int'>), ('z', <class 'int'>)])
>>>
```

In this partial binding, you will notice that missing arguments are simply ignored (i.e., there is no binding for argument y). However, the most important part of the binding is the creation of the ordered dictionary bound_types.arguments. This dictionary maps the argument names to the supplied values in the same order as the function signature. In the case of our decorator, this mapping contains the type assertions that we're going to enforce.

In the actual wrapper function made by the decorator, the sig.bind() method is used. bind() is like bind_partial() except that it does not allow for missing arguments. So, here is what happens:

```
>>> bound_values = sig.bind(1, 2, 3)
>>> bound_values.arguments
OrderedDict([('x', 1), ('y', 2), ('z', 3)])
>>>
```

Using this mapping, it is relatively easy to enforce the required assertions.

```
>>> for name, value in bound_values.arguments.items():
...     if name in bound_types.arguments:
...         if not isinstance(value, bound_types.arguments[name]):
...             raise TypeError()
...
>>>
```

A somewhat subtle aspect of the solution is that the assertions do not get applied to unsupplied arguments with default values. For example, this code works, even though the default value of items is of the "wrong" type:

```
>>> @typeassert(int, list)
... def bar(x, items=None):
...     if items is None:
...         items = []
...     items.append(x)
...     return items
>>> bar(2)
[2]
>>> bar(2,3)
Traceback (most recent call last):
  File "<stdin>", line 1, in <module>
  File "contract.py", line 33, in wrapper
TypeError: Argument items must be <class 'list'>
>>> bar(4, [1, 2, 3])
[1, 2, 3, 4]
>>>
```

A final point of design discussion might be the use of decorator arguments versus function annotations. For example, why not write the decorator to look at annotations like this?

```
@typeassert
def spam(x:int, y, z:int = 42):
    print(x,y,z)
```

One possible reason for not using annotations is that each argument to a function can only have a single annotation assigned. Thus, if the annotations are used for type assertions, they can't really be used for anything else. Likewise, the `@typeassert` decorator won't work with functions that use annotations for a different purpose. By using decorator arguments, as shown in the solution, the decorator becomes a lot more general purpose and can be used with any function whatsoever—even functions that use annotations.

More information about function signature objects can be found in PEP 362 (*http://www.python.org/dev/peps/pep-0362*), as well as the documentation for the `inspect` module (*http://docs.python.org/3/library/inspect.html*). Recipe 9.16 also has an additional example.

9.8. Defining Decorators As Part of a Class

Problem

You want to define a decorator inside a class definition and apply it to other functions or methods.

Solution

Defining a decorator inside a class is straightforward, but you first need to sort out the manner in which the decorator will be applied. Specifically, whether it is applied as an instance or a class method. Here is an example that illustrates the difference:

```
from functools import wraps

class A:
    # Decorator as an instance method
    def decorator1(self, func):
        @wraps(func)
        def wrapper(*args, **kwargs):
            print('Decorator 1')
            return func(*args, **kwargs)
        return wrapper

    # Decorator as a class method
    @classmethod
    def decorator2(cls, func):
        @wraps(func)
        def wrapper(*args, **kwargs):
            print('Decorator 2')
```

```
        return func(*args, **kwargs)
    return wrapper
```

Here is an example of how the two decorators would be applied:

```
# As an instance method
a = A()

@a.decorator1
def spam():
    pass

# As a class method
@A.decorator2
def grok():
    pass
```

If you look carefully, you'll notice that one is applied from an instance a and the other is applied from the class A.

Discussion

Defining decorators in a class might look odd at first glance, but there are examples of this in the standard library. In particular, the built-in @property decorator is actually a class with getter(), setter(), and deleter() methods that each act as a decorator. For example:

```
class Person:
    # Create a property instance
    first_name = property()

    # Apply decorator methods
    @first_name.getter
    def first_name(self):
        return self._first_name

    @first_name.setter
    def first_name(self, value):
        if not isinstance(value, str):
            raise TypeError('Expected a string')
        self._first_name = value
```

The key reason why it's defined in this way is that the various decorator methods are manipulating state on the associated property instance. So, if you ever had a problem where decorators needed to record or combine information behind the scenes, it's a sensible approach.

A common confusion when writing decorators in classes is getting tripped up by the proper use of the extra self or cls arguments in the decorator code itself. Although the outermost decorator function, such as decorator1() or decorator2(), needs to

---

provide a self or cls argument (since they're part of a class), the wrapper function created inside doesn't generally need to include an extra argument. This is why the `wrapper()` function created in both decorators doesn't include a self argument. The only time you would ever need this argument is in situations where you actually needed to access parts of an instance in the wrapper. Otherwise, you just don't have to worry about it.

A final subtle facet of having decorators defined in a class concerns their potential use with inheritance. For example, suppose you want to apply one of the decorators defined in class A to methods defined in a subclass B. To do that, you would need to write code like this:

```
class B(A):
    @A.decorator2
    def bar(self):
        pass
```

In particular, the decorator in question has to be defined as a class method and you have to explicitly use the name of the superclass A when applying it. You can't use a name such as `@B.decorator2`, because at the time of method definition, class B has not yet been created.

9.9. Defining Decorators As Classes

Problem

You want to wrap functions with a decorator, but the result is going to be a callable instance. You need your decorator to work both inside and outside class definitions.

Solution

To define a decorator as an instance, you need to make sure it implements the `__call__()` and `__get__()` methods. For example, this code defines a class that puts a simple profiling layer around another function:

```
import types
from functools import wraps

class Profiled:
    def __init__(self, func):
        wraps(func)(self)
        self.ncalls = 0

    def __call__(self, *args, **kwargs):
        self.ncalls += 1
        return self.__wrapped__(*args, **kwargs)
```

```
    def __get__(self, instance, cls):
        if instance is None:
            return self
        else:
            return types.MethodType(self, instance)
```

To use this class, you use it like a normal decorator, either inside or outside of a class:

```
@Profiled
def add(x, y):
    return x + y

class Spam:
    @Profiled
    def bar(self, x):
        print(self, x)
```

Here is an interactive session that shows how these functions work:

```
>>> add(2, 3)
5
>>> add(4, 5)
9
>>> add.ncalls
2
>>> s = Spam()
>>> s.bar(1)
<__main__.Spam object at 0x10069e9d0> 1
>>> s.bar(2)
<__main__.Spam object at 0x10069e9d0> 2
>>> s.bar(3)
<__main__.Spam object at 0x10069e9d0> 3
>>> Spam.bar.ncalls
3
```

Discussion

Defining a decorator as a class is usually straightforward. However, there are some rather subtle details that deserve more explanation, especially if you plan to apply the decorator to instance methods.

First, the use of the functools.wraps() function serves the same purpose here as it does in normal decorators—namely to copy important metadata from the wrapped function to the callable instance.

Second, it is common to overlook the __get__() method shown in the solution. If you omit the __get__() and keep all of the other code the same, you'll find that bizarre things happen when you try to invoke decorated instance methods. For example:

```
>>> s = Spam()
>>> s.bar(3)
Traceback (most recent call last):
```

```
...
TypeError: spam() missing 1 required positional argument: 'x'
```

The reason it breaks is that whenever functions implementing methods are looked up in a class, their __get__() method is invoked as part of the descriptor protocol, which is described in Recipe 8.9. In this case, the purpose of __get__() is to create a bound method object (which ultimately supplies the self argument to the method). Here is an example that illustrates the underlying mechanics:

```
>>> s = Spam()
>>> def grok(self, x):
...     pass
...
>>> grok.__get__(s, Spam)
<bound method Spam.grok of <__main__.Spam object at 0x100671e90>>
>>>
```

In this recipe, the __get__() method is there to make sure bound method objects get created properly. type.MethodType() creates a bound method manually for use here. Bound methods only get created if an instance is being used. If the method is accessed on a class, the instance argument to __get__() is set to None and the Profiled instance itself is just returned. This makes it possible for someone to extract its ncalls attribute, as shown.

If you want to avoid some of this of this mess, you might consider an alternative formulation of the decorator using closures and nonlocal variables, as described in Recipe 9.5. For example:

```
import types
from functools import wraps

def profiled(func):
    ncalls = 0
    @wraps(func)
    def wrapper(*args, **kwargs):
        nonlocal ncalls
        ncalls += 1
        return func(*args, **kwargs)
    wrapper.ncalls = lambda: ncalls
    return wrapper

# Example
@profiled
def add(x, y):
    return x + y
```

This example almost works in exactly the same way except that access to ncalls is now provided through a function attached as a function attribute. For example:

```
>>> add(2, 3)
5
```

```
>>> add(4, 5)
9
>>> add.ncalls()
2
>>>
```

9.10. Applying Decorators to Class and Static Methods

Problem

You want to apply a decorator to a class or static method.

Solution

Applying decorators to class and static methods is straightforward, but make sure that your decorators are applied before @classmethod or @staticmethod. For example:

```python
import time
from functools import wraps

# A simple decorator
def timethis(func):
    @wraps(func)
    def wrapper(*args, **kwargs):
        start = time.time()
        r = func(*args, **kwargs)
        end = time.time()
        print(end-start)
        return r
    return wrapper

# Class illustrating application of the decorator to different kinds of methods
class Spam:
    @timethis
    def instance_method(self, n):
        print(self, n)
        while n > 0:
            n -= 1

    @classmethod
    @timethis
    def class_method(cls, n):
        print(cls, n)
        while n > 0:
            n -= 1

    @staticmethod
    @timethis
    def static_method(n):
        print(n)
```

```
    while n > 0:
        n -= 1
```

The resulting class and static methods should operate normally, but have the extra timing:

```
>>> s = Spam()
>>> s.instance_method(1000000)
<__main__.Spam object at 0x1006a6050> 1000000
0.11817407608032227
>>> Spam.class_method(1000000)
<class '__main__.Spam'> 1000000
0.11334395408630371
>>> Spam.static_method(1000000)
1000000
0.11740279197692871
>>>
```

Discussion

If you get the order of decorators wrong, you'll get an error. For example, if you use the following:

```
class Spam:
    ...
    @timethis
    @staticmethod
    def static_method(n):
        print(n)
        while n > 0:
            n -= 1
```

Then the static method will crash:

```
>>> Spam.static_method(1000000)
Traceback (most recent call last):
  File "<stdin>", line 1, in <module>
  File "timethis.py", line 6, in wrapper
    start = time.time()
TypeError: 'staticmethod' object is not callable
>>>
```

The problem here is that @classmethod and @staticmethod don't actually create objects that are directly callable. Instead, they create special descriptor objects, as described in Recipe 8.9. Thus, if you try to use them like functions in another decorator, the decorator will crash. Making sure that these decorators appear first in the decorator list fixes the problem.

One situation where this recipe is of critical importance is in defining class and static methods in abstract base classes, as described in Recipe 8.12. For example, if you want to define an abstract class method, you can use this code:

```
from abc import ABCMeta, abstractmethod

class A(metaclass=ABCMeta):
    @classmethod
    @abstractmethod
    def method(cls):
        pass
```

In this code, the order of @classmethod and @abstractmethod matters. If you flip the two decorators around, everything breaks.

9.11. Writing Decorators That Add Arguments to Wrapped Functions

Problem

You want to write a decorator that adds an extra argument to the calling signature of the wrapped function. However, the added argument can't interfere with the existing calling conventions of the function.

Solution

Extra arguments can be injected into the calling signature using keyword-only arguments. Consider the following decorator:

```
from functools import wraps

def optional_debug(func):
    @wraps(func)
    def wrapper(*args, debug=False, **kwargs):
        if debug:
            print('Calling', func.__name__)
        return func(*args, **kwargs)
    return wrapper
```

Here is an example of how the decorator works:

```
>>> @optional_debug
... def spam(a,b,c):
...     print(a,b,c)
...
>>> spam(1,2,3)
1 2 3
>>> spam(1,2,3, debug=True)
Calling spam
1 2 3
>>>
```

Discussion

Adding arguments to the signature of wrapped functions is not the most common example of using decorators. However, it might be a useful technique in avoiding certain kinds of code replication patterns. For example, if you have code like this:

```python
def a(x, debug=False):
    if debug:
        print('Calling a')
    ...

def b(x, y, z, debug=False):
    if debug:
        print('Calling b')
    ...

def c(x, y, debug=False):
    if debug:
        print('Calling c')
    ...
```

You can refactor it into the following:

```python
@optional_debug
def a(x):
    ...

@optional_debug
def b(x, y, z):
    ...

@optional_debug
def c(x, y):
    ...
```

The implementation of this recipe relies on the fact that keyword-only arguments are easy to add to functions that also accept *args and **kwargs parameters. By using a keyword-only argument, it gets singled out as a special case and removed from subsequent calls that only use the remaining positional and keyword arguments.

One tricky part here concerns a potential name clash between the added argument and the arguments of the function being wrapped. For example, if the @optional_debug decorator was applied to a function that already had a debug argument, then it would break. If that's a concern, an extra check could be added:

```python
from functools import wraps
import inspect

def optional_debug(func):
    if 'debug' in inspect.getargspec(func).args:
        raise TypeError('debug argument already defined')
```

```
    @wraps(func)
    def wrapper(*args, debug=False, **kwargs):
        if debug:
            print('Calling', func.__name__)
        return func(*args, **kwargs)
    return wrapper
```

A final refinement to this recipe concerns the proper management of function signatures. An astute programmer will realize that the signature of wrapped functions is wrong. For example:

```
>>> @optional_debug
... def add(x,y):
...     return x+y
...
>>> import inspect
>>> print(inspect.signature(add))
(x, y)
>>>
```

This can be fixed by making the following modification:

```
from functools import wraps
import inspect

def optional_debug(func):
    if 'debug' in inspect.getargspec(func).args:
        raise TypeError('debug argument already defined')

    @wraps(func)
    def wrapper(*args, debug=False, **kwargs):
        if debug:
            print('Calling', func.__name__)
        return func(*args, **kwargs)

    sig = inspect.signature(func)
    parms = list(sig.parameters.values())
    parms.append(inspect.Parameter('debug',
                                   inspect.Parameter.KEYWORD_ONLY,
                                   default=False))
    wrapper.__signature__ = sig.replace(parameters=parms)
    return wrapper
```

With this change, the signature of the wrapper will now correctly reflect the presence of the debug argument. For example:

```
>>> @optional_debug
... def add(x,y):
...     return x+y
...
>>> print(inspect.signature(add))
(x, y, *, debug=False)
>>> add(2,3)
```

```
        5
>>>
```

See Recipe 9.16 for more information about function signatures.

9.12. Using Decorators to Patch Class Definitions

Problem

You want to inspect or rewrite portions of a class definition to alter its behavior, but without using inheritance or metaclasses.

Solution

This might be a perfect use for a class decorator. For example, here is a class decorator that rewrites the __getattribute__ special method to perform logging.

```
def log_getattribute(cls):
    # Get the original implementation
    orig_getattribute = cls.__getattribute__

    # Make a new definition
    def new_getattribute(self, name):
        print('getting:', name)
        return orig_getattribute(self, name)

    # Attach to the class and return
    cls.__getattribute__ = new_getattribute
    return cls

# Example use
@log_getattribute
class A:
    def __init__(self,x):
        self.x = x
    def spam(self):
        pass
```

Here is what happens if you try to use the class in the solution:

```
>>> a = A(42)
>>> a.x
getting: x
42
>>> a.spam()
getting: spam
>>>
```

Discussion

Class decorators can often be used as a straightforward alternative to other more advanced techniques involving mixins or metaclasses. For example, an alternative implementation of the solution might involve inheritance, as in the following:

```python
class LoggedGetattribute:
    def __getattribute__(self, name):
        print('getting:', name)
        return super().__getattribute__(name)

# Example:
class A(LoggedGetattribute):
    def __init__(self,x):
        self.x = x
    def spam(self):
        pass
```

This works, but to understand it, you have to have some awareness of the method resolution order, super(), and other aspects of inheritance, as described in Recipe 8.7. In some sense, the class decorator solution is much more direct in how it operates, and it doesn't introduce new dependencies into the inheritance hierarchy. As it turns out, it's also just a bit faster, due to not relying on the super() function.

If you are applying multiple class decorators to a class, the application order might matter. For example, a decorator that replaces a method with an entirely new implementation would probably need to be applied before a decorator that simply wraps an existing method with some extra logic.

See Recipe 8.13 for another example of class decorators in action.

9.13. Using a Metaclass to Control Instance Creation

Problem

You want to change the way in which instances are created in order to implement singletons, caching, or other similar features.

Solution

As Python programmers know, if you define a class, you call it like a function to create instances. For example:

```python
class Spam:
    def __init__(self, name):
        self.name = name

a = Spam('Guido')
b = Spam('Diana')
```

If you want to customize this step, you can do it by defining a metaclass and reimplementing its __call__() method in some way. To illustrate, suppose that you didn't want anyone creating instances at all:

```
class NoInstances(type):
    def __call__(self, *args, **kwargs):
        raise TypeError("Can't instantiate directly")

# Example
class Spam(metaclass=NoInstances):
    @staticmethod
    def grok(x):
        print('Spam.grok')
```

In this case, users can call the defined static method, but it's impossible to create an instance in the normal way. For example:

```
>>> Spam.grok(42)
Spam.grok
>>> s = Spam()
Traceback (most recent call last):
  File "<stdin>", line 1, in <module>
  File "example1.py", line 7, in __call__
    raise TypeError("Can't instantiate directly")
TypeError: Can't instantiate directly
>>>
```

Now, suppose you want to implement the singleton pattern (i.e., a class where only one instance is ever created). That is also relatively straightforward, as shown here:

```
class Singleton(type):
    def __init__(self, *args, **kwargs):
        self.__instance = None
        super().__init__(*args, **kwargs)

    def __call__(self, *args, **kwargs):
        if self.__instance is None:
            self.__instance = super().__call__(*args, **kwargs)
            return self.__instance
        else:
            return self.__instance

# Example
class Spam(metaclass=Singleton):
    def __init__(self):
        print('Creating Spam')
```

In this case, only one instance ever gets created. For example:

```
>>> a = Spam()
Creating Spam
>>> b = Spam()
>>> a is b
```

```
True
>>> c = Spam()
>>> a is c
True
>>>
```

Finally, suppose you want to create cached instances, as described in Recipe 8.25. Here's a metaclass that implements it:

```python
import weakref

class Cached(type):
    def __init__(self, *args, **kwargs):
        super().__init__(*args, **kwargs)
        self.__cache = weakref.WeakValueDictionary()

    def __call__(self, *args):
        if args in self.__cache:
            return self.__cache[args]
        else:
            obj = super().__call__(*args)
            self.__cache[args] = obj
            return obj

# Example
class Spam(metaclass=Cached):
    def __init__(self, name):
        print('Creating Spam({!r})'.format(name))
        self.name = name
```

Here's an example showing the behavior of this class:

```
>>> a = Spam('Guido')
Creating Spam('Guido')
>>> b = Spam('Diana')
Creating Spam('Diana')
>>> c = Spam('Guido')          # Cached
>>> a is b
False
>>> a is c                     # Cached value returned
True
>>>
```

Discussion

Using a metaclass to implement various instance creation patterns can often be a much more elegant approach than other solutions not involving metaclasses. For example, if you didn't use a metaclass, you might have to hide the classes behind some kind of extra factory function. For example, to get a singleton, you might use a hack such as the following:

```
class _Spam:
    def __init__(self):
        print('Creating Spam')

_spam_instance = None
def Spam():
    global _spam_instance
    if _spam_instance is not None:
        return _spam_instance
    else:
        _spam_instance = _Spam()
        return _spam_instance
```

Although the solution involving metaclasses involves a much more advanced concept, the resulting code feels cleaner and less hacked together.

See Recipe 8.25 for more information on creating cached instances, weak references, and other details.

9.14. Capturing Class Attribute Definition Order

Problem

You want to automatically record the order in which attributes and methods are defined inside a class body so that you can use it in various operations (e.g., serializing, mapping to databases, etc.).

Solution

Capturing information about the body of class definition is easily accomplished through the use of a metaclass. Here is an example of a metaclass that uses an OrderedDict to capture definition order of descriptors:

```
from collections import OrderedDict

# A set of descriptors for various types
class Typed:
    _expected_type = type(None)
    def __init__(self, name=None):
        self._name = name

    def __set__(self, instance, value):
        if not isinstance(value, self._expected_type):
            raise TypeError('Expected ' + str(self._expected_type))
        instance.__dict__[self._name] = value

class Integer(Typed):
    _expected_type = int
```

```
class Float(Typed):
    _expected_type = float

class String(Typed):
    _expected_type = str

# Metaclass that uses an OrderedDict for class body
class OrderedMeta(type):
    def __new__(cls, clsname, bases, clsdict):
        d = dict(clsdict)
        order = []
        for name, value in clsdict.items():
            if isinstance(value, Typed):
                value._name = name
                order.append(name)
        d['_order'] = order
        return type.__new__(cls, clsname, bases, d)

    @classmethod
    def __prepare__(cls, clsname, bases):
        return OrderedDict()
```

In this metaclass, the definition order of descriptors is captured by using an Ordered
Dict during the execution of the class body. The resulting order of names is then extracted from the dictionary and stored into a class attribute _order. This can then be
used by methods of the class in various ways. For example, here is a simple class that
uses the ordering to implement a method for serializing the instance data as a line of
CSV data:

```
class Structure(metaclass=OrderedMeta):
    def as_csv(self):
        return ','.join(str(getattr(self,name)) for name in self._order)

# Example use
class Stock(Structure):
    name = String()
    shares = Integer()
    price = Float()
    def __init__(self, name, shares, price):
        self.name = name
        self.shares = shares
        self.price = price
```

Here is an interactive session illustrating the use of the Stock class in the example:

```
>>> s = Stock('GOOG',100,490.1)
>>> s.name
'GOOG'
>>> s.as_csv()
'GOOG,100,490.1'
>>> t = Stock('AAPL','a lot', 610.23)
Traceback (most recent call last):
```

```
    File "<stdin>", line 1, in <module>
    File "dupmethod.py", line 34, in __init__
TypeError: shares expects <class 'int'>
>>>
```

Discussion

The entire key to this recipe is the __prepare__() method, which is defined in the OrderedMeta metaclass. This method is invoked immediately at the start of a class definition with the class name and base classes. It must then return a mapping object to use when processing the class body. By returning an OrderedDict instead of a normal dictionary, the resulting definition order is easily captured.

It is possible to extend this functionality even further if you are willing to make your own dictionary-like objects. For example, consider this variant of the solution that rejects duplicate definitions:

```python
from collections import OrderedDict

class NoDupOrderedDict(OrderedDict):
    def __init__(self, clsname):
        self.clsname = clsname
        super().__init__()
    def __setitem__(self, name, value):
        if name in self:
            raise TypeError('{} already defined in {}'.format(name, self.clsname))
        super().__setitem__(name, value)

class OrderedMeta(type):
    def __new__(cls, clsname, bases, clsdict):
        d = dict(clsdict)
        d['_order'] = [name for name in clsdict if name[0] != '_']
        return type.__new__(cls, clsname, bases, d)

    @classmethod
    def __prepare__(cls, clsname, bases):
        return NoDupOrderedDict(clsname)
```

Here's what happens if you use this metaclass and make a class with duplicate entries:

```
>>> class A(metaclass=OrderedMeta):
...     def spam(self):
...             pass
...     def spam(self):
...             pass
...
Traceback (most recent call last):
  File "<stdin>", line 1, in <module>
  File "<stdin>", line 4, in A
  File "dupmethod2.py", line 25, in __setitem__
    (name, self.clsname))
```

```
TypeError: spam already defined in A
>>>
```

A final important part of this recipe concerns the treatment of the modified dictionary in the metaclass __new__() method. Even though the class was defined using an alternative dictionary, you still have to convert this dictionary to a proper dict instance when making the final class object. This is the purpose of the d = dict(clsdict) statement.

Being able to capture definition order is a subtle but important feature for certain kinds of applications. For instance, in an object relational mapper, classes might be written in a manner similar to that shown in the example:

```
class Stock(Model):
    name = String()
    shares = Integer()
    price = Float()
```

Underneath the covers, the code might want to capture the definition order to map objects to tuples or rows in a database table (e.g., similar to the functionality of the as_csv() method in the example). The solution shown is very straightforward and often simpler than alternative approaches (which typically involve maintaining hidden counters within the descriptor classes).

9.15. Defining a Metaclass That Takes Optional Arguments

Problem

You want to define a metaclass that allows class definitions to supply optional arguments, possibly to control or configure aspects of processing during type creation.

Solution

When defining classes, Python allows a metaclass to be specified using the metaclass keyword argument in the class statement. For example, with abstract base classes:

```
from abc import ABCMeta, abstractmethod

class IStream(metaclass=ABCMeta):
    @abstractmethod
    def read(self, maxsize=None):
        pass

    @abstractmethod
    def write(self, data):
        pass
```

However, in custom metaclasses, additional keyword arguments can be supplied, like this:

```
class Spam(metaclass=MyMeta, debug=True, synchronize=True):
    ...
```

To support such keyword arguments in a metaclass, make sure you define them on the __prepare__(), __new__(), and __init__() methods using keyword-only arguments, like this:

```
class MyMeta(type):
    # Optional
    @classmethod
    def __prepare__(cls, name, bases, *, debug=False, synchronize=False):
        # Custom processing
        ...
        return super().__prepare__(name, bases)

    # Required
    def __new__(cls, name, bases, ns, *, debug=False, synchronize=False):
        # Custom processing
        ...
        return super().__new__(cls, name, bases, ns)

    # Required
    def __init__(self, name, bases, ns, *, debug=False, synchronize=False):
        # Custom processing
        ...
        super().__init__(name, bases, ns)
```

Discussion

Adding optional keyword arguments to a metaclass requires that you understand all of the steps involved in class creation, because the extra arguments are passed to every method involved. The __prepare__() method is called first and used to create the class namespace prior to the body of any class definition being processed. Normally, this method simply returns a dictionary or other mapping object. The __new__() method is used to instantiate the resulting type object. It is called after the class body has been fully executed. The __init__() method is called last and used to perform any additional initialization steps.

When writing metaclasses, it is somewhat common to only define a __new__() or __init__() method, but not both. However, if extra keyword arguments are going to be accepted, then both methods must be provided and given compatible signatures. The default __prepare__() method accepts any set of keyword arguments, but ignores them. You only need to define it yourself if the extra arguments would somehow affect management of the class namespace creation.

The use of keyword-only arguments in this recipe reflects the fact that such arguments will only be supplied by keyword during class creation.

The specification of keyword arguments to configure a metaclass might be viewed as an alternative to using class variables for a similar purpose. For example:

```
class Spam(metaclass=MyMeta):
    debug = True
    synchronize = True
    ...
```

The advantage to supplying such parameters as an argument is that they don't pollute the class namespace with extra names that only pertain to class creation and not the subsequent execution of statements in the class. In addition, they are available to the __prepare__() method, which runs prior to processing any statements in the class body. Class variables, on the other hand, would only be accessible in the __new__() and __init__() methods of a metaclass.

9.16. Enforcing an Argument Signature on *args and **kwargs

Problem

You've written a function or method that uses *args and **kwargs, so that it can be general purpose, but you would also like to check the passed arguments to see if they match a specific function calling signature.

Solution

For any problem where you want to manipulate function calling signatures, you should use the signature features found in the inspect module. Two classes, Signature and Parameter, are of particular interest here. Here is an interactive example of creating a function signature:

```
>>> from inspect import Signature, Parameter
>>> # Make a signature for a func(x, y=42, *, z=None)
>>> parms = [ Parameter('x', Parameter.POSITIONAL_OR_KEYWORD),
...           Parameter('y', Parameter.POSITIONAL_OR_KEYWORD, default=42),
...           Parameter('z', Parameter.KEYWORD_ONLY, default=None) ]
>>> sig = Signature(parms)
>>> print(sig)
(x, y=42, *, z=None)
>>>
```

Once you have a signature object, you can easily bind it to *args and **kwargs using the signature's bind() method, as shown in this simple example:

```
>>> def func(*args, **kwargs):
...     bound_values = sig.bind(*args, **kwargs)
...     for name, value in bound_values.arguments.items():
...         print(name,value)
...
>>> # Try various examples
>>> func(1, 2, z=3)
x 1
y 2
z 3
>>> func(1)
x 1
>>> func(1, z=3)
x 1
z 3
>>> func(y=2, x=1)
x 1
y 2
>>> func(1, 2, 3, 4)
Traceback (most recent call last):
...
  File "/usr/local/lib/python3.3/inspect.py", line 1972, in _bind
    raise TypeError('too many positional arguments')
TypeError: too many positional arguments
>>> func(y=2)
Traceback (most recent call last):
...
  File "/usr/local/lib/python3.3/inspect.py", line 1961, in _bind
    raise TypeError(msg) from None
TypeError: 'x' parameter lacking default value
>>> func(1, y=2, x=3)
Traceback (most recent call last):
...
  File "/usr/local/lib/python3.3/inspect.py", line 1985, in _bind
    '{arg!r}'.format(arg=param.name))
TypeError: multiple values for argument 'x'
>>>
```

As you can see, the binding of a signature to the passed arguments enforces all of the usual function calling rules concerning required arguments, defaults, duplicates, and so forth.

Here is a more concrete example of enforcing function signatures. In this code, a base class has defined an extremely general-purpose version of __init__(), but subclasses are expected to supply an expected signature.

```
from inspect import Signature, Parameter

def make_sig(*names):
    parms = [Parameter(name, Parameter.POSITIONAL_OR_KEYWORD)
             for name in names]
    return Signature(parms)
```

```
class Structure:
    __signature__ = make_sig()
    def __init__(self, *args, **kwargs):
        bound_values = self.__signature__.bind(*args, **kwargs)
        for name, value in bound_values.arguments.items():
            setattr(self, name, value)

# Example use
class Stock(Structure):
    __signature__ = make_sig('name', 'shares', 'price')

class Point(Structure):
    __signature__ = make_sig('x', 'y')
```

Here is an example of how the Stock class works:

```
>>> import inspect
>>> print(inspect.signature(Stock))
(name, shares, price)
>>> s1 = Stock('ACME', 100, 490.1)
>>> s2 = Stock('ACME', 100)
Traceback (most recent call last):
...
TypeError: 'price' parameter lacking default value
>>> s3 = Stock('ACME', 100, 490.1, shares=50)
Traceback (most recent call last):
...
TypeError: multiple values for argument 'shares'
>>>
```

Discussion

The use of functions involving *args and **kwargs is very common when trying to make general-purpose libraries, write decorators or implement proxies. However, one downside of such functions is that if you want to implement your own argument checking, it can quickly become an unwieldy mess. As an example, see Recipe 8.11. The use of a signature object simplifies this.

In the last example of the solution, it might make sense to create signature objects through the use of a custom metaclass. Here is an alternative implementation that shows how to do this:

```
from inspect import Signature, Parameter

def make_sig(*names):
    parms = [Parameter(name, Parameter.POSITIONAL_OR_KEYWORD)
                for name in names]
    return Signature(parms)

class StructureMeta(type):
```

```
    def __new__(cls, clsname, bases, clsdict):
        clsdict['__signature__'] = make_sig(*clsdict.get('_fields',[]))
        return super().__new__(cls, clsname, bases, clsdict)

class Structure(metaclass=StructureMeta):
    _fields = []
    def __init__(self, *args, **kwargs):
        bound_values = self.__signature__.bind(*args, **kwargs)
        for name, value in bound_values.arguments.items():
            setattr(self, name, value)

# Example
class Stock(Structure):
    _fields = ['name', 'shares', 'price']

class Point(Structure):
    _fields = ['x', 'y']
```

When defining custom signatures, it is often useful to store the signature in a special attribute __signature__, as shown. If you do this, code that uses the inspect module to perform introspection will see the signature and report it as the calling convention. For example:

```
>>> import inspect
>>> print(inspect.signature(Stock))
(name, shares, price)
>>> print(inspect.signature(Point))
(x, y)
>>>
```

9.17. Enforcing Coding Conventions in Classes

Problem

Your program consists of a large class hierarchy and you would like to enforce certain kinds of coding conventions (or perform diagnostics) to help maintain programmer sanity.

Solution

If you want to monitor the definition of classes, you can often do it by defining a metaclass. A basic metaclass is usually defined by inheriting from type and redefining its __new__() method or __init__() method. For example:

```
class MyMeta(type):
    def __new__(self, clsname, bases, clsdict):
        # clsname is name of class being defined
        # bases is tuple of base classes
```

```
        # clsdict is class dictionary
        return super().__new__(cls, clsname, bases, clsdict)
```

Alternatively, if __init__() is defined:

```
class MyMeta(type):
    def __init__(self, clsname, bases, clsdict):
        super().__init__(clsname, bases, clsdict)
        # clsname is name of class being defined
        # bases is tuple of base classes
        # clsdict is class dictionary
```

To use a metaclass, you would generally incorporate it into a top-level base class from which other objects inherit. For example:

```
class Root(metaclass=MyMeta):
    pass

class A(Root):
    pass

class B(Root):
    pass
```

A key feature of a metaclass is that it allows you to examine the contents of a class at the time of definition. Inside the redefined __init__() method, you are free to inspect the class dictionary, base classes, and more. Moreover, once a metaclass has been specified for a class, it gets inherited by all of the subclasses. Thus, a sneaky framework builder can specify a metaclass for one of the top-level classes in a large hierarchy and capture the definition of all classes under it.

As a concrete albeit whimsical example, here is a metaclass that rejects any class definition containing methods with mixed-case names (perhaps as a means for annoying Java programmers):

```
class NoMixedCaseMeta(type):
    def __new__(cls, clsname, bases, clsdict):
        for name in clsdict:
            if name.lower() != name:
                raise TypeError('Bad attribute name: ' + name)
        return super().__new__(cls, clsname, bases, clsdict)

class Root(metaclass=NoMixedCaseMeta):
    pass

class A(Root):
    def foo_bar(self):      # Ok
        pass

class B(Root):
    def fooBar(self):       # TypeError
        pass
```

As a more advanced and useful example, here is a metaclass that checks the definition of redefined methods to make sure they have the same calling signature as the original method in the superclass.

```
from inspect import signature
import logging

class MatchSignaturesMeta(type):
    def __init__(self, clsname, bases, clsdict):
        super().__init__(clsname, bases, clsdict)
        sup = super(self, self)
        for name, value in clsdict.items():
            if name.startswith('_') or not callable(value):
                continue
            # Get the previous definition (if any) and compare the signatures
            prev_dfn = getattr(sup,name,None)
            if prev_dfn:
                prev_sig = signature(prev_dfn)
                val_sig = signature(value)
                if prev_sig != val_sig:
                    logging.warning('Signature mismatch in %s. %s != %s',
                                    value.__qualname__, prev_sig, val_sig)

# Example
class Root(metaclass=MatchSignaturesMeta):
    pass

class A(Root):
    def foo(self, x, y):
        pass

    def spam(self, x, *, z):
        pass

# Class with redefined methods, but slightly different signatures
class B(A):
    def foo(self, a, b):
        pass

    def spam(self,x,z):
        pass
```

If you run this code, you will get output such as the following:

```
WARNING:root:Signature mismatch in B.spam. (self, x, *, z) != (self, x, z)
WARNING:root:Signature mismatch in B.foo. (self, x, y) != (self, a, b)
```

Such warnings might be useful in catching subtle program bugs. For example, code that relies on keyword argument passing to a method will break if a subclass changes the argument names.

Discussion

In large object-oriented programs, it can sometimes be useful to put class definitions under the control of a metaclass. The metaclass can observe class definitions and be used to alert programmers to potential problems that might go unnoticed (e.g., using slightly incompatible method signatures).

One might argue that such errors would be better caught by program analysis tools or IDEs. To be sure, such tools are useful. However, if you're creating a framework or library that's going to be used by others, you often don't have any control over the rigor of their development practices. Thus, for certain kinds of applications, it might make sense to put a bit of extra checking in a metaclass if such checking would result in a better user experience.

The choice of redefining __new__() or __init__() in a metaclass depends on how you want to work with the resulting class. __new__() is invoked prior to class creation and is typically used when a metaclass wants to alter the class definition in some way (by changing the contents of the class dictionary). The __init__() method is invoked after a class has been created, and is useful if you want to write code that works with the fully formed class object. In the last example, this is essential since it is using the super() function to search for prior definitions. This only works once the class instance has been created and the underlying method resolution order has been set.

The last example also illustrates the use of Python's function signature objects. Essentially, the metaclass takes each callable definition in a class, searches for a prior definition (if any), and then simply compares their calling signatures using inspect.signature().

Last, but not least, the line of code that uses super(self, self) is not a typo. When working with a metaclass, it's important to realize that the self is actually a class object. So, that statement is actually being used to find definitions located further up the class hierarchy that make up the parents of self.

9.18. Defining Classes Programmatically

Problem

You're writing code that ultimately needs to create a new class object. You've thought about emitting emit class source code to a string and using a function such as exec() to evaluate it, but you'd prefer a more elegant solution.

Solution

You can use the function `types.new_class()` to instantiate new class objects. All you need to do is provide the name of the class, tuple of parent classes, keyword arguments, and a callback that populates the class dictionary with members. For example:

```
# stock.py
# Example of making a class manually from parts

# Methods
def __init__(self, name, shares, price):
    self.name = name
    self.shares = shares
    self.price = price

def cost(self):
    return self.shares * self.price

cls_dict = {
    '__init__' : __init__,
    'cost' : cost,
}

# Make a class
import types

Stock = types.new_class('Stock', (), {}, lambda ns: ns.update(cls_dict))
Stock.__module__ = __name__
```

This makes a normal class object that works just like you expect:

```
>>> s = Stock('ACME', 50, 91.1)
>>> s
<stock.Stock object at 0x1006a9b10>
>>> s.cost()
4555.0
>>>
```

A subtle facet of the solution is the assignment to `Stock.__module__` after the call to `types.new_class()`. Whenever a class is defined, its `__module__` attribute contains the name of the module in which it was defined. This name is used to produce the output made by methods such as `__repr__()`. It's also used by various libraries, such as `pickle`. Thus, in order for the class you make to be "proper," you need to make sure this attribute is set accordingly.

If the class you want to create involves a different metaclass, it would be specified in the third argument to `types.new_class()`. For example:

```
>>> import abc
>>> Stock = types.new_class('Stock', (), {'metaclass': abc.ABCMeta},
...                         lambda ns: ns.update(cls_dict))
...
```

```
>>> Stock.__module__ = __name__
>>> Stock
<class '__main__.Stock'>
>>> type(Stock)
<class 'abc.ABCMeta'>
>>>
```

The third argument may also contain other keyword arguments. For example, a class definition like this

```
class Spam(Base, debug=True, typecheck=False):
    ...
```

would translate to a `new_class()` call similar to this:

```
Spam = types.new_class('Spam', (Base,),
                       {'debug': True, 'typecheck': False},
                       lambda ns: ns.update(cls_dict))
```

The fourth argument to `new_class()` is the most mysterious, but it is a function that receives the mapping object being used for the class namespace as input. This is normally a dictionary, but it's actually whatever object gets returned by the `__prepare__()` method, as described in Recipe 9.14. This function should add new entries to the namespace using the `update()` method (as shown) or other mapping operations.

Discussion

Being able to manufacture new class objects can be useful in certain contexts. One of the more familiar examples involves the `collections.namedtuple()` function. For example:

```
>>> Stock = collections.namedtuple('Stock', ['name', 'shares', 'price'])
>>> Stock
<class '__main__.Stock'>
>>>
```

`namedtuple()` uses `exec()` instead of the technique shown here. However, here is a simple variant that creates a class directly:

```
import operator
import types
import sys

def named_tuple(classname, fieldnames):
    # Populate a dictionary of field property accessors
    cls_dict = { name: property(operator.itemgetter(n))
                 for n, name in enumerate(fieldnames) }

    # Make a __new__ function and add to the class dict
    def __new__(cls, *args):
        if len(args) != len(fieldnames):
            raise TypeError('Expected {} arguments'.format(len(fieldnames)))
```

```
        return tuple.__new__(cls, args)

    cls_dict['__new__'] = __new__

    # Make the class
    cls = types.new_class(classname, (tuple,), {},
                          lambda ns: ns.update(cls_dict))

    # Set the module to that of the caller
    cls.__module__ = sys._getframe(1).f_globals['__name__']
    return cls
```

The last part of this code uses a so-called "frame hack" involving sys._getframe() to obtain the module name of the caller. Another example of frame hacking appears in Recipe 2.15.

The following example shows how the preceding code works:

```
>>> Point = named_tuple('Point', ['x', 'y'])
>>> Point
<class '__main__.Point'>
>>> p = Point(4, 5)
>>> len(p)
2
>>> p.x
4
>>> p.y
5
>>> p.x = 2
Traceback (most recent call last):
  File "<stdin>", line 1, in <module>
AttributeError: can't set attribute
>>> print('%s %s' % p)
4 5
>>>
```

One important aspect of the technique used in this recipe is its proper support for metaclasses. You might be inclined to create a class directly by instantiating a metaclass directly. For example:

```
Stock = type('Stock', (), cls_dict)
```

The problem is that this approach skips certain critical steps, such as invocation of the metaclass __prepare__() method. By using types.new_class() instead, you ensure that all of the necessary initialization steps get carried out. For instance, the callback function that's given as the fourth argument to types.new_class() receives the mapping object that's returned by the __prepare__() method.

If you only want to carry out the preparation step, use types.prepare_class(). For example:

```
import types

metaclass, kwargs, ns = types.prepare_class('Stock', (), {'metaclass': type})
```

This finds the appropriate metaclass and invokes its __prepare__() method. The metaclass, remaining keyword arguments, and prepared namespace are then returned.

For more information, see PEP 3115 (*http://www.python.org/dev/peps/pep-3115*), as well as the Python documentation (*http://docs.python.org/3/reference/datamo del.html#metaclasses*).

9.19. Initializing Class Members at Definition Time

Problem

You want to initialize parts of a class definition once at the time a class is defined, not when instances are created.

Solution

Performing initialization or setup actions at the time of class definition is a classic use of metaclasses. Essentially, a metaclass is triggered at the point of a definition, at which point you can perform additional steps.

Here is an example that uses this idea to create classes similar to named tuples from the collections module:

```
import operator

class StructTupleMeta(type):
    def __init__(cls, *args, **kwargs):
        super().__init__(*args, **kwargs)
        for n, name in enumerate(cls._fields):
            setattr(cls, name, property(operator.itemgetter(n)))

class StructTuple(tuple, metaclass=StructTupleMeta):
    _fields = []
    def __new__(cls, *args):
        if len(args) != len(cls._fields):
            raise ValueError('{} arguments required'.format(len(cls._fields)))
        return super().__new__(cls,args)
```

This code allows simple tuple-based data structures to be defined, like this:

```
class Stock(StructTuple):
    _fields = ['name', 'shares', 'price']

class Point(StructTuple):
    _fields = ['x', 'y']
```

Here's how they work:

```
>>> s = Stock('ACME', 50, 91.1)
>>> s
('ACME', 50, 91.1)
>>> s[0]
'ACME'
>>> s.name
'ACME'
>>> s.shares * s.price
4555.0
>>> s.shares = 23
Traceback (most recent call last):
  File "<stdin>", line 1, in <module>
AttributeError: can't set attribute
>>>
```

Discussion

In this recipe, the StructTupleMeta class takes the listing of attribute names in the _fields class attribute and turns them into property methods that access a particular tuple slot. The operator.itemgetter() function creates an accessor function and the property() function turns it into a property.

The trickiest part of this recipe is knowing when the different initialization steps occur. The __init__() method in StructTupleMeta is only called once for each class that is defined. The cls argument is the class that has just been defined. Essentially, the code is using the _fields class variable to take the newly defined class and add some new parts to it.

The StructTuple class serves as a common base class for users to inherit from. The __new__() method in that class is responsible for making new instances. The use of __new__() here is a bit unusual, but is partly related to the fact that we're modifying the calling signature of tuples so that we can create instances with code that uses a normal-looking calling convention like this:

```
s = Stock('ACME', 50, 91.1)        # OK
s = Stock(('ACME', 50, 91.1))      # Error
```

Unlike __init__(), the __new__() method gets triggered before an instance is created. Since tuples are immutable, it's not possible to make any changes to them once they have been created. An __init__() function gets triggered too late in the instance creation process to do what we want. That's why __new__() has been defined.

Although this is a short recipe, careful study will reward the reader with a deep insight about how Python classes are defined, how instances are created, and the points at which different methods of metaclasses and classes are invoked.

PEP 422 (*http://www.python.org/dev/peps/pep-0422*) may provide an alternative means for performing the task described in this recipe. However, as of this writing, it has not been adopted or accepted. Nevertheless, it might be worth a look in case you're working with a version of Python newer than Python 3.3.

9.20. Implementing Multiple Dispatch with Function Annotations

Problem

You've learned about function argument annotations and you have a thought that you might be able to use them to implement multiple-dispatch (method overloading) based on types. However, you're not quite sure what's involved (or if it's even a good idea).

Solution

This recipe is based on a simple observation—namely, that since Python allows arguments to be annotated, perhaps it might be possible to write code like this:

```
class Spam:
    def bar(self, x:int, y:int):
        print('Bar 1:', x, y)
    def bar(self, s:str, n:int = 0):
        print('Bar 2:', s, n)

s = Spam()
s.bar(2, 3)      # Prints Bar 1: 2 3
s.bar('hello')   # Prints Bar 2: hello 0
```

Here is the start of a solution that does just that, using a combination of metaclasses and descriptors:

```
# multiple.py

import inspect
import types

class MultiMethod:
    '''
    Represents a single multimethod.
    '''
    def __init__(self, name):
        self._methods = {}
        self.__name__ = name

    def register(self, meth):
        '''
        Register a new method as a multimethod
        '''
```

```python
        sig = inspect.signature(meth)

        # Build a type signature from the method's annotations
        types = []
        for name, parm in sig.parameters.items():
            if name == 'self':
                continue
            if parm.annotation is inspect.Parameter.empty:
                raise TypeError(
                    'Argument {} must be annotated with a type'.format(name)
                )
            if not isinstance(parm.annotation, type):
                raise TypeError(
                    'Argument {} annotation must be a type'.format(name)
                )
            if parm.default is not inspect.Parameter.empty:
                self._methods[tuple(types)] = meth
            types.append(parm.annotation)

        self._methods[tuple(types)] = meth

    def __call__(self, *args):
        '''
        Call a method based on type signature of the arguments
        '''
        types = tuple(type(arg) for arg in args[1:])
        meth = self._methods.get(types, None)
        if meth:
            return meth(*args)
        else:
            raise TypeError('No matching method for types {}'.format(types))

    def __get__(self, instance, cls):
        '''
        Descriptor method needed to make calls work in a class
        '''
        if instance is not None:
            return types.MethodType(self, instance)
        else:
            return self

class MultiDict(dict):
    '''
    Special dictionary to build multimethods in a metaclass
    '''
    def __setitem__(self, key, value):
        if key in self:
            # If key already exists, it must be a multimethod or callable
            current_value = self[key]
            if isinstance(current_value, MultiMethod):
                current_value.register(value)
            else:
```

```
                mvalue = MultiMethod(key)
                mvalue.register(current_value)
                mvalue.register(value)
                super().__setitem__(key, mvalue)
        else:
            super().__setitem__(key, value)

class MultipleMeta(type):
    '''
    Metaclass that allows multiple dispatch of methods
    '''
    def __new__(cls, clsname, bases, clsdict):
        return type.__new__(cls, clsname, bases, dict(clsdict))

    @classmethod
    def __prepare__(cls, clsname, bases):
        return MultiDict()
```

To use this class, you write code like this:

```
class Spam(metaclass=MultipleMeta):
    def bar(self, x:int, y:int):
        print('Bar 1:', x, y)
    def bar(self, s:str, n:int = 0):
        print('Bar 2:', s, n)

# Example: overloaded __init__
import time
class Date(metaclass=MultipleMeta):
    def __init__(self, year: int, month:int, day:int):
        self.year = year
        self.month = month
        self.day = day

    def __init__(self):
        t = time.localtime()
        self.__init__(t.tm_year, t.tm_mon, t.tm_mday)
```

Here is an interactive session that verifies that it works:

```
>>> s = Spam()
>>> s.bar(2, 3)
Bar 1: 2 3
>>> s.bar('hello')
Bar 2: hello 0
>>> s.bar('hello', 5)
Bar 2: hello 5
>>> s.bar(2, 'hello')
Traceback (most recent call last):
  File "<stdin>", line 1, in <module>
  File "multiple.py", line 42, in __call__
    raise TypeError('No matching method for types {}'.format(types))
TypeError: No matching method for types (<class 'int'>, <class 'str'>)
```

```
>>> # Overloaded __init__
>>> d = Date(2012, 12, 21)
>>> # Get today's date
>>> e = Date()
>>> e.year
2012
>>> e.month
12
>>> e.day
3
>>>
```

Discussion

Honestly, there might be too much magic going on in this recipe to make it applicable to real-world code. However, it does dive into some of the inner workings of metaclasses and descriptors, and reinforces some of their concepts. Thus, even though you might not apply this recipe directly, some of its underlying ideas might influence other programming techniques involving metaclasses, descriptors, and function annotations.

The main idea in the implementation is relatively simple. The MutipleMeta metaclass uses its __prepare__() method to supply a custom class dictionary as an instance of MultiDict. Unlike a normal dictionary, MultiDict checks to see whether entries already exist when items are set. If so, the duplicate entries get merged together inside an instance of MultiMethod.

Instances of MultiMethod collect methods by building a mapping from type signatures to functions. During construction, function annotations are used to collect these signatures and build the mapping. This takes place in the MultiMethod.register() method. One critical part of this mapping is that for multimethods, types must be specified on all of the arguments or else an error occurs.

To make MultiMethod instances emulate a callable, the __call__() method is implemented. This method builds a type tuple from all of the arguments except self, looks up the method in the internal map, and invokes the appropriate method. The __get__() is required to make MultiMethod instances operate correctly inside class definitions. In the implementation, it's being used to create proper bound methods. For example:

```
>>> b = s.bar
>>> b
<bound method Spam.bar of <__main__.Spam object at 0x1006a46d0>>
>>> b.__self__
<__main__.Spam object at 0x1006a46d0>
>>> b.__func__
<__main__.MultiMethod object at 0x1006a4d50>
>>> b(2, 3)
Bar 1: 2 3
>>> b('hello')
```

```
Bar 2: hello 0
>>>
```

To be sure, there are a lot of moving parts to this recipe. However, it's all a little unfortunate considering how many limitations there are. For one, the solution doesn't work with keyword arguments: For example:

```
>>> s.bar(x=2, y=3)
Traceback (most recent call last):
  File "<stdin>", line 1, in <module>
TypeError: __call__() got an unexpected keyword argument 'y'

>>> s.bar(s='hello')
Traceback (most recent call last):
  File "<stdin>", line 1, in <module>
TypeError: __call__() got an unexpected keyword argument 's'
>>>
```

There might be some way to add such support, but it would require a completely different approach to method mapping. The problem is that the keyword arguments don't arrive in any kind of particular order. When mixed up with positional arguments, you simply get a jumbled mess of arguments that you have to somehow sort out in the __call__() method.

This recipe is also severely limited in its support for inheritance. For example, something like this doesn't work:

```
class A:
    pass

class B(A):
    pass

class C:
    pass

class Spam(metaclass=MultipleMeta):
    def foo(self, x:A):
        print('Foo 1:', x)

    def foo(self, x:C):
        print('Foo 2:', x)
```

The reason it fails is that the x:A annotation fails to match instances that are subclasses (such as instances of B). For example:

```
>>> s = Spam()
>>> a = A()
>>> s.foo(a)
Foo 1: <__main__.A object at 0x1006a5310>
>>> c = C()
>>> s.foo(c)
```

```
Foo 2: <__main__.C object at 0x1007a1910>
>>> b = B()
>>> s.foo(b)
Traceback (most recent call last):
  File "<stdin>", line 1, in <module>
  File "multiple.py", line 44, in __call__
    raise TypeError('No matching method for types {}'.format(types))
TypeError: No matching method for types (<class '__main__.B'>,)
>>>
```

As an alternative to using metaclasses and annotations, it is possible to implement a similar recipe using decorators. For example:

```python
import types

class multimethod:
    def __init__(self, func):
        self._methods = {}
        self.__name__ = func.__name__
        self._default = func

    def match(self, *types):
        def register(func):
            ndefaults = len(func.__defaults__) if func.__defaults__ else 0
            for n in range(ndefaults+1):
                self._methods[types[:len(types) - n]] = func
            return self
        return register

    def __call__(self, *args):
        types = tuple(type(arg) for arg in args[1:])
        meth = self._methods.get(types, None)
        if meth:
            return meth(*args)
        else:
            return self._default(*args)

    def __get__(self, instance, cls):
        if instance is not None:
            return types.MethodType(self, instance)
        else:
            return self
```

To use the decorator version, you would write code like this:

```python
class Spam:
    @multimethod
    def bar(self, *args):
        # Default method called if no match
        raise TypeError('No matching method for bar')

    @bar.match(int, int)
    def bar(self, x, y):
```

```
        print('Bar 1:', x, y)

    @bar.match(str, int)
    def bar(self, s, n = 0):
        print('Bar 2:', s, n)
```

The decorator solution also suffers the same limitations as the previous implementation (namely, no support for keyword arguments and broken inheritance).

All things being equal, it's probably best to stay away from multiple dispatch in general-purpose code. There are special situations where it might make sense, such as in programs that are dispatching methods based on some kind of pattern matching. For example, perhaps the visitor pattern described in Recipe 8.21 could be recast into a class that used multiple dispatch in some way. However, other than that, it's usually never a bad idea to stick with a more simple approach (simply use methods with different names).

Ideas concerning different ways to implement multiple dispatch have floated around the Python community for years. As a decent starting point for that discussion, see Guido van Rossum's blog post "Five-Minute Multimethods in Python" (*http://www.arti ma.com/weblogs/viewpost.jsp?thread=101605*).

9.21. Avoiding Repetitive Property Methods

Problem

You are writing classes where you are repeatedly having to define property methods that perform common tasks, such as type checking. You would like to simplify the code so there is not so much code repetition.

Solution

Consider a simple class where attributes are being wrapped by property methods:

```
class Person:
    def __init__(self, name ,age):
        self.name = name
        self.age = age

    @property
    def name(self):
        return self._name

    @name.setter
    def name(self, value):
        if not isinstance(value, str):
            raise TypeError('name must be a string')
        self._name = value
```

```
@property
def age(self):
    return self._age

@age.setter
def age(self, value):
    if not isinstance(value, int):
        raise TypeError('age must be an int')
    self._age = value
```

As you can see, a lot of code is being written simply to enforce some type assertions on attribute values. Whenever you see code like this, you should explore different ways of simplifying it. One possible approach is to make a function that simply defines the property for you and returns it. For example:

```
def typed_property(name, expected_type):
    storage_name = '_' + name

    @property
    def prop(self):
        return getattr(self, storage_name)

    @prop.setter
    def prop(self, value):
        if not isinstance(value, expected_type):
            raise TypeError('{} must be a {}'.format(name, expected_type))
        setattr(self, storage_name, value)
    return prop

# Example use
class Person:
    name = typed_property('name', str)
    age = typed_property('age', int)
    def __init__(self, name, age):
        self.name = name
        self.age = age
```

Discussion

This recipe illustrates an important feature of inner function or closures—namely, their use in writing code that works a lot like a macro. The `typed_property()` function in this example may look a little weird, but it's really just generating the property code for you and returning the resulting property object. Thus, when it's used in a class, it operates exactly as if the code appearing inside `typed_property()` was placed into the class definition itself. Even though the property getter and setter methods are accessing local variables such as `name`, `expected_type`, and `storage_name`, that is fine—those values are held behind the scenes in a closure.

This recipe can be tweaked in an interesting manner using the `functools.partial()` function. For example, you can do this:

```
from functools import partial

String = partial(typed_property, expected_type=str)
Integer = partial(typed_property, expected_type=int)

# Example:
class Person:
    name = String('name')
    age = Integer('age')
    def __init__(self, name, age):
        self.name = name
        self.age = age
```

Here the code is starting to look a lot like some of the type system descriptor code shown in Recipe 8.13.

9.22. Defining Context Managers the Easy Way

Problem

You want to implement new kinds of context managers for use with the `with` statement.

Solution

One of the most straightforward ways to write a new context manager is to use the `@contextmanager` decorator in the `contextlib` module. Here is an example of a context manager that times the execution of a code block:

```
import time
from contextlib import contextmanager

@contextmanager
def timethis(label):
    start = time.time()
    try:
        yield
    finally:
        end = time.time()
        print('{}: {}'.format(label, end - start))

# Example use
with timethis('counting'):
    n = 10000000
    while n > 0:
        n -= 1
```

In the timethis() function, all of the code prior to the yield executes as the __en
ter__() method of a context manager. All of the code after the yield executes as the
__exit__() method. If there was an exception, it is raised at the yield statement.

Here is a slightly more advanced context manager that implements a kind of transaction
on a list object:

```
@contextmanager
def list_transaction(orig_list):
    working = list(orig_list)
    yield working
    orig_list[:] = working
```

The idea here is that changes made to a list only take effect if an entire code block runs
to completion with no exceptions. Here is an example that illustrates:

```
>>> items = [1, 2, 3]
>>> with list_transaction(items) as working:
...     working.append(4)
...     working.append(5)
...
>>> items
[1, 2, 3, 4, 5]
>>> with list_transaction(items) as working:
...     working.append(6)
...     working.append(7)
...     raise RuntimeError('oops')
...
Traceback (most recent call last):
  File "<stdin>", line 4, in <module>
RuntimeError: oops
>>> items
[1, 2, 3, 4, 5]
>>>
```

Discussion

Normally, to write a context manager, you define a class with an __enter__() and
__exit__() method, like this:

```
import time

class timethis:
    def __init__(self, label):
        self.label = label
    def __enter__(self):
        self.start = time.time()
    def __exit__(self, exc_ty, exc_val, exc_tb):
        end = time.time()
        print('{}: {}'.format(self.label, end - self.start))
```

Although this isn't hard, it's a lot more tedious than writing a simple function using @contextmanager.

@contextmanager is really only used for writing self-contained context-management functions. If you have some object (e.g., a file, network connection, or lock) that needs to support the with statement, you still need to implement the __enter__() and __exit__() methods separately.

9.23. Executing Code with Local Side Effects

Problem

You are using exec() to execute a fragment of code in the scope of the caller, but after execution, none of its results seem to be visible.

Solution

To better understand the problem, try a little experiment. First, execute a fragment of code in the global namespace:

```
>>> a = 13
>>> exec('b = a + 1')
>>> print(b)
14
>>>
```

Now, try the same experiment inside a function:

```
>>> def test():
...     a = 13
...     exec('b = a + 1')
...     print(b)
...
>>> test()
Traceback (most recent call last):
  File "<stdin>", line 1, in <module>
  File "<stdin>", line 4, in test
NameError: global name 'b' is not defined
>>>
```

As you can see, it fails with a NameError almost as if the exec() statement never actually executed. This can be a problem if you ever want to use the result of the exec() in a later calculation.

To fix this kind of problem, you need to use the locals() function to obtain a dictionary of the local variables prior to the call to exec(). Immediately afterward, you can extract modified values from the locals dictionary. For example:

```
>>> def test():
...     a = 13
...     loc = locals()
...     exec('b = a + 1')
...     b = loc['b']
...     print(b)
...
>>> test()
14
>>>
```

Discussion

Correct use of exec() is actually quite tricky in practice. In fact, in most situations where you might be considering the use of exec(), a more elegant solution probably exists (e.g., decorators, closures, metaclasses, etc.).

However, if you still must use exec(), this recipe outlines some subtle aspects of using it correctly. By default, exec() executes code in the local and global scope of the caller. However, inside functions, the local scope passed to exec() is a dictionary that is a copy of the actual local variables. Thus, if the code in exec() makes any kind of modification, that modification is never reflected in the actual local variables. Here is another example that shows this effect:

```
>>> def test1():
...     x = 0
...     exec('x += 1')
...     print(x)
...
>>> test1()
0
>>>
```

When you call locals() to obtain the local variables, as shown in the solution, you get the copy of the locals that is passed to exec(). By inspecting the value of the dictionary after execution, you can obtain the modified values. Here is an experiment that shows this:

```
>>> def test2():
...     x = 0
...     loc = locals()
...     print('before:', loc)
...     exec('x += 1')
...     print('after:', loc)
...     print('x =', x)
...
>>> test2()
before: {'x': 0}
after: {'loc': {...}, 'x': 1}
```

```
x = 0
>>>
```

Carefully observe the output of the last step. Unless you copy the modified value from loc back to x, the variable remains unchanged.

With any use of locals(), you need to be careful about the order of operations. Each time it is invoked, locals() will take the current value of local variables and overwrite the corresponding entries in the dictionary. Observe the outcome of this experiment:

```
>>> def test3():
...     x = 0
...     loc = locals()
...     print(loc)
...     exec('x += 1')
...     print(loc)
...     locals()
...     print(loc)
...
>>> test3()
{'x': 0}
{'loc': {...}, 'x': 1}
{'loc': {...}, 'x': 0}
>>>
```

Notice how the last call to locals() caused x to be overwritten.

As an alternative to using locals(), you might make your own dictionary and pass it to exec(). For example:

```
>>> def test4():
...     a = 13
...     loc = { 'a' : a }
...     glb = { }
...     exec('b = a + 1', glb, loc)
...     b = loc['b']
...     print(b)
...
>>> test4()
14
>>>
```

For most uses of exec(), this is probably good practice. You just need to make sure that the global and local dictionaries are properly initialized with names that the executed code will access.

Last, but not least, before using exec(), you might ask yourself if other alternatives are available. Many problems where you might consider the use of exec() can be replaced by closures, decorators, metaclasses, or other metaprogramming features.

9.24. Parsing and Analyzing Python Source

Problem

You want to write programs that parse and analyze Python source code.

Solution

Most programmers know that Python can evaluate or execute source code provided in the form of a string. For example:

```
>>> x = 42
>>> eval('2 + 3*4 + x')
56
>>> exec('for i in range(10): print(i)')
0
1
2
3
4
5
6
7
8
9
>>>
```

However, the `ast` module can be used to compile Python source code into an abstract syntax tree (AST) that can be analyzed. For example:

```
>>> import ast
>>> ex = ast.parse('2 + 3*4 + x', mode='eval')
>>> ex
<_ast.Expression object at 0x1007473d0>
>>> ast.dump(ex)
"Expression(body=BinOp(left=BinOp(left=Num(n=2), op=Add(),
right=BinOp(left=Num(n=3), op=Mult(), right=Num(n=4))), op=Add(),
right=Name(id='x', ctx=Load())))"

>>> top = ast.parse('for i in range(10): print(i)', mode='exec')
>>> top
<_ast.Module object at 0x100747390>
>>> ast.dump(top)
"Module(body=[For(target=Name(id='i', ctx=Store()),
iter=Call(func=Name(id='range', ctx=Load()), args=[Num(n=10)],
keywords=[], starargs=None, kwargs=None),
body=[Expr(value=Call(func=Name(id='print', ctx=Load()),
args=[Name(id='i', ctx=Load())], keywords=[], starargs=None,
kwargs=None))], orelse=[])])"
>>>
```

Analyzing the source tree requires a bit of study on your part, but it consists of a collection of AST nodes. The easiest way to work with these nodes is to define a visitor class that implements various visit_NodeName() methods where NodeName() matches the node of interest. Here is an example of such a class that records information about which names are loaded, stored, and deleted.

```python
import ast

class CodeAnalyzer(ast.NodeVisitor):
    def __init__(self):
        self.loaded = set()
        self.stored = set()
        self.deleted = set()
    def visit_Name(self, node):
        if isinstance(node.ctx, ast.Load):
            self.loaded.add(node.id)
        elif isinstance(node.ctx, ast.Store):
            self.stored.add(node.id)
        elif isinstance(node.ctx, ast.Del):
            self.deleted.add(node.id)

# Sample usage
if __name__ == '__main__':
    # Some Python code
    code = '''
for i in range(10):
    print(i)
del i
'''

    # Parse into an AST
    top = ast.parse(code, mode='exec')

    # Feed the AST to analyze name usage
    c = CodeAnalyzer()
    c.visit(top)
    print('Loaded:', c.loaded)
    print('Stored:', c.stored)
    print('Deleted:', c.deleted)
```

If you run this program, you'll get output like this:

```
Loaded: {'i', 'range', 'print'}
Stored: {'i'}
Deleted: {'i'}
```

Finally, ASTs can be compiled and executed using the compile() function. For example:

```
>>> exec(compile(top,'<stdin>', 'exec'))
0
1
2
3
4
```

```
5
6
7
8
9
>>>
```

Discussion

The fact that you can analyze source code and get information from it could be the start of writing various code analysis, optimization, or verification tools. For instance, instead of just blindly passing some fragment of code into a function like exec(), you could turn it into an AST first and look at it in some detail to see what it's doing. You could also write tools that look at the entire source code for a module and perform some sort of static analysis over it.

It should be noted that it is also possible to rewrite the AST to represent new code if you really know what you're doing. Here is an example of a decorator that lowers globally accessed names into the body of a function by reparsing the function body's source code, rewriting the AST, and recreating the function's code object:

```python
# namelower.py
import ast
import inspect

# Node visitor that lowers globally accessed names into
# the function body as local variables.
class NameLower(ast.NodeVisitor):
    def __init__(self, lowered_names):
        self.lowered_names = lowered_names

    def visit_FunctionDef(self, node):
        # Compile some assignments to lower the constants
        code = '__globals = globals()\n'
        code += '\n'.join("{0} = __globals['{0}']".format(name)
                          for name in self.lowered_names)

        code_ast = ast.parse(code, mode='exec')

        # Inject new statements into the function body
        node.body[:0] = code_ast.body

        # Save the function object
        self.func = node

# Decorator that turns global names into locals
def lower_names(*namelist):
    def lower(func):
        srclines = inspect.getsource(func).splitlines()
        # Skip source lines prior to the @lower_names decorator
```

```
    for n, line in enumerate(srclines):
        if '@lower_names' in line:
            break

    src = '\n'.join(srclines[n+1:])
    # Hack to deal with indented code
    if src.startswith((' ','\t')):
        src = 'if 1:\n' + src
    top = ast.parse(src, mode='exec')

    # Transform the AST
    cl = NameLower(namelist)
    cl.visit(top)

    # Execute the modified AST
    temp = {}
    exec(compile(top,'','exec'), temp, temp)

    # Pull out the modified code object
    func.__code__ = temp[func.__name__].__code__
    return func
return lower
```

To use this code, you would write code such as the following:

```
INCR = 1

@lower_names('INCR')
def countdown(n):
    while n > 0:
        n -= INCR
```

The decorator rewrites the source code of the countdown() function to look like this:

```
def countdown(n):
    __globals = globals()
    INCR = __globals['INCR']
    while n > 0:
        n -= INCR
```

In a performance test, it makes the function run about 20% faster.

Now, should you go applying this decorator to all of your functions? Probably not. However, it's a good illustration of some very advanced things that might be possible through AST manipulation, source code manipulation, and other techniques.

This recipe was inspired by a similar recipe at ActiveState (*http://code.activestate.com/recipes/277940-decorator-for-bindingconstants-at-compile-time*) that worked by manipulating Python's byte code. Working with the AST is a higher-level approach that might be a bit more straightforward. See the next recipe for more information about byte code.

9.25. Disassembling Python Byte Code

Problem

You want to know in detail what your code is doing under the covers by disassembling it into lower-level byte code used by the interpreter.

Solution

The `dis` module can be used to output a disassembly of any Python function. For example:

```
>>> def countdown(n):
...     while n > 0:
...         print('T-minus', n)
...         n -= 1
...     print('Blastoff!')
...
>>> import dis
>>> dis.dis(countdown)
  2           0 SETUP_LOOP              39 (to 42)
        >>    3 LOAD_FAST                0 (n)
              6 LOAD_CONST               1 (0)
              9 COMPARE_OP               4 (>)
             12 POP_JUMP_IF_FALSE       41

  3          15 LOAD_GLOBAL              0 (print)
             18 LOAD_CONST               2 ('T-minus')
             21 LOAD_FAST                0 (n)
             24 CALL_FUNCTION            2 (2 positional, 0 keyword pair)
             27 POP_TOP

  4          28 LOAD_FAST                0 (n)
             31 LOAD_CONST               3 (1)
             34 INPLACE_SUBTRACT
             35 STORE_FAST               0 (n)
             38 JUMP_ABSOLUTE            3
        >>   41 POP_BLOCK

  5     >>   42 LOAD_GLOBAL              0 (print)
             45 LOAD_CONST               4 ('Blastoff!')
             48 CALL_FUNCTION            1 (1 positional, 0 keyword pair)
             51 POP_TOP
             52 LOAD_CONST               0 (None)
             55 RETURN_VALUE
>>>
```

Discussion

The dis module can be useful if you ever need to study what's happening in your program at a very low level (e.g., if you're trying to understand performance characteristics).

The raw byte code interpreted by the dis() function is available on functions as follows:

```
>>> countdown.__code__.co_code
b"x'\x00|\x00\x00d\x01\x00k\x04\x00r)\x00t\x00\x00d\x02\x00|\x00\x00\x83
\x02\x00\x01|\x00\x00d\x03\x008}\x00\x00q\x03\x00Wt\x00\x00d\x04\x00\x83
\x01\x00\x01d\x00\x00S"
>>>
```

If you ever want to interpret this code yourself, you would need to use some of the constants defined in the opcode module. For example:

```
>>> c = countdown.__code__.co_code
>>> import opcode
>>> opcode.opname[c[0]]
>>> opcode.opname[c[0]]
'SETUP_LOOP'
>>> opcode.opname[c[3]]
'LOAD_FAST'
>>>
```

Ironically, there is no function in the dis module that makes it easy for you to process the byte code in a programmatic way. However, this generator function will take the raw byte code sequence and turn it into opcodes and arguments.

```
import opcode

def generate_opcodes(codebytes):
    extended_arg = 0
    i = 0
    n = len(codebytes)
    while i < n:
        op = codebytes[i]
        i += 1
        if op >= opcode.HAVE_ARGUMENT:
            oparg = codebytes[i] + codebytes[i+1]*256 + extended_arg
            extended_arg = 0
            i += 2
            if op == opcode.EXTENDED_ARG:
                extended_arg = oparg * 65536
                continue
        else:
            oparg = None
        yield (op, oparg)
```

To use this function, you would use code like this:

```
>>> for op, oparg in generate_opcodes(countdown.__code__.co_code):
...         print(op, opcode.opname[op], oparg)
```

```
...
120 SETUP_LOOP 39
124 LOAD_FAST 0
100 LOAD_CONST 1
107 COMPARE_OP 4
114 POP_JUMP_IF_FALSE 41
116 LOAD_GLOBAL 0
100 LOAD_CONST 2
124 LOAD_FAST 0
131 CALL_FUNCTION 2
1 POP_TOP None
124 LOAD_FAST 0
100 LOAD_CONST 3
56 INPLACE_SUBTRACT None
125 STORE_FAST 0
113 JUMP_ABSOLUTE 3
87 POP_BLOCK None
116 LOAD_GLOBAL 0
100 LOAD_CONST 4
131 CALL_FUNCTION 1
1 POP_TOP None
100 LOAD_CONST 0
83 RETURN_VALUE None
>>>
```

It's a little-known fact, but you can replace the raw byte code of any function that you
want. It takes a bit of work to do it, but here's an example of what's involved:

```
>>> def add(x, y):
...     return x + y
...
>>> c = add.__code__
>>> c
<code object add at 0x1007beed0, file "<stdin>", line 1>
>>> c.co_code
b'|\x00\x00|\x01\x00\x17S'
>>>
>>> # Make a completely new code object with bogus byte code
>>> import types
>>> newbytecode = b'xxxxxxx'
>>> nc = types.CodeType(c.co_argcount, c.co_kwonlyargcount,
...     c.co_nlocals, c.co_stacksize, c.co_flags, newbytecode, c.co_consts,
...     c.co_names, c.co_varnames, c.co_filename, c.co_name,
...     c.co_firstlineno, c.co_lnotab)
>>> nc
<code object add at 0x10069fe40, file "<stdin>", line 1>
>>> add.__code__ = nc
>>> add(2,3)
Segmentation fault
```

Having the interpreter crash is a pretty likely outcome of pulling a crazy stunt like this.
However, developers working on advanced optimization and metaprogramming tools

might be inclined to rewrite byte code for real. This last part illustrates how to do it. See this code on ActiveState (*http://code.activestate.com/recipes/277940-decorator-for-bindingconstants-at-compile-time*) for another example of such code in action.

CHAPTER 10

Modules and Packages

Modules and packages are the core of any large project, and the Python installation itself. This chapter focuses on common programming techniques involving modules and packages, such as how to organize packages, splitting large modules into multiple files, and creating namespace packages. Recipes that allow you to customize the operation of the `import` statement itself are also given.

10.1. Making a Hierarchical Package of Modules

Problem

You want to organize your code into a package consisting of a hierarchical collection of modules.

Solution

Making a package structure is simple. Just organize your code as you wish on the filesystem and make sure that every directory defines an *__init__.py* file. For example:

```
graphics/
    __init__.py
    primitive/
        __init__.py
        line.py
        fill.py
        text.py
    formats/
        __init__.py
        png.py
        jpg.py
```

Once you have done this, you should be able to perform various `import` statements, such as the following:

```
import graphics.primitive.line
from graphics.primitive import line
import graphics.formats.jpg as jpg
```

Discussion

Defining a hierarchy of modules is as easy as making a directory structure on the file-system. The purpose of the *__init__.py* files is to include optional initialization code that runs as different levels of a package are encountered. For example, if you have the statement `import graphics`, the file *graphics/__init__.py* will be imported and form the contents of the `graphics` namespace. For an import such as `import graphics.for mats.jpg`, the files *graphics/__init__.py* and *graphics/formats/__init__.py* will both be imported prior to the final import of the *graphics/formats/jpg.py* file.

More often that not, it's fine to just leave the *__init__.py* files empty. However, there are certain situations where they might include code. For example, an *__init__.py* file can be used to automatically load submodules like this:

```
# graphics/formats/__init__.py

from . import jpg
from . import png
```

For such a file, a user merely has to use a single `import graphics.formats` instead of a separate import for `graphics.formats.jpg` and `graphics.formats.png`.

Other common uses of *__init__.py* include consolidating definitions from multiple files into a single logical namespace, as is sometimes done when splitting modules. This is discussed in Recipe 10.4.

Astute programmers will notice that Python 3.3 still seems to perform package imports even if no *__init__.py* files are present. If you don't define *__init__.py*, you actually create what's known as a "namespace package," which is described in Recipe 10.5. All things being equal, include the *__init__.py* files if you're just starting out with the creation of a new package.

10.2. Controlling the Import of Everything

Problem

You want precise control over the symbols that are exported from a module or package when a user uses the `from module import *` statement.

Solution

Define a variable __all__ in your module that explicitly lists the exported names. For example:

```
# somemodule.py

def spam():
    pass

def grok():
    pass

blah = 42

# Only export 'spam' and 'grok'
__all__ = ['spam', 'grok']
```

Discussion

Although the use of `from module import *` is strongly discouraged, it still sees frequent use in modules that define a large number of names. If you don't do anything, this form of import will export all names that don't start with an underscore. On the other hand, if __all__ is defined, then only the names explicitly listed will be exported.

If you define __all__ as an empty list, then nothing will be exported. An `AttributeError` is raised on import if __all__ contains undefined names.

10.3. Importing Package Submodules Using Relative Names

Problem

You have code organized as a package and want to import a submodule from one of the other package submodules without hardcoding the package name into the import statement.

Solution

To import modules of a package from other modules in the same package, use a package-relative import. For example, suppose you have a package `mypackage` organized as follows on the filesystem:

```
mypackage/
    __init__.py
    A/
        __init__.py
```

```
        spam.py
        grok.py
    B/
        __init__.py
        bar.py
```

If the module mypackage.A.spam wants to import the module grok located in the same directory, it should include an import statement like this:

```
# mypackage/A/spam.py

from . import grok
```

If the same module wants to import the module B.bar located in a different directory, it can use an import statement like this:

```
# mypackage/A/spam.py

from ..B import bar
```

Both of the import statements shown operate relative to the location of the *spam.py* file and do not include the top-level package name.

Discussion

Inside packages, imports involving modules in the same package can either use fully specified absolute names or a relative imports using the syntax shown. For example:

```
# mypackage/A/spam.py

from mypackage.A import grok      # OK
from . import grok               # OK
import grok                      # Error (not found)
```

The downside of using an absolute name, such as mypackage.A, is that it hardcodes the top-level package name into your source code. This, in turn, makes your code more brittle and hard to work with if you ever want to reorganize it. For example, if you ever changed the name of the package, you would have to go through all of your files and fix the source code. Similarly, hardcoded names make it difficult for someone else to move the code around. For example, perhaps someone wants to install two different versions of a package, differentiating them only by name. If relative imports are used, it would all work fine, whereas everything would break with absolute names.

The . and .. syntax on the import statement might look funny, but think of it as specifying a directory name. . means look in the current directory and ..B means look in the ../B directory. This syntax only works with the from form of import. For example:

```
from . import grok      # OK
import .grok            # ERROR
```

Although it looks like you could navigate the filesystem using a relative import, they are not allowed to escape the directory in which a package is defined. That is, combinations of dotted name patterns that would cause an import to occur from a non-package directory cause an error.

Finally, it should be noted that relative imports only work for modules that are located inside a proper package. In particular, they do not work inside simple modules located at the top level of scripts. They also won't work if parts of a package are executed directly as a script. For example:

```
% python3 mypackage/A/spam.py      # Relative imports fail
```

On the other hand, if you execute the preceding script using the -m option to Python, the relative imports will work properly. For example:

```
% python3 -m mypackage.A.spam      # Relative imports work
```

For more background on relative package imports, see PEP 328 (*http://www.python.org/dev/peps/pep-0328*).

10.4. Splitting a Module into Multiple Files

Problem

You have a module that you would like to split into multiple files. However, you would like to do it without breaking existing code by keeping the separate files unified as a single logical module.

Solution

A program module can be split into separate files by turning it into a package. Consider the following simple module:

```
# mymodule.py

class A:
    def spam(self):
        print('A.spam')

class B(A):
    def bar(self):
        print('B.bar')
```

Suppose you want to split *mymodule.py* into two files, one for each class definition. To do that, start by replacing the *mymodule.py* file with a directory called *mymodule*. In that directory, create the following files:

```
mymodule/
    __init__.py
    a.py
    b.py
```

In the *a.py* file, put this code:

```
# a.py

class A:
    def spam(self):
        print('A.spam')
```

In the *b.py* file, put this code:

```
# b.py

from .a import A

class B(A):
    def bar(self):
        print('B.bar')
```

Finally, in the *__init__.py* file, glue the two files together:

```
# __init__.py

from .a import A
from .b import B
```

If you follow these steps, the resulting mymodule package will appear to be a single logical module:

```
>>> import mymodule
>>> a = mymodule.A()
>>> a.spam()
A.spam
>>> b = mymodule.B()
>>> b.bar()
B.bar
>>>
```

Discussion

The primary concern in this recipe is a design question of whether or not you want users to work with a lot of small modules or just a single module. For example, in a large code base, you could just break everything up into separate files and make users use a lot of import statements like this:

```
from mymodule.a import A
from mymodule.b import B
...
```

This works, but it places more of a burden on the user to know where the different parts are located. Often, it's just easier to unify things and allow a single import like this:

```
from mymodule import A, B
```

For this latter case, it's most common to think of `mymodule` as being one large source file. However, this recipe shows how to stitch multiple files together into a single logical namespace. The key to doing this is to create a package directory and to use the *__init__.py* file to glue the parts together.

When a module gets split, you'll need to pay careful attention to cross-filename references. For instance, in this recipe, class B needs to access class A as a base class. A package-relative import `from .a import A` is used to get it.

Package-relative imports are used throughout the recipe to avoid hardcoding the top-level module name into the source code. This makes it easier to rename the module or move it around elsewhere later (see Recipe 10.3).

One extension of this recipe involves the introduction of "lazy" imports. As shown, the *__init__.py* file imports all of the required subcomponents all at once. However, for a very large module, perhaps you only want to load components as they are needed. To do that, here is a slight variation of *__init__.py*:

```
# __init__.py

def A():
    from .a import A
    return A()

def B():
    from .b import B
    return B()
```

In this version, classes A and B have been replaced by functions that load the desired classes when they are first accessed. To a user, it won't look much different. For example:

```
>>> import mymodule
>>> a = mymodule.A()
>>> a.spam()
A.spam
>>>
```

The main downside of lazy loading is that inheritance and type checking might break. For example, you might have to change your code slightly:

```
if isinstance(x, mymodule.A):        # Error
    ...

if isinstance(x, mymodule.a.A):      # Ok
    ...
```

For a real-world example of lazy loading, look at the source code for *multiprocessing/ __init__.py* in the standard library.

10.5. Making Separate Directories of Code Import Under a Common Namespace

Problem

You have a large base of code with parts possibly maintained and distributed by different people. Each part is organized as a directory of files, like a package. However, instead of having each part installed as a separated named package, you would like all of the parts to join together under a common package prefix.

Solution

Essentially, the problem here is that you would like to define a top-level Python package that serves as a namespace for a large collection of separately maintained subpackages. This problem often arises in large application frameworks where the framework developers want to encourage users to distribute plug-ins or add-on packages.

To unify separate directories under a common namespace, you organize the code just like a normal Python package, but you omit *__init__.py* files in the directories where the components are going to join together. To illustrate, suppose you have two different directories of Python code like this:

```
foo-package/
    spam/
        blah.py

bar-package/
    spam/
        grok.py
```

In these directories, the name spam is being used as a common namespace. Observe that there is no *__init__.py* file in either directory.

Now watch what happens if you add both foo-package and bar-package to the Python module path and try some imports:

```
>>> import sys
>>> sys.path.extend(['foo-package', 'bar-package'])
>>> import spam.blah
>>> import spam.grok
>>>
```

You'll observe that, by magic, the two different package directories merge together and you can import either spam.blah or spam.grok. It just works.

Discussion

The mechanism at work here is a feature known as a "namespace package." Essentially, a namespace package is a special kind of package designed for merging different directories of code together under a common namespace, as shown. For large frameworks, this can be useful, since it allows parts of a framework to be broken up into separately installed downloads. It also enables people to easily make third-party add-ons and other extensions to such frameworks.

The key to making a namespace package is to make sure there are no __init__.py files in the top-level directory that is to serve as the common namespace. The missing __init__.py file causes an interesting thing to happen on package import. Instead of causing an error, the interpreter instead starts creating a list of all directories that happen to contain a matching package name. A special namespace package module is then created and a read-only copy of the list of directories is stored in its __path__ variable. For example:

```
>>> import spam
>>> spam.__path__
_NamespacePath(['foo-package/spam', 'bar-package/spam'])
>>>
```

The directories on __path__ are used when locating further package subcomponents (e.g., when importing spam.grok or spam.blah).

An important feature of namespace packages is that anyone can extend the namespace with their own code. For example, suppose you made your own directory of code like this:

```
my-package/
    spam/
        custom.py
```

If you added your directory of code to sys.path along with the other packages, it would just seamlessly merge together with the other spam package directories:

```
>>> import spam.custom
>>> import spam.grok
>>> import spam.blah
>>>
```

As a debugging tool, the main way that you can tell if a package is serving as a namespace package is to check its __file__ attribute. If it's missing altogether, the package is a namespace. This will also be indicated in the representation string by the word "namespace":

```
>>> spam.__file__
Traceback (most recent call last):
  File "<stdin>", line 1, in <module>
AttributeError: 'module' object has no attribute '__file__'
```

```
>>> spam
<module 'spam' (namespace)>
>>>
```

Further information about namespace packages can be found in PEP 420 (*http://www.python.org/dev/peps/pep-0420*).

10.6. Reloading Modules

Problem

You want to reload an already loaded module because you've made changes to its source.

Solution

To reload a previously loaded module, use `imp.reload()`. For example:

```
>>> import spam
>>> import imp
>>> imp.reload(spam)
<module 'spam' from './spam.py'>
>>>
```

Discussion

Reloading a module is something that is often useful during debugging and development, but which is generally never safe in production code due to the fact that it doesn't always work as you expect.

Under the covers, the `reload()` operation wipes out the contents of a module's underlying dictionary and refreshes it by re-executing the module's source code. The identity of the module object itself remains unchanged. Thus, this operation updates the module everywhere that it has been imported in a program.

However, `reload()` does not update definitions that have been imported using statements such as `from module import name`. To illustrate, consider the following code:

```
# spam.py

def bar():
    print('bar')

def grok():
    print('grok')
```

Now start an interactive session:

```
>>> import spam
>>> from spam import grok
>>> spam.bar()
```

```
bar
>>> grok()
grok
>>>
```

Without quitting Python, go edit the source code to *spam.py* so that the function grok()
looks like this:

```
def grok():
    print('New grok')
```

Now go back to the interactive session, perform a reload, and try this experiment:

```
>>> import imp
>>> imp.reload(spam)
<module 'spam' from './spam.py'>
>>> spam.bar()
bar
>>> grok()              # Notice old output
grok
>>> spam.grok()         # Notice new output
New grok
>>>
```

In this example, you'll observe that there are two versions of the grok() function loaded.
Generally, this is not what you want, and is just the sort of thing that eventually leads
to massive headaches.

For this reason, reloading of modules is probably something to be avoided in production
code. Save it for debugging or for interactive sessions where you're experimenting with
the interpreter and trying things out.

10.7. Making a Directory or Zip File Runnable As a Main Script

Problem

You have a program that has grown beyond a simple script into an application involving
multiple files. You'd like to have some easy way for users to run the program.

Solution

If your application program has grown into multiple files, you can put it into its own
directory and add a *__main__.py* file. For example, you can create a directory like this:

```
myapplication/
    spam.py
    bar.py
    grok.py
    __main__.py
```

If *__main__.py* is present, you can simply run the Python interpreter on the top-level directory like this:

```
bash % python3 myapplication
```

The interpreter will execute the *__main__.py* file as the main program.

This technique also works if you package all of your code up into a zip file. For example:

```
bash % ls
spam.py    bar.py   grok.py    __main__.py
bash % zip -r myapp.zip *.py
bash % python3 myapp.zip
... output from __main__.py ...
```

Discussion

Creating a directory or zip file and adding a *__main__.py* file is one possible way to package a larger Python application. It's a little bit different than a package in that the code isn't meant to be used as a standard library module that's installed into the Python library. Instead, it's just this bundle of code that you want to hand someone to execute.

Since directories and zip files are a little different than normal files, you may also want to add a supporting shell script to make execution easier. For example, if the code was in a file named *myapp.zip*, you could make a top-level script like this:

```
#!/usr/bin/env python3 /usr/local/bin/myapp.zip
```

10.8. Reading Datafiles Within a Package

Problem

Your package includes a datafile that your code needs to read. You need to do this in the most portable way possible.

Solution

Suppose you have a package with files organized as follows:

```
mypackage/
    __init__.py
    somedata.dat
    spam.py
```

Now suppose the file *spam.py* wants to read the contents of the file *somedata.dat*. To do it, use the following code:

```
# spam.py

import pkgutil
data = pkgutil.get_data(__package__, 'somedata.dat')
```

The resulting variable `data` will be a byte string containing the raw contents of the file.

Discussion

To read a datafile, you might be inclined to write code that uses built-in I/O functions, such as `open()`. However, there are several problems with this approach.

First, a package has very little control over the current working directory of the interpreter. Thus, any I/O operations would have to be programmed to use absolute filenames. Since each module includes a `__file__` variable with the full path, it's not impossible to figure out the location, but it's messy.

Second, packages are often installed as *.zip* or *.egg* files, which don't preserve the files in the same way as a normal directory on the filesystem. Thus, if you tried to use `open()` on a datafile contained in an archive, it wouldn't work at all.

The `pkgutil.get_data()` function is meant to be a high-level tool for getting a datafile regardless of where or how a package has been installed. It will simply "work" and return the file contents back to you as a byte string.

The first argument to `get_data()` is a string containing the package name. You can either supply it directly or use a special variable, such as `__package__`. The second argument is the relative name of the file within the package. If necessary, you can navigate into different directories using standard Unix filename conventions as long as the final directory is still located within the package.

10.9. Adding Directories to sys.path

Problem

You have Python code that can't be imported because it's not located in a directory listed in `sys.path`. You would like to add new directories to Python's path, but don't want to hardwire it into your code.

Solution

There are two common ways to get new directories added to `sys.path`. First, you can add them through the use of the `PYTHONPATH` environment variable. For example:

```
bash % env PYTHONPATH=/some/dir:/other/dir python3
Python 3.3.0 (default, Oct  4 2012, 10:17:33)
[GCC 4.2.1 (Apple Inc. build 5666) (dot 3)] on darwin
```

```
Type "help", "copyright", "credits" or "license" for more information.
>>> import sys
>>> sys.path
['', '/some/dir', '/other/dir', ...]
>>>
```

In a custom application, this environment variable could be set at program startup or through a shell script of some kind.

The second approach is to create a *.pth* file that lists the directories like this:

```
# myapplication.pth
/some/dir
/other/dir
```

This *.pth* file needs to be placed into one of Python's *site-packages* directories, which are typically located at */usr/local/lib/python3.3/site-packages* or *~/.local/lib/python3.3/site-packages*. On interpreter startup, the directories listed in the *.pth* file will be added to *sys.path* as long as they exist on the filesystem. Installation of a *.pth* file might require administrator access if it's being added to the system-wide Python interpreter.

Discussion

Faced with trouble locating files, you might be inclined to write code that manually adjusts the value of sys.path. For example:

```
import sys
sys.path.insert(0, '/some/dir')
sys.path.insert(0, '/other/dir')
```

Although this "works," it is extremely fragile in practice and should be avoided if possible. Part of the problem with this approach is that it adds hardcoded directory names to your source. This can cause maintenance problems if your code ever gets moved around to a new location. It's usually much better to configure the path elsewhere in a manner that can be adjusted without making source code edits.

You can sometimes work around the problem of hardcoded directories if you carefully construct an appropriate absolute path using module-level variables, such as __file__. For example:

```
import sys
from os.path import abspath, join, dirname
sys.path.insert(0, abspath(dirname('__file__'), 'src'))
```

This adds an *src* directory to the path where that directory is located in the same directory as the code that's executing the insertion step.

The *site-packages* directories are the locations where third-party modules and packages normally get installed. If your code was installed in that manner, that's where it would be placed. Although *.pth* files for configuring the path must appear in *site-packages*, they can refer to any directories on the system that you wish. Thus, you can elect to have your code in a completely different set of directories as long as those directories are included in a *.pth* file.

10.10. Importing Modules Using a Name Given in a String

Problem

You have the name of a module that you would like to import, but it's being held in a string. You would like to invoke the import command on the string.

Solution

Use the `importlib.import_module()` function to manually import a module or part of a package where the name is given as a string. For example:

```
>>> import importlib
>>> math = importlib.import_module('math')
>>> math.sin(2)
0.9092974268256817
>>> mod = importlib.import_module('urllib.request')
>>> u = mod.urlopen('http://www.python.org')
>>>
```

`import_module` simply performs the same steps as `import`, but returns the resulting module object back to you as a result. You just need to store it in a variable and use it like a normal module afterward.

If you are working with packages, `import_module()` can also be used to perform relative imports. However, you need to give it an extra argument. For example:

```
import importlib

# Same as 'from . import b'
b = importlib.import_module('.b', __package__)
```

Discussion

The problem of manually importing modules with `import_module()` most commonly arises when writing code that manipulates or wraps around modules in some way. For example, perhaps you're implementing a customized importing mechanism of some kind where you need to load a module by name and perform patches to the loaded code.

In older code, you will sometimes see the built-in `__import__()` function used to perform imports. Although this works, `importlib.import_module()` is usually easier to use.

See Recipe 10.11 for an advanced example of customizing the import process.

10.11. Loading Modules from a Remote Machine Using Import Hooks

Problem

You would like to customize Python's import statement so that it can transparently load modules from a remote machine.

Solution

First, a serious disclaimer about security. The idea discussed in this recipe would be wholly bad without some kind of extra security and authentication layer. That said, the main goal is actually to take a deep dive into the inner workings of Python's import statement. If you get this recipe to work and understand the inner workings, you'll have a solid foundation of customizing import for almost any other purpose. With that out of the way, let's carry on.

At the core of this recipe is a desire to extend the functionality of the import statement. There are several approaches for doing this, but for the purposes of illustration, start by making the following directory of Python code:

```
testcode/
    spam.py
    fib.py
    grok/
        __init__.py
        blah.py
```

The content of these files doesn't matter, but put a few simple statements and functions in each file so you can test them and see output when they're imported. For example:

```
# spam.py
print("I'm spam")

def hello(name):
    print('Hello %s' % name)

# fib.py
print("I'm fib")

def fib(n):
    if n < 2:
        return 1
    else:
        return fib(n-1) + fib(n-2)

# grok/__init__.py
print("I'm grok.__init__")
```

```
# grok/blah.py
print("I'm grok.blah")
```

The goal here is to allow remote access to these files as modules. Perhaps the easiest way to do this is to publish them on a web server. Simply go to the *testcode* directory and run Python like this:

```
bash % cd testcode
bash % python3 -m http.server 15000
Serving HTTP on 0.0.0.0 port 15000 ...
```

Leave that server running and start up a separate Python interpreter. Make sure you can access the remote files using urllib. For example:

```
>>> from urllib.request import urlopen
>>> u = urlopen('http://localhost:15000/fib.py')
>>> data = u.read().decode('utf-8')
>>> print(data)
# fib.py
print("I'm fib")

def fib(n):
    if n < 2:
        return 1
    else:
        return fib(n-1) + fib(n-2)

>>>
```

Loading source code from this server is going to form the basis for the remainder of this recipe. Specifically, instead of manually grabbing a file of source code using urlopen(), the import statement will be customized to do it transparently behind the scenes.

The first approach to loading a remote module is to create an explicit loading function for doing it. For example:

```
import imp
import urllib.request
import sys

def load_module(url):
    u = urllib.request.urlopen(url)
    source = u.read().decode('utf-8')
    mod = sys.modules.setdefault(url, imp.new_module(url))
    code = compile(source, url, 'exec')
    mod.__file__ = url
    mod.__package__ = ''
    exec(code, mod.__dict__)
    return mod
```

This function merely downloads the source code, compiles it into a code object using compile(), and executes it in the dictionary of a newly created module object. Here's how you would use the function:

```
>>> fib = load_module('http://localhost:15000/fib.py')
I'm fib
>>> fib.fib(10)
89
>>> spam = load_module('http://localhost:15000/spam.py')
I'm spam
>>> spam.hello('Guido')
Hello Guido
>>> fib
<module 'http://localhost:15000/fib.py' from 'http://localhost:15000/fib.py'>
>>> spam
<module 'http://localhost:15000/spam.py' from 'http://localhost:15000/spam.py'>
>>>
```

As you can see, it "works" for simple modules. However, it's not plugged into the usual import statement, and extending the code to support more advanced constructs, such as packages, would require additional work.

A much slicker approach is to create a custom importer. The first way to do this is to create what's known as a meta path importer. Here is an example:

```
# urlimport.py

import sys
import importlib.abc
import imp
from urllib.request import urlopen
from urllib.error import HTTPError, URLError
from html.parser import HTMLParser

# Debugging
import logging
log = logging.getLogger(__name__)

# Get links from a given URL
def _get_links(url):
    class LinkParser(HTMLParser):
        def handle_starttag(self, tag, attrs):
            if tag == 'a':
                attrs = dict(attrs)
                links.add(attrs.get('href').rstrip('/'))

    links = set()
    try:
        log.debug('Getting links from %s' % url)
        u = urlopen(url)
        parser = LinkParser()
        parser.feed(u.read().decode('utf-8'))
```

```
        except Exception as e:
            log.debug('Could not get links. %s', e)
        log.debug('links: %r', links)
        return links

class UrlMetaFinder(importlib.abc.MetaPathFinder):
    def __init__(self, baseurl):
        self._baseurl = baseurl
        self._links   = { }
        self._loaders = { baseurl : UrlModuleLoader(baseurl) }

    def find_module(self, fullname, path=None):
        log.debug('find_module: fullname=%r, path=%r', fullname, path)
        if path is None:
            baseurl = self._baseurl
        else:
            if not path[0].startswith(self._baseurl):
                return None
            baseurl = path[0]

        parts = fullname.split('.')
        basename = parts[-1]
        log.debug('find_module: baseurl=%r, basename=%r', baseurl, basename)

        # Check link cache
        if basename not in self._links:
            self._links[baseurl] = _get_links(baseurl)

        # Check if it's a package
        if basename in self._links[baseurl]:
            log.debug('find_module: trying package %r', fullname)
            fullurl = self._baseurl + '/' + basename
            # Attempt to load the package (which accesses __init__.py)
            loader = UrlPackageLoader(fullurl)
            try:
                loader.load_module(fullname)
                self._links[fullurl] = _get_links(fullurl)
                self._loaders[fullurl] = UrlModuleLoader(fullurl)
                log.debug('find_module: package %r loaded', fullname)
            except ImportError as e:
                log.debug('find_module: package failed. %s', e)
                loader = None
            return loader

        # A normal module
        filename = basename + '.py'
        if filename in self._links[baseurl]:
            log.debug('find_module: module %r found', fullname)
            return self._loaders[baseurl]
        else:
            log.debug('find_module: module %r not found', fullname)
            return None
```

```python
    def invalidate_caches(self):
        log.debug('invalidating link cache')
        self._links.clear()

# Module Loader for a URL
class UrlModuleLoader(importlib.abc.SourceLoader):
    def __init__(self, baseurl):
        self._baseurl = baseurl
        self._source_cache = {}

    def module_repr(self, module):
        return '<urlmodule %r from %r>' % (module.__name__, module.__file__)

    # Required method
    def load_module(self, fullname):
        code = self.get_code(fullname)
        mod = sys.modules.setdefault(fullname, imp.new_module(fullname))
        mod.__file__ = self.get_filename(fullname)
        mod.__loader__ = self
        mod.__package__ = fullname.rpartition('.')[0]
        exec(code, mod.__dict__)
        return mod

    # Optional extensions
    def get_code(self, fullname):
        src = self.get_source(fullname)
        return compile(src, self.get_filename(fullname), 'exec')

    def get_data(self, path):
        pass

    def get_filename(self, fullname):
        return self._baseurl + '/' + fullname.split('.')[-1] + '.py'

    def get_source(self, fullname):
        filename = self.get_filename(fullname)
        log.debug('loader: reading %r', filename)
        if filename in self._source_cache:
            log.debug('loader: cached %r', filename)
            return self._source_cache[filename]
        try:
            u = urlopen(filename)
            source = u.read().decode('utf-8')
            log.debug('loader: %r loaded', filename)
            self._source_cache[filename] = source
            return source
        except (HTTPError, URLError) as e:
            log.debug('loader: %r failed.  %s', filename, e)
            raise ImportError("Can't load %s" % filename)
```

```
        def is_package(self, fullname):
            return False

    # Package loader for a URL
    class UrlPackageLoader(UrlModuleLoader):
        def load_module(self, fullname):
            mod = super().load_module(fullname)
            mod.__path__ = [ self._baseurl ]
            mod.__package__ = fullname

        def get_filename(self, fullname):
            return self._baseurl + '/' + '__init__.py'

        def is_package(self, fullname):
            return True

    # Utility functions for installing/uninstalling the loader
    _installed_meta_cache = { }
    def install_meta(address):
        if address not in _installed_meta_cache:
            finder = UrlMetaFinder(address)
            _installed_meta_cache[address] = finder
            sys.meta_path.append(finder)
            log.debug('%r installed on sys.meta_path', finder)

    def remove_meta(address):
        if address in _installed_meta_cache:
            finder = _installed_meta_cache.pop(address)
            sys.meta_path.remove(finder)
            log.debug('%r removed from sys.meta_path', finder)
```

Here is an interactive session showing how to use the preceding code:

```
>>> # importing currently fails
>>> import fib
Traceback (most recent call last):
  File "<stdin>", line 1, in <module>
ImportError: No module named 'fib'

>>> # Load the importer and retry (it works)
>>> import urlimport
>>> urlimport.install_meta('http://localhost:15000')
>>> import fib
I'm fib
>>> import spam
I'm spam
>>> import grok.blah
I'm grok.__init__
I'm grok.blah
>>> grok.blah.__file__
'http://localhost:15000/grok/blah.py'
>>>
```

This particular solution involves installing an instance of a special finder object UrlMetaFinder as the last entry in sys.meta_path. Whenever modules are imported, the finders in sys.meta_path are consulted in order to locate the module. In this example, the UrlMetaFinder instance becomes a finder of last resort that's triggered when a module can't be found in any of the normal locations.

As for the general implementation approach, the UrlMetaFinder class wraps around a user-specified URL. Internally, the finder builds sets of valid links by scraping them from the given URL. When imports are made, the module name is compared against this set of known links. If a match can be found, a separate UrlModuleLoader class is used to load source code from the remote machine and create the resulting module object. One reason for caching the links is to avoid unnecessary HTTP requests on repeated imports.

The second approach to customizing import is to write a hook that plugs directly into the sys.path variable, recognizing certain directory naming patterns. Add the following class and support functions to *urlimport.py*:

```
# urlimport.py

# ... include previous code above ...


# Path finder class for a URL
class UrlPathFinder(importlib.abc.PathEntryFinder):
    def __init__(self, baseurl):
        self._links = None
        self._loader = UrlModuleLoader(baseurl)
        self._baseurl = baseurl

    def find_loader(self, fullname):
        log.debug('find_loader: %r', fullname)
        parts = fullname.split('.')
        basename = parts[-1]
        # Check link cache
        if self._links is None:
            self._links = []        # See discussion
            self._links = _get_links(self._baseurl)

        # Check if it's a package
        if basename in self._links:
            log.debug('find_loader: trying package %r', fullname)
            fullurl = self._baseurl + '/' + basename
            # Attempt to load the package (which accesses __init__.py)
            loader = UrlPackageLoader(fullurl)
            try:
                loader.load_module(fullname)
                log.debug('find_loader: package %r loaded', fullname)
            except ImportError as e:
                log.debug('find_loader: %r is a namespace package', fullname)
```

```
            loader = None
        return (loader, [fullurl])

        # A normal module
        filename = basename + '.py'
        if filename in self._links:
            log.debug('find_loader: module %r found', fullname)
            return (self._loader, [])
        else:
            log.debug('find_loader: module %r not found', fullname)
            return (None, [])

    def invalidate_caches(self):
        log.debug('invalidating link cache')
        self._links = None

# Check path to see if it looks like a URL
_url_path_cache = {}
def handle_url(path):
    if path.startswith(('http://', 'https://')):
        log.debug('Handle path? %s. [Yes]', path)
        if path in _url_path_cache:
            finder = _url_path_cache[path]
        else:
            finder = UrlPathFinder(path)
            _url_path_cache[path] = finder
        return finder
    else:
        log.debug('Handle path? %s. [No]', path)

def install_path_hook():
    sys.path_hooks.append(handle_url)
    sys.path_importer_cache.clear()
    log.debug('Installing handle_url')

def remove_path_hook():
    sys.path_hooks.remove(handle_url)
    sys.path_importer_cache.clear()
    log.debug('Removing handle_url')
```

To use this path-based finder, you simply add URLs to sys.path. For example:

```
>>> # Initial import fails
>>> import fib
Traceback (most recent call last):
  File "<stdin>", line 1, in <module>
ImportError: No module named 'fib'

>>> # Install the path hook
>>> import urlimport
>>> urlimport.install_path_hook()

>>> # Imports still fail (not on path)
```

```
>>> import fib
Traceback (most recent call last):
  File "<stdin>", line 1, in <module>
ImportError: No module named 'fib'

>>> # Add an entry to sys.path and watch it work
>>> import sys
>>> sys.path.append('http://localhost:15000')
>>> import fib
I'm fib
>>> import grok.blah
I'm grok.__init__
I'm grok.blah
>>> grok.blah.__file__
'http://localhost:15000/grok/blah.py'
>>>
```

The key to this last example is the handle_url() function, which is added to the sys.path_hooks variable. When the entries on sys.path are being processed, the functions in sys.path_hooks are invoked. If any of those functions return a finder object, that finder is used to try to load modules for that entry on sys.path.

It should be noted that the remotely imported modules work exactly like any other module. For instance:

```
>>> fib
<urlmodule 'fib' from 'http://localhost:15000/fib.py'>
>>> fib.__name__
'fib'
>>> fib.__file__
'http://localhost:15000/fib.py'
>>> import inspect
>>> print(inspect.getsource(fib))
# fib.py
print("I'm fib")

def fib(n):
    if n < 2:
        return 1
    else:
        return fib(n-1) + fib(n-2)

>>>
```

Discussion

Before discussing this recipe in further detail, it should be emphasized that Python's module, package, and import mechanism is one of the most complicated parts of the entire language—often poorly understood by even the most seasoned Python programmers unless they've devoted effort to peeling back the covers. There are several critical documents that are worth reading, including the documentation for the importlib (*http://docs.python.org/3/library/importlib.html*) module and PEP 302 (*http://www.python.org/dev/peps/pep-0302*). That documentation won't be repeated here, but some essential highlights will be discussed.

First, if you want to create a new module object, you use the `imp.new_module()` function. For example:

```
>>> import imp
>>> m = imp.new_module('spam')
>>> m
<module 'spam'>
>>> m.__name__
'spam'
>>>
```

Module objects usually have a few expected attributes, including __file__ (the name of the file that the module was loaded from) and __package__ (the name of the enclosing package, if any).

Second, modules are cached by the interpreter. The module cache can be found in the dictionary `sys.modules`. Because of this caching, it's common to combine caching and module creation together into a single step. For example:

```
>>> import sys
>>> import imp
>>> m = sys.modules.setdefault('spam', imp.new_module('spam'))
>>> m
<module 'spam'>
>>>
```

The main reason for doing this is that if a module with the given name already exists, you'll get the already created module instead. For example:

```
>>> import math
>>> m = sys.modules.setdefault('math', imp.new_module('math'))
>>> m
<module 'math' from '/usr/local/lib/python3.3/lib-dynload/math.so'>
>>> m.sin(2)
0.9092974268256817
>>> m.cos(2)
-0.4161468365471424
>>>
```

Since creating modules is easy, it is straightforward to write simple functions, such as the `load_module()` function in the first part of this recipe. A downside of this approach is that it is actually rather tricky to handle more complicated cases, such as package imports. In order to handle a package, you would have to reimplement much of the underlying logic that's already part of the normal import statement (e.g., checking for directories, looking for *__init__.py* files, executing those files, setting up paths, etc.).

This complexity is one of the reasons why it's often better to extend the import statement directly rather than defining a custom function.

Extending the import statement is straightforward, but involves a number of moving parts. At the highest level, import operations are processed by a list of "meta-path" finders that you can find in the list sys.meta_path. If you output its value, you'll see the following:

```
>>> from pprint import pprint
>>> pprint(sys.meta_path)
[<class '_frozen_importlib.BuiltinImporter'>,
 <class '_frozen_importlib.FrozenImporter'>,
 <class '_frozen_importlib.PathFinder'>]
>>>
```

When executing a statement such as import fib, the interpreter walks through the finder objects on sys.meta_path and invokes their find_module() method in order to locate an appropriate module loader. It helps to see this by experimentation, so define the following class and try the following:

```
>>> class Finder:
...     def find_module(self, fullname, path):
...             print('Looking for', fullname, path)
...             return None
...
>>> import sys
>>> sys.meta_path.insert(0, Finder())   # Insert as first entry
>>> import math
Looking for math None
>>> import types
Looking for types None
>>> import threading
Looking for threading None
Looking for time None
Looking for traceback None
Looking for linecache None
Looking for tokenize None
Looking for token None
>>>
```

Notice how the find_module() method is being triggered on every import. The role of the path argument in this method is to handle packages. When packages are imported, it is a list of the directories that are found in the package's __path__ attribute. These are the paths that need to be checked to find package subcomponents. For example, notice the path setting for xml.etree and xml.etree.ElementTree:

```
>>> import xml.etree.ElementTree
Looking for xml None
Looking for xml.etree ['/usr/local/lib/python3.3/xml']
Looking for xml.etree.ElementTree ['/usr/local/lib/python3.3/xml/etree']
Looking for warnings None
```

```
Looking for contextlib None
Looking for xml.etree.ElementPath ['/usr/local/lib/python3.3/xml/etree']
Looking for _elementtree None
Looking for copy None
Looking for org None
Looking for pyexpat None
Looking for ElementC14N None
>>>
```

The placement of the finder on sys.meta_path is critical. Remove it from the front of the list to the end of the list and try more imports:

```
>>> del sys.meta_path[0]
>>> sys.meta_path.append(Finder())
>>> import urllib.request
>>> import datetime
```

Now you don't see any output because the imports are being handled by other entries in sys.meta_path. In this case, you would only see it trigger when nonexistent modules are imported:

```
>>> import fib
Looking for fib None
Traceback (most recent call last):
  File "<stdin>", line 1, in <module>
ImportError: No module named 'fib'
>>> import xml.superfast
Looking for xml.superfast ['/usr/local/lib/python3.3/xml']
Traceback (most recent call last):
  File "<stdin>", line 1, in <module>
ImportError: No module named 'xml.superfast'
>>>
```

The fact that you can install a finder to catch unknown modules is the key to the UrlMetaFinder class in this recipe. An instance of UrlMetaFinder is added to the end of sys.meta_path, where it serves as a kind of importer of last resort. If the requested module name can't be located by any of the other import mechanisms, it gets handled by this finder. Some care needs to be taken when handling packages. Specifically, the value presented in the path argument needs to be checked to see if it starts with the URL registered in the finder. If not, the submodule must belong to some other finder and should be ignored.

Additional handling of packages is found in the UrlPackageLoader class. This class, rather than importing the package name, tries to load the underlying *__init__*.py file. It also sets the module __path__ attribute. This last part is critical, as the value set will be passed to subsequent find_module() calls when loading package submodules.

The path-based import hook is an extension of these ideas, but based on a somewhat different mechanism. As you know, sys.path is a list of directories where Python looks for modules. For example:

```
>>> from pprint import pprint
>>> import sys
>>> pprint(sys.path)
['',
 '/usr/local/lib/python33.zip',
 '/usr/local/lib/python3.3',
 '/usr/local/lib/python3.3/plat-darwin',
 '/usr/local/lib/python3.3/lib-dynload',
 '/usr/local/lib/...3.3/site-packages']
>>>
```

Each entry in sys.path is additionally attached to a finder object. You can view these finders by looking at sys.path_importer_cache:

```
>>> pprint(sys.path_importer_cache)
{'.': FileFinder('.'),
 '/usr/local/lib/python3.3': FileFinder('/usr/local/lib/python3.3'),
 '/usr/local/lib/python3.3/': FileFinder('/usr/local/lib/python3.3/'),
 '/usr/local/lib/python3.3/collections': FileFinder('...python3.3/collections'),
 '/usr/local/lib/python3.3/encodings': FileFinder('...python3.3/encodings'),
 '/usr/local/lib/python3.3/lib-dynload': FileFinder('...python3.3/lib-dynload'),
 '/usr/local/lib/python3.3/plat-darwin': FileFinder('...python3.3/plat-darwin'),
 '/usr/local/lib/python3.3/site-packages': FileFinder('...python3.3/site-packages'),
 '/usr/local/lib/python33.zip': None}
>>>
```

sys.path_importer_cache tends to be much larger than sys.path because it records finders for all known directories where code is being loaded. This includes subdirectories of packages which usually aren't included on sys.path.

To execute import fib, the directories on sys.path are checked in order. For each directory, the name fib is presented to the associated finder found in sys.path_importer_cache. This is also something that you can investigate by making your own finder and putting an entry in the cache. Try this experiment:

```
>>> class Finder:
...     def find_loader(self, name):
...             print('Looking for', name)
...             return (None, [])
...
>>> import sys
>>> # Add a "debug" entry to the importer cache
>>> sys.path_importer_cache['debug'] = Finder()
>>> # Add a "debug" directory to sys.path
>>> sys.path.insert(0, 'debug')
>>> import threading
Looking for threading
Looking for time
Looking for traceback
Looking for linecache
Looking for tokenize
```

```
Looking for token
>>>
```

Here, you've installed a new cache entry for the name debug and installed the name
debug as the first entry on sys.path. On all subsequent imports, you see your finder
being triggered. However, since it returns (None, []), processing simply continues to the
next entry.

The population of sys.path_importer_cache is controlled by a list of functions stored
in sys.path_hooks. Try this experiment, which clears the cache and adds a new path
checking function to sys.path_hooks:

```
>>> sys.path_importer_cache.clear()
>>> def check_path(path):
...     print('Checking', path)
...     raise ImportError()
...
>>> sys.path_hooks.insert(0, check_path)
>>> import fib
Checked debug
Checking .
Checking /usr/local/lib/python33.zip
Checking /usr/local/lib/python3.3
Checking /usr/local/lib/python3.3/plat-darwin
Checking /usr/local/lib/python3.3/lib-dynload
Checking /Users/beazley/.local/lib/python3.3/site-packages
Checking /usr/local/lib/python3.3/site-packages
Looking for fib
Traceback (most recent call last):
  File "<stdin>", line 1, in <module>
ImportError: No module named 'fib'
>>>
```

As you can see, the check_path() function is being invoked for every entry on
sys.path. However, since an ImportError exception is raised, nothing else happens
(checking just moves to the next function on sys.path_hooks).

Using this knowledge of how sys.path is processed, you can install a custom path
checking function that looks for filename patterns, such as URLs. For instance:

```
>>> def check_url(path):
...     if path.startswith('http://'):
...             return Finder()
...     else:
...             raise ImportError()
...
>>> sys.path.append('http://localhost:15000')
>>> sys.path_hooks[0] = check_url
>>> import fib
Looking for fib            # Finder output!
Traceback (most recent call last):
```

```
  File "<stdin>", line 1, in <module>
ImportError: No module named 'fib'

>>> # Notice installation of Finder in sys.path_importer_cache
>>> sys.path_importer_cache['http://localhost:15000']
<__main__.Finder object at 0x10064c850>
>>>
```

This is the key mechanism at work in the last part of this recipe. Essentially, a custom path checking function has been installed that looks for URLs in sys.path. When they are encountered, a new UrlPathFinder instance is created and installed into sys.path_importer_cache. From that point forward, all import statements that pass through that part of sys.path will try to use your custom finder.

Package handling with a path-based importer is somewhat tricky, and relates to the return value of the find_loader() method. For simple modules, find_loader() returns a tuple (loader, None) where loader is an instance of a loader that will import the module.

For a normal package, find_loader() returns a tuple (loader, path) where loader is the loader instance that will import the package (and execute __init__.py) and path is a list of the directories that will make up the initial setting of the package's __path__ attribute. For example, if the base URL was http://localhost:15000 and a user executed import grok, the path returned by find_loader() would be ['http://local host:15000/grok'].

The find_loader() must additionally account for the possibility of a namespace package. A namespace package is a package where a valid package directory name exists, but no __init__.py file can be found. For this case, find_loader() must return a tuple (None, path) where path is a list of directories that would have made up the package's __path__ attribute had it defined an __init__.py file. For this case, the import mechanism moves on to check further directories on sys.path. If more namespace packages are found, all of the resulting paths are joined together to make a final namespace package. See Recipe 10.5 for more information on namespace packages.

There is a recursive element to package handling that is not immediately obvious in the solution, but also at work. All packages contain an internal path setting, which can be found in __path__ attribute. For example:

```
>>> import xml.etree.ElementTree
>>> xml.__path__
['/usr/local/lib/python3.3/xml']
>>> xml.etree.__path__
['/usr/local/lib/python3.3/xml/etree']
>>>
```

As mentioned, the setting of __path__ is controlled by the return value of the find_load er() method. However, the subsequent processing of __path__ is also handled by the functions in sys.path_hooks. Thus, when package subcomponents are loaded, the entries in __path__ are checked by the handle_url() function. This causes new instances of UrlPathFinder to be created and added to sys.path_importer_cache.

One remaining tricky part of the implementation concerns the behavior of the han dle_url() function and its interaction with the _get_links() function used internally. If your implementation of a finder involves the use of other modules (e.g., urllib.re quest), there is a possibility that those modules will attempt to make further imports in the middle of the finder's operation. This can actually cause handle_url() and other parts of the finder to get executed in a kind of recursive loop. To account for this possibility, the implementation maintains a cache of created finders (one per URL). This avoids the problem of creating duplicate finders. In addition, the following fragment of code ensures that the finder doesn't respond to any import requests while it's in the processs of getting the initial set of links:

```
# Check link cache
if self._links is None:
    self._links = []      # See discussion
    self._links = _get_links(self._baseurl)
```

You may not need this checking in other implementations, but for this example involving URLs, it was required.

Finally, the invalidate_caches() method of both finders is a utility method that is supposed to clear internal caches should the source code change. This method is triggered when a user invokes importlib.invalidate_caches(). You might use it if you want the URL importers to reread the list of links, possibly for the purpose of being able to access newly added files.

In comparing the two approaches (modifying sys.meta_path or using a path hook), it helps to take a high-level view. Importers installed using sys.meta_path are free to handle modules in any manner that they wish. For instance, they could load modules out of a database or import them in a manner that is radically different than normal module/package handling. This freedom also means that such importers need to do more bookkeeping and internal management. This explains, for instance, why the implementation of UrlMetaFinder needs to do its own caching of links, loaders, and other details. On the other hand, path-based hooks are more narrowly tied to the processing of sys.path. Because of the connection to sys.path, modules loaded with such extensions will tend to have the same features as normal modules and packages that programmers are used to.

Assuming that your head hasn't completely exploded at this point, a key to understanding and experimenting with this recipe may be the added logging calls. You can enable logging and try experiments such as this:

```
>>> import logging
>>> logging.basicConfig(level=logging.DEBUG)
>>> import urlimport
>>> urlimport.install_path_hook()
DEBUG:urlimport:Installing handle_url
>>> import fib
DEBUG:urlimport:Handle path? /usr/local/lib/python33.zip. [No]
Traceback (most recent call last):
  File "<stdin>", line 1, in <module>
ImportError: No module named 'fib'
>>> import sys
>>> sys.path.append('http://localhost:15000')
>>> import fib
DEBUG:urlimport:Handle path? http://localhost:15000. [Yes]
DEBUG:urlimport:Getting links from http://localhost:15000
DEBUG:urlimport:links: {'spam.py', 'fib.py', 'grok'}
DEBUG:urlimport:find_loader: 'fib'
DEBUG:urlimport:find_loader: module 'fib' found
DEBUG:urlimport:loader: reading 'http://localhost:15000/fib.py'
DEBUG:urlimport:loader: 'http://localhost:15000/fib.py' loaded
I'm fib
>>>
```

Last, but not least, spending some time sleeping with PEP 302 (*http://www.python.org/dev/peps/pep-0302*) and the documentation for `importlib` under your pillow may be advisable.

10.12. Patching Modules on Import

Problem

You want to patch or apply decorators to functions in an existing module. However, you only want to do it if the module actually gets imported and used elsewhere.

Solution

The essential problem here is that you would like to carry out actions in response to a module being loaded. Perhaps you want to trigger some kind of callback function that would notify you when a module was loaded.

This problem can be solved using the same import hook machinery discussed in Recipe 10.11. Here is a possible solution:

```python
# postimport.py

import importlib
import sys
from collections import defaultdict

_post_import_hooks = defaultdict(list)

class PostImportFinder:
    def __init__(self):
        self._skip = set()

    def find_module(self, fullname, path=None):
        if fullname in self._skip:
            return None
        self._skip.add(fullname)
        return PostImportLoader(self)

class PostImportLoader:
    def __init__(self, finder):
        self._finder = finder

    def load_module(self, fullname):
        importlib.import_module(fullname)
        module = sys.modules[fullname]
        for func in _post_import_hooks[fullname]:
            func(module)
        self._finder._skip.remove(fullname)
        return module

def when_imported(fullname):
    def decorate(func):
        if fullname in sys.modules:
            func(sys.modules[fullname])
        else:
            _post_import_hooks[fullname].append(func)
        return func
    return decorate

sys.meta_path.insert(0, PostImportFinder())
```

To use this code, you use the when_imported() decorator. For example:

```
>>> from postimport import when_imported
>>> @when_imported('threading')
... def warn_threads(mod):
...     print('Threads?  Are you crazy?')
...
>>>
>>> import threading
Threads?  Are you crazy?
>>>
```

As a more practical example, maybe you want to apply decorators to existing definitions, such as shown here:

```
from functools import wraps
from postimport import when_imported

def logged(func):
    @wraps(func)
    def wrapper(*args, **kwargs):
        print('Calling', func.__name__, args, kwargs)
        return func(*args, **kwargs)
    return wrapper

# Example
@when_imported('math')
def add_logging(mod):
    mod.cos = logged(mod.cos)
    mod.sin = logged(mod.sin)
```

Discussion

This recipe relies on the import hooks that were discussed in Recipe 10.11, with a slight twist.

First, the role of the `@when_imported` decorator is to register handler functions that get triggered on import. The decorator checks `sys.modules` to see if a module was already loaded. If so, the handler is invoked immediately. Otherwise, the handler is added to a list in the `_post_import_hooks` dictionary. The purpose of `_post_import_hooks` is simply to collect all handler objects that have been registered for each module. In principle, more than one handler could be registered for a given module.

To trigger the pending actions in `_post_import_hooks` after module import, the `Post ImportFinder` class is installed as the first item in `sys.meta_path`. If you recall from Recipe 10.11, `sys.meta_path` contains a list of finder objects that are consulted in order to locate modules. By installing `PostImportFinder` as the first item, it captures all module imports.

In this recipe, however, the role of `PostImportFinder` is not to load modules, but to trigger actions upon the completion of an import. To do this, the actual import is delegated to the other finders on `sys.meta_path`. Rather than trying to do this directly, the function `imp.import_module()` is called recursively in the `PostImportLoader` class. To avoid getting stuck in an infinite loop, `PostImportFinder` keeps a set of all the modules that are currently in the process of being loaded. If a module name is part of this set, it is simply ignored by `PostImportFinder`. This is what causes the import request to pass to the other finders on `sys.meta_path`.

After a module has been loaded with `imp.import_module()`, all handlers currently registered in `_post_import_hooks` are called with the newly loaded module as an argument. From this point forward, the handlers are free to do what they want with the module.

A major feature of the approach shown in this recipe is that the patching of a module occurs in a seamless fashion, regardless of where or how a module of interest is actually loaded. You simply write a handler function that's decorated with `@when_imported()` and it all just magically works from that point forward.

One caution about this recipe is that it does not work for modules that have been explicitly reloaded using `imp.reload()`. That is, if you reload a previously loaded module, the post import handler function doesn't get triggered again (all the more reason to not use `reload()` in production code). On the other hand, if you delete the module from `sys.modules` and redo the import, you'll see the handler trigger again.

More information about post-import hooks can be found in PEP 369 (*http://www.python.org/dev/peps/pep-0369*). As of this writing, the PEP has been withdrawn by the author due to it being out of date with the current implementation of the `importlib` module. However, it is easy enough to implement your own solution using this recipe.

10.13. Installing Packages Just for Yourself

Problem

You want to install a third-party package, but you don't have permission to install packages into the system Python. Alternatively, perhaps you just want to install a package for your own use, not all users on the system.

Solution

Python has a per-user installation directory that's typically located in a directory such as *~/.local/lib/python3.3/site-packages*. To force packages to install in this directory, give the `--user` option to the installation command. For example:

```
python3 setup.py install --user
```

or

```
pip install --user packagename
```

The user *site-packages* directory normally appears before the system *site-packages* directory on `sys.path`. Thus, packages you install using this technique take priority over the packages already installed on the system (although this is not always the case depending on the behavior of third-party package managers, such as `distribute` or `pip`).

Discussion

Normally, packages get installed into the system-wide *site-packages* directory, which is found in a location such as */usr/local/lib/python3.3/site-packages*. However, doing so typically requires administrator permissions and use of the sudo command. Even if you have permission to execute such a command, using sudo to install a new, possibly un-proven, package might give you some pause.

Installing packages into the per-user directory is often an effective workaround that allows you to create a custom installation.

As an alternative, you can also create a virtual environment, which is discussed in the next recipe.

10.14. Creating a New Python Environment

Problem

You want to create a new Python environment in which you can install modules and packages. However, you want to do this without installing a new copy of Python or making changes that might affect the system Python installation.

Solution

You can make a new "virtual" environment using the pyvenv command. This command is installed in the same directory as the Python interpreter or possibly in the *Scripts* directory on Windows. Here is an example:

```
bash % pyvenv Spam
bash %
```

The name supplied to pyvenv is the name of a directory that will be created. Upon creation, the *Spam* directory will look something like this:

```
bash % cd Spam
bash % ls
bin             include         lib         pyvenv.cfg
bash %
```

In the *bin* directory, you'll find a Python interpreter that you can use. For example:

```
bash % Spam/bin/python3
Python 3.3.0 (default, Oct  6 2012, 15:45:22)
[GCC 4.2.1 (Apple Inc. build 5666) (dot 3)] on darwin
Type "help", "copyright", "credits" or "license" for more information.
>>> from pprint import pprint
>>> import sys
>>> pprint(sys.path)
['',
```

```
    '/usr/local/lib/python33.zip',
    '/usr/local/lib/python3.3',
    '/usr/local/lib/python3.3/plat-darwin',
    '/usr/local/lib/python3.3/lib-dynload',
    '/Users/beazley/Spam/lib/python3.3/site-packages']
>>>
```

A key feature of this interpreter is that its *site-packages* directory has been set to the newly created environment. Should you decide to install third-party packages, they will be installed here, not in the normal system *site-packages* directory.

Discussion

The creation of a virtual environment mostly pertains to the installation and management of third-party packages. As you can see in the example, the `sys.path` variable contains directories from the normal system Python, but the *site-packages* directory has been relocated to a new directory.

With a new virtual environment, the next step is often to install a package manager, such as `distribute` or `pip`. When installing such tools and subsequent packages, you just need to make sure you use the interpreter that's part of the virtual environment. This should install the packages into the newly created *site-packages* directory.

Although a virtual environment might look like a copy of the Python installation, it really only consists of a few files and symbolic links. All of the standard library files and interpreter executables come from the original Python installation. Thus, creating such environments is easy, and takes almost no machine resources.

By default, virtual environments are completely clean and contain no third-party add-ons. If you would like to include already installed packages as part of a virtual environment, create the environment using the `--system-site-packages` option. For example:

```
bash % pyvenv --system-site-packages Spam
bash %
```

More information about `pyvenv` and virtual environments can be found in PEP 405 (*http://www.python.org/dev/peps/pep-0405*).

10.15. Distributing Packages

Problem

You've written a useful library, and you want to be able to give it away to others.

Solution

If you're going to start giving code away, the first thing to do is to give it a unique name and clean up its directory structure. For example, a typical library package might look something like this:

```
projectname/
    README.txt
    Doc/
        documentation.txt
    projectname/
        __init__.py
        foo.py
        bar.py
        utils/
            __init__.py
            spam.py
            grok.py
    examples/
        helloworld.py
        ...
```

To make the package something that you can distribute, first write a *setup.py* file that looks like this:

```
# setup.py
from distutils.core import setup

setup(name='projectname',
      version='1.0',
      author='Your Name',
      author_email='you@youraddress.com',
      url='http://www.you.com/projectname',
      packages=['projectname', 'projectname.utils'],
)
```

Next, make a file *MANIFEST.in* that lists various nonsource files that you want to include in your package:

```
# MANIFEST.in
include *.txt
recursive-include examples *
recursive-include Doc *
```

Make sure the *setup.py* and *MANIFEST.in* files appear in the top-level directory of your package. Once you have done this, you should be able to make a source distribution by typing a command such as this:

```
% bash python3 setup.py sdist
```

This will create a file such as *projectname-1.0.zip* or *projectname-1.0.tar.gz*, depending on the platform. If it all works, this file is suitable for giving to others or uploading to the Python Package Index (*http://pypi.python.org*).

Discussion

For pure Python code, writing a plain *setup.py* file is usually straightforward. One potential gotcha is that you have to manually list every subdirectory that makes up the packages source code. A common mistake is to only list the top-level directory of a package and to forget to include package subcomponents. This is why the specification for `packages` in *setup.py* includes the list `packages=['projectname', 'project name.utils']`.

As most Python programmers know, there are many third-party packaging options, including setuptools, distribute, and so forth. Some of these are replacements for the `distutils` library found in the standard library. Be aware that if you rely on these packages, users may not be able to install your software unless they also install the required package manager first. Because of this, you can almost never go wrong by keeping things as simple as possible. At a bare minimum, make sure your code can be installed using a standard Python 3 installation. Additional features can be supported as an option if additional packages are available.

Packaging and distribution of code involving C extensions can get considerably more complicated. Chapter 15 on C extensions has a few details on this. In particular, see Recipe 15.2.

## CHAPTER 11

Network and Web Programming

This chapter is about various topics related to using Python in networked and distributed applications. Topics are split between using Python as a client to access existing services and using Python to implement networked services as a server. Common techniques for writing code involving cooperating or communicating with interpreters are also given.

11.1. Interacting with HTTP Services As a Client

Problem

You need to access various services via HTTP as a client. For example, downloading data or interacting with a REST-based API.

Solution

For simple things, it's usually easy enough to use the `urllib.request` module. For example, to send a simple HTTP GET request to a remote service, do something like this:

```python
from urllib import request, parse

# Base URL being accessed
url = 'http://httpbin.org/get'

# Dictionary of query parameters (if any)
parms = {
    'name1' : 'value1',
    'name2' : 'value2'
}

# Encode the query string
querystring = parse.urlencode(parms)
```

```
# Make a GET request and read the response
u = request.urlopen(url+'?' + querystring)
resp = u.read()
```

If you need to send the query parameters in the request body using a POST method, encode them and supply them as an optional argument to urlopen() like this:

```
from urllib import request, parse

# Base URL being accessed
url = 'http://httpbin.org/post'

# Dictionary of query parameters (if any)
parms = {
   'name1' : 'value1',
   'name2' : 'value2'
}

# Encode the query string
querystring = parse.urlencode(parms)

# Make a POST request and read the response
u = request.urlopen(url, querystring.encode('ascii'))
resp = u.read()
```

If you need to supply some custom HTTP headers in the outgoing request such as a change to the user-agent field, make a dictionary containing their value and create a Request instance and pass it to urlopen() like this:

```
from urllib import request, parse
...

# Extra headers
headers = {
    'User-agent' : 'none/ofyourbusiness',
    'Spam' : 'Eggs'
}

req = request.Request(url, querystring.encode('ascii'), headers=headers)

# Make a request and read the response
u = request.urlopen(req)
resp = u.read()
```

If your interaction with a service is more complicated than this, you should probably look at the requests library (*http://pypi.python.org/pypi/requests*). For example, here is equivalent requests code for the preceding operations:

```
import requests

# Base URL being accessed
url = 'http://httpbin.org/post'
```

```
# Dictionary of query parameters (if any)
parms = {
    'name1' : 'value1',
    'name2' : 'value2'
}

# Extra headers
headers = {
    'User-agent' : 'none/ofyourbusiness',
    'Spam' : 'Eggs'
}

resp = requests.post(url, data=parms, headers=headers)

# Decoded text returned by the request
text = resp.text
```

A notable feature of `requests` is how it returns the resulting response content from a request. As shown, the `resp.text` attribute gives you the Unicode decoded text of a request. However, if you access `resp.content`, you get the raw binary content instead. On the other hand, if you access `resp.json`, then you get the response content interpreted as JSON.

Here is an example of using `requests` to make a HEAD request and extract a few fields of header data from the response:

```
import requests

resp = requests.head('http://www.python.org/index.html')

status = resp.status_code
last_modified = resp.headers['last-modified']
content_type = resp.headers['content-type']
content_length = resp.headers['content-length']
```

Here is a `requests` example that executes a login into the Python Package index using basic authentication:

```
import requests

resp = requests.get('http://pypi.python.org/pypi?:action=login',
                    auth=('user','password'))
```

Here is an example of using `requests` to pass HTTP cookies from one request to the next:

```
import requests

# First request
resp1 = requests.get(url)
...
```

```
# Second requests with cookies received on first requests
resp2 = requests.get(url, cookies=resp1.cookies)
```

Last, but not least, here is an example of using `requests` to upload content:

```
import requests
url = 'http://httpbin.org/post'
files = { 'file': ('data.csv', open('data.csv', 'rb')) }

r = requests.post(url, files=files)
```

Discussion

For really simple HTTP client code, using the built-in `urllib` module is usually fine. However, if you have to do anything other than simple `GET` or `POST` requests, you really can't rely on its functionality. This is where a third-party module, such as `requests`, comes in handy.

For example, if you decided to stick entirely with the standard library instead of a library like `requests`, you might have to implement your code using the low-level `http.cli ent` module instead. For example, this code shows how to execute a `HEAD` request:

```
from http.client import HTTPConnection
from urllib import parse

c = HTTPConnection('www.python.org', 80)
c.request('HEAD', '/index.html')
resp = c.getresponse()

print('Status', resp.status)
for name, value in resp.getheaders():
    print(name, value)
```

Similarly, if you have to write code involving proxies, authentication, cookies, and other details, using `urllib` is awkward and verbose. For example, here is a sample of code that authenticates to the Python package index:

```
import urllib.request

auth = urllib.request.HTTPBasicAuthHandler()
auth.add_password('pypi','http://pypi.python.org','username','password')
opener = urllib.request.build_opener(auth)

r = urllib.request.Request('http://pypi.python.org/pypi?:action=login')
u = opener.open(r)
resp = u.read()

# From here. You can access more pages using opener
...
```

Frankly, all of this is much easier in `requests`.

Testing HTTP client code during development can often be frustrating because of all the tricky details you need to worry about (e.g., cookies, authentication, headers, encodings, etc.). To do this, consider using the httpbin service (*http://httpbin.org*). This site receives requests and then echoes information back to you in the form a JSON response. Here is an interactive example:

```
>>> import requests
>>> r = requests.get('http://httpbin.org/get?name=Dave&n=37',
...     headers = { 'User-agent': 'goaway/1.0' })
>>> resp = r.json
>>> resp['headers']
{'User-Agent': 'goaway/1.0', 'Content-Length': '', 'Content-Type': '',
'Accept-Encoding': 'gzip, deflate, compress', 'Connection':
'keep-alive', 'Host': 'httpbin.org', 'Accept': '*/*'}
>>> resp['args']
{'name': 'Dave', 'n': '37'}
>>>
```

Working with a site such as *httpbin.org* is often preferable to experimenting with a real site—especially if there's a risk it might shut down your account after three failed login attempts (i.e., don't try to learn how to write an HTTP authentication client by logging into your bank).

Although it's not discussed here, `requests` provides support for many more advanced HTTP-client protocols, such as OAuth. The `requests` documentation (*http://docs.python-requests.org*) is excellent (and frankly better than anything that could be provided in this short space). Go there for more information.

11.2. Creating a TCP Server

Problem

You want to implement a server that communicates with clients using the TCP Internet protocol.

Solution

An easy way to create a TCP server is to use the `socketserver` library. For example, here is a simple echo server:

```
from socketserver import BaseRequestHandler, TCPServer

class EchoHandler(BaseRequestHandler):
    def handle(self):
        print('Got connection from', self.client_address)
        while True:
```

```
                    msg = self.request.recv(8192)
                    if not msg:
                        break
                    self.request.send(msg)

        if __name__ == '__main__':
            serv = TCPServer(('', 20000), EchoHandler)
            serv.serve_forever()
```

In this code, you define a special handler class that implements a handle() method for servicing client connections. The request attribute is the underlying client socket and client_address has client address.

To test the server, run it and then open a separate Python process that connects to it:

```
>>> from socket import socket, AF_INET, SOCK_STREAM
>>> s = socket(AF_INET, SOCK_STREAM)
>>> s.connect(('localhost', 20000))
>>> s.send(b'Hello')
5
>>> s.recv(8192)
b'Hello'
>>>
```

In many cases, it may be easier to define a slightly different kind of handler. Here is an example that uses the StreamRequestHandler base class to put a file-like interface on the underlying socket:

```
from socketserver import StreamRequestHandler, TCPServer

class EchoHandler(StreamRequestHandler):
    def handle(self):
        print('Got connection from', self.client_address)
        # self.rfile is a file-like object for reading
        for line in self.rfile:
            # self.wfile is a file-like object for writing
            self.wfile.write(line)

if __name__ == '__main__':
    serv = TCPServer(('', 20000), EchoHandler)
    serv.serve_forever()
```

Discussion

socketserver makes it relatively easy to create simple TCP servers. However, you should be aware that, by default, the servers are single threaded and can only serve one client at a time. If you want to handle multiple clients, either instantiate a ForkingTCP Server or ThreadingTCPServer object instead. For example:

```
from socketserver import ThreadingTCPServer
...
```

```
if __name__ == '__main__':
    serv = ThreadingTCPServer(('', 20000), EchoHandler)
    serv.serve_forever()
```

One issue with forking and threaded servers is that they spawn a new process or thread on each client connection. There is no upper bound on the number of allowed clients, so a malicious hacker could potentially launch a large number of simultaneous connections in an effort to make your server explode.

If this is a concern, you can create a pre-allocated pool of worker threads or processes. To do this, you create an instance of a normal nonthreaded server, but then launch the serve_forever() method in a pool of multiple threads. For example:

```
...
if __name__ == '__main__':
    from threading import Thread
    NWORKERS = 16
    serv = TCPServer(('', 20000), EchoHandler)
    for n in range(NWORKERS):
        t = Thread(target=serv.serve_forever)
        t.daemon = True
        t.start()
    serv.serve_forever()
```

Normally, a TCPServer binds and activates the underlying socket upon instantiation. However, sometimes you might want to adjust the underlying socket by setting options. To do this, supply the bind_and_activate=False argument, like this:

```
if __name__ == '__main__':
    serv = TCPServer(('', 20000), EchoHandler, bind_and_activate=False)
    # Set up various socket options
    serv.socket.setsockopt(socket.SOL_SOCKET, socket.SO_REUSEADDR, True)
    # Bind and activate
    serv.server_bind()
    serv.server_activate()
    serv.serve_forever()
```

The socket option shown is actually a very common setting that allows the server to rebind to a previously used port number. It's actually so common that it's a class variable that can be set on TCPServer. Set it before instantiating the server, as shown in this example:

```
...
if __name__ == '__main__':
    TCPServer.allow_reuse_address = True
    serv = TCPServer(('', 20000), EchoHandler)
    serv.serve_forever()
```

In the solution, two different handler base classes were shown (BaseRequestHandler and StreamRequestHandler). The StreamRequestHandler class is actually a bit more flexible, and supports some features that can be enabled through the specification of additional class variables. For example:

```python
import socket

class EchoHandler(StreamRequestHandler):
    # Optional settings (defaults shown)
    timeout = 5                            # Timeout on all socket operations
    rbufsize = -1                          # Read buffer size
    wbufsize = 0                           # Write buffer size
    disable_nagle_algorithm = False  # Sets TCP_NODELAY socket option
    def handle(self):
        print('Got connection from', self.client_address)
        try:
            for line in self.rfile:
                # self.wfile is a file-like object for writing
                self.wfile.write(line)
        except socket.timeout:
            print('Timed out!')
```

Finally, it should be noted that most of Python's higher-level networking modules (e.g., HTTP, XML-RPC, etc.) are built on top of the socketserver functionality. That said, it is also not difficult to implement servers directly using the socket library as well. Here is a simple example of directly programming a server with Sockets:

```python
from socket import socket, AF_INET, SOCK_STREAM

def echo_handler(address, client_sock):
    print('Got connection from {}'.format(address))
    while True:
        msg = client_sock.recv(8192)
        if not msg:
            break
        client_sock.sendall(msg)
    client_sock.close()

def echo_server(address, backlog=5):
    sock = socket(AF_INET, SOCK_STREAM)
    sock.bind(address)
    sock.listen(backlog)
    while True:
        client_sock, client_addr = sock.accept()
        echo_handler(client_addr, client_sock)

if __name__ == '__main__':
    echo_server(('', 20000))
```

11.3. Creating a UDP Server

Problem

You want to implement a server that communicates with clients using the UDP Internet protocol.

Solution

As with TCP, UDP servers are also easy to create using the socketserver library. For example, here is a simple time server:

```
from socketserver import BaseRequestHandler, UDPServer
import time

class TimeHandler(BaseRequestHandler):
    def handle(self):
        print('Got connection from', self.client_address)
        # Get message and client socket
        msg, sock = self.request
        resp = time.ctime()
        sock.sendto(resp.encode('ascii'), self.client_address)

if __name__ == '__main__':
    serv = UDPServer(('', 20000), TimeHandler)
    serv.serve_forever()
```

As before, you define a special handler class that implements a handle() method for servicing client connections. The request attribute is a tuple that contains the incoming datagram and underlying socket object for the server. The client_address contains the client address.

To test the server, run it and then open a separate Python process that sends messages to it:

```
>>> from socket import socket, AF_INET, SOCK_DGRAM
>>> s = socket(AF_INET, SOCK_DGRAM)
>>> s.sendto(b'', ('localhost', 20000))
0
>>> s.recvfrom(8192)
(b'Wed Aug 15 20:35:08 2012', ('127.0.0.1', 20000))
>>>
```

Discussion

A typical UDP server receives an incoming datagram (message) along with a client address. If the server is to respond, it sends a datagram back to the client. For transmission of datagrams, you should use the sendto() and recvfrom() methods of a socket. Although the traditional `send()` and `recv()` methods also might work, the former two methods are more commonly used with UDP communication.

Given that there is no underlying connection, UDP servers are often much easier to write than a TCP server. However, UDP is also inherently unreliable (e.g., no "connection" is established and messages might be lost). Thus, it would be up to you to figure out how to deal with lost messages. That's a topic beyond the scope of this book, but typically you might need to introduce sequence numbers, retries, timeouts, and other mechanisms to ensure reliability if it matters for your application. UDP is often used in cases where the requirement of reliable delivery can be relaxed. For instance, in real-time applications such as multimedia streaming and games where there is simply no option to go back in time and recover a lost packet (the program simply skips it and keeps moving forward).

The `UDPServer` class is single threaded, which means that only one request can be serviced at a time. In practice, this is less of an issue with UDP than with TCP connections. However, should you want concurrent operation, instantiate a `ForkingUDPServer` or `ThreadingUDPServer` object instead:

```python
from socketserver import ThreadingUDPServer
...
if __name__ == '__main__':
    serv = ThreadingUDPServer(('',20000), TimeHandler)
    serv.serve_forever()
```

Implementing a UDP server directly using sockets is also not difficult. Here is an example:

```python
from socket import socket, AF_INET, SOCK_DGRAM
import time

def time_server(address):
    sock = socket(AF_INET, SOCK_DGRAM)
    sock.bind(address)
    while True:
        msg, addr = sock.recvfrom(8192)
        print('Got message from', addr)
        resp = time.ctime()
        sock.sendto(resp.encode('ascii'), addr)

if __name__ == '__main__':
    time_server(('', 20000))
```

11.4. Generating a Range of IP Addresses from a CIDR Address

Problem

You have a CIDR network address such as "123.45.67.89/27," and you want to generate a range of all the IP addresses that it represents (e.g., "123.45.67.64," "123.45.67.65," ..., "123.45.67.95").

Solution

The `ipaddress` module can be easily used to perform such calculations. For example:

```
>>> import ipaddress
>>> net = ipaddress.ip_network('123.45.67.64/27')
>>> net
IPv4Network('123.45.67.64/27')
>>> for a in net:
...     print(a)
...
123.45.67.64
123.45.67.65
123.45.67.66
123.45.67.67
123.45.67.68
...
123.45.67.95
>>>

>>> net6 = ipaddress.ip_network('12:3456:78:90ab:cd:ef01:23:30/125')
>>> net6
IPv6Network('12:3456:78:90ab:cd:ef01:23:30/125')
>>> for a in net6:
...     print(a)
...
12:3456:78:90ab:cd:ef01:23:30
12:3456:78:90ab:cd:ef01:23:31
12:3456:78:90ab:cd:ef01:23:32
12:3456:78:90ab:cd:ef01:23:33
12:3456:78:90ab:cd:ef01:23:34
12:3456:78:90ab:cd:ef01:23:35
12:3456:78:90ab:cd:ef01:23:36
12:3456:78:90ab:cd:ef01:23:37
>>>
```

Network objects also allow indexing like arrays. For example:

```
>>> net.num_addresses
32
>>> net[0]
```

```
IPv4Address('123.45.67.64')
>>> net[1]
IPv4Address('123.45.67.65')
>>> net[-1]
IPv4Address('123.45.67.95')
>>> net[-2]
IPv4Address('123.45.67.94')
>>>
```

In addition, you can perform operations such as a check for network membership:

```
>>> a = ipaddress.ip_address('123.45.67.69')
>>> a in net
True
>>> b = ipaddress.ip_address('123.45.67.123')
>>> b in net
False
>>>
```

An IP address and network address can be specified together as an IP interface. For example:

```
>>> inet = ipaddress.ip_interface('123.45.67.73/27')
>>> inet.network
IPv4Network('123.45.67.64/27')
>>> inet.ip
IPv4Address('123.45.67.73')
>>>
```

Discussion

The ipaddress module has classes for representing IP addresses, networks, and interfaces. This can be especially useful if you want to write code that needs to manipulate network addresses in some way (e.g., parsing, printing, validating, etc.).

Be aware that there is only limited interaction between the ipaddress module and other network-related modules, such as the socket library. In particular, it is usually not possible to use an instance of IPv4Address as a substitute for address string. Instead, you have to explicitly convert it using str() first. For example:

```
>>> a = ipaddress.ip_address('127.0.0.1')
>>> from socket import socket, AF_INET, SOCK_STREAM
>>> s = socket(AF_INET, SOCK_STREAM)
>>> s.connect((a, 8080))
Traceback (most recent call last):
  File "<stdin>", line 1, in <module>
TypeError: Can't convert 'IPv4Address' object to str implicitly
>>> s.connect((str(a), 8080))
>>>
```

See "An Introduction to the ipaddress Module" (*http://docs.python.org/3/howto/ipad dress.html*) for more information and advanced usage.

11.5. Creating a Simple REST-Based Interface

Problem

You want to be able to control or interact with your program remotely over the network using a simple REST-based interface. However, you don't want to do it by installing a full-fledged web programming framework.

Solution

One of the easiest ways to build REST-based interfaces is to create a tiny library based on the WSGI standard, as described in PEP 3333 (*http://www.python.org/dev/peps/pep-3333*). Here is an example:

```python
# resty.py

import cgi

def notfound_404(environ, start_response):
    start_response('404 Not Found', [ ('Content-type', 'text/plain') ])
    return [b'Not Found']

class PathDispatcher:
    def __init__(self):
        self.pathmap = { }

    def __call__(self, environ, start_response):
        path = environ['PATH_INFO']
        params = cgi.FieldStorage(environ['wsgi.input'],
                                  environ=environ)
        method = environ['REQUEST_METHOD'].lower()
        environ['params'] = { key: params.getvalue(key) for key in params }
        handler = self.pathmap.get((method,path), notfound_404)
        return handler(environ, start_response)

    def register(self, method, path, function):
        self.pathmap[method.lower(), path] = function
        return function
```

To use this dispatcher, you simply write different handlers, such as the following:

```python
import time

_hello_resp = '''\
<html>
  <head>
     <title>Hello {name}</title>
  </head>
  <body>
     <h1>Hello {name}!</h1>
  </body>
```

```
</html>'''

def hello_world(environ, start_response):
    start_response('200 OK', [ ('Content-type','text/html')])
    params = environ['params']
    resp = _hello_resp.format(name=params.get('name'))
    yield resp.encode('utf-8')

_localtime_resp = '''\
<?xml version="1.0"?>
<time>
  <year>{t.tm_year}</year>
  <month>{t.tm_mon}</month>
  <day>{t.tm_mday}</day>
  <hour>{t.tm_hour}</hour>
  <minute>{t.tm_min}</minute>
  <second>{t.tm_sec}</second>
</time>'''

def localtime(environ, start_response):
    start_response('200 OK', [ ('Content-type', 'application/xml') ])
    resp = _localtime_resp.format(t=time.localtime())
    yield resp.encode('utf-8')

if __name__ == '__main__':
    from resty import PathDispatcher
    from wsgiref.simple_server import make_server

    # Create the dispatcher and register functions
    dispatcher = PathDispatcher()
    dispatcher.register('GET', '/hello', hello_world)
    dispatcher.register('GET', '/localtime', localtime)

    # Launch a basic server
    httpd = make_server('', 8080, dispatcher)
    print('Serving on port 8080...')
    httpd.serve_forever()
```

To test your server, you can interact with it using a browser or urllib. For example:

```
>>> u = urlopen('http://localhost:8080/hello?name=Guido')
>>> print(u.read().decode('utf-8'))
<html>
  <head>
     <title>Hello Guido</title>
  </head>
  <body>
     <h1>Hello Guido!</h1>
  </body>
</html>
>>> u = urlopen('http://localhost:8080/localtime')
>>> print(u.read().decode('utf-8'))
<?xml version="1.0"?>
```

```
<time>
  <year>2012</year>
  <month>11</month>
  <day>24</day>
  <hour>14</hour>
  <minute>49</minute>
  <second>17</second>
</time>
>>>
```

Discussion

In REST-based interfaces, you are typically writing programs that respond to common HTTP requests. However, unlike a full-fledged website, you're often just pushing data around. This data might be encoded in a variety of standard formats such as XML, JSON, or CSV. Although it seems minimal, providing an API in this manner can be a very useful thing for a wide variety of applications.

For example, long-running programs might use a REST API to implement monitoring or diagnostics. Big data applications can use REST to build a query/data extraction system. REST can even be used to control hardware devices, such as robots, sensors, mills, or lightbulbs. What's more, REST APIs are well supported by various client-side programming environments, such as Javascript, Android, iOS, and so forth. Thus, having such an interface can be a way to encourage the development of more complex applications that interface with your code.

For implementing a simple REST interface, it is often easy enough to base your code on the Python WSGI standard. WSGI is supported by the standard library, but also by most third-party web frameworks. Thus, if you use it, there is a lot of flexibility in how your code might be used later.

In WSGI, you simply implement applications in the form of a callable that accepts this calling convention:

```
import cgi

def wsgi_app(environ, start_response):
    ...
```

The environ argument is a dictionary that contains values inspired by the CGI interface provided by various web servers such as Apache [see Internet RFC 3875 (*http://tools.ietf.org/html/rfc3875*)]. To extract different fields, you would write code like this:

```
def wsgi_app(environ, start_response):
    method = environ['REQUEST_METHOD']
    path = environ['PATH_INFO']
    # Parse the query parameters
    params = cgi.FieldStorage(environ['wsgi.input'], environ=environ)
    ...
```

A few common values are shown here. environ['REQUEST_METHOD'] is the type of request (e.g., GET, POST, HEAD, etc.). environ['PATH_INFO'] is the path or the resource being requested. The call to cgi.FieldStorage() extracts supplied query parameters from the request and puts them into a dictionary-like object for later use.

The start_response argument is a function that must be called to initiate a response. The first argument is the resulting HTTP status. The second argument is a list of (name, value) tuples that make up the HTTP headers of the response. For example:

```python
def wsgi_app(environ, start_response):
    ...
    start_response('200 OK', [('Content-type', 'text/plain')])
```

To return data, an WSGI application must return a sequence of byte strings. This can be done using a list like this:

```python
def wsgi_app(environ, start_response):
    ...
    start_response('200 OK', [('Content-type', 'text/plain')])
    resp = []
    resp.append(b'Hello World\n')
    resp.append(b'Goodbye!\n')
    return resp
```

Alternatively, you can use yield:

```python
def wsgi_app(environ, start_response):
    ...
    start_response('200 OK', [('Content-type', 'text/plain')])
    yield b'Hello World\n'
    yield b'Goodbye!\n'
```

It's important to emphasize that byte strings must be used in the result. If the response consists of text, it will need to be encoded into bytes first. Of course, there is no requirement that the returned value be text—you could easily write an application function that creates images.

Although WSGI applications are commonly defined as a function, as shown, an instance may also be used as long as it implements a suitable __call__() method. For example:

```python
class WSGIApplication:
    def __init__(self):
        ...
    def __call__(self, environ, start_response)
        ...
```

This technique has been used to create the PathDispatcher class in the recipe. The dispatcher does nothing more than manage a dictionary mapping (method, path) pairs to handler functions. When a request arrives, the method and path are extracted and used to dispatch to a handler. In addition, any query variables are parsed and put into a dictionary that is stored as `environ['params']` (this latter step is so common, it makes a lot of sense to simply do it in the dispatcher in order to avoid a lot of replicated code).

To use the dispatcher, you simply create an instance and register various WSGI-style application functions with it, as shown in the recipe. Writing these functions should be extremely straightforward, as you follow the rules concerning the `start_response()` function and produce output as byte strings.

One thing to consider when writing such functions is the careful use of string templates. Nobody likes to work with code that is a tangled mess of `print()` functions, XML, and various formatting operations. In the solution, triple-quoted string templates are being defined and used internally. This particular approach makes it easier to change the format of the output later (just change the template as opposed to any of the code that uses it).

Finally, an important part of using WSGI is that nothing in the implementation is specific to a particular web server. That is actually the whole idea—since the standard is server and framework neutral, you should be able to plug your application into a wide variety of servers. In the recipe, the following code is used for testing:

```python
if __name__ == '__main__':
    from wsgiref.simple_server import make_server

    # Create the dispatcher and register functions
    dispatcher = PathDispatcher()
    ...

    # Launch a basic server
    httpd = make_server('', 8080, dispatcher)
    print('Serving on port 8080...')
    httpd.serve_forever()
```

This will create a simple server that you can use to see if your implementation works. Later on, when you're ready to scale things up to a larger level, you will change this code to work with a particular server.

WSGI is an intentionally minimal specification. As such, it doesn't provide any support for more advanced concepts such as authentication, cookies, redirection, and so forth. These are not hard to implement yourself. However, if you want just a bit more support, you might consider third-party libraries, such as WebOb (*http://webob.org*) or Paste (*http://pythonpaste.org*).

11.6. Implementing a Simple Remote Procedure Call with XML-RPC

Problem

You want an easy way to execute functions or methods in Python programs running on remote machines.

Solution

Perhaps the easiest way to implement a simple remote procedure call mechanism is to use XML-RPC. Here is an example of a simple server that implements a simple key-value store:

```python
from xmlrpc.server import SimpleXMLRPCServer

class KeyValueServer:
    _rpc_methods_ = ['get', 'set', 'delete', 'exists', 'keys']
    def __init__(self, address):
        self._data = {}
        self._serv = SimpleXMLRPCServer(address, allow_none=True)
        for name in self._rpc_methods_:
            self._serv.register_function(getattr(self, name))

    def get(self, name):
        return self._data[name]

    def set(self, name, value):
        self._data[name] = value

    def delete(self, name):
        del self._data[name]

    def exists(self, name):
        return name in self._data

    def keys(self):
        return list(self._data)

    def serve_forever(self):
        self._serv.serve_forever()

# Example
if __name__ == '__main__':
    kvserv = KeyValueServer(('', 15000))
    kvserv.serve_forever()
```

Here is how you would access the server remotely from a client:

```
>>> from xmlrpc.client import ServerProxy
>>> s = ServerProxy('http://localhost:15000', allow_none=True)
>>> s.set('foo', 'bar')
>>> s.set('spam', [1, 2, 3])
>>> s.keys()
['spam', 'foo']
>>> s.get('foo')
'bar'
>>> s.get('spam')
[1, 2, 3]
>>> s.delete('spam')
>>> s.exists('spam')
False
>>>
```

Discussion

XML-RPC can be an extremely easy way to set up a simple remote procedure call service. All you need to do is create a server instance, register functions with it using the `regis ter_function()` method, and then launch it using the `serve_forever()` method. This recipe packages it up into a class to put all of the code together, but there is no such requirement. For example, you could create a server by trying something like this:

```
from xmlrpc.server import SimpleXMLRPCServer
def add(x,y):
    return x+y

serv = SimpleXMLRPCServer(('', 15000))
serv.register_function(add)
serv.serve_forever()
```

Functions exposed via XML-RPC only work with certain kinds of data such as strings, numbers, lists, and dictionaries. For everything else, some study is required. For instance, if you pass an instance through XML-RPC, only its instance dictionary is handled:

```
>>> class Point:
...     def __init__(self, x, y):
...             self.x = x
...             self.y = y
...
>>> p = Point(2, 3)
>>> s.set('foo', p)
>>> s.get('foo')
{'x': 2, 'y': 3}
>>>
```

Similarly, handling of binary data is a bit different than you expect:

```
>>> s.set('foo', b'Hello World')
>>> s.get('foo')
<xmlrpc.client.Binary object at 0x10131d410>
```

```
>>> _.data
b'Hello World'
>>>
```

As a general rule, you probably shouldn't expose an XML-RPC service to the rest of the world as a public API. It often works best on internal networks where you might want to write simple distributed programs involving a few different machines.

A downside to XML-RPC is its performance. The `SimpleXMLRPCServer` implementation is only single threaded, and wouldn't be appropriate for scaling a large application, although it can be made to run multithreaded, as shown in Recipe 11.2. Also, since XML-RPC serializes all data as XML, it's inherently slower than other approaches. However, one benefit of this encoding is that it's understood by a variety of other programming languages. By using it, clients written in languages other than Python will be able to access your service.

Despite its limitations, XML-RPC is worth knowing about if you ever have the need to make a quick and dirty remote procedure call system. Oftentimes, the simple solution is good enough.

11.7. Communicating Simply Between Interpreters

Problem

You are running multiple instances of the Python interpreter, possibly on different machines, and you would like to exchange data between interpreters using messages.

Solution

It is easy to communicate between interpreters if you use the `multiprocessing.con nection` module. Here is a simple example of writing an echo server:

```
from multiprocessing.connection import Listener
import traceback

def echo_client(conn):
    try:
        while True:
            msg = conn.recv()
            conn.send(msg)
    except EOFError:
        print('Connection closed')

def echo_server(address, authkey):
    serv = Listener(address, authkey=authkey)
    while True:
        try:
            client = serv.accept()
```

```
            echo_client(client)
        except Exception:
            traceback.print_exc()

    echo_server(('', 25000), authkey=b'peekaboo')
```

Here is a simple example of a client connecting to the server and sending various messages:

```
>>> from multiprocessing.connection import Client
>>> c = Client(('localhost', 25000), authkey=b'peekaboo')
>>> c.send('hello')
>>> c.recv()
'hello'
>>> c.send(42)
>>> c.recv()
42
>>> c.send([1, 2, 3, 4, 5])
>>> c.recv()
[1, 2, 3, 4, 5]
>>>
```

Unlike a low-level socket, messages are kept intact (each object sent using send() is received in its entirety with recv()). In addition, objects are serialized using pickle. So, any object compatible with pickle can be sent or received over the connection.

Discussion

There are many packages and libraries related to implementing various forms of message passing, such as ZeroMQ, Celery, and so forth. As an alternative, you might also be inclined to implement a message layer on top of low-level sockets. However, sometimes you just want a simple solution. The multiprocessing.connection library is just that—using a few simple primitives, you can easily connect interpreters together and have them exchange messages.

If you know that the interpreters are going to be running on the same machine, you can use alternative forms of networking, such as UNIX domain sockets or Windows named pipes. To create a connection using a UNIX domain socket, simply change the address to a filename such as this:

```
    s = Listener('/tmp/myconn', authkey=b'peekaboo')
```

To create a connection using a Windows named pipe, use a filename such as this:

```
    s = Listener(r'\\.\pipe\myconn', authkey=b'peekaboo')
```

As a general rule, you would not be using multiprocessing to implement public-facing services. The authkey parameter to Client() and Listener() is there to help authenticate the end points of the connection. Connection attempts with a bad key raise an exception. In addition, the module is probably best suited for long-running connections (not a large number of short connections). For example, two interpreters might establish a connection at startup and keep the connection active for the entire duration of a problem.

Don't use `multiprocessing` if you need more low-level control over aspects of the connection. For example, if you needed to support timeouts, nonblocking I/O, or anything similar, you're probably better off using a different library or implementing such features on top of sockets instead.

11.8. Implementing Remote Procedure Calls

Problem

You want to implement simple remote procedure call (RPC) on top of a message passing layer, such as sockets, multiprocessing connections, or ZeroMQ.

Solution

RPC is easy to implement by encoding function requests, arguments, and return values using `pickle`, and passing the pickled byte strings between interpreters. Here is an example of a simple RPC handler that could be incorporated into a server:

```
# rpcserver.py

import pickle
class RPCHandler:
    def __init__(self):
        self._functions = { }

    def register_function(self, func):
        self._functions[func.__name__] = func

    def handle_connection(self, connection):
        try:
            while True:
                # Receive a message
                func_name, args, kwargs = pickle.loads(connection.recv())
                # Run the RPC and send a response
                try:
                    r = self._functions[func_name](*args,**kwargs)
                    connection.send(pickle.dumps(r))
                except Exception as e:
                    connection.send(pickle.dumps(e))
        except EOFError:
            pass
```

To use this handler, you need to add it into a messaging server. There are many possible choices, but the multiprocessing library provides a simple option. Here is an example RPC server:

```
from multiprocessing.connection import Listener
from threading import Thread

def rpc_server(handler, address, authkey):
    sock = Listener(address, authkey=authkey)
    while True:
        client = sock.accept()
        t = Thread(target=handler.handle_connection, args=(client,))
        t.daemon = True
        t.start()

# Some remote functions
def add(x, y):
    return x + y

def sub(x, y):
    return x - y

# Register with a handler
handler = RPCHandler()
handler.register_function(add)
handler.register_function(sub)

# Run the server
rpc_server(handler, ('localhost', 17000), authkey=b'peekaboo')
```

To access the server from a remote client, you need to create a corresponding RPC proxy class that forwards requests. For example:

```
import pickle

class RPCProxy:
    def __init__(self, connection):
        self._connection = connection
    def __getattr__(self, name):
        def do_rpc(*args, **kwargs):
            self._connection.send(pickle.dumps((name, args, kwargs)))
            result = pickle.loads(self._connection.recv())
            if isinstance(result, Exception):
                raise result
            return result
        return do_rpc
```

To use the proxy, you wrap it around a connection to the server. For example:

```
>>> from multiprocessing.connection import Client
>>> c = Client(('localhost', 17000), authkey=b'peekaboo')
>>> proxy = RPCProxy(c)
>>> proxy.add(2, 3)
```

```
5
>>> proxy.sub(2, 3)
-1
>>> proxy.sub([1, 2], 4)
Traceback (most recent call last):
  File "<stdin>", line 1, in <module>
  File "rpcserver.py", line 37, in do_rpc
    raise result
TypeError: unsupported operand type(s) for -: 'list' and 'int'
>>>
```

It should be noted that many messaging layers (such as multiprocessing) already serialize data using pickle. If this is the case, the pickle.dumps() and pickle.loads()
calls can be eliminated.

Discussion

The general idea of the RPCHandler and RPCProxy classes is relatively simple. If a client
wants to call a remote function, such as foo(1, 2, z=3), the proxy class creates a tuple
('foo', (1, 2), {'z': 3}) that contains the function name and arguments. This
tuple is pickled and sent over the connection. This is performed in the do_rpc() closure
that's returned by the __getattr__() method of RPCProxy. The server receives and
unpickles the message, looks up the function name to see if it's registered, and executes
it with the given arguments. The result (or exception) is then pickled and sent back.

As shown, the example relies on multiprocessing for communication. However, this
approach could be made to work with just about any other messaging system. For example, if you want to implement RPC over ZeroMQ, just replace the connection objects
with an appropriate ZeroMQ socket object.

Given the reliance on pickle, security is a major concern (because a clever hacker can
create messages that make arbitrary functions execute during unpickling). In particular,
you should never allow RPC from untrusted or unauthenticated clients. In particular,
you definitely don't want to allow access from just any machine on the Internet—this
should really only be used internally, behind a firewall, and not exposed to the rest of
the world.

As an alternative to pickle, you might consider the use of JSON, XML, or some other
data encoding for serialization. For example, this recipe is fairly easy to adapt to JSON
encoding if you simply replace pickle.loads() and pickle.dumps() with
json.loads() and json.dumps(). For example:

```
# jsonrpcserver.py
import json

class RPCHandler:
    def __init__(self):
        self._functions = { }
```

```python
    def register_function(self, func):
        self._functions[func.__name__] = func

    def handle_connection(self, connection):
        try:
            while True:
                # Receive a message
                func_name, args, kwargs = json.loads(connection.recv())
                # Run the RPC and send a response
                try:
                    r = self._functions[func_name](*args,**kwargs)
                    connection.send(json.dumps(r))
                except Exception as e:
                    connection.send(json.dumps(str(e)))
        except EOFError:
            pass

# jsonrpcclient.py
import json

class RPCProxy:
    def __init__(self, connection):
        self._connection = connection
    def __getattr__(self, name):
        def do_rpc(*args, **kwargs):
            self._connection.send(json.dumps((name, args, kwargs)))
            result = json.loads(self._connection.recv())
            return result
        return do_rpc
```

One complicated factor in implementing RPC is how to handle exceptions. At the very least, the server shouldn't crash if an exception is raised by a method. However, the means by which the exception gets reported back to the client requires some study. If you're using pickle, exception instances can often be serialized and reraised in the client. If you're using some other protocol, you might have to think of an alternative approach. At the very least, you would probably want to return the exception string in the response. This is the approach taken in the JSON example.

For another example of an RPC implementation, it can be useful to look at the implementation of the SimpleXMLRPCServer and ServerProxy classes used in XML-RPC, as described in Recipe 11.6.

11.9. Authenticating Clients Simply

Problem

You want a simple way to authenticate the clients connecting to servers in a distributed system, but don't need the complexity of something like SSL.

Solution

Simple but effective authentication can be performed by implementing a connection handshake using the hmac module. Here is sample code:

```
import hmac
import os

def client_authenticate(connection, secret_key):
    '''
    Authenticate client to a remote service.
    connection represents a network connection.
    secret_key is a key known only to both client/server.
    '''
    message = connection.recv(32)
    hash = hmac.new(secret_key, message)
    digest = hash.digest()
    connection.send(digest)

def server_authenticate(connection, secret_key):
    '''
    Request client authentication.
    '''
    message = os.urandom(32)
    connection.send(message)
    hash = hmac.new(secret_key, message)
    digest = hash.digest()
    response = connection.recv(len(digest))
    return hmac.compare_digest(digest,response)
```

The general idea is that upon connection, the server presents the client with a message of random bytes (returned by os.urandom(), in this case). The client and server both compute a cryptographic hash of the random data using hmac and a secret key known only to both ends. The client sends its computed digest back to the server, where it is compared and used to decide whether or not to accept or reject the connection.

Comparison of resulting digests should be performed using the hmac.compare_di gest() function. This function has been written in a way that avoids timing-analysis-based attacks and should be used instead of a normal comparison operator (==).

To use these functions, you would incorporate them into existing networking or messaging code. For example, with sockets, the server code might look something like this:

```
from socket import socket, AF_INET, SOCK_STREAM

secret_key = b'peekaboo'
def echo_handler(client_sock):
    if not server_authenticate(client_sock, secret_key):
        client_sock.close()
        return
    while True:
```

```
            msg = client_sock.recv(8192)
            if not msg:
                break
            client_sock.sendall(msg)

    def echo_server(address):
        s = socket(AF_INET, SOCK_STREAM)
        s.bind(address)
        s.listen(5)
        while True:
            c,a = s.accept()
            echo_handler(c)

    echo_server(('', 18000))
```

Within a client, you would do this:

```
from socket import socket, AF_INET, SOCK_STREAM

secret_key = b'peekaboo'

s = socket(AF_INET, SOCK_STREAM)
s.connect(('localhost', 18000))
client_authenticate(s, secret_key)
s.send(b'Hello World')
resp = s.recv(1024)
...
```

Discussion

A common use of hmac authentication is in internal messaging systems and interprocess communication. For example, if you are writing a system that involves multiple processes communicating across a cluster of machines, you can use this approach to make sure that only allowed processes are allowed to connect to one another. In fact, HMAC-based authentication is used internally by the multiprocessing library when it sets up communication with subprocesses.

It's important to stress that authenticating a connection is not the same as encryption. Subsequent communication on an authenticated connection is sent in the clear, and would be visible to anyone inclined to sniff the traffic (although the secret key known to both sides is never transmitted).

The authentication algorithm used by hmac is based on cryptographic hashing functions, such as MD5 and SHA-1, and is described in detail in IETF RFC 2104 (*http://tools.ietf.org/html/rfc2104.html*).

11.10. Adding SSL to Network Services

Problem

You want to implement a network service involving sockets where servers and clients authenticate themselves and encrypt the transmitted data using SSL.

Solution

The `ssl` module provides support for adding SSL to low-level socket connections. In particular, the `ssl.wrap_socket()` function takes an existing socket and wraps an SSL layer around it. For example, here's an example of a simple echo server that presents a server certificate to connecting clients:

```python
from socket import socket, AF_INET, SOCK_STREAM
import ssl

KEYFILE = 'server_key.pem'   # Private key of the server
CERTFILE = 'server_cert.pem' # Server certificate (given to client)

def echo_client(s):
    while True:
        data = s.recv(8192)
        if data == b'':
            break
        s.send(data)
    s.close()
    print('Connection closed')

def echo_server(address):
    s = socket(AF_INET, SOCK_STREAM)
    s.bind(address)
    s.listen(1)

    # Wrap with an SSL layer requiring client certs
    s_ssl = ssl.wrap_socket(s,
                            keyfile=KEYFILE,
                            certfile=CERTFILE,
                            server_side=True
                            )
    # Wait for connections
    while True:
        try:
            c,a = s_ssl.accept()
            print('Got connection', c, a)
            echo_client(c)
        except Exception as e:
            print('{}: {}'.format(e.__class__.__name__, e))

echo_server(('', 20000))
```

Here's an interactive session that shows how to connect to the server as a client. The client requires the server to present its certificate and verifies it:

```
>>> from socket import socket, AF_INET, SOCK_STREAM
>>> import ssl
>>> s = socket(AF_INET, SOCK_STREAM)
>>> s_ssl = ssl.wrap_socket(s,
...                         cert_reqs=ssl.CERT_REQUIRED,
...                         ca_certs = 'server_cert.pem')
>>> s_ssl.connect(('localhost', 20000))
>>> s_ssl.send(b'Hello World?')
12
>>> s_ssl.recv(8192)
b'Hello World?'
>>>
```

The problem with all of this low-level socket hacking is that it doesn't play well with existing network services already implemented in the standard library. For example, most server code (HTTP, XML-RPC, etc.) is actually based on the socketserver library. Client code is also implemented at a higher level. It is possible to add SSL to existing services, but a slightly different approach is needed.

First, for servers, SSL can be added through the use of a mixin class like this:

```
import ssl

class SSLMixin:
    '''
    Mixin class that adds support for SSL to existing servers based
    on the socketserver module.
    '''
    def __init__(self, *args,
                 keyfile=None, certfile=None, ca_certs=None,
                 cert_reqs=ssl.NONE,
                 **kwargs):
        self._keyfile = keyfile
        self._certfile = certfile
        self._ca_certs = ca_certs
        self._cert_reqs = cert_reqs
        super().__init__(*args, **kwargs)

    def get_request(self):
        client, addr = super().get_request()
        client_ssl = ssl.wrap_socket(client,
                                     keyfile = self._keyfile,
                                     certfile = self._certfile,
                                     ca_certs = self._ca_certs,
                                     cert_reqs = self._cert_reqs,
                                     server_side = True)
        return client_ssl, addr
```

To use this mixin class, you can mix it with other server classes. For example, here's an example of defining an XML-RPC server that operates over SSL:

```
# XML-RPC server with SSL

from xmlrpc.server import SimpleXMLRPCServer

class SSLSimpleXMLRPCServer(SSLMixin, SimpleXMLRPCServer):
    pass
```

Here's the XML-RPC server from Recipe 11.6 modified only slightly to use SSL:

```
import ssl
from xmlrpc.server import SimpleXMLRPCServer
from sslmixin import SSLMixin

class SSLSimpleXMLRPCServer(SSLMixin, SimpleXMLRPCServer):
    pass

class KeyValueServer:
    _rpc_methods_ = ['get', 'set', 'delete', 'exists', 'keys']
    def __init__(self, *args, **kwargs):
        self._data = {}
        self._serv = SSLSimpleXMLRPCServer(*args, allow_none=True, **kwargs)
        for name in self._rpc_methods_:
            self._serv.register_function(getattr(self, name))

    def get(self, name):
        return self._data[name]

    def set(self, name, value):
        self._data[name] = value

    def delete(self, name):
        del self._data[name]

    def exists(self, name):
        return name in self._data

    def keys(self):
        return list(self._data)

    def serve_forever(self):
        self._serv.serve_forever()

if __name__ == '__main__':
    KEYFILE='server_key.pem'    # Private key of the server
    CERTFILE='server_cert.pem'  # Server certificate
    kvserv = KeyValueServer(('', 15000),
                            keyfile=KEYFILE,
                            certfile=CERTFILE),
    kvserv.serve_forever()
```

To use this server, you can connect using the normal `xmlrpc.client` module. Just specify a `https:` in the URL. For example:

```
>>> from xmlrpc.client import ServerProxy
>>> s = ServerProxy('https://localhost:15000', allow_none=True)
>>> s.set('foo','bar')
>>> s.set('spam', [1, 2, 3])
>>> s.keys()
['spam', 'foo']
>>> s.get('foo')
'bar'
>>> s.get('spam')
[1, 2, 3]
>>> s.delete('spam')
>>> s.exists('spam')
False
>>>
```

One complicated issue with SSL clients is performing extra steps to verify the server certificate or to present a server with client credentials (such as a client certificate). Unfortunately, there seems to be no standardized way to accomplish this, so research is often required. However, here is an example of how to set up a secure XML-RPC connection that verifies the server's certificate:

```
from xmlrpc.client import SafeTransport, ServerProxy
import ssl

class VerifyCertSafeTransport(SafeTransport):
    def __init__(self, cafile, certfile=None, keyfile=None):
        SafeTransport.__init__(self)
        self._ssl_context = ssl.SSLContext(ssl.PROTOCOL_TLSv1)
        self._ssl_context.load_verify_locations(cafile)
        if cert:
            self._ssl_context.load_cert_chain(certfile, keyfile)
        self._ssl_context.verify_mode = ssl.CERT_REQUIRED

    def make_connection(self, host):
        # Items in the passed dictionary are passed as keyword
        # arguments to the http.client.HTTPSConnection() constructor.
        # The context argument allows an ssl.SSLContext instance to
        # be passed with information about the SSL configuration
        s = super().make_connection((host, {'context': self._ssl_context}))

        return s

# Create the client proxy
s = ServerProxy('https://localhost:15000',
                transport=VerifyCertSafeTransport('server_cert.pem'),
                allow_none=True)
```

As shown, the server presents a certificate to the client and the client verifies it. This verification can go both directions. If the server wants to verify the client, change the server startup to the following:

```
if __name__ == '__main__':
    KEYFILE='server_key.pem'    # Private key of the server
    CERTFILE='server_cert.pem'  # Server certificate
    CA_CERTS='client_cert.pem'  # Certificates of accepted clients

    kvserv = KeyValueServer(('', 15000),
                            keyfile=KEYFILE,
                            certfile=CERTFILE,
                            ca_certs=CA_CERTS,
                            cert_reqs=ssl.CERT_REQUIRED,
                            )
    kvserv.serve_forever()
```

To make the XML-RPC client present its certificates, change the `ServerProxy` initialization to this:

```
# Create the client proxy
s = ServerProxy('https://localhost:15000',
                transport=VerifyCertSafeTransport('server_cert.pem',
                                                  'client_cert.pem',
                                                  'client_key.pem'),
                allow_none=True)
```

Discussion

Getting this recipe to work will test your system configuration skills and understanding of SSL. Perhaps the biggest challenge is simply getting the initial configuration of keys, certificates, and other matters in order.

To clarify what's required, each endpoint of an SSL connection typically has a private key and a signed certificate file. The certificate file contains the public key and is presented to the remote peer on each connection. For public servers, certificates are normally signed by a certificate authority such as Verisign, Equifax, or similar organization (something that costs money). To verify server certificates, clients maintain a file containing the certificates of trusted certificate authorities. For example, web browsers maintain certificates corresponding to the major certificate authorities and use them to verify the integrity of certificates presented by web servers during HTTPS connections.

For the purposes of this recipe, you can create what's known as a self-signed certificate. Here's how you do it:

```
bash % openssl req -new -x509 -days 365 -nodes -out server_cert.pem \
         -keyout server_key.pem
Generating a 1024 bit RSA private key
..........................................++++++
...++++++
```

```
writing new private key to 'server_key.pem'
 -----
You are about to be asked to enter information that will be incorporated
into your certificate request.
What you are about to enter is what is called a Distinguished Name or a DN.
There are quite a few fields but you can leave some blank
For some fields there will be a default value,
If you enter '.', the field will be left blank.
 -----
Country Name (2 letter code) [AU]:US
State or Province Name (full name) [Some-State]:Illinois
Locality Name (eg, city) []:Chicago
Organization Name (eg, company) [Internet Widgits Pty Ltd]:Dabeaz, LLC
Organizational Unit Name (eg, section) []:
Common Name (eg, YOUR name) []:localhost
Email Address []:
bash %
```

When creating the certificate, the values for the various fields are often arbitrary. However, the "Common Name" field often contains the DNS hostname of servers. If you're just testing things out on your own machine, use "localhost." Otherwise, use the domain name of the machine that's going to run the server.

As a result of this configuration, you will have a *server_key.pem* file that contains the private key. It looks like this:

```
-----BEGIN RSA PRIVATE KEY-----
MIICXQIBAAKBgQCZrCNLoEyAKF+f9UNcFaz5Osa6jf7qkbUl8si5xQrY3ZYC7juu
nL1dZLn/VbEFIITaUOgvBtPv1qUWTJGwga62VSG1oFE0ODIx3g2Nh4sRf+rySsx2
L4442nx0z4O5vJQ7k6eRNHAZUUnCL50+YvjyLyt7ryLSjSuKhCcJsbZgPwIDAQAB
AoGAB5evrr7eyL4160tM5rHTeATlaLY3UBOe5Z8XN8Z6gLiB/ucSX9AysviVD/6F
3oD6z2aL8jbeJc1vHqjt0dC2dwwm32vVl8mRdyoAsQpWmiqXrkvP4Bsl04VpBeHw
Qt8xNSW9SFhceL3LEvw9M8i9MV39viih1ILyH8OuHdvJyFECQQDLEjl2d2ppxND9
PoLqVFAirDfX2JnLTdWbc+M11a9Jdn3hKF8TcxfEnFVs5Gav1MusicY5KB0ylYPb
YbTvqKc7AkEAwbnRBO2VYEZsJZp2X0IZqP9ovWokkpYx+PE4+c6MySDgaMcigL7v
WDIIIJG1CHudD09GhqFNasDzyb2HAIW4CzQJBAKDdkv+xoW6gJx42Auc2WzTcUHCA
eXR/+BLpPrhKykzbvOQ8YvS5W764SUO1u1LWs3G+wnRMvrRvlMCZKgggDjkCQQCG
Jewto2+a+WkOKQXrNNScCDE5aPTmZQc5waCYq4UmCZQcOjkUOiN3ST1U5iuxRqfb
V/yX6fw0qh+fLWtkOs/JAkA+okMSxZwqRtfgOFGBfwQ8/iKrnizeanTQ3L6scFXI
CHZXdJ3XQ6qUmNxNn7iJ7S/LDawo1QfWkCfD9FYoxBlg
-----END RSA PRIVATE KEY-----
```

The server certificate in `server_cert.pem` looks similar:

```
-----BEGIN CERTIFICATE-----
MIIC+DCCAmGgAwIBAgIJAPMd+vi45js3MA0GCSqGSIb3DQEBBQUAMFwxCzAJBgNV
BAYTAlVTMREwDwYDVQQIEwhJbGxpbm9pczEQMA4GA1UEBxMHQ2hpY2FnbzEUMBIG
A1UEChMLRGFiZWF6LCBMTEMxEjAQBgNVBAMTCWxvY2FsaG9zdDAeFw0xMzAxMTEx
ODQyMjdaFw0xNDAxMTExODQyMjdaMFwxCzAJBgNVBAYTAlVTMREwDwYDVQQIEwhJ
bGxpbm9pczEQMA4GA1UEBxMHQ2hpY2FnbzEUMBIGA1UEChMLRGFiZWF6LCBMTEMx
EjAQBgNVBAMTCWxvY2FsaG9zdDCBnzANBgkqhkiG9w0BAQEFAAOBjQAwgYkCgYEA
mawjS6BMgChfn/VDXBWs+TrGuo3+6pG1JfLIucUK2N2WAu47rpy9XWS5/1WxBSCE
2lDoLwbT79alFkyRsIGutlUhtaBRNDgyMd4NjYeLEX/q8krMdi+OONp8dM+DubyU
```

```
O5OnkTRwGVFJwi+dPmL48i8re68i0o0rioQnCbG2YD8CAwEAAaOBwTCBvjAdBgNV
HQ4EFgQUrtoLHHgXiDZTr26NMmgKJLJLFtIwgY4GA1UdIwSBhjCBg4AUrtoLHHgX
iDZTr26NMmgKJLJLFtKhYKReMFwxCzAJBgNVBAYTAlVTMREwDwYDVQQIEwhJbGxp
bm9pczEQMA4GA1UEBxMHQ2hpY2FnbzEUMBIGA1UEChMLRGFiWF6LCBMTEMxEjAQ
BgNVBAMTCWxvY2FsaG9zdIIJAPMd+vi45js3MAwGA1UdEwQFMAMBAf8wDQYJKoZI
hvcNAQEFBQADgYEAFci+dqvMG4xF8UTnbGVvZJPIzJDRee6Nbt6AHQo9pOdAIMAu
WsGCplSOaDNdKKzl+b2UT2Zp3AIW4Qd51bouSNnR4M/gnr9ZD1ZctFd3jS+C5XRp
D3vvcW5lAnCCC80P6rXy7d7hTeFu5EYKtRGXNvVNd/06NALGDflrrOwxF3Y=
-----END CERTIFICATE-----
```

In server-related code, both the private key and certificate file will be presented to the various SSL-related wrapping functions. The certificate is what gets presented to clients. The private key should be protected and remains on the server.

In client-related code, a special file of valid certificate authorities needs to be maintained to verify the server's certificate. If you have no such file, then at the very least, you can put a copy of the server's certificate on the client machine and use that as a means for verification. During connection, the server will present its certificate, and then you'll use the stored certificate you already have to verify that it's correct.

Servers can also elect to verify the identity of clients. To do that, clients need to have their own private key and certificate key. The server would also need to maintain a file of trusted certificate authorities for verifying the client certificates.

If you intend to add SSL support to a network service for real, this recipe really only gives a small taste of how to set it up. You will definitely want to consult the documentation (*http://docs.python.org/3/library/ssl.html*) for more of the finer points. Be prepared to spend a significant amount of time experimenting with it to get things to work.

11.11. Passing a Socket File Descriptor Between Processes

Problem

You have multiple Python interpreter processes running and you want to pass an open file descriptor from one interpreter to the other. For instance, perhaps there is a server process that is responsible for receiving connections, but the actual servicing of clients is to be handled by a different interpreter.

Solution

To pass a file descriptor between processes, you first need to connect the processes together. On Unix machines, you might use a Unix domain socket, whereas on Windows, you could use a named pipe. However, rather than deal with such low-level mechanics, it is often easier to use the multiprocessing module to set up such a connection.

Once a connection is established, you can use the send_handle() and recv_handle()
functions in multiprocessing.reduction to send file descriptors between processes.

The following example illustrates the basics:

```python
import multiprocessing
from multiprocessing.reduction import recv_handle, send_handle
import socket

def worker(in_p, out_p):
    out_p.close()
    while True:
        fd = recv_handle(in_p)
        print('CHILD: GOT FD', fd)
        with socket.socket(socket.AF_INET, socket.SOCK_STREAM, fileno=fd) as s:
            while True:
                msg = s.recv(1024)
                if not msg:
                    break
                print('CHILD: RECV {!r}'.format(msg))
                s.send(msg)

def server(address, in_p, out_p, worker_pid):
    in_p.close()
    s = socket.socket(socket.AF_INET, socket.SOCK_STREAM)
    s.setsockopt(socket.SOL_SOCKET, socket.SO_REUSEADDR, True)
    s.bind(address)
    s.listen(1)
    while True:
        client, addr = s.accept()
        print('SERVER: Got connection from', addr)
        send_handle(out_p, client.fileno(), worker_pid)
        client.close()

if __name__ == '__main__':
    c1, c2 = multiprocessing.Pipe()
    worker_p = multiprocessing.Process(target=worker, args=(c1,c2))
    worker_p.start()

    server_p = multiprocessing.Process(target=server,
                args=(('', 15000), c1, c2, worker_p.pid))
    server_p.start()

    c1.close()
    c2.close()
```

In this example, two processes are spawned and connected by a multiprocessing Pipe
object. The server process opens a socket and waits for client connections. The worker
process merely waits to receive a file descriptor on the pipe using recv_handle(). When
the server receives a connection, it sends the resulting socket file descriptor to the worker

using send_handle(). The worker takes over the socket and echoes data back to the client until the connection is closed.

If you connect to the running server using Telnet or a similar tool, here is an example of what you might see:

```
bash % python3 passfd.py
SERVER: Got connection from ('127.0.0.1', 55543)
CHILD: GOT FD 7
CHILD: RECV b'Hello\r\n'
CHILD: RECV b'World\r\n'
```

The most important part of this example is the fact that the client socket accepted in the server is actually serviced by a completely different process. The server merely hands it off, closes it, and waits for the next connection.

Discussion

Passing file descriptors between processes is something that many programmers don't even realize is possible. However, it can sometimes be a useful tool in building scalable systems. For example, on a multicore machine, you could have multiple instances of the Python interpreter and use file descriptor passing to more evenly balance the number of clients being handled by each interpreter.

The send_handle() and recv_handle() functions shown in the solution really only work with multiprocessing connections. Instead of using a pipe, you can connect interpreters as shown in Recipe 11.7, and it will work as long as you use UNIX domain sockets or Windows pipes. For example, you could implement the server and worker as completely separate programs to be started separately. Here is the implementation of the server:

```
# servermp.py
from multiprocessing.connection import Listener
from multiprocessing.reduction import send_handle
import socket

def server(work_address, port):
    # Wait for the worker to connect
    work_serv = Listener(work_address, authkey=b'peekaboo')
    worker = work_serv.accept()
    worker_pid = worker.recv()

    # Now run a TCP/IP server and send clients to worker
    s = socket.socket(socket.AF_INET, socket.SOCK_STREAM)
    s.setsockopt(socket.SOL_SOCKET, socket.SO_REUSEADDR, True)
    s.bind(('', port))
    s.listen(1)
    while True:
        client, addr = s.accept()
        print('SERVER: Got connection from', addr)
```

```
            send_handle(worker, client.fileno(), worker_pid)
            client.close()

    if __name__ == '__main__':
        import sys
        if len(sys.argv) != 3:
            print('Usage: server.py server_address port', file=sys.stderr)
            raise SystemExit(1)

        server(sys.argv[1], int(sys.argv[2]))
```

To run this server, you would run a command such as `python3 servermp.py /tmp/servconn 15000`. Here is the corresponding client code:

```
# workermp.py

from multiprocessing.connection import Client
from multiprocessing.reduction import recv_handle
import os
from socket import socket, AF_INET, SOCK_STREAM

def worker(server_address):
    serv = Client(server_address, authkey=b'peekaboo')
    serv.send(os.getpid())
    while True:
        fd = recv_handle(serv)
        print('WORKER: GOT FD', fd)
        with socket(AF_INET, SOCK_STREAM, fileno=fd) as client:
            while True:
                msg = client.recv(1024)
                if not msg:
                    break
                print('WORKER: RECV {!r}'.format(msg))
                client.send(msg)

if __name__ == '__main__':
    import sys
    if len(sys.argv) != 2:
        print('Usage: worker.py server_address', file=sys.stderr)
        raise SystemExit(1)

    worker(sys.argv[1])
```

To run the worker, you would type `python3 workermp.py /tmp/servconn`. The resulting operation should be exactly the same as the example that used `Pipe()`.

Under the covers, file descriptor passing involves creating a UNIX domain socket and the `sendmsg()` method of sockets. Since this technique is not widely known, here is a different implementation of the server that shows how to pass descriptors using sockets:

```
# server.py
import socket
```

```
    import struct

def send_fd(sock, fd):
    '''
    Send a single file descriptor.
    '''
    sock.sendmsg([b'x'],
                 [(socket.SOL_SOCKET, socket.SCM_RIGHTS, struct.pack('i', fd))])
    ack = sock.recv(2)
    assert ack == b'OK'

def server(work_address, port):
    # Wait for the worker to connect
    work_serv = socket.socket(socket.AF_UNIX, socket.SOCK_STREAM)
    work_serv.bind(work_address)
    work_serv.listen(1)
    worker, addr = work_serv.accept()

    # Now run a TCP/IP server and send clients to worker
    s = socket.socket(socket.AF_INET, socket.SOCK_STREAM)
    s.setsockopt(socket.SOL_SOCKET, socket.SO_REUSEADDR, True)
    s.bind(('',port))
    s.listen(1)
    while True:
        client, addr = s.accept()
        print('SERVER: Got connection from', addr)
        send_fd(worker, client.fileno())
        client.close()

if __name__ == '__main__':
    import sys
    if len(sys.argv) != 3:
        print('Usage: server.py server_address port', file=sys.stderr)
        raise SystemExit(1)

    server(sys.argv[1], int(sys.argv[2]))
```

Here is an implementation of the worker using sockets:

```
# worker.py
import socket
import struct

def recv_fd(sock):
    '''
    Receive a single file descriptor
    '''
    msg, ancdata, flags, addr = sock.recvmsg(1,
                                    socket.CMSG_LEN(struct.calcsize('i')))

    cmsg_level, cmsg_type, cmsg_data = ancdata[0]
    assert cmsg_level == socket.SOL_SOCKET and cmsg_type == socket.SCM_RIGHTS
    sock.sendall(b'OK')
```

```
        return struct.unpack('i', cmsg_data)[0]

def worker(server_address):
    serv = socket.socket(socket.AF_UNIX, socket.SOCK_STREAM)
    serv.connect(server_address)
    while True:
        fd = recv_fd(serv)
        print('WORKER: GOT FD', fd)
        with socket.socket(socket.AF_INET, socket.SOCK_STREAM, fileno=fd) as client:
            while True:
                msg = client.recv(1024)
                if not msg:
                    break
                print('WORKER: RECV {!r}'.format(msg))
                client.send(msg)

if __name__ == '__main__':
    import sys
    if len(sys.argv) != 2:
        print('Usage: worker.py server_address', file=sys.stderr)
        raise SystemExit(1)

    worker(sys.argv[1])
```

If you are going to use file-descriptor passing in your program, it is advisable to read more about it in an advanced text, such as *Unix Network Programming* by W. Richard Stevens (Prentice Hall, 1990). Passing file descriptors on Windows uses a different technique than Unix (not shown). For that platform, it is advisable to study the source code to `multiprocessing.reduction` in close detail to see how it works.

11.12. Understanding Event-Driven I/O

Problem

You have heard about packages based on "event-driven" or "asynchronous" I/O, but you're not entirely sure what it means, how it actually works under the covers, or how it might impact your program if you use it.

Solution

At a fundamental level, event-driven I/O is a technique that takes basic I/O operations (e.g., reads and writes) and converts them into events that must be handled by your program. For example, whenever data was received on a socket, it turns into a "receive" event that is handled by some sort of callback method or function that you supply to respond to it. As a possible starting point, an event-driven framework might start with a base class that implements a series of basic event handler methods like this:

```
class EventHandler:
    def fileno(self):
        'Return the associated file descriptor'
        raise NotImplemented('must implement')

    def wants_to_receive(self):
        'Return True if receiving is allowed'
        return False

    def handle_receive(self):
        'Perform the receive operation'
        pass

    def wants_to_send(self):
        'Return True if sending is requested'
        return False

    def handle_send(self):
        'Send outgoing data'
        pass
```

Instances of this class then get plugged into an event loop that looks like this:

```
import select

def event_loop(handlers):
    while True:
        wants_recv = [h for h in handlers if h.wants_to_receive()]
        wants_send = [h for h in handlers if h.wants_to_send()]
        can_recv, can_send, _ = select.select(wants_recv, wants_send, [])
        for h in can_recv:
            h.handle_receive()
        for h in can_send:
            h.handle_send()
```

That's it! The key to the event loop is the select() call, which polls file descriptors for activity. Prior to calling select(), the event loop simply queries all of the handlers to see which ones want to receive or send. It then supplies the resulting lists to select(). As a result, select() returns the list of objects that are ready to receive or send. The corresponding handle_receive() or handle_send() methods are triggered.

To write applications, specific instances of EventHandler classes are created. For example, here are two simple handlers that illustrate two UDP-based network services:

```
import socket
import time

class UDPServer(EventHandler):
    def __init__(self, address):
        self.sock = socket.socket(socket.AF_INET, socket.SOCK_DGRAM)
        self.sock.bind(address)
```

```python
    def fileno(self):
        return self.sock.fileno()

    def wants_to_receive(self):
        return True

class UDPTimeServer(UDPServer):
    def handle_receive(self):
        msg, addr = self.sock.recvfrom(1)
        self.sock.sendto(time.ctime().encode('ascii'), addr)

class UDPEchoServer(UDPServer):
    def handle_receive(self):
        msg, addr = self.sock.recvfrom(8192)
        self.sock.sendto(msg, addr)

if __name__ == '__main__':
    handlers = [ UDPTimeServer(('',14000)), UDPEchoServer(('',15000)) ]
    event_loop(handlers)
```

To test this code, you can try connecting to it from another Python interpreter:

```python
>>> from socket import *
>>> s = socket(AF_INET, SOCK_DGRAM)
>>> s.sendto(b'',('localhost',14000))
0
>>> s.recvfrom(128)
(b'Tue Sep 18 14:29:23 2012', ('127.0.0.1', 14000))
>>> s.sendto(b'Hello',('localhost',15000))
5
>>> s.recvfrom(128)
(b'Hello', ('127.0.0.1', 15000))
>>>
```

Implementing a TCP server is somewhat more complex, since each client involves the instantiation of a new handler object. Here is an example of a TCP echo client.

```python
class TCPServer(EventHandler):
    def __init__(self, address, client_handler, handler_list):
        self.sock = socket.socket(socket.AF_INET, socket.SOCK_STREAM)
        self.sock.setsockopt(socket.SOL_SOCKET, socket.SO_REUSEADDR, True)
        self.sock.bind(address)
        self.sock.listen(1)
        self.client_handler = client_handler
        self.handler_list = handler_list

    def fileno(self):
        return self.sock.fileno()

    def wants_to_receive(self):
        return True
```

```python
    def handle_receive(self):
        client, addr = self.sock.accept()
        # Add the client to the event loop's handler list
        self.handler_list.append(self.client_handler(client, self.handler_list))

class TCPClient(EventHandler):
    def __init__(self, sock, handler_list):
        self.sock = sock
        self.handler_list = handler_list
        self.outgoing = bytearray()

    def fileno(self):
        return self.sock.fileno()

    def close(self):
        self.sock.close()
        # Remove myself from the event loop's handler list
        self.handler_list.remove(self)

    def wants_to_send(self):
        return True if self.outgoing else False

    def handle_send(self):
        nsent = self.sock.send(self.outgoing)
        self.outgoing = self.outgoing[nsent:]

class TCPEchoClient(TCPClient):
    def wants_to_receive(self):
        return True

    def handle_receive(self):
        data = self.sock.recv(8192)
        if not data:
            self.close()
        else:
            self.outgoing.extend(data)

if __name__ == '__main__':
    handlers = []
    handlers.append(TCPServer(('',16000), TCPEchoClient, handlers))
    event_loop(handlers)
```

The key to the TCP example is the addition and removal of clients from the handler list. On each connection, a new handler is created for the client and added to the list. When the connection is closed, each client must take care to remove themselves from the list.

If you run this program and try connecting with Telnet or some similar tool, you'll see it echoing received data back to you. It should easily handle multiple clients.

Discussion

Virtually all event-driven frameworks operate in a manner that is similar to that shown in the solution. The actual implementation details and overall software architecture might vary greatly, but at the core, there is a polling loop that checks sockets for activity and which performs operations in response.

One potential benefit of event-driven I/O is that it can handle a very large number of simultaneous connections without ever using threads or processes. That is, the `se lect()` call (or equivalent) can be used to monitor hundreds or thousands of sockets and respond to events occuring on any of them. Events are handled one at a time by the event loop, without the need for any other concurrency primitives.

The downside to event-driven I/O is that there is no true concurrency involved. If any of the event handler methods blocks or performs a long-running calculation, it blocks the progress of everything. There is also the problem of calling out to library functions that aren't written in an event-driven style. There is always the risk that some library call will block, causing the event loop to stall.

Problems with blocking or long-running calculations can be solved by sending the work out to a separate thread or process. However, coordinating threads and processes with an event loop is tricky. Here is an example of code that will do it using the `concur rent.futures` module:

```
from concurrent.futures import ThreadPoolExecutor
import os

class ThreadPoolHandler(EventHandler):
    def __init__(self, nworkers):
        if os.name == 'posix':
            self.signal_done_sock, self.done_sock = socket.socketpair()
        else:
            server = socket.socket(socket.AF_INET, socket.SOCK_STREAM)
            server.bind(('127.0.0.1', 0))
            server.listen(1)
            self.signal_done_sock = socket.socket(socket.AF_INET,
                                                  socket.SOCK_STREAM)
            self.signal_done_sock.connect(server.getsockname())
            self.done_sock, _ = server.accept()
            server.close()

        self.pending = []
        self.pool = ThreadPoolExecutor(nworkers)

    def fileno(self):
        return self.done_sock.fileno()

    # Callback that executes when the thread is done
    def _complete(self, callback, r):
```

```
        self.pending.append((callback, r.result()))
        self.signal_done_sock.send(b'x')

    # Run a function in a thread pool
    def run(self, func, args=(), kwargs={},*,callback):
        r = self.pool.submit(func, *args, **kwargs)
        r.add_done_callback(lambda r: self._complete(callback, r))

    def wants_to_receive(self):
        return True

    # Run callback functions of completed work
    def handle_receive(self):
        # Invoke all pending callback functions
        for callback, result in self.pending:
            callback(result)
            self.done_sock.recv(1)
        self.pending = []
```

In this code, the run() method is used to submit work to the pool along with a callback function that should be triggered upon completion. The actual work is then submitted to a ThreadPoolExecutor instance. However, a really tricky problem concerns the co-ordination of the computed result and the event loop. To do this, a pair of sockets are created under the covers and used as a kind of signaling mechanism. When work is completed by the thread pool, it executes the _complete() method in the class. This method queues up the pending callback and result before writing a byte of data on one of these sockets. The fileno() method is programmed to return the other socket. Thus, when this byte is written, it will signal to the event loop that something has happened. The handle_receive() method, when triggered, will then execute all of the callback functions for previously submitted work. Frankly, it's enough to make one's head spin.

Here is a simple server that shows how to use the thread pool to carry out a long-running calculation:

```
    # A really bad Fibonacci implementation
    def fib(n):
        if n < 2:
            return 1
        else:
            return fib(n - 1) + fib(n - 2)

    class UDPFibServer(UDPServer):
        def handle_receive(self):
            msg, addr = self.sock.recvfrom(128)
            n = int(msg)
            pool.run(fib, (n,), callback=lambda r: self.respond(r, addr))

        def respond(self, result, addr):
            self.sock.sendto(str(result).encode('ascii'), addr)
```

```
if __name__ == '__main__':
    pool = ThreadPoolHandler(16)
    handlers = [ pool, UDPFibServer(('',16000))]
    event_loop(handlers)
```

To try this server, simply run it and try some experiments with another Python program:

```
from socket import *
sock = socket(AF_INET, SOCK_DGRAM)
for x in range(40):
    sock.sendto(str(x).encode('ascii'), ('localhost', 16000))
    resp = sock.recvfrom(8192)
    print(resp[0])
```

You should be able to run this program repeatedly from many different windows and have it operate without stalling other programs, even though it gets slower and slower as the numbers get larger.

Having gone through this recipe, should you use its code? Probably not. Instead, you should look for a more fully developed framework that accomplishes the same task. However, if you understand the basic concepts presented here, you'll understand the core techniques used to make such frameworks operate. As an alternative to callback-based programming, event-driven code will sometimes use coroutines. See Recipe 12.12 for an example.

11.13. Sending and Receiving Large Arrays

Problem

You want to send and receive large arrays of contiguous data across a network connection, making as few copies of the data as possible.

Solution

The following functions utilize memoryviews to send and receive large arrays:

```
# zerocopy.py

def send_from(arr, dest):
    view = memoryview(arr).cast('B')
    while len(view):
        nsent = dest.send(view)
        view = view[nsent:]

def recv_into(arr, source):
    view = memoryview(arr).cast('B')
    while len(view):
        nrecv = source.recv_into(view)
        view = view[nrecv:]
```

To test the program, first create a server and client program connected over a socket. In the server:

```
>>> from socket import *
>>> s = socket(AF_INET, SOCK_STREAM)
>>> s.bind(('', 25000))
>>> s.listen(1)
>>> c,a = s.accept()
>>>
```

In the client (in a separate interpreter):

```
>>> from socket import *
>>> c = socket(AF_INET, SOCK_STREAM)
>>> c.connect(('localhost', 25000))
>>>
```

Now, the whole idea of this recipe is that you can blast a huge array through the connection. In this case, arrays might be created by the array module or perhaps numpy. For example:

```
# Server
>>> import numpy
>>> a = numpy.arange(0.0, 50000000.0)
>>> send_from(a, c)
>>>
```

```
# Client
>>> import numpy
>>> a = numpy.zeros(shape=50000000, dtype=float)
>>> a[0:10]
array([ 0.,  0.,  0.,  0.,  0.,  0.,  0.,  0.,  0.,  0.])
>>> recv_into(a, c)
>>> a[0:10]
array([ 0.,  1.,  2.,  3.,  4.,  5.,  6.,  7.,  8.,  9.])
>>>
```

Discussion

In data-intensive distributed computing and parallel programming applications, it's not uncommon to write programs that need to send/receive large chunks of data. However, to do this, you somehow need to reduce the data down to raw bytes for use with low-level network functions. You may also need to slice the data into chunks, since most network-related functions aren't able to send or receive huge blocks of data entirely all at once.

One approach is to serialize the data in some way—possibly by converting into a byte string. However, this usually ends up making a copy of the data. Even if you do this piecemeal, your code still ends up making a lot of little copies.

This recipe gets around this by playing a sneaky trick with memoryviews. Essentially, a memoryview is an overlay of an existing array. Not only that, memoryviews can be cast to different types to allow interpretation of the data in a different manner. This is the purpose of the following statement:

```
view = memoryview(arr).cast('B')
```

It takes an array arr and casts into a memoryview of unsigned bytes.

In this form, the view can be passed to socket-related functions, such as sock.send() or send.recv_into(). Under the covers, those methods are able to work directly with the memory region. For example, sock.send() sends data directly from memory without a copy. send.recv_into() uses the memoryview as the input buffer for the receive operation.

The remaining complication is the fact that the socket functions may only work with partial data. In general, it will take many different send() and recv_into() calls to transmit the entire array. Not to worry. After each operation, the view is sliced by the number of sent or received bytes to produce a new view. The new view is also a memory overlay. Thus, no copies are made.

One issue here is that the receiver has to know in advance how much data will be sent so that it can either preallocate an array or verify that it can receive the data into an existing array. If this is a problem, the sender could always arrange to send the size first, followed by the array data.

## CHAPTER 12

Concurrency

Python has long supported different approaches to concurrent programming, including programming with threads, launching subprocesses, and various tricks involving generator functions. In this chapter, recipes related to various aspects of concurrent programming are presented, including common thread programming techniques and approaches for parallel processing.

As experienced programmers know, concurrent programming is fraught with potential peril. Thus, a major focus of this chapter is on recipes that tend to lead to more reliable and debuggable code.

12.1. Starting and Stopping Threads

Problem

You want to create and destroy threads for concurrent execution of code.

Solution

The `threading` library can be used to execute any Python callable in its own thread. To do this, you create a `Thread` instance and supply the callable that you wish to execute as a target. Here is a simple example:

```
# Code to execute in an independent thread
import time
def countdown(n):
    while n > 0:
        print('T-minus', n)
        n -= 1
        time.sleep(5)
```

```
# Create and launch a thread
from threading import Thread
t = Thread(target=countdown, args=(10,))
t.start()
```

When you create a thread instance, it doesn't start executing until you invoke its start()
method (which invokes the target function with the arguments you supplied).

Threads are executed in their own system-level thread (e.g., a POSIX thread or Windows
threads) that is fully managed by the host operating system. Once started, threads run
independently until the target function returns. You can query a thread instance to see
if it's still running:

```
if t.is_alive():
    print('Still running')
else:
    print('Completed')
```

You can also request to join with a thread, which waits for it to terminate:

```
t.join()
```

The interpreter remains running until all threads terminate. For long-running threads
or background tasks that run forever, you should consider making the thread daemonic.
For example:

```
t = Thread(target=countdown, args=(10,), daemon=True)
t.start()
```

Daemonic threads can't be joined. However, they are destroyed automatically when the
main thread terminates.

Beyond the two operations shown, there aren't many other things you can do with
threads. For example, there are no operations to terminate a thread, signal a thread,
adjust its scheduling, or perform any other high-level operations. If you want these
features, you need to build them yourself.

If you want to be able to terminate threads, the thread must be programmed to poll for
exit at selected points. For example, you might put your thread in a class such as this:

```
class CountdownTask:
    def __init__(self):
        self._running = True

    def terminate(self):
        self._running = False

    def run(self, n):
        while self._running and n > 0:
            print('T-minus', n)
            n -= 1
            time.sleep(5)
```

```
c = CountdownTask()
t = Thread(target=c.run, args=(10,))
t.start()
...
c.terminate() # Signal termination
t.join()      # Wait for actual termination (if needed)
```

Polling for thread termination can be tricky to coordinate if threads perform blocking operations such as I/O. For example, a thread blocked indefinitely on an I/O operation may never return to check if it's been killed. To correctly deal with this case, you'll need to carefully program thread to utilize timeout loops. For example:

```
class IOTask:
    def terminate(self):
        self._running = False

    def run(self, sock):
        # sock is a socket
        sock.settimeout(5)          # Set timeout period
        while self._running:
            # Perform a blocking I/O operation w/ timeout
            try:
                data = sock.recv(8192)
                break
            except socket.timeout:
                continue
            # Continued processing
            ...
        # Terminated
        return
```

Discussion

Due to a global interpreter lock (GIL), Python threads are restricted to an execution model that only allows one thread to execute in the interpreter at any given time. For this reason, Python threads should generally not be used for computationally intensive tasks where you are trying to achieve parallelism on multiple CPUs. They are much better suited for I/O handling and handling concurrent execution in code that performs blocking operations (e.g., waiting for I/O, waiting for results from a database, etc.).

Sometimes you will see threads defined via inheritance from the Thread class. For example:

```
from threading import Thread

class CountdownThread(Thread):
    def __init__(self, n):
        super().__init__()
        self.n = 0
    def run(self):
        while self.n > 0:
```

```
        print('T-minus', self.n)
        self.n -= 1
        time.sleep(5)

c = CountdownThread(5)
c.start()
```

Although this works, it introduces an extra dependency between the code and the threading library. That is, you can only use the resulting code in the context of threads, whereas the technique shown earlier involves writing code with no explicit dependency on threading. By freeing your code of such dependencies, it becomes usable in other contexts that may or may not involve threads. For instance, you might be able to execute your code in a separate process using the multiprocessing module using code like this:

```
import multiprocessing
c = CountdownTask(5)
p = multiprocessing.Process(target=c.run)
p.start()
...
```

Again, this only works if the CountdownTask class has been written in a manner that is neutral to the actual means of concurrency (threads, processes, etc.).

12.2. Determining If a Thread Has Started

Problem

You've launched a thread, but want to know when it actually starts running.

Solution

A key feature of threads is that they execute independently and nondeterministically. This can present a tricky synchronization problem if other threads in the program need to know if a thread has reached a certain point in its execution before carrying out further operations. To solve such problems, use the Event object from the threading library.

Event instances are similar to a "sticky" flag that allows threads to wait for something to happen. Initially, an event is set to 0. If the event is unset and a thread waits on the event, it will block (i.e., go to sleep) until the event gets set. A thread that sets the event will wake up all of the threads that happen to be waiting (if any). If a thread waits on an event that has already been set, it merely moves on, continuing to execute.

Here is some sample code that uses an Event to coordinate the startup of a thread:

```
from threading import Thread, Event
import time
```

```
# Code to execute in an independent thread
def countdown(n, started_evt):
    print('countdown starting')
    started_evt.set()
    while n > 0:
        print('T-minus', n)
        n -= 1
        time.sleep(5)

# Create the event object that will be used to signal startup
started_evt = Event()

# Launch the thread and pass the startup event
print('Launching countdown')
t = Thread(target=countdown, args=(10,started_evt))
t.start()

# Wait for the thread to start
started_evt.wait()
print('countdown is running')
```

When you run this code, the "countdown is running" message will always appear after the "countdown starting" message. This is coordinated by the event that makes the main thread wait until the countdown() function has first printed the startup message.

Discussion

Event objects are best used for one-time events. That is, you create an event, threads wait for the event to be set, and once set, the Event is discarded. Although it is possible to clear an event using its clear() method, safely clearing an event and waiting for it to be set again is tricky to coordinate, and can lead to missed events, deadlock, or other problems (in particular, you can't guarantee that a request to clear an event after setting it will execute before a released thread cycles back to wait on the event again).

If a thread is going to repeatedly signal an event over and over, you're probably better off using a Condition object instead. For example, this code implements a periodic timer that other threads can monitor to see whenever the timer expires:

```
import threading
import time

class PeriodicTimer:
    def __init__(self, interval):
        self._interval = interval
        self._flag = 0
        self._cv = threading.Condition()

    def start(self):
        t = threading.Thread(target=self.run)
        t.daemon = True
```

```
        t.start()

    def run(self):
        '''
        Run the timer and notify waiting threads after each interval
        '''
        while True:
            time.sleep(self._interval)
            with self._cv:
                self._flag ^= 1
                self._cv.notify_all()

    def wait_for_tick(self):
        '''
        Wait for the next tick of the timer
        '''
        with self._cv:
            last_flag = self._flag
            while last_flag == self._flag:
                self._cv.wait()

# Example use of the timer
ptimer = PeriodicTimer(5)
ptimer.start()

# Two threads that synchronize on the timer
def countdown(nticks):
    while nticks > 0:
        ptimer.wait_for_tick()
        print('T-minus', nticks)
        nticks -= 1

def countup(last):
    n = 0
    while n < last:
        ptimer.wait_for_tick()
        print('Counting', n)
        n += 1

threading.Thread(target=countdown, args=(10,)).start()
threading.Thread(target=countup, args=(5,)).start()
```

A critical feature of Event objects is that they wake all waiting threads. If you are writing a program where you only want to wake up a single waiting thread, it is probably better to use a Semaphore or Condition object instead.

For example, consider this code involving semaphores:

```
# Worker thread
def worker(n, sema):
    # Wait to be signaled
    sema.acquire()
```

```
    # Do some work
    print('Working', n)

# Create some threads
sema = threading.Semaphore(0)
nworkers = 10
for n in range(nworkers):
    t = threading.Thread(target=worker, args=(n, sema,))
    t.start()
```

If you run this, a pool of threads will start, but nothing happens because they're all blocked waiting to acquire the semaphore. Each time the semaphore is released, only one worker will wake up and run. For example:

```
>>> sema.release()
Working 0
>>> sema.release()
Working 1
>>>
```

Writing code that involves a lot of tricky synchronization between threads is likely to make your head explode. A more sane approach is to thread threads as communicating tasks using queues or as actors. Queues are described in the next recipe. Actors are described in Recipe 12.10.

12.3. Communicating Between Threads

Problem

You have multiple threads in your program and you want to safely communicate or exchange data between them.

Solution

Perhaps the safest way to send data from one thread to another is to use a Queue from the queue library. To do this, you create a Queue instance that is shared by the threads. Threads then use put() or get() operations to add or remove items from the queue. For example:

```
from queue import Queue
from threading import Thread

# A thread that produces data
def producer(out_q):
    while True:
        # Produce some data
        ...
        out_q.put(data)
```

```
# A thread that consumes data
def consumer(in_q):
    while True:
        # Get some data
        data = in_q.get()
        # Process the data
        ...

# Create the shared queue and launch both threads
q = Queue()
t1 = Thread(target=consumer, args=(q,))
t2 = Thread(target=producer, args=(q,))
t1.start()
t2.start()
```

Queue instances already have all of the required locking, so they can be safely shared by as many threads as you wish.

When using queues, it can be somewhat tricky to coordinate the shutdown of the producer and consumer. A common solution to this problem is to rely on a special sentinel value, which when placed in the queue, causes consumers to terminate. For example:

```
from queue import Queue
from threading import Thread

# Object that signals shutdown
_sentinel = object()

# A thread that produces data
def producer(out_q):
    while running:
        # Produce some data
        ...
        out_q.put(data)

    # Put the sentinel on the queue to indicate completion
    out_q.put(_sentinel)

# A thread that consumes data
def consumer(in_q):
    while True:
        # Get some data
        data = in_q.get()

        # Check for termination
        if data is _sentinel:
            in_q.put(_sentinel)
            break

        # Process the data
        ...
```

A subtle feature of this example is that the consumer, upon receiving the special sentinel value, immediately places it back onto the queue. This propagates the sentinel to other consumers threads that might be listening on the same queue—thus shutting them all down one after the other.

Although queues are the most common thread communication mechanism, you can build your own data structures as long as you add the required locking and synchronization. The most common way to do this is to wrap your data structures with a condition variable. For example, here is how you might build a thread-safe priority queue, as discussed in Recipe 1.5.

```python
import heapq
import threading

class PriorityQueue:
    def __init__(self):
        self._queue = []
        self._count = 0
        self._cv = threading.Condition()
    def put(self, item, priority):
        with self._cv:
            heapq.heappush(self._queue, (-priority, self._count, item))
            self._count += 1
            self._cv.notify()

    def get(self):
        with self._cv:
            while len(self._queue) == 0:
                self._cv.wait()
            return heapq.heappop(self._queue)[-1]
```

Thread communication with a queue is a one-way and nondeterministic process. In general, there is no way to know when the receiving thread has actually received a message and worked on it. However, Queue objects do provide some basic completion features, as illustrated by the task_done() and join() methods in this example:

```python
from queue import Queue
from threading import Thread

# A thread that produces data
def producer(out_q):
    while running:
        # Produce some data
        ...
        out_q.put(data)

# A thread that consumes data
def consumer(in_q):
    while True:
        # Get some data
        data = in_q.get()
```

```
            # Process the data
            ...
            # Indicate completion
            in_q.task_done()

    # Create the shared queue and launch both threads
    q = Queue()
    t1 = Thread(target=consumer, args=(q,))
    t2 = Thread(target=producer, args=(q,))
    t1.start()
    t2.start()

    # Wait for all produced items to be consumed
    q.join()
```

If a thread needs to know immediately when a consumer thread has processed a particular item of data, you should pair the sent data with an Event object that allows the producer to monitor its progress. For example:

```
from queue import Queue
from threading import Thread, Event

# A thread that produces data
def producer(out_q):
    while running:
        # Produce some data
        ...
        # Make an (data, event) pair and hand it to the consumer
        evt = Event()
        out_q.put((data, evt))
        ...
        # Wait for the consumer to process the item
        evt.wait()

# A thread that consumes data
def consumer(in_q):
    while True:
        # Get some data
        data, evt = in_q.get()
        # Process the data
        ...
        # Indicate completion
        evt.set()
```

Discussion

Writing threaded programs based on simple queuing is often a good way to maintain sanity. If you can break everything down to simple thread-safe queuing, you'll find that you don't need to litter your program with locks and other low-level synchronization. Also, communicating with queues often leads to designs that can be scaled up to other kinds of message-based communication patterns later on. For instance, you might be able to split your program into multiple processes, or even a distributed system, without changing much of its underlying queuing architecture.

One caution with thread queues is that putting an item in a queue doesn't make a copy of the item. Thus, communication actually involves passing an object reference between threads. If you are concerned about shared state, it may make sense to only pass immutable data structures (e.g., integers, strings, or tuples) or to make deep copies of the queued items. For example:

```python
from queue import Queue
from threading import Thread
import copy

# A thread that produces data
def producer(out_q):
    while True:
        # Produce some data
        ...
        out_q.put(copy.deepcopy(data))

# A thread that consumes data
def consumer(in_q):
    while True:
        # Get some data
        data = in_q.get()
        # Process the data
        ...
```

Queue objects provide a few additional features that may prove to be useful in certain contexts. If you create a Queue with an optional size, such as Queue(N), it places a limit on the number of items that can be enqueued before the put() blocks the producer. Adding an upper bound to a queue might make sense if there is mismatch in speed between a producer and consumer. For instance, if a producer is generating items at a much faster rate than they can be consumed. On the other hand, making a queue block when it's full can also have an unintended cascading effect throughout your program, possibly causing it to deadlock or run poorly. In general, the problem of "flow control" between communicating threads is a much harder problem than it seems. If you ever find yourself trying to fix a problem by fiddling with queue sizes, it could be an indicator of a fragile design or some other inherent scaling problem.

Both the get() and put() methods support nonblocking and timeouts. For example:

```python
import queue
q = queue.Queue()

try:
    data = q.get(block=False)
except queue.Empty:
    ...
```

```
try:
    q.put(item, block=False)
except queue.Full:
    ...

try:
    data = q.get(timeout=5.0)
except queue.Empty:
    ...
```

Both of these options can be used to avoid the problem of just blocking indefinitely on a particular queuing operation. For example, a nonblocking `put()` could be used with a fixed-sized queue to implement different kinds of handling code for when a queue is full. For example, issuing a log message and discarding:

```
def producer(q):
    ...
    try:
        q.put(item, block=False)
    except queue.Full:
        log.warning('queued item %r discarded!', item)
```

A timeout is useful if you're trying to make consumer threads periodically give up on operations such as `q.get()` so that they can check things such as a termination flag, as described in Recipe 12.1.

```
_running = True

def consumer(q):
    while _running:
        try:
            item = q.get(timeout=5.0)
            # Process item
            ...
        except queue.Empty:
            pass
```

Lastly, there are utility methods `q.qsize()`, `q.full()`, `q.empty()` that can tell you the current size and status of the queue. However, be aware that all of these are unreliable in a multithreaded environment. For example, a call to `q.empty()` might tell you that the queue is empty, but in the time that has elapsed since making the call, another thread could have added an item to the queue. Frankly, it's best to write your code not to rely on such functions.

12.4. Locking Critical Sections

Problem

Your program uses threads and you want to lock critical sections of code to avoid race conditions.

Solution

To make mutable objects safe to use by multiple threads, use `Lock` objects in the `threading` library, as shown here:

```
import threading

class SharedCounter:
    '''
    A counter object that can be shared by multiple threads.
    '''
    def __init__(self, initial_value = 0):
        self._value = initial_value
        self._value_lock = threading.Lock()

    def incr(self,delta=1):
        '''
        Increment the counter with locking
        '''
        with self._value_lock:
            self._value += delta

    def decr(self,delta=1):
        '''
        Decrement the counter with locking
        '''
        with self._value_lock:
            self._value -= delta
```

A `Lock` guarantees mutual exclusion when used with the `with` statement—that is, only one thread is allowed to execute the block of statements under the `with` statement at a time. The `with` statement acquires the lock for the duration of the indented statements and releases the lock when control flow exits the indented block.

Discussion

Thread scheduling is inherently nondeterministic. Because of this, failure to use locks in threaded programs can result in randomly corrupted data and bizarre behavior known as a "race condition." To avoid this, locks should always be used whenever shared mutable state is accessed by multiple threads.

In older Python code, it is common to see locks explicitly acquired and released. For example, in this variant of the last example:

```python
import threading

class SharedCounter:
    '''
    A counter object that can be shared by multiple threads.
    '''
    def __init__(self, initial_value = 0):
        self._value = initial_value
        self._value_lock = threading.Lock()

    def incr(self,delta=1):
        '''
        Increment the counter with locking
        '''
        self._value_lock.acquire()
        self._value += delta
        self._value_lock.release()

    def decr(self,delta=1):
        '''
        Decrement the counter with locking
        '''
        self._value_lock.acquire()
        self._value -= delta
        self._value_lock.release()
```

The with statement is more elegant and less prone to error—especially in situations where a programmer might forget to call the release() method or if a program happens to raise an exception while holding a lock (the with statement guarantees that locks are always released in both cases).

To avoid the potential for deadlock, programs that use locks should be written in a way such that each thread is only allowed to acquire one lock at a time. If this is not possible, you may need to introduce more advanced deadlock avoidance into your program, as described in Recipe 12.5.

In the threading library, you'll find other synchronization primitives, such as RLock and Semaphore objects. As a general rule of thumb, these are more special purpose and should not be used for simple locking of mutable state. An RLock or re-entrant lock object is a lock that can be acquired multiple times by the same thread. It is primarily used to implement code based locking or synchronization based on a construct known as a "monitor." With this kind of locking, only one thread is allowed to use an entire function or the methods of a class while the lock is held. For example, you could implement the SharedCounter class like this:

```python
import threading

class SharedCounter:
    '''
    A counter object that can be shared by multiple threads.
    '''
    _lock = threading.RLock()
    def __init__(self, initial_value = 0):
        self._value = initial_value

    def incr(self,delta=1):
        '''
        Increment the counter with locking
        '''
        with SharedCounter._lock:
            self._value += delta

    def decr(self,delta=1):
        '''
        Decrement the counter with locking
        '''
        with SharedCounter._lock:
            self.incr(-delta)
```

In this variant of the code, there is just a single class-level lock shared by all instances of the class. Instead of the lock being tied to the per-instance mutable state, the lock is meant to synchronize the methods of the class. Specifically, this lock ensures that only one thread is allowed to be using the methods of the class at once. However, unlike a standard lock, it is OK for methods that already have the lock to call other methods that also use the lock (e.g., see the decr() method).

One feature of this implementation is that only one lock is created, regardless of how many counter instances are created. Thus, it is much more memory-efficient in situations where there are a large number of counters. However, a possible downside is that it may cause more lock contention in programs that use a large number of threads and make frequent counter updates.

A Semaphore object is a synchronization primitive based on a shared counter. If the counter is nonzero, the with statement decrements the count and a thread is allowed to proceed. The counter is incremented upon the conclusion of the with block. If the counter is zero, progress is blocked until the counter is incremented by another thread. Although a semaphore can be used in the same manner as a standard Lock, the added complexity in implementation negatively impacts performance. Instead of simple locking, Semaphore objects are more useful for applications involving signaling between threads or throttling. For example, if you want to limit the amount of concurrency in a part of code, you might use a semaphore, as follows:

```python
from threading import Semaphore
import urllib.request
```

```
# At most, five threads allowed to run at once
_fetch_url_sema = Semaphore(5)

def fetch_url(url):
    with _fetch_url_sema:
        return urllib.request.urlopen(url)
```

If you're interested in the underlying theory and implementation of thread synchronization primitives, consult almost any textbook on operating systems.

12.5. Locking with Deadlock Avoidance

Problem

You're writing a multithreaded program where threads need to acquire more than one lock at a time while avoiding deadlock.

Solution

In multithreaded programs, a common source of deadlock is due to threads that attempt to acquire multiple locks at once. For instance, if a thread acquires the first lock, but then blocks trying to acquire the second lock, that thread can potentially block the progress of other threads and make the program freeze.

One solution to deadlock avoidance is to assign each lock in the program a unique number, and to enforce an ordering rule that only allows multiple locks to be acquired in ascending order. This is surprisingly easy to implement using a context manager as follows:

```
import threading
from contextlib import contextmanager

# Thread-local state to stored information on locks already acquired
_local = threading.local()

@contextmanager
def acquire(*locks):
    # Sort locks by object identifier
    locks = sorted(locks, key=lambda x: id(x))

    # Make sure lock order of previously acquired locks is not violated
    acquired = getattr(_local,'acquired',[])
    if acquired and max(id(lock) for lock in acquired) >= id(locks[0]):
        raise RuntimeError('Lock Order Violation')

    # Acquire all of the locks
    acquired.extend(locks)
    _local.acquired = acquired
```

```
try:
    for lock in locks:
        lock.acquire()
    yield
finally:
    # Release locks in reverse order of acquisition
    for lock in reversed(locks):
        lock.release()
    del acquired[-len(locks):]
```

To use this context manager, you simply allocate lock objects in the normal way, but use the `acquire()` function whenever you want to work with one or more locks. For example:

```
import threading
x_lock = threading.Lock()
y_lock = threading.Lock()

def thread_1():
    while True:
        with acquire(x_lock, y_lock):
            print('Thread-1')

def thread_2():
    while True:
        with acquire(y_lock, x_lock):
            print('Thread-2')

t1 = threading.Thread(target=thread_1)
t1.daemon = True
t1.start()

t2 = threading.Thread(target=thread_2)
t2.daemon = True
t2.start()
```

If you run this program, you'll find that it happily runs forever without deadlock—even though the acquisition of locks is specified in a different order in each function.

The key to this recipe lies in the first statement that sorts the locks according to object identifier. By sorting the locks, they always get acquired in a consistent order regardless of how the user might have provided them to `acquire()`.

The solution uses thread-local storage to solve a subtle problem with detecting potential deadlock if multiple `acquire()` operations are nested. For example, suppose you wrote the code like this:

```
import threading
x_lock = threading.Lock()
y_lock = threading.Lock()

def thread_1():
```

```
        while True:
            with acquire(x_lock):
                with acquire(y_lock):
                    print('Thread-1')

    def thread_2():
        while True:
            with acquire(y_lock):
                with acquire(x_lock):
                    print('Thread-2')

    t1 = threading.Thread(target=thread_1)
    t1.daemon = True
    t1.start()

    t2 = threading.Thread(target=thread_2)
    t2.daemon = True
    t2.start()
```

If you run this version of the program, one of the threads will crash with an exception such as this:

```
Exception in thread Thread-1:
Traceback (most recent call last):
  File "/usr/local/lib/python3.3/threading.py", line 639, in _bootstrap_inner
    self.run()
  File "/usr/local/lib/python3.3/threading.py", line 596, in run
    self._target(*self._args, **self._kwargs)
  File "deadlock.py", line 49, in thread_1
    with acquire(y_lock):
  File "/usr/local/lib/python3.3/contextlib.py", line 48, in __enter__
    return next(self.gen)
  File "deadlock.py", line 15, in acquire
    raise RuntimeError("Lock Order Violation")
RuntimeError: Lock Order Violation
>>>
```

This crash is caused by the fact that each thread remembers the locks it has already acquired. The acquire() function checks the list of previously acquired locks and enforces the ordering constraint that previously acquired locks must have an object ID that is less than the new locks being acquired.

Discussion

The issue of deadlock is a well-known problem with programs involving threads (as well as a common subject in textbooks on operating systems). As a rule of thumb, as long as you can ensure that threads can hold only one lock at a time, your program will be deadlock free. However, once multiple locks are being acquired at the same time, all bets are off.

Detecting and recovering from deadlock is an extremely tricky problem with few elegant solutions. For example, a common deadlock detection and recovery scheme involves the use of a watchdog timer. As threads run, they periodically reset the timer, and as long as everything is running smoothly, all is well. However, if the program deadlocks, the watchdog timer will eventually expire. At that point, the program "recovers" by killing and then restarting itself.

Deadlock avoidance is a different strategy where locking operations are carried out in a manner that simply does not allow the program to enter a deadlocked state. The solution in which locks are always acquired in strict order of ascending object ID can be mathematically proven to avoid deadlock, although the proof is left as an exercise to the reader (the gist of it is that by acquiring locks in a purely increasing order, you can't get cyclic locking dependencies, which are a necessary condition for deadlock to occur).

As a final example, a classic thread deadlock problem is the so-called "dining philosopher's problem." In this problem, five philosophers sit around a table on which there are five bowls of rice and five chopsticks. Each philosopher represents an independent thread and each chopstick represents a lock. In the problem, philosophers either sit and think or they eat rice. However, in order to eat rice, a philosopher needs two chopsticks. Unfortunately, if all of the philosophers reach over and grab the chopstick to their left, they'll all just sit there with one stick and eventually starve to death. It's a gruesome scene.

Using the solution, here is a simple deadlock free implementation of the dining philosopher's problem:

```python
import threading

# The philosopher thread
def philosopher(left, right):
    while True:
        with acquire(left,right):
            print(threading.currentThread(), 'eating')

# The chopsticks (represented by locks)
NSTICKS = 5
chopsticks = [threading.Lock() for n in range(NSTICKS)]

# Create all of the philosophers
for n in range(NSTICKS):
    t = threading.Thread(target=philosopher,
                         args=(chopsticks[n],chopsticks[(n+1) % NSTICKS]))
    t.start()
```

Last, but not least, it should be noted that in order to avoid deadlock, all locking operations must be carried out using our acquire() function. If some fragment of code decided to acquire a lock directly, then the deadlock avoidance algorithm wouldn't work.

12.6. Storing Thread-Specific State

Problem

You need to store state that's specific to the currently executing thread and not visible to other threads.

Solution

Sometimes in multithreaded programs, you need to store data that is only specific to the currently executing thread. To do this, create a thread-local storage object using `threading.local()`. Attributes stored and read on this object are only visible to the executing thread and no others.

As an interesting practical example of using thread-local storage, consider the `LazyCon nection` context-manager class that was first defined in Recipe 8.3. Here is a slightly modified version that safely works with multiple threads:

```python
from socket import socket, AF_INET, SOCK_STREAM
import threading

class LazyConnection:
    def __init__(self, address, family=AF_INET, type=SOCK_STREAM):
        self.address = address
        self.family = AF_INET
        self.type = SOCK_STREAM
        self.local = threading.local()

    def __enter__(self):
        if hasattr(self.local, 'sock'):
            raise RuntimeError('Already connected')
        self.local.sock = socket(self.family, self.type)
        self.local.sock.connect(self.address)
        return self.local.sock

    def __exit__(self, exc_ty, exc_val, tb):
        self.local.sock.close()
        del self.local.sock
```

In this code, carefully observe the use of the `self.local` attribute. It is initialized as an instance of `threading.local()`. The other methods then manipulate a socket that's stored as `self.local.sock`. This is enough to make it possible to safely use an instance of `LazyConnection` in multiple threads. For example:

```python
from functools import partial
def test(conn):
    with conn as s:
        s.send(b'GET /index.html HTTP/1.0\r\n')
        s.send(b'Host: www.python.org\r\n')
```

```
            s.send(b'\r\n')
            resp = b''.join(iter(partial(s.recv, 8192), b''))

        print('Got {} bytes'.format(len(resp)))

    if __name__ == '__main__':
        conn = LazyConnection(('www.python.org', 80))

        t1 = threading.Thread(target=test, args=(conn,))
        t2 = threading.Thread(target=test, args=(conn,))
        t1.start()
        t2.start()
        t1.join()
        t2.join()
```

The reason it works is that each thread actually creates its own dedicated socket connection (stored as self.local.sock). Thus, when the different threads perform socket operations, they don't interfere with one another as they are being performed on different sockets.

Discussion

Creating and manipulating thread-specific state is not a problem that often arises in most programs. However, when it does, it commonly involves situations where an object being used by multiple threads needs to manipulate some kind of dedicated system resource, such as a socket or file. You can't just have a single socket object shared by everyone because chaos would ensue if multiple threads ever started reading and writing on it at the same time. Thread-local storage fixes this by making such resources only visible in the thread where they're being used.

In this recipe, the use of threading.local() makes the LazyConnection class support one connection per thread, as opposed to one connection for the entire process. It's a subtle but interesting distinction.

Under the covers, an instance of threading.local() maintains a separate instance dictionary for each thread. All of the usual instance operations of getting, setting, and deleting values just manipulate the per-thread dictionary. The fact that each thread uses a separate dictionary is what provides the isolation of data.

12.7. Creating a Thread Pool

Problem

You want to create a pool of worker threads for serving clients or performing other kinds of work.

Solution

The concurrent.futures library has a ThreadPoolExecutor class that can be used for this purpose. Here is an example of a simple TCP server that uses a thread-pool to serve clients:

```python
from socket import AF_INET, SOCK_STREAM, socket
from concurrent.futures import ThreadPoolExecutor

def echo_client(sock, client_addr):
    '''
    Handle a client connection
    '''
    print('Got connection from', client_addr)
    while True:
        msg = sock.recv(65536)
        if not msg:
            break
        sock.sendall(msg)
    print('Client closed connection')
    sock.close()

def echo_server(addr):
    pool = ThreadPoolExecutor(128)
    sock = socket(AF_INET, SOCK_STREAM)
    sock.bind(addr)
    sock.listen(5)
    while True:
        client_sock, client_addr = sock.accept()
        pool.submit(echo_client, client_sock, client_addr)

echo_server(('',15000))
```

If you want to manually create your own thread pool, it's usually easy enough to do it using a Queue. Here is a slightly different, but manual implementation of the same code:

```python
from socket import socket, AF_INET, SOCK_STREAM
from threading import Thread
from queue import Queue

def echo_client(q):
    '''
    Handle a client connection
    '''
    sock, client_addr = q.get()
    print('Got connection from', client_addr)
    while True:
        msg = sock.recv(65536)
        if not msg:
            break
        sock.sendall(msg)
    print('Client closed connection')
```

```
        sock.close()

    def echo_server(addr, nworkers):
        # Launch the client workers
        q = Queue()
        for n in range(nworkers):
            t = Thread(target=echo_client, args=(q,))
            t.daemon = True
            t.start()

        # Run the server
        sock = socket(AF_INET, SOCK_STREAM)
        sock.bind(addr)
        sock.listen(5)
        while True:
            client_sock, client_addr = sock.accept()
            q.put((client_sock, client_addr))

    echo_server(('',15000), 128)
```

One advantage of using ThreadPoolExecutor over a manual implementation is that it makes it easier for the submitter to receive results from the called function. For example, you could write code like this:

```
from concurrent.futures import ThreadPoolExecutor
import urllib.request

def fetch_url(url):
    u = urllib.request.urlopen(url)
    data = u.read()
    return data

pool = ThreadPoolExecutor(10)
# Submit work to the pool
a = pool.submit(fetch_url, 'http://www.python.org')
b = pool.submit(fetch_url, 'http://www.pypy.org')

# Get the results back
x = a.result()
y = b.result()
```

The result objects in the example handle all of the blocking and coordination needed to get data back from the worker thread. Specifically, the operation a.result() blocks until the corresponding function has been executed by the pool and returned a value.

Discussion

Generally, you should avoid writing programs that allow unlimited growth in the number of threads. For example, take a look at the following server:

```
from threading import Thread
from socket import socket, AF_INET, SOCK_STREAM
```

```
def echo_client(sock, client_addr):
    '''
    Handle a client connection
    '''
    print('Got connection from', client_addr)
    while True:
        msg = sock.recv(65536)
        if not msg:
            break
        sock.sendall(msg)
    print('Client closed connection')
    sock.close()

def echo_server(addr, nworkers):
    # Run the server
    sock = socket(AF_INET, SOCK_STREAM)
    sock.bind(addr)
    sock.listen(5)
    while True:
        client_sock, client_addr = sock.accept()
        t = Thread(target=echo_client, args=(client_sock, client_addr))
        t.daemon = True
        t.start()

echo_server(('',15000))
```

Although this works, it doesn't prevent some asynchronous hipster from launching an attack on the server that makes it create so many threads that your program runs out of resources and crashes (thus further demonstrating the "evils" of using threads). By using a pre-initialized thread pool, you can carefully put an upper limit on the amount of supported concurrency.

You might be concerned with the effect of creating a large number of threads. However, modern systems should have no trouble creating pools of a few thousand threads. Moreover, having a thousand threads just sitting around waiting for work isn't going to have much, if any, impact on the performance of other code (a sleeping thread does just that—nothing at all). Of course, if all of those threads wake up at the same time and start hammering on the CPU, that's a different story—especially in light of the Global Interpreter Lock (GIL). Generally, you only want to use thread pools for I/O-bound processing.

One possible concern with creating large thread pools might be memory use. For example, if you create 2,000 threads on OS X, the system shows the Python process using up more than 9 GB of virtual memory. However, this is actually somewhat misleading. When creating a thread, the operating system reserves a region of virtual memory to hold the thread's execution stack (often as large as 8 MB). Only a small fragment of this memory is actually mapped to real memory, though. Thus, if you look a bit closer, you might find the Python process is using far less real memory (e.g., for 2,000 threads, only

70 MB of real memory is used, not 9 GB). If the size of the virtual memory is a concern, you can dial it down using the `threading.stack_size()` function. For example:

```
import threading
threading.stack_size(65536)
```

If you add this call and repeat the experiment of creating 2,000 threads, you'll find that the Python process is now only using about 210 MB of virtual memory, although the amount of real memory in use remains about the same. Note that the thread stack size must be at least 32,768 bytes, and is usually restricted to be a multiple of the system memory page size (4096, 8192, etc.).

12.8. Performing Simple Parallel Programming

Problem

You have a program that performs a lot of CPU-intensive work, and you want to make it run faster by having it take advantage of multiple CPUs.

Solution

The `concurrent.futures` library provides a `ProcessPoolExecutor` class that can be used to execute computationally intensive functions in a separately running instance of the Python interpreter. However, in order to use it, you first need to have some computationally intensive work. Let's illustrate with a simple yet practical example.

Suppose you have an entire directory of gzip-compressed Apache web server logs:

```
logs/
   20120701.log.gz
   20120702.log.gz
   20120703.log.gz
   20120704.log.gz
   20120705.log.gz
   20120706.log.gz
   ...
```

Further suppose each log file contains lines like this:

```
124.115.6.12 - - [10/Jul/2012:00:18:50 -0500] "GET /robots.txt ..." 200 71
210.212.209.67 - - [10/Jul/2012:00:18:51 -0500] "GET /ply/ ..." 200 11875
210.212.209.67 - - [10/Jul/2012:00:18:51 -0500] "GET /favicon.ico ..." 404 369
61.135.216.105 - - [10/Jul/2012:00:20:04 -0500] "GET /blog/atom.xml ..." 304 -
...
```

Here is a simple script that takes this data and identifies all hosts that have accessed the *robots.txt* file:

```
# findrobots.py

import gzip
import io
import glob

def find_robots(filename):
    '''
    Find all of the hosts that access robots.txt in a single log file
    '''
    robots = set()
    with gzip.open(filename) as f:
        for line in io.TextIOWrapper(f,encoding='ascii'):
            fields = line.split()
            if fields[6] == '/robots.txt':
                robots.add(fields[0])
    return robots

def find_all_robots(logdir):
    '''
    Find all hosts across and entire sequence of files
    '''
    files = glob.glob(logdir+'/*.log.gz')
    all_robots = set()
    for robots in map(find_robots, files):
        all_robots.update(robots)
    return all_robots

if __name__ == '__main__':
    robots = find_all_robots('logs')
    for ipaddr in robots:
        print(ipaddr)
```

The preceding program is written in the commonly used map-reduce style. The function find_robots() is mapped across a collection of filenames and the results are combined into a single result (the all_robots set in the find_all_robots() function).

Now, suppose you want to modify this program to use multiple CPUs. It turns out to be easy—simply replace the map() operation with a similar operation carried out on a process pool from the concurrent.futures library. Here is a slightly modified version of the code:

```
# findrobots.py

import gzip
import io
import glob
from concurrent import futures

def find_robots(filename):
    '''
    Find all of the hosts that access robots.txt in a single log file
```

```
    '''
    robots = set()
    with gzip.open(filename) as f:
        for line in io.TextIOWrapper(f,encoding='ascii'):
            fields = line.split()
            if fields[6] == '/robots.txt':
                robots.add(fields[0])
    return robots

def find_all_robots(logdir):
    '''
    Find all hosts across and entire sequence of files
    '''
    files = glob.glob(logdir+'/*.log.gz')
    all_robots = set()
    with futures.ProcessPoolExecutor() as pool:
        for robots in pool.map(find_robots, files):
            all_robots.update(robots)
    return all_robots

if __name__ == '__main__':
    robots - find_all_robots('logs')
    for ipaddr in robots:
        print(ipaddr)
```

With this modification, the script produces the same result but runs about 3.5 times faster on our quad-core machine. The actual performance will vary according to the number of CPUs available on your machine.

Discussion

Typical usage of a `ProcessPoolExecutor` is as follows:

```
from concurrent.futures import ProcessPoolExecutor

with ProcessPoolExecutor() as pool:
    ...
    do work in parallel using pool
    ...
```

Under the covers, a `ProcessPoolExecutor` creates N independent running Python interpreters where N is the number of available CPUs detected on the system. You can change the number of processes created by supplying an optional argument to `ProcessPoolExecutor(N)`. The pool runs until the last statement in the `with` block is executed, at which point the process pool is shut down. However, the program will wait until all submitted work has been processed.

Work to be submitted to a pool must be defined in a function. There are two methods for submission. If you are are trying to parallelize a list comprehension or a `map()` operation, you use `pool.map()`:

```
# A function that performs a lot of work
def work(x):
    ...
    return result

# Nonparallel code
results = map(work, data)

# Parallel implementation
with ProcessPoolExecutor() as pool:
    results = pool.map(work, data)
```

Alternatively, you can manually submit single tasks using the `pool.submit()` method:

```
# Some function
def work(x):
    ...
    return result

with ProcessPoolExecutor() as pool:
    ...
    # Example of submitting work to the pool
    future_result = pool.submit(work, arg)

    # Obtaining the result (blocks until done)
    r = future_result.result()
    ...
```

If you manually submit a job, the result is an instance of `Future`. To obtain the actual result, you call its `result()` method. This blocks until the result is computed and returned by the pool.

Instead of blocking, you can also arrange to have a callback function triggered upon completion instead. For example:

```
def when_done(r):
    print('Got:', r.result())

with ProcessPoolExecutor() as pool:
    future_result = pool.submit(work, arg)
    future_result.add_done_callback(when_done)
```

The user-supplied callback function receives an instance of `Future` that must be used to obtain the actual result (i.e., by calling its `result()` method).

Although process pools can be easy to use, there are a number of important considerations to be made in designing larger programs. In no particular order:

- This technique for parallelization only works well for problems that can be trivially decomposed into independent parts.

- Work must be submitted in the form of simple functions. Parallel execution of instance methods, closures, or other kinds of constructs are not supported.

- Function arguments and return values must be compatible with `pickle`. Work is carried out in a separate interpreter using interprocess communication. Thus, data exchanged between interpreters has to be serialized.

- Functions submitted for work should not maintain persistent state or have side effects. With the exception of simple things such as logging, you don't really have any control over the behavior of child processes once started. Thus, to preserve your sanity, it is probably best to keep things simple and carry out work in pure-functions that don't alter their environment.

- Process pools are created by calling the `fork()` system call on Unix. This makes a clone of the Python interpreter, including all of the program state at the time of the fork. On Windows, an independent copy of the interpreter that does not clone state is launched. The actual forking process does not occur until the first `pool.map()` or `pool.submit()` method is called.

- Great care should be made when combining process pools and programs that use threads. In particular, you should probably create and launch process pools prior to the creation of any threads (e.g., create the pool in the main thread at program startup).

12.9. Dealing with the GIL (and How to Stop Worrying About It)

Problem

You've heard about the Global Interpreter Lock (GIL), and are worried that it might be affecting the performance of your multithreaded program.

Solution

Although Python fully supports thread programming, parts of the C implementation of the interpreter are not entirely thread safe to a level of allowing fully concurrent execution. In fact, the interpreter is protected by a so-called Global Interpreter Lock (GIL) that only allows one Python thread to execute at any given time. The most noticeable effect of the GIL is that multithreaded Python programs are not able to fully take advantage of multiple CPU cores (e.g., a computationally intensive application using more than one thread only runs on a single CPU).

Before discussing common GIL workarounds, it is important to emphasize that the GIL tends to only affect programs that are heavily CPU bound (i.e., dominated by computation). If your program is mostly doing I/O, such as network communication, threads are often a sensible choice because they're mostly going to spend their time sitting around waiting. In fact, you can create thousands of Python threads with barely a concern. Modern operating systems have no trouble running with that many threads, so it's simply not something you should worry much about.

For CPU-bound programs, you really need to study the nature of the computation being performed. For instance, careful choice of the underlying algorithm may produce a far greater speedup than trying to parallelize an unoptimal algorithm with threads. Similarly, given that Python is interpreted, you might get a far greater speedup simply by moving performance-critical code into a C extension module. Extensions such as NumPy (*http://www.numpy.org*) are also highly effective at speeding up certain kinds of calculations involving array data. Last, but not least, you might investigate alternative implementations, such as PyPy, which features optimizations such as a JIT compiler (although, as of this writing, it does not yet support Python 3).

It's also worth noting that threads are not necessarily used exclusively for performance. A CPU-bound program might be using threads to manage a graphical user interface, a network connection, or provide some other kind of service. In this case, the GIL can actually present more of a problem, since code that holds it for an excessively long period will cause annoying stalls in the non-CPU-bound threads. In fact, a poorly written C extension can actually make this problem worse, even though the computation part of the code might run faster than before.

Having said all of this, there are two common strategies for working around the limitations of the GIL. First, if you are working entirely in Python, you can use the multiprocessing module to create a process pool and use it like a co-processor. For example, suppose you have the following thread code:

```
# Performs a large calculation (CPU bound)
def some_work(args):
    ...
    return result

# A thread that calls the above function
def some_thread():
    while True:
        ...
        r = some_work(args)
        ...
```

Here's how you would modify the code to use a pool:

```
# Processing pool (see below for initiazation)
pool = None
```

```
# Performs a large calculation (CPU bound)
def some_work(args):
    ...
    return result

# A thread that calls the above function
def some_thread():
    while True:
        ...
        r = pool.apply(some_work, (args))
        ...

# Initiaze the pool
if __name__ == '__main__':
    import multiprocessing
    pool = multiprocessing.Pool()
```

This example with a pool works around the GIL using a neat trick. Whenever a thread
wants to perform CPU-intensive work, it hands the work to the pool. The pool, in turn,
hands the work to a separate Python interpreter running in a different process. While
the thread is waiting for the result, it releases the GIL. Moreover, because the calculation
is being performed in a separate interpreter, it's no longer bound by the restrictions of
the GIL. On a multicore system, you'll find that this technique easily allows you to take
advantage of all the CPUs.

The second strategy for working around the GIL is to focus on C extension programming. The general idea is to move computationally intensive tasks to C, independent of
Python, and have the C code release the GIL while it's working. This is done by inserting
special macros into the C code like this:

```
#include "Python.h"
...

PyObject *pyfunc(PyObject *self, PyObject *args) {
    ...
    Py_BEGIN_ALLOW_THREADS
    // Threaded C code
    ...
    Py_END_ALLOW_THREADS
    ...
}
```

If you are using other tools to access C, such as the ctypes library or Cython, you may
not need to do anything. For example, ctypes releases the GIL when calling into C by
default.

Discussion

Many programmers, when faced with thread performance problems, are quick to blame
the GIL for all of their ills. However, doing so is shortsighted and naive. Just as a real-

world example, mysterious "stalls" in a multithreaded network program might be caused by something entirely different (e.g., a stalled DNS lookup) rather than anything related to the GIL. The bottom line is that you really need to study your code to know if the GIL is an issue or not. Again, realize that the GIL is mostly concerned with CPU-bound processing, not I/O.

If you are going to use a process pool as a workaround, be aware that doing so involves data serialization and communication with a different Python interpreter. For this to work, the operation to be performed needs to be contained within a Python function defined by the def statement (i.e., no lambdas, closures, callable instances, etc.), and the function arguments and return value must be compatible with pickle. Also, the amount of work to be performed must be sufficiently large to make up for the extra communication overhead.

Another subtle aspect of pools is that mixing threads and process pools together can be a good way to make your head explode. If you are going to use both of these features together, it is often best to create the process pool as a singleton at program startup, prior to the creation of any threads. Threads will then use the same process pool for all of their computationally intensive work.

For C extensions, the most important feature is maintaining isolation from the Python interpreter process. That is, if you're going to offload work from Python to C, you need to make sure the C code operates independently of Python. This means using no Python data structures and making no calls to Python's C API. Another consideration is that you want to make sure your C extension does enough work to make it all worthwhile. That is, it's much better if the extension can perform millions of calculations as opposed to just a few small calculations.

Needless to say, these solutions to working around the GIL don't apply to all possible problems. For instance, certain kinds of applications don't work well if separated into multiple processes, nor may you want to code parts in C. For these kinds of applications, you may have to come up with your own solution (e.g., multiple processes accessing shared memory regions, multiple interpreters running in the same process, etc.). Alternatively, you might look at some other implementations of the interpreter, such as PyPy.

See Recipes 15.7 and 15.10 for additional information on releasing the GIL in C extensions.

12.10. Defining an Actor Task

Problem

You'd like to define tasks with behavior similar to "actors" in the so-called "actor model."

Solution

The "actor model" is one of the oldest and most simple approaches to concurrency and distributed computing. In fact, its underlying simplicity is part of its appeal. In a nutshell, an actor is a concurrently executing task that simply acts upon messages sent to it. In response to these messages, it may decide to send further messages to other actors. Communication with actors is one way and asynchronous. Thus, the sender of a message does not know when a message actually gets delivered, nor does it receive a response or acknowledgment that the message has been processed.

Actors are straightforward to define using a combination of a thread and a queue. For example:

```python
from queue import Queue
from threading import Thread, Event

# Sentinel used for shutdown
class ActorExit(Exception):
    pass

class Actor:
    def __init__(self):
        self._mailbox = Queue()

    def send(self, msg):
        '''
        Send a message to the actor
        '''
        self._mailbox.put(msg)

    def recv(self):
        '''
        Receive an incoming message
        '''
        msg = self._mailbox.get()
        if msg is ActorExit:
            raise ActorExit()
        return msg

    def close(self):
        '''
        Close the actor, thus shutting it down
        '''
        self.send(ActorExit)

    def start(self):
        '''
        Start concurrent execution
        '''
        self._terminated = Event()
        t = Thread(target=self._bootstrap)
```

```
        t.daemon = True
        t.start()

    def _bootstrap(self):
        try:
            self.run()
        except ActorExit:
            pass
        finally:
            self._terminated.set()

    def join(self):
        self._terminated.wait()

    def run(self):
        '''
        Run method to be implemented by the user
        '''
        while True:
            msg = self.recv()

# Sample ActorTask
class PrintActor(Actor):
    def run(self):
        while True:
            msg = self.recv()
            print('Got:', msg)

# Sample use
p = PrintActor()
p.start()
p.send('Hello')
p.send('World')
p.close()
p.join()
```

In this example, `Actor` instances are things that you simply send a message to using their `send()` method. Under the covers, this places the message on a queue and hands it off to an internal thread that runs to process the received messages. The `close()` method is programmed to shut down the actor by placing a special sentinel value (`ActorExit`) on the queue. Users define new actors by inheriting from `Actor` and redefining the `run()` method to implement their custom processing. The usage of the `ActorExit` exception is such that user-defined code can be programmed to catch the termination request and handle it if appropriate (the exception is raised by the `get()` method and propagated).

If you relax the requirement of concurrent and asynchronous message delivery, actor-like objects can also be minimally defined by generators. For example:

```
def print_actor():
    while True:
```

```
        try:
            msg = yield        # Get a message
            print('Got:', msg)
        except GeneratorExit:
            print('Actor terminating')

# Sample use
p = print_actor()
next(p)      # Advance to the yield (ready to receive)
p.send('Hello')
p.send('World')
p.close()
```

Discussion

Part of the appeal of actors is their underlying simplicity. In practice, there is just one core operation, send(). Plus, the general concept of a "message" in actor-based systems is something that can be expanded in many different directions. For example, you could pass tagged messages in the form of tuples and have actors take different courses of action like this:

```
class TaggedActor(Actor):
    def run(self):
        while True:
            tag, *payload = self.recv()
            getattr(self,'do_'+tag)(*payload)

    # Methods correponding to different message tags
    def do_A(self, x):
        print('Running A', x)

    def do_B(self, x, y):
        print('Running B', x, y)

# Example
a = TaggedActor()
a.start()
a.send(('A', 1))      # Invokes do_A(1)
a.send(('B', 2, 3))   # Invokes do_B(2,3)
```

As another example, here is a variation of an actor that allows arbitrary functions to be executed in a worker and results to be communicated back using a special Result object:

```
from threading import Event
class Result:
    def __init__(self):
        self._evt = Event()
        self._result = None

    def set_result(self, value):
        self._result = value
```

```
            self._evt.set()

        def result(self):
            self._evt.wait()
            return self._result

    class Worker(Actor):
        def submit(self, func, *args, **kwargs):
            r = Result()
            self.send((func, args, kwargs, r))
            return r

        def run(self):
            while True:
                func, args, kwargs, r = self.recv()
                r.set_result(func(*args, **kwargs))

    # Example use
    worker = Worker()
    worker.start()
    r = worker.submit(pow, 2, 3)
    print(r.result())
```

Last, but not least, the concept of "sending" a task a message is something that can be scaled up into systems involving multiple processes or even large distributed systems. For example, the send() method of an actor-like object could be programmed to transmit data on a socket connection or deliver it via some kind of messaging infrastructure (e.g., AMQP, ZMQ, etc.).

12.11. Implementing Publish/Subscribe Messaging

Problem

You have a program based on communicating threads and want them to implement publish/subscribe messaging.

Solution

To implement publish/subscribe messaging, you typically introduce a separate "exchange" or "gateway" object that acts as an intermediary for all messages. That is, instead of directly sending a message from one task to another, a message is sent to the exchange and it delivers it to one or more attached tasks. Here is one example of a very simple exchange implementation:

```
from collections import defaultdict

class Exchange:
    def __init__(self):
        self._subscribers = set()
```

```
    def attach(self, task):
        self._subscribers.add(task)

    def detach(self, task):
        self._subscribers.remove(task)

    def send(self, msg):
        for subscriber in self._subscribers:
            subscriber.send(msg)

# Dictionary of all created exchanges
_exchanges = defaultdict(Exchange)

# Return the Exchange instance associated with a given name
def get_exchange(name):
    return _exchanges[name]
```

An exchange is really nothing more than an object that keeps a set of active subscribers and provides methods for attaching, detaching, and sending messages. Each exchange is identified by a name, and the get_exchange() function simply returns the Ex change instance associated with a given name.

Here is a simple example that shows how to use an exchange:

```
# Example of a task.  Any object with a send() method

class Task:
    ...
    def send(self, msg):
        ...

task_a = Task()
task_b = Task()

# Example of getting an exchange
exc = get_exchange('name')

# Examples of subscribing tasks to it
exc.attach(task_a)
exc.attach(task_b)

# Example of sending messages
exc.send('msg1')
exc.send('msg2')

# Example of unsubscribing
exc.detach(task_a)
exc.detach(task_b)
```

Although there are many different variations on this theme, the overall idea is the same. Messages will be delivered to an exchange and the exchange will deliver them to attached subscribers.

Discussion

The concept of tasks or threads sending messages to one another (often via queues) is easy to implement and quite popular. However, the benefits of using a public/subscribe (pub/sub) model instead are often overlooked.

First, the use of an exchange can simplify much of the plumbing involved in setting up communicating threads. Instead of trying to wire threads together across multiple program modules, you only worry about connecting them to a known exchange. In some sense, this is similar to how the logging library works. In practice, it can make it easier to decouple various tasks in the program.

Second, the ability of the exchange to broadcast messages to multiple subscribers opens up new communication patterns. For example, you could implement systems with redundant tasks, broadcasting, or fan-out. You could also build debugging and diagnostic tools that attach themselves to exchanges as ordinary subscribers. For example, here is a simple diagnostic class that would display sent messages:

```python
class DisplayMessages:
    def __init__(self):
        self.count = 0
    def send(self, msg):
        self.count += 1
        print('msg[{}]: {!r}'.format(self.count, msg))

exc = get_exchange('name')
d = DisplayMessages()
exc.attach(d)
```

Last, but not least, a notable aspect of the implementation is that it works with a variety of task-like objects. For example, the receivers of a message could be actors (as described in Recipe 12.10), coroutines, network connections, or just about anything that implements a proper send() method.

One potentially problematic aspect of an exchange concerns the proper attachment and detachment of subscribers. In order to properly manage resources, every subscriber that attaches must eventually detach. This leads to a programming model similar to this:

```python
exc = get_exchange('name')
exc.attach(some_task)
try:
    ...
finally:
    exc.detach(some_task)
```

In some sense, this is similar to the usage of files, locks, and similar objects. Experience has shown that it is quite easy to forget the final detach() step. To simplify this, you might consider the use of the context-management protocol. For example, adding a subscribe() method to the exchange like this:

```
from contextlib import contextmanager
from collections import defaultdict

class Exchange:
    def __init__(self):
        self._subscribers = set()

    def attach(self, task):
        self._subscribers.add(task)

    def detach(self, task):
        self._subscribers.remove(task)

    @contextmanager
    def subscribe(self, *tasks):
        for task in tasks:
            self.attach(task)
        try:
            yield
        finally:
            for task in tasks:
                self.detach(task)

    def send(self, msg):
        for subscriber in self._subscribers:
            subscriber.send(msg)

# Dictionary of all created exchanges
_exchanges = defaultdict(Exchange)

# Return the Exchange instance associated with a given name
def get_exchange(name):
    return _exchanges[name]

# Example of using the subscribe() method
exc = get_exchange('name')
with exc.subscribe(task_a, task_b):
    ...
    exc.send('msg1')
    exc.send('msg2')
    ...

# task_a and task_b detached here
```

Finally, it should be noted that there are numerous possible extensions to the exchange idea. For example, exchanges could implement an entire collection of message channels or apply pattern matching rules to exchange names. Exchanges can also be extended into distributed computing applications (e.g., routing messages to tasks on different machines, etc.).

12.12. Using Generators As an Alternative to Threads

Problem

You want to implement concurrency using generators (coroutines) as an alternative to system threads. This is sometimes known as user-level threading or green threading.

Solution

To implement your own concurrency using generators, you first need a fundamental insight concerning generator functions and the yield statement. Specifically, the fundamental behavior of yield is that it causes a generator to suspend its execution. By suspending execution, it is possible to write a scheduler that treats generators as a kind of "task" and alternates their execution using a kind of cooperative task switching.

To illustrate this idea, consider the following two generator functions using a simple yield:

```
# Two simple generator functions
def countdown(n):
    while n > 0:
        print('T-minus', n)
        yield
        n -= 1
    print('Blastoff!')

def countup(n):
    x = 0
    while x < n:
        print('Counting up', x)
        yield
        x += 1
```

These functions probably look a bit funny using yield all by itself. However, consider the following code that implements a simple task scheduler:

```
from collections import deque

class TaskScheduler:
    def __init__(self):
        self._task_queue = deque()

    def new_task(self, task):
        '''
        Admit a newly started task to the scheduler
```

```
        '''
        self._task_queue.append(task)

    def run(self):
        '''
        Run until there are no more tasks
        '''
        while self._task_queue:
            task = self._task_queue.popleft()
            try:
                # Run until the next yield statement
                next(task)
                self._task_queue.append(task)
            except StopIteration:
                # Generator is no longer executing
                pass

# Example use
sched = TaskScheduler()
sched.new_task(countdown(10))
sched.new_task(countdown(5))
sched.new_task(countup(15))
sched.run()
```

In this code, the `TaskScheduler` class runs a collection of generators in a round-robin manner—each one running until they reach a `yield` statement. For the sample, the output will be as follows:

```
T-minus 10
T-minus 5
Counting up 0
T-minus 9
T-minus 4
Counting up 1
T-minus 8
T-minus 3
Counting up 2
T-minus 7
T-minus 2
...
```

At this point, you've essentially implemented the tiny core of an "operating system" if you will. Generator functions are the tasks and the `yield` statement is how tasks signal that they want to suspend. The scheduler simply cycles over the tasks until none are left executing.

In practice, you probably wouldn't use generators to implement concurrency for something as simple as shown. Instead, you might use generators to replace the use of threads when implementing actors (see Recipe 12.10) or network servers.

The following code illustrates the use of generators to implement a thread-free version of actors:

```python
from collections import deque

class ActorScheduler:
    def __init__(self):
        self._actors = { }          # Mapping of names to actors
        self._msg_queue = deque()   # Message queue

    def new_actor(self, name, actor):
        '''
        Admit a newly started actor to the scheduler and give it a name
        '''
        self._msg_queue.append((actor,None))
        self._actors[name] = actor

    def send(self, name, msg):
        '''
        Send a message to a named actor
        '''
        actor = self._actors.get(name)
        if actor:
            self._msg_queue.append((actor,msg))

    def run(self):
        '''
        Run as long as there are pending messages.
        '''
        while self._msg_queue:
            actor, msg = self._msg_queue.popleft()
            try:
                actor.send(msg)
            except StopIteration:
                pass

# Example use
if __name__ == '__main__':
    def printer():
        while True:
            msg = yield
            print('Got:', msg)

    def counter(sched):
        while True:
            # Receive the current count
            n = yield
            if n == 0:
                break
            # Send to the printer task
            sched.send('printer', n)
            # Send the next count to the counter task (recursive)
```

```
        sched.send('counter', n-1)

    sched = ActorScheduler()
    # Create the initial actors
    sched.new_actor('printer', printer())
    sched.new_actor('counter', counter(sched))

    # Send an initial message to the counter to initiate
    sched.send('counter', 10000)
    sched.run()
```

The execution of this code might take a bit of study, but the key is the queue of pending messages. Essentially, the scheduler runs as long as there are messages to deliver. A remarkable feature is that the counter generator sends messages to itself and ends up in a recursive cycle not bound by Python's recursion limit.

Here is an advanced example showing the use of generators to implement a concurrent network application:

```
from collections import deque
from select import select

# This class represents a generic yield event in the scheduler
class YieldEvent:
    def handle_yield(self, sched, task):
        pass
    def handle_resume(self, sched, task):
        pass

# Task Scheduler
class Scheduler:
    def __init__(self):
        self._numtasks = 0       # Total num of tasks
        self._ready = deque()    # Tasks ready to run
        self._read_waiting = {}  # Tasks waiting to read
        self._write_waiting = {} # Tasks waiting to write

    # Poll for I/O events and restart waiting tasks
    def _iopoll(self):
        rset,wset,eset = select(self._read_waiting,
                                self._write_waiting,[])
        for r in rset:
            evt, task = self._read_waiting.pop(r)
            evt.handle_resume(self, task)
        for w in wset:
            evt, task = self._write_waiting.pop(w)
            evt.handle_resume(self, task)

    def new(self,task):
        '''
        Add a newly started task to the scheduler
        '''
```

```
        self._ready.append((task, None))
        self._numtasks += 1

    def add_ready(self, task, msg=None):
        '''
        Append an already started task to the ready queue.
        msg is what to send into the task when it resumes.
        '''
        self._ready.append((task, msg))

    # Add a task to the reading set
    def _read_wait(self, fileno, evt, task):
        self._read_waiting[fileno] = (evt, task)

    # Add a task to the write set
    def _write_wait(self, fileno, evt, task):
        self._write_waiting[fileno] = (evt, task)

    def run(self):
        '''
        Run the task scheduler until there are no tasks
        '''
        while self._numtasks:
            if not self._ready:
                self._iopoll()
            task, msg = self._ready.popleft()
            try:
                # Run the coroutine to the next yield
                r = task.send(msg)
                if isinstance(r, YieldEvent):
                    r.handle_yield(self, task)
                else:
                    raise RuntimeError('unrecognized yield event')
            except StopIteration:
                self._numtasks -= 1

# Example implementation of coroutine-based socket I/O
class ReadSocket(YieldEvent):
    def __init__(self, sock, nbytes):
        self.sock = sock
        self.nbytes = nbytes
    def handle_yield(self, sched, task):
        sched._read_wait(self.sock.fileno(), self, task)
    def handle_resume(self, sched, task):
        data = self.sock.recv(self.nbytes)
        sched.add_ready(task, data)

class WriteSocket(YieldEvent):
    def __init__(self, sock, data):
        self.sock = sock
        self.data = data
    def handle_yield(self, sched, task):
```

```python
            sched._write_wait(self.sock.fileno(), self, task)
    def handle_resume(self, sched, task):
        nsent = self.sock.send(self.data)
        sched.add_ready(task, nsent)

class AcceptSocket(YieldEvent):
    def __init__(self, sock):
        self.sock = sock
    def handle_yield(self, sched, task):
        sched._read_wait(self.sock.fileno(), self, task)
    def handle_resume(self, sched, task):
        r = self.sock.accept()
        sched.add_ready(task, r)

# Wrapper around a socket object for use with yield
class Socket(object):
    def __init__(self, sock):
        self._sock = sock
    def recv(self, maxbytes):
        return ReadSocket(self._sock, maxbytes)
    def send(self, data):
        return WriteSocket(self._sock, data)
    def accept(self):
        return AcceptSocket(self._sock)
    def __getattr__(self, name):
        return getattr(self._sock, name)

if __name__ == '__main__':
    from socket import socket, AF_INET, SOCK_STREAM
    import time

    # Example of a function involving generators.  This should
    # be called using line = yield from readline(sock)
    def readline(sock):
        chars = []
        while True:
            c = yield sock.recv(1)
            if not c:
                break
            chars.append(c)
            if c == b'\n':
                break
        return b''.join(chars)

    # Echo server using generators
    class EchoServer:
        def __init__(self,addr,sched):
            self.sched = sched
            sched.new(self.server_loop(addr))

        def server_loop(self,addr):
            s = Socket(socket(AF_INET,SOCK_STREAM))
```

```
            s.bind(addr)
            s.listen(5)
            while True:
                c,a = yield s.accept()
                print('Got connection from ', a)
                self.sched.new(self.client_handler(Socket(c)))

        def client_handler(self,client):
            while True:
                line = yield from readline(client)
                if not line:
                    break
                line = b'GOT:' + line
                while line:
                    nsent = yield client.send(line)
                    line = line[nsent:]
            client.close()
            print('Client closed')

    sched = Scheduler()
    EchoServer(('',16000),sched)
    sched.run()
```

This code will undoubtedly require a certain amount of careful study. However, it is essentially implementing a small operating system. There is a queue of tasks ready to run and there are waiting areas for tasks sleeping for I/O. Much of the scheduler involves moving tasks between the ready queue and the I/O waiting area.

Discussion

When building generator-based concurrency frameworks, it is most common to work with the more general form of yield:

```
def some_generator():
    ...
    result = yield data
    ...
```

Functions that use yield in this manner are more generally referred to as "coroutines." Within a scheduler, the yield statement gets handled in a loop as follows:

```
f = some_generator()

# Initial result. Is None to start since nothing has been computed
result = None
while True:
    try:
        data = f.send(result)
        result = ... do some calculation ...
    except StopIteration:
        break
```

The logic concerning the result is a bit convoluted. However, the value passed to send() defines what gets returned when the yield statement wakes back up. So, if a yield is going to return a result in response to data that was previously yielded, it gets returned on the next send() operation. If a generator function has just started, sending in a value of None simply makes it advance to the first yield statement.

In addition to sending in values, it is also possible to execute a close() method on a generator. This causes a silent GeneratorExit exception to be raised at the yield statement, which stops execution. If desired, a generator can catch this exception and perform cleanup actions. It's also possible to use the throw() method of a generator to raise an arbitrary execution at the yield statement. A task scheduler might use this to communicate errors into running generators.

The yield from statement used in the last example is used to implement coroutines that serve as subroutines or procedures to be called from other generators. Essentially, control transparently transfers to the new function. Unlike normal generators, a function that is called using yield from can return a value that becomes the result of the yield from statement. More information about yield from can be found in PEP 380 (*http://www.python.org/dev/peps/pep-0380*).

Finally, if programming with generators, it is important to stress that there are some major limitations. In particular, you get none of the benefits that threads provide. For instance, if you execute any code that is CPU bound or which blocks for I/O, it will suspend the entire task scheduler until the completion of that operation. To work around this, your only real option is to delegate the operation to a separate thread or process where it can run independently. Another limitation is that most Python libraries have not been written to work well with generator-based threading. If you take this approach, you may find that you need to write replacements for many standard library functions.

As basic background on coroutines and the techniques utilized in this recipe, see PEP 342 (*http://www.python.org/dev/peps/pep-0342*) and "A Curious Course on Coroutines and Concurrency" (*http://www.dabeaz.com/coroutines*).

PEP 3156 (*http://www.python.org/dev/peps/pep-3156*) also has a modern take on asynchronous I/O involving coroutines. In practice, it is extremelyunlikely that you will write a low-level coroutine scheduler yourself. However, ideas surrounding coroutines are the basis for many popular libraries, including gevent (*http://www.gevent.org*), greenlet (*http://pypi.python.org/pypi/greenlet*), Stackless Python (*http://www.stackless.com*), and similar projects.

12.13. Polling Multiple Thread Queues

Problem

You have a collection of thread queues, and you would like to be able to poll them for incoming items, much in the same way as you might poll a collection of network connections for incoming data.

Solution

A common solution to polling problems involves a little-known trick involving a hidden loopback network connection. Essentially, the idea is as follows: for each queue (or any object) that you want to poll, you create a pair of connected sockets. You then write on one of the sockets to signal the presence of data. The other sockect is then passed to `select()` or a similar function to poll for the arrival of data. Here is some sample code that illustrates this idea:

```python
import queue
import socket
import os

class PollableQueue(queue.Queue):
    def __init__(self):
        super().__init__()
        # Create a pair of connected sockets
        if os.name == 'posix':
            self._putsocket, self._getsocket = socket.socketpair()
        else:
            # Compatibility on non-POSIX systems
            server = socket.socket(socket.AF_INET, socket.SOCK_STREAM)
            server.bind(('127.0.0.1', 0))
            server.listen(1)
            self._putsocket = socket.socket(socket.AF_INET, socket.SOCK_STREAM)
            self._putsocket.connect(server.getsockname())
            self._getsocket, _ = server.accept()
            server.close()

    def fileno(self):
        return self._getsocket.fileno()

    def put(self, item):
        super().put(item)
        self._putsocket.send(b'x')

    def get(self):
        self._getsocket.recv(1)
        return super().get()
```

In this code, a new kind of Queue instance is defined where there is an underlying pair of connected sockets. The socketpair() function on Unix machines can establish such sockets easily. On Windows, you have to fake it using code similar to that shown (it looks a bit weird, but a server socket is created and a client immediately connects to it afterward). The normal get() and put() methods are then redefined slightly to perform a small bit of I/O on these sockets. The put() method writes a single byte of data to one of the sockets after putting data on the queue. The get() method reads a single byte of data from the other socket when removing an item from the queue.

The fileno() method is what makes the queue pollable using a function such as select(). Essentially, it just exposes the underlying file descriptor of the socket used by the get() function.

Here is an example of some code that defines a consumer which monitors multiple queues for incoming items:

```python
import select
import threading

def consumer(queues):
    '''
    Consumer that reads data on multiple queues simultaneously
    '''
    while True:
        can_read, _, _ = select.select(queues,[],[])
        for r in can_read:
            item = r.get()
            print('Got:', item)

q1 = PollableQueue()
q2 = PollableQueue()
q3 = PollableQueue()
t = threading.Thread(target=consumer, args=([q1,q2,q3],))
t.daemon = True
t.start()

# Feed data to the queues
q1.put(1)
q2.put(10)
q3.put('hello')
q2.put(15)
...
```

If you try it, you'll find that the consumer indeed receives all of the put items, regardless of which queues they are placed in.

Discussion

The problem of polling non-file-like objects, such as queues, is often a lot trickier than it looks. For instance, if you don't use the socket technique shown, your only option is to write code that cycles through the queues and uses a timer, like this:

```
import time
def consumer(queues):
    while True:
        for q in queues:
            if not q.empty():
                item = q.get()
                print('Got:', item)
        # Sleep briefly to avoid 100% CPU
        time.sleep(0.01)
```

This might work for certain kinds of problems, but it's clumsy and introduces other weird performance problems. For example, if new data is added to a queue, it won't be detected for as long as 10 milliseconds (an eternity on a modern processor).

You run into even further problems if the preceding polling is mixed with the polling of other objects, such as network sockets. For example, if you want to poll both sockets and queues at the same time, you might have to use code like this:

```
import select

def event_loop(sockets, queues):
    while True:
        # polling with a timeout
        can_read, _, _ = select.select(sockets, [], [], 0.01)
        for r in can_read:
            handle_read(r)
        for q in queues:
            if not q.empty():
                item = q.get()
                print('Got:', item)
```

The solution shown solves a lot of these problems by simply putting queues on equal status with sockets. A single select() call can be used to poll for activity on both. It is not necessary to use timeouts or other time-based hacks to periodically check. Moreover, if data gets added to a queue, the consumer will be notified almost instantaneously. Although there is a tiny amount of overhead associated with the underlying I/O, it often is worth it to have better response time and simplified coding.

12.14. Launching a Daemon Process on Unix

Problem

You would like to write a program that runs as a proper daemon process on Unix or Unix-like systems.

Solution

Creating a proper daemon process requires a precise sequence of system calls and careful attention to detail. The following code shows how to define a daemon process along with the ability to easily stop it once launched:

```python
#!/usr/bin/env python3
# daemon.py

import os
import sys
import atexit
import signal

def daemonize(pidfile, *, stdin='/dev/null',
                          stdout='/dev/null',
                          stderr='/dev/null'):

    if os.path.exists(pidfile):
        raise RuntimeError('Already running')

    # First fork (detaches from parent)
    try:
        if os.fork() > 0:
            raise SystemExit(0)   # Parent exit
    except OSError as e:
        raise RuntimeError('fork #1 failed.')

    os.chdir('/')
    os.umask(0)
    os.setsid()
    # Second fork (relinquish session leadership)
    try:
        if os.fork() > 0:
            raise SystemExit(0)
    except OSError as e:
        raise RuntimeError('fork #2 failed.')

    # Flush I/O buffers
    sys.stdout.flush()
    sys.stderr.flush()

    # Replace file descriptors for stdin, stdout, and stderr
```

```python
    with open(stdin, 'rb', 0) as f:
        os.dup2(f.fileno(), sys.stdin.fileno())
    with open(stdout, 'ab', 0) as f:
        os.dup2(f.fileno(), sys.stdout.fileno())
    with open(stderr, 'ab', 0) as f:
        os.dup2(f.fileno(), sys.stderr.fileno())

    # Write the PID file
    with open(pidfile,'w') as f:
        print(os.getpid(),file=f)

    # Arrange to have the PID file removed on exit/signal
    atexit.register(lambda: os.remove(pidfile))

    # Signal handler for termination (required)
    def sigterm_handler(signo, frame):
        raise SystemExit(1)

    signal.signal(signal.SIGTERM, sigterm_handler)

def main():
    import time
    sys.stdout.write('Daemon started with pid {}\n'.format(os.getpid()))
    while True:
        sys.stdout.write('Daemon Alive! {}\n'.format(time.ctime()))
        time.sleep(10)

if __name__ == '__main__':
    PIDFILE = '/tmp/daemon.pid'

    if len(sys.argv) != 2:
        print('Usage: {} [start|stop]'.format(sys.argv[0]), file=sys.stderr)
        raise SystemExit(1)

    if sys.argv[1] == 'start':
        try:
            daemonize(PIDFILE,
                        stdout='/tmp/daemon.log',
                        stderr='/tmp/dameon.log')
        except RuntimeError as e:
            print(e, file=sys.stderr)
            raise SystemExit(1)

        main()

    elif sys.argv[1] == 'stop':
        if os.path.exists(PIDFILE):
            with open(PIDFILE) as f:
                os.kill(int(f.read()), signal.SIGTERM)
        else:
            print('Not running', file=sys.stderr)
            raise SystemExit(1)
```

```
else:
    print('Unknown command {!r}'.format(sys.argv[1]), file=sys.stderr)
    raise SystemExit(1)
```

To launch the daemon, the user would use a command like this:

```
bash % daemon.py start
bash % cat /tmp/daemon.pid
2882
bash % tail -f /tmp/daemon.log
Daemon started with pid 2882
Daemon Alive! Fri Oct 12 13:45:37 2012
Daemon Alive! Fri Oct 12 13:45:47 2012
...
```

Daemon processes run entirely in the background, so the command returns immediately. However, you can view its associated pid file and log, as just shown. To stop the daemon, use:

```
bash % daemon.py stop
bash %
```

Discussion

This recipe defines a function `daemonize()` that should be called at program startup to make the program run as a daemon. The signature to `daemonize()` is using keyword-only arguments to make the purpose of the optional arguments more clear when used. This forces the user to use a call such as this:

```
daemonize('daemon.pid',
          stdin='/dev/null,
          stdout='/tmp/daemon.log',
          stderr='/tmp/daemon.log')
```

As opposed to a more cryptic call such as:

```
# Illegal. Must use keyword arguments
daemonize('daemon.pid',
          '/dev/null', '/tmp/daemon.log','/tmp/daemon.log')
```

The steps involved in creating a daemon are fairly cryptic, but the general idea is as follows. First, a daemon has to detach itself from its parent process. This is the purpose of the first `os.fork()` operation and immediate termination by the parent.

After the child has been orphaned, the call to `os.setsid()` creates an entirely new process session and sets the child as the leader. This also sets the child as the leader of a new process group and makes sure there is no controlling terminal. If this all sounds a bit too magical, it has to do with getting the daemon to detach properly from the terminal and making sure that things like signals don't interfere with its operation.

The calls to `os.chdir()` and `os.umask(0)` change the current working directory and reset the file mode mask. Changing the directory is usually a good idea so that the daemon is no longer working in the directory from which it was launched.

The second call to `os.fork()` is by far the more mysterious operation here. This step makes the daemon process give up the ability to acquire a new controlling terminal and provides even more isolation (essentially, the daemon gives up its session leadership and thus no longer has the permission to open controlling terminals). Although you could probably omit this step, it's typically recommended.

Once the daemon process has been properly detached, it performs steps to reinitialize the standard I/O streams to point at files specified by the user. This part is actually somewhat tricky. References to file objects associated with the standard I/O streams are found in multiple places in the interpreter (`sys.stdout`, `sys.__stdout__`, etc.). Simply closing `sys.stdout` and reassigning it is not likely to work correctly, because there's no way to know if it will fix all uses of `sys.stdout`. Instead, a separate file object is opened, and the `os.dup2()` call is used to have it replace the file descriptor currently being used by `sys.stdout`. When this happens, the original file for `sys.stdout` will be closed and the new one takes its place. It must be emphasized that any file encoding or text handling already applied to the standard I/O streams will remain in place.

A common practice with daemon processes is to write the process ID of the daemon in a file for later use by other programs. The last part of the `daemonize()` function writes this file, but also arranges to have the file removed on program termination. The `atexit.register()` function registers a function to execute when the Python interpreter terminates. The definition of a signal handler for `SIGTERM` is also required for a graceful termination. The signal handler merely raises `SystemExit()` and nothing more. This might look unnecessary, but without it, termination signals kill the interpreter without performing the cleanup actions registered with `atexit.register()`. An example of code that kills the daemon can be found in the handling of the `stop` command at the end of the program.

More information about writing daemon processes can be found in *Advanced Programming in the UNIX Environment,* 2nd Edition, by W. Richard Stevens and Stephen A. Rago (Addison-Wesley, 2005). Although focused on C programming, all of the material is easily adapted to Python, since all of the required POSIX functions are available in the standard library.

CHAPTER 13
Utility Scripting and System Administration

A lot of people use Python as a replacement for shell scripts, using it to automate common system tasks, such as manipulating files, configuring systems, and so forth. The main goal of this chapter is to describe features related to common tasks encountered when writing scripts. For example, parsing command-line options, manipulating files on the filesystem, getting useful system configuration data, and so forth. Chapter 5 also contains general information related to files and directories.

13.1. Accepting Script Input via Redirection, Pipes, or Input Files

Problem

You want a script you've written to be able to accept input using whatever mechanism is easiest for the user. This should include piping output from a command to the script, redirecting a file into the script, or just passing a filename, or list of filenames, to the script on the command line.

Solution

Python's built-in `fileinput` module makes this very simple and concise. If you have a script that looks like this:

```
#!/usr/bin/env python3
import fileinput

with fileinput.input() as f_input:
    for line in f_input:
        print(line, end='')
```

Then you can already accept input to the script in all of the previously mentioned ways. If you save this script as *filein.py* and make it executable, you can do all of the following and get the expected output:

```
$ ls | ./filein.py        # Prints a directory listing to stdout.
$ ./filein.py /etc/passwd  # Reads /etc/passwd to stdout.
$ ./filein.py < /etc/passwd # Reads /etc/passwd to stdout.
```

Discussion

The `fileinput.input()` function creates and returns an instance of the `FileInput` class. In addition to containing a few handy helper methods, the instance can also be used as a context manager. So, to put all of this together, if we wrote a script that expected to be printing output from several files at once, we might have it include the filename and line number in the output, like this:

```
>>> import fileinput
>>> with fileinput.input('/etc/passwd') as f:
>>>     for line in f:
...         print(f.filename(), f.lineno(), line, end='')
...
/etc/passwd 1 ##
/etc/passwd 2 # User Database
/etc/passwd 3 #

<other output omitted>
```

Using it as a context manager ensures that the file is closed when it's no longer being used, and we leveraged a few handy `FileInput` helper methods here to get some extra information in the output.

13.2. Terminating a Program with an Error Message

Problem

You want your program to terminate by printing a message to standard error and returning a nonzero status code.

Solution

To have a program terminate in this manner, raise a `SystemExit` exception, but supply the error message as an argument. For example:

```
raise SystemExit('It failed!')
```

This will cause the supplied message to be printed to `sys.stderr` and the program to exit with a status code of 1.

Discussion

This is a small recipe, but it solves a common problem that arises when writing scripts. Namely, to terminate a program, you might be inclined to write code like this:

```
import sys
sys.stderr.write('It failed!\n')
raise SystemExit(1)
```

None of the extra steps involving `import` or writing to `sys.stderr` are neccessary if you simply supply the message to `SystemExit()` instead.

13.3. Parsing Command-Line Options

Problem

You want to write a program that parses options supplied on the command line (found in `sys.argv`).

Solution

The `argparse` module can be used to parse command-line options. A simple example will help to illustrate the essential features:

```
# search.py
'''
Hypothetical command-line tool for searching a collection of
files for one or more text patterns.
'''
import argparse
parser = argparse.ArgumentParser(description='Search some files')

parser.add_argument(dest='filenames',metavar='filename', nargs='*')

parser.add_argument('-p', '--pat',metavar='pattern', required=True,
                    dest='patterns', action='append',
                    help='text pattern to search for')

parser.add_argument('-v', dest='verbose', action='store_true',
                    help='verbose mode')

parser.add_argument('-o', dest='outfile', action='store',
                    help='output file')

parser.add_argument('--speed', dest='speed', action='store',
                    choices={'slow','fast'}, default='slow',
                    help='search speed')

args = parser.parse_args()
```

```
# Output the collected arguments
print(args.filenames)
print(args.patterns)
print(args.verbose)
print(args.outfile)
print(args.speed)
```

This program defines a command-line parser with the following usage:

```
bash % python3 search.py -h
usage: search.py [-h] [-p pattern] [-v] [-o OUTFILE] [--speed {slow,fast}]
                 [filename [filename ...]]

Search some files

positional arguments:
  filename

optional arguments:
  -h, --help            show this help message and exit
  -p pattern, --pat pattern
                        text pattern to search for
  -v                    verbose mode
  -o OUTFILE            output file
  --speed {slow,fast}   search speed
```

The following session shows how data shows up in the program. Carefully observe the output of the print() statements.

```
bash % python3 search.py foo.txt bar.txt
usage: search.py [-h] -p pattern [-v] [-o OUTFILE] [--speed {fast,slow}]
                 [filename [filename ...]]
search.py: error: the following arguments are required: -p/--pat

bash % python3 search.py -v -p spam --pat=eggs foo.txt bar.txt
filenames = ['foo.txt', 'bar.txt']
patterns  = ['spam', 'eggs']
verbose   = True
outfile   = None
speed     = slow

bash % python3 search.py -v -p spam --pat=eggs foo.txt bar.txt -o results
filenames = ['foo.txt', 'bar.txt']
patterns  = ['spam', 'eggs']
verbose   = True
outfile   = results
speed     = slow

bash % python3 search.py -v -p spam --pat=eggs foo.txt bar.txt -o results \
           --speed=fast
filenames = ['foo.txt', 'bar.txt']
patterns  = ['spam', 'eggs']
verbose   = True
outfile   = results
speed     = fast
```

Further processing of the options is up to the program. Replace the `print()` functions with something more interesting.

Discussion

The `argparse` module is one of the largest modules in the standard library, and has a huge number of configuration options. This recipe shows an essential subset that can be used and extended to get started.

To parse options, you first create an `ArgumentParser` instance and add declarations for the options you want to support it using the `add_argument()` method. In each `add_ar gument()` call, the `dest` argument specifies the name of an attribute where the result of parsing will be placed. The `metavar` argument is used when generating help messages. The `action` argument specifies the processing associated with the argument and is often `store` for storing a value or `append` for collecting multiple argument values into a list.

The following argument collects all of the extra command-line arguments into a list. It's being used to make a list of filenames in the example:

```
parser.add_argument(dest='filenames',metavar='filename', nargs='*')
```

The following argument sets a Boolean flag depending on whether or not the argument was provided:

```
parser.add_argument('-v', dest='verbose', action='store_true',
                    help='verbose mode')
```

The following argument takes a single value and stores it as a string:

```
parser.add_argument('-o', dest='outfile', action='store',
                    help='output file')
```

The following argument specification allows an argument to be repeated multiple times and all of the values append into a list. The `required` flag means that the argument must be supplied at least once. The use of `-p` and `--pat` mean that either argument name is acceptable.

```
parser.add_argument('-p', '--pat',metavar='pattern', required=True,
                    dest='patterns', action='append',
                    help='text pattern to search for')
```

Finally, the following argument specification takes a value, but checks it against a set of possible choices.

```
parser.add_argument('--speed', dest='speed', action='store',
                    choices={'slow','fast'}, default='slow',
                    help='search speed')
```

Once the options have been given, you simply execute the `parser.parse()` method. This will process the `sys.argv` value and return an instance with the results. The results for each argument are placed into an attribute with the name given in the `dest` parameter to `add_argument()`.

There are several other approaches for parsing command-line options. For example, you might be inclined to manually process `sys.argv` yourself or use the `getopt` module (which is modeled after a similarly named C library). However, if you take this approach, you'll simply end up replicating much of the code that `argparse` already provides. You may also encounter code that uses the `optparse` library to parse options. Although `optparse` is very similar to `argparse`, the latter is more modern and should be preferred in new projects.

13.4. Prompting for a Password at Runtime

Problem

You've written a script that requires a password, but since the script is meant for interactive use, you'd like to prompt the user for a password rather than hardcode it into the script.

Solution

Python's `getpass` module is precisely what you need in this situation. It will allow you to very easily prompt for a password without having the keyed-in password displayed on the user's terminal. Here's how it's done:

```
import getpass

user = getpass.getuser()
passwd = getpass.getpass()

if svc_login(user, passwd):    # You must write svc_login()
    print('Yay!')
else:
    print('Boo!')
```

In this code, the `svc_login()` function is code that you must write to further process the password entry. Obviously, the exact handling is application-specific.

Discussion

Note in the preceding code that `getpass.getuser()` doesn't prompt the user for their username. Instead, it uses the current user's login name, according to the user's shell environment, or as a last resort, according to the local system's password database (on platforms that support the `pwd` module).

If you want to explicitly prompt the user for their username, which can be more reliable, use the built-in `input` function:

```
user = input('Enter your username: ')
```

It's also important to remember that some systems may not support the hiding of the typed password input to the `getpass()` method. In this case, Python does all it can to forewarn you of problems (i.e., it alerts you that passwords will be shown in cleartext) before moving on.

13.5. Getting the Terminal Size

Problem

You need to get the terminal size in order to properly format the output of your program.

Solution

Use the `os.get_terminal_size()` function to do this:

```
>>> import os
>>> sz = os.get_terminal_size()
>>> sz
os.terminal_size(columns=80, lines=24)
>>> sz.columns
80
>>> sz.lines
24
>>>
```

Discussion

There are many other possible approaches for obtaining the terminal size, ranging from reading environment variables to executing low-level system calls involving `ioctl()` and TTYs. Frankly, why would you bother with that when this one simple call will suffice?

13.6. Executing an External Command and Getting Its Output

Problem

You want to execute an external command and collect its output as a Python string.

Solution

Use the `subprocess.check_output()` function. For example:

```
import subprocess
out_bytes = subprocess.check_output(['netstat','-a'])
```

This runs the specified command and returns its output as a byte string. If you need to interpret the resulting bytes as text, add a further decoding step. For example:

```
out_text = out_bytes.decode('utf-8')
```

If the executed command returns a nonzero exit code, an exception is raised. Here is an example of catching errors and getting the output created along with the exit code:

```
try:
    out_bytes = subprocess.check_output(['cmd','arg1','arg2'])
except subprocess.CalledProcessError as e:
    out_bytes = e.output       # Output generated before error
    code      = e.returncode   # Return code
```

By default, `check_output()` only returns output written to standard output. If you want both standard output and error collected, use the `stderr` argument:

```
out_bytes = subprocess.check_output(['cmd','arg1','arg2'],
                                    stderr=subprocess.STDOUT)
```

If you need to execute a command with a timeout, use the `timeout` argument:

```
try:
    out_bytes = subprocess.check_output(['cmd','arg1','arg2'], timeout=5)
except subprocess.TimeoutExpired as e:
    ...
```

Normally, commands are executed without the assistance of an underlying shell (e.g., sh, bash, etc.). Instead, the list of strings supplied are given to a low-level system command, such as `os.execve()`. If you want the command to be interpreted by a shell, supply it using a simple string and give the `shell=True` argument. This is sometimes useful if you're trying to get Python to execute a complicated shell command involving pipes, I/O redirection, and other features. For example:

```
out_bytes = subprocess.check_output('grep python | wc > out', shell=True)
```

Be aware that executing commands under the shell is a potential security risk if arguments are derived from user input. The `shlex.quote()` function can be used to properly quote arguments for inclusion in shell commands in this case.

Discussion

The `check_output()` function is the easiest way to execute an external command and get its output. However, if you need to perform more advanced communication with a

---

subprocess, such as sending it input, you'll need to take a difference approach. For that, use the subprocess.Popen class directly. For example:

```
import subprocess

# Some text to send
text = b'''
hello world
this is a test
goodbye
'''

# Launch a command with pipes
p = subprocess.Popen(['wc'],
        stdout = subprocess.PIPE,
        stdin = subprocess.PIPE)

# Send the data and get the output
stdout, stderr = p.communicate(text)

# To interpret as text, decode
out = stdout.decode('utf-8')
err = stderr.decode('utf-8')
```

The subprocess module is not suitable for communicating with external commands that expect to interact with a proper TTY. For example, you can't use it to automate tasks that ask the user to enter a password (e.g., a ssh session). For that, you would need to turn to a third-party module, such as those based on the popular "expect" family of tools (e.g., pexpect or similar).

13.7. Copying or Moving Files and Directories

Problem

You need to copy or move files and directories around, but you don't want to do it by calling out to shell commands.

Solution

The shutil module has portable implementations of functions for copying files and directories. The usage is extremely straightforward. For example:

```
import shutil

# Copy src to dst. (cp src dst)
shutil.copy(src, dst)

# Copy files, but preserve metadata (cp -p src dst)
shutil.copy2(src, dst)
```

```
# Copy directory tree (cp -R src dst)
shutil.copytree(src, dst)

# Move src to dst (mv src dst)
shutil.move(src, dst)
```

The arguments to these functions are all strings supplying file or directory names. The underlying semantics try to emulate that of similar Unix commands, as shown in the comments.

By default, symbolic links are followed by these commands. For example, if the source file is a symbolic link, then the destination file will be a copy of the file the link points to. If you want to copy the symbolic link instead, supply the follow_symlinks keyword argument like this:

```
shutil.copy2(src, dst, follow_symlinks=False)
```

If you want to preserve symbolic links in copied directories, do this:

```
shutil.copytree(src, dst, symlinks=True)
```

The copytree() optionally allows you to ignore certain files and directories during the copy process. To do this, you supply an ignore function that takes a directory name and filename listing as input, and returns a list of names to ignore as a result. For example:

```
def ignore_pyc_files(dirname, filenames):
    return [name in filenames if name.endswith('.pyc')]

shutil.copytree(src, dst, ignore=ignore_pyc_files)
```

Since ignoring filename patterns is common, a utility function ignore_patterns() has already been provided to do it. For example:

```
shutil.copytree(src, dst, ignore=shutil.ignore_patterns('*~','*.pyc'))
```

Discussion

Using shutil to copy files and directories is mostly straightforward. However, one caution concerning file metadata is that functions such as copy2() only make a best effort in preserving this data. Basic information, such as access times, creation times, and permissions, will always be preserved, but preservation of owners, ACLs, resource forks, and other extended file metadata may or may not work depending on the underlying operating system and the user's own access permissions. You probably wouldn't want to use a function like shutil.copytree() to perform system backups.

When working with filenames, make sure you use the functions in os.path for the greatest portability (especially if working with both Unix and Windows). For example:

```
>>> filename = '/Users/guido/programs/spam.py'
>>> import os.path
>>> os.path.basename(filename)
'spam.py'
>>> os.path.dirname(filename)
'/Users/guido/programs'
>>> os.path.split(filename)
('/Users/guido/programs', 'spam.py')
>>> os.path.join('/new/dir', os.path.basename(filename))
'/new/dir/spam.py'
>>> os.path.expanduser('~/guido/programs/spam.py')
'/Users/guido/programs/spam.py'
>>>
```

One tricky bit about copying directories with copytree() is the handling of errors. For example, in the process of copying, the function might encounter broken symbolic links, files that can't be accessed due to permission problems, and so on. To deal with this, all exceptions encountered are collected into a list and grouped into a single exception that gets raised at the end of the operation. Here is how you would handle it:

```
try:
    shutil.copytree(src, dst)
except shutil.Error as e:
    for src, dst, msg in e.args[0]:
        # src is source name
        # dst is destination name
        # msg is error message from exception
        print(dst, src, msg)
```

If you supply the ignore_dangling_symlinks=True keyword argument, then copy tree() will ignore dangling symlinks.

The functions shown in this recipe are probably the most commonly used. However, shutil has many more operations related to copying data. The documentation is definitely worth a further look. See the Python documentation (*http://docs.python.org/3/ library/shutil.html*).

13.8. Creating and Unpacking Archives

Problem

You need to create or unpack archives in common formats (e.g., *.tar*, *.tgz*, or *.zip*).

Solution

The shutil module has two functions—make_archive() and unpack_archive()—that do exactly what you want. For example:

```
>>> import shutil
>>> shutil.unpack_archive('Python-3.3.0.tgz')
>>> shutil.make_archive('py33','zip','Python-3.3.0')
'/Users/beazley/Downloads/py33.zip'
>>>
```

The second argument to make_archive() is the desired output format. To get a list of supported archive formats, use get_archive_formats(). For example:

```
>>> shutil.get_archive_formats()
[('bztar', "bzip2'ed tar-file"), ('gztar', "gzip'ed tar-file"),
 ('tar', 'uncompressed tar file'), ('zip', 'ZIP file')]
>>>
```

Discussion

Python has other library modules for dealing with the low-level details of various archive formats (e.g., tarfile, zipfile, gzip, bz2, etc.). However, if all you're trying to do is make or extract an archive, there's really no need to go so low level. You can just use these high-level functions in shutil instead.

The functions have a variety of additional options for logging, dryruns, file permissions, and so forth. Consult the shutil library documentation for further details.

13.9. Finding Files by Name

Problem

You need to write a script that involves finding files, like a file renaming script or a log archiver utility, but you'd rather not have to call shell utilities from within your Python script, or you want to provide specialized behavior not easily available by "shelling out."

Solution

To search for files, use the os.walk() function, supplying it with the top-level directory. Here is an example of a function that finds a specific filename and prints out the full path of all matches:

```
#!/usr/bin/env python3.3
import os

def findfile(start, name):
    for relpath, dirs, files in os.walk(start):
        if name in files:
            full_path = os.path.join(start, relpath, name)
            print(os.path.normpath(os.path.abspath(full_path)))
```

```
if __name__ == '__main__':
    findfile(sys.argv[1], sys.argv[2])
```

Save this script as *findfile.py* and run it from the command line, feeding in the starting point and the name as positional arguments, like this:

```
bash % ./findfile.py . myfile.txt
```

Discussion

The os.walk() method traverses the directory hierarchy for us, and for each directory it enters, it returns a 3-tuple, containing the relative path to the directory it's inspecting, a list containing all of the directory names in that directory, and a list of filenames in that directory.

For each tuple, you simply check if the target filename is in the files list. If it is, os.path.join() is used to put together a path. To avoid the possibility of weird looking paths like *././foo//bar*, two additional functions are used to fix the result. The first is os.path.abspath(), which takes a path that might be relative and forms the absolute path, and the second is os.path.normpath(), which will normalize the path, thereby resolving issues with double slashes, multiple references to the current directory, and so on.

Although this script is pretty simple compared to the features of the find utility found on UNIX platforms, it has the benefit of being cross-platform. Furthermore, a lot of additional functionality can be added in a portable manner without much more work. To illustrate, here is a function that prints out all of the files that have a recent modification time:

```
#!/usr/bin/env python3.3

import os
import time

def modified_within(top, seconds):
    now = time.time()
    for path, dirs, files in os.walk(top):
        for name in files:
            fullpath = os.path.join(path, name)
            if os.path.exists(fullpath):
                mtime = os.path.getmtime(fullpath)
                if mtime > (now - seconds):
                    print(fullpath)

if __name__ == '__main__':
    import sys
    if len(sys.argv) != 3:
        print('Usage: {} dir seconds'.format(sys.argv[0]))
        raise SystemExit(1)
```

```
modified_within(sys.argv[1], float(sys.argv[2]))
```

It wouldn't take long for you to build far more complex operations on top of this little function using various features of the os, os.path, glob, and similar modules. See Recipes 5.11 and 5.13 for related recipes.

13.10. Reading Configuration Files

Problem

You want to read configuration files written in the common *.ini* configuration file format.

Solution

The configparser module can be used to read configuration files. For example, suppose you have this configuration file:

```
; config.ini
; Sample configuration file

[installation]
library=%(prefix)s/lib
include=%(prefix)s/include
bin=%(prefix)s/bin
prefix=/usr/local

# Setting related to debug configuration
[debug]
log_errors=true
show_warnings=False

[server]
port: 8080
nworkers: 32
pid-file=/tmp/spam.pid
root=/www/root
signature:
    =================================
    Brought to you by the Python Cookbook
    =================================
```

Here is an example of how to read it and extract values:

```
>>> from configparser import ConfigParser
>>> cfg = ConfigParser()
>>> cfg.read('config.ini')
['config.ini']
>>> cfg.sections()
['installation', 'debug', 'server']
>>> cfg.get('installation','library')
```

```
'/usr/local/lib'
>>> cfg.getboolean('debug','log_errors')
True
>>> cfg.getint('server','port')
8080
>>> cfg.getint('server','nworkers')
32
>>> print(cfg.get('server','signature'))

==================================
Brought to you by the Python Cookbook
==================================
>>>
```

If desired, you can also modify the configuration and write it back to a file using the
cfg.write() method. For example:

```
>>> cfg.set('server','port','9000')
>>> cfg.set('debug','log_errors','False')
>>> import sys
>>> cfg.write(sys.stdout)
[installation]
library = %(prefix)s/lib
include = %(prefix)s/include
bin = %(prefix)s/bin
prefix = /usr/local

[debug]
log_errors = False
show_warnings = False

[server]
port = 9000
nworkers = 32
pid-file = /tmp/spam.pid
root = /www/root
signature =
        ■■■■■■■■----------------============
        Brought to you by the Python Cookbook
        ==================================
>>>
```

Discussion

Configuration files are well suited as a human-readable format for specifying configuration data to your program. Within each config file, values are grouped into different
sections (e.g., "installation," "debug," and "server," in the example). Each section then
specifies values for various variables in that section.

There are several notable differences between a config file and using a Python source file for the same purpose. First, the syntax is much more permissive and "sloppy." For example, both of these assignments are equivalent:

```
prefix=/usr/local
prefix: /usr/local
```

The names used in a config file are also assumed to be case-insensitive. For example:

```
>>> cfg.get('installation','PREFIX')
'/usr/local'
>>> cfg.get('installation','prefix')
'/usr/local'
>>>
```

When parsing values, methods such as `getboolean()` look for any reasonable value. For example, these are all equivalent:

```
log_errors = true
log_errors = TRUE
log_errors = Yes
log_errors = 1
```

Perhaps the most significant difference between a config file and Python code is that, unlike scripts, configuration files are not executed in a top-down manner. Instead, the file is read in its entirety. If variable substitutions are made, they are done after the fact. For example, in this part of the config file, it doesn't matter that the `prefix` variable is assigned after other variables that happen to use it:

```
[installation]
library=%(prefix)s/lib
include=%(prefix)s/include
bin=%(prefix)s/bin
prefix=/usr/local
```

An easily overlooked feature of `ConfigParser` is that it can read multiple configuration files together and merge their results into a single configuration. For example, suppose a user made their own configuration file that looked like this:

```
; ~/.config.ini
[installation]
prefix=/Users/beazley/test

[debug]
log_errors=False
```

This file can be merged with the previous configuration by reading it separately. For example:

```
>>> # Previously read configuration
>>> cfg.get('installation', 'prefix')
'/usr/local'
```

```
>>> # Merge in user-specific configuration
>>> import os
>>> cfg.read(os.path.expanduser('~/.config.ini'))
['/Users/beazley/.config.ini']
>>> cfg.get('installation', 'prefix')
'/Users/beazley/test'
>>> cfg.get('installation', 'library')
'/Users/beazley/test/lib'
>>> cfg.getboolean('debug', 'log_errors')
False
>>>
```

Observe how the override of the prefix variable affects other related variables, such as the setting of library. This works because variable interpolation is performed as late as possible. You can see this by trying the following experiment:

```
>>> cfg.get('installation','library')
'/Users/beazley/test/lib'
>>> cfg.set('installation','prefix','/tmp/dir')
>>> cfg.get('installation','library')
'/tmp/dir/lib'
>>>
```

Finally, it's important to note that Python does not support the full range of features you might find in an *.ini* file used by other programs (e.g., applications on Windows). Make sure you consult the configparser documentation for the finer details of the syntax and supported features.

13.11. Adding Logging to Simple Scripts

Problem

You want scripts and simple programs to write diagnostic information to log files.

Solution

The easiest way to add logging to simple programs is to use the logging module. For example:

```
import logging

def main():
    # Configure the logging system
    logging.basicConfig(
        filename='app.log',
        level=logging.ERROR
    )

    # Variables (to make the calls that follow work)
    hostname = 'www.python.org'
```

```
    item = 'spam'
    filename = 'data.csv'
    mode = 'r'

    # Example logging calls (insert into your program)
    logging.critical('Host %s unknown', hostname)
    logging.error("Couldn't find %r", item)
    logging.warning('Feature is deprecated')
    logging.info('Opening file %r, mode=%r', filename, mode)
    logging.debug('Got here')

if __name__ == '__main__':
    main()
```

The five logging calls (critical(), error(), warning(), info(), debug()) represent different severity levels in decreasing order. The level argument to basicConfig() is a filter. All messages issued at a level lower than this setting will be ignored.

The argument to each logging operation is a message string followed by zero or more arguments. When making the final log message, the % operator is used to format the message string using the supplied arguments.

If you run this program, the contents of the file *app.log* will be as follows:

```
CRITICAL:root:Host www.python.org unknown
ERROR:root:Could not find 'spam'
```

If you want to change the output or level of output, you can change the parameters to the basicConfig() call. For example:

```
logging.basicConfig(
    filename='app.log',
    level=logging.WARNING,
    format='%(levelname)s:%(asctime)s:%(message)s')
```

As a result, the output changes to the following:

```
CRITICAL:2012-11-20 12:27:13,595:Host www.python.org unknown
ERROR:2012-11-20 12:27:13,595:Could not find 'spam'
WARNING:2012-11-20 12:27:13,595:Feature is deprecated
```

As shown, the logging configuration is hardcoded directly into the program. If you want to configure it from a configuration file, change the basicConfig() call to the following:

```
import logging
import logging.config

def main():
    # Configure the logging system
    logging.config.fileConfig('logconfig.ini')
    ...
```

Now make a configuration file *logconfig.ini* that looks like this:

```
[loggers]
keys=root

[handlers]
keys=defaultHandler

[formatters]
keys=defaultFormatter

[logger_root]
level=INFO
handlers=defaultHandler
qualname=root

[handler_defaultHandler]
class=FileHandler
formatter=defaultFormatter
args=('app.log', 'a')

[formatter_defaultFormatter]
format=%(levelname)s:%(name)s:%(message)s
```

If you want to make changes to the configuration, you can simply edit the *logconfig.ini* file as appropriate.

Discussion

Ignoring for the moment that there are about a million advanced configuration options for the `logging` module, this solution is quite sufficient for simple programs and scripts. Simply make sure that you execute the `basicConfig()` call prior to making any logging calls, and your program will generate logging output.

If you want the logging messages to route to standard error instead of a file, don't supply any filename information to `basicConfig()`. For example, simply do this:

```
logging.basicConfig(level=logging.INFO)
```

One subtle aspect of `basicConfig()` is that it can only be called once in your program. If you later need to change the configuration of the logging module, you need to obtain the root logger and make changes to it directly. For example:

```
logging.getLogger().level = logging.DEBUG
```

It must be emphasized that this recipe only shows a basic use of the `logging` module. There are significantly more advanced customizations that can be made. An excellent resource for such customization is the "Logging Cookbook" (*http://docs.python.org/3/ howto/logging-cookbook.html*).

13.12. Adding Logging to Libraries

Problem

You would like to add a logging capability to a library, but don't want it to interfere with programs that don't use logging.

Solution

For libraries that want to perform logging, you should create a dedicated logger object, and initially configure it as follows:

```
# somelib.py

import logging
log = logging.getLogger(__name__)
log.addHandler(logging.NullHandler())

# Example function (for testing)
def func():
    log.critical('A Critical Error!')
    log.debug('A debug message')
```

With this configuration, no logging will occur by default. For example:

```
>>> import somelib
>>> somelib.func()
>>>
```

However, if the logging system gets configured, log messages will start to appear. For example:

```
>>> import logging
>>> logging.basicConfig()
>>> somelib.func()
CRITICAL:somelib:A Critical Error!
>>>
```

Discussion

Libraries present a special problem for logging, since information about the environment in which they are used isn't known. As a general rule, you should never write library code that tries to configure the logging system on its own or which makes assumptions about an already existing logging configuration. Thus, you need to take great care to provide isolation.

The call to `getLogger(__name__)` creates a logger module that has the same name as the calling module. Since all modules are unique, this creates a dedicated logger that is likely to be separate from other loggers.

The `log.addHandler(logging.NullHandler())` operation attaches a null handler to the just created logger object. A null handler ignores all logging messages by default. Thus, if the library is used and logging is never configured, no messages or warnings will appear.

One subtle feature of this recipe is that the logging of individual libraries can be independently configured, regardless of other logging settings. For example, consider the following code:

```
>>> import logging
>>> logging.basicConfig(level=logging.ERROR)
>>> import somelib
>>> somelib.func()
CRITICAL:somelib:A Critical Error!

>>> # Change the logging level for 'somelib' only
>>> logging.getLogger('somelib').level=logging.DEBUG
>>> somelib.func()
CRITICAL:somelib:A Critical Error!
DEBUG:somelib:A debug message
>>>
```

Here, the root logger has been configured to only output messages at the ERROR level or higher. However, the level of the logger for `somelib` has been separately configured to output debugging messages. That setting takes precedence over the global setting.

The ability to change the logging settings for a single module like this can be a useful debugging tool, since you don't have to change any of the global logging settings—simply change the level for the one module where you want more output.

The "Logging HOWTO" (*http://docs.python.org/3/howto/logging.html*) has more information about configuring the `logging` module and other useful tips.

13.13. Making a Stopwatch Timer

Problem

You want to be able to record the time it takes to perform various tasks.

Solution

The `time` module contains various functions for performing timing-related functions. However, it's often useful to put a higher-level interface on them that mimics a stop watch. For example:

```
import time

class Timer:
    def __init__(self, func=time.perf_counter):
        self.elapsed = 0.0
        self._func = func
        self._start = None

    def start(self):
        if self._start is not None:
            raise RuntimeError('Already started')
        self._start = self._func()

    def stop(self):
        if self._start is None:
            raise RuntimeError('Not started')
        end = self._func()
        self.elapsed += end - self._start
        self._start = None

    def reset(self):
        self.elapsed = 0.0

    @property
    def running(self):
        return self._start is not None

    def __enter__(self):
        self.start()
        return self

    def __exit__(self, *args):
        self.stop()
```

This class defines a timer that can be started, stopped, and reset as needed by the user. It keeps track of the total elapsed time in the elapsed attribute. Here is an example that shows how it can be used:

```
def countdown(n):
    while n > 0:
        n -= 1

# Use 1: Explicit start/stop
t = Timer()
t.start()
countdown(1000000)
t.stop()
print(t.elapsed)

# Use 2: As a context manager
with t:
    countdown(1000000)
```

```
print(t.elapsed)

with Timer() as t2:
    countdown(1000000)
print(t2.elapsed)
```

Discussion

This recipe provides a simple yet very useful class for making timing measurements and tracking elapsed time. It's also a nice illustration of how to support the context-management protocol and the with statement.

One issue in making timing measurements concerns the underlying time function used to do it. As a general rule, the accuracy of timing measurements made with functions such as time.time() or time.clock() varies according to the operating system. In contrast, the time.perf_counter() function always uses the highest-resolution timer available on the system.

As shown, the time recorded by the Timer class is made according to wall-clock time, and includes all time spent sleeping. If you only want the amount of CPU time used by the process, use time.process_time() instead. For example:

```
t = Timer(time.process_time)
with t:
    countdown(1000000)
print(t.elapsed)
```

Both the time.perf_counter() and time.process_time() return a "time" in fractional seconds. However, the actual value of the time doesn't have any particular meaning. To make sense of the results, you have to call the functions twice and compute a time difference.

More examples of timing and profiling are given in Recipe 14.13.

13.14. Putting Limits on Memory and CPU Usage

Problem

You want to place some limits on the memory or CPU use of a program running on Unix system.

Solution

The resource module can be used to perform both tasks. For example, to restrict CPU time, do the following:

```
import signal
import resource
import os

def time_exceeded(signo, frame):
    print("Time's up!")
    raise SystemExit(1)

def set_max_runtime(seconds):
    # Install the signal handler and set a resource limit
    soft, hard = resource.getrlimit(resource.RLIMIT_CPU)
    resource.setrlimit(resource.RLIMIT_CPU, (seconds, hard))
    signal.signal(signal.SIGXCPU, time_exceeded)

if __name__ == '__main__':
    set_max_runtime(15)
    while True:
        pass
```

When this runs, the SIGXCPU signal is generated when the time expires. The program can then clean up and exit.

To restrict memory use, put a limit on the total address space in use. For example:

```
import resource

def limit_memory(maxsize):
    soft, hard = resource.getrlimit(resource.RLIMIT_AS)
    resource.setrlimit(resource.RLIMIT_AS, (maxsize, hard))
```

With a memory limit in place, programs will start generating MemoryError exceptions when no more memory is available.

Discussion

In this recipe, the setrlimit() function is used to set a soft and hard limit on a particular resource. The soft limit is a value upon which the operating system will typically restrict or notify the process via a signal. The hard limit represents an upper bound on the values that may be used for the soft limit. Typically, this is controlled by a system-wide parameter set by the system administrator. Although the hard limit can be lowered, it can never be raised by user processes (even if the process lowered itself).

The setrlimit() function can additionally be used to set limits on things such as the number of child processes, number of open files, and similar system resources. Consult the documentation for the resource module for further details.

Be aware that this recipe only works on Unix systems, and that it might not work on all of them. For example, when tested, it works on Linux but not on OS X.

13.15. Launching a Web Browser

Problem

You want to launch a browser from a script and have it point to some URL that you specify.

Solution

The `webbrowser` module can be used to launch a browser in a platform-independent manner. For example:

```
>>> import webbrowser
>>> webbrowser.open('http://www.python.org')
True
>>>
```

This opens the requested page using the default browser. If you want a bit more control over how the page gets opened, you can use one of the following functions:

```
>>> # Open the page in a new browser window
>>> webbrowser.open_new('http://www.python.org')
True
>>>

>>> # Open the page in a new browser tab
>>> webbrowser.open_new_tab('http://www.python.org')
True
>>>
```

These will try to open the page in a new browser window or tab, if possible and supported by the browser.

If you want to open a page in a specific browser, you can use the `webbrowser.get()` function to specify a particular browser. For example:

```
>>> c = webbrowser.get('firefox')
>>> c.open('http://www.python.org')
True
>>> c.open_new_tab('http://docs.python.org')
True
>>>
```

A full list of supported browser names can be found in the Python documentation (*http://docs.python.org/3/library/webbrowser.html*).

Discussion

Being able to easily launch a browser can be a useful operation in many scripts. For example, maybe a script performs some kind of deployment to a server and you'd like to have it quickly launch a browser so you can verify that it's working. Or maybe a program writes data out in the form of HTML pages and you'd just like to fire up a browser to see the result. Either way, the webbrowser module is a simple solution.

## CHAPTER 14

Testing, Debugging, and Exceptions

Testing rocks, but debugging? Not so much. The fact that there's no compiler to analyze your code before Python executes it makes testing a critical part of development. The goal of this chapter is to discuss some common problems related to testing, debugging, and exception handling. It is not meant to be a gentle introduction to test-driven development or the `unittest` module. Thus, some familiarity with testing concepts is assumed.

14.1. Testing Output Sent to stdout

Problem

You have a program that has a method whose output goes to standard Output (`sys.stdout`). This almost always means that it emits text to the screen. You'd like to write a test for your code to prove that, given the proper input, the proper output is displayed.

Solution

Using the `unittest.mock` module's `patch()` function, it's pretty simple to mock out `sys.stdout` for just a single test, and put it back again, without messy temporary variables or leaking mocked-out state between test cases.

Consider, as an example, the following function in a module `mymodule`:

```
# mymodule.py

def urlprint(protocol, host, domain):
    url = '{}://{}.{}'.format(protocol, host, domain)
    print(url)
```

The built-in print function, by default, sends output to sys.stdout. In order to test that output is actually getting there, you can mock it out using a stand-in object, and then make assertions about what happened. Using the unittest.mock module's patch() method makes it convenient to replace objects only within the context of a running test, returning things to their original state immediately after the test is complete. Here's the test code for mymodule:

```
from io import StringIO
from unittest import TestCase
from unittest.mock import patch
import mymodule

class TestURLPrint(TestCase):
    def test_url_gets_to_stdout(self):
        protocol = 'http'
        host = 'www'
        domain = 'example.com'
        expected_url = '{}://{}.{}\n'.format(protocol, host, domain)

        with patch('sys.stdout', new=StringIO()) as fake_out:
            mymodule.urlprint(protocol, host, domain)
            self.assertEqual(fake_out.getvalue(), expected_url)
```

Discussion

The urlprint() function takes three arguments, and the test starts by setting up dummy arguments for each one. The expected_url variable is set to a string containing the expected output.

To run the test, the unittest.mock.patch() function is used as a context manager to replace the value of sys.stdout with a StringIO object as a substitute. The fake_out variable is the mock object that's created in this process. This can be used inside the body of the with statement to perform various checks. When the with statement completes, patch conveniently puts everything back the way it was before the test ever ran.

It's worth noting that certain C extensions to Python may write directly to standard output, bypassing the setting of sys.stdout. This recipe won't help with that scenario, but it should work fine with pure Python code (if you need to capture I/O from such C extensions, you can do it by opening a temporary file and performing various tricks involving file descriptors to have standard output temporarily redirected to that file).

More information about capturing IO in a string and StringIO objects can be found in Recipe 5.6.

14.2. Patching Objects in Unit Tests

Problem

You're writing unit tests and need to apply patches to selected objects in order to make assertions about how they were used in the test (e.g., assertions about being called with certain parameters, access to selected attributes, etc.).

Solution

The `unittest.mock.patch()` function can be used to help with this problem. It's a little unusual, but `patch()` can be used as a decorator, a context manager, or stand-alone. For example, here's an example of how it's used as a decorator:

```
from unittest.mock import patch
import example

@patch('example.func')
def test1(x, mock_func):
    example.func(x)        # Uses patched example.func
    mock_func.assert_called_with(x)
```

It can also be used as a context manager:

```
with patch('example.func') as mock_func:
    example.func(x)        # Uses patched example.func
    mock_func.assert_called_with(x)
```

Last, but not least, you can use it to patch things manually:

```
p = patch('example.func')
mock_func = p.start()
example.func(x)
mock_func.assert_called_with(x)
p.stop()
```

If necessary, you can stack decorators and context managers to patch multiple objects. For example:

```
@patch('example.func1')
@patch('example.func2')
@patch('example.func3')
def test1(mock1, mock2, mock3):
    ...

def test2():
    with patch('example.patch1') as mock1, \
         patch('example.patch2') as mock2, \
         patch('example.patch3') as mock3:
    ...
```

Discussion

patch() works by taking an existing object with the fully qualified name that you provide and replacing it with a new value. The original value is then restored after the completion of the decorated function or context manager. By default, values are replaced with MagicMock instances. For example:

```
>>> x = 42
>>> with patch('__main__.x'):
...     print(x)
...
<MagicMock name='x' id='4314230032'>
>>> x
42
>>>
```

However, you can actually replace the value with anything that you wish by supplying it as a second argument to patch():

```
>>> x
42
>>> with patch('__main__.x', 'patched_value'):
...     print(x)
...
patched_value
>>> x
42
>>>
```

The MagicMock instances that are normally used as replacement values are meant to mimic callables and instances. They record information about usage and allow you to make assertions. For example:

```
>>> from unittest.mock import MagicMock
>>> m = MagicMock(return_value = 10)
>>> m(1, 2, debug=True)
10
>>> m.assert_called_with(1, 2, debug=True)
>>> m.assert_called_with(1, 2)
Traceback (most recent call last):
  File "<stdin>", line 1, in <module>
  File ".../unittest/mock.py", line 726, in assert_called_with
    raise AssertionError(msg)
AssertionError: Expected call: mock(1, 2)
Actual call: mock(1, 2, debug=True)
>>>

>>> m.upper.return_value = 'HELLO'
>>> m.upper('hello')
'HELLO'
>>> assert m.upper.called
```

```
>>> m.split.return_value = ['hello', 'world']
>>> m.split('hello world')
['hello', 'world']
>>> m.split.assert_called_with('hello world')
>>>

>>> m['blah']
<MagicMock name='mock.__getitem__()' id='4314412048'>
>>> m.__getitem__.called
True
>>> m.__getitem__.assert_called_with('blah')
>>>
```

Typically, these kinds of operations are carried out in a unit test. For example, suppose you have some function like this:

```
# example.py
from urllib.request import urlopen
import csv

def dowprices():
    u = urlopen('http://finance.yahoo.com/d/quotes.csv?s=@^DJI&f=sl1')
    lines = (line.decode('utf-8') for line in u)
    rows = (row for row in csv.reader(lines) if len(row) == 2)
    prices = { name:float(price) for name, price in rows }
    return prices
```

Normally, this function uses urlopen() to go fetch data off the Web and parse it. To unit test it, you might want to give it a more predictable dataset of your own creation, however. Here's an example using patching:

```
import unittest
from unittest.mock import patch
import io
import example

sample_data = io.BytesIO(b'''\
"IBM",91.1\r
"AA",13.25\r
"MSFT",27.72\r
\r
''')

class Tests(unittest.TestCase):
    @patch('example.urlopen', return_value=sample_data)
    def test_dowprices(self, mock_urlopen):
        p = example.dowprices()
        self.assertTrue(mock_urlopen.called)
        self.assertEqual(p,
                         {'IBM': 91.1,
                          'AA': 13.25,
                          'MSFT' : 27.72})
```

```
if __name__ == '__main__':
    unittest.main()
```

In this example, the urlopen() function in the example module is replaced with a mock object that returns a BytesIO() containing sample data as a substitute.

An important but subtle facet of this test is the patching of example.urlopen instead of urllib.request.urlopen. When you are making patches, you have to use the names as they are used in the code being tested. Since the example code uses from urllib.request import urlopen, the urlopen() function used by the dowprices() function is actually located in example.

This recipe has really only given a very small taste of what's possible with the unittest.mock module. The official documentation (*http://docs.python.org/3/library/unittest.mock*) is a must-read for more advanced features.

14.3. Testing for Exceptional Conditions in Unit Tests

Problem

You want to write a unit test that cleanly tests if an exception is raised.

Solution

To test for exceptions, use the assertRaises() method. For example, if you want to test that a function raised a ValueError exception, use this code:

```
import unittest

# A simple function to illustrate
def parse_int(s):
    return int(s)

class TestConversion(unittest.TestCase):
    def test_bad_int(self):
        self.assertRaises(ValueError, parse_int, 'N/A')
```

If you need to test the exception's value in some way, then a different approach is needed. For example:

```
import errno

class TestIO(unittest.TestCase):
    def test_file_not_found(self):
        try:
            f = open('/file/not/found')
        except IOError as e:
            self.assertEqual(e.errno, errno.ENOENT)
```

```
        else:
            self.fail('IOError not raised')
```

Discussion

The `assertRaises()` method provides a convenient way to test for the presence of an exception. A common pitfall is to write tests that manually try to do things with exceptions on their own. For instance:

```
class TestConversion(unittest.TestCase):
    def test_bad_int(self):
        try:
            r = parse_int('N/A')
        except ValueError as e:
            self.assertEqual(type(e), ValueError)
```

The problem with such approaches is that it is easy to forget about corner cases, such as that when no exception is raised at all. To do that, you need to add an extra check for that situation, as shown here:

```
class TestConversion(unittest.TestCase):
    def test_bad_int(self):
        try:
            r = parse_int('N/A')
        except ValueError as e:
            self.assertEqual(type(e), ValueError)
        else:
            self.fail('ValueError not raised')
```

The `assertRaises()` method simply takes care of these details, so you should prefer to use it.

The one limitation of `assertRaises()` is that it doesn't provide a means for testing the value of the exception object that's created. To do that, you have to manually test it, as shown. Somewhere in between these two extremes, you might consider using the `assertRaisesRegex()` method, which allows you to test for an exception and perform a regular expression match against the exception's string representation at the same time. For example:

```
class TestConversion(unittest.TestCase):
    def test_bad_int(self):
        self.assertRaisesRegex(ValueError, 'invalid literal .*',
                               parse_int, 'N/A')
```

A little-known fact about `assertRaises()` and `assertRaisesRegex()` is that they can also be used as context managers:

```
class TestConversion(unittest.TestCase):
    def test_bad_int(self):
        with self.assertRaisesRegex(ValueError, 'invalid literal .*'):
            r = parse_int('N/A')
```

This form can be useful if your test involves multiple steps (e.g., setup) besides that of simply executing a callable.

14.4. Logging Test Output to a File

Problem

You want the results of running unit tests written to a file instead of printed to standard output.

Solution

A very common technique for running unit tests is to include a small code fragment like this at the bottom of your testing file:

```
import unittest

class MyTest(unittest.TestCase):
    ...

if __name__ == '__main__':
    unittest.main()
```

This makes the test file executable, and prints the results of running tests to standard output. If you would like to redirect this output, you need to unwind the main() call a bit and write your own main() function like this:

```
import sys
def main(out=sys.stderr, verbosity=2):
    loader = unittest.TestLoader()
    suite = loader.loadTestsFromModule(sys.modules[__name__])
    unittest.TextTestRunner(out,verbosity=verbosity).run(suite)

if __name__ == '__main__':
    with open('testing.out', 'w') as f:
        main(f)
```

Discussion

The interesting thing about this recipe is not so much the task of getting test results redirected to a file, but the fact that doing so exposes some notable inner workings of the unittest module.

At a basic level, the unittest module works by first assembling a test suite. This test suite consists of the different testing methods you defined. Once the suite has been assembled, the tests it contains are executed.

These two parts of unit testing are separate from each other. The `unittest.TestLoad`er instance created in the solution is used to assemble a test suite. The `loadTestsFrom`Module() is one of several methods it defines to gather tests. In this case, it scans a module for `TestCase` classes and extracts test methods from them. If you want something more fine-grained, the `loadTestsFromTestCase()` method (not shown) can be used to pull test methods from an individual class that inherits from `TestCase`.

The `TextTestRunner` class is an example of a test runner class. The main purpose of this class is to execute the tests contained in a test suite. This class is the same test runner that sits behind the `unittest.main()` function. However, here we're giving it a bit of low-level configuration, including an output file and an elevated verbosity level.

Although this recipe only consists of a few lines of code, it gives a hint as to how you might further customize the `unittest` framework. To customize how test suites are assembled, you would perform various operations using the `TestLoader` class. To customize how tests execute, you could make custom test runner classes that emulate the functionality of `TextTestRunner`. Both topics are beyond the scope of what can be covered here. However, documentation for the `unittest` module has extensive coverage of the underlying protocols.

14.5. Skipping or Anticipating Test Failures

Problem

You want to skip or mark selected tests as an anticipated failure in your unit tests.

Solution

The `unittest` module has decorators that can be applied to selected test methods to control their handling. For example:

```
import unittest
import os
import platform

class Tests(unittest.TestCase):
    def test_0(self):
        self.assertTrue(True)

    @unittest.skip('skipped test')
    def test_1(self):
        self.fail('should have failed!')

    @unittest.skipIf(os.name=='posix', 'Not supported on Unix')
    def test_2(self):
        import winreg
```

```
@unittest.skipUnless(platform.system() == 'Darwin', 'Mac specific test')
def test_3(self):
    self.assertTrue(True)

@unittest.expectedFailure
def test_4(self):
    self.assertEqual(2+2, 5)

if __name__ == '__main__':
    unittest.main()
```

If you run this code on a Mac, you'll get this output:

```
bash % python3 testsample.py -v
test_0 (__main__.Tests) ... ok
test_1 (__main__.Tests) ... skipped 'skipped test'
test_2 (__main__.Tests) ... skipped 'Not supported on Unix'
test_3 (__main__.Tests) ... ok
test_4 (__main__.Tests) ... expected failure

----------------------------------------------------------------------
Ran 5 tests in 0.002s

OK (skipped=2, expected failures=1)
```

Discussion

The `skip()` decorator can be used to skip over a test that you don't want to run at all. `skipIf()` and `skipUnless()` can be a useful way to write tests that only apply to certain platforms or Python versions, or which have other dependencies. Use the `@expected Failure` decorator to mark tests that are known failures, but for which you don't want the test framework to report more information.

The decorators for skipping methods can also be applied to entire testing classes. For example:

```
@unittest.skipUnless(platform.system() == 'Darwin', 'Mac specific tests')
class DarwinTests(unittest.TestCase):
    ...
```

14.6. Handling Multiple Exceptions

Problem

You have a piece of code that can throw any of several different exceptions, and you need to account for all of the potential exceptions that could be raised without creating duplicate code or long, meandering code passages.

Solution

If you can handle different exceptions all using a single block of code, they can be grouped together in a tuple like this:

```
try:
    client_obj.get_url(url)
except (URLError, ValueError, SocketTimeout):
    client_obj.remove_url(url)
```

In the preceding example, the remove_url() method will be called if any one of the listed exceptions occurs. If, on the other hand, you need to handle one of the exceptions differently, put it into its own except clause:

```
try:
    client_obj.get_url(url)
except (URLError, ValueError):
    client_obj.remove_url(url)
except SocketTimeout:
    client_obj.handle_url_timeout(url)
```

Many exceptions are grouped into an inheritance hierarchy. For such exceptions, you can catch all of them by simply specifying a base class. For example, instead of writing code like this:

```
try:
    f = open(filename)
except (FileNotFoundError, PermissionError):
    ...
```

you could rewrite the except statement as:

```
try:
    f = open(filename)
except OSError:
    ...
```

This works because OSError is a base class that's common to both the FileNotFound Errorand PermissionError exceptions.

Discussion

Although it's not specific to handling *multiple* exceptions per se, it's worth noting that you can get a handle to the thrown exception using the as keyword:

```
try:
    f = open(filename)
except OSError as e:
    if e.errno == errno.ENOENT:
        logger.error('File not found')
    elif e.errno == errno.EACCES:
        logger.error('Permission denied')
```

```
    else:
        logger.error('Unexpected error: %d', e.errno)
```

In this example, the e variable holds an instance of the raised OSError. This is useful if you need to inspect the exception further, such as processing it based on the value of an additional status code.

Be aware that except clauses are checked in the order listed and that the first match executes. It may be a bit pathological, but you can easily create situations where multiple except clauses might match. For example:

```
>>> f = open('missing')
Traceback (most recent call last):
  File "<stdin>", line 1, in <module>
FileNotFoundError: [Errno 2] No such file or directory: 'missing'
>>> try:
...     f = open('missing')
... except OSError:
...     print('It failed')
... except FileNotFoundError:
...     print('File not found')
...
It failed
>>>
```

Here the except FileNotFoundError clause doesn't execute because the OSError is more general, matches the FileNotFoundError exception, and was listed first.

As a debugging tip, if you're not entirely sure about the class hierarchy of a particular exception, you can quickly view it by inspecting the exception's __mro__ attribute. For example:

```
>>> FileNotFoundError.__mro__
(<class 'FileNotFoundError'>, <class 'OSError'>, <class 'Exception'>,
 <class 'BaseException'>, <class 'object'>)
>>>
```

Any one of the listed classes up to BaseException can be used with the except statement.

14.7. Catching All Exceptions

Problem

You want to write code that catches all exceptions.

Solution

To catch all exceptions, write an exception handler for Exception, as shown here:

```
try:
    ...
except Exception as e:
    ...
    log('Reason:', e)        # Important!
```

This will catch all exceptions save `SystemExit`, `KeyboardInterrupt`, and `GeneratorExit`. If you also want to catch those exceptions, change `Exception` to `BaseException`.

Discussion

Catching all exceptions is sometimes used as a crutch by programmers who can't remember all of the possible exceptions that might occur in complicated operations. As such, it is also a very good way to write undebuggable code if you are not careful.

Because of this, if you choose to catch all exceptions, it is absolutely critical to log or report the actual reason for the exception somewhere (e.g., log file, error message printed to screen, etc.). If you don't do this, your head will likely explode at some point. Consider this example:

```
def parse_int(s):
    try:
        n = int(v)
    except Exception:
        print("Couldn't parse")
```

If you try this function, it behaves like this:

```
>>> parse_int('n/a')
Couldn't parse
>>> parse_int('42')
Couldn't parse
>>>
```

At this point, you might be left scratching your head as to why it doesn't work. Now suppose the function had been written like this:

```
def parse_int(s):
    try:
        n = int(v)
    except Exception as e:
        print("Couldn't parse")
        print('Reason:', e)
```

In this case, you get the following output, which indicates that a programming mistake has been made:

```
>>> parse_int('42')
Couldn't parse
Reason: global name 'v' is not defined
>>>
```

All things being equal, it's probably better to be as precise as possible in your exception handling. However, if you must catch all exceptions, just make sure you give good diagnostic information or propagate the exception so that cause doesn't get lost.

14.8. Creating Custom Exceptions

Problem

You're building an application and would like to wrap lower-level exceptions with custom ones that have more meaning in the context of your application.

Solution

Creating new exceptions is easy—just define them as classes that inherit from Exception (or one of the other existing exception types if it makes more sense). For example, if you are writing code related to network programming, you might define some custom exceptions like this:

```
class NetworkError(Exception):
    pass

class HostnameError(NetworkError):
    pass

class TimeoutError(NetworkError):
    pass

class ProtocolError(NetworkError):
    pass
```

Users could then use these exceptions in the normal way. For example:

```
try:
    msg = s.recv()
except TimeoutError as e:
    ...
except ProtocolError as e:
    ...
```

Discussion

Custom exception classes should almost always inherit from the built-in Exception class, or inherit from some locally defined base exception that itself inherits from Exception. Although all exceptions also derive from BaseException, you should not use this as a base class for new exceptions. BaseException is reserved for system-exiting exceptions, such as KeyboardInterrupt or SystemExit, and other exceptions that should signal the application to exit. Therefore, catching these exceptions is not the intended use case. Assuming you follow this convention, it follows that inheriting from `BaseException` causes your custom exceptions to not be caught and to signal an imminent application shutdown!

Having custom exceptions in your application and using them as shown makes your application code tell a more coherent story to whoever may need to read the code. One design consideration involves the grouping of custom exceptions via inheritance. In complicated applications, it may make sense to introduce further base classes that group different classes of exceptions together. This gives the user a choice of catching a narrowly specified error, such as this:

```
try:
    s.send(msg)
except ProtocolError:
    ...
```

It also gives the ability to catch a broad range of errors, such as the following:

```
try:
    s.send(msg)
except NetworkError:
    ...
```

If you are going to define a new exception that overrides the `__init__()` method of `Exception`, make sure you always call `Exception.__init__()` with all of the passed arguments. For example:

```
class CustomError(Exception):
    def __init__(self, message, status):
        super().__init__(message, status)
        self.message = message
        self.status = status
```

This might look a little weird, but the default behavior of `Exception` is to accept all arguments passed and to store them in the `.args` attribute as a tuple. Various other libraries and parts of Python expect all exceptions to have the `.args` attribute, so if you skip this step, you might find that your new exception doesn't behave quite right in certain contexts. To illustrate the use of `.args`, consider this interactive session with the built-in `RuntimeError` exception, and notice how any number of arguments can be used with the `raise` statement:

```
>>> try:
...     raise RuntimeError('It failed')
... except RuntimeError as e:
...     print(e.args)
...
('It failed',)
>>> try:
...     raise RuntimeError('It failed', 42, 'spam')
... except RuntimeError as e:
```

```
...        print(e.args)
...
('It failed', 42, 'spam')
>>>
```

For more information on creating your own exceptions, see the Python documentation (*http://docs.python.org/3/tutorial/errors.html*).

14.9. Raising an Exception in Response to Another Exception

Problem

You want to raise an exception in response to catching a different exception, but want to include information about both exceptions in the traceback.

Solution

To chain exceptions, use the `raise from` statement instead of a simple `raise` statement. This will give you information about both errors. For example:

```
>>> def example():
...     try:
...             int('N/A')
...     except ValueError as e:
...             raise RuntimeError('A parsing error occurred') from e
...
>>> example()
Traceback (most recent call last):
  File "<stdin>", line 3, in example
ValueError: invalid literal for int() with base 10: 'N/A'

The above exception was the direct cause of the following exception:

Traceback (most recent call last):
  File "<stdin>", line 1, in <module>
  File "<stdin>", line 5, in example
RuntimeError: A parsing error occurred
>>>
```

As you can see in the traceback, both exceptions are captured. To catch such an exception, you would use a normal except statement. However, you can look at the __cause__ attribute of the exception object to follow the exception chain should you wish. For example:

```
try:
    example()
except RuntimeError as e:
    print("It didn't work:", e)
```

```
        if e.__cause__:
            print('Cause:', e.__cause__)
```

An implicit form of chained exceptions occurs when another exception gets raised inside an except block. For example:

```
>>> def example2():
...     try:
...             int('N/A')
...     except ValueError as e:
...             print("Couldn't parse:", err)
...
>>>
>>> example2()
Traceback (most recent call last):
  File "<stdin>", line 3, in example2
ValueError: invalid literal for int() with base 10: 'N/A'

During handling of the above exception, another exception occurred:

Traceback (most recent call last):
  File "<stdin>", line 1, in <module>
  File "<stdin>", line 5, in example2
NameError: global name 'err' is not defined
>>>
```

In this example, you get information about both exceptions, but the interpretation is a bit different. In this case, the NameError exception is raised as the result of a programming error, not in direct response to the parsing error. For this case, the __cause__ attribute of an exception is not set. Instead, a __context__ attribute is set to the prior exception.

If, for some reason, you want to suppress chaining, use raise from None:

```
>>> def example3():
...     try:
...             int('N/A')
...     except ValueError:
...             raise RuntimeError('A parsing error occurred') from None
...
>>> example3()
Traceback (most recent call last):
  File "<stdin>", line 1, in <module>
  File "<stdin>", line 5, in example3
RuntimeError: A parsing error occurred
>>>
```

Discussion

In designing code, you should give careful attention to use of the `raise` statement inside of other `except` blocks. In most cases, such `raise` statements should probably be changed to `raise from` statements. That is, you should prefer this style:

```
try:
    ...
except SomeException as e:
    raise DifferentException() from e
```

The reason for doing this is that you are explicitly chaining the causes together. That is, the `DifferentException` is being raised in direct response to getting a `SomeException`. This relationship will be explicitly stated in the resulting traceback.

If you write your code in the following style, you still get a chained exception, but it's often not clear if the exception chain was intentional or the result of an unforeseen programming error:

```
try:
    ...
except SomeException:
    raise DifferentException()
```

When you use `raise from`, you're making it clear that you meant to raise the second exception.

Resist the urge to suppress exception information, as shown in the last example. Although suppressing exception information can lead to smaller tracebacks, it also discards information that might be useful for debugging. All things being equal, it's often best to keep as much information as possible.

14.10. Reraising the Last Exception

Problem

You caught an exception in an `except` block, but now you want to reraise it.

Solution

Simply use the `raise` statement all by itself. For example:

```
>>> def example():
...     try:
...             int('N/A')
...     except ValueError:
...             print("Didn't work")
...             raise
...
```

```
>>> example()
Didn't work
Traceback (most recent call last):
  File "<stdin>", line 1, in <module>
  File "<stdin>", line 3, in example
ValueError: invalid literal for int() with base 10: 'N/A'
>>>
```

Discussion

This problem typically arises when you need to take some kind of action in response to
an exception (e.g., logging, cleanup, etc.), but afterward, you simply want to propagate
the exception along. A very common use might be in catch-all exception handlers:

```
try:
    ...
except Exception as e:
    # Process exception information in some way
    ...

    # Propagate the exception
    raise
```

14.11. Issuing Warning Messages

Problem

You want to have your program issue warning messages (e.g., about deprecated features
or usage problems).

Solution

To have your program issue a warning message, use the warnings.warn() function. For
example:

```
import warnings

def func(x, y, logfile=None, debug=False):
    if logfile is not None:
        warnings.warn('logfile argument deprecated', DeprecationWarning)
    ...
```

The arguments to warn() are a warning message along with a warning class, which is
typically one of the following: UserWarning, DeprecationWarning, SyntaxWarning,
RuntimeWarning, ResourceWarning, or FutureWarning.

The handling of warnings depends on how you have executed the interpreter and other
configuration. For example, if you run Python with the -W all option, you'll get output
such as the following:

```
bash % python3 -W all example.py
example.py:5: DeprecationWarning: logfile argument is deprecated
    warnings.warn('logfile argument is deprecated', DeprecationWarning)
```

Normally, warnings just produce output messages on standard error. If you want to turn warnings into exceptions, use the -W error option:

```
bash % python3 -W error example.py
Traceback (most recent call last):
  File "example.py", line 10, in <module>
    func(2, 3, logfile='log.txt')
  File "example.py", line 5, in func
    warnings.warn('logfile argument is deprecated', DeprecationWarning)
DeprecationWarning: logfile argument is deprecated
bash %
```

Discussion

Issuing a warning message is often a useful technique for maintaining software and assisting users with issues that don't necessarily rise to the level of being a full-fledged exception. For example, if you're going to change the behavior of a library or framework, you can start issuing warning messages for the parts that you're going to change while still providing backward compatibility for a time. You can also warn users about problematic usage issues in their code.

As another example of a warning in the built-in library, here is an example of a warning message generated by destroying a file without closing it:

```
>>> import warnings
>>> warnings.simplefilter('always')
>>> f = open('/etc/passwd')
>>> del f
__main__:1: ResourceWarning: unclosed file <_io.TextIOWrapper name='/etc/passwd'
 mode='r' encoding='UTF-8'>
>>>
```

By default, not all warning messages appear. The -W option to Python can control the output of warning messages. -W all will output all warning messages, -W ignore ignores all warnings, and -W error turns warnings into exceptions. As an alternative, you can can use the warnings.simplefilter() function to control output, as just shown. An argument of always makes all warning messages appear, ignore ignores all warnings, and error turns warnings into exceptions.

For simple cases, this is all you really need to issue warning messages. The warnings module provides a variety of more advanced configuration options related to the filtering and handling of warning messages. See the Python documentation (*http:// docs.python.org/3/library/warnings.html*) for more information.

14.12. Debugging Basic Program Crashes

Problem

Your program is broken and you'd like some simple strategies for debugging it.

Solution

If your program is crashing with an exception, running your program as `python3 -i` `someprogram.py` can be a useful tool for simply looking around. The `-i` option starts an interactive shell as soon as a program terminates. From there, you can explore the environment. For example, suppose you have this code:

```
# sample.py

def func(n):
    return n + 10

func('Hello')
```

Running `python3 -i` produces the following:

```
bash % python3 -i sample.py
Traceback (most recent call last):
  File "sample.py", line 6, in <module>
    func('Hello')
  File "sample.py", line 4, in func
    return n + 10
TypeError: Can't convert 'int' object to str implicitly
>>> func(10)
20
>>>
```

If you don't see anything obvious, a further step is to launch the Python debugger after a crash. For example:

```
>>> import pdb
>>> pdb.pm()
> sample.py(4)func()
-> return n + 10
(Pdb) w
  sample.py(6)<module>()
-> func('Hello')
> sample.py(4)func()
-> return n + 10
(Pdb) print n
'Hello'
(Pdb) q
>>>
```

If your code is deeply buried in an environment where it is difficult to obtain an interactive shell (e.g., in a server), you can often catch errors and produce tracebacks yourself. For example:

```
import traceback
import sys

try:
    func(arg)
except:
    print('**** AN ERROR OCCURRED ****')
    traceback.print_exc(file=sys.stderr)
```

If your program isn't crashing, but it's producing wrong answers or you're mystified by how it works, there is often nothing wrong with just injecting a few print() calls in places of interest. However, if you're going to do that, there are a few related techniques of interest. First, the traceback.print_stack() function will create a stack track of your program immediately at that point. For example:

```
>>> def sample(n):
...     if n > 0:
...             sample(n-1)
...     else:
...             traceback.print_stack(file=sys.stderr)
...
>>> sample(5)
  File "<stdin>", line 1, in <module>
  File "<stdin>", line 3, in sample
  File "<stdin>", line 3, in sample
  File "<stdin>", line 3, in sample
  File "<stdin>", line 3, in sample
  File "<stdin>", line 3, in sample
  File "<stdin>", line 5, in sample
>>>
```

Alternatively, you can also manually launch the debugger at any point in your program using pdb.set_trace() like this:

```
import pdb

def func(arg):
    ...
    pdb.set_trace()
    ...
```

This can be a useful technique for poking around in the internals of a large program and answering questions about the control flow or arguments to functions. For instance, once the debugger starts, you can inspect variables using print or type a command such as w to get the stack traceback.

Discussion

Don't make debugging more complicated than it needs to be. Simple errors can often be resolved by merely knowing how to read program tracebacks (e.g., the actual error is usually the last line of the traceback). Inserting a few selected print() functions in your code can also work well if you're in the process of developing it and you simply want some diagnostics (just remember to remove the statements later).

A common use of the debugger is to inspect variables inside a function that has crashed. Knowing how to enter the debugger after such a crash has occurred is a useful skill to know.

Inserting statements such as pdb.set_trace() can be useful if you're trying to unravel an extremely complicated program where the underlying control flow isn't obvious. Essentially, the program will run until it hits the set_trace() call, at which point it will immediately enter the debugger. From there, you can try to make more sense of it.

If you're using an IDE for Python development, the IDE will typically provide its own debugging interface on top of or in place of pdb. Consult the manual for your IDE for more information.

14.13. Profiling and Timing Your Program

Problem

You would like to find out where your program spends its time and make timing measurements.

Solution

If you simply want to time your whole program, it's usually easy enough to use something like the Unix time command. For example:

```
bash % time python3 someprogram.py
real 0m13.937s
user 0m12.162s
sys  0m0.098s
bash %
```

On the other extreme, if you want a detailed report showing what your program is doing, you can use the cProfile module:

```
bash % python3 -m cProfile someprogram.py
         859647 function calls in 16.016 CPU seconds

   Ordered by: standard name


   ncalls  tottime  percall  cumtime  percall filename:lineno(function)
   263169    0.080    0.000    0.080    0.000 someprogram.py:16(frange)
      513    0.001    0.000    0.002    0.000 someprogram.py:30(generate_mandel)
   262656    0.194    0.000   15.295    0.000 someprogram.py:32(<genexpr>)
        1    0.036    0.036   16.077   16.077 someprogram.py:4(<module>)
   262144   15.021    0.000   15.021    0.000 someprogram.py:4(in_mandelbrot)
        1    0.000    0.000    0.000    0.000 os.py:746(urandom)
        1    0.000    0.000    0.000    0.000 png.py:1056(_readable)
        1    0.000    0.000    0.000    0.000 png.py:1073(Reader)
        1    0.227    0.227    0.438    0.438 png.py:163(<module>)
      512    0.010    0.000    0.010    0.000 png.py:200(group)
     ...
bash %
```

More often than not, profiling your code lies somewhere in between these two extremes. For example, you may already know that your code spends most of its time in a few selected functions. For selected profiling of functions, a short decorator can be useful. For example:

```python
# timethis.py

import time
from functools import wraps

def timethis(func):
    @wraps(func)
    def wrapper(*args, **kwargs):
        start = time.perf_counter()
        r = func(*args, **kwargs)
        end = time.perf_counter()
        print('{}.{} : {}'.format(func.__module__, func.__name__, end - start))
        return r
    return wrapper
```

To use this decorator, you simply place it in front of a function definition to get timings from it. For example:

```python
>>> @timethis
... def countdown(n):
...     while n > 0:
...             n -= 1
...
>>> countdown(10000000)
__main__.countdown : 0.803001880645752
>>>
```

To time a block of statements, you can define a context manager. For example:

```
from contextlib import contextmanager

@contextmanager
def timeblock(label):
    start = time.perf_counter()
    try:
        yield
    finally:
        end = time.perf_counter()
        print('{} : {}'.format(label, end - start))
```

Here is an example of how the context manager works:

```
>>> with timeblock('counting'):
...     n = 10000000
...     while n > 0:
...         n -= 1
...
counting : 1.5551159381866455
>>>
```

For studying the performance of small code fragments, the timeit module can be useful. For example:

```
>>> from timeit import timeit
>>> timeit('math.sqrt(2)', 'import math')
0.1432319980012835
>>> timeit('sqrt(2)', 'from math import sqrt')
0.10836604500218527
>>>
```

timeit works by executing the statement specified in the first argument a million times and measuring the time. The second argument is a setup string that is executed to set up the environment prior to running the test. If you need to change the number of iterations, supply a number argument like this:

```
>>> timeit('math.sqrt(2)', 'import math', number=10000000)
1.434852126003534
>>> timeit('sqrt(2)', 'from math import sqrt', number=10000000)
1.0270336690009572
>>>
```

Discussion

When making performance measurements, be aware that any results you get are approximations. The time.perf_counter() function used in the solution provides the highest-resolution timer possible on a given platform. However, it still measures wall-clock time, and can be impacted by many different factors, such as machine load.

If you are interested in process time as opposed to wall-clock time, use time.pro cess_time() instead. For example:

```
from functools import wraps
def timethis(func):
    @wraps(func)
    def wrapper(*args, **kwargs):
        start = time.process_time()
        r = func(*args, **kwargs)
        end = time.process_time()
        print('{}.{} : {}'.format(func.__module__, func.__name__, end - start))
        return r
    return wrapper
```

Last, but not least, if you're going to perform detailed timing analysis, make sure to read the documentation for the `time`, `timeit`, and other associated modules, so that you have an understanding of important platform-related differences and other pitfalls.

See Recipe 13.13 for a related recipe on creating a stopwatch timer class.

14.14. Making Your Programs Run Faster

Problem

Your program runs too slow and you'd like to speed it up without the assistance of more extreme solutions, such as C extensions or a just-in-time (JIT) compiler.

Solution

While the first rule of optimization might be to "not do it," the second rule is almost certainly "don't optimize the unimportant." To that end, if your program is running slow, you might start by profiling your code as discussed in Recipe 14.13.

More often than not, you'll find that your program spends its time in a few hotspots, such as inner data processing loops. Once you've identified those locations, you can use the no-nonsense techniques presented in the following sections to make your program run faster.

Use functions

A lot of programmers start using Python as a language for writing simple scripts. When writing scripts, it is easy to fall into a practice of simply writing code with very little structure. For example:

```
# somescript.py

import sys
import csv

with open(sys.argv[1]) as f:
    for row in csv.reader(f):
```

```
# Some kind of processing
...
```

A little-known fact is that code defined in the global scope like this runs slower than code defined in a function. The speed difference has to do with the implementation of local versus global variables (operations involving locals are faster). So, if you want to make the program run faster, simply put the scripting statements in a function:

```
# somescript.py
import sys
import csv

def main(filename):
    with open(filename) as f:
        for row in csv.reader(f):
            # Some kind of processing
            ...

main(sys.argv[1])
```

The speed difference depends heavily on the processing being performed, but in our experience, speedups of 15-30% are not uncommon.

Selectively eliminate attribute access

Every use of the dot (.) operator to access attributes comes with a cost. Under the covers, this triggers special methods, such as __getattribute__() and __getattr__(), which often lead to dictionary lookups.

You can often avoid attribute lookups by using the from module import name form of import as well as making selected use of bound methods. To illustrate, consider the following code fragment:

```
import math

def compute_roots(nums):
    result = []
    for n in nums:
        result.append(math.sqrt(n))
    return result

# Test
nums = range(1000000)
for n in range(100):
    r = compute_roots(nums)
```

When tested on our machine, this program runs in about 40 seconds. Now change the compute_roots() function as follows:

```
from math import sqrt

def compute_roots(nums):
```

```
result = []
result_append = result.append
for n in nums:
    result_append(sqrt(n))
return result
```

This version runs in about 29 seconds. The only difference between the two versions of code is the elimination of attribute access. Instead of using `math.sqrt()`, the code uses `sqrt()`. The `result.append()` method is additionally placed into a local variable `re sult_append` and reused in the inner loop.

However, it must be emphasized that these changes only make sense in frequently executed code, such as loops. So, this optimization really only makes sense in carefully selected places.

Understand locality of variables

As previously noted, local variables are faster than global variables. For frequently accessed names, speedups can be obtained by making those names as local as possible. For example, consider this modified version of the `compute_roots()` function just discussed:

```
import math

def compute_roots(nums):
    sqrt = math.sqrt
    result = []
    result_append = result.append
    for n in nums:
        result_append(sqrt(n))
    return result
```

In this version, `sqrt` has been lifted from the `math` module and placed into a local variable. If you run this code, it now runs in about 25 seconds (an improvement over the previous version, which took 29 seconds). That additional speedup is due to a local lookup of `sqrt` being a bit faster than a global lookup of `sqrt`.

Locality arguments also apply when working in classes. In general, looking up a value such as `self.name` will be considerably slower than accessing a local variable. In inner loops, it might pay to lift commonly accessed attributes into a local variable. For example:

```
# Slower
class SomeClass:
    ...
    def method(self):
        for x in s:
            op(self.value)

# Faster
class SomeClass:
```

```
...
def method(self):
    value = self.value
    for x in s:
        op(value)
```

Avoid gratuitous abstraction

Any time you wrap up code with extra layers of processing, such as decorators, properties, or descriptors, you're going to make it slower. As an example, consider this class:

```
class A:
    def __init__(self, x, y):
        self.x = x
        self.y = y
    @property
    def y(self):
        return self._y
    @y.setter
    def y(self, value):
        self._y = value
```

Now, try a simple timing test:

```
>>> from timeit import timeit
>>> a = A(1,2)
>>> timeit('a.x', 'from __main__ import a')
0.07817923510447145
>>> timeit('a.y', 'from __main__ import a')
0.35766440676525235
>>>
```

As you can observe, accessing the property y is not just slightly slower than a simple attribute x, it's about 4.5 times slower. If this difference matters, you should ask yourself if the definition of y as a property was really necessary. If not, simply get rid of it and go back to using a simple attribute instead. Just because it might be common for programs in another programming language to use getter/setter functions, that doesn't mean you should adopt that programming style for Python.

Use the built-in containers

Built-in data types such as strings, tuples, lists, sets, and dicts are all implemented in C, and are rather fast. If you're inclined to make your own data structures as a replacement (e.g., linked lists, balanced trees, etc.), it may be rather difficult if not impossible to match the speed of the built-ins. Thus, you're often better off just using them.

Avoid making unnecessary data structures or copies

Sometimes programmers get carried away with making unnecessary data structures when they just don't have to. For example, someone might write code like this:

```
values = [x for x in sequence]
squares = [x*x for x in values]
```

Perhaps the thinking here is to first collect a bunch of values into a list and then to start applying operations such as list comprehensions to it. However, the first list is completely unnecessary. Simply write the code like this:

```
squares = [x*x for x in sequence]
```

Related to this, be on the lookout for code written by programmers who are overly paranoid about Python's sharing of values. Overuse of functions such as copy.deep copy() may be a sign of code that's been written by someone who doesn't fully understand or trust Python's memory model. In such code, it may be safe to eliminate many of the copies.

Discussion

Before optimizing, it's usually worthwhile to study the algorithms that you're using first. You'll get a much bigger speedup by switching to an O(n log n) algorithm than by trying to tweak the implementation of an an O(n**2) algorithm.

If you've decided that you still must optimize, it pays to consider the big picture. As a general rule, you don't want to apply optimizations to every part of your program, because such changes are going to make the code hard to read and understand. Instead, focus only on known performance bottlenecks, such as inner loops.

You need to be especially wary interpreting the results of micro-optimizations. For example, consider these two techniques for creating a dictionary:

```
a = {
    'name' : 'AAPL',
    'shares' : 100,
    'price' : 534.22
}

b = dict(name='AAPL', shares=100, price=534.22)
```

The latter choice has the benefit of less typing (you don't need to quote the key names). However, if you put the two code fragments in a head-to-head performance battle, you'll find that using dict() runs three times slower! With this knowledge, you might be inclined to scan your code and replace every use of dict() with its more verbose alternative. However, a smart programmer will only focus on parts of a program where it might actually matter, such as an inner loop. In other places, the speed difference just isn't going to matter at all.

If, on the other hand, your performance needs go far beyond the simple techniques in this recipe, you might investigate the use of tools based on just-in-time (JIT) compilation techniques. For example, the PyPy project (*http://pypy.org*) is an alternate implementation of the Python interpreter that analyzes the execution of your program and generates native machine code for frequently executed parts. It can sometimes make Python programs run an order of magnitude faster, often approaching (or even exceeding) the speed of code written in C. Unfortunately, as of this writing, PyPy does not yet fully support Python 3. So, that is something to look for in the future. You might also consider the Numba project (*http://numba.pydata.org*). Numba is a dynamic compiler where you annotate selected Python functions that you want to optimize with a decorator. Those functions are then compiled into native machine code through the use of LLVM (*http://llvm.org*). It too can produce signficant performance gains. However, like PyPy, support for Python 3 should be viewed as somewhat experimental.

Last, but not least, the words of John Ousterhout come to mind: "The best performance improvement is the transition from the nonworking to the working state." Don't worry about optimization until you need to. Making sure your program works correctly is usually more important than making it run fast (at least initially).

## CHAPTER 15

C Extensions

This chapter looks at the problem of accessing C code from Python. Many of Python's built-in libraries are written in C, and accessing C is an important part of making Python talk to existing libraries. It's also an area that might require the most study if you're faced with the problem of porting extension code from Python 2 to 3.

Although Python provides an extensive C programming API, there are actually many different approaches for dealing with C. Rather than trying to give an exhaustive reference for every possible tool or technique, the approach is to focus on a small fragment of C code along with some representative examples of how to work with the code. The goal is to provide a series of programming templates that experienced programmers can expand upon for their own use.

Here is the C code we will work with in most of the recipes:

```c
/* sample.c */_method
#include <math.h>

/* Compute the greatest common divisor */
int gcd(int x, int y) {
    int g = y;
    while (x > 0) {
        g = x;
        x = y % x;
        y = g;
    }
    return g;
}

/* Test if (x0,y0) is in the Mandelbrot set or not */
int in_mandel(double x0, double y0, int n) {
  double x=0,y=0,xtemp;
  while (n > 0) {
    xtemp = x*x - y*y + x0;
    y = 2*x*y + y0;
```

```
        x = xtemp;
        n -= 1;
        if (x*x + y*y > 4) return 0;
    }
    return 1;
}

/* Divide two numbers */
int divide(int a, int b, int *remainder) {
    int quot = a / b;
    *remainder = a % b;
    return quot;
}

/* Average values in an array */
double avg(double *a, int n) {
    int i;
    double total = 0.0;
    for (i = 0; i < n; i++) {
        total += a[i];
    }
    return total / n;
}

/* A C data structure */
typedef struct Point {
    double x,y;
} Point;

/* Function involving a C data structure */
double distance(Point *p1, Point *p2) {
    return hypot(p1->x - p2->x, p1->y - p2->y);
}
```

This code contains a number of different C programming features. First, there are a few simple functions such as gcd() and is_mandel(). The divide() function is an example of a C function returning multiple values, one through a pointer argument. The avg() function performs a data reduction across a C array. The Point and distance() function involve C structures.

For all of the recipes that follow, assume that the preceding code is found in a file named *sample.c*, that definitions are found in a file named *sample.h* and that it has been compiled into a library libsample that can be linked to other C code. The exact details of compilation and linking vary from system to system, but that is not the primary focus. It is assumed that if you're working with C code, you've already figured that out.

15.1. Accessing C Code Using ctypes

Problem

You have a small number of C functions that have been compiled into a shared library or DLL. You would like to call these functions purely from Python without having to write additional C code or using a third-party extension tool.

Solution

For small problems involving C code, it is often easy enough to use the `ctypes` module that is part of Python's standard library. In order to use `ctypes`, you must first make sure the C code you want to access has been compiled into a shared library that is compatible with the Python interpreter (e.g., same architecture, word size, compiler, etc.). For the purposes of this recipe, assume that a shared library, `libsample.so`, has been created and that it contains nothing more than the code shown in the chapter introduction. Further assume that the *libsample.so* file has been placed in the same directory as the *sample.py* file shown next.

To access the resulting library, you make a Python module that wraps around it, such as the following:

```python
# sample.py
import ctypes
import os

# Try to locate the .so file in the same directory as this file
_file = 'libsample.so'
_path = os.path.join(*(os.path.split(__file__)[:-1] + (_file,)))
_mod = ctypes.cdll.LoadLibrary(_path)

# int gcd(int, int)
gcd = _mod.gcd
gcd.argtypes = (ctypes.c_int, ctypes.c_int)
gcd.restype = ctypes.c_int

# int in_mandel(double, double, int)
in_mandel = _mod.in_mandel
in_mandel.argtypes = (ctypes.c_double, ctypes.c_double, ctypes.c_int)
in_mandel.restype = ctypes.c_int

# int divide(int, int, int *)
_divide = _mod.divide
_divide.argtypes = (ctypes.c_int, ctypes.c_int, ctypes.POINTER(ctypes.c_int))
_divide.restype = ctypes.c_int

def divide(x, y):
    rem = ctypes.c_int()
    quot = _divide(x, y, rem)
```

```
        return quot,rem.value

    # void avg(double *, int n)
    # Define a special type for the 'double *' argument
    class DoubleArrayType:
        def from_param(self, param):
            typename = type(param).__name__
            if hasattr(self, 'from_' + typename):
                return getattr(self, 'from_' + typename)(param)
            elif isinstance(param, ctypes.Array):
                return param
            else:
                raise TypeError("Can't convert %s" % typename)

        # Cast from array.array objects
        def from_array(self, param):
            if param.typecode != 'd':
                raise TypeError('must be an array of doubles')
            ptr, _ = param.buffer_info()
            return ctypes.cast(ptr, ctypes.POINTER(ctypes.c_double))

        # Cast from lists/tuples
        def from_list(self, param):
            val = ((ctypes.c_double)*len(param))(*param)
            return val

        from_tuple = from_list

        # Cast from a numpy array
        def from_ndarray(self, param):
            return param.ctypes.data_as(ctypes.POINTER(ctypes.c_double))

    DoubleArray = DoubleArrayType()
    _avg = _mod.avg
    _avg.argtypes = (DoubleArray, ctypes.c_int)
    _avg.restype = ctypes.c_double

    def avg(values):
        return _avg(values, len(values))

    # struct Point { }
    class Point(ctypes.Structure):
        _fields_ = [('x', ctypes.c_double),
                    ('y', ctypes.c_double)]

    # double distance(Point *, Point *)
    distance = _mod.distance
    distance.argtypes = (ctypes.POINTER(Point), ctypes.POINTER(Point))
    distance.restype = ctypes.c_double
```

If all goes well, you should be able to load the module and use the resulting C functions. For example:

```
>>> import sample
>>> sample.gcd(35,42)
7
>>> sample.in_mandel(0,0,500)
1
>>> sample.in_mandel(2.0,1.0,500)
0
>>> sample.divide(42,8)
(5, 2)
>>> sample.avg([1,2,3])
2.0
>>> p1 = sample.Point(1,2)
>>> p2 = sample.Point(4,5)
>>> sample.distance(p1,p2)
4.242640687119285
>>>
```

Discussion

There are several aspects of this recipe that warrant some discussion. The first issue concerns the overall packaging of C and Python code together. If you are using `ctypes` to access C code that you have compiled yourself, you will need to make sure that the shared library gets placed in a location where the `sample.py` module can find it. One possibility is to put the resulting *.so* file in the same directory as the supporting Python code. This is what's shown at the first part of this recipe—*sample.py* looks at the `__file__` variable to see where it has been installed, and then constructs a path that points to a *libsample.so* file in the same directory.

If the C library is going to be installed elsewhere, then you'll have to adjust the path accordingly. If the C library is installed as a standard library on your machine, you might be able to use the `ctypes.util.find_library()` function. For example:

```
>>> from ctypes.util import find_library
>>> find_library('m')
'/usr/lib/libm.dylib'
>>> find_library('pthread')
'/usr/lib/libpthread.dylib'
>>> find_library('sample')
'/usr/local/lib/libsample.so'
>>>
```

Again, `ctypes` won't work at all if it can't locate the library with the C code. Thus, you'll need to spend a few minutes thinking about how you want to install things.

Once you know where the C library is located, you use `ctypes.cdll.LoadLibrary()` to load it. The following statement in the solution does this where _path is the full pathname to the shared library:

```
_mod = ctypes.cdll.LoadLibrary(_path)
```

Once a library has been loaded, you need to write statements that extract specific symbols and put type signatures on them. This is what's happening in code fragments such as this:

```
# int in_mandel(double, double, int)
in_mandel = _mod.in_mandel
in_mandel.argtypes = (ctypes.c_double, ctypes.c_double, ctypes.c_int)
in_mandel.restype = ctypes.c_int
```

In this code, the .argtypes attribute is a tuple containing the input arguments to a function, and .restype is the return type. ctypes defines a variety of type objects (e.g., c_double, c_int, c_short, c_float, etc.) that represent common C data types. Attaching the type signatures is critical if you want to make Python pass the right kinds of arguments and convert data correctly (if you don't do this, not only will the code not work, but you might cause the entire interpreter process to crash).

A somewhat tricky part of using ctypes is that the original C code may use idioms that don't map cleanly to Python. The divide() function is a good example because it returns a value through one of its arguments. Although that's a common C technique, it's often not clear how it's supposed to work in Python. For example, you can't do anything straightforward like this:

```
>>> divide = _mod.divide
>>> divide.argtypes = (ctypes.c_int, ctypes.c_int, ctypes.POINTER(ctypes.c_int))
>>> x = 0
>>> divide(10, 3, x)
Traceback (most recent call last):
  File "<stdin>", line 1, in <module>
ctypes.ArgumentError: argument 3: <class 'TypeError'>: expected LP_c_int
instance instead of int
>>>
```

Even if this did work, it would violate Python's immutability of integers and probably cause the entire interpreter to be sucked into a black hole. For arguments involving pointers, you usually have to construct a compatible ctypes object and pass it in like this:

```
>>> x = ctypes.c_int()
>>> divide(10, 3, x)
3
>>> x.value
1
>>>
```

Here an instance of a ctypes.c_int is created and passed in as the pointer object. Unlike a normal Python integer, a c_int object can be mutated. The .value attribute can be used to either retrieve or change the value as desired.

For cases where the C calling convention is "un-Pythonic," it is common to write a small wrapper function. In the solution, this code makes the `divide()` function return the two results using a tuple instead:

```
# int divide(int, int, int *)
_divide = _mod.divide
_divide.argtypes = (ctypes.c_int, ctypes.c_int, ctypes.POINTER(ctypes.c_int))
_divide.restype = ctypes.c_int

def divide(x, y):
    rem = ctypes.c_int()
    quot = _divide(x,y,rem)
    return quot, rem.value
```

The `avg()` function presents a new kind of challenge. The underlying C code expects to receive a pointer and a length representing an array. However, from the Python side, we must consider the following questions: What is an array? Is it a list? A tuple? An array from the `array` module? A numpy array? Is it all of these? In practice, a Python "array" could take many different forms, and maybe you would like to support multiple possibilities.

The `DoubleArrayType` class shows how to handle this situation. In this class, a single method `from_param()` is defined. The role of this method is to take a single parameter and narrow it down to a compatible `ctypes` object (a pointer to a `ctypes.c_double`, in the example). Within `from_param()`, you are free to do anything that you wish. In the solution, the typename of the parameter is extracted and used to dispatch to a more specialized method. For example, if a list is passed, the typename is `list` and a method `from_list()` is invoked.

For lists and tuples, the `from_list()` method performs a conversion to a `ctypes` array object. This looks a little weird, but here is an interactive example of converting a list to a `ctypes` array:

```
>>> nums = [1, 2, 3]
>>> a = (ctypes.c_double * len(nums))(*nums)
>>> a
<__main__.c_double_Array_3 object at 0x10069cd40>
>>> a[0]
1.0
>>> a[1]
2.0
>>> a[2]
3.0
>>>
```

For `array` objects, the `from_array()` method extracts the underlying memory pointer and casts it to a `ctypes` pointer object. For example:

```
>>> import array
>>> a = array.array('d',[1,2,3])
>>> a
array('d', [1.0, 2.0, 3.0])
>>> ptr_ = a.buffer_info()
>>> ptr
4298687200
>>> ctypes.cast(ptr, ctypes.POINTER(ctypes.c_double))
<__main__.LP_c_double object at 0x10069cd40>
>>>
```

The from_ndarray() shows comparable conversion code for numpy arrays.

By defining the DoubleArrayType class and using it in the type signature of avg(), as shown, the function can accept a variety of different array-like inputs:

```
>>> import sample
>>> sample.avg([1,2,3])
2.0
>>> sample.avg((1,2,3))
2.0
>>> import array
>>> sample.avg(array.array('d',[1,2,3]))
2.0
>>> import numpy
>>> sample.avg(numpy.array([1.0,2.0,3.0]))
2.0
>>>
```

The last part of this recipe shows how to work with a simple C structure. For structures, you simply define a class that contains the appropriate fields and types like this:

```
class Point(ctypes.Structure):
    _fields_ = [('x', ctypes.c_double),
                ('y', ctypes.c_double)]
```

Once defined, you can use the class in type signatures as well as in code that needs to instantiate and work with the structures. For example:

```
>>> p1 = sample.Point(1,2)
>>> p2 = sample.Point(4,5)
>>> p1.x
1.0
>>> p1.y
2.0
>>> sample.distance(p1,p2)
4.242640687119285
>>>
```

A few final comments: ctypes is a useful library to know about if all you're doing is accessing a few C functions from Python. However, if you're trying to access a large library, you might want to look at alternative approaches, such as Swig (described in Recipe 15.9) or Cython (described in Recipe 15.10).

The main problem with a large library is that since `ctypes` isn't entirely automatic, you'll have to spend a fair bit of time writing out all of the type signatures, as shown in the example. Depending on the complexity of the library, you might also have to write a large number of small wrapper functions and supporting classes. Also, unless you fully understand all of the low-level details of the C interface, including memory management and error handling, it is often quite easy to make Python catastrophically crash with a segmentation fault, access violation, or some similar error.

As an alternative to `ctypes`, you might also look at CFFI (*http://cffi.readthedocs.org/en/latest*). CFFI provides much of the same functionality, but uses C syntax and supports more advanced kinds of C code. As of this writing, CFFI is still a relatively new project, but its use has been growing rapidly. There has even been some discussion of including it in the Python standard library in some future release. Thus, it's definitely something to keep an eye on.

15.2. Writing a Simple C Extension Module

Problem

You want to write a simple C extension module directly using Python's extension API and no other tools.

Solution

For simple C code, it is straightforward to make a handcrafted extension module. As a preliminary step, you probably want to make sure your C code has a proper header file. For example,

```c
/* sample.h */

#include <math.h>

extern int gcd(int, int);
extern int in_mandel(double x0, double y0, int n);
extern int divide(int a, int b, int *remainder);
extern double avg(double *a, int n);

typedef struct Point {
    double x,y;
} Point;

extern double distance(Point *p1, Point *p2);
```

Typically, this header would correspond to a library that has been compiled separately. With that assumption, here is a sample extension module that illustrates the basics of writing extension functions:

```c
#include "Python.h"
#include "sample.h"

/* int gcd(int, int) */
static PyObject *py_gcd(PyObject *self, PyObject *args) {
  int x, y, result;

  if (!PyArg_ParseTuple(args,"ii", &x, &y)) {
    return NULL;
  }
  result = gcd(x,y);
  return Py_BuildValue("i", result);
}

/* int in_mandel(double, double, int) */
static PyObject *py_in_mandel(PyObject *self, PyObject *args) {
  double x0, y0;
  int n;
  int result;

  if (!PyArg_ParseTuple(args, "ddi", &x0, &y0, &n)) {
    return NULL;
  }
  result = in_mandel(x0,y0,n);
  return Py_BuildValue("i", result);
}

/* int divide(int, int, int *) */
static PyObject *py_divide(PyObject *self, PyObject *args) {
  int a, b, quotient, remainder;
  if (!PyArg_ParseTuple(args, "ii", &a, &b)) {
    return NULL;
  }
  quotient = divide(a,b, &remainder);
  return Py_BuildValue("(ii)", quotient, remainder);
}

/* Module method table */
static PyMethodDef SampleMethods[] = {
  {"gcd",  py_gcd, METH_VARARGS, "Greatest common divisor"},
  {"in_mandel", py_in_mandel, METH_VARARGS, "Mandelbrot test"},
  {"divide", py_divide, METH_VARARGS, "Integer division"},
  { NULL, NULL, 0, NULL}
};

/* Module structure */
static struct PyModuleDef samplemodule = {
  PyModuleDef_HEAD_INIT,
```

```
  "sample",            /* name of module */
  "A sample module",   /* Doc string (may be NULL) */
  -1,                  /* Size of per-interpreter state or -1 */
  SampleMethods        /* Method table */
};

/* Module initialization function */
PyMODINIT_FUNC
PyInit_sample(void) {
  return PyModule_Create(&samplemodule);
}
```

For building the extension module, create a *setup.py* file that looks like this:

```
# setup.py
from distutils.core import setup, Extension

setup(name='sample',
      ext_modules=[
        Extension('sample',
                  ['pysample.c'],
                  include_dirs = ['/some/dir'],
                  define_macros = [('FOO','1')],
                  undef_macros = ['BAR'],
                  library_dirs = ['/usr/local/lib'],
                  libraries = ['sample']
                  )
        ]
)
```

Now, to build the resulting library, simply use python3 buildlib.py build_ext --
inplace. For example:

```
bash % python3 setup.py build_ext --inplace
running build_ext
building 'sample' extension
gcc -fno-strict-aliasing -DNDEBUG -g -fwrapv -O3 -Wall -Wstrict-prototypes
 -I/usr/local/include/python3.3m -c pysample.c
 -o build/temp.macosx-10.6-x86_64-3.3/pysample.o
gcc -bundle -undefined dynamic_lookup
build/temp.macosx-10.6-x86_64-3.3/pysample.o \
 -L/usr/local/lib -lsample -o sample.so
bash %
```

As shown, this creates a shared library called sample.so. When compiled, you should
be able to start importing it as a module:

```
>>> import sample
>>> sample.gcd(35, 42)
7
>>> sample.in_mandel(0, 0, 500)
1
>>> sample.in_mandel(2.0, 1.0, 500)
```

```
0
>>> sample.divide(42, 8)
(5, 2)
>>>
```

If you are attempting these steps on Windows, you may need to spend some time fiddling with your environment and the build environment to get extension modules to build correctly. Binary distributions of Python are typically built using Microsoft Visual Studio. To get extensions to work, you may have to compile them using the same or compatible tools. See the Python documentation (*http://docs.python.org/3/extending/windows.html*).

Discussion

Before attempting any kind of handwritten extension, it is absolutely critical that you consult Python's documentation on "Extending and Embedding the Python Interpreter" (*http://docs.python.org/3/extending/index.html*). Python's C extension API is large, and repeating all of it here is simply not practical. However, the most important parts can be easily discussed.

First, in extension modules, functions that you write are all typically written with a common prototype such as this:

```
static PyObject *py_func(PyObject *self, PyObject *args) {
    ...
}
```

PyObject is the C data type that represents any Python object. At a very high level, an extension function is a C function that receives a tuple of Python objects (in PyObject *args) and returns a new Python object as a result. The self argument to the function is unused for simple extension functions, but comes into play should you want to define new classes or object types in C (e.g., if the extension function were a method of a class, then self would hold the instance).

The PyArg_ParseTuple() function is used to convert values from Python to a C representation. As input, it takes a format string that indicates the required values, such as "i" for integer and "d" for double, as well as the addresses of C variables in which to place the converted results. PyArg_ParseTuple() performs a variety of checks on the number and type of arguments. If there is any mismatch with the format string, an exception is raised and NULL is returned. By checking for this and simply returning NULL, an appropriate exception will have been raised in the calling code.

The Py_BuildValue() function is used to create Python objects from C data types. It also accepts a format code to indicate the desired type. In the extension functions, it is used to return results back to Python. One feature of Py_BuildValue() is that it can build more complicated kinds of objects, such as tuples and dictionaries. In the code for `py_divide()`, an example showing the return of a tuple is shown. However, here are a few more examples:

```
return Py_BuildValue("i", 34);      // Return an integer
return Py_BuildValue("d", 3.4);     // Return a double
return Py_BuildValue("s", "Hello"); // Null-terminated UTF-8 string
return Py_BuildValue("(ii)", 3, 4); // Tuple (3, 4)
```

Near the bottom of any extension module, you will find a function table such as the `SampleMethods` table shown in this recipe. This table lists C functions, the names to use in Python, as well as doc strings. All modules are required to specify such a table, as it gets used in the initialization of the module.

The final function `PyInit_sample()` is the module initialization function that executes when the module is first imported. The primary job of this function is to register the module object with the interpreter.

As a final note, it must be stressed that there is considerably more to extending Python with C functions than what is shown here (in fact, the C API contains well over 500 functions in it). You should view this recipe simply as a stepping stone for getting started. To do more, start with the documentation on the `PyArg_ParseTuple()` and `Py_Build Value()` functions, and expand from there.

15.3. Writing an Extension Function That Operates on Arrays

Problem

You want to write a C extension function that operates on contiguous arrays of data, as might be created by the array module or libraries like NumPy. However, you would like your function to be general purpose and not specific to any one array library.

Solution

To receive and process arrays in a portable manner, you should write code that uses the Buffer Protocol (*http://docs.python.org/3/c-api/buffer.html*). Here is an example of a handwritten C extension function that receives array data and calls the `avg(double *buf, int len)` function from this chapter's introduction:

```
/* Call double avg(double *, int) */
static PyObject *py_avg(PyObject *self, PyObject *args) {
  PyObject *bufobj;
  Py_buffer view;
  double result;
  /* Get the passed Python object */
  if (!PyArg_ParseTuple(args, "O", &bufobj)) {
    return NULL;
```

```
    }

    /* Attempt to extract buffer information from it */
    if (PyObject_GetBuffer(bufobj, &view,
        PyBUF_ANY_CONTIGUOUS | PyBUF_FORMAT) == -1) {
      return NULL;
    }

    if (view.ndim != 1) {
      PyErr_SetString(PyExc_TypeError, "Expected a 1-dimensional array");
      PyBuffer_Release(&view);
      return NULL;
    }

    /* Check the type of items in the array */
    if (strcmp(view.format,"d") != 0) {
      PyErr_SetString(PyExc_TypeError, "Expected an array of doubles");
      PyBuffer_Release(&view);
      return NULL;
    }

    /* Pass the raw buffer and size to the C function */
    result = avg(view.buf, view.shape[0]);

    /* Indicate we're done working with the buffer */
    PyBuffer_Release(&view);
    return Py_BuildValue("d", result);
}
```

Here is an example that shows how this extension function works:

```
>>> import array
>>> avg(array.array('d',[1,2,3]))
2.0
>>> import numpy
>>> avg(numpy.array([1.0,2.0,3.0]))
2.0
>>> avg([1,2,3])
Traceback (most recent call last):
  File "<stdin>", line 1, in <module>
TypeError: 'list' does not support the buffer interface
>>> avg(b'Hello')
Traceback (most recent call last):
  File "<stdin>", line 1, in <module>
TypeError: Expected an array of doubles
>>> a = numpy.array([[1.,2.,3.],[4.,5.,6.]])
>>> avg(a[:,2])
Traceback (most recent call last):
  File "<stdin>", line 1, in <module>
ValueError: ndarray is not contiguous
>>> sample.avg(a)
Traceback (most recent call last):
  File "<stdin>", line 1, in <module>
```

```
TypeError: Expected a 1-dimensional array
>>> sample.avg(a[0])
2.0
>>>
```

Discussion

Passing array objects to C functions might be one of the most common things you would want to do with a extension function. A large number of Python applications, ranging from image processing to scientific computing, are based on high-performance array processing. By writing code that can accept and operate on arrays, you can write customized code that plays nicely with those applications as opposed to having some sort of custom solution that only works with your own code.

The key to this code is the PyBuffer_GetBuffer() function. Given an arbitrary Python object, it tries to obtain information about the underlying memory representation. If it's not possible, as is the case with most normal Python objects, it simply raises an exception and returns -1. The special flags passed to PyBuffer_GetBuffer() give additional hints about the kind of memory buffer that is requested. For example, PyBUF_ANY_CONTIGUOUS specifies that a contiguous region of memory is required.

For arrays, byte strings, and other similar objects, a Py_buffer structure is filled with information about the underlying memory. This includes a pointer to the memory, size, itemsize, format, and other details. Here is the definition of this structure:

```
typedef struct bufferinfo {
    void *buf;               /* Pointer to buffer memory */
    PyObject *obj;           /* Python object that is the owner */
    Py_ssize_t len;          /* Total size in bytes */
    Py_ssize_t itemsize;     /* Size in bytes of a single item */
    int readonly;            /* Read-only access flag */
    int ndim;                /* Number of dimensions */
    char *format;            /* struct code of a single item */
    Py_ssize_t *shape;       /* Array containing dimensions */
    Py_ssize_t *strides;     /* Array containing strides */
    Py_ssize_t *suboffsets;  /* Array containing suboffsets */
} Py_buffer;
```

In this recipe, we are simply concerned with receiving a contiguous array of doubles. To check if items are a double, the format attribute is checked to see if the string is "d". This is the same code that the struct module uses when encoding binary values. As a general rule, format could be any format string that's compatible with the struct module and might include multiple items in the case of arrays containing C structures.

Once we have verified the underlying buffer information, we simply pass it to the C function, which treats it as a normal C array. For all practical purposes, it is not concerned with what kind of array it is or what library created it. This is how the function is able to work with arrays created by the array module or by numpy.

Before returning a final result, the underlying buffer view must be released using PyBuffer_Release(). This step is required to properly manage reference counts of objects.

Again, this recipe only shows a tiny fragment of code that receives an array. If working with arrays, you might run into issues with multidimensional data, strided data, different data types, and more that will require study. Make sure you consult the official documentation (*http://docs.python.org/3/c-api/buffer.html*) to get more details.

If you need to write many extensions involving array handling, you may find it easier to implement the code in Cython. See Recipe 15.11.

15.4. Managing Opaque Pointers in C Extension Modules

Problem

You have an extension module that needs to handle a pointer to a C data structure, but you don't want to expose any internal details of the structure to Python.

Solution

Opaque data structures are easily handled by wrapping them inside capsule objects. Consider this fragment of C code from our sample code:

```
typedef struct Point {
    double x,y;
} Point;

extern double distance(Point *p1, Point *p2);
```

Here is an example of extension code that wraps the Point structure and distance() function using capsules:

```
/* Destructor function for points */
static void del_Point(PyObject *obj) {
  free(PyCapsule_GetPointer(obj,"Point"));
}

/* Utility functions */
static Point *PyPoint_AsPoint(PyObject *obj) {
  return (Point *) PyCapsule_GetPointer(obj, "Point");
}

static PyObject *PyPoint_FromPoint(Point *p, int must_free) {
  return PyCapsule_New(p, "Point", must_free ? del_Point : NULL);
}

/* Create a new Point object */
static PyObject *py_Point(PyObject *self, PyObject *args) {
```

```
    Point *p;
    double x,y;
    if (!PyArg_ParseTuple(args,"dd",&x,&y)) {
      return NULL;
    }
    p = (Point *) malloc(sizeof(Point));
    p->x = x;
    p->y = y;
    return PyPoint_FromPoint(p, 1);
  }

  static PyObject *py_distance(PyObject *self, PyObject *args) {
    Point *p1, *p2;
    PyObject *py_p1, *py_p2;
    double result;

    if (!PyArg_ParseTuple(args,"OO",&py_p1, &py_p2)) {
      return NULL;
    }
    if (!(p1 = PyPoint_AsPoint(py_p1))) {
      return NULL;
    }
    if (!(p2 = PyPoint_AsPoint(py_p2))) {
      return NULL;
    }
    result = distance(p1,p2);
    return Py_BuildValue("d", result);
  }
```

Using these functions from Python looks like this:

```
>>> import sample
>>> p1 = sample.Point(2,3)
>>> p2 = sample.Point(4,5)
>>> p1
<capsule object "Point" at 0x1004ea330>
>>> p2
<capsule object "Point" at 0x1005d1db0>
>>> sample.distance(p1,p2)
2.8284271247461903
>>>
```

Discussion

Capsules are similar to a typed C pointer. Internally, they hold a generic pointer along with an identifying name and can be easily created using the PyCapsule_New() function. In addition, an optional destructor function can be attached to a capsule to release the underlying memory when the capsule object is garbage collected.

To extract the pointer contained inside a capsule, use the `PyCapsule_GetPointer()` function and specify the name. If the supplied name doesn't match that of the capsule or some other error occurs, an exception is raised and NULL is returned.

In this recipe, a pair of utility functions—`PyPoint_FromPoint()` and `PyPoint_As Point()`—have been written to deal with the mechanics of creating and unwinding `Point` instances from capsule objects. In any extension functions, we'll use these functions instead of working with capsules directly. This design choice makes it easier to deal with possible changes to the wrapping of `Point` objects in the future. For example, if you decided to use something other than a capsule later, you would only have to change these two functions.

One tricky part about capsules concerns garbage collection and memory management. The `PyPoint_FromPoint()` function accepts a `must_free` argument that indicates whether the underlying `Point *` structure is to be collected when the capsule is destroyed. When working with certain kinds of C code, ownership issues can be difficult to handle (e.g., perhaps a `Point` structure is embedded within a larger data structure that is managed separately). Rather than making a unilateral decision to garbage collect, this extra argument gives control back to the programmer. It should be noted that the destructor associated with an existing capsule can also be changed using the `PyCap sule_SetDestructor()` function.

Capsules are a sensible solution to interfacing with certain kinds of C code involving structures. For instance, sometimes you just don't care about exposing the internals of a structure or turning it into a full-fledged extension type. With a capsule, you can put a lightweight wrapper around it and easily pass it around to other extension functions.

15.5. Defining and Exporting C APIs from Extension Modules

Problem

You have a C extension module that internally defines a variety of useful functions that you would like to export as a public C API for use elsewhere. You would like to use these functions inside other extension modules, but don't know how to link them together, and doing it with the C compiler/linker seems excessively complicated (or impossible).

Solution

This recipe focuses on the code written to handle `Point` objects, which were presented in Recipe 15.4. If you recall, that C code included some utility functions like this:

```
/* Destructor function for points */
static void del_Point(PyObject *obj) {
```

```
  free(PyCapsule_GetPointer(obj,"Point"));
}

/* Utility functions */
static Point *PyPoint_AsPoint(PyObject *obj) {
  return (Point *) PyCapsule_GetPointer(obj, "Point");
}

static PyObject *PyPoint_FromPoint(Point *p, int must_free) {
  return PyCapsule_New(p, "Point", must_free ? del_Point : NULL);
}
```

The problem now addressed is how to export the PyPoint_AsPoint() and Py
Point_FromPoint() functions as an API that other extension modules could use and
link to (e.g., if you have other extensions that also want to use the wrapped Point
objects).

To solve this problem, start by introducing a new header file for the "sample" extension
called *pysample.h.* Put the following code in it:

```
/* pysample.h */
#include "Python.h"
#include "sample.h"
#ifdef __cplusplus
extern "C" {
#endif

/* Public API Table */
typedef struct {
  Point *(*aspoint)(PyObject *);
  PyObject *(*frompoint)(Point *, int);
} _PointAPIMethods;

#ifndef PYSAMPLE_MODULE
/* Method table in external module */
static _PointAPIMethods *_point_api = 0;

/* Import the API table from sample */
static int import_sample(void) {
  _point_api = (_PointAPIMethods *) PyCapsule_Import("sample._point_api",0);
  return (_point_api != NULL) ? 1 : 0;
}

/* Macros to implement the programming interface */
#define PyPoint_AsPoint(obj) (_point_api->aspoint)(obj)
#define PyPoint_FromPoint(obj) (_point_api->frompoint)(obj)
#endif

#ifdef __cplusplus
}
#endif
```

The most important feature here is the `_PointAPIMethods` table of function pointers. It will be initialized in the exporting module and found by importing modules.

Change the original extension module to populate the table and export it as follows:

```c
/* pysample.c */

#include "Python.h"
#define PYSAMPLE_MODULE
#include "pysample.h"


...
/* Destructor function for points */
static void del_Point(PyObject *obj) {
  printf("Deleting point\n");
  free(PyCapsule_GetPointer(obj,"Point"));
}

/* Utility functions */
static Point *PyPoint_AsPoint(PyObject *obj) {
  return (Point *) PyCapsule_GetPointer(obj, "Point");
}

static PyObject *PyPoint_FromPoint(Point *p, int free) {
  return PyCapsule_New(p, "Point", free ? del_Point : NULL);
}

static _PointAPIMethods _point_api = {
  PyPoint_AsPoint,
  PyPoint_FromPoint
};
...

/* Module initialization function */
PyMODINIT_FUNC
PyInit_sample(void) {
  PyObject *m;
  PyObject *py_point_api;

  m = PyModule_Create(&samplemodule);
  if (m == NULL)
    return NULL;

  /* Add the Point C API functions */
  py_point_api = PyCapsule_New((void *) &_point_api, "sample._point_api", NULL);
  if (py_point_api) {
    PyModule_AddObject(m, "_point_api", py_point_api);
  }
  return m;
}
```

Finally, here is an example of a new extension module that loads and uses these API functions:

```
/* ptexample.c */

/* Include the header associated with the other module */
#include "pysample.h"

/* An extension function that uses the exported API */
static PyObject *print_point(PyObject *self, PyObject *args) {
  PyObject *obj;
  Point *p;
  if (!PyArg_ParseTuple(args,"O", &obj)) {
    return NULL;
  }

  /* Note: This is defined in a different module */
  p = PyPoint_AsPoint(obj);
  if (!p) {
    return NULL;
  }
  printf("%f %f\n", p->x, p->y);
  return Py_BuildValue("");
}

static PyMethodDef PtExampleMethods[] = {
  {"print_point", print_point, METH_VARARGS, "output a point"},
  { NULL, NULL, 0, NULL}
};

static struct PyModuleDef ptexamplemodule = {
  PyModuleDef_HEAD_INIT,
  "ptexample",           /* name of module */
  "A module that imports an API",  /* Doc string (may be NULL) */
  -1,                    /* Size of per-interpreter state or -1 */
  PtExampleMethods       /* Method table */
};

/* Module initialization function */
PyMODINIT_FUNC
PyInit_ptexample(void) {
  PyObject *m;

  m = PyModule_Create(&ptexamplemodule);
  if (m == NULL)
    return NULL;

  /* Import sample, loading its API functions */
  if (!import_sample()) {
    return NULL;
  }
```

```
    return m;
}
```

When compiling this new module, you don't even need to bother to link against any of the libraries or code from the other module. For example, you can just make a simple *setup.py* file like this:

```
# setup.py
from distutils.core import setup, Extension

setup(name='ptexample',
      ext_modules=[
        Extension('ptexample',
                  ['ptexample.c'],
                  include_dirs = [],  # May need pysample.h directory
                  )
          ]
)
```

If it all works, you'll find that your new extension function works perfectly with the C API functions defined in the other module:

```
>>> import sample
>>> p1 = sample.Point(2,3)
>>> p1
<capsule object "Point *" at 0x1004ea330>
>>> import ptexample
>>> ptexample.print_point(p1)
2.000000 3.000000
>>>
```

Discussion

This recipe relies on the fact that capsule objects can hold a pointer to anything you wish. In this case, the defining module populates a structure of function pointers, creates a capsule that points to it, and saves the capsule in a module-level attribute (e.g., `sample._point_api`).

Other modules can be programmed to pick up this attribute when imported and extract the underlying pointer. In fact, Python provides the `PyCapsule_Import()` utility function, which takes care of all the steps for you. You simply give it the name of the attribute (e.g., `sample._point_api`), and it will find the capsule and extract the pointer all in one step.

There are some C programming tricks involved in making exported functions look normal in other modules. In the *pysample.h* file, a pointer `_point_api` is used to point to the method table that was initialized in the exporting module. A related function `import_sample()` is used to perform the required capsule import and initialize this pointer. This function must be called before any functions are used. Normally, it would be called in during module initialization. Finally, a set of C preprocessor macros have been defined to transparently dispatch the API functions through the method table. The user just uses the original function names, but doesn't know about the extra indirection through these macros.

Finally, there is another important reason why you might use this technique to link modules together—it's actually easier and it keeps modules more cleanly decoupled. If you didn't want to use this recipe as shown, you might be able to cross-link modules using advanced features of shared libraries and the dynamic loader. For example, putting common API functions into a shared library and making sure that all extension modules link against that shared library. Yes, this works, but it can be tremendously messy in large systems. Essentially, this recipe cuts out all of that magic and allows modules to link to one another through Python's normal import mechanism and just a tiny number of capsule calls. For compilation of modules, you only need to worry about header files, not the hairy details of shared libraries.

Further information about providing C APIs for extension modules can be found in the Python documentation (*http://docs.python.org/3/extending/extending.html*).

15.6. Calling Python from C

Problem

You want to safely execute a Python callable from C and return a result back to C. For example, perhaps you are writing C code that wants to use a Python function as a callback.

Solution

Calling Python from C is mostly straightforward, but involves a number of tricky parts. The following C code shows an example of how to do it safely:

```
#include <Python.h>

/* Execute func(x,y) in the Python interpreter.  The
   arguments and return result of the function must
   be Python floats */

double call_func(PyObject *func, double x, double y) {
  PyObject *args;
  PyObject *kwargs;
  PyObject *result = 0;
  double retval;

  /* Make sure we own the GIL */
  PyGILState_STATE state = PyGILState_Ensure();
```

```
    /* Verify that func is a proper callable */
    if (!PyCallable_Check(func)) {
      fprintf(stderr,"call_func: expected a callable\n");
      goto fail;
    }
    /* Build arguments */
    args = Py_BuildValue("(dd)", x, y);
    kwargs = NULL;

    /* Call the function */
    result = PyObject_Call(func, args, kwargs);
    Py_DECREF(args);
    Py_XDECREF(kwargs);

    /* Check for Python exceptions (if any) */
    if (PyErr_Occurred()) {
      PyErr_Print();
      goto fail;
    }

    /* Verify the result is a float object */
    if (!PyFloat_Check(result)) {
      fprintf(stderr,"call_func: callable didn't return a float\n");
      goto fail;
    }

    /* Create the return value */
    retval = PyFloat_AsDouble(result);
    Py_DECREF(result);

    /* Restore previous GIL state and return */
    PyGILState_Release(state);
    return retval;

fail:
    Py_XDECREF(result);
    PyGILState_Release(state);
    abort();    // Change to something more appropriate
  }
```

To use this function, you need to have obtained a reference to an existing Python callable to pass in. There are many ways that you can go about doing that, such as having a callable object passed into an extension module or simply writing C code to extract a symbol from an existing module.

Here is a simple example that shows calling a function from an embedded Python interpreter:

```
#include <Python.h>

/* Definition of call_func() same as above */
...
```

```c
/* Load a symbol from a module */
PyObject *import_name(const char *modname, const char *symbol) {
  PyObject *u_name, *module;
  u_name = PyUnicode_FromString(modname);
  module = PyImport_Import(u_name);
  Py_DECREF(u_name);
  return PyObject_GetAttrString(module, symbol);
}

/* Simple embedding example */
int main() {
  PyObject *pow_func;
  double x;

  Py_Initialize();
  /* Get a reference to the math.pow function */
  pow_func = import_name("math","pow");

  /* Call it using our call_func() code */
  for (x = 0.0; x < 10.0; x += 0.1) {
    printf("%0.2f %0.2f\n", x, call_func(pow_func,x,2.0));
  }
  /* Done */
  Py_DECREF(pow_func);
  Py_Finalize();
  return 0;
}
```

To build this last example, you'll need to compile the C and link against the Python interpreter. Here is a Makefile that shows how you might do it (this is something that might require some amount of fiddling with on your machine):

```
all::
        cc -g embed.c -I/usr/local/include/python3.3m \
          -L/usr/local/lib/python3.3/config-3.3m -lpython3.3m
```

Compiling and running the resulting executable should produce output similar to this:

```
0.00 0.00
0.10 0.01
0.20 0.04
0.30 0.09
0.40 0.16
...
```

Here is a slightly different example that shows an extension function that receives a callable and some arguments and passes them to `call_func()` for the purposes of testing:

```c
/* Extension function for testing the C-Python callback */
PyObject *py_call_func(PyObject *self, PyObject *args) {
  PyObject *func;
```

```
    double x, y, result;
    if (!PyArg_ParseTuple(args,"Odd", &func,&x,&y)) {
      return NULL;
    }
    result = call_func(func, x, y);
    return Py_BuildValue("d", result);
}
```

Using this extension function, you could test it as follows:

```
>>> import sample
>>> def add(x,y):
...       return x+y
...
>>> sample.call_func(add,3,4)
7.0
>>>
```

Discussion

If you are calling Python from C, the most important thing to keep in mind is that C is generally going to be in charge. That is, C has the responsibility of creating the arguments, calling the Python function, checking for exceptions, checking types, extracting return values, and more.

As a first step, it is critical that you have a Python object representing the callable that you're going to invoke. This could be a function, class, method, built-in method, or anything that implements the __call__() operation. To verify that it's callable, use PyCallable_Check() as shown in this code fragment:

```
double call_func(PyObject *func, double x, double y) {
  ...
  /* Verify that func is a proper callable */
  if (!PyCallable_Check(func)) {
    fprintf(stderr,"call_func: expected a callable\n");
    goto fail;
  }
  ...
```

As an aside, handling errors in the C code is something that you will need to carefully study. As a general rule, you can't just raise a Python exception. Instead, errors will have to be handled in some other manner that makes sense to your C code. In the solution, we're using goto to transfer control to an error handling block that calls abort(). This causes the whole program to die, but in real code you would probably want to do something more graceful (e.g., return a status code). Keep in mind that C is in charge here, so there isn't anything comparable to just raising an exception. Error handling is something you'll have to engineer into the program somehow.

Calling a function is relatively straightforward—simply use PyObject_Call(), supplying it with the callable object, a tuple of arguments, and an optional dictionary of keyword arguments. To build the argument tuple or dictionary, you can use Py_Build Value(), as shown.

```
double call_func(PyObject *func, double x, double y) {
  PyObject *args;
  PyObject *kwargs;

  ...
  /* Build arguments */
  args = Py_BuildValue("(dd)", x, y);
  kwargs = NULL;

  /* Call the function */
  result = PyObject_Call(func, args, kwargs);
  Py_DECREF(args);
  Py_XDECREF(kwargs);
  ...
```

If there are no keyword arguments, you can pass NULL, as shown. After making the function call, you need to make sure that you clean up the arguments using Py_DE CREF() or Py_XDECREF(). The latter function safely allows the NULL pointer to be passed (which is ignored), which is why we're using it for cleaning up the optional keyword arguments.

After calling the Python function, you must check for the presence of exceptions. The PyErr_Occurred() function can be used to do this. Knowing what to do in response to an exception is tricky. Since you're working from C, you really don't have the exception machinery that Python has. Thus, you would have to set an error status code, log the error, or do some kind of sensible processing. In the solution, abort() is called for lack of a simpler alternative (besides, hardened C programmers will appreciate the abrupt crash):

```
  ...
  /* Check for Python exceptions (if any) */
  if (PyErr_Occurred()) {
    PyErr_Print();
    goto fail;
  }
  ...
fail:
  PyGILState_Release(state);
  abort();
```

Extracting information from the return value of calling a Python function is typically going to involve some kind of type checking and value extraction. To do this, you may have to use functions in the Python concrete objects layer (*http://docs.python.org/3/c-api/concrete.html*). In the solution, the code checks for and extracts the value of a Python float using PyFloat_Check() and PyFloat_AsDouble().

A final tricky part of calling into Python from C concerns the management of Python's global interpreter lock (GIL). Whenever Python is accessed from C, you need to make sure that the GIL is properly acquired and released. Otherwise, you run the risk of having the interpreter corrupt data or crash. The calls to `PyGILState_Ensure()` and `PyGIL State_Release()` make sure that it's done correctly:

```
double call_func(PyObject *func, double x, double y) {
  ...
  double retval;

  /* Make sure we own the GIL */
  PyGILState_STATE state = PyGILState_Ensure();
  ...
  /* Code that uses Python C API functions */
  ...
  /* Restore previous GIL state and return */
  PyGILState_Release(state);
  return retval;

fail:
  PyGILState_Release(state);
  abort();
}
```

Upon return, `PyGILState_Ensure()` always guarantees that the calling thread has exclusive access to the Python interpreter. This is true even if the calling C code is running a different thread that is unknown to the interpreter. At this point, the C code is free to use any Python C-API functions that it wants. Upon successful completion, `PyGIL State_Release()` is used to restore the interpreter back to its original state.

It is critical to note that every `PyGILState_Ensure()` call must be followed by a matching `PyGILState_Release()` call—even in cases where errors have occurred. In the solution, the use of a `goto` statement might look like a horrible design, but we're actually using it to transfer control to a common exit block that performs this required step. Think of the code after the `fail:` lable as serving the same purpose as code in a Python `final ly:` block.

If you write your C code using all of these conventions including management of the GIL, checking for exceptions, and thorough error checking, you'll find that you can reliably call into the Python interpreter from C—even in very complicated programs that utilize advanced programming techniques such as multithreading.

15.7. Releasing the GIL in C Extensions

Problem

You have C extension code in that you want to execute concurrently with other threads in the Python interpreter. To do this, you need to release and reacquire the global interpreter lock (GIL).

Solution

In C extension code, the GIL can be released and reacquired by inserting the following macros in the code:

```
#include "Python.h"
...

PyObject *pyfunc(PyObject *self, PyObject *args) {
    ...
    Py_BEGIN_ALLOW_THREADS
    // Threaded C code.  Must not use Python API functions
    ...
    Py_END_ALLOW_THREADS
    ...
    return result;
}
```

Discussion

The GIL can only safely be released if you can guarantee that no Python C API functions will be executed in the C code. Typical examples where the GIL might be released are in computationally intensive code that performs calculations on C arrays (e.g., in extensions such as numpy) or in code where blocking I/O operations are going to be performed (e.g., reading or writing on a file descriptor).

While the GIL is released, other Python threads are allowed to execute in the interpreter. The Py_END_ALLOW_THREADS macro blocks execution until the calling threads reacquires the GIL in the interpreter.

15.8. Mixing Threads from C and Python

Problem

You have a program that involves a mix of C, Python, and threads, but some of the threads are created from C outside the control of the Python interpreter. Moreover, certain threads utilize functions in the Python C API.

Solution

If you're going to mix C, Python, and threads together, you need to make sure you properly initialize and manage Python's global interpreter lock (GIL). To do this, include the following code somewhere in your C code and make sure it's called prior to creation of any threads:

```
#include <Python.h>

...
if (!PyEval_ThreadsInitialized()) {
  PyEval_InitThreads();
}
...
```

For any C code that involves Python objects or the Python C API, make sure you properly acquire and release the GIL first. This is done using `PyGILState_Ensure()` and `PyGILState_Release()`, as shown in the following:

```
...
/* Make sure we own the GIL */
PyGILState_STATE state = PyGILState_Ensure();

/* Use functions in the interpreter */
...
/* Restore previous GIL state and return */
PyGILState_Release(state);
...
```

Every call to `PyGILState_Ensure()` must have a matching call to `PyGILState_Release()`.

Discussion

In advanced applications involving C and Python, it is not uncommon to have many things going on at once—possibly involving a mix of a C code, Python code, C threads, and Python threads. As long as you diligently make sure the interpreter is properly initialized and that C code involving the interpreter has the proper GIL management calls, it all should work.

Be aware that the `PyGILState_Ensure()` call does not immediately preempt or interrupt the interpreter. If other code is currently executing, this function will block until that code decides to release the GIL. Internally, the interpreter performs periodic thread switching, so even if another thread is executing, the caller will eventually get to run (although it may have to wait for a while first).

15.9. Wrapping C Code with Swig

Problem

You have existing C code that you would like to access as a C extension module. You would like to do this using the Swig wrapper generator (*http://www.swig.org*).

Solution

Swig operates by parsing C header files and automatically creating extension code. To use it, you first need to have a C header file. For example, this header file for our sample code:

```
/* sample.h */

#include <math.h>
extern int gcd(int, int);
extern int in_mandel(double x0, double y0, int n);
extern int divide(int a, int b, int *remainder);
extern double avg(double *a, int n);

typedef struct Point {
    double x,y;
} Point;

extern double distance(Point *p1, Point *p2);
```

Once you have the header files, the next step is to write a Swig "interface" file. By convention, these files have a *.i* suffix and might look similar to the following:

```
// sample.i - Swig interface
%module sample
%{
#include "sample.h"
%}

/* Customizations */
%extend Point {
    /* Constructor for Point objects */
    Point(double x, double y) {
        Point *p = (Point *) malloc(sizeof(Point));
        p->x = x;
        p->y = y;
        return p;
    };
};

/* Map int *remainder as an output argument */
%include typemaps.i
%apply int *OUTPUT { int * remainder };
```

```
    /* Map the argument pattern (double *a, int n) to arrays */
    %typemap(in) (double *a, int n)(Py_buffer view) {
      view.obj = NULL;
      if (PyObject_GetBuffer($input, &view, PyBUF_ANY_CONTIGUOUS | PyBUF_FORMAT) == -1) {
        SWIG_fail;
      }
      if (strcmp(view.format,"d") != 0) {
        PyErr_SetString(PyExc_TypeError, "Expected an array of doubles");
        SWIG_fail;
      }
      $1 = (double *) view.buf;
      $2 = view.len / sizeof(double);
    }

    %typemap(freearg) (double *a, int n) {
      if (view$argnum.obj) {
        PyBuffer_Release(&view$argnum);
      }
    }

    /* C declarations to be included in the extension module */

    extern int gcd(int, int);
    extern int in_mandel(double x0, double y0, int n);
    extern int divide(int a, int b, int *remainder);
    extern double avg(double *a, int n);

    typedef struct Point {
        double x,y;
    } Point;

    extern double distance(Point *p1, Point *p2);
```

Once you have written the interface file, Swig is invoked as a command-line tool:

```
bash % swig -python -py3 sample.i
bash %
```

The output of swig is two files, *sample_wrap.c* and *sample.py*. The latter file is what users import. The *sample_wrap.c* file is C code that needs to be compiled into a supporting module called _sample. This is done using the same techniques as for normal extension modules. For example, you create a *setup.py* file like this:

```
# setup.py
from distutils.core import setup, Extension

setup(name='sample',
      py_modules=['sample.py'],
      ext_modules=[
        Extension('_sample',
                  ['sample_wrap.c'],
                  include_dirs = [],
                  define_macros = [],
```

```
                         undef_macros = [],
                         library_dirs = [],
                         libraries = ['sample']
                         )
             ]
    )
```

To compile and test, run python3 on the *setup.py* file like this:

```
bash % python3 setup.py build_ext --inplace
running build_ext
building '_sample' extension
gcc -fno-strict-aliasing -DNDEBUG -g -fwrapv -O3 -Wall -Wstrict-prototypes
-I/usr/local/include/python3.3m -c sample_wrap.c
 -o build/temp.macosx-10.6-x86_64-3.3/sample_wrap.o
sample_wrap.c: In function 'SWIG_InitializeModule':
sample_wrap.c:3589: warning: statement with no effect
gcc -bundle -undefined dynamic_lookup build/temp.macosx-10.6-x86_64-3.3/sample.o
 build/temp.macosx-10.6-x86_64-3.3/sample_wrap.o -o _sample.so -lsample
bash %
```

If all of this works, you'll find that you can use the resulting C extension module in a straightforward way. For example:

```
>>> import sample
>>> sample.gcd(42,8)
2
>>> sample.divide(42,8)
[5, 2]
>>> p1 = sample.Point(2,3)
>>> p2 = sample.Point(4,5)
>>> sample.distance(p1,p2)
2.8284271247461903
>>> p1.x
2.0
>>> p1.y
3.0
>>> import array
>>> a = array.array('d',[1,2,3])
>>> sample.avg(a)
2.0
>>>
```

Discussion

Swig is one of the oldest tools for building extension modules, dating back to Python 1.4. However, recent versions currently support Python 3. The primary users of Swig tend to have large existing bases of C that they are trying to access using Python as a high-level control language. For instance, a user might have C code containing thousands of functions and various data structures that they would like to access from Python. Swig can automate much of the wrapper generation process.

All Swig interfaces tend to start with a short preamble like this:

```
%module sample
%{
#include "sample.h"
%}
```

This merely declares the name of the extension module and specifies C header files that must be included to make everything compile (the code enclosed in %{ and %} is pasted directly into the output code so this is where you put all included files and other definitions needed for compilation).

The bottom part of a Swig interface is a listing of C declarations that you want to be included in the extension. This is often just copied from the header files. In our example, we just pasted in the header file directly like this:

```
%module sample
%{
#include "sample.h"
%}
...
extern int gcd(int, int);
extern int in_mandel(double x0, double y0, int n);
extern int divide(int a, int b, int *remainder);
extern double avg(double *a, int n);

typedef struct Point {
    double x,y;
} Point;

extern double distance(Point *p1, Point *p2);
```

It is important to stress that these declarations are telling Swig what you want to include in the Python module. It is quite common to edit the list of declarations or to make modifications as appropriate. For example, if you didn't want certain declarations to be included, you would remove them from the declaration list.

The most complicated part of using Swig is the various customizations that it can apply to the C code. This is a huge topic that can't be covered in great detail here, but a number of such customizations are shown in this recipe.

The first customization involving the %extend directive allows methods to be attached to existing structure and class definitions. In the example, this is used to add a constructor method to the Point structure. This customization makes it possible to use the structure like this:

```
>>> p1 = sample.Point(2,3)
>>>
```

If omitted, then Point objects would have to be created in a much more clumsy manner like this:

```
>>> # Usage if %extend Point is omitted
>>> p1 = sample.Point()
>>> p1.x = 2.0
>>> p1.y = 3
```

The second customization involving the inclusion of the `typemaps.i` library and the `%apply` directive is instructing Swig that the argument signature `int *remainder` is to be treated as an output value. This is actually a pattern matching rule. In all declarations that follow, any time `int *remainder` is encountered, it is handled as output. This customization is what makes the `divide()` function return two values:

```
>>> sample.divide(42,8)
[5, 2]
>>>
```

The last customization involving the `%typemap` directive is probably the most advanced feature shown here. A typemap is a rule that gets applied to specific argument patterns in the input. In this recipe, a typemap has been written to match the argument pattern (`double *a, int n`). Inside the typemap is a fragment of C code that tells Swig how to convert a Python object into the associated C arguments. The code in this recipe has been written using Python's buffer protocol in an attempt to match any input argument that looks like an array of doubles (e.g., NumPy arrays, arrays created by the `array` module, etc.). See Recipe 15.3.

Within the typemap code, substitutions such as $1 and $2 refer to variables that hold the converted values of the C arguments in the typemap pattern (e.g., $1 maps to `double *a` and $2 maps to `int n`). $input refers to a `PyObject *` argument that was supplied as an input argument. $argnum is the argument number.

Writing and understanding typemaps is often the bane of programmers using Swig. Not only is the code rather cryptic, but you need to understand the intricate details of both the Python C API and the way in which Swig interacts with it. The Swig documentation has many more examples and detailed information.

Nevertheless, if you have a lot of a C code to expose as an extension module, Swig can be a very powerful tool for doing it. The key thing to keep in mind is that Swig is basically a compiler that processes C declarations, but with a powerful pattern matching and customization component that lets you change the way in which specific declarations and types get processed. More information can be found at Swig's website (*http://www.swig.org*), including Python-specific documentation (*http://www.swig.org/Doc2.0/Python.html*).

15.10. Wrapping Existing C Code with Cython

Problem

You want to use Cython (*http://cython.org*) to make a Python extension module that wraps around an existing C library.

Solution

Making an extension module with Cython looks somewhat similar to writing a hand-written extension, in that you will be creating a collection of wrapper functions. However, unlike previous recipes, you won't be doing this in C—the code will look a lot more like Python.

As preliminaries, assume that the sample code shown in the introduction to this chapter has been compiled into a C library called `libsample`. Start by creating a file named *csample.pxd* that looks like this:

```
# csample.pxd
#
# Declarations of "external" C functions and structures

cdef extern from "sample.h":
    int gcd(int, int)
    bint in_mandel(double, double, int)
    int divide(int, int, int *)
    double avg(double *, int) nogil

    ctypedef struct Point:
        double x
        double y

    double distance(Point *, Point *)
```

This file serves the same purpose in Cython as a C header file. The initial declaration `cdef extern from "sample.h"` declares the required C header file. Declarations that follow are taken from that header. The name of this file is *csample.pxd*, not *sample.pxd*—this is important.

Next, create a file named *sample.pyx*. This file will define wrappers that bridge the Python interpreter to the underlying C code declared in the *csample.pxd* file:

```
# sample.pyx

# Import the low-level C declarations
cimport csample

# Import some functionality from Python and the C stdlib
from cpython.pycapsule cimport *
```

```
from libc.stdlib cimport malloc, free

# Wrappers
def gcd(unsigned int x, unsigned int y):
    return csample.gcd(x, y)

def in_mandel(x, y, unsigned int n):
    return csample.in_mandel(x, y, n)

def divide(x, y):
    cdef int rem
    quot = csample.divide(x, y, &rem)
    return quot, rem

def avg(double[:] a):
    cdef:
        int sz
        double result

    sz = a.size
    with nogil:
        result = csample.avg(<double *> &a[0], sz)
    return result

# Destructor for cleaning up Point objects
cdef del_Point(object obj):
    pt = <csample.Point *> PyCapsule_GetPointer(obj,"Point")
    free(<void *> pt)

# Create a Point object and return as a capsule
def Point(double x,double y):
    cdef csample.Point *p
    p = <csample.Point *> malloc(sizeof(csample.Point))
    if p == NULL:
        raise MemoryError("No memory to make a Point")
    p.x = x
    p.y = y
    return PyCapsule_New(<void *>p,"Point",<PyCapsule_Destructor>del_Point)

def distance(p1, p2):
    pt1 = <csample.Point *> PyCapsule_GetPointer(p1,"Point")
    pt2 = <csample.Point *> PyCapsule_GetPointer(p2,"Point")
    return csample.distance(pt1,pt2)
```

Various details of this file will be covered further in the discussion section. Finally, to
build the extension module, create a *setup.py* file that looks like this:

```
from distutils.core import setup
from distutils.extension import Extension
from Cython.Distutils import build_ext

ext_modules = [
    Extension('sample',
```

```
                    ['sample.pyx'],
                    libraries=['sample'],
                    library_dirs=['.'])]
    setup(
      name = 'Sample extension module',
      cmdclass = {'build_ext': build_ext},
      ext_modules = ext_modules
    )
```

To build the resulting module for experimentation, type this:

```
bash % python3 setup.py build_ext --inplace
running build_ext
cythoning sample.pyx to sample.c
building 'sample' extension
gcc -fno-strict-aliasing -DNDEBUG -g -fwrapv -O3 -Wall -Wstrict-prototypes
  -I/usr/local/include/python3.3m -c sample.c
  -o build/temp.macosx-10.6-x86_64-3.3/sample.o
gcc -bundle -undefined dynamic_lookup build/temp.macosx-10.6-x86_64-3.3/sample.o
  -L. -lsample -o sample.so
bash %
```

If it works, you should have an extension module sample.so that can be used as shown
in the following example:

```
>>> import sample
>>> sample.gcd(42,10)
2
>>> sample.in_mandel(1,1,400)
False
>>> sample.in_mandel(0,0,400)
True
>>> sample.divide(42,10)
(4, 2)
>>> import array
>>> a = array.array('d',[1,2,3])
>>> sample.avg(a)
2.0
>>> p1 = sample.Point(2,3)
>>> p2 = sample.Point(4,5)
>>> p1
<capsule object "Point" at 0x1005d1e70>
>>> p2
<capsule object "Point" at 0x1005d1ea0>
>>> sample.distance(p1,p2)
2.8284271247461903
>>>
```

Discussion

This recipe incorporates a number of advanced features discussed in prior recipes, including manipulation of arrays, wrapping opaque pointers, and releasing the GIL. Each of these parts will be discussed in turn, but it may help to review earlier recipes first.

At a high level, using Cython is modeled after C. The *.pxd* files merely contain C definitions (similar to *.h* files) and the *.pyx* files contain implementation (similar to a *.c* file). The cimport statement is used by Cython to import definitions from a *.pxd* file. This is different than using a normal Python import statement, which would load a regular Python module.

Although *.pxd* files contain definitions, they are not used for the purpose of automatically creating extension code. Thus, you still have to write simple wrapper functions. For example, even though the *csample.pxd* file declares int gcd(int, int) as a function, you still have to write a small wrapper for it in *sample.pyx*. For instance:

```
cimport csample

def gcd(unsigned int x, unsigned int y):
    return csample.gcd(x,y)
```

For simple functions, you don't have to do too much. Cython will generate wrapper code that properly converts the arguments and return value. The C data types attached to the arguments are optional. However, if you include them, you get additional error checking for free. For example, if someone calls this function with negative values, an exception is generated:

```
>>> sample.gcd(-10,2)
Traceback (most recent call last):
  File "<stdin>", line 1, in <module>
  File "sample.pyx", line 7, in sample.gcd (sample.c:1284)
    def gcd(unsigned int x,unsigned int y):
OverflowError: can't convert negative value to unsigned int
>>>
```

If you want to add additional checking to the wrapper, just use additional wrapper code. For example:

```
def gcd(unsigned int x, unsigned int y):
    if x <= 0:
        raise ValueError("x must be > 0")
    if y <= 0:
        raise ValueError("y must be > 0")
    return csample.gcd(x,y)
```

The declaration of in_mandel() in the *csample.pxd* file has an interesting, but subtle definition. In that file, the function is declared as returning a bint instead of an int. This causes the function to create a proper Boolean value from the result instead of a simple integer. So, a return value of 0 gets mapped to False and 1 to True.

Within the Cython wrappers, you have the option of declaring C data types in addition to using all of the usual Python objects. The wrapper for `divide()` shows an example of this as well as how to handle a pointer argument.

```
def divide(x,y):
    cdef int rem
    quot = csample.divide(x,y,&rem)
    return quot, rem
```

Here, the `rem` variable is explicitly declared as a C `int` variable. When passed to the underlying `divide()` function, `&rem` makes a pointer to it just as in C.

The code for the `avg()` function illustrates some more advanced features of Cython. First the declaration `def avg(double[:] a)` declares `avg()` as taking a one-dimensional memoryview of `double` values. The amazing part about this is that the resulting function will accept any compatible array object, including those created by libraries such as `numpy`. For example:

```
>>> import array
>>> a = array.array('d',[1,2,3])
>>> import numpy
>>> b = numpy.array([1., 2., 3.])
>>> import sample
>>> sample.avg(a)
2.0
>>> sample.avg(b)
2.0
>>>
```

In the wrapper, `a.size` and `&a[0]` refer to the number of array items and underlying pointer, respectively. The syntax `<double *> &a[0]` is how you type cast pointers to a different type if necessary. This is needed to make sure the C `avg()` receives a pointer of the correct type. Refer to the next recipe for some more advanced usage of Cython memoryviews.

In addition to working with general arrays, the `avg()` example also shows how to work with the global interpreter lock. The statement `with nogil:` declares a block of code as executing without the GIL. Inside this block, it is illegal to work with any kind of normal Python object—only objects and functions declared as `cdef` can be used. In addition to that, external functions must explicitly declare that they can execute without the GIL. Thus, in the *csample.pxd* file, the `avg()` is declared as `double avg(double *, int) nogil`.

The handling of the `Point` structure presents a special challenge. As shown, this recipe treats `Point` objects as opaque pointers using capsule objects, as described in Recipe 15.4. However, to do this, the underlying Cython code is a bit more complicated. First, the following imports are being used to bring in definitions of functions from the C library and Python C API:

```
from cpython.pycapsule cimport *
from libc.stdlib cimport malloc, free
```

The function del_Point() and Point() use this functionality to create a capsule object that wraps around a Point * pointer. The declaration cdef del_Point() declares del_Point() as a function that is only accessible from Cython and not Python. Thus, this function will not be visible to the outside—instead, it's used as a callback function to clean up memory allocated by the capsule. Calls to functions such as PyCapsule_New(), PyCapsule_GetPointer() are directly from the Python C API and are used in the same way.

The distance() function has been written to extract pointers from the capsule objects created by Point(). One notable thing here is that you simply don't have to worry about exception handling. If a bad object is passed, PyCapsule_GetPointer() raises an exception, but Cython already knows to look for it and propagate it out of the distance() function if it occurs.

A downside to the handling of Point structures is that they will be completely opaque in this implementation. You won't be able to peek inside or access any of their attributes. There is an alternative approach to wrapping, which is to define an extension type, as shown in this code:

```
# sample.pyx

cimport csample
from libc.stdlib cimport malloc, free
...

cdef class Point:
    cdef csample.Point *_c_point
    def __cinit__(self, double x, double y):
        self._c_point = <csample.Point *> malloc(sizeof(csample.Point))
        self._c_point.x = x
        self._c_point.y = y

    def __dealloc__(self):
        free(self._c_point)

    property x:
        def __get__(self):
            return self._c_point.x
        def __set__(self, value):
            self._c_point.x = value

    property y:
        def __get__(self):
            return self._c_point.y
        def __set__(self, value):
            self._c_point.y = value
```

```
def distance(Point p1, Point p2):
    return csample.distance(p1._c_point, p2._c_point)
```

Here, the cdef class Point is declaring Point as an extension type. The class variable cdef csample.Point *_c_point is declaring an instance variable that holds a pointer to an underlying Point structure in C. The __cinit__() and __dealloc__() methods create and destroy the underlying C structure using malloc() and free() calls. The property x and property y declarations give code that gets and sets the underlying structure attributes. The wrapper for distance() has also been suitably modified to accept instances of the Point extension type as arguments, but pass the underlying pointer to the C function.

Making this change, you will find that the code for manipulating Point objects is more natural:

```
>>> import sample
>>> p1 = sample.Point(2,3)
>>> p2 = sample.Point(4,5)
>>> p1
<sample.Point object at 0x100447288>
>>> p2
<sample.Point object at 0x1004472a0>
>>> p1.x
2.0
>>> p1.y
3.0
>>> sample.distance(p1,p2)
2.8284271247461903
>>>
```

This recipe has illustrated many of Cython's core features that you might be able to extrapolate to more complicated kinds of wrapping. However, you will definitely want to read more of the official documentation (*http://docs.cython.org*) to do more.

The next few recipes also illustrate a few additional Cython features.

15.11. Using Cython to Write High-Performance Array Operations

Problem

You would like to write some high-performance array processing functions to operate on arrays from libraries such as NumPy. You've heard that tools such as Cython can make this easier, but aren't sure how to do it.

Solution

As an example, consider the following code which shows a Cython function for clipping the values in a simple one-dimensional array of doubles:

```
# sample.pyx (Cython)

cimport cython

@cython.boundscheck(False)
@cython.wraparound(False)
cpdef clip(double[:] a, double min, double max, double[:] out):
    '''
    Clip the values in a to be between min and max. Result in out
    '''
    if min > max:
        raise ValueError("min must be <= max")
    if a.shape[0] != out.shape[0]:
        raise ValueError("input and output arrays must be the same size")
    for i in range(a.shape[0]):
        if a[i] < min:
            out[i] = min
        elif a[i] > max:
            out[i] = max
        else:
            out[i] = a[i]
```

To compile and build the extension, you'll need a *setup.py* file such as the following (use `python3 setup.py build_ext --inplace` to build it):

```
from distutils.core import setup
from distutils.extension import Extension
from Cython.Distutils import build_ext

ext_modules = [
    Extension('sample',
              ['sample.pyx'])
]

setup(
  name = 'Sample app',
  cmdclass = {'build_ext': build_ext},
  ext_modules = ext_modules
)
```

You will find that the resulting function clips arrays, and that it works with many different kinds of array objects. For example:

```
>>> # array module example
>>> import sample
>>> import array
>>> a = array.array('d',[1,-3,4,7,2,0])
>>> a
```

```
array('d', [1.0, -3.0, 4.0, 7.0, 2.0, 0.0])
>>> sample.clip(a,1,4,a)
>>> a
array('d', [1.0, 1.0, 4.0, 4.0, 2.0, 1.0])

>>> # numpy example
>>> import numpy
>>> b = numpy.random.uniform(-10,10,size=1000000)
>>> b
array([-9.55546017,  7.45599334,  0.69248932, ...,  0.69583148,
        -3.86290931,  2.37266888])
>>> c = numpy.zeros_like(b)
>>> c
array([ 0.,  0.,  0., ...,  0.,  0.,  0.])
>>> sample.clip(b,-5,5,c)
>>> c
array([-5.        ,  5.        ,  0.69248932, ...,  0.69583148,
        -3.86290931,  2.37266888])
>>> min(c)
-5.0
>>> max(c)
5.0
>>>
```

You will also find that the resulting code is fast. The following session puts our implementation in a head-to-head battle with the clip() function already present in numpy:

```
>>> timeit('numpy.clip(b,-5,5,c)','from __main__ import b,c,numpy',number=1000)
8.093049556000551
>>> timeit('sample.clip(b,-5,5,c)','from __main__ import b,c,sample',
...         number=1000)
3.760528204000366
>>>
```

As you can see, it's quite a bit faster—an interesting result considering the core of the NumPy version is written in C.

Discussion

This recipe utilizes Cython typed memoryviews, which greatly simplify code that operates on arrays. The declaration cpdef clip() declares clip() as both a C-level and Python-level function. In Cython, this is useful, because it means that the function call is more efficently called by other Cython functions (e.g., if you want to invoke clip() from a different Cython function).

The typed parameters double[:] a and double[:] out declare those parameters as one-dimensional arrays of doubles. As input, they will access any array object that properly implements the memoryview interface, as described in PEP 3118 (*http://www.python.org/dev/peps/pep-3118*). This includes arrays from NumPy and from the built-in array library.

When writing code that produces a result that is also an array, you should follow the convention shown of having an output parameter as shown. This places the responsibility of creating the output array on the caller and frees the code from having to know too much about the specific details of what kinds of arrays are being manipulated (it just assumes the arrays are already in-place and only needs to perform a few basic sanity checks such as making sure their sizes are compatible). In libraries such as NumPy, it is relatively easy to create output arrays using functions such as numpy.zeros() or numpy.zeros_like(). Alternatively, to create uninitialized arrays, you can use num py.empty() or numpy.empty_like(). This will be slightly faster if you're about to over-write the array contents with a result.

In the implementation of your function, you simply write straightforward looking array processing code using indexing and array lookups (e.g., a[i], out[i], and so forth). Cython will take steps to make sure these produce efficient code.

The two decorators that precede the definition of clip() are a few optional performance optimizations. @cython.boundscheck(False) eliminates all array bounds checking and can be used if you know the indexing won't go out of range. @cython.wrap around(False) eliminates the handling of negative array indices as wrapping around to the end of the array (like with Python lists). The inclusion of these decorators can make the code run substantially faster (almost 2.5 times faster on this example when tested).

Whenever working with arrays, careful study and experimentation with the underlying algorithm can also yield large speedups. For example, consider this variant of the clip() function that uses conditional expressions:

```
@cython.boundscheck(False)
@cython.wraparound(False)
cpdef clip(double[:] a, double min, double max, double[:] out):
    if min > max:
        raise ValueError("min must be <= max")
    if a.shape[0] != out.shape[0]:
        raise ValueError("input and output arrays must be the same size")
    for i in range(a.shape[0]):
        out[i] = (a[i] if a[i] < max else max) if a[i] > min else min
```

When tested, this version of the code runs over 50% faster (2.44s versus 3.76s on the timeit() test shown earlier).

At this point, you might be wondering how this code would stack up against a hand-written C version. For example, perhaps you write the following C function and craft a handwritten extension to using techniques shown in earlier recipes:

```
void clip(double *a, int n, double min, double max, double *out) {
    double x;
    for (; n >= 0; n--, a++, out++) {
        x = *a;
```

```
        *out = x > max ? max : (x < min ? min : x);
    }
}
```

The extension code for this isn't shown, but after experimenting, we found that a hand-crafted C extension ran more than 10% slower than the version created by Cython. The bottom line is that the code runs a lot faster than you might think.

There are several extensions that can be made to the solution code. For certain kinds of array operations, it might make sense to release the GIL so that multiple threads can run in parallel. To do that, modify the code to include the with nogil: statement:

```
@cython.boundscheck(False)
@cython.wraparound(False)
cpdef clip(double[:] a, double min, double max, double[:] out):
    if min > max:
        raise ValueError("min must be <= max")
    if a.shape[0] != out.shape[0]:
        raise ValueError("input and output arrays must be the same size")
    with nogil:
        for i in range(a.shape[0]):
            out[i] = (a[i] if a[i] < max else max) if a[i] > min else min
```

If you want to write a version of the code that operates on two-dimensional arrays, here is what it might look like:

```
@cython.boundscheck(False)
@cython.wraparound(False)
cpdef clip2d(double[:,:] a, double min, double max, double[:,:] out):
    if min > max:
        raise ValueError("min must be <= max")
    for n in range(a.ndim):
        if a.shape[n] != out.shape[n]:
            raise TypeError("a and out have different shapes")
    for i in range(a.shape[0]):
        for j in range(a.shape[1]):
            if a[i,j] < min:
                out[i,j] = min
            elif a[i,j] > max:
                out[i,j] = max
            else:
                out[i,j] = a[i,j]
```

Hopefully it's not lost on the reader that all of the code in this recipe is not tied to any specific array library (e.g., NumPy). That gives the code a great deal of flexibility. However, it's also worth noting that dealing with arrays can be significantly more complicated once multiple dimensions, strides, offsets, and other factors are introduced. Those topics are beyond the scope of this recipe, but more information can be found in PEP 3118 (*http://www.python.org/dev/peps/pep-3118*). The Cython documentation on "typed memoryviews" (*http://docs.cython.org/src/userguide/memoryviews.html*) is also essential reading.

15.12. Turning a Function Pointer into a Callable

Problem

You have (somehow) obtained the memory address of a compiled function, but want to turn it into a Python callable that you can use as an extension function.

Solution

The `ctypes` module can be used to create Python callables that wrap around arbitrary memory addresses. The following example shows how to obtain the raw, low-level address of a C function and how to turn it back into a callable object:

```
>>> import ctypes
>>> lib = ctypes.cdll.LoadLibrary(None)
>>> # Get the address of sin() from the C math library
>>> addr = ctypes.cast(lib.sin, ctypes.c_void_p).value
>>> addr
140735505915760

>>> # Turn the address into a callable function
>>> functype = ctypes.CFUNCTYPE(ctypes.c_double, ctypes.c_double)
>>> func = functype(addr)
>>> func
<CFunctionType object at 0x1006816d0>

>>> # Call the resulting function
>>> func(2)
0.9092974268256817
>>> func(0)
0.0
>>>
```

Discussion

To make a callable, you must first create a `CFUNCTYPE` instance. The first argument to `CFUNCTYPE()` is the return type. Subsequent arguments are the types of the arguments. Once you have defined the function type, you wrap it around an integer memory address to create a callable object. The resulting object is used like any normal function accessed through `ctypes`.

This recipe might look rather cryptic and low level. However, it is becoming increasingly common for programs and libraries to utilize advanced code generation techniques like just in-time compilation, as found in libraries such as LLVM.

For example, here is a simple example that uses the `llvmpy` extension (*http://www.llvmpy.org*) to make a small assembly function, obtain a function pointer to it, and turn it into a Python callable:

```
>>> from llvm.core import Module, Function, Type, Builder
>>> mod = Module.new('example')
>>> f = Function.new(mod,Type.function(Type.double(), \
                    [Type.double(), Type.double()], False), 'foo')
>>> block = f.append_basic_block('entry')
>>> builder = Builder.new(block)
>>> x2 = builder.fmul(f.args[0],f.args[0])
>>> y2 = builder.fmul(f.args[1],f.args[1])
>>> r = builder.fadd(x2,y2)
>>> builder.ret(r)
<llvm.core.Instruction object at 0x10078e990>
>>> from llvm.ee import ExecutionEngine
>>> engine = ExecutionEngine.new(mod)
>>> ptr = engine.get_pointer_to_function(f)
>>> ptr
4325863440
>>> foo = ctypes.CFUNCTYPE(ctypes.c_double, ctypes.c_double, ctypes.c_double)(ptr)

>>> # Call the resulting function
>>> foo(2,3)
13.0
>>> foo(4,5)
41.0
>>> foo(1,2)
5.0
>>>
```

It goes without saying that doing anything wrong at this level will probably cause the Python interpreter to die a horrible death. Keep in mind that you're directly working with machine-level memory addresses and native machine code—not Python functions.

15.13. Passing NULL-Terminated Strings to C Libraries

Problem

You are writing an extension module that needs to pass a NULL-terminated string to a C library. However, you're not entirely sure how to do it with Python's Unicode string implementation.

Solution

Many C libraries include functions that operate on NULL-terminated strings declared as type char *. Consider the following C function that we will use for the purposes of illustration and testing:

```
void print_chars(char *s) {
    while (*s) {
        printf("%2x ", (unsigned char) *s);
```

```
        s++;
    }
    printf("\n");
}
```

This function simply prints out the hex representation of individual characters so that the passed strings can be easily debugged. For example:

```
print_chars("Hello");   // Outputs: 48 65 6c 6c 6f
```

For calling such a C function from Python, you have a few choices. First, you could restrict it to only operate on bytes using "y" conversion code to PyArg_ParseTuple() like this:

```
static PyObject *py_print_chars(PyObject *self, PyObject *args) {
    char *s;

    if (!PyArg_ParseTuple(args, "y", &s)) {
        return NULL;
    }
    print_chars(s);
    Py_RETURN_NONE;
}
```

The resulting function operates as follows. Carefully observe how bytes with embedded NULL bytes and Unicode strings are rejected:

```
>>> print_chars(b'Hello World')
48 65 6c 6c 6f 20 57 6f 72 6c 64
>>> print_chars(b'Hello\x00World')
Traceback (most recent call last):
  File "<stdin>", line 1, in <module>
TypeError: must be bytes without null bytes, not bytes
>>> print_chars('Hello World')
Traceback (most recent call last):
  File "<stdin>", line 1, in <module>
TypeError: 'str' does not support the buffer interface
>>>
```

If you want to pass Unicode strings instead, use the "s" format code to PyArg_Parse Tuple() such as this:

```
static PyObject *py_print_chars(PyObject *self, PyObject *args) {
    char *s;

    if (!PyArg_ParseTuple(args, "s", &s)) {
        return NULL;
    }
    print_chars(s);
    Py_RETURN_NONE;
}
```

When used, this will automatically convert all strings to a NULL-terminated UTF-8 encoding. For example:

```
>>> print_chars('Hello World')
48 65 6c 6c 6f 20 57 6f 72 6c 64
>>> print_chars('Spicy Jalape\u00f1o')  # Note: UTF-8 encoding
53 70 69 63 79 20 4a 61 6c 61 70 65 c3 b1 6f
>>> print_chars('Hello\x00World')
Traceback (most recent call last):
  File "<stdin>", line 1, in <module>
TypeError: must be str without null characters, not str
>>> print_chars(b'Hello World')
Traceback (most recent call last):
  File "<stdin>", line 1, in <module>
TypeError: must be str, not bytes
>>>
```

If for some reason, you are working directly with a PyObject * and can't use PyArg_Par seTuple( ), the following code samples show how you can check and extract a suitable char * reference, from both a bytes and string object:

```
/* Some Python Object (obtained somehow) */
PyObject *obj;

/* Conversion from bytes */
{
   char *s;
   s = PyBytes_AsString(o);
   if (!s) {
      return NULL;    /* TypeError already raised */
   }
   print_chars(s);
}

/* Conversion to UTF-8 bytes from a string */
{
   PyObject *bytes;
   char *s;
   if (!PyUnicode_Check(obj)) {
      PyErr_SetString(PyExc_TypeError, "Expected string");
      return NULL;
   }
   bytes = PyUnicode_AsUTF8String(obj);
   s = PyBytes_AsString(bytes);
   print_chars(s);
   Py_DECREF(bytes);
}
```

Both of the preceding conversions guarantee NULL-terminated data, but they do not check for embedded NULL bytes elsewhere inside the string. Thus, that's something that you would need to check yourself if it's important.

Discussion

If it all possible, you should try to avoid writing code that relies on NULL-terminated strings since Python has no such requirement. It is almost always better to handle strings using the combination of a pointer and a size if possible. Nevertheless, sometimes you have to work with legacy C code that presents no other option.

Although it is easy to use, there is a hidden memory overhead associated with using the "s" format code to PyArg_ParseTuple() that is easy to overlook. When you write code that uses this conversion, a UTF-8 string is created and permanently attached to the original string object. If the original string contains non-ASCII characters, this makes the size of the string increase until it is garbage collected. For example:

```
>>> import sys
>>> s = 'Spicy Jalape\u00f1o'
>>> sys.getsizeof(s)
87
>>> print_chars(s)      # Passing string
53 70 69 63 79 20 4a 61 6c 61 70 65 c3 b1 6f
>>> sys.getsizeof(s)    # Notice increased size
103
>>>
```

If this growth in memory use is a concern, you should rewrite your C extension code to use the PyUnicode_AsUTF8String() function like this:

```
static PyObject *py_print_chars(PyObject *self, PyObject *args) {
  PyObject *o, *bytes;
  char *s;

  if (!PyArg_ParseTuple(args, "U", &o)) {
    return NULL;
  }
  bytes = PyUnicode_AsUTF8String(o);
  s = PyBytes_AsString(bytes);
  print_chars(s);
  Py_DECREF(bytes);
  Py_RETURN_NONE;
}
```

With this modification, a UTF-8 encoded string is created if needed, but then discarded after use. Here is the modified behavior:

```
>>> import sys
>>> s = 'Spicy Jalape\u00f1o'
>>> sys.getsizeof(s)
87
>>> print_chars(s)
53 70 69 63 79 20 4a 61 6c 61 70 65 c3 b1 6f
>>> sys.getsizeof(s)
87
>>>
```

If you are trying to pass NULL-terminated strings to functions wrapped via `ctypes`, be aware that `ctypes` only allows bytes to be passed and that it does not check for embedded NULL bytes. For example:

```
>>> import ctypes
>>> lib = ctypes.cdll.LoadLibrary("./libsample.so")
>>> print_chars = lib.print_chars
>>> print_chars.argtypes = (ctypes.c_char_p,)
>>> print_chars(b'Hello World')
48 65 6c 6c 6f 20 57 6f 72 6c 64
>>> print_chars(b'Hello\x00World')
48 65 6c 6c 6f
>>> print_chars('Hello World')
Traceback (most recent call last):
  File "<stdin>", line 1, in <module>
ctypes.ArgumentError: argument 1: <class 'TypeError'>: wrong type
>>>
```

If you want to pass a string instead of bytes, you need to perform a manual UTF-8 encoding first. For example:

```
>>> print_chars('Hello World'.encode('utf-8'))
48 65 6c 6c 6f 20 57 6f 72 6c 64
>>>
```

For other extension tools (e.g., Swig, Cython), careful study is probably in order should you decide to use them to pass strings to C code.

15.14. Passing Unicode Strings to C Libraries

Problem

You are writing an extension module that needs to pass a Python string to a C library function that may or may not know how to properly handle Unicode.

Solution

There are many issues to be concerned with here, but the main one is that existing C libraries won't understand Python's native representation of Unicode. Therefore, your challenge is to convert the Python string into a form that can be more easily understood by C libraries.

For the purposes of illustration, here are two C functions that operate on string data and output it for the purposes of debugging and experimentation. One uses bytes provided in the form `char *`, `int`, whereas the other uses wide characters in the form `wchar_t *`, `int`:

```
void print_chars(char *s, int len) {
    int n = 0;
```

```
    while (n < len) {
      printf("%2x ", (unsigned char) s[n]);
      n++;
    }
    printf("\n");
}

void print_wchars(wchar_t *s, int len) {
  int n = 0;
  while (n < len) {
    printf("%x ", s[n]);
    n++;
  }
  printf("\n");
}
```

For the byte-oriented function print_chars(), you need to convert Python strings into a suitable byte encoding such as UTF-8. Here is a sample extension function that does this:

```
static PyObject *py_print_chars(PyObject *self, PyObject *args) {
  char *s;
  Py_ssize_t  len;

  if (!PyArg_ParseTuple(args, "s#", &s, &len)) {
    return NULL;
  }
  print_chars(s, len);
  Py_RETURN_NONE;
}
```

For library functions that work with the machine native wchar_t type, you can write extension code such as this:

```
static PyObject *py_print_wchars(PyObject *self, PyObject *args) {
  wchar_t *s;
  Py_ssize_t  len;

  if (!PyArg_ParseTuple(args, "u#", &s, &len)) {
    return NULL;
  }
  print_wchars(s,len);
  Py_RETURN_NONE;
}
```

Here is an interactive session that illustrates how these functions work:

```
>>> s = 'Spicy Jalape\u00f1o'
>>> print_chars(s)
53 70 69 63 79 20 4a 61 6c 61 70 65 c3 b1 6f
>>> print_wchars(s)
53 70 69 63 79 20 4a 61 6c 61 70 65 f1 6f
>>>
```

Carefully observe how the byte-oriented function `print_chars()` is receiving UTF-8 encoded data, whereas `print_wchars()` is receiving the Unicode code point values.

Discussion

Before considering this recipe, you should first study the nature of the C library that you're accessing. For many C libraries, it might make more sense to pass bytes instead of a string. To do that, use this conversion code instead:

```
static PyObject *py_print_chars(PyObject *self, PyObject *args) {
  char *s;
  Py_ssize_t  len;

  /* accepts bytes, bytearray, or other byte-like object */
  if (!PyArg_ParseTuple(args, "y#", &s, &len)) {
    return NULL;
  }
  print_chars(s, len);
  Py_RETURN_NONE;
}
```

If you decide that you still want to pass strings, you need to know that Python 3 uses an adaptable string representation that is not entirely straightforward to map directly to C libraries using the standard types `char *` or `wchar_t *` See PEP 393 (*http://www.python.org/dev/peps/pep-0393*) for details. Thus, to present string data to C, some kind of conversion is almost always necessary. The s# and u# format codes to `PyArg_ParseTuple()` safely perform such conversions.

One potential downside is that such conversions cause the size of the original string object to permanently increase. Whenever a conversion is made, a copy of the converted data is kept and attached to the original string object so that it can be reused later. You can observe this effect:

```
>>> import sys
>>> s = 'Spicy Jalape\u00f1o'
>>> sys.getsizeof(s)
87
>>> print_chars(s)
53 70 69 63 79 20 4a 61 6c 61 70 65 c3 b1 6f
>>> sys.getsizeof(s)
103
>>> print_wchars(s)
53 70 69 63 79 20 4a 61 6c 61 70 65 f1 6f
>>> sys.getsizeof(s)
163
>>>
```

For small amounts of string data, this might not matter, but if you're doing large amounts of text processing in extensions, you may want to avoid the overhead. Here is an alternative implementation of the first extension function that avoids these memory inefficiencies:

```
static PyObject *py_print_chars(PyObject *self, PyObject *args) {
  PyObject *obj, *bytes;
  char *s;
  Py_ssize_t   len;

  if (!PyArg_ParseTuple(args, "U", &obj)) {
    return NULL;
  }
  bytes = PyUnicode_AsUTF8String(obj);
  PyBytes_AsStringAndSize(bytes, &s, &len);
  print_chars(s, len);
  Py_DECREF(bytes);
  Py_RETURN_NONE;
}
```

Avoiding memory overhead for wchar_t handling is much more tricky. Internally, Python stores strings using the most efficient representation possible. For example, strings containing nothing but ASCII are stored as arrays of bytes, whereas strings containing characters in the range U+0000 to U+FFFF use a two-byte representation. Since there isn't a single representation of the data, you can't just cast the internal array to wchar_t * and hope that it works. Instead, a wchar_t array has to be created and text copied into it. The "u#" format code to PyArg_ParseTuple() does this for you at the cost of efficiency (it attaches the resulting copy to the string object).

If you want to avoid this long-term memory overhead, your only real choice is to copy the Unicode data into a temporary array, pass it to the C library function, and then deallocate the array. Here is one possible implementation:

```
static PyObject *py_print_wchars(PyObject *self, PyObject *args) {
  PyObject *obj;
  wchar_t *s;
  Py_ssize_t len;

  if (!PyArg_ParseTuple(args, "U", &obj)) {
    return NULL;
  }
  if ((s = PyUnicode_AsWideCharString(obj, &len)) == NULL) {
    return NULL;
  }
  print_wchars(s, len);
  PyMem_Free(s);
  Py_RETURN_NONE;
}
```

In this implementation, PyUnicode_AsWideCharString() creates a temporary buffer of wchar_t characters and copies data into it. That buffer is passed to C and then released afterward. As of this writing, there seems to be a possible bug related to this behavior, as described at the Python issues page (*http://bugs.python.org/issue16254*).

If, for some reason you know that the C library takes the data in a different byte encoding than UTF-8, you can force Python to perform an appropriate conversion using extension code such as the following:

```
static PyObject *py_print_chars(PyObject *self, PyObject *args) {
  char *s = 0;
  int   len;
  if (!PyArg_ParseTuple(args, "es#", "encoding-name", &s, &len)) {
    return NULL;
  }
  print_chars(s, len);
  PyMem_Free(s);
  Py_RETURN_NONE;
}
```

Last, but not least, if you want to work directly with the characters in a Unicode string, here is an example that illustrates low-level access:

```
static PyObject *py_print_wchars(PyObject *self, PyObject *args) {
  PyObject *obj;
  int n, len;
  int kind;
  void *data;

  if (!PyArg_ParseTuple(args, "U", &obj)) {
    return NULL;
  }
  if (PyUnicode_READY(obj) < 0) {
    return NULL;
  }

  len = PyUnicode_GET_LENGTH(obj);
  kind = PyUnicode_KIND(obj);
  data = PyUnicode_DATA(obj);

  for (n = 0; n < len; n++) {
    Py_UCS4 ch = PyUnicode_READ(kind, data, n);
    printf("%x ", ch);
  }
  printf("\n");
  Py_RETURN_NONE;
}
```

In this code, the PyUnicode_KIND() and PyUnicode_DATA() macros are related to the variable-width storage of Unicode, as described in PEP 393 (*http://www.python.org/dev/peps/pep-0393*). The kind variable encodes information about the underlying storage (8-bit, 16-bit, or 32-bit) and data points the buffer. In reality, you don't need to do anything with these values as long as you pass them to the `PyUnicode_READ()` macro when extracting characters.

A few final words: when passing Unicode strings from Python to C, you should probably try to make it as simple as possible. If given the choice between an encoding such as UTF-8 or wide characters, choose UTF-8. Support for UTF-8 seems to be much more common, less trouble-prone, and better supported by the interpreter. Finally, make sure your review the documentation on Unicode handling (*http://docs.python.org/3/c-api/unicode.html*).

15.15. Converting C Strings to Python

Problem

You want to convert strings from C to Python bytes or a string object.

Solution

For C strings represented as a pair `char *`, `int`, you must decide whether or not you want the string presented as a raw byte string or as a Unicode string. Byte objects can be built using `Py_BuildValue()` as follows:

```
char *s;      /* Pointer to C string data */
int   len;    /* Length of data */

/* Make a bytes object */
PyObject *obj = Py_BuildValue("y#", s, len);
```

If you want to create a Unicode string and you know that s points to data encoded as UTF-8, you can use the following:

```
PyObject *obj = Py_BuildValue("s#", s, len);
```

If s is encoded in some other known encoding, you can make a string using `PyUnicode_Decode()` as follows:

```
PyObject *obj = PyUnicode_Decode(s, len, "encoding", "errors");

/* Examples /*
obj = PyUnicode_Decode(s, len, "latin-1", "strict");
obj = PyUnicode_Decode(s, len, "ascii", "ignore");
```

If you happen to have a wide string represented as a `wchar_t *`, `len` pair, there are a few options. First, you could use `Py_BuildValue()` as follows:

```
wchar_t *w;   /* Wide character string */
int len;      /* Length */

PyObject *obj = Py_BuildValue("u#", w, len);
```

Alternatively, you can use PyUnicode_FromWideChar():

```
PyObject *obj = PyUnicode_FromWideChar(w, len);
```

For wide character strings, no interpretation is made of the character data—it is assumed to be raw Unicode code points which are directly converted to Python.

Discussion

Conversion of strings from C to Python follow the same principles as I/O. Namely, the data from C must be explicitly decoded into a string according to some codec. Common encodings include ASCII, Latin-1, and UTF-8. If you're not entirely sure of the encoding or the data is binary, you're probably best off encoding the string as bytes instead.

When making an object, Python always copies the string data you provide. If necessary, it's up to you to release the C string afterward (if required). Also, for better reliability, you should try to create strings using both a pointer and a size rather than relying on NULL-terminated data.

15.16. Working with C Strings of Dubious Encoding

Problem

You are converting strings back and forth between C and Python, but the C encoding is of a dubious or unknown nature. For example, perhaps the C data is supposed to be UTF-8, but it's not being strictly enforced. You would like to write code that can handle malformed data in a graceful way that doesn't crash Python or destroy the string data in the process.

Solution

Here is some C data and a function that illustrates the nature of this problem:

```c
/* Some dubious string data (malformed UTF-8) */
const char *sdata = "Spicy Jalape\xc3\xb1o\xae";
int slen = 16;

/* Output character data */
void print_chars(char *s, int len) {
  int n = 0;
  while (n < len) {
    printf("%2x ", (unsigned char) s[n]);
    n++;
  }
  printf("\n");
}
```

In this code, the string `sdata` contains a mix of UTF-8 and malformed data. Nevertheless, if a user calls `print_chars(sdata, slen)` in C, it works fine.

Now suppose you want to convert the contents of `sdata` into a Python string. Further suppose you want to later pass that string to the `print_chars()` function through an extension. Here's how to do it in a way that exactly preserves the original data even though there are encoding problems:

```
/* Return the C string back to Python */
static PyObject *py_retstr(PyObject *self, PyObject *args) {
  if (!PyArg_ParseTuple(args, "")) {
    return NULL;
  }
  return PyUnicode_Decode(sdata, slen, "utf-8", "surrogateescape");
}

/* Wrapper for the print_chars() function */
static PyObject *py_print_chars(PyObject *self, PyObject *args) {
  PyObject *obj, *bytes;
  char *s = 0;
  Py_ssize_t   len;

  if (!PyArg_ParseTuple(args, "U", &obj)) {
    return NULL;
  }

  if ((bytes = PyUnicode_AsEncodedString(obj,"utf-8","surrogateescape"))
        == NULL) {
    return NULL;
  }
  PyBytes_AsStringAndSize(bytes, &s, &len);
  print_chars(s, len);
  Py_DECREF(bytes);
  Py_RETURN_NONE;
}
```

If you try these functions from Python, here's what happens:

```
>>> s = retstr()
>>> s
'Spicy Jalapeño\udcae'
>>> print_chars(s)
53 70 69 63 79 20 4a 61 6c 61 70 65 c3 b1 6f ae
>>>
```

Careful observation will reveal that the malformed string got encoded into a Python string without errors, and that when passed back into C, it turned back into a byte string that exactly encoded the same bytes as the original C string.

Discussion

This recipe addresses a subtle, but potentially annoying problem with string handling in extension modules. Namely, the fact that C strings in extensions might not follow the strict Unicode encoding/decoding rules that Python normally expects. Thus, it's possible that some malformed C data would pass to Python. A good example might be C strings associated with low-level system calls such as filenames. For instance, what happens if a system call returns a broken string back to the interpreter that can't be properly decoded.

Normally, Unicode errors are often handled by specifying some sort of error policy, such as strict, ignore, replace, or something similar. However, a downside of these policies is that they irreparably destroy the original string content. For example, if the malformed data in the example was decoded using one of these polices, you would get results such as this:

```
>>> raw = b'Spicy Jalape\xc3\xb1o\xae'
>>> raw.decode('utf-8','ignore')
'Spicy Jalapeño'
>>> raw.decode('utf-8','replace')
'Spicy Jalapeño?'
>>>
```

The surrogateescape error handling policies takes all nondecodable bytes and turns them into the low-half of a surrogate pair (\udcXX where XX is the raw byte value). For example:

```
>>> raw.decode('utf-8','surrogateescape')
'Spicy Jalapeño\udcae'
>>>
```

Isolated low surrogate characters such as \udcae never appear in valid Unicode. Thus, this string is technically an illegal representation. In fact, if you ever try to pass it to functions that perform output, you'll get encoding errors:

```
>>> s = raw.decode('utf-8', 'surrogateescape')
>>> print(s)
Traceback (most recent call last):
  File "<stdin>", line 1, in <module>
UnicodeEncodeError: 'utf-8' codec can't encode character '\udcae'
in position 14: surrogates not allowed
>>>
```

However, the main point of allowing the surrogate escapes is to allow malformed strings to pass from C to Python and back into C without any data loss. When the string is encoded using surrogateescape again, the surrogate characters are turned back into their original bytes. For example:

```
>>> s
'Spicy Jalapeño\udcae'
```

```
>>> s.encode('utf-8','surrogateescape')
b'Spicy Jalape\xc3\xb1o\xae'
>>>
```

As a general rule, it's probably best to avoid surrogate encoding whenever possible—
your code will be much more reliable if it uses proper encodings. However, sometimes
there are situations where you simply don't have control over the data encoding and
you aren't free to ignore or replace the bad data because other functions may need to
use it. This recipe shows how to do it.

As a final note, many of Python's system-oriented functions, especially those related to
filenames, environment variables, and command-line options, use surrogate encoding.
For example, if you use a function such as os.listdir() on a directory containing a
undecodable filename, it will be returned as a string with surrogate escapes. See
Recipe 5.15 for a related recipe.

PEP 383 (*http://www.python.org/dev/peps/pep-0383*) has more information about the
problem addressed by this recipe and surrogateescape error handling.

15.17. Passing Filenames to C Extensions

Problem

You need to pass filenames to C library functions, but need to make sure the filename
has been encoded according to the system's expected filename encoding.

Solution

To write an extension function that receives a filename, use code such as this:

```
static PyObject *py_get_filename(PyObject *self, PyObject *args) {
  PyObject *bytes;
  char *filename;
  Py_ssize_t len;
  if (!PyArg_ParseTuple(args,"O&", PyUnicode_FSConverter, &bytes)) {
    return NULL;
  }
  PyBytes_AsStringAndSize(bytes, &filename, &len);
  /* Use filename */
  ...

  /* Cleanup and return */
  Py_DECREF(bytes)
  Py_RETURN_NONE;
}
```

If you already have a PyObject * that you want to convert as a filename, use code such
as the following:

```
PyObject *obj;      /* Object with the filename */
PyObject *bytes;
char *filename;
Py_ssize_t len;

bytes = PyUnicode_EncodeFSDefault(obj);
PyBytes_AsStringAndSize(bytes, &filename, &len);
/* Use filename */
...
/* Cleanup */
Py_DECREF(bytes);
```

If you need to return a filename back to Python, use the following code:

```
/* Turn a filename into a Python object */

char *filename;        /* Already set */
int  filename_len;     /* Already set */

PyObject *obj = PyUnicode_DecodeFSDefaultAndSize(filename, filename_len);
```

Discussion

Dealing with filenames in a portable way is a tricky problem that is best left to Python. If you use this recipe in your extension code, filenames will be handled in a manner that is consistent with filename handling in the rest of Python. This includes encoding/decoding of bytes, dealing with bad characters, surrogate escapes, and other complications.

15.18. Passing Open Files to C Extensions

Problem

You have an open file object in Python, but need to pass it to C extension code that will use the file.

Solution

To convert a file to an integer file descriptor, use `PyFile_FromFd()`, as shown:

```
PyObject *fobj;       /* File object (already obtained somehow) */
int fd = PyObject_AsFileDescriptor(fobj);
if (fd < 0) {
   return NULL;
}
```

The resulting file descriptor is obtained by calling the `fileno()` method on `fobj`. Thus, any object that exposes a descriptor in this manner should work (e.g., file, socket, etc.).

Once you have the descriptor, it can be passed to various low-level C functions that expect to work with files.

If you need to convert an integer file descriptor back into a Python object, use PyFile_FromFd() as follows:

```
int fd;      /* Existing file descriptor (already open) */
PyObject *fobj = PyFile_FromFd(fd, "filename","r",-1,NULL,NULL,NULL,1);
```

The arguments to PyFile_FromFd() mirror those of the built-in open() function. NULL values simply indicate that the default settings for the encoding, errors, and newline arguments are being used.

Discussion

If you are passing file objects from Python to C, there are a few tricky issues to be concerned about. First, Python performs its own I/O buffering through the io module. Prior to passing any kind of file descriptor to C, you should first flush the I/O buffers on the associated file objects. Otherwise, you could get data appearing out of order on the file stream.

Second, you need to pay careful attention to file ownership and the responsibility of closing the file in particular. If a file descriptor is passed to C, but still used in Python, you need to make sure C doesn't accidentally close the file. Likewise, if a file descriptor is being turned into a Python file object, you need to be clear about who is responsible for closing it. The last argument to PyFile_FromFd() is set to 1 to indicate that Python should close the file.

If you need to make a different kind of file object such as a FILE * object from the C standard I/O library using a function such as fdopen(), you'll need to be especially careful. Doing so would introduce two completely different I/O buffering layers into the I/O stack (one from Python's io module and one from C stdio). Operations such as fclose() in C could also inadvertently close the file for further use in Python. If given a choice, you should probably make extension code work with the low-level integer file descriptors as opposed to using a higher-level abstraction such as that provided by <stdio.h>.

15.19. Reading File-Like Objects from C

Problem

You want to write C extension code that consumes data from any Python file-like object (e.g., normal files, StringIO objects, etc.).

Solution

To consume data on a file-like object, you need to repeatedly invoke its `read()` method and take steps to properly decode the resulting data.

Here is a sample C extension function that merely consumes all of the data on a file-like object and dumps it to standard output so you can see it:

```
#define CHUNK_SIZE 8192

/* Consume a "file-like" object and write bytes to stdout */
static PyObject *py_consume_file(PyObject *self, PyObject *args) {
  PyObject *obj;
  PyObject *read_meth;
  PyObject *result = NULL;
  PyObject *read_args;

  if (!PyArg_ParseTuple(args,"O", &obj)) {
    return NULL;
  }

  /* Get the read method of the passed object */
  if ((read_meth = PyObject_GetAttrString(obj, "read")) == NULL) {
    return NULL;
  }

  /* Build the argument list to read() */
  read_args = Py_BuildValue("(i)", CHUNK_SIZE);
  while (1) {
    PyObject *data;
    PyObject *enc_data;
    char *buf;
    Py_ssize_t len;

    /* Call read() */
    if ((data = PyObject_Call(read_meth, read_args, NULL)) == NULL) {
      goto final;
    }

    /* Check for EOF */
    if (PySequence_Length(data) == 0) {
      Py_DECREF(data);
      break;
    }

    /* Encode Unicode as Bytes for C */
    if ((enc_data=PyUnicode_AsEncodedString(data,"utf-8","strict"))==NULL) {
      Py_DECREF(data);
      goto final;
    }

    /* Extract underlying buffer data */
```

```
    PyBytes_AsStringAndSize(enc_data, &buf, &len);

    /* Write to stdout (replace with something more useful) */
    write(1, buf, len);

    /* Cleanup */
    Py_DECREF(enc_data);
    Py_DECREF(data);
  }
  result = Py_BuildValue("");

 final:
  /* Cleanup */
  Py_DECREF(read_meth);
  Py_DECREF(read_args);
  return result;
}
```

To test the code, try making a file-like object such as a `StringIO` instance and pass it in:

```
>>> import io
>>> f = io.StringIO('Hello\nWorld\n')
>>> import sample
>>> sample.consume_file(f)
Hello
World
>>>
```

Discussion

Unlike a normal system file, a file-like object is not necessarily built around a low-level file descriptor. Thus, you can't use normal C library functions to access it. Instead, you need to use Python's C API to manipulate the file-like object much like you would in Python.

In the solution, the `read()` method is extracted from the passed object. An argument list is built and then repeatedly passed to `PyObject_Call()` to invoke the method. To detect end-of-file (EOF), `PySequence_Length()` is used to see if the returned result has zero length.

For all I/O operations, you'll need to concern yourself with the underlying encoding and distinction between bytes and Unicode. This recipe shows how to read a file in text mode and decode the resulting text into a bytes encoding that can be used by C. If you want to read the file in binary mode, only minor changes will be made. For example:

```
  ...
    /* Call read() */
    if ((data = PyObject_Call(read_meth, read_args, NULL)) == NULL) {
      goto final;
    }
```

```
/* Check for EOF */
if (PySequence_Length(data) == 0) {
  Py_DECREF(data);
  break;
}
if (!PyBytes_Check(data)) {
  Py_DECREF(data);
  PyErr_SetString(PyExc_IOError, "File must be in binary mode");
  goto final;
}

/* Extract underlying buffer data */
PyBytes_AsStringAndSize(data, &buf, &len);
...
```

The trickiest part of this recipe concerns proper memory management. When working with PyObject * variables, careful attention needs to be given to managing reference counts and cleaning up values when no longer needed. The various Py_DECREF() calls are doing this.

The recipe is written in a general-purpose manner so that it can be adapted to other file operations, such as writing. For example, to write data, merely obtain the write() method of the file-like object, convert data into an appropriate Python object (bytes or Unicode), and invoke the method to have it written to the file.

Finally, although file-like objects often provide other methods (e.g., readline(), read_into()), it is probably best to just stick with the basic read() and write() methods for maximal portability. Keeping things as simple as possible is often a good policy for C extensions.

15.20. Consuming an Iterable from C

Problem

You want to write C extension code that consumes items from any iterable object such as a list, tuple, file, or generator.

Solution

Here is a sample C extension function that shows how to consume the items on an iterable:

```
static PyObject *py_consume_iterable(PyObject *self, PyObject *args) {
  PyObject *obj;
  PyObject *iter;
  PyObject *item;

  if (!PyArg_ParseTuple(args, "O", &obj)) {
```

```
        return NULL;
    }
    if ((iter = PyObject_GetIter(obj)) == NULL) {
        return NULL;
    }
    while ((item = PyIter_Next(iter)) != NULL) {
        /* Use item */
        ...
        Py_DECREF(item);
    }
    Py_DECREF(iter);
    return Py_BuildValue("");
}
```

Discussion

The code in this recipe mirrors similar code in Python. The `PyObject_GetIter()` call is the same as calling `iter()` to get an iterator. The `PyIter_Next()` function invokes the next method on the iterator returning the next item or NULL if there are no more items. Make sure you're careful with memory management—`Py_DECREF()` needs to be called on both the produced items and the iterator object itself to avoid leaking memory.

15.21. Diagnosing Segmentation Faults

Problem

The interpreter violently crashes with a segmentation fault, bus error, access violation, or other fatal error. You would like to get a Python traceback that shows you where your program was running at the point of failure.

Solution

The `faulthandler` module can be used to help you solve this problem. Include the following code in your program:

```
import faulthandler
faulthandler.enable()
```

Alternatively, run Python with the `-Xfaulthandler` option such as this:

```
bash % python3 -Xfaulthandler program.py
```

Last, but not least, you can set the PYTHONFAULTHANDLER environment variable.

With `faulthandler` enabled, fatal errors in C extensions will result in a Python traceback being printed on failures. For example:

```
Fatal Python error: Segmentation fault
```

```
Current thread 0x00007fff71106cc0:
  File "example.py", line 6 in foo
  File "example.py", line 10 in bar
  File "example.py", line 14 in spam
  File "example.py", line 19 in <module>
Segmentation fault
```

Although this won't tell you where in the C code things went awry, at least it can tell you how it got there from Python.

Discussion

The `faulthandler` will show you the stack traceback of the Python code executing at the time of failure. At the very least, this will show you the top-level extension function that was invoked. With the aid of pdb or other Python debugger, you can investigate the flow of the Python code leading to the error.

`faulthandler` will not tell you anything about the failure from C. For that, you will need to use a traditional C debugger, such as gdb. However, the information from the `faulthandler` traceback may give you a better idea of where to direct your attention.

It should be noted that certain kinds of errors in C may not be easily recoverable. For example, if a C extension trashes the stack or program heap, it may render `faulthandler` inoperable and you'll simply get no output at all (other than a crash). Obviously, your mileage may vary.

Further Reading

There are a large number of books and online resources available for learning and programming Python. However, if like this book, your focus is on the use of Python 3, finding reliable information is made a bit more difficult simply due to the sheer volume of existing material written for earlier Python versions.

In this appendix, we provide a few selected links to material that may be particularly useful in the context of Python 3 programming and the recipes contained in this book. This is by no means an exhaustive list of resources, so you should definitely check to see if new titles or more up-to-date editions of these books have been published.

Online Resources

http://docs.python.org

> It goes without saying that Python's own online documentation is an excellent resource if you need to delve into the finer details of the language and modules. Just make sure you're looking at the documentation for Python 3 and not earlier versions.

http://www.python.org/dev/peps

> Python Enhancement Proposals (PEPs) are invaluable if you want to understand the motivation for adding new features to the Python language as well as subtle implementation details. This is especially true for some of the more advanced language features. In writing this book, the PEPs were often more useful than the official documentation.

http://pyvideo.org

> This is a large collection of video presentations and tutorials from past PyCon conferences, user group meetings, and more. It can be an invaluable resource for learning about modern Python development. Many of the videos feature Python core developers talking about the new features being added in Python 3.

http://code.activestate.com/recipes/langs/python

> The ActiveState Python recipes site has long been a resource for finding the solution to thousands of specific programming problems. As of this writing, it contains approximately 300 recipes specific to Python 3. You'll find that many of its recipes either expand upon topics covered in this book or focus on more narrowly defined tasks. As such, it's a good companion.

http://stackoverflow.com/questions/tagged/python

> Stack Overflow currently has more than 175,000 questions tagged as Python-related (and almost 5000 questions specific to Python 3). Although the quality of the questions and answers varies, there is a lot of good material to be found.

Books for Learning Python

The following books provide an introduction to Python with a focus on Python 3:

- *Learning Python*, 4th Edition, by Mark Lutz, O'Reilly & Associates (2009).
- *The Quick Python Book*, 2nd Edition, by Vernon Ceder, Manning (2010).
- *Python Programming for the Absolute Beginner*, 3rd Edition, by Michael Dawson, Course Technology PTR (2010).
- *Beginning Python: From Novice to Professional*, 2nd Edition, by Magnus Lie Hetland, Apress (2008).
- *Programming in Python 3*, 2nd Edition, by Mark Summerfield, Addison-Wesley (2010).

Advanced Books

The following books provide more advanced coverage and include Python 3 topics:

- *Programming Python*, 4th Edition, by Mark Lutz, O'Reilly & Associates (2010).
- *Python Essential Reference*, 4th Edition, by David Beazley, Addison-Wesley (2009).
- *Core Python Applications Programming*, 3rd Edition, by Wesley Chun, Prentice Hall (2012).
- *The Python Standard Library by Example*, by Doug Hellmann, Addison-Wesley (2011).
- *Python 3 Object Oriented Programming*, by Dusty Phillips, Packt Publishing (2010).
- *Porting to Python 3*, by Lennart Regebro, CreateSpace (2011), *http://python3port ing.com*.

Index

Symbols

!r formatting code, 244

% (percent) operator, 58, 556
    format() function vs., 88

* (star) operator
    EBNFs and, 70

**kwargs, 218
    decorators and, 331
    enforcing signature on, 364–367
    help function and, 219
    wrapped functions and, 353

*args, 217
    decorators and, 331
    enforcing signature on, 364–367
    wrapped functions and, 353

+ (plus) operator, 48, 59

-O option (interpreter), 343

-OO option (interpreter), 343

-W (warnings), 584
    all option, 583
    error option, 584
    ignore option, 584

. (dot) operator, 49, 591

< (less than) operator, date comparisons with, 108

== operator, 462

? (question mark) modifier in regular expressions, 48

\$ (end-marker) in regular expressions, 44

_ (single underscore)
    avoiding clashes with reserved words, 251
    naming convention and, 250

__ (double underscore), naming conventions and, 250

A

abc module, 274

abspath() (os.path module), 551

abstract base classes, 274–276
    collections module and, 283–286
    predefined, 276

abstract syntax tree, 389–392

abstraction, gratuitous, 593

@abstractmethod decorator (abc module), 275

accepting script via input files, 539

accessor functions, 238–241
    adjusting decorators with, 336–339

ACCESS_COPY (mmap module), 155

ACLs, 548

actor model, 516–520

addHandler() operation (logging module), 559

add_argument() method (ArgumentParser module), 543, 544

Advanced Programming in the Unix Environment, 2e (Stevens, Rago), 538

algorithms, 1–35
    filtering sequence elements, 26–28

We'd like to hear your suggestions for improving our indexes. Send email to index@oreilly.com.

dict() function, 29, 594
dictionaries
    comparing, 15–16
    converting to XML, 189–191
    Counter objects and, 21
    defaultdict vs., 12
    grouping records based on field, 24–26
    JSON support for, 179
    keeping in order, 12–13
    multiple values for a single key in, 11–12
    removing duplicates from, 17
    sorting, 13–15
    sorting list of, by common key, 21–23
    subsets, extracting, 28–29
dictionary comprehension, 29
dining philosophers problem (deadlocks), 503
directories
    as runnable scripts, 407–408
    copying, 547
    moving, 547
    temporary, 167–170
directory listings, 158–159
dis module, 393–396
discarding vs. filtering iterables, 124
distributed systems and property calls, 255
domain sockets (Unix), 457, 470
    connecting interpreters with, 472
DOTALL flag (re module), 49
dropwhile() function (itertools module), 123
dump() function (pickle module), 171
dumps() function (json module), 179
    indent argument, 181
    sort_keys argument, 182
dumps() function (pickle module), 171
dup2() function (os module), 538

E

EBNF, 69
ElementTree module (xml.etree), 66, 183–186
    creating XML documents with, 189–191
    iterparse() function, 188
    parse() function, 185
    parse_and_remove() function, 189
    parsing namespaces and, 194
    parsing/modifying/rewriting files with, 191–193
empty() method (queue module), 496
encode() method (str type), 56

encoding text data, 141–144
    changing in open files, 163–165
    passing to C libraries, 648–653
    pickling and, 174
encryption vs. authentication, 463
end argument (print() function), 144
endswith() method (str type), 38
    pattern matching with, 42
__enter__() method (with statements), 246–248
enumerate() function, 127–128
environ argument (WSGI), 451
error messages, terminating program with, 540
error() function (logging module), 556
escape() function (html module), 65
escape() function (xml.sax.saxutils module), 191
Event object (threading module), 488–491
event-driven I/O, 475–481
except statement, 576, 580
    chained exceptions and, 581
    reraising exceptions caught by, 582
Exception class, 579
    handler for, 576
exceptions
    catching all, 576
    creating custom, 578
    handling multiple, 574
    raising in response to another exception, 580
    reraising, 582
    SystemExit, 540
    testing for, 570
    with statements and, 247
exec() function, 386–388
execve() function (os module), 546
__exit__() method (with statements), 246–248
@expectedFailure decorator, 574
exponential notation, 87
%extend directive (Swig), 630
external command
    executing, 545
    getting output, 545

F

factory functions, 323
faulthandler module, 663–664
fdel attribute (properties), 253
fget attribute (properties), 253
FieldStorage() class (cgi module), 452
file descriptor
    passing between processes, 470–475

mkstemp() function (tempfile module), 169
mmap module, 153–156
mock module (unittest module), 565, 570
module import * statement, 398–399
modules, 397–435
    controlling import of, 398–399
    from module import * statement, 398
    hierarchical packages of, 397–398
    import hooks, using, 412–428
    importing with relative names, 399–401
    importing, using string as name, 411
    importlib module, 421
    import_module() function (importlib module), 411
    invalidate_caches() function (importlib module), 427
    meta path importer, 414–418
    new_module() function (imp module), 421
    objects, creating, 421
    patching on import, 428–431
    relative imports vs. absolute names, 400
    reloading, 406–407
    remote machines, loading from, 412–428
    splitting into multiple files, 401–404
    sys.path, adding directories to, 409–411
    sys.path_importer_cache object, 424
    virtual environments and, 432–433
    __all__ variable in, 398–399
    __init__.py file, 397
    __main__.py files, 407–408
monthrange() function (calendar module), 108
months, finding date ranges of, 107–109
moving directories/files, 547
__mro__ attribute, 576
multidicts, 11–12
multiple-dispatch, 376–382
multiprocessing module, 488
    GIL and, 514
    passing file descriptors with, 470–475
    reduction module, 470–475
    RPCs and, 459
mutable buffers, reading into, 152–153
MutableMapping class (collections module), 283
MutableSequence class (collections module), 283
MutableSet class (collections module), 283

N

named pipes (Windows), 457, 470, 472
NamedTemporaryFile() function (tempfile module), 169
namedtuple() function (collections module), 30
namedtuple() method (collections module)
    new_class() function and, 372
    unpacking binary data and, 203
NameError exception, 581
namespace package, checking for, 426
namespaces (XML), parsing, 193–195
namespaces, multiple directories in, 404–406
naming conventions
    for private data, 250–251
    __ (double underscore) and, 250
NaN (not a number) values, 94–95
    in JSON, 183
    isnan() function and, 95
nested sequences, flattening, 135–136
network programming, 437–483
    connection (multiprocessing module), 456–458
    event-driven I/O, 475–481
    hmac module, 461–463
    interpreters, communication between, 456–458
    large arrays, sending/receiving, 481–483
    passing file descriptors, 470–475
    remote procedure calls, 454–456, 458–461
    simple authentication, 461–463
    socketserver module, 441–444
    SSL, implementing, 464–470
    TCP servers, 441–444
    UDP server, implementing, 445–446
    UDPServer class, 446
    XML-RPC, 454–456
__new__() method (classes)
    coding conventions and, 367–370
    optional arguments and, 363
newlines, 142
new_class() function (types module), 370–374
new_module() function (imp module), 421
next() function (iterators), 113
nlargest() function (heapq module), 7–8
nonblocking, supporting with queues, 495
noncapture groups (regular expressions), 49
nonlocal declarations, 239
    adjusting decorators with, 336–339

About the Authors

David Beazley is an independent software developer and book author living in the city of Chicago. He primarily works on programming tools, providing custom software development, and teaching practical programming courses for software developers, scientists, and engineers. He is best known for his work with the Python programming language, for which he has created several open source packages (e.g., Swig and PLY) and authored the acclaimed *Python Essential Reference*. He also has significant experience with systems programming in C, C++, and assembly language.

Brian K. Jones is a system administrator in the department of computer science at Princeton University.

Colophon

The animal on the cover of *Python Cookbook*, Third Edition is a springhaas (*Pedetes capensis*), also known as a spring hare. Springhaas are not hares at all, but rather the only member of the family *Pedetidae* in the order Rodentia. They are not marsupials, but they are vaguely kangaroo-like, with small front legs, powerful hind legs designed for hopping, jumping, and leaping, and long, strong, bushy (but not prehensile) tails used for balance and as a brace when sitting. They grow to be about 14 to 18 inches long, with tails as long as their bodies, and can weigh approximately eight pounds. Springhaas have rich, glossy, tawny, or golden-reddish coats with long, soft fur and white underbellies. Their heads are disproportionately large, and they have long ears (with a flap of skin at the base they can close to prevent sand from getting inside while they are digging) and large, dark brown eyes.

Springhaas mate throughout the year and have a gestation period of about 78 to 82 days. Females generally give birth to only one baby (which stays with its mother until it is approximately seven weeks old) per litter but have three or four litters each year. Babies are born with teeth and are fully furred, with their eyes closed and ears open.

Springhaas are terrestrial and well-adapted for digging, and they tend to spend their days in the small networks of their burrows and tunnels. They are nocturnal and primarily herbivorous, feeding on bulbs, roots, grains, and occasionally insects. While they are foraging, they move about on all fours, but they are able to move 10 to 25 feet in a single horizontal leap and are capable of quick getaways when frightened. Although they are often seen foraging in groups in the wild, they do not form an organized social unit and usually nest alone or in breeding pairs. Springhaas can live up to 15 years in captivity. They are found in Zaire, Kenya, and South Africa, in dry, desert, or semiarid areas, and they are a favorite and important food source in South Africa.

The cover image is from *Animal Creation: Mammalia*. The cover font is Adobe ITC Garamond. The text font is Adobe Minion Pro; the heading font is Adobe Myriad Condensed; and the code font is Dalton Maag's Ubuntu Mono.

Have it your way.

CPSIA information can be obtained at www.ICGtesting.com
Printed in the USA
BVOW07s1414120214

344746BV00009B/216/P